Gary Cambers and Steve Sibley

Cambridge IGCSE®
Geography
Coursebook

Completely Cambridge – Cambridge resources for Cambridge qualifications

Cambridge University Press works closely with University of Cambridge International Examinations (CIE) as parts of the University of Cambridge. We enable thousands of students to pass their CIE exams by providing comprehensive, high-quality, endorsed resources.

To find out more about University of Cambridge International Examinations visit www.cie.org.uk

To find out more about Cambridge University Press visit www.cambridge.org/cie

CAMBRIDGE UNIVERSITY PRESS
Cambridge, New York, Melbourne, Madrid, Cape Town,
Singapore, São Paulo, Delhi, Mexico City

Cambridge University Press
The Edinburgh Building, Cambridge CB2 8RU, UK

www.cambridge.org
Information on this title: www.cambridge.org/9780521757843

First published 2010
5th printing 2012

Printed in India by Replika Press Pvt. Ltd

A catalogue record for this publication is available from the British Library

ISBN 978-0-521-75784-3 Paperback with CD-ROM for Windows and Mac

Cover image: Boaz Rottem / Alamy
Illustrations: Kathy Baxendale and Pete Smith
Photo research: Suzanne Williams

TERMS AND CONDITIONS OF USE FOR THE CD-ROM

The CD-ROM at the back of this book is provided on the following terms and conditions:

- The CD-ROM is made available for the use of current teachers and students within a purchasing institution, or for private purchasers, only. A purchase of at least one copy of the book must be made in respect of each teacher, student or private purchaser who uses the CD-ROM. The CD-ROM may be installed on individual computers or networks for use as above.
- Subject to the above, the material on the CD-ROM, in whole or in part, may not be passed in an electronic form to another party, and may not be copied (except for making one copy of the CD-ROM solely for backup or archival purposes), distributed or stored electronically. It may not be posted on a public website, and may not be altered for any reason without the permission of Cambridge University Press.
- Permission is explicitly granted for use of the materials on a data projector, interactive whiteboard or other public display in the context of classroom teaching at a purchasing institution.
- Once a teacher or student ceases to be a member of the purchasing institution all copies of the material on the CD-ROM stored on his/her personal computer must be destroyed and the CD-ROM returned to the purchasing institution.
- All material contained within the CD-ROM is protected by copyright and other intellectual property laws. You may not alter, remove or destroy any copyright notice or other material placed on or with this CD-ROM.
- The CD-ROM is supplied 'as-is' with no express guarantee as to its suitability.

CONTENTS

Theme 2 The Natural Environment 61

The *Cambridge IGCSE Geography* coursebook and CD-ROM have been written specifically to prepare students for Papers 1, 2 and 4 of the CIE examination.

Part A: Geographical Themes – Preparing for Paper 1

Part A deals with the syllabus themes in the order of the syllabus. As the contents page illustrates, there is a close and deliberate link in Part A to the syllabus. The following three themes are covered:

Theme 1: Population and Settlement

Theme 2: The Natural Environment

Theme 3: Economic Development and the Use of Resources.

The authors have translated the syllabus themes into 31 generic topics, each of which is covered on a double-page spread to introduce the topic. Twenty-nine of these topics are then followed by at least one but usually two case studies of topical and relevant examples from over 40 different countries, most of which have CIE centres where candidates take the IGCSE Geography examination. The three case study questions on Paper 1 are worth 21 out of 75 marks, so centres that have been requesting resources to prepare candidates more effectively for this part of the examination will find a wide range of examples to use. All are resource-based and involve problem-solving and free-response writing as required. At the end of each set of case studies there is a sample case study question provided for students to attempt, based on the examples provided or from others they have been taught. A global issue is studied at the end of each theme, and a full world map showing countries covered by the case studies is provided at the start (on page 2).

Part B: Geographical Skills – Preparing for Paper 2

This paper is mainly skills-based and tests a candidate's ability to handle various ways of depicting geographical information without requiring specific place-knowledge as in Paper 1. As one examination question will be based on a large-scale (1:25 000 or 1:50 000) topographical map of a tropical area, Part B of the textbook provides six examples of such maps, from Peru, Zimbabwe, Kenya, Jamaica, Indonesia and Reunion Island. Teachers will find previous examinations have used maps of the Caribbean, Zimbabwe, and Mauritius. For each country an extract of a map is provided with examples of map skills questions. Further work continues developing map skills as well as dealing with topics of relevance within each country that relates to the map extract. The authors are well aware how difficult it is to obtain international maps of tropical areas at the two scales needed; the six map extracts provided here will supplement those obtained from previous examinations.

Part C: The Alternative to Coursework – Preparing for Paper 4

Paper 3 is the coursework component and is not dealt with in detail here, although aspects of fieldwork and coursework are touched on in Part C. Paper 4 is taken by candidates as a written examination instead of carrying out coursework and/or fieldwork. Four topics – two physical and two human – are covered with investigations into the Central Business District (CBD), Rivers, Tourism, and the Weather – all topics that previously have been set on Paper 4. Each investigation begins with a double-page spread that illustrates how fieldwork could be carried out on each of these topics. Then, taking a recent question on the topic, there is a detailed analysis of candidate answers with examination tips provided, as well as opportunities for students to assess answers. The final exercise provides examples of coursework topics that are undertaken in several CIE centres in different countries. These suggest the type of fieldwork or coursework that teachers might consider introducing. Although the majority of centres do choose Paper 4 as an alternative to coursework, it is important that teachers try to carry out some local fieldwork, which Part C attempts to encourage.

The CD

Outline maps: These are always useful for teachers to use with several tasks. Eleven outline maps are provided covering the major regions of the world. In addition a sheet of triangular graph paper is provided as it can be difficult to obtain in many countries.

Support sheets: Forty-two photocopiable support sheets – at least one per topic and one for each map work section – are provided here. In most cases they provide help with sketches and graph work and supplement the topics and case studies.

Sample questions: Thirty-one full sample questions are provided in exactly the same style and format as they occur on Paper 1. Each question has a part **a** and **b** with resources to respond to; the case study, which is provided in the textbook, is added to complete a full question. Mark schemes are also provided for teachers to use.

Glossary: The glossary used in the textbook is repeated here for reference or for copying to issue to students.

Gary Cambers and Steve Sibley

Part A Geographical Themes

Preparing for Paper 1

Paper 1 is a compulsory paper taken by all candidates. It consists of 6 questions – 2 on each Theme. Candidates must choose any 3 questions to answer. Each is worth 25 marks giving a total of 75 marks. Part A of the book focuses on case studies and attempts to provide topical examples for the final part of each question which is a case study question. Here candidates must use a real place they have studied. Some topics are followed by more than one example of a case study and there is one typical case study examination question with almost all topics in the book. The CD contains typical complete questions, including the case studies from Part A, with mark schemes. Support worksheets can also be found on the CD.

From June 2010 there will be three different versions of Paper 1, numbered 11, 12 and 13. The Paper the centre receives will depend on which of the three international time zones it is allocated to. A recent past paper and mark scheme for Paper 1 is available for reference at www.cie.org.uk

The location of case studies used in PART A: GEOGRAPHICAL THEMES

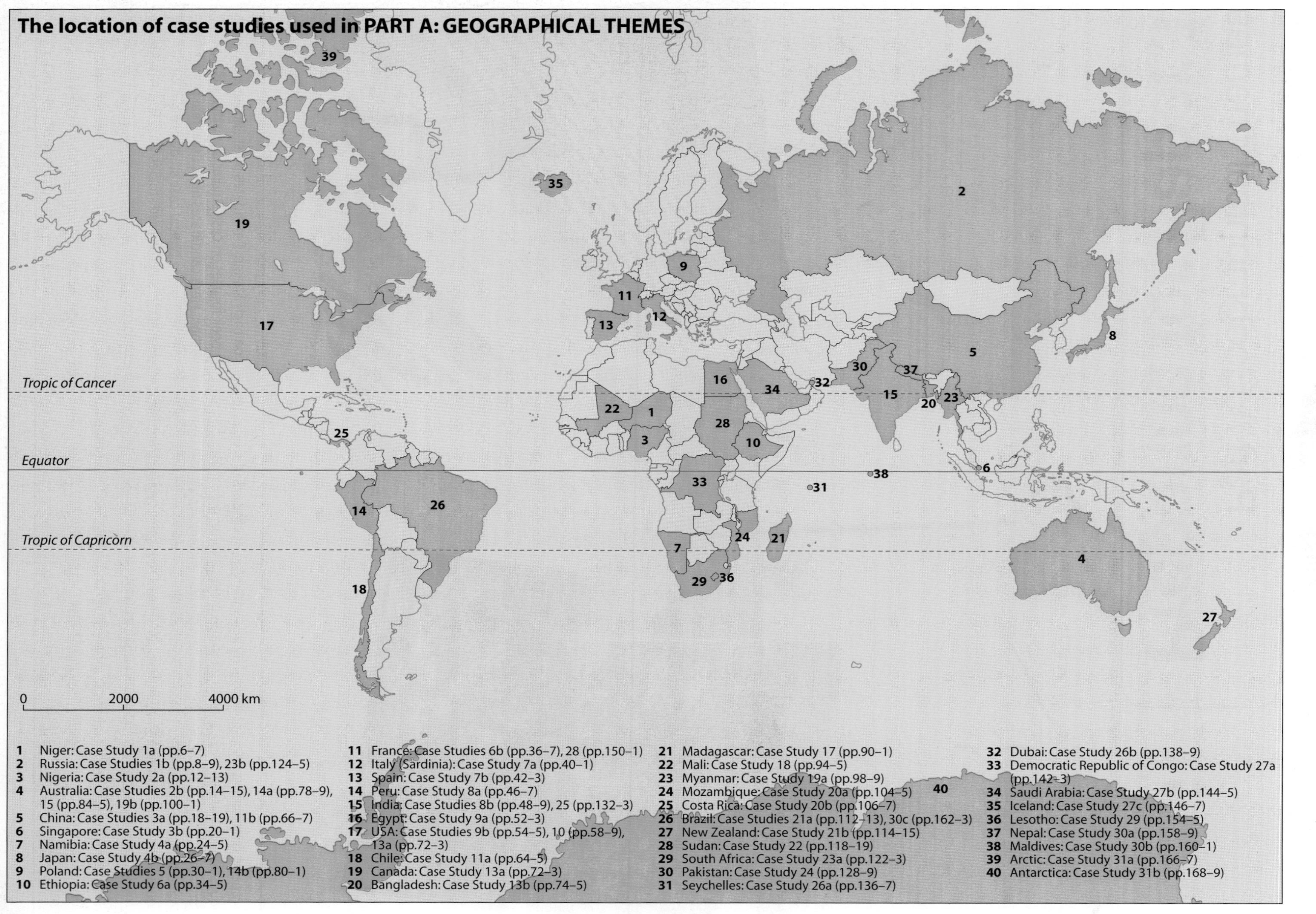

1 Niger: Case Study 1a (pp.6–7)
2 Russia: Case Studies 1b (pp.8–9), 23b (pp.124–5)
3 Nigeria: Case Study 2a (pp.12–13)
4 Australia: Case Studies 2b (pp.14–15), 14a (pp.78–9), 15 (pp.84–5), 19b (pp.100–1)
5 China: Case Studies 3a (pp.18–19), 11b (pp.66–7)
6 Singapore: Case Study 3b (pp.20–1)
7 Namibia: Case Study 4a (pp.24–5)
8 Japan: Case Study 4b (pp.26–7)
9 Poland: Case Studies 5 (pp.30–1), 14b (pp.80–1)
10 Ethiopia: Case Study 6a (pp.34–5)
11 France: Case Studies 6b (pp.36–7), 28 (pp.150–1)
12 Italy (Sardinia): Case Study 7a (pp.40–1)
13 Spain: Case Study 7b (pp.42–3)
14 Peru: Case Study 8a (pp.46–7)
15 India: Case Studies 8b (pp.48–9), 25 (pp.132–3)
16 Egypt: Case Study 9a (pp.52–3)
17 USA: Case Studies 9b (pp.54–5), 10 (pp.58–9), 13a (pp.72–3)
18 Chile: Case Study 11a (pp.64–5)
19 Canada: Case Study 13a (pp.72–3)
20 Bangladesh: Case Study 13b (pp.74–5)
21 Madagascar: Case Study 17 (pp.90–1)
22 Mali: Case Study 18 (pp.94–5)
23 Myanmar: Case Study 19a (pp.98–9)
24 Mozambique: Case Study 20a (pp.104–5)
25 Costa Rica: Case Study 20b (pp.106–7)
26 Brazil: Case Studies 21a (pp.112–13), 30c (pp.162–3)
27 New Zealand: Case Study 21b (pp.114–15)
28 Sudan: Case Study 22 (pp.118–19)
29 South Africa: Case Study 23a (pp.122–3)
30 Pakistan: Case Study 24 (pp.128–9)
31 Seychelles: Case Study 26a (pp.136–7)
32 Dubai: Case Study 26b (pp.138–9)
33 Democratic Republic of Congo: Case Study 27a (pp.142–3)
34 Saudi Arabia: Case Study 27b (pp.144–5)
35 Iceland: Case Study 27c (pp.146–7)
36 Lesotho: Case Study 29 (pp.154–5)
37 Nepal: Case Study 30a (pp.158–9)
38 Maldives: Case Study 30b (pp.160–1)
39 Arctic: Case Study 31a (pp.166–7)
40 Antarctica: Case Study 31b (pp.168–9)

Theme 1
Population and Settlement

The Oshadi Market in Lagos, Nigeria

Population growth

A World population

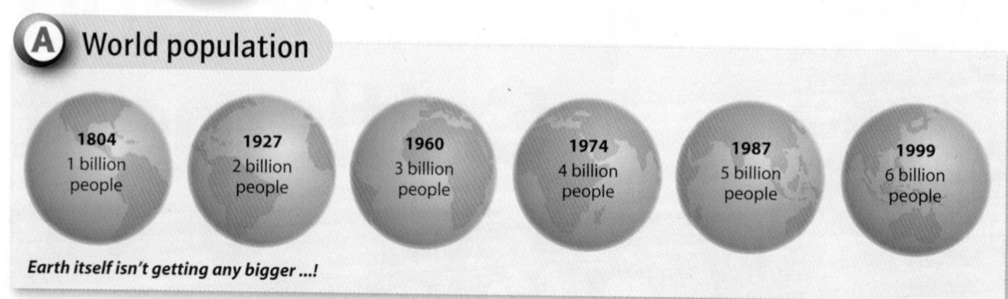

Earth itself isn't getting any bigger ...!

B Population growth rates

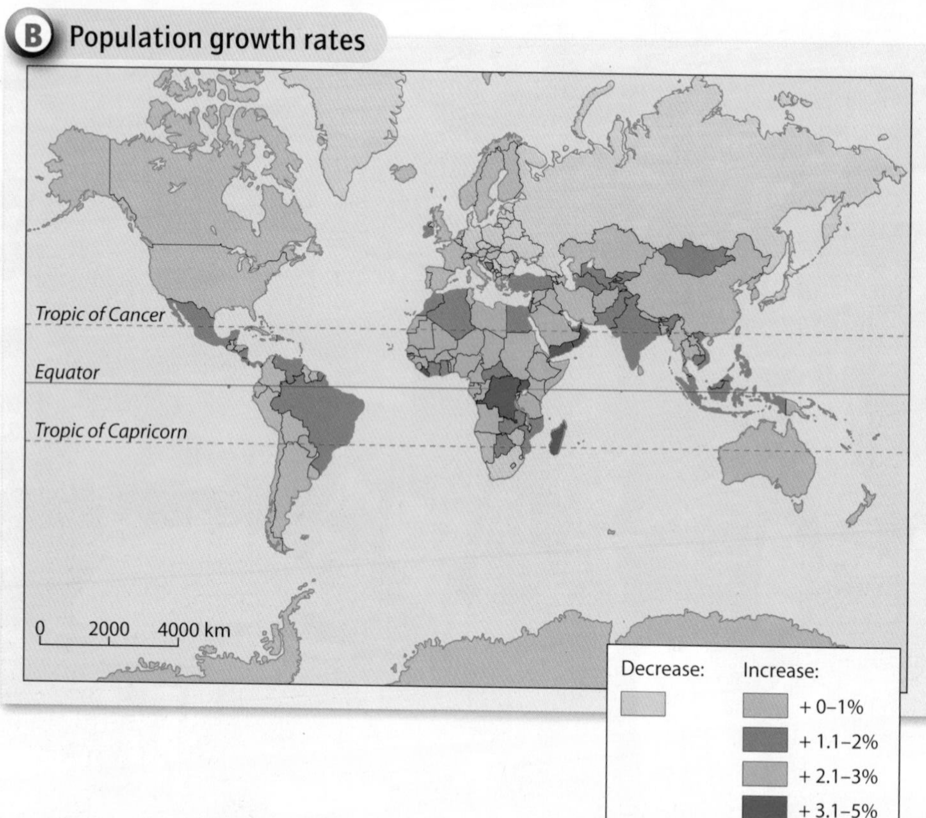

Population explosion

The population of the world is growing by 88 million people every year, which means an extra 241 095 people every day. There are 167 more people now than there were one minute ago! If there are 30 people in your class, the world's population increases by this amount every 10 seconds.

This rapid growth of world population, called the population explosion, is slowing down. Estimates suggest that by the end of this century it may have stabilised at around 10 billion.

Not all countries have the same rates of population growth. Some are still growing rapidly, whilst others have low growth rates or are even declining.

Task 1

Study **Source A**.

a Draw a line graph to show the growth of the world population (in billions) between 1804 and 1999. Your horizontal axis should go from 1800 to 2100.

b Continue the line to show the estimated (projected) increase up to the end of this century using the following figures:

2013	7 billion
2028	8 billion
2054	9 billion
2100	10 billion

Task 2

Study **Source B**.

a Use an atlas to put the following countries into rank order from the highest to the lowest rate of population growth.

- Canada
- Oman
- India
- Paraguay
- Romania

b Write a paragraph to compare rates of growth in African countries with those in Europe. Give examples of countries and growth rates to back up the points you are making.

C Population change

Country	Birth rate (per 1000 people)	Death rate (per 1000 people)	Net migration (per 1000 people)
Malta	10.3	8.3	+2.0
Morocco	21.3	5.5	–0.8
Poland	10.0	9.9	–0.5

Natural population change is calculated by subtracting the **death rate** from the **birth rate**. So Malta's natural population change is 10.3 – 8.3 = 2.0 per 1000 people.

To calculate the overall population change the amount of **migration** must be considered. If more people move into the country than move out of it, this is added. If more move out of the country than into it this is subtracted. So Malta's **overall population change** is 10.3 – 8.3 + 2.0 = 4.0 per 1000 people. This can be worked out as a percentage (i.e. 0.4%).

Task 3

Study **Source C**.

- **a** Calculate the natural population change of Morocco per 1000 people.
- **b** Calculate the overall population change of Poland per 1000 people.
- **c** Calculate the overall rate of population change of the country in which you live, as a percentage. You will need to find out the birth rate, death rate and net migration. For any country this information can be found at: www.cia.gov/library/publications/the-world-factbook/

D The Demographic Transition Model

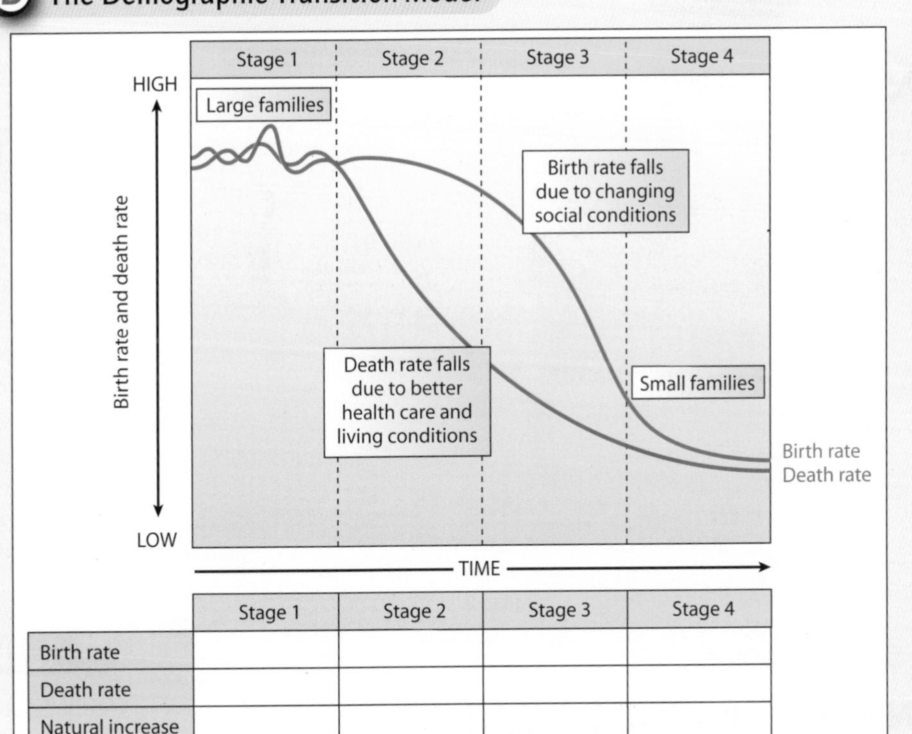

	Stage 1	Stage 2	Stage 3	Stage 4
Birth rate				
Death rate				
Natural increase				

The Demographic Transition Model

The Demographic Transition Model is a model of the way that population growth can be divided into four stages as birth and death rates change over time. It is based on what has happened in Europe and North America. The part of the graph representing population growth is the area between the lines, where birth rate is higher than death rate.

Task 4

- **a** Make a copy of the Demographic Transition Model in **Source D**. Shade in the natural increase.
- **b** Make a copy of the table under the graph. Complete the first two rows of the table using the words *high*, *low* or *decreasing*. Complete the third row using the phrases *small increase*, *large increase*, *slower increase* and *fluctuating*.
- **c** Today some countries have birth rates that are lower than death rates, so their population is declining. On your copy of the Demographic Transition Model, add an extra stage to show this and label it 'Stage 5'.

E Living in Dhaka, Bangladesh

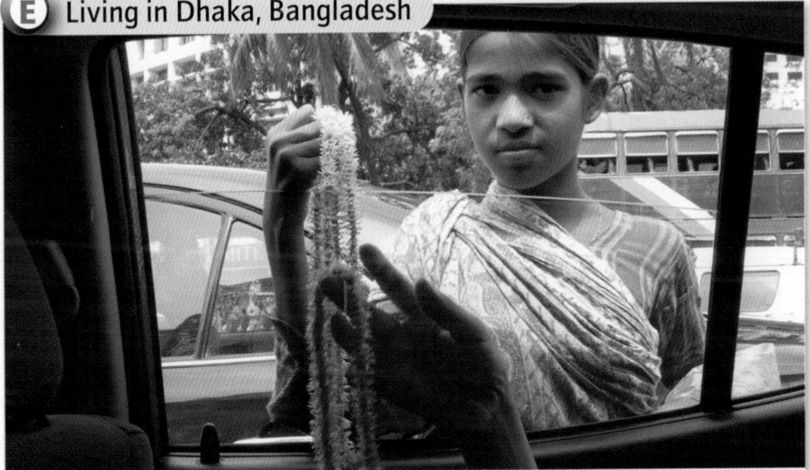

This photograph was taken in Dhaka, the capital city of Bangladesh, which is in Stage 3 of the Demographic Transition Model. Nasrin, the girl shown in the photograph, is 10 years old. She has three sisters who are aged 15, 7 and 3, and two brothers aged 12 and 5, and her mother is expecting another baby. The family live in a two-roomed house which they have built themselves. Nasrin went to school until she was 8 years old, but now she spends her days selling home-made necklaces at one of the main road junctions in the city, to earn money to buy food for her family.

Task 5

Read **Source E**. Compare your family and your lifestyle with those of Nasrin. You should write a paragraph and try to identify the main similarities and differences.

CASE STUDY 1a Rapid population growth in Niger

A Where is Niger?

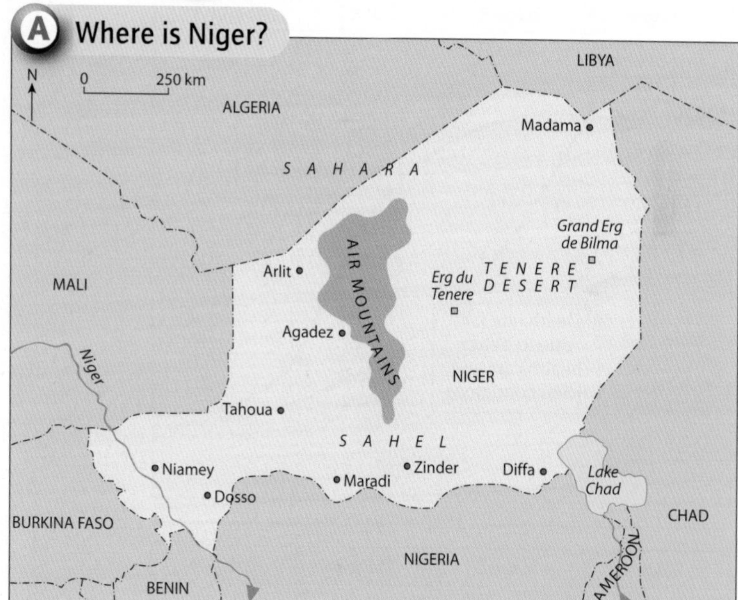

B Niger factfile

Total population	13.3 million
Population growth rate	2.9%
Life expectancy	44.3 years
Literacy	28.7%
GDP per capita	US$ 700
Population below poverty line	63%
Workforce	
• Agriculture	90%
• Industry	6%
• Services	4%

Niger – an LEDC in West Africa

The Republic of Niger is a land-locked country in West Africa, named after the Niger river which flows through the south-west. Its climate is mainly very hot and dry, with many desert areas. It is an LEDC and is one of the poorest countries in the world.

The largest ethnic groups in Niger are the Hausa and Djerma-Songhai, sedentary farmers who live in the southern part of the country. The rest are nomadic or semi-nomadic livestock-raising peoples – Fulani, Tuareg, Kanuri, Arabs, and Toubou.

The population of Niger has grown from 1.7 million in 1960 to over 13 million in 2008. With a high population growth rate of 2.9% it is expected to reach 56 million by 2050. Niger has the highest fertility rate in the world (7.1 births per woman). This means that nearly half of the population is under 15 years old.

Task 1

Study **Source A**.

Describe the size and location of Niger. Refer to distance and direction.

Task 2

a Make a copy of **Source B**. Draw an extra column and fill this in with information about the country in which you are living. For any country this information can be found at: www.cia.gov/library/publications/the-world-factbook/

b Use the information about Niger and your own country to write a paragraph to show that Niger is one of the poorest countries in the world.

Task 3

Study **Source C**.

a Draw a graph to show the birth and death rates of Niger between 2000 and 2008. Use different coloured lines for each of the birth and death rates and shade in the area in between them that represents the natural population growth.

b Choose the correct words or phrases to complete the four sentences below about Niger:

- Birth rates and death rates *increased/decreased* between 2000 and 2008.
- Birth rates between 2000 and 2008 were always *higher/lower* than death rates.
- Natural population growth in 2008 was *20.2/28.4/29.3* per 1000 people.
- This was *higher/lower* in 2008 than it was in 2000.

C Birth and death rates in Niger

Year	Birth rate (per 1000 people)	Death rate (per 1000 people)
2000	51.5	23.1
2001	50.7	22.7
2002	49.9	22.3
2003	49.5	21.7
2004	48.3	21.3
2005	51.3	21.2
2006	50.7	20.9
2007	50.2	20.6
2008	49.6	20.3

Falling death rates

Over the past 100 years death rates have been falling in many parts of the world.

There are now lower death rates because:

- babies are inoculated against diseases
- there are better supplies of clean water
- people eat a better diet
- there are more clinics and hospitals
- there is better health education
- people enjoy better living conditions
- women are becoming better educated.

NIGER: POPULATION EXPLOSION THREATENS DEVELOPMENT GAINS

If the people of Niger remain uninformed about family planning and keep reproducing at the current rate, the country's population will more than quadruple by 2050, according to research by Niger's national statistics agency. Niger's population will make it impossible for the government to provide adequate health, education, jobs and water – tasks that it is already finding difficult, with a fraction of the population.

'We surveyed the country and found that the average number of children per mother is 7.1. However, we also asked them how many they would like to have – women said 9 and men said 12, but some families said they would like 40 or 50 children,' said Adamou Soumana. For poor families children are a source of wealth. They work on the land, go into the towns to earn money and look after their parents when they are old.

Just 5% of the people of Niger use family planning and contraception. 'People aren't informed enough about the negative consequences of having so many children,' Soumana added.

An action plan

GOVERNMENT ACTION PLAN

Niger's government has put in place a plan to slow down population growth.

The government wants the number using family planning to increase from 5 to 20% by 2015. The plan also calls for information campaigns to educate religious leaders and especially women about the availability and importance of family planning. It proposes that the number of early marriages be cut. Many girls in Niger marry before the age of 15. Raising the marriage age to 18 would take up to four years off a woman's reproductive life.

Task 4

Working in groups, discuss the reasons why death rates have been reduced in many countries. Put the reasons in order of importance and explain your group's order to the rest of the class.

Task 5

Study **Source D**.

Draw a spider diagram to show reasons why birth rates are still high in Niger. To do this:

a Draw a circle in the middle of your page. Write in it 'Why birth rates are high in Niger.'
b Draw lines radiating from the circle.
c Write a reason at the end of each line.

Task 6

Study **Source E**.

a The government of Niger has an action plan to slow down population growth. Design a poster that shows how it is attempting to do this.
b Explain why it will be difficult to persuade people in Niger to have smaller families.

What is happening to Russia's population?

Source A shows Russia and the other countries which, up to 1991, used to form the Union of Soviet Socialist Republics (USSR). Russia's population is likely to decline from 143 million in 2007 to 111 million in 2050. The main causes of this are a high death rate, low birth rate and a low level of immigration. Alcohol-related deaths in Russia are very high and life expectancy is low. Russian women, who are highly educated, do not want large numbers of children. Immigration into Russia is low, and many emigrants are moving away from Russia, particularly to Western Europe to look for a better lifestyle.

A Birth and death rates in the former USSR

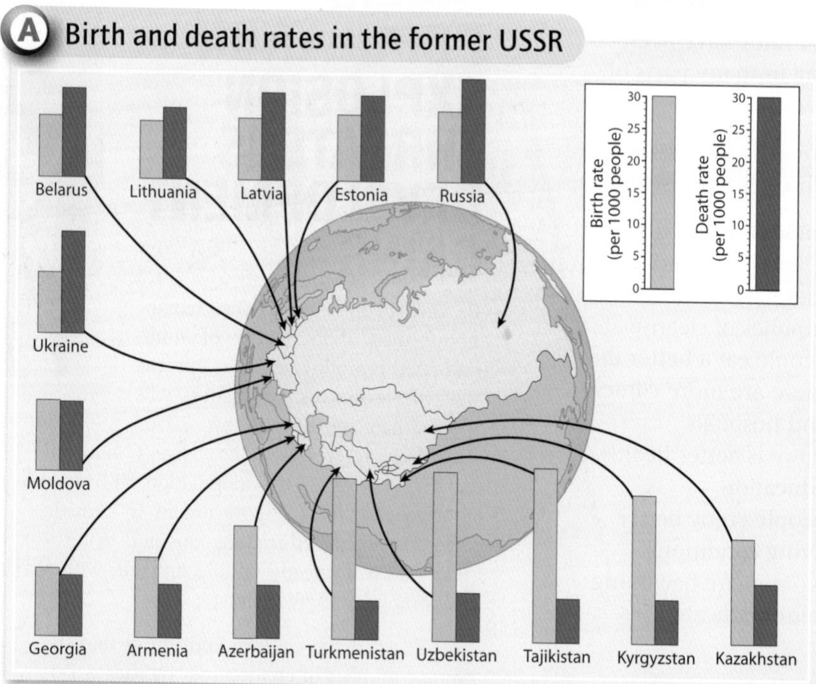

B Russia's population

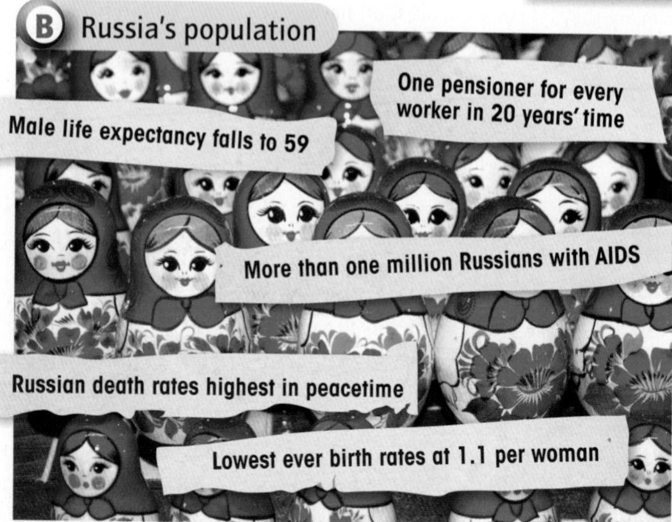

One pensioner for every worker in 20 years' time
Male life expectancy falls to 59
More than one million Russians with AIDS
Russian death rates highest in peacetime
Lowest ever birth rates at 1.1 per woman

C Russian birth and death rates

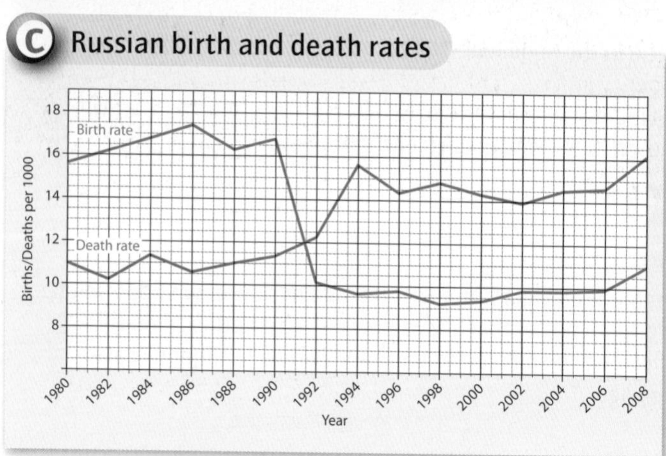

Task 1

Study **Source A**.

a Name the country shown on the map with the highest rate of natural population growth.
b Work out the population decline of Russia per 1000 people.
c Name **three** other countries shown on the map that are experiencing population decline.

Task 2

Study **Source C**.

a Describe how birth rates and death rates changed in Russia between 1980 and 2008.
b Identify the years when the total population:
- increased
- remained the same
- decreased.

Task 3

Match the following beginnings and endings of sentences to complete **three** sentences which explain why Russia's population is now declining.

Death rates are high …	… because Russian women prefer to have a career rather than large numbers of children.
Birth rates are low …	… as more people move out of Russia than into the country.
Population is lost through migration …	… because of high levels of alcoholism, heart disease and accidents.

D Population graphs for the G8 countries

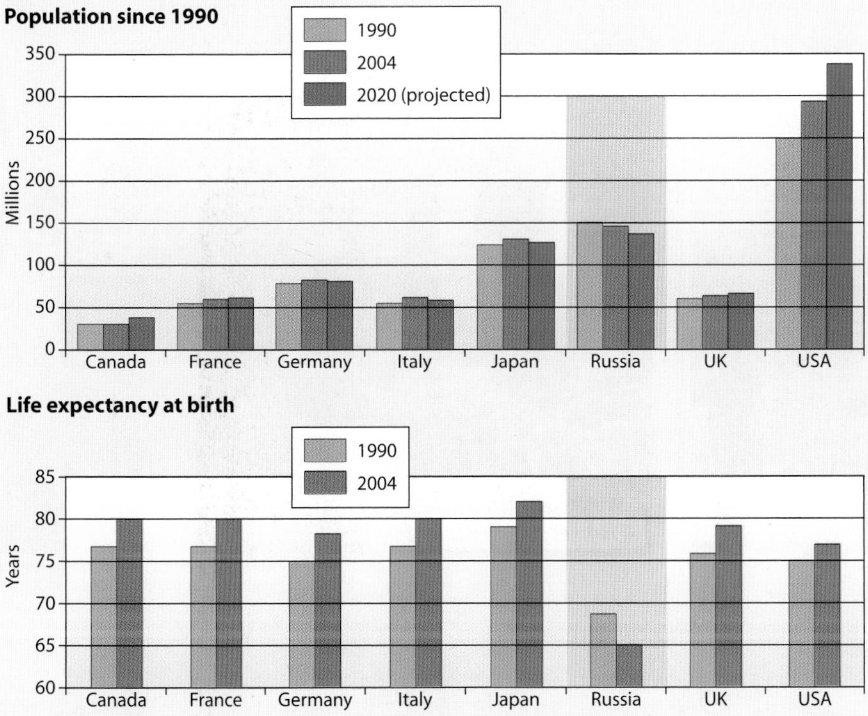

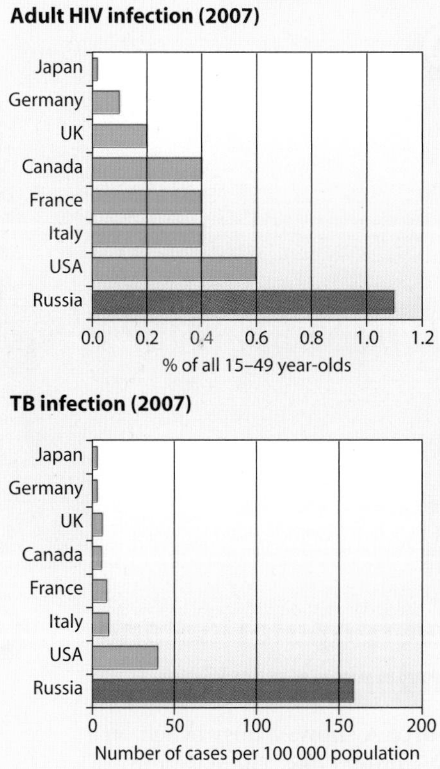

Population since 1990

1990
2004
2020 (projected)

Millions: 0, 50, 100, 150, 200, 250, 300, 350

Canada, France, Germany, Italy, Japan, Russia, UK, USA

Adult HIV infection (2007)

Japan, Germany, UK, Canada, France, Italy, USA, Russia

0.0, 0.2, 0.4, 0.6, 0.8, 1.0, 1.2

% of all 15–49 year-olds

Life expectancy at birth

1990
2004

Years: 60, 65, 70, 75, 80, 85

Canada, France, Germany, Italy, Japan, Russia, UK, USA

TB infection (2007)

Japan, Germany, UK, Canada, France, Italy, USA, Russia

0, 50, 100, 150, 200

Number of cases per 100 000 population

Russia is one of the G8 countries – of the world's most powerful nations.

Task 4

Study **Sources B and D.**

a Use **Source D** to identify the main differences between Russia and the other G8 countries. Use figures and examples in your answer.

b Use **Source B** to suggest reasons for these differences.

Task 5

Study **Source E.**

A Russian couple are trying to decide whether to have a second child. Write a conversation between them which includes information about the advantages and problems of having another child.

E Cash for more babies!

A second baby? Russia's mothers aren't persuaded

19 May 2006

President Vladimir Putin last week promised to spend some of the country's oil profits on efforts to solve the population problem. He ordered parliament to more than double monthly child support payments to 1500 roubles (about US$55) and added that women who choose to have a second baby will receive 250,000 roubles (US$9200); a very large amount in a country where average monthly incomes are close to US$330.

On Monday, young women at the Family Planning Youth Centre in Moscow said they liked the sound of more money, but suggested that Mr Putin has no idea about their lives. 'A child is not an easy project, and in this world a woman is expected to get an education, find a job, and make a career,' says Svetlana Romanicheva, a student who says she won't consider having a baby for at least five years.

Others say Putin is right. 'Russian women typically have one child ... but many of my patients would like a second if they felt they had enough support,' says Galina Dedova, a doctor at Happy Families, a private Moscow clinic. 'Most of my patients count their roubles ... If they could get more money, some might have more children.'

Sample case study question

For a country that you have studied, explain why it has a high rate of natural population growth.

TOPIC 2 Too many or too few?

A

A beach in Mumbai, India

B

A market stall in Rome, Italy

Overpopulation and underpopulation

Source A shows a busy beach on a hot summer day. There isn't much space for people to lie on the sand to enjoy the sunshine or to play football and cricket, and for those who want to cool down in the sea there isn't even much space there. There are too many people on the beach for the families to enjoy it – the beach is overpopulated. The sellers of ice creams and cold drinks are happy though!

Source B shows a market place. The stalls have lots of produce to sell but where are all the customers? People certainly have plenty of space to browse around but there are not enough people for the stallholders to make a living – the market is underpopulated.

C Population and resources

RICE OIL COAL

Overpopulation

RICE OIL COAL
RICE OIL COAL

Optimum population

OIL
RICE OIL COAL
RICE OIL COAL

Underpopulation

Task 1

Study **Sources A and B**.

a The beach is *overpopulated*. Make a list of the problems this might cause for visitors and the people who live and work in the resort.

b The market is *underpopulated*. Why is this a problem?

c Look at the photo on page 3. Describe how the 'population' might change during the day. Refer to *overpopulation* and *underpopulation*

Task 2

Study **Source C**.

Use the diagrams to explain what is meant by:

- optimum population
- overpopulation
- underpopulation.

What is overpopulation?

If the number of people living in an area is greater than the resources available to support that population, it is overpopulated. A large population in a country does not mean that it is overpopulated. For example, there are many people living in Germany but it has enough resources to support its population. However, some rural communities in parts of Africa are overpopulated. This isn't because they are crowded with people but because there are not enough resources to support the population living there.

What is underpopulation?

If the number of people living in an area is less than is needed to make full use of the resources available, then the area can be described as underpopulated. For example, Australia has many resources but it is not using them fully. The country could support a higher population, which means that it is underpopulated.

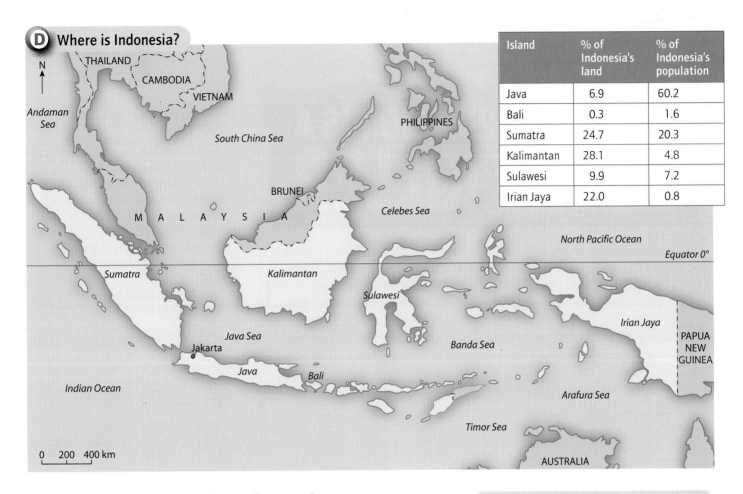

D Where is Indonesia?

Island	% of Indonesia's land	% of Indonesia's population
Java	6.9	60.2
Bali	0.3	1.6
Sumatra	24.7	20.3
Kalimantan	28.1	4.8
Sulawesi	9.9	7.2
Irian Jaya	22.0	0.8

N
THAILAND
CAMBODIA
VIETNAM
Andaman Sea
South China Sea
PHILIPPINES
BRUNEI
M A L A Y S I A
Celebes Sea
North Pacific Ocean
Equator 0°
Sumatra
Kalimantan
Sulawesi
Irian Jaya
Java Sea
Jakarta
Banda Sea
PAPUA NEW GUINEA
Java
Bali
Indian Ocean
Arafura Sea
Timor Sea
AUSTRALIA
0 200 400 km

Indonesia's Transmigration Scheme

Indonesia is a country which consists of over 17 000 islands, about 9000 of which are inhabited. On some islands many people are crowded into a relatively small area, whilst other inhabited islands are underpopulated. During the late 20th century the Indonesian government gave people incentives to move from the overpopulated islands of Java and Bali to the islands of Irian Jaya, Kalimantan, Sumatra and Sulawesi. The purpose of this transmigration was to:

- reduce the poverty and overpopulation on Java
- provide opportunities for hard-working poor people
- provide a workforce to make better use of the natural resources of the underpopulated outer islands.

Task 3

Study **Source D**.

a Draw a graph using the statistics about the percentage of population and area of the six Indonesian islands.

b What does the graph show about the imbalance between population and land in Indonesia?

E Problems in Jakarta, Java

Task 4

Study **Source E**.

a Java is overpopulated. Use evidence from the photograph to list the problems this may cause in cities like Jakarta.

b Rural parts of Java are also overpopulated. What problems could overpopulation cause in rural areas?

Task 5

Imagine you are an unemployed person living in Jakarta with a young family.

With a partner, discuss the advantages and disadvantages to you and your family of migrating to Kalimantan as part of the government's Transmigration Scheme.

You may want to carry out some research about transmigration in Indonesia, and the island of Kalimantan, to help you answer the question.

Overpopulation in Nigeria

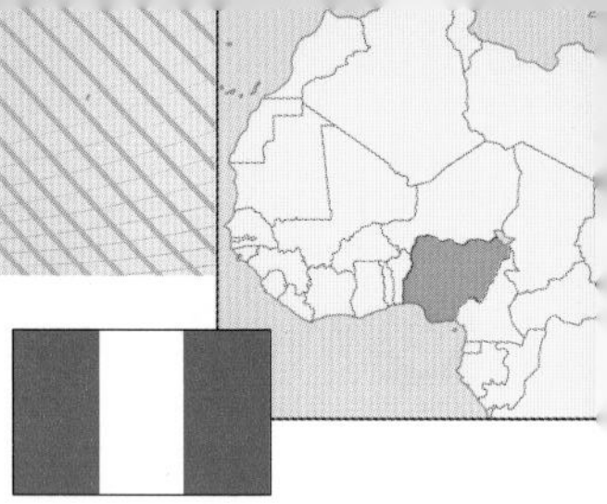

A

NIGERIA'S POPULATION IS A SILENT KILLER

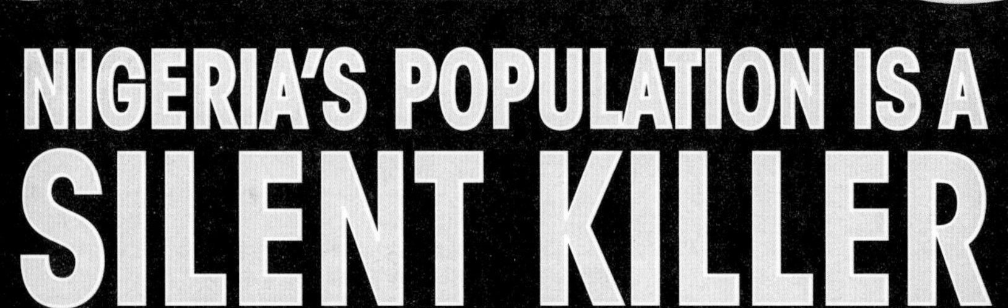

Nigeria has a population of 140 million people with over 70% living on less than one dollar a day. It occupies only 3% of Africa but has 15% of its people. Overpopulation means depletion of natural resources, increased levels of air and water pollution, and lack of essential services such as health care and education. Overcrowding has resulted in increased disease levels, inadequate sanitation and scarcity of resources for medical care and education. Desperation to survive has increased the crime rate and the country now experiences serious over-congestion of public transport, roads and bridges.

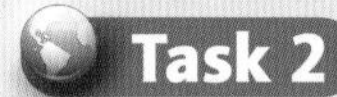

Task 1

Study **Source A**.

a Using your own words, write **two** sentences using Nigeria's population statistics to show that the country is overpopulated.

b Define the following terms:
- depletion of natural resources
- lack of essential services
- inadequate sanitation.

Task 2

Study **Source B**.

Look at the six problems shown on the spider diagram.

For each problem explain how it can be caused by overpopulation.

B **Problems caused by overpopulation**

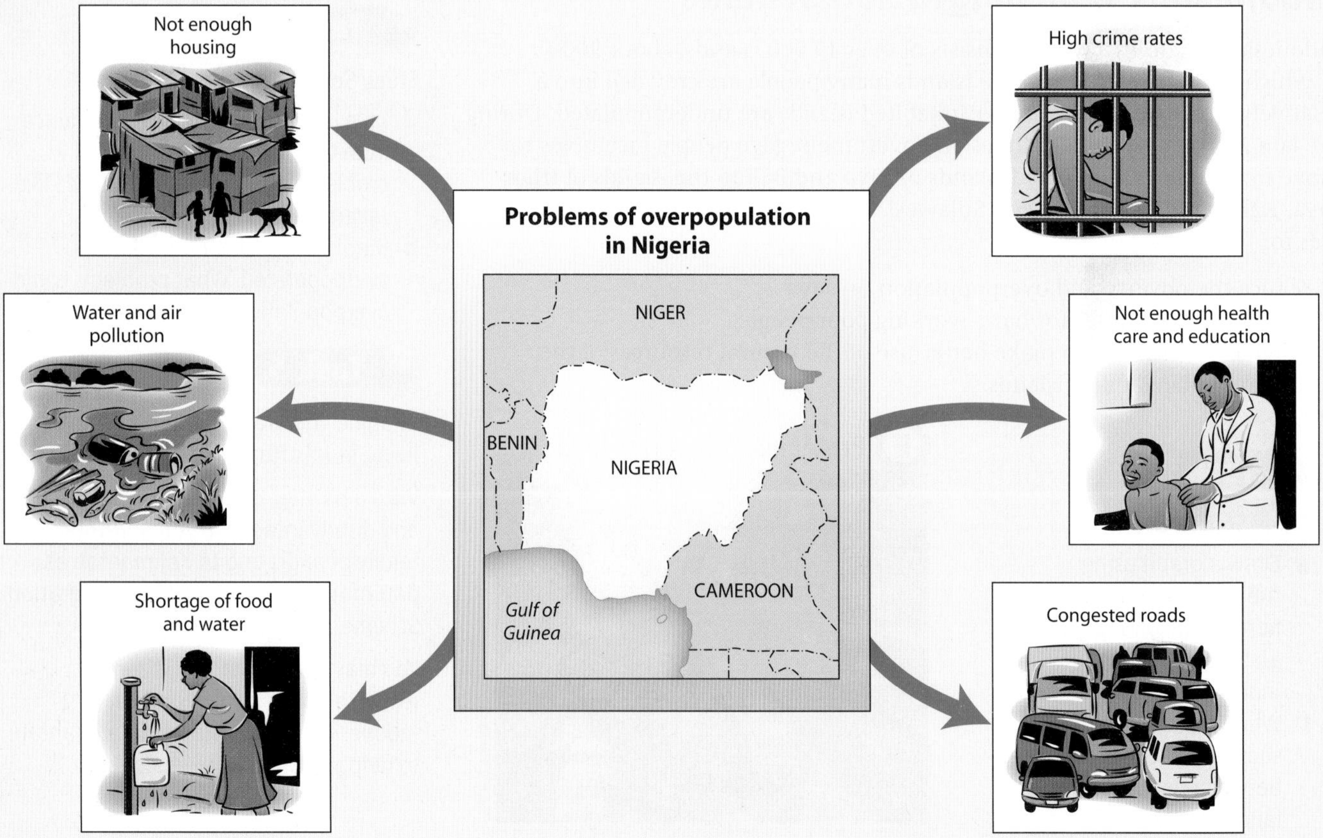

C Education and food supply in selected African countries

Children under 5 who are underweight (%)

0 5 10 15 20 25 30

Nigeria
Ivory Coast
Ghana
Botswana
South Africa
Mali
Egypt
Kenya

50 55 60 65 70 75 80 85 90 95 100

Enrolment at primary school (%)

Study **Source C**.

a What percentage of:
- children attend primary school in Nigeria
- children aged under 5 are underweight in Nigeria?

b Which countries are being described below?
- 79% of children attend primary school and 4% of children are underweight.
- 62% of children attend primary school and 20% of children are underweight.

c What relationship is shown on the graph between the percentage of children who attend primary school and the percentage of children who are underweight?

d What do the statistics on the graph tell you about overpopulation in Nigeria compared with the other seven African countries?

Study **Sources D and E**.

Use the evidence in the photographs and extract to write a short newspaper article about how overpopulation in Nigeria affects the quality of life of its people.

D Life in Lagos, Nigeria

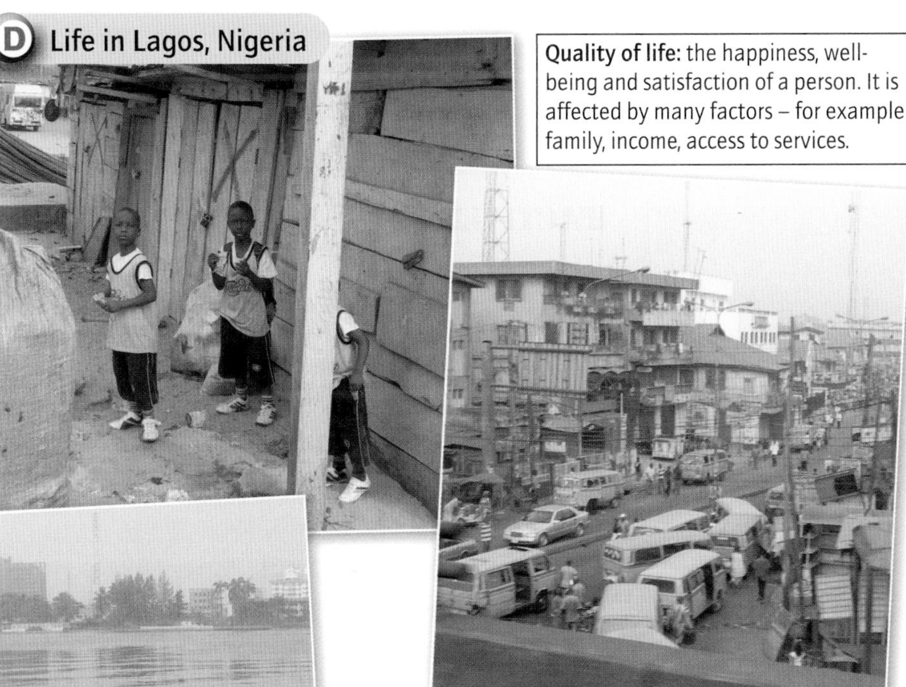

Quality of life: the happiness, well-being and satisfaction of a person. It is affected by many factors – for example family, income, access to services.

E Nigerian elections, April 2007

Nigerian polls bring hope of change in chaotic Lagos

Plagued by crime, residents of Nigeria's sprawling commercial capital Lagos hope that elections will bring change. In the last ten months 273 civilians and 84 policemen have been killed by criminals who have been stealing cars, robbing banks and breaking into homes.

Many of Lagos's 9 million inhabitants live in shanties, with no running water or sanitation, beneath the skyscrapers of some of Africa's biggest firms.

'We have no running water and the power cuts are getting worse. I want things to change,' said Osita Mgbafule, 30, a trader, standing by an open sewer close to a polling station in the Surulere district. Despite record oil prices which have helped to pay off most of Nigeria's foreign debt, the overpopulated West African nation of 140 million people is suffering the worst electricity crisis in decades, while education and transport are shambolic.

CASE STUDY

2b Underpopulation in Australia

A Australia

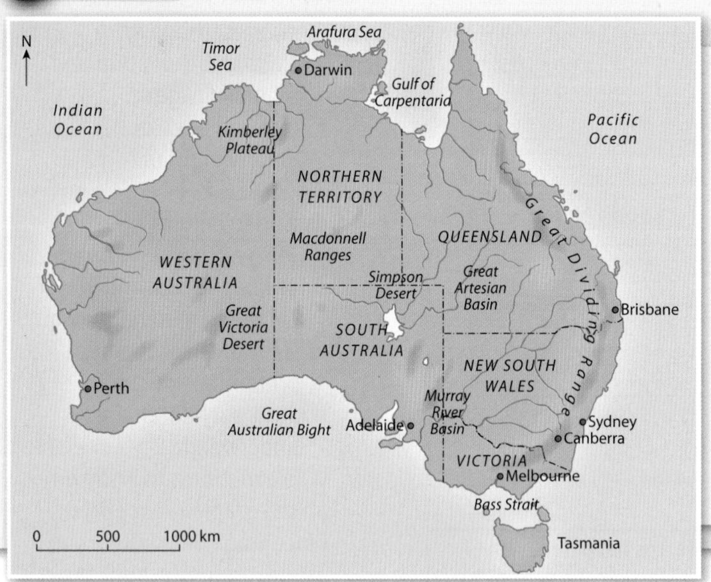

FACTFILE AUSTRALIA

Area: 7 686 850 km²

Population: 20 600 856

Main agricultural products: wheat, barley, sugarcane, fruits; cattle, sheep, poultry

Main industries: mining, industrial and transportation equipment, food processing, chemicals, steel

Oil production: 572 400 billion barrels/day

Natural gas production: 38.62 billion m³

Value of exports: US$141.7 billion

B USA

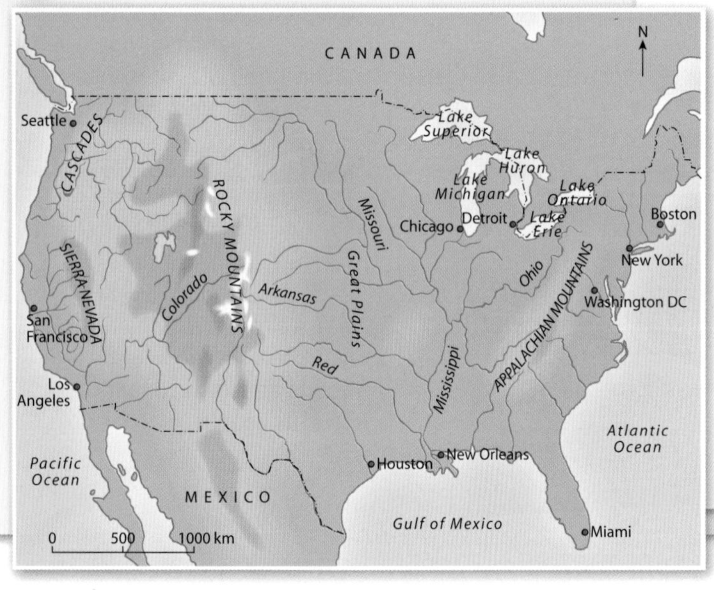

FACTFILE USA

Area: 9 826 630 km²

Population: 303 824 646

Main agricultural products: wheat, corn, other grains, fruits, vegetables, cotton; beef, pork, poultry, dairy products; fish; forest products

Main industries: petroleum, steel, motor vehicles, aerospace, telecommunications, chemicals, electronics, food processing, consumer goods, timber, mining

Oil production: 8.322 million billion barrels/day

Natural gas production: 490.8 billion m³

Value of exports: US$1.149 trillion

Underpopulated Australia

The USA and Australia are not very different in size, but the USA has over 300 million people and Australia only 20 million. Many areas of Australia are empty and the resources are not being used fully. The country could support a higher population. This means that Australia is underpopulated. Indeed, successive Australian governments have tried to increase its population, to develop the country economically and to protect it from foreign influence. From only 3.7 million in 1901, the population has increased to its current 20 million.

Task 1

Study **Sources A and B**.

Use the evidence in the maps and factfiles to explain why Australia can be considered to be underpopulated compared with the USA.

C Underpopulated Australia?

We're in a drought, so to invite more people to share in the limited water supply on the driest continent on Earth doesn't make much sense.
Give benefits to people having children and the benefits should increase depending on the number of children.
Who says Australia is underpopulated? Sure, it's a whole continent but most of it's desert where no one wants to live. And there's not all that much land for farming.

Australia is a beautiful country, and one of its great attractions is that there are so many wide open spaces, and so few people in them. I would hate Australia to become like China or the USA! We already have heaps of people here from other countries who can't speak English, and this causes problems in many areas.

How should Australia solve its underpopulation problem? By relaxing the visa rules so that more immigrants can get citizenship, and by expanding the economy. If the economy is prosperous more people will move here for job opportunities.

Task 2

Study **Source C.**

a Identify **three** methods which could be used to solve the underpopulation problem in Australia.

b Identify **three** problems which may be caused if more people are encouraged to migrate to Australia.

c Explain why some people think that Australia is not underpopulated.

Sample case study question

Explain how underpopulation has caused problems in a country or area you have studied.

Planning for population change

The rapid growth in the world's population has been called a population explosion. Over the past 150 years improvements in health care and sanitation around the world have caused a fall in death rates. While birth rates have fallen in **MEDCs**, they are still high in LEDCs. So, overall, there are more people being born and more are living longer.

Task 1

Study **Source A**.

a Why do some governments carry out a census?

b Why is it difficult to compare the census data from different countries?

c Give **three** reasons why census data might be unreliable.

d Do you have censuses in your country? When was the last census? When is the next census?

A Counting the people

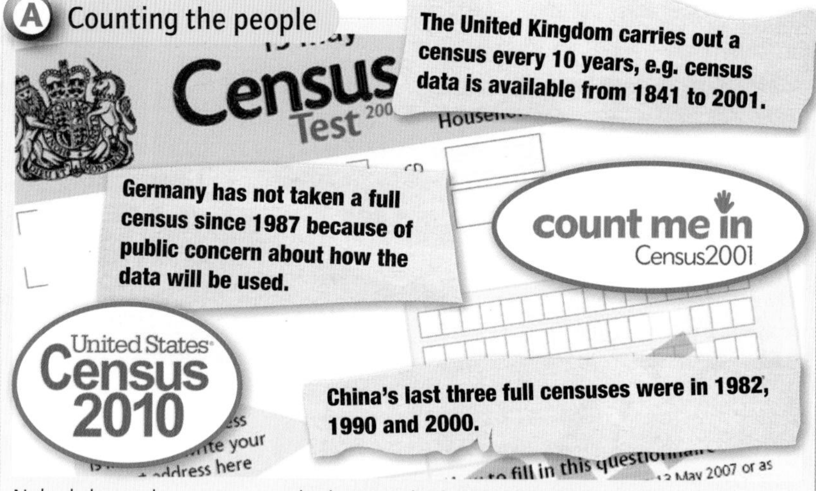

Census
Test
The United Kingdom carries out a census every 10 years, e.g. census data is available from 1841 to 2001.
Germany has not taken a full census since 1987 because of public concern about how the data will be used.
count me in
Census2001
United States
Census
2010
China's last three full censuses were in 1982, 1990 and 2000.

Nobody knows how many people there are in the world. Censuses take place at different times. Some countries cannot afford censuses. Country boundaries change, so census data cannot be compared. People do not always complete the forms. Even in MEDCs it can take over a year for the data to be published, by which time it is already out of date! So a world population figure is an estimate – but we do know it is growing.

B Age varies across the world

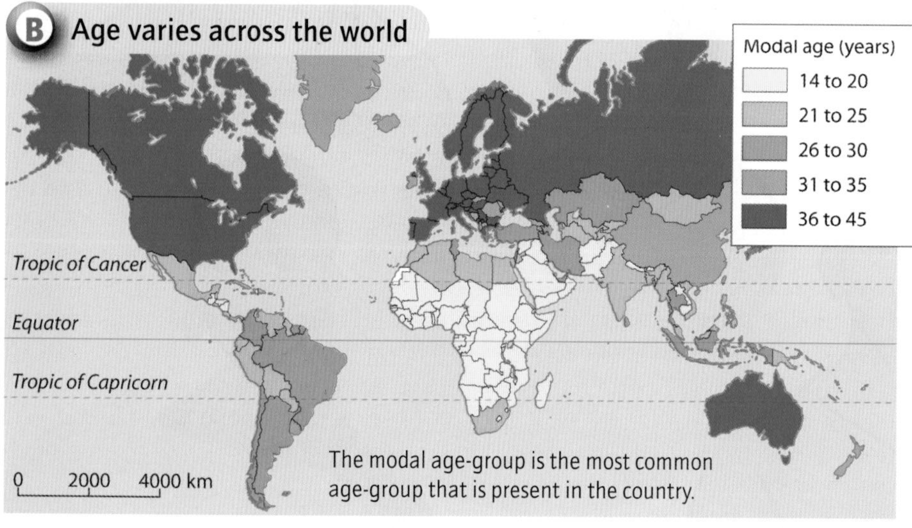

The modal age-group is the most common age-group that is present in the country.

Task 2

Study **Source B**.

a Describe and compare the modal age-groups in MEDCs and LEDCs.

b Name a country with a high modal age-group and a country with a low modal age-group. Use an atlas to help you.

c Suggest different problems that these age groups may present to governments.

Task 3

Study **Source C**.

a Which **two** MEDCs will have the highest percentage of population over 65 in 2025? Suggest **two** problems this will cause for each government.

b Name **two** LEDCs from the graph. What difficulties will they have in caring for their elderly population in the next few years?

C More old people in future

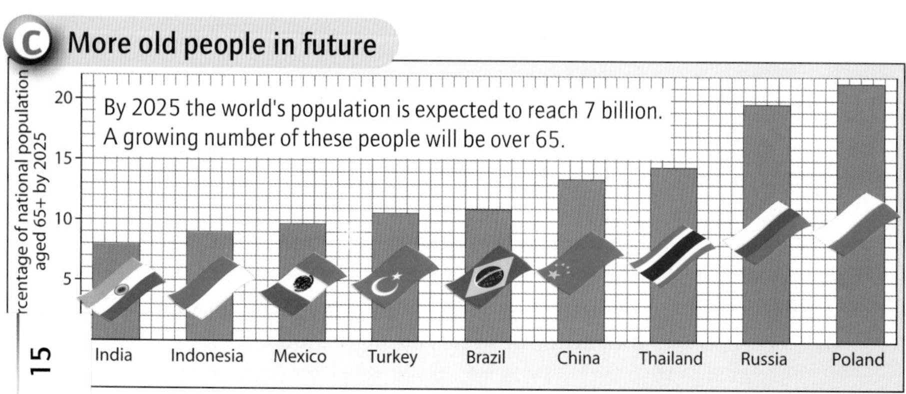

By 2025 the world's population is expected to reach 7 billion. A growing number of these people will be over 65.

Population structure

Demography is the study of people or populations. Population pyramids are very useful for demographers. They are created from census data. The population structure can be clearly shown as a population pyramid.

Governments can identify where there may be population issues that need policies and money to resolve them. Perhaps too many babies are being born and the birth rate needs reducing; or it could be the opposite. Maybe there are not going to be enough workers – so one answer may be to encourage immigration. If there are going to be many old people in ten years' time, their care needs planning for.

D Population pyramids

Daily exercise at Dujiangyan School, Sichuan, China

Secondary schools in China can still have up to 10 000 pupils in them despite a reduction in birth rates.

Features of a population pyramid

Population pyramids can give you information about three different groups of people.

- The youngest age group of 0–15 are dependants as they are usually of school age and depend on others for resources.
- The 15–64 age group are usually working and young and elderly groups are dependent on them. They provide resources that the other groups depend on.
- The elderly group from 65 upwards are dependants as they are not usually in work.

An LEDC population pyramid

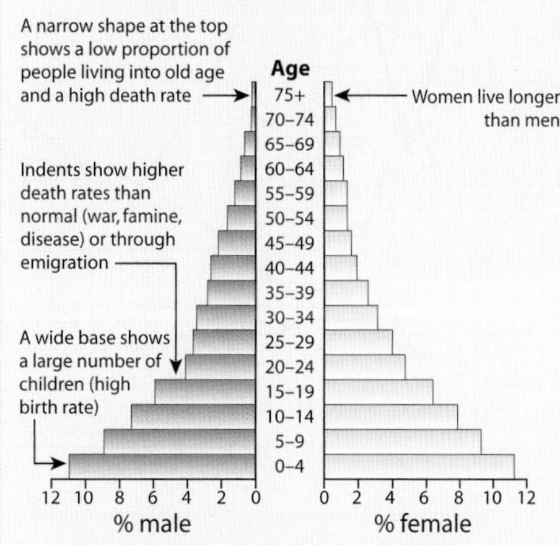

An MEDC population pyramid

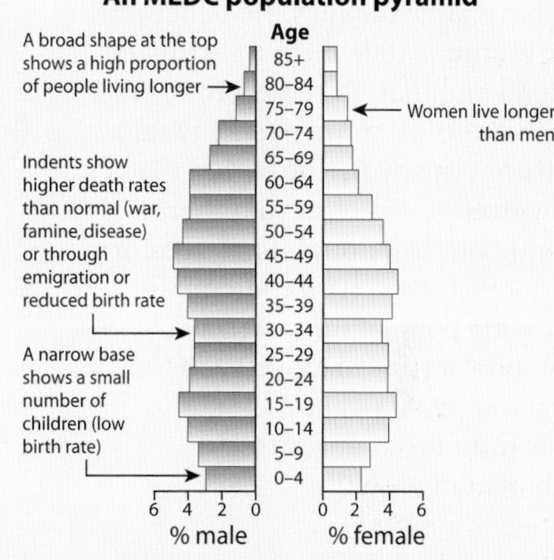

Some causes of different population structures in LEDCs and MEDCs

Typical of LEDCS – expanding	Typical of MEDCs – reducing
High death rate	Low death rate
High birth rate	Low birth rate
Low life expectancy	High life expectancy

Task 4

Study **Source D**.

a List **three** differences in the shape and structure of the two population pyramids.

b How do the issues facing the government of the LEDC pyramid differ from those illustrated on the MEDC pyramid?

E Controlling population

China 2000

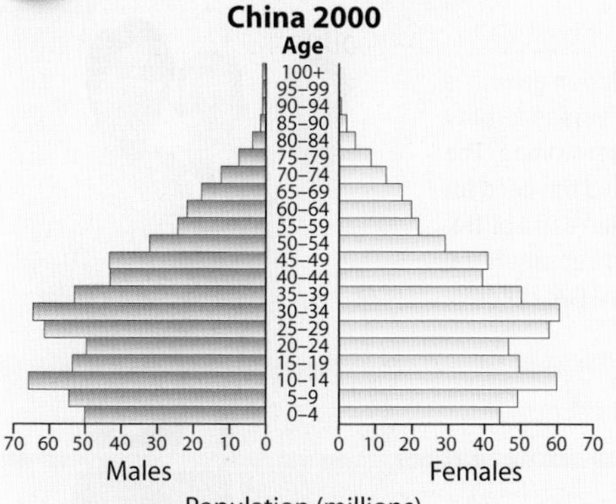

China is a country that has controlled its population growth by limiting most parents to one child only. This policy was introduced in 1980.

Task 5

Study **Source E**.

a Describe the pattern of the China 2000 pyramid from ages 30 to 94. Why was China becoming very concerned about birth rates in the 1970s?

b What evidence is there of a declining birth rate from 1970? Suggest a year when the 'one-child' policy might have been relaxed.

c Look at the China 2025 pyramid. Does the one-child policy appear to have been successful? What other issues will China's government face?

China 2025

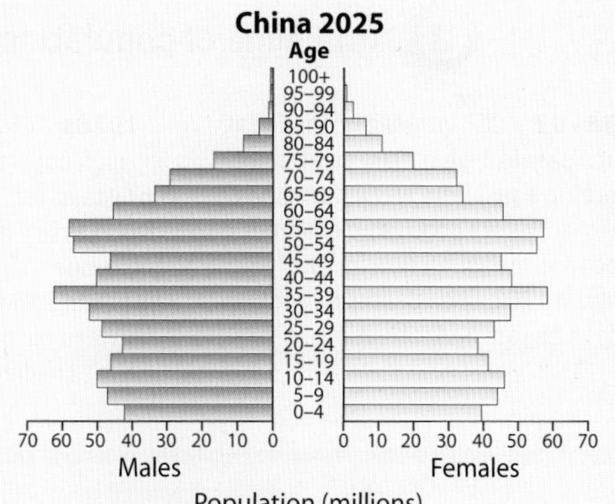

Task 6

Imagine you were asked to carry out a census of your school. Discuss in groups how you would do this.

Reducing population in China

The population problem

Since 1949 the Chinese Communist Party (CCP) has ruled China. Until the early 1970s the CCP showed little interest in controlling population growth. Indeed between 1960 and 1970 the Chinese leader, Mao Zedong, encouraged his people to have large families. He believed that more people meant a stronger China and that, in the event of war with the USA, more people would ensure victory. By the early 1970s, however, it was clear that there would not be enough food, jobs or services to cope with the rapidly growing population. A drastic solution was needed. In 1980 the first one-child policy was introduced to control population growth.

A Demographic transition in China, 1950–2020

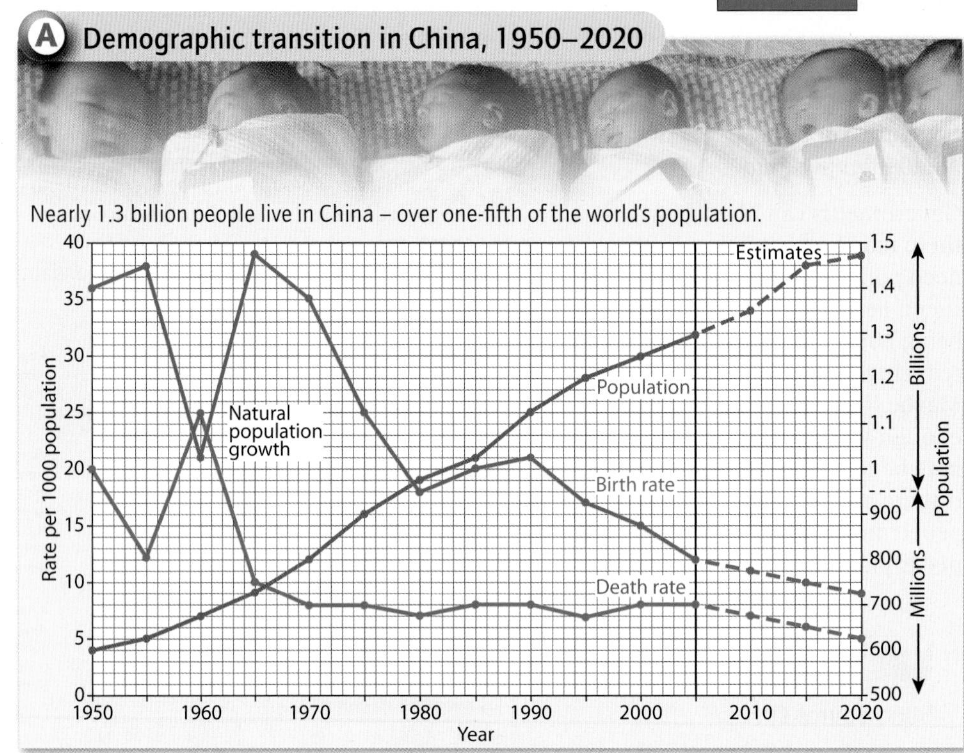

Task 1

Study **Source A**.

- **a** State the birth rate, death rate and natural population change for 1965.
- **b** How had these changed by 2005? Use data in your answer.
- **c** How did China's population change between 1950 and 2005? How might it change between 2005 and 2020?

Task 2

Study **Sources A and B**.

- **a** Describe the changes in population 1959 to 1961.
- **b** Suggest reasons for these changes.
- **c** Give **three** reasons why the CCP encouraged large families after 1963.
- **d** What did the 'Later, Longer, Fewer' policy aim to do?

B A timeline of population 'events'

1950s No major influence by CCP ruling party on population.

1958–63 CCP introduces 'The Great Leap Forward' 5-year plan: an attempt to reform agriculture and industry, but the changes are poorly implemented. Floods and drought follow in 1959–62, causing 20 million deaths through disease and starvation.

1963–70 Government encourages large families to make China stronger. Average fertility in 1963 is 5.8 children per woman. In 1965 birth rate reaches almost 40 per 1000.

1970s China realises that high population growth is unsustainable. The 'Later, Longer, Fewer' policy is introduced. This encourages parents to delay their first child, allow a longer interval between births and have fewer children in total.

1978–83 'One family, one child' policy emerges. Rapid population growth seen as barrier to development. China wants to modernise four key areas: industry, agriculture, defence, science and technology.

1984–2006 Population growth is reduced from 2.4% to 1%. Average fertility in 2006 down to 1.7 children per woman. The one-child policy has precluded the need for China to cope with 300 million extra births. Some relaxing of policy in 21st century. Rural families may have two children.

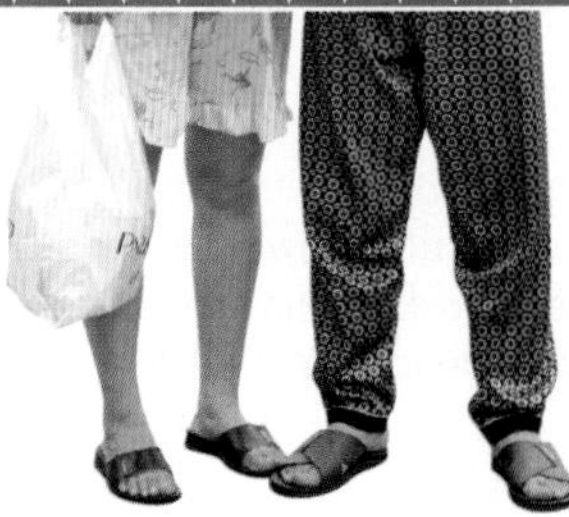

Consequences of the 'One family, one child' policy

China has the world's biggest national population, with 1.3 billion people. But the population is not balanced. There are about 86 girls to every 100 boys in China. The desire for a boy is part of Chinese culture. The belief that only a son can carry on the family line and lead proper ceremonies of remembrance of ancestors dates back thousands of years. In rural areas boys are also preferred for farm work and looking after their ageing parents.

C Where are the girls?

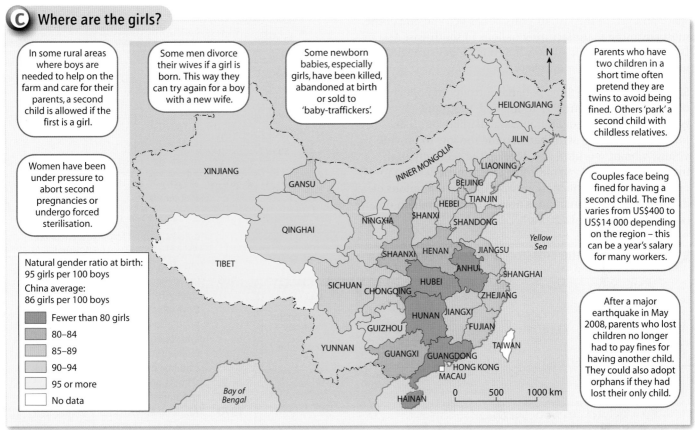

In some rural areas where boys are needed to help on the farm and care for their parents, a second child is allowed if the first is a girl.

Some men divorce their wives if a girl is born. This way they can try again for a boy with a new wife.

Some newborn babies, especially girls, have been killed, abandoned at birth or sold to 'baby-traffickers'.

Parents who have two children in a short time often pretend they are twins to avoid being fined. Others 'park' a second child with childless relatives.

Women have been under pressure to abort second pregnancies or undergo forced sterilisation.

Couples face being fined for having a second child. The fine varies from US$400 to US$14 000 depending on the region – this can be a year's salary for many workers.

After a major earthquake in May 2008, parents who lost children no longer had to pay fines for having another child. They could also adopt orphans if they had lost their only child.

Natural gender ratio at birth: 95 girls per 100 boys
China average: 86 girls per 100 boys

- Fewer than 80 girls
- 80–84
- 85–89
- 90–94
- 95 or more
- No data

HEILONGJIANG, JILIN, LIAONING, INNER MONGOLIA, BEIJING, TIANJIN, HEBEI, XINJIANG, GANSU, NINGXIA, SHANXI, SHANDONG, QINGHAI, TIBET, SHAANXI, HENAN, JIANGSU, ANHUI, SHANGHAI, SICHUAN, CHONGQING, HUBEI, ZHEJIANG, HUNAN, JIANGXI, GUIZHOU, FUJIAN, YUNNAN, GUANGXI, GUANGDONG, TAIWAN, HONG KONG, MACAU, HAINAN, Yellow Sea, Bay of Bengal, N, 0, 500, 1000 km

D China's population by age-group (est. millions)

Age	1950	1995	2010	2025	2050
50+	87	209	332	526	631
20–49	228	594	665	597	529
5–19	165	320	290	278	247
0–4	76	103	93	86	78
Total	556	1226	1380	1487	1485

Task 3

Study **Source C**.

a Name **one** province with:
- fewer than 80 girls per 100 boys
- more than 90 girls per 100 boys.

b How does the distribution of provinces with the fewest girls compare with those with the most girls?

c The areas with the most girls are often rural farming areas. What problems might this cause for farming traditions in China?

Task 4

Study **Source D**.

a Draw a graph to represent this data.

b By how much is it estimated that population will grow between 1950 and 2050? Is there evidence that the population will achieve stability?

c What is expected to happen to the 0–4 and the 50+ age-groups over this period?

d Suggest problems that China's rulers will face in 2050 if these estimates are correct. How could these be overcome?

Task 5

Write down **three** statements that support the 'One family, one child' policy, and **three** that are against it as a way of controlling population. What do you think? Justify your answer.

CASE STUDY 3b

Increasing population in Singapore

Singapore: one island, many people

Once a British colony, Singapore has been an independent city state since 1965. It has limited natural resources and space and yet, in the last 40 years, it has become one of the most advanced manufacturing nations in south-east Asia. Despite this economic success the country has struggled to manage its population numbers.

Since independence Singapore has introduced population control policies. From 1957 to the mid-1980s the government tried to discourage large families but then found population growth had become too low to provide a young, vibrant workforce to develop the economy of the future. In a reversal of policy the government decided to encourage rapid population growth. Despite limitations of living space, the population is now almost 4.7 million on an island with an area of 620 km².

A Singapore – the crossroads of south-east Asia

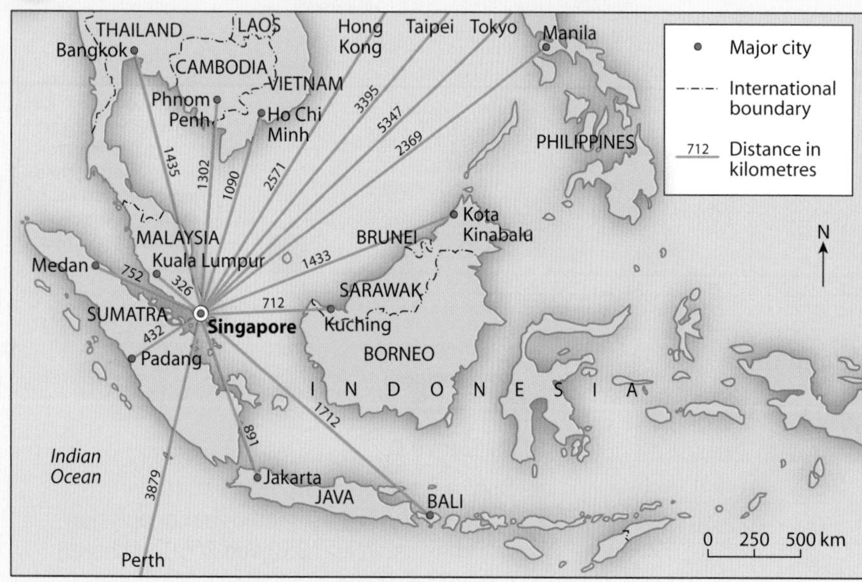

B Population change in Singapore, 1901–2000

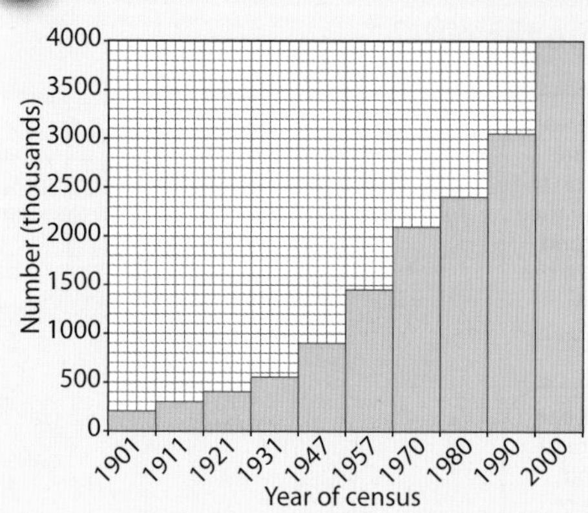

1957 Population of 1.47 million but growing quickly. Annual fertility rate (children per woman) peaks at 6.4. Family planning offered in 1959.

1965 Independence – no longer a British colony. Fertility rate down to 4.8. Government wanted to reduce population as large numbers of children and young people are seen as a threat to living standards and political stability: there would not be enough schools, hospitals and jobs, leading to civil unrest.

1970 Abortion and voluntary sterilisation made legal. The 'Stop at Two" campaign introduced population 'disincentives' such as:

- extra taxes for a 3rd child
- no paid maternity leave for 3rd child
- parents with more than 2 children could not enrol in best schools.

Successful policies reduced fertility rate to less than 2 by 1980s.

C Population pyramid, 2000

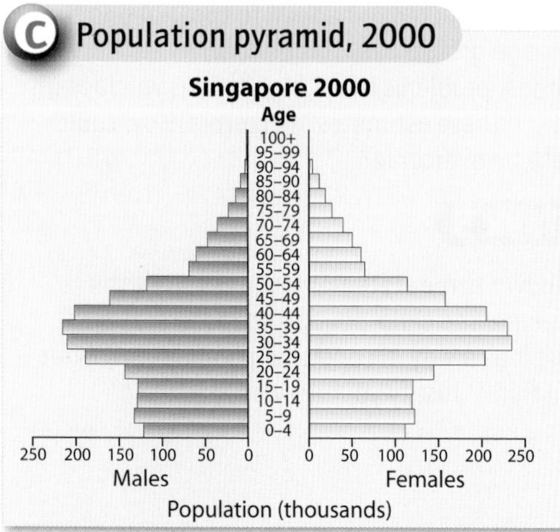

Task 1

Study **Source A**.

a Describe the location of Singapore. Why is it called 'the crossroads of Asia'?

b Calculate the average number of people per square kilometre in Singapore.

c Suggest **three** problems that an increasing population might cause for the island.

Task 2

Study **Source B**.

a What is unusual about the year interval on the horizontal axis? Explain this.

b Describe how population changed between 1901 and 2000.

c Give **two** examples of policies used in the 'Stop at Two' campaign.

Increasing the population

By the 1980s the low rate of population growth was causing the government some concern. Also, the most educated citizens were having fewer children. In 1983 Prime Minister Lee Yuan Kew expressed his concern that male university graduates preferred less well educated wives, so female graduates were not getting married and bearing children. In the mid-1980s Singapore completely reversed its population policies. Not only did it actively pursue policies to increase population through natural growth and immigration. It also developed policies to influence the type of people who had children. In 1984, children of female university graduates were offered places at the best schools, and a grant of 10 000 SGD* was given to less well educated women who agreed to be sterilised after the birth of their second child.

* 1000 Singapore dollars (SGD) = 700 US dollars

Task 3

Study **Source C**.

a How can you tell that policies to reduce the birth rate were in operation after 1965?

b Suggest why the government reversed its policies and encouraged population growth from the mid-1980s.

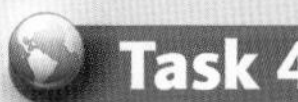

Task 4

Study **Source D**.

a List **three** incentives of the 'Have Three or More' scheme.

b Suggest which income groups this was aimed at. Why?

c What evidence shows that the scheme did not increase birth rates? Suggest why.

d Give **two** reasons why Singapore's population continued to grow.

D Mid-1980s to the 21st century: population too low ...

HAVE THREE OR MORE, IF YOU CAN AFFORD IT

If you have three or more babies, look what you can get.

* Tax rebates for the third child.
* Subsidies for day-care.
* Priority in enrolling at the best schools.
* Priority in gaining housing for large families.
* Extended sick leave.
* Up to 4 years' maternity leave for civil servants.

Contact our counselling service if you are considering abortion or sterilisation.

DON'T PASSIVELY WATCH OURSELVES GO EXTINCT!

Year	Children per woman
1957	6.4
1965	4.8
1975	2.0
1985	1.6
1995	1.7
2005	1.4

Unfortunately, despite all the incentives, the birth rate stayed at its lowest level of 1.4 children per woman in 1987 – far less than needed to maintain the population. Working people wanted more material assets and men and women were keen to pursue careers. Marriages were later too. The government tried other means such as a campaign to promote the joys of marriage and parenthood and a matchmaking agency for those with A levels. It also offered a 20 000 SGD tax rebate for the fourth child. But the birth rate remained low. However, 20 000 people enter Singapore each year to work and the population continues to increase due to the large numbers born before the mid-1980s. The problems facing the government will be a large elderly population to be housed on limited land as well as a small working population supporting a large number of old people.

Demographer at the University of Singapore

E The next 50 years ...

Singapore predicts population will expand to 6.5 million in 40–50 years!

Singapore's land planners are exploring new ways of creating space to accommodate a possible population increase of 40% over the next 40 to 50 years.

Faced with a declining birth rate, Singapore has embarked on an aggressive drive to increase its population. There are incentives to have more children. Immigration will be encouraged. In 2006 the birth rate fell to a record low of 1.3 children per female. This is the 28th consecutive year it has dropped below the 'replacement rate' needed to maintain the population.

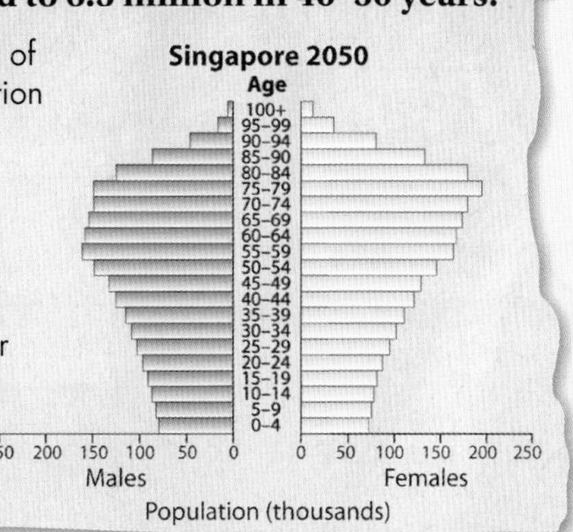

Task 5

Study **Source E**.

a How will Singapore's projected population change by 2050?

b Look at the projected pyramid for 2050. Imagine you are the Minister of Housing Development. Write a short paper (maximum 150 words) outlining:

* **three** problems facing the government
* **three** possible solutions to these problems.

Present your views to your classmates.

Sample case study question

For a country you have studied, describe the policies used by the government to reduce rates of population growth.

TOPIC 4 Population density

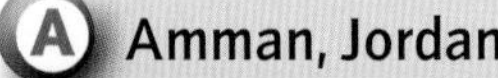

A Amman, Jordan

B The Alps, France

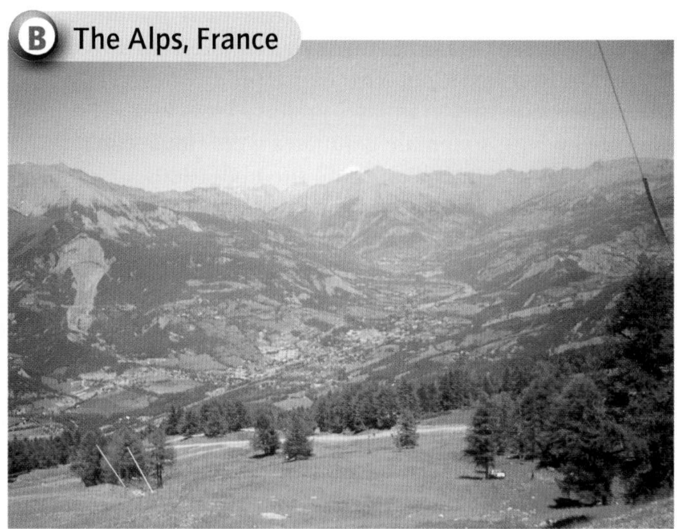

Where do people live?

Source A shows part of Amman, in Jordan, where the population is over 2.5 million. The large amount of work that is available there makes it possible for many people to make a living. There is a great variety of different types of jobs, for example in offices, shops, factories, transport and hotels.

Source B shows part of the Alps, in France, where few people live. This range of fold mountains, the highest in Europe, rises to 4810 metres above sea level. These mountains are so high and steep that it is hard to make a living there. The slopes are difficult to build on, access is limited and winters are long and cold.

Task 1

Study **Sources A and B.**

Describe differences between the two areas shown. Refer to:

- relief
- accessibility
- employment opportunities
- climate.

Task 2

Study **Source C.**

a Find a picture of your own of an area where lots of people live. Add labels to it to explain why many people live there.

b Find a picture of your own of an area where very few people live. Add labels to it to describe the difficulties of living there.

C Factors influencing where people live

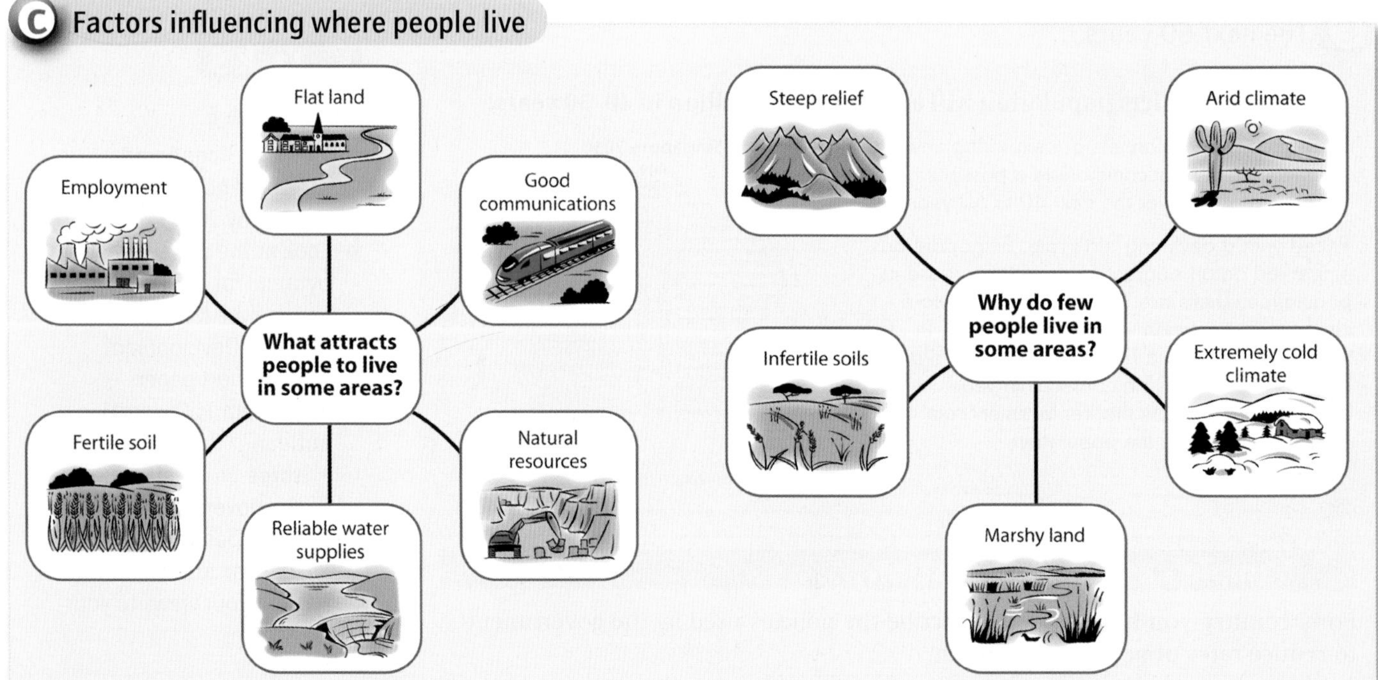

D World population density

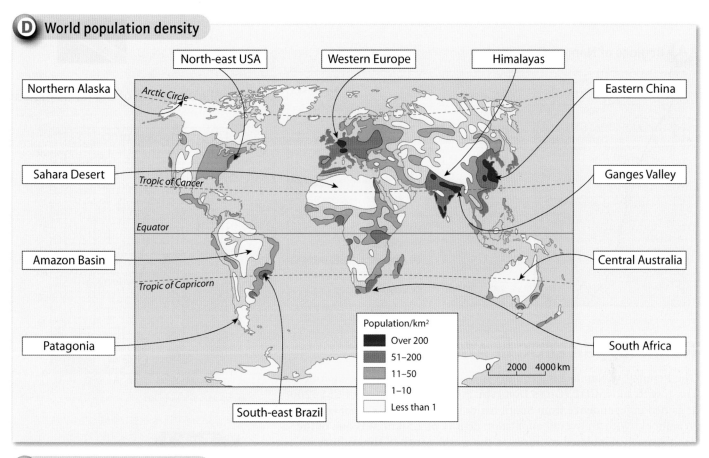

North-east USA
Western Europe
Himalayas
Northern Alaska
Eastern China
Arctic Circle
Sahara Desert
Ganges Valley
Tropic of Cancer
Equator
Amazon Basin
Central Australia
Tropic of Capricorn
Patagonia
South Africa
South-east Brazil

Population/km²
Over 200
51–200
11–50
1–10
Less than 1

0 2000 4000 km

E Areas of extreme climate

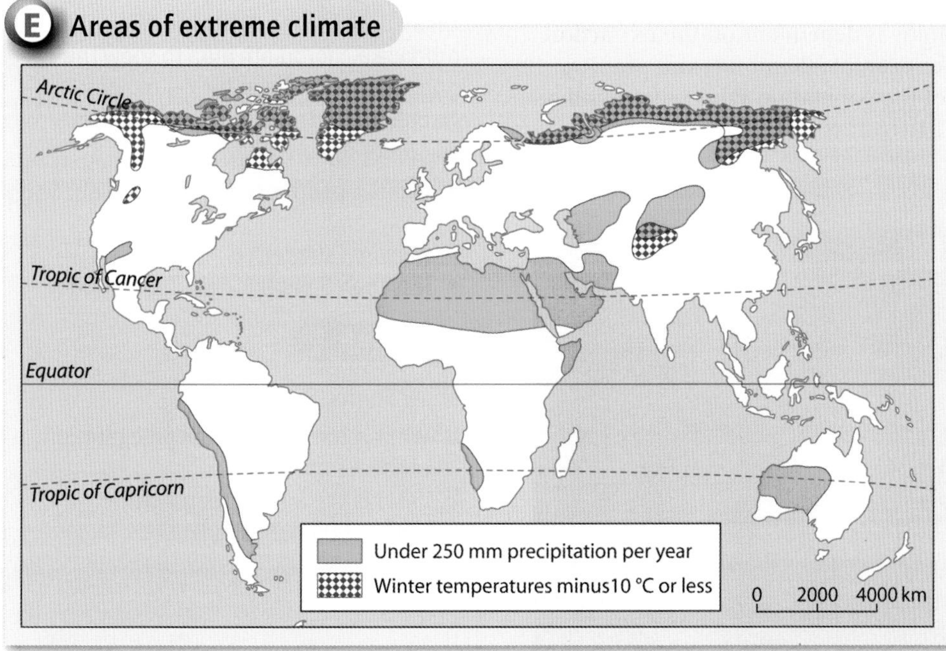

Population density

Population density describes the average number of people living in a given area (this is usually a square kilometre, or km²). It is calculated by dividing the total population by the area of land. If all the people living in the world were evenly spread over the surface of the land there would be about 6 people living in every square kilometre. But, as you have seen, in some areas lots of people live close together in large urban areas (towns and cities). These are densely populated or have a high population density, e.g. north-east USA.

There are other areas where few or no people live, such as in mountainous regions and deserts. These are sparsely populated or have a low population density, e.g. central Australia.

Task 3

Study **Sources D and E**.

a Use the information on the maps to explain the link between population density and climate. Give examples in your answer.

b Many densely populated areas have a temperate climate. Find out what a temperate climate is and write down its main features.

Low population density in Namibia

A Regions of Namibia

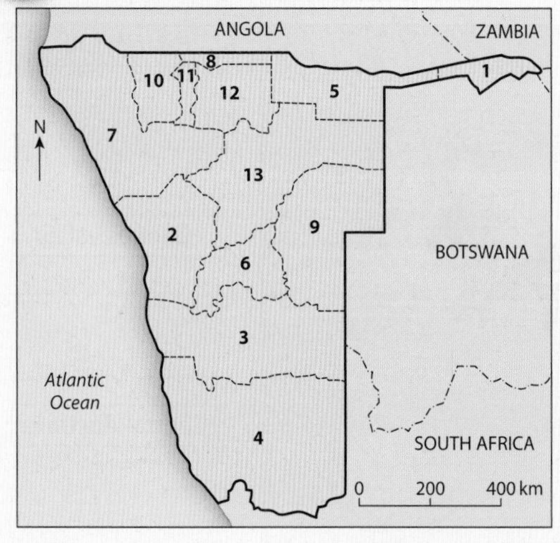

	Region	Population density/km²
1	Caprivi	5.5
2	Erongo	1.7
3	Hardap	0.6
4	Karas	0.4
5	Kavango	4.2
6	Khomas	6.8
7	Kunene	0.6
8	Ohangwena	21.3
9	Omaheke	0.8
10	Omusati	8.6
11	Oshana	18.7
12	Oshikoto	4.2
13	Otjozondjupa	1.3

B Climate graph of the Karas region

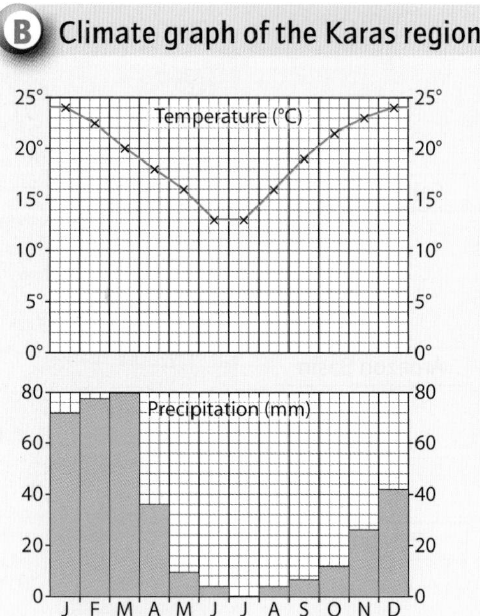

Namibia – an LEDC in Africa

The Republic of Namibia is a country in southern Africa on the Atlantic coast, with a low GDP (Gross Domestic Product) per person of US$ 5200. It gained independence from South Africa in 1990 and its capital city is Windhoek. With an overall population density of 2.5/km² it is one of the most sparsely populated countries in the world. Much of the country is desert, with a hot, dry climate. Rainfall is sparse and erratic and there are prolonged periods of drought. The economy is dependent on the extraction and processing of minerals for export, for example diamonds and uranium. Mining employs only about 3 per cent of the population while about half of the population depend on subsistence agriculture.

C The Karas region of Namibia

X

Y

Z

Task 1

On an outline map of **Source A** produce a choropleth map to show the population density of the 13 regions of Namibia. Use three shades of the same colour for regions with:

- over 15 people /km² (*dark shade*)
- between 5 and 15 people /km² (*medium shade*)
- less than 5 people /km² (*light shade*).

Task 2

Study **Source B**.

a What is the total annual precipitation of the Karas region?

b What is the annual temperature range of the Karas region?

D Part of the Karas region

15°E 16°E 17°E 18°E
26°S 27°S 28°S 29°S

Koichab Pan
Z
Lüderitz
Kolmanskop
Aus
Bethanie
Goageb
Kosis
Seeheim
Konkiep
Fish
X
Y
DIAMOND AREA 1
(RESTRICTED AREA)
Rosh Pinah
Ai Ais
Sendelingsdrif
Oranjemund
Noordoewer
Atlantic Ocean
Part of South Africa
B4 C13 C14 C10
0 50 100 km

- Tarred road
- Gravel trunk and main road
- Gravel district road
- B8 Major route
- C27 Minor road route
- 123 Distance in km
- Nature or game park
- River
- Airport landing strip
- International border
- Railway
- Major town
- Very small place

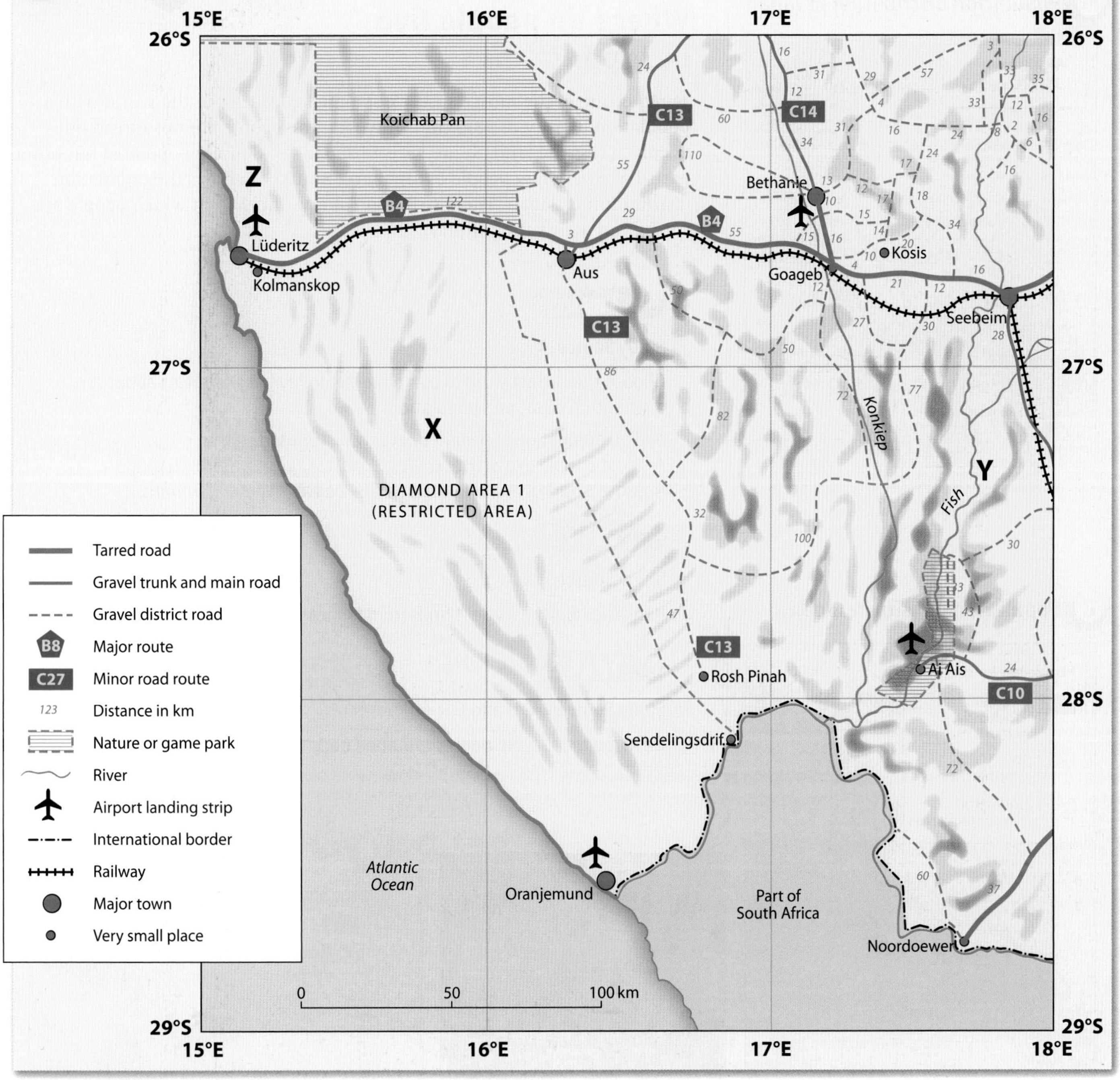

Task 3

Study **Sources C and D**.

The map shows part of the Karas region in southern Namibia, the most sparsely populated region in the country. The locations where the photographs were taken are shown on the map.

a Use latitude and longitude to give references for the position of each photograph. (Note that 1°= 60'. The symbol ' is called a minute.)

b Write **one** sentence about each photo which clearly describes its main features.

Task 4

Explain why the Karas region is sparsely populated. Support your answer by referring to evidence from the sources.

High population density in Japan

Where do people live in Japan?

Japan is one of the most densely populated countries in the world with a population density of 339/km². However, the people are not spread out evenly across the land. Some parts of Japan are densely populated but other parts have very few people living there. **Source A** shows the population distribution of Japan. The distribution shows the way in which people are spread out across the country.

Task 1

Study **Source A**.

Choose the correct word to complete the following sentences about the distribution of Japan's population:

- The population is *evenly/unevenly* distributed.
- Most people live on *Hokkaido/Honshu/Kyushu/Shikoku* Island.
- Most people live along the *borders/coast/rivers/mountains.*

Task 2

Study **Source B**.

Rank the four Japanese islands from highest to lowest population density.

Task 3

Study **Sources A, B and C**.

Describe the link between population density and relief in Japan.

A Population distribution in Japan

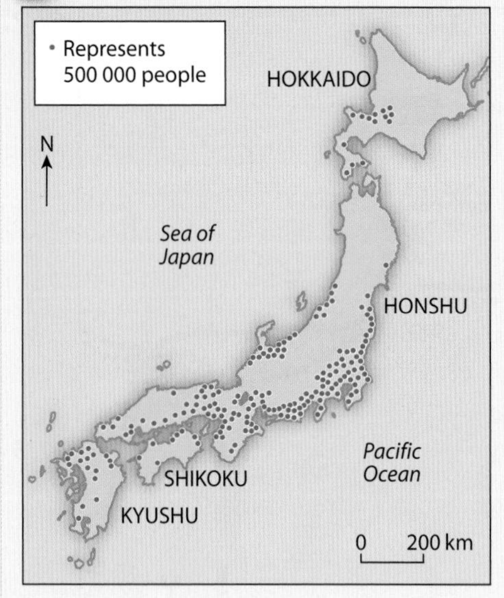

B Population density in Japan

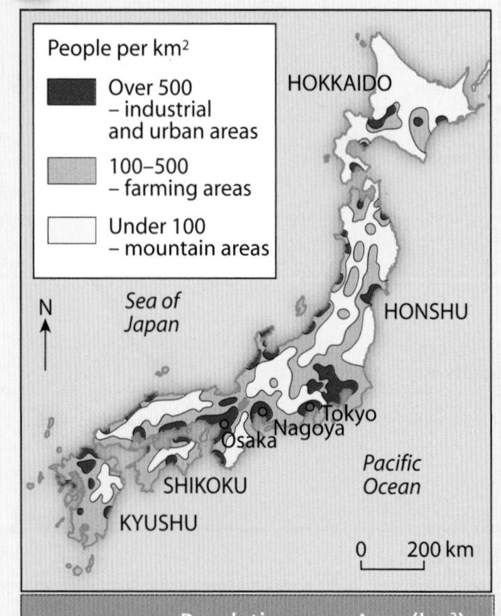

	Population	Area (km²)
Hokkaido	5 601 000	83 500
Honshu	103 423 000	230 500
Kyushu	13 316 000	42 150
Shikoku	4 063 000	18 800

Tokyo is a crowded capital city

C Relief of Japan

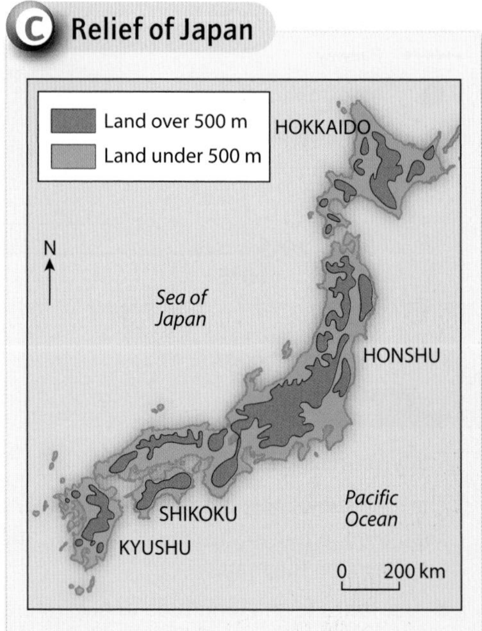

D Different population densities

Northern Japanese Alps

A village in Gifu prefecture, Japan

Tokyo cityscape

Low-density rural areas

Over two-thirds of Japan is mountainous, with high land and steep slopes. These areas include the central part of Honshu Island and the southern part of Shikoku Island. Few people live here because:

- there is not enough flat land to grow food on
- soils are thin, acidic and infertile
- many areas are isolated and remote as the winding roads are poor and there are few if any other communications
- there is little work except forestry as there are few natural resources
- the climate is often extreme, with long cold winters and heavy rain or snow.

High-density rural areas

Outside the urban areas, on the flat valley floors and gently sloping lower slopes of Honshu and Kyushu Islands, many people live in villages or small towns, between which there are many farms. Some people are farmers but others commute daily to the large cities where they work. These areas are densely populated because:

- crops can easily be grown on the fertile soils of the flat or gently sloping land
- it is easy to use farm machinery on flat land
- the warm temperate climate means a variety of crops can be grown
- good roads and railways make it possible to live in the countryside and work in the cities.

High-density urban areas

Towns and cities stretch along the coasts, particularly on Honshu Island. Almost a half of Japan's population live in the areas around Tokyo, Nagoya and Osaka. These areas are densely populated because:

- on the flat land it is easy to build
  - towns and cities
  - factories, offices and other commercial buildings
  - road and rail networks
  - airports
- on the coast there are many ports and harbours which have led to
  - the import of raw materials
  - the export of manufactured goods
  - the development of a fishing industry.

Task 4

Study **Source D**.

Draw a table like the one below and fill in the details.

	Low-density rural areas	High-density rural areas	High-density urban areas
Relief			
Communications			
Economy			

Task 5

A large part of Japan's population lives in the Tokyo, Nagoya and Osaka areas.

Working in groups, carry out research on why so many people live in these areas.

You may want to use the Internet or other sources to prepare a presentation. In your presentation you should include information about:

- relief
- climate
- employment.

Sample case study question

For a named area that you have studied, explain why it has a high population density.

International migration

A Important definitions

Immigration Reception Centre

Type of migrant	Definition	Example
Asylum seeker	A person who has left their country of origin for fear of persecution. They have asked for permission to stay in another country and are waiting for a decision on this.	People leaving conflicts in South-east Asia arriving by boat from Indonesia to seek asylum in Australia.
Refugee	A person who has been forced to leave their country of origin in fear of their lives. They run away often with no idea where they will end up and with no permission to stay in another country.	Movement of Georgians out of South Ossetia due to occupation by Russian troops.
International migrant	A person who moves to live and work in a different country for at least a year. If they move for better work they are called economic migrants.	Polish workers moving within the European Union (EU) into the UK.
National migrant	A person who moves to live and work in another place within the same country.	Moving from a rural village in West Bengal to live and work in Kolkata, India.
Illegal immigrant	A person who enters a country to live and work there without permission.	People smuggled by boats from Morocco into Fuerteventura, a Spanish island off the African coast.

B On the move – migration in the news!

Holiday island spoilt by seaborne immigrant invasion

Another boatload arrives from north Africa

The tiny island of Lampeduza, just off the north African coast, is known as the 'European tropics'. It is a hot, arid land of palm trees, cacti and coral. But, through the heat haze, you can see the Italian coastguards bringing in boatloads of exhausted and dehydrated would-be immigrants from north Africa. Between January and August 2008 over 15 000 have arrived on the Italian island but over 400 died on the journey across the Mediterranean Sea. Each migrant has paid about US$ 3000 for the chance to travel in an overloaded, ramshackle boat to the 'Promised Land' from Libya and Tunisia.

Task 1

Study **Source A**. Write down the differences between:

- an asylum seeker and a refugee
- an international and a national migrant.

Task 2

Study **Sources A and B**.

Make a table showing origin and destination countries of **three** migrations. Add any other international migrations you know of.

C Push and pull factors

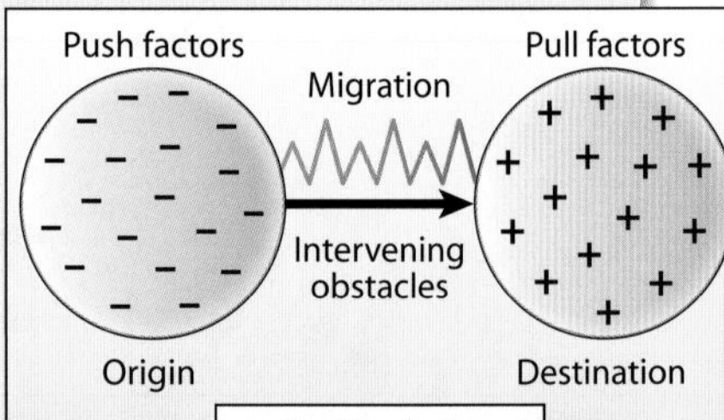

Push factors are to do with where people are living. These are reasons to move away from that place, e.g. there is no work available due to drought.

Pull factors are to do with where people wish to move to. These are reasons that attract people to the new place, e.g. freedom from persecution.

Intervening obstacles may be many, e.g. cost of moving, passport/visa issues, physical obstacles.

Migration changes population distribution

The distribution of the world's population is constantly changing. One reason for this is the number of people moving to live and work in a new country from another country. This is called international migration.

Today immigration (moving in to live and work in another country) and emigration (moving out to live and work in another country) are much easier to achieve than many years ago. Aeroplanes, railways, ferries and cars make migration possible. Many people choose to migrate for positive reasons. Some people, however, are forced to move out of countries and are not always welcome at their destinations. Whether forced (involuntary) or voluntary, migration is an issue that affects many countries.

The European Union and migration

After the Second World War in Western Europe (1939–45) many countries wanted peace and stability. They began to work together and trade together. From small beginnings in 1948, with Belgium, the Netherlands and Luxembourg working together (known as Benelux), the European Union (EU) has grown to 27 countries – known as member states – with others applying to join. The EU represents almost 500 million people. One of the impacts of working more closely with each other is that people can move within the EU without the need to show their passport or get a visa. This has caused a great deal of movement, or migration, between the EU countries.

D Several countries, one Europe

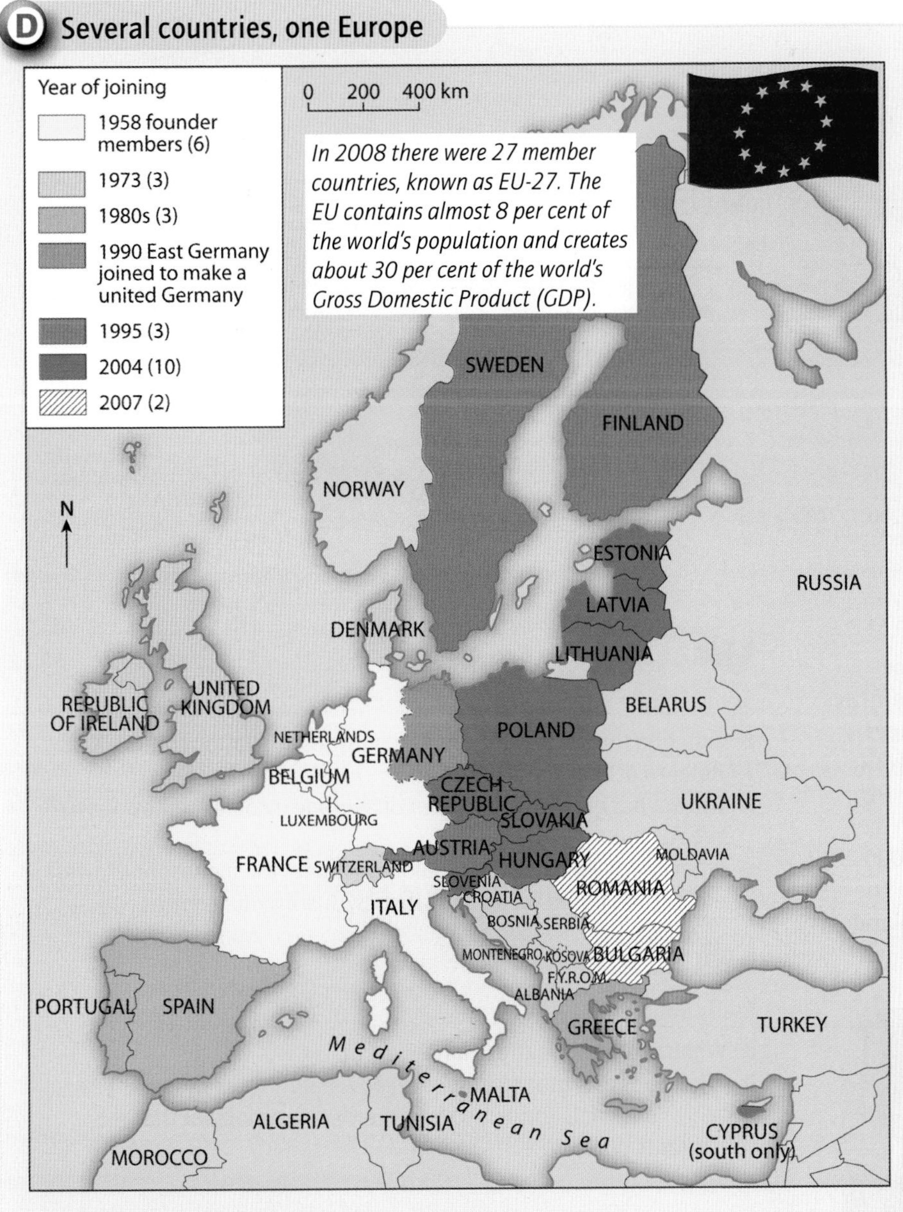

Task 3

Study **Source C**.

a How are *push* and *pull* factors different?

b Below are two examples of push and pull factors. List them in a table and write down which is *push* and which is *pull*. Add **two** other examples of each – but avoid opposites.

- Drought means crops cannot grow.
- Chance of a better education in a nearby town.

Task 4

Study **Source D**.

a How many countries made up the EU before 2004?

b Describe the EU expansion that took place after and including 2004.

c How has the EU made it easier to move between countries to live and work?

Task 5

Study **Source E.**

a Discuss the advantages and disadvantages of increasing freedom of movement within the EU.

b How has your country been affected by migration?

E The EU – some migration issues

	Advantages	Disadvantages
1	Encourages greater mixing of European cultures.	Countries may lose their distinctive culture.
2	Freedom of movement means that workers can easily move to other countries to fill job vacancies.	Large movements of workers from poor to rich countries may cause resentment, racism and conflict.
3	EU funds can be used to improve transport and infrastructure in poorer countries.	Large companies from the richer countries may move into poorer countries, forcing local businesses to close.

CASE STUDY 5

Polish workers move into the UK

A The A8 countries and the UK

A8 country	Average income (US$)	Unemployment in 2005 (% of labour force)
Czech Republic	9130	8
Estonia	7080	10
Hungary	8370	5
Latvia	5580	11
Lithuania	5740	12
Poland	6100	19
Slovakia	6480	18
Slovenia	14770	7
UK	**33630**	**5**

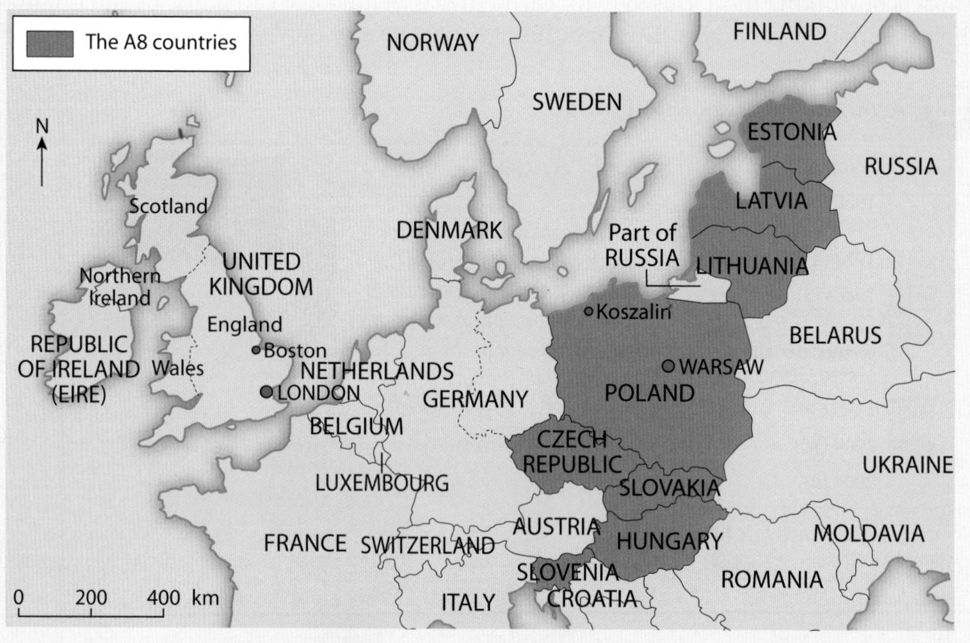

In come the A8 countries …

In 2004 eight countries from eastern Europe joined the European Union. All of these countries had relatively high unemployment and wages around 40 per cent of the EU average. With the freedom of movement available within the EU, many workers from these countries migrated to work in other EU countries. Nearly 600 000 migrants chose to work in the UK in 2004. The largest number (62 per cent) were from Poland.

Task 1

Study **Source A**.

a Describe the location of the A8 countries in relation to the UK. Refer to distance and direction.

b Draw a bar graph in rank order of average income (highest first) for the A8 countries.

c From which A8 countries would you expect the highest and lowest emigration based on these statistics? Justify your choices.

Task 2

Study **Source B**.

a What and where is the Sciana Placzu?

b What suggests that most jobs are low-paid?

c Which unskilled and skilled jobs are the most popular that the migrants do?

B Working in the UK

The Sciana Placzu – the so-called Wailing Wall – is in King Street, Hammersmith, London. Here Poles gather to look for work in the UK. It is better known in Poland than in the UK. Here you will find qualified doctors scribbling down details of work in catering and cleaning or giving out restaurant leaflets. But the rate of pay is hardly ever mentioned!

Examples of jobs being done by east Europeans in the UK (2006)

UNSKILLED	Numbers	SKILLED	Numbers
Factory worker	40270	Lorry driver	1920
Kitchen assistant	11800	Bricklayer	445
Packer	11650	Computing/IT	130
Farm worker	9145	Plumber	95
Cleaner/domestic staff	8895	Barrister	10
Building labourer	4585	Circus performers	10

C Positive and negative impacts

For the UK		For the Poles	
Positive	Negative	Positive	Negative
Jobs filled that UK workers do not want	Fewer jobs for unskilled UK workers	Chance of a job	May leave family at home
Can pay low wages	May move back once earned money	Better pay than in Poland	May encounter hostility in UK
Will work long hours	Anti-immigration issues and racism	Can save money and return to improve life in Poland	Language and cultural issues in the UK
Increased population will spend more in local economy	Services such as hospitals and schools cannot cope with extra numbers	Chance to get away from living with parents as they cannot afford to move out	May struggle to obtain housing in the UK; some end up homeless

D Johanna's journey

Boomerang Migrants Chase Dreams in UK

Behind the 19th-century town centre buildings, Koszalin (population 140 000) is crumbling. Its industry has died, investment is crumbling and unemployment at 23% is among the worst in Poland. Since joining the EU in 2004 hundreds of young Poles have left their families to 'catch our dreams'. Johanna Rosinska (25) is one of them. She is known as a 'boomerang migrant' – one who migrates overseas to work hard, saves hard and then returns home to use the money to set up a business. She eventually plans to run a florist shop in Koszalin so has found work as a gardener. Although Johanna is a graduate in agricultural studies, Poland cannot provide work for most graduates so she has to migrate overseas.

E Polish migration into Boston, UK

In 2001 the population of Boston was 55 700. Seven years later it was estimated at 70 000 – a rise of over 25 per cent. Most of these are migrant workers from eastern Europe, especially Poland. They do make a vital contribution to the local economy and there is plenty of work on the farms and in factories. But rapid migration brings problems, for example there are 65 different languages spoken here – you sometimes feel there are more foreigners now than English people! Pressure is also put on public services – houses and hospitals can't be provided that quickly – and, anyhow, we can't be certain that the migrants will stay in Boston.

Boston Councillor

Task 3

Study **Sources C and D.**

a Give **one** advantage and **one** disadvantage of Polish migration into the UK. Do this for the UK and then for Polish migrants.
b Give **two push** and **two pull** factors which explain why young people are leaving Koszalin in Poland to work in the UK.
c Why is Johanna Rosinska a 'boomerang migrant'?

Task 4

Read **Source E.**

a By how much did the population of Boston rise between 2001 and 2008?
b What types of jobs were the migrants recruited to do?
c How have Polish migrants changed the community?
d Imagine you were migrating to Boston to live and work.
- What sorts of problems might you come across?
- How might you solve them?

Task 5

In 2008 many Poles decided to return to their home country using money earned in the UK to settle there. Suggest some advantages and disadvantages of Poles returning to Poland, for the home country and for the UK.

Sample case study question

Name two countries between which people have migrated. Explain why migration has taken place between these countries.

Rural settlements

Locating settlements

Unless you live a nomadic life, you will be living in a fixed place such as a village or a town or city. If you live in an MEDC you are likely to be living in a town or city – an urban area. Over 85 per cent of people in MEDCs live in towns or cities. However, in LEDCs the pattern is different. In many LEDCs over 75 per cent of people still live as nomads or villagers in the countryside – in rural areas – despite the growth of large cities. This is partly because most of them have to provide their own food through farming.

Why did people begin to live here?

When did people begin to live here?

How has the settlement changed in my lifetime?

How will it change in the future?

A Questions about where you live

B Africa's urban and rural population

North Africa is the area of the continent that includes much of the Sahara Desert and borders the Mediterranean Sea. These countries are part of the Arab world.

Sub-Saharan Africa is the area of the continent that lies south of the Sahara Desert. It includes those countries that are entirely south of the Sahara Desert and those that are partly in the southern section of the desert.

The African population is mostly rural. Only around 40 per cent live in urban areas. East Africa, with 23 per cent, is far less urbanised than West Africa (with 40 per cent) or southern Africa (with 43 per cent).

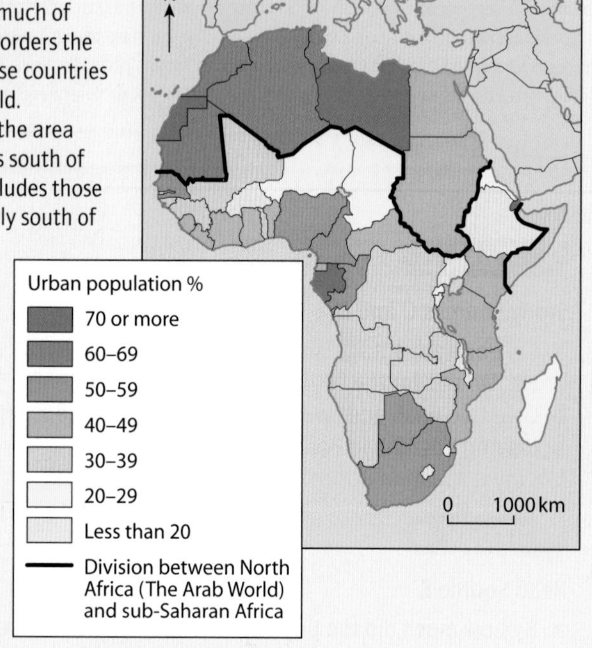

Task 1

a In which country do you live? Is this an MEDC or an LEDC? Explain your choice.

b Do you live in an urban or a rural area?

c Describe the location of your home in relation to your school.

d Discuss your answers to the questions in **Source A**. Add **three** other questions.

C World poverty facts and figures

* 1.2 billion people – one in five of the global population – live in absolute poverty (on income of less than US$ 1 per day).
* 75% of these people live in rural areas and 60% of the people who live in absolute poverty will still live in rural areas by 2025.
* Over 50% of the poor depend directly on agriculture for their livelihood.
* Over 70% of the poor live in south-east Asia and sub-Saharan Africa.

Task 2

Study **Source B**.

a On an outline map of Africa create your own map showing rural population. You will need to change the key in **Source B** to do this. Use choropleth shading to complete your map.

b Use either map to identify:
- **two** countries with a low rural population
- **two** countries with a high rural population.

c Compare the rural population of north Africa with that of sub-Saharan Africa.
Suggest reasons for any differences.

Task 3

Study **Source C**.

a What proportion of people live on less than US$ 1 per day? Find out the current exchange rate for US$ 1 in your currency. Could you live on this?

b Do most of these people live in rural or urban areas? Suggest reasons why the poorest people live in these areas.

Rural settlement patterns vary

Villages have usually grown over hundreds of years. They were not planned but there were usually good reasons for people to create a village community at a particular place. Types of rural settlement range from isolated farms to hamlets to villages.

Task 4

Study **Source D**.

a Compare the settlement density of the two areas.

b How are the settlement patterns in Kisumu East and Mdungu Kebbe different?

D Contrasting patterns in sub-Saharan Africa

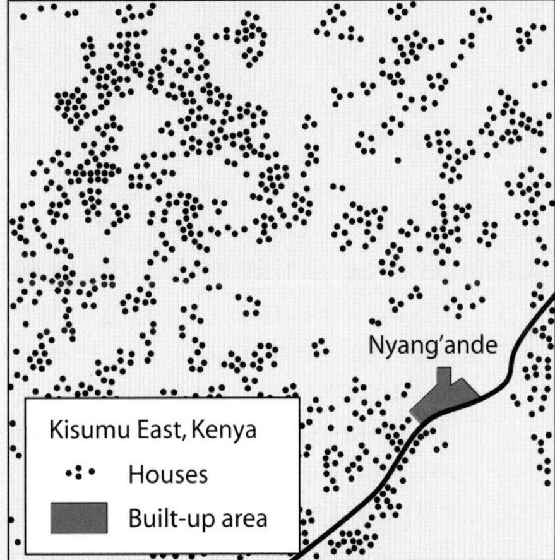

Nucleated settlements have their buildings clustered together, usually around a central point. They can vary in shape. A small number of clustered houses form a hamlet, a large number form a village.

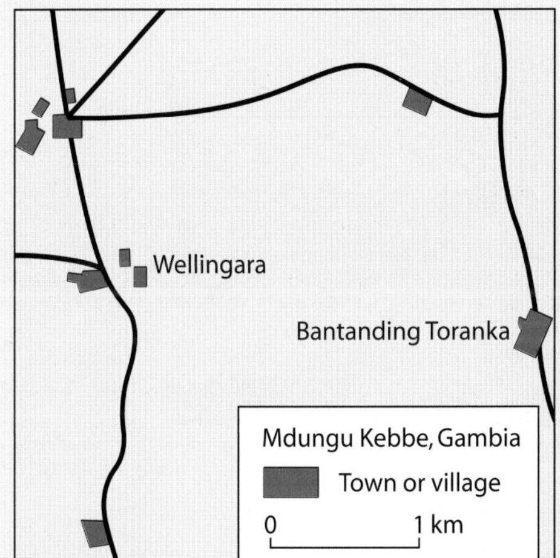

Dispersed settlements, such as farms and isolated buildings, are scattered across the countryside, often in highland areas. Villages are often surrounded by dispersed settlements.

E Selecting a settlement site

The area is divided into six zones. Each zone offers a different opportunity for settlement.

A	Part of low-lying marshland
B	Low ridge of limestone
C	Part of low-lying marshland
D	A gently sloping area at the foot of hills
E	A steeply sloping west-facing hillside
F	The exposed upland surface of the hills

0 1 km
E F
N
River
River
River
225
265
269
150
45
45
15
15
30
A B C D

Task 5

Study **Source E**. This is a contoured sketch map of the relief and drainage of an area.

a Assess the attractiveness of each zone for settlement using the five factors in the table (right). You should copy this table and insert either 0 or 1 against each factor. For example, in Zone A there is a stream so it scores 1 for 'available water'. Complete the scoring for Zones B–F.

b Add the total positive and negative scores for each zone. Subtract the negative from the positive for each zone. This gives you the overall score of attractiveness for each zone. Zone A has been completed for you.

c Put your zones in order of attractiveness and then compare your table with those of others in your class. Discuss any differences.

d Discuss and list other information you would need before you made a final decision on the best site.

Calculating the Attractiveness Index

Positive factors	A	B	C	D	E	F	Negative factors	A	B	C	D	E	F
Water available	1	1	1	1	0	0	Lack of water	0	0	0	0	1	1
Gentle slopes	1						Steep slopes	0					
Low altitude	1						High altitude	0					
Good natural drainage	1						Poor natural drainage	0					
No flood hazard	0						Flood hazard	1					
TOTALS	4						TOTALS	1					

Attractiveness Index for Zone A = Positive total – Negative total = 3

CASE STUDY 6a

Rural settlement in Ethiopia

Rural settlement

Ethiopia lives off the land. More than 75 per cent of the population depends on agriculture for a living but only 13 per cent of the land can be used for crop production. The rest is forest, mountain, savanna and pasture land. The majority of people live in villages or roam the desert as nomadic pastoralists. Small communities have been created where there is the possibility of growing crops and the availability of water. Many of these are in the Ethiopian Highlands where, despite the steep slopes, rainfall is plentiful and the plateaus provide flat ground.

Ethiopia is the most mountainous country in Africa. Some 85% of Ethiopians live in the highlands in small villages.

The flat plateaus, with fertile soils and terraced slopes, are intensively cultivated, but soil is washed into the Blue Nile due to deforestation. Barley, wheat, maize, peas and beans are grown.

Heavy rainfall (over 1500 mm a year) and high temperatures in the mountains are good for crops. But the rain does not always arrive on time, so planning is difficult.

Task 1

Study **Source A**.

a Imagine you were taking this photograph from an aeroplane. Write a two-minute description of the scene to be used on your local radio station.

b Draw an outline sketch of this photograph. Label the following:
- steep slopes
- flat plateaus
- fields
- huts and settlements.

c Describe the location of the settlements. Include references to site and situation from **Source B**.

A Rural settlement in the Ethiopian Highlands

B What interests geographers about settlements?

Site: the actual land occupied by the settlement, e.g. on flat land, on fertile soils, on a hilltop, at a bridging point, in a gap between hills.

Situation: the location of the settlement in relation to the area around it, e.g. close to a reliable water supply, close to a main route, close to other settlements for trade and services.

Shape: the shape of the village, e.g. linear (along a river valley or road) or nucleated (around a crossroads or on a hilltop).

Function: the main activities of the settlement, e.g. defence, farming, mining.

C A lowland village near Addis Ababa

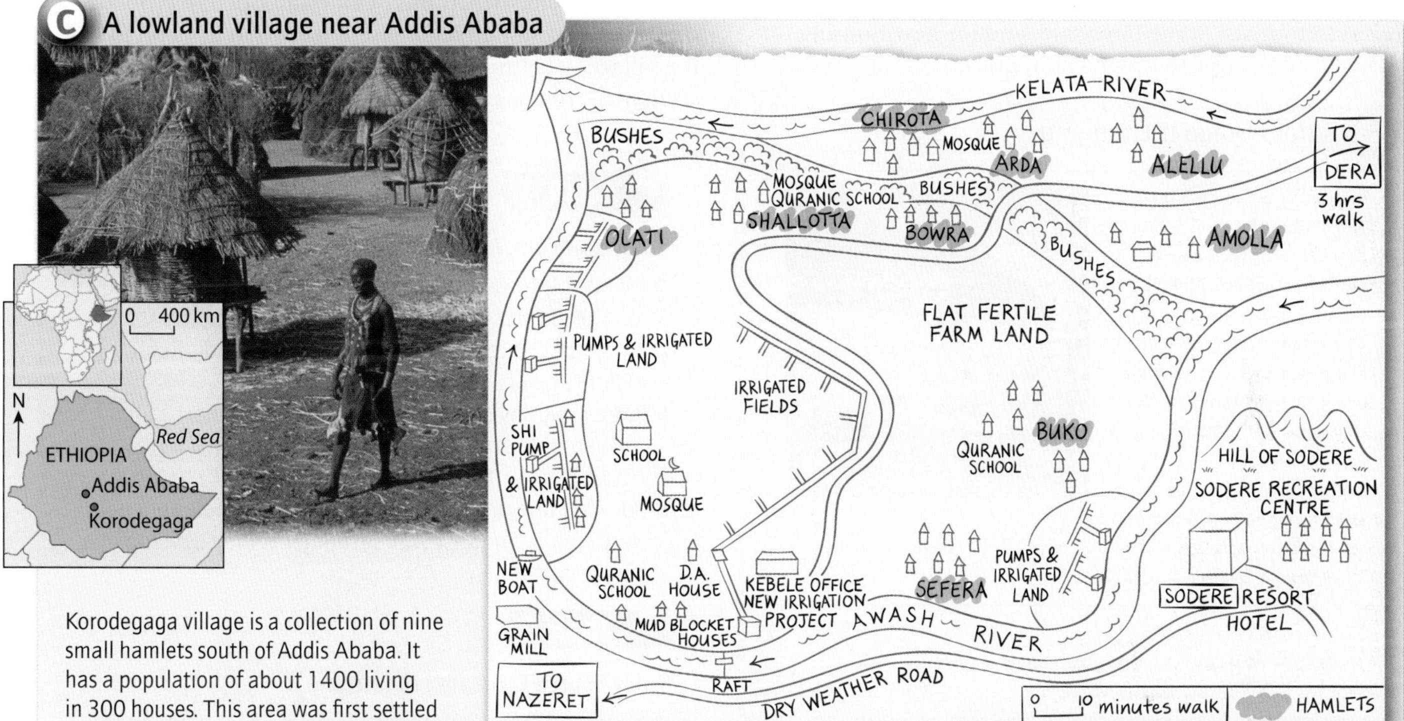

Korodegaga village is a collection of nine small hamlets south of Addis Ababa. It has a population of about 1400 living in 300 houses. This area was first settled in the early 20th century by nomadic pastoralists. There were many advantages for settlement. It had access to water from two rivers, flat fertile soil, and forests for building and firewood. Here maize, tef* and beans could be grown and cattle, sheep, goats and hens kept.

The main disadvantage is lack of rain all year. Drought is a major problem and hunger and starvation are common. Korodegaga is more fortunate than other nearby villages. It receives around 600 mm of rain from June to August but then has a nine-month dry season. However, irrigation is practised and the rivers do not dry up. This is important as the sandy soil does not hold water for long. One other problem is that the heavy rain can wash away soil into the rivers.

In recent years a number of changes have taken place. Deforestation since 1980 for firewood and housing is a problem as it encourages soil erosion by wind and rain. Also, extra settlers have moved in here since 1990. The services are an attraction with schools, mosques, rafts to cross the river and a grain mill. Self-Help International (an NGO based in the USA) has also sponsored an irrigation scheme since 2001 providing water for 130 households using pumps running on diesel. Although there is no market or shop here, villagers walk to Dera (25 km), Bofa (10 km) or Awash Melkase (8 km) to access these services.

* *tef: an important grain crop only grown in Ethiopia from which a form of bread is made*

Adapted from Ethiopian Village Studies – *University of Bath*

Task 2

Study **Source C**.

- **a** Describe the location of the village in relation to Addis Ababa.
- **b** Describe the site and function of this village.
- **c** Give **three** advantages for the villagers of this location.
- **d** How have problems caused by the dry season been overcome?
- **e** How has the village changed in the last 30 years?
- **f** What part has Self-Help International played in changing the village?

Task 3

Self Help International (SHI) is advertising for an 18-year-old student to spend a 'gap year' helping people in villages like Korodegaga. The job is voluntary but all expenses are paid.

- **a** Suggest different ways in which SHI could advertise the post.
- **b** Choose **one** way and create the job advert.

CASE STUDY 6b

Rural settlement in France

Normandy
Brittany

Countryside changes

Dramatic changes have affected the French countryside in the past 50 years. Changes in farming activity, often driven by the European Union (EU), have led to larger fields, fewer hedgerows and different crops being grown. Farmers have also diversified into using their land for other activities such as caravan parks and renting out barns and cottages (*gites*) to tourists. Some have sold land for new housing on the edge of villages to urban commuters.

Rural populations have changed too. Young people have moved to urban areas, leaving an ageing population facing a decline in services. Replacing these younger people are people from other countries who often buy a second home, and tourists. Despite these changes, the pattern of rural settlement, which has been established over many centuries, can still be recognised. It is what goes on in the village – its function – and where it takes place – its structure – that is changing.

A Rural France is changing

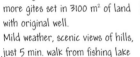

FOR SALE: Silfiac, BRITTANY
160 000 euros*
Beautiful large farmhouse for sale, fully renovated, centrally heated, 4 beds, 2 baths, wood-burning stove and original beams. Planning permission for 2 gites with large stone barn ideal for more gites set in 3100 m² of land with original well.
Mild weather, scenic views of hills, just 5 min. walk from fishing lake and bar/crêperie, not on a main road, surrounded by open fields.
* 1000 euro is approximately US$ 1500

Hedgerowed pastures, gorse heaths, dense forests, and vineyards roll away inland where there are scattered sleepy slate-roofed villages, elegant manor houses and hidden castles – this is Brittany's countryside or *pays*. But change is happening in rural areas. Silfiac (pop. 449), in central Brittany, is a village that typifies such changes. Due to the ageing population the school at Silfiac is now closed. The village has lost local people, especially the younger generation, who have moved to urban areas for work or other services.

Villagers now visit superstores in nearby towns like Pontivy; small shops such as boulangeries* and post offices have closed. The café, a garage and Le Relais Armoricain restaurant remain but rely on passing tourist trade more than local people. Urban commuters, however, are moving into new houses being built on the edge of the village where farmers have sold land.

Near to Silfiac another change is taking place. At Lanouan some local owners and migrants from the UK are renovating nine old farmhouses and barns. Of the four UK owners, two have migrated permanently and two use them as second homes. French owners may rent them out as gites for tourists. Tourists can also stay at the Arts and Language Centre which used to be a French Catholic school but is now English-owned and run. With Silfiac being only a one-hour drive from ferry ports to England, such as Roscoff, UK owners and tourists are a common sight here.

* *boulangerie* = baker

Task 1

Study **Source B**, an area of Normandy.

a What is the scale of this map? Calculate the area shown on the extract to the nearest square kilometre.

b Describe the relief of this area of Normandy. Refer to heights given.

c On an overlay or tracing paper, mark off the settlements and name them.

d To what extent is this pattern 'nucleated'?

e Identify **one** grid square that shows examples of linear settlement. Suggest why settlements may develop in a linear pattern.

Task 2

Study **Source C**, an area of Brittany.

a Give a six-figure reference for the highest point on this map.

b Compare the relief of this area with that in Normandy.

c In what ways is the pattern and size of settlements different to Normandy?

Task 3

Silfiac in Brittany is a village that has undergone change. Study **Sources A and C**.

a In which four-figure grid-square is Silfiac? Describe the location of Lanouan.

b How has the village and the area around it changed in the last 20 years? Write about people, services and the environment.

c Suggest why the area is attractive to people from the UK. Suggest any advantages and disadvantages that people from other countries have brought to Silfiac and the area around the village.

Sample case study question

For a named area that you have studied in an LEDC, explain why rural depopulation has occurred.

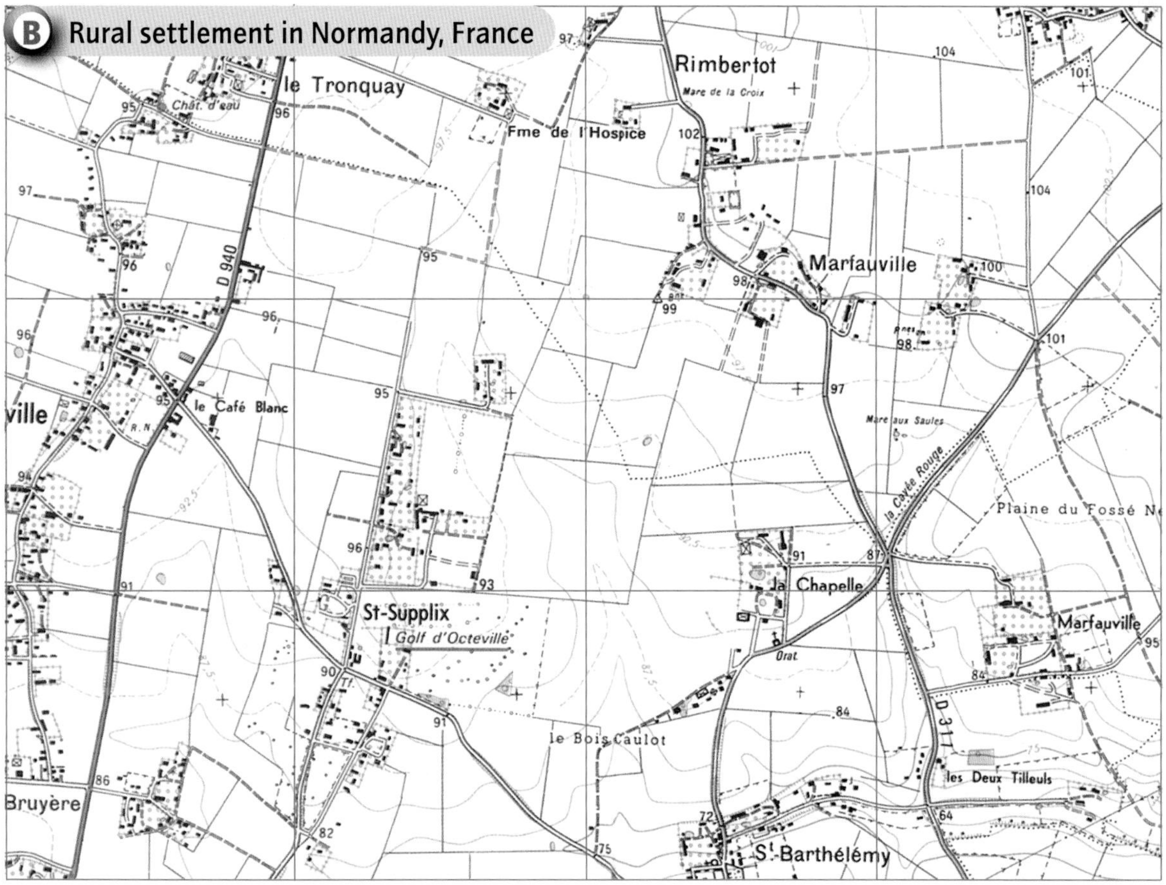

B Rural settlement in Normandy, France

Nucleated settlements have often developed in lowland areas where land is fertile. These areas attracted people many years ago to settle here and farm. Each parish farmed a similar amount of land around it to feed a similar population. This led to a pattern of clustered villages at fairly equal intervals across the landscape. Sometimes, within nucleated settlements, there is an important road or a narrow river valley. In these cases settlements often develop along the road or valley in a linear (or ribbon) shape.

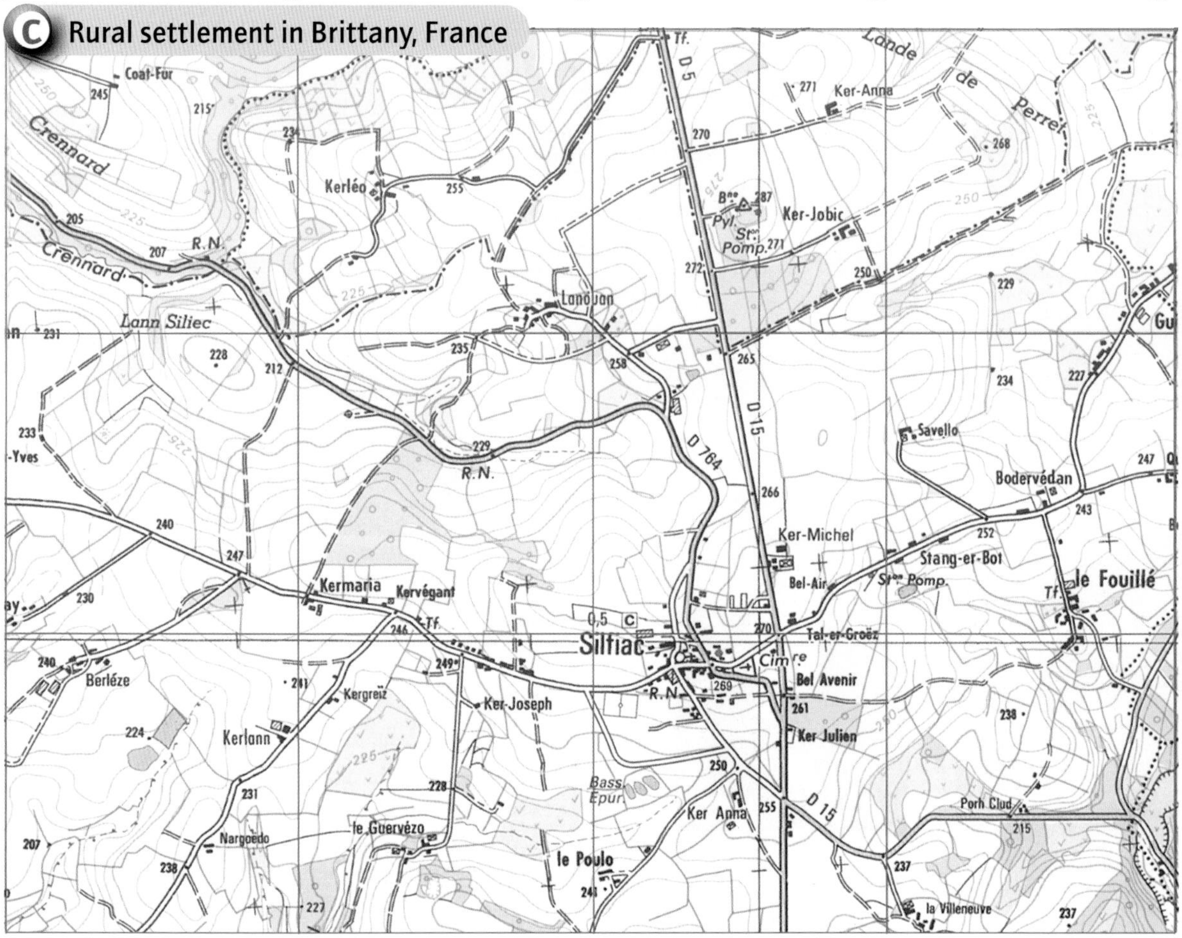

C Rural settlement in Brittany, France

Dispersed patterns are often found in upland areas where settlement is difficult. Here people settled in small farms and hamlets in areas which may be sheltered, or provide a route through the hills or have some potential for growing crops or grazing livestock. Settlements are small, randomly located and isolated due to the difficulties of living here.

Scale for both maps is 1:25 000 (4 cm = 1 km)

Urban settlements

Settlement hierarchy

A settlement hierarchy shows how settlements in any area can be put in order based on their size or the services that they provide. Higher up the hierarchy the population size and number of services in the settlement increases, although in any area there are fewer large settlements than small ones.

Settlements in an area depend on each other as people will use a variety of services found in different settlements. The area served by a settlement is known as its sphere of influence. The size of this will depend on the type and number of services offered by the settlement and the transport links to it.

Rural settlements only have a few services, which are low order services. Low order services are those that are used often, for example a small general store which sells convenience goods. Urban settlements have a greater number and variety of services, including both low order and high order services. High order services are not needed so often. They may sell comparison goods, such as furniture or clothing, and people are usually prepared to travel further to buy them. The distance that people are prepared to travel to use a service is known as its range.

In order to make a profit a shop or service needs a minimum number of potential customers, which is known as its threshold population. Services providing low order goods or services need a lower threshold population (as the service is used daily) than high order services, which need many more potential customers and thus have a higher threshold population.

A A settlement hierarchy

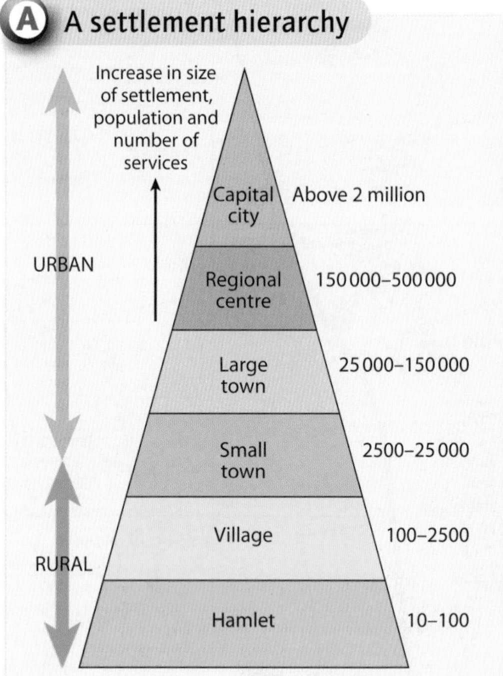

Task 1

Study **Source A** and a map of the country in which you live.

Draw a settlement hierarchy diagram for your country. In your diagram you should name examples of the settlements of different sizes.

B Different types of services

Mumbai, India

Gdansk, Poland

Lexington, North Carolina, USA

Madrid, Spain

Georgia, USA

Task 2

Study **Source B**.

Identify the services in the photographs which are:

- high order services selling comparison goods
- services that could be found in villages, towns or cities
- services with a large sphere of influence
- services that need a high threshold population.

C Functions of urban settlements

Newark, UK

Market town: where farmers buy and sell goods. These:

- are found in farming areas
- have many services, e.g. shops and offices
- have good transport links – often they are route centres
- are often near bridges over rivers (mills to process farm produce were built on the river)
- have a market place in the town centre.

Olbia, Sardinia

Port: where goods are loaded and unloaded by ship. These:

- are found where there are sheltered harbours, such as on an estuary, at the mouth of a river or in a bay
- have flat land for building or storage close to the water
- have deep water for large ships
- may be close to major industrial areas inland to import and export their goods.

Leicester, UK

Industrial town: where many people work in factories, processing raw materials or assembling products. These:

- may be found on or near coalfields
- may have old factories near to the centre of the urban area, close to railways or canals
- may have old housing areas and factories built close to each other
- may have new industrial estates on the outskirts, near main roads for transport.

Nice, France

Resort: a place where tourists visit to enjoy themselves. These:

- may be on the coast with beaches or in scenic inland areas
- may be large historical cities
- may be close to industrial areas with large populations, with good rail and road links
- have hotels and entertainments of various types.

The function of a settlement is its main economic activity or purpose.

The functions of many settlements have changed over time.

Example: Marmaris (Turkey)

In the 1960s Marmaris was a small, attractive fishing village. Few people visited it despite the attractive scenery and warm summers. However, over the next 30 years travellers discovered the lovely little village and began to flock there.

By 1990 Marmaris had been transformed from a small fishing village to a sprawling mass of hotels based around the needs of tourists. The town had changed its functions completely.

D Identifying the functions of a settlement

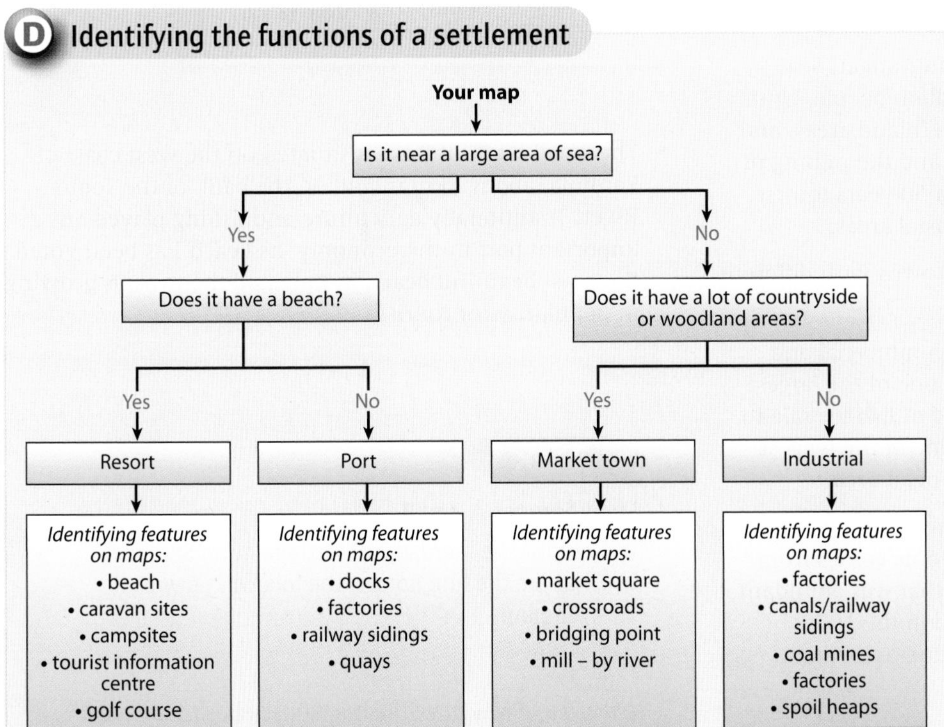

Task 3

Study **Sources C and D** along with the maps in Part B of this book (pages 171–208).

a Find **one** example of each of the following:
- Market town
- Port
- Industrial town
- Coastal resort

For each example you should:
- name the settlement
- give the page number of the map on which you found it
- give a four-figure grid reference for the square where the settlement is.

b Give examples from your own country of settlements with different functions.

Urban settlements in Sardinia

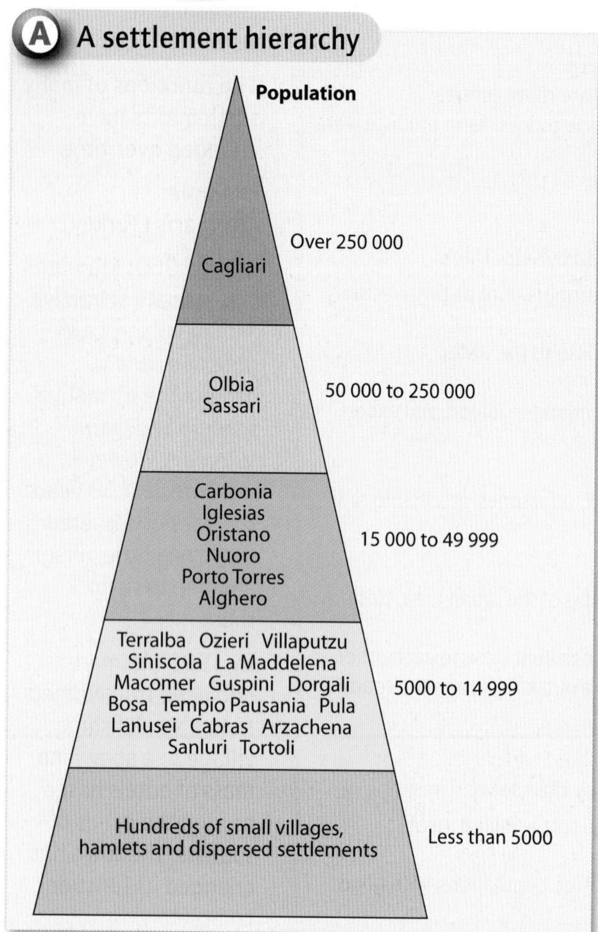

Sardinia – a Mediterranean island

Sardinia is an Italian island in the Mediterranean Sea with a total population of about 1.7 million people. Until recently most of the population lived in inland areas, and the economy was based on agriculture and the mining of coal, lead and zinc. However, in the last 50 years tourist development has taken place in the coastal areas.

There are a number of large and small towns with different functions. Three examples are:

- Cagliari, the capital city, is the main commercial and industrial centre of the island. It has one of the largest fish markets in Italy with a vast array of fish for sale to both the public and trade. It is also one of the biggest container terminals in the Mediterranean area.
- Carbonia was built to provide housing for the workforce of the nearby mines. The name Carbonia comes from the Italian word for coal, a resource that was abundant in this region. Since the mines closed in the 1970s, Carbonia has had to deal with high unemployment.
- The small town of Bosa is situated on the west coast of Sardinia, about 3 km inland on the bank of the Temo River. Traditionally agriculture and fishing played an important part in the economy. Its beach has been voted the most beautiful beach in Italy and the town is growing in popularity for tourism.

Task 1

Study **Sources A and B.**

a Describe the hierarchy of settlements in Sardinia.

b What are the functions of the following towns:
- Cagliari
- Carbonia
- Bosa?

c How and why have the functions of Bosa changed?

C The port of Olbia

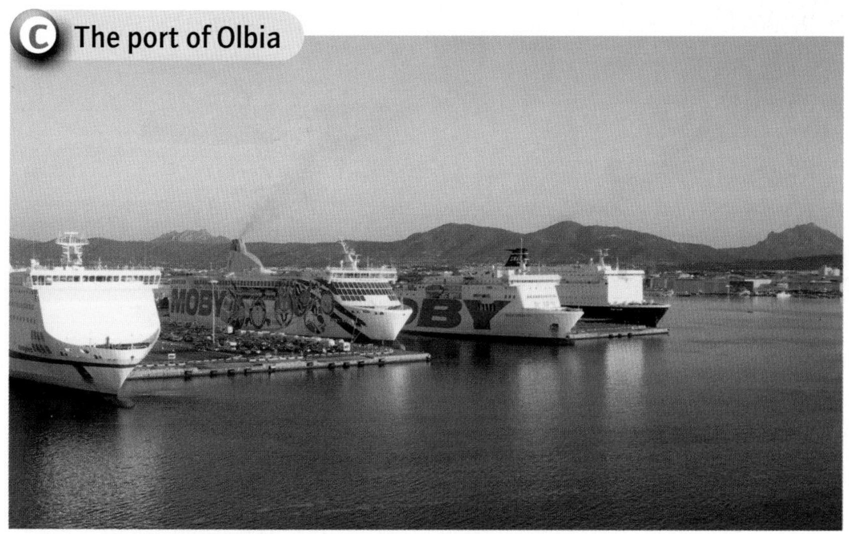

D Where is Olbia?

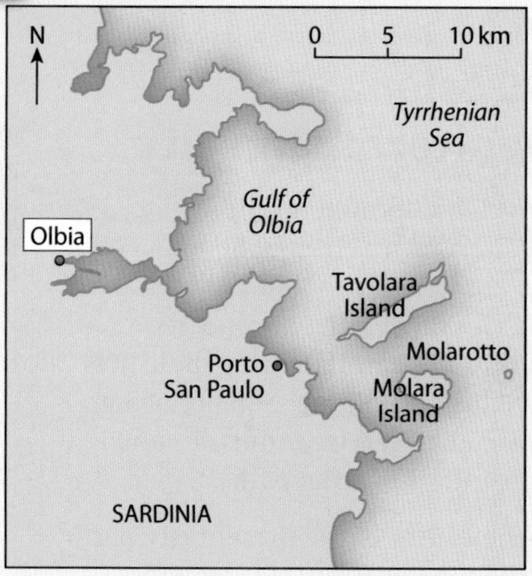

N
0 5 10 km
Tyrrhenian Sea
Gulf of Olbia
Olbia
Tavolara Island
Molarotto
Porto San Paulo
Molara Island
SARDINIA

An important port

Olbia is a town of over 50 000 inhabitants in north-east Sardinia. It is the main connection between Sardinia and the Italian mainland, with an airport, a passenger port, and a railway to Porto Torres and Cagliari. There is an expressway to Nuoro and Cagliari and main roads to Sassari, Tempio Pausania and Palau.

Task 2

Study **Sources C and D.**

Suggest reasons why Olbia has become an important port.

E Services in Sardinia

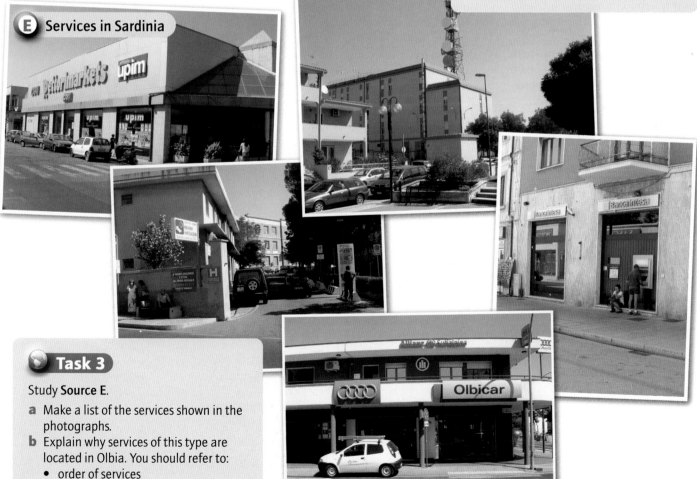

Task 3

Study **Source E.**

a Make a list of the services shown in the photographs.

b Explain why services of this type are located in Olbia. You should refer to:

- order of services
- sphere of influence
- threshold population.

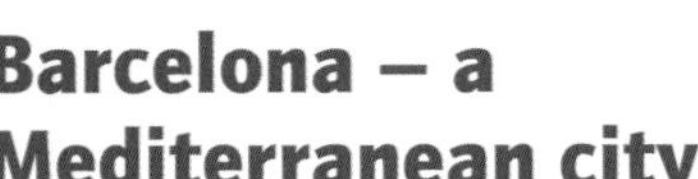

Barcelona – urban land use

Barcelona – a Mediterranean city

Barcelona, located on the Mediterranean coast of Spain, has many features that are typical of a city in western Europe. Its traditional manufacturing industries have been declining, and are being replaced by service industries and high-tech industrial parks.

In the centre of the present city part of the medieval city still remains with narrow streets, alleyways and small squares.

The area to the south of the medieval city is El Raval. It was the area where factories and high-rise tenement blocks were constructed during the Industrial Revolution but now much improvement is taking place. During the 19th century the city grew with planned housing development in a grid-iron pattern. This connected Barcelona to nearby smaller towns (e.g. Gracia), which became a part of the main city.

To the north, on the slopes of the hills, a number of large villas were built in the late 19th and early 20th centuries. These formed a high-class residential zone. Between 1945 and 1975, large areas of high-rise apartments were built along the major routeways and on the edges of the city (e.g. La Mina) for migrants from other parts of Spain seeking work in the city.

A Population statistics

District	Population density (people per km²)	Average life expectancy (years)	Population with higher qualifications (%)	Population born overseas (%)
Cuitat Vella	19757	73.2	11.4	22.7
Eixample	33275	79.7	23.9	8.1
Gracia	27237	79.2	21.6	6.8
Les Corts	13675	80.4	26.9	6.7
Nou Barris	20422	78.2	6.2	4.6
Sant Marti	19118	78.9	10.6	5.2
Horta Guinado	13879	79.0	12.1	4.7
Sants Montjuic	7832	78.4	11.1	7.2
Sant Andreu	20610	79.1	10.5	4.6
Sarria Sant Gervasi	6612	80.5	36.7	7.8

In the last 20 years, two major events – the 1992 Olympic Games and the Universal Forum of Cultures 2004 – have led to massive changes. For example, in the Poblenou district, an area of old manufacturing industry, an Olympic village was constructed on an abandoned factory site. Remaining factories and workshops in the Poblenou district are being changed into a zone for new technologies.

B Districts of Barcelona

N
Sarria Sant Gervasi
Horta Guinardo
Nou Barris
Les Corts
Gracia
Sant Andreu
Eixample
Sant Marti
Cuitat Vella
Sants Montjuic
0 1 2 km

C Land use in Barcelona

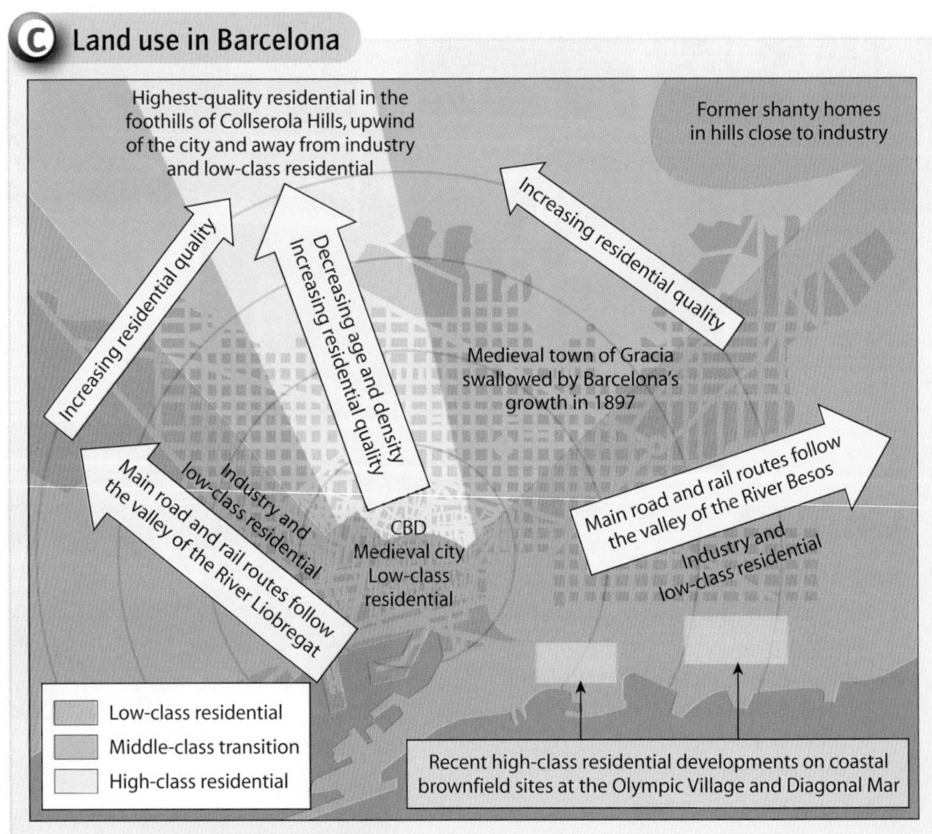

Urban zones

It is possible in many cities to identify zones where you can find a particular type of land use, e.g. a residential zone.

Land use models are theories that attempt to explain the layout of urban areas. A model is used to simplify complex, real-world situations, and make them easier to explain and understand.

Source D shows two different land use models that apply to urban areas in MEDCs.

The Burgess model is based on the idea that land values are highest in the centre of a town or city. This is because competition is high in the central parts of the settlement. This leads to high-rise, high-density buildings being found near the CBD, with low-density, sparse developments on the edge of the town or city.

The Hoyt model is based on the circles on the Burgess model, but adds sectors of similar land uses, e.g. the industrial zones that radiate out from the CBD. These could be following a main road or a railway line.

Task 1

Study **Sources A and B.**

a On a copy of the map show the information about population density, using choropleth shading. Use different shades for less than 10 000, 10 000 to 19 999, 20 000 to 29 999 and 30 000 or more. Remember to include a key.

b Draw a scatter graph to show the relationship between the percentage of the population with higher qualifications and the percentage who were born overseas.

c Does the pattern on the graph suggest a relationship between these two statistics? Comment on any pattern shown.

Task 2

Study **Sources A, B and C.**

High-cost housing areas are likely to have:

- lower population densities
- a greater percentage of the population with higher qualifications
- a lower percentage of foreign-born population than low- cost housing areas.

Produce a map of Barcelona showing high-cost and low-cost housing areas.

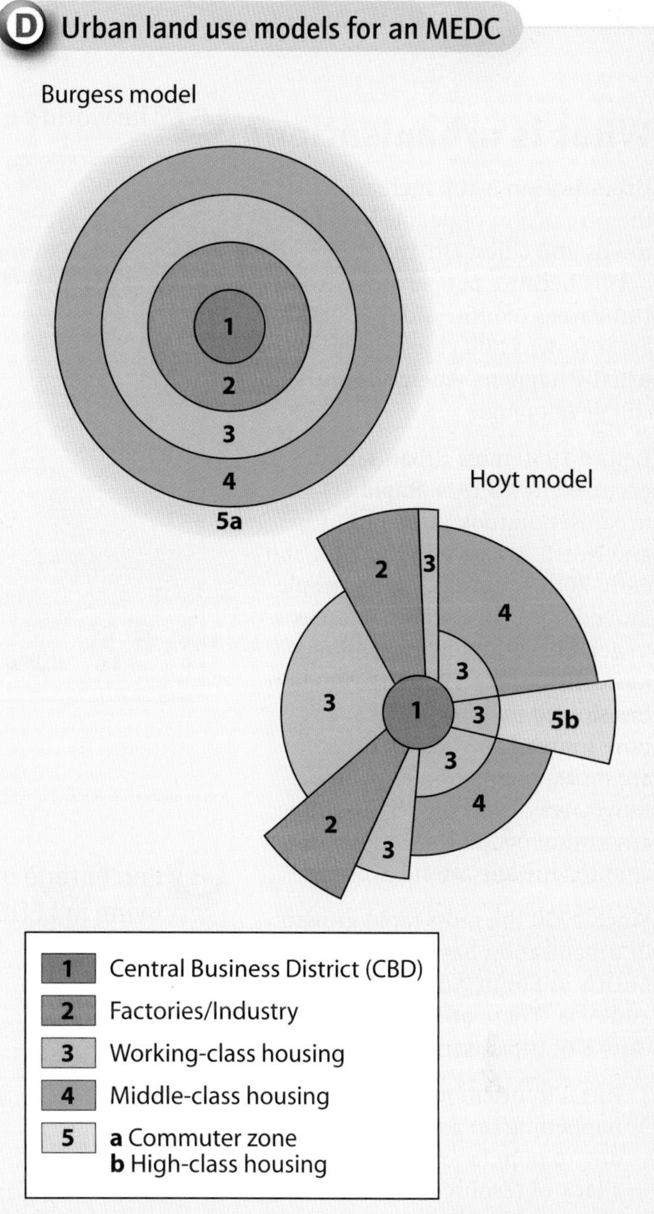

Task 3

Study **Sources C and D.**

a Describe the similarities and differences between the Burgess and Hoyt models of urban land use.

b Suggest reasons why in a typical MEDC city:

- high-cost, modern housing is on the outskirts
- traditional industry is close to railway lines.

c How well does Barcelona fit with the two models of urban land use?

Sample case study question

For a town or city that you have studied, explain the reasons for its growth and functions.

Urbanisation

What is urbanisation?

Urbanisation is the increase in the proportion of people living in towns and cities. Urbanisation occurs because people move from rural areas (countryside) to urban areas (towns and cities). This usually happens when a country is still developing.

Before 1950 most urbanisation occurred in MEDCs. Rapid urbanisation took place in Europe and North America in the 19th and early 20th centuries. Many people moved from rural to urban areas to get jobs in rapidly expanding industries. Since 1950 urbanisation has slowed in most MEDCs, and now some of the biggest cities are losing population as people move away from the city to rural environments. This is known as counter-urbanisation.

Since 1950 the most rapid growth in urbanisation has occurred in LEDCs in South America, Africa and Asia. There are two main causes of urbanisation in LEDCs.

1 Rural to urban migration is happening on a massive scale due to population pressure and a lack of resources in rural areas. These are known as 'push' factors.
2 People living in rural areas believe that the standard of living in urban areas will be much better than in rural areas. They hope for well-paid jobs, greater opportunities to find 'informal' work, and better health care and education.

A The world's urban population

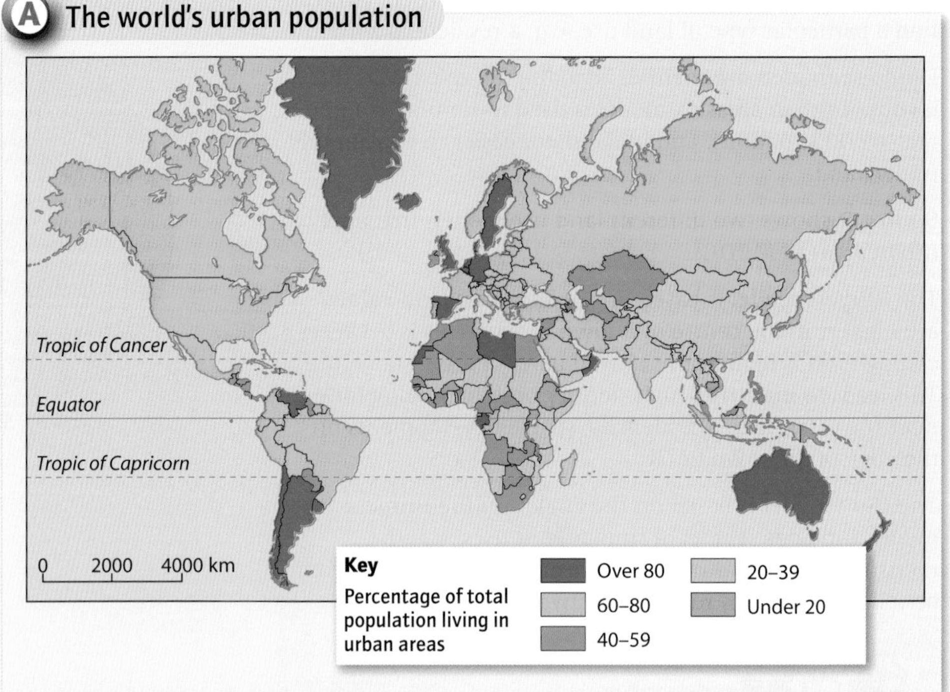

B Percentage of total population living in LEDC cities

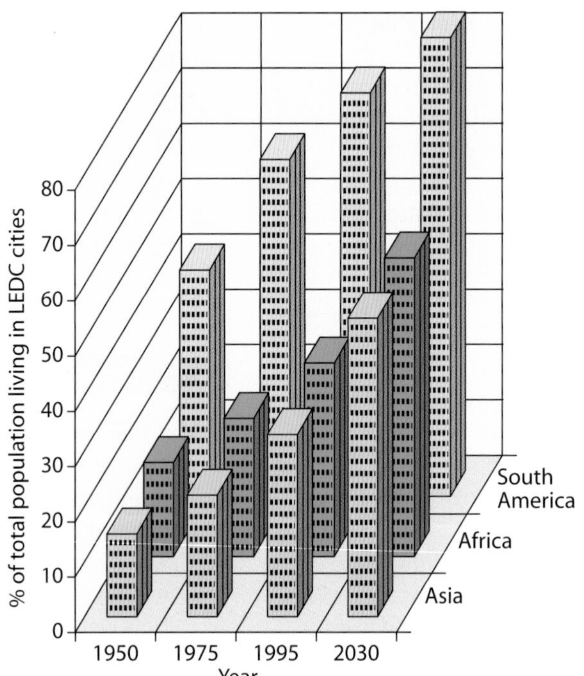

Task 1

Study **Source A** and an atlas.

a Name a continent where over 60 per cent of the population live in urban areas in all the countries.

b What percentage of the population live in urban areas in:
- Brazil
- Egypt
- India?

Task 2

Study **Source B**.

Compare the rates of urbanisation in Africa, South America and Asia.

C Pushes and pulls ... and the reality ...

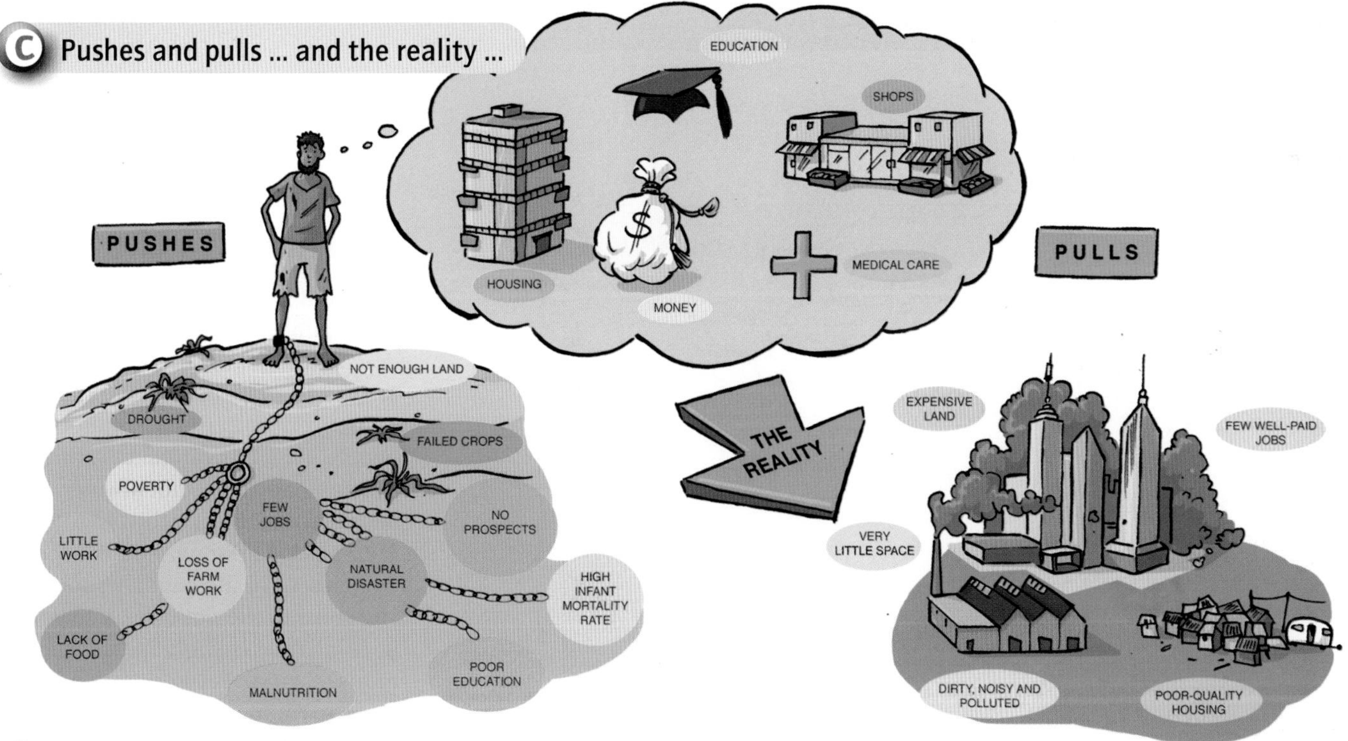

D Moving to the city

You don't seem local?
No , I was born in the countryside.

My father ran a farm but there was a drought and my brothers took the best land.

So what made you come here?

I wanted a better way of life…

E Slum crisis?

'Slumdog Millionaire' highlights global crisis

Toronto, February 25 (IANS)

A Canadian NGO working in the slums of India hailed multiple Oscars for 'Slumdog Millionaire' as the film has highlighted the hard life of people in urban slums the world over.

'Slumdog Millionaire' has put the hard truth about urban slums before world audiences.

'Although the film is set in India, similar living conditions can be found in most countries,' said Pat Ferguson, president of Operation Eyesight which funds projects in Mumbai and other Indian cities.

'Almost a billion people live in squalid slums scattered across the globe, and it's a growing problem.

'The UN predicts the number of slum dwellers will double to 2 billion by 2030 if no action is taken,' she said.

REPORT REVEALS GLOBAL SLUM CRISIS

Slum-dwellers who make up a third of the world's urban population often live no better – if not worse – than rural people, a United Nations report says. Worst hit is sub-Saharan Africa where 72% of urban inhabitants live in slums rising to nearly 100% in some states. More than one billion people live in slums now and, if no action is taken, the world's slum population could rise to 1.4 bn by 2020.

Task 3

Study **Source C**.

a Identify **three** reasons why people want to leave rural areas in LEDCs.

b Identify **three** attractions of urban areas for people who live in the countryside in LEDCs.

Task 4

Study **Sources D and E**.

Many people move to urban areas in LEDCs for a better quality of life.

Do you think they achieve this? Give reasons for your answer.

CASE STUDY 8a Urbanisation in Peru – Lima

A Peru – an LEDC in South America

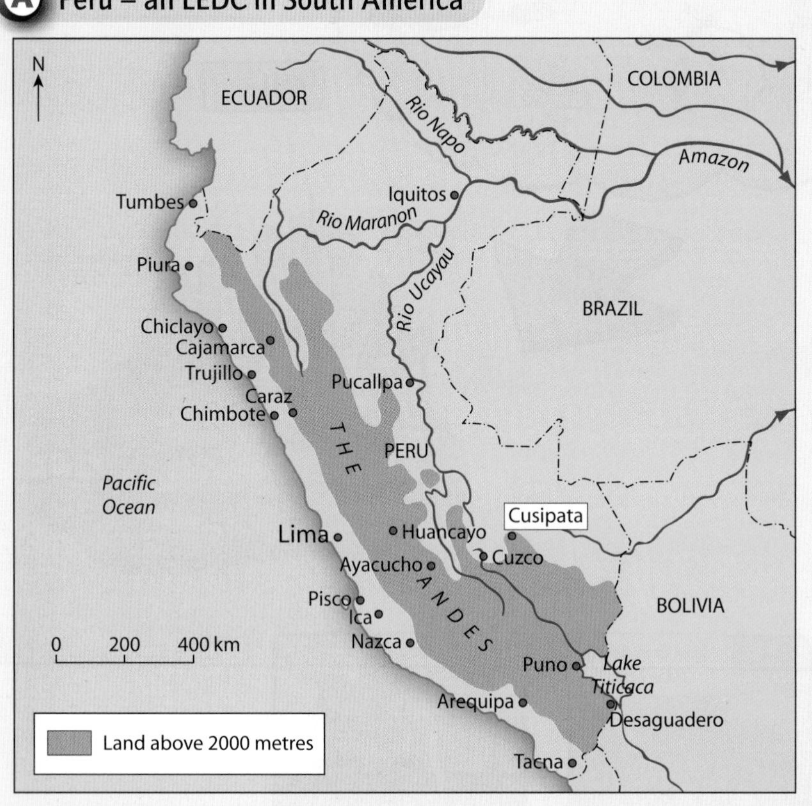

Task 1

Study **Source A**.

a Describe the location within Peru of Lima and Cusipata.
b What is the distance from Cusipata to Lima?

Task 2

Study **Sources B and D**.

Use evidence from the photographs to describe differences between the housing in the village and Lima.

B Housing in Lima

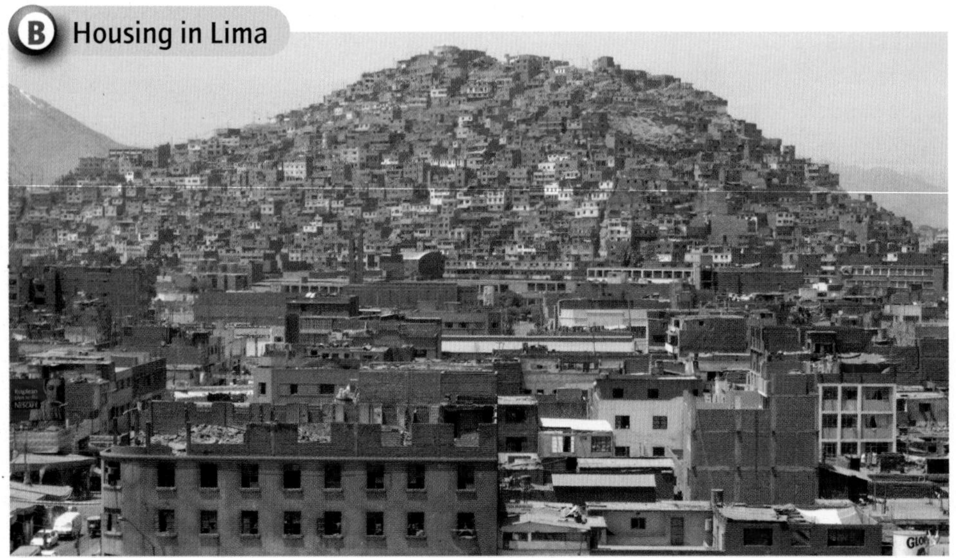

Moving into the city

Source B shows housing in Lima, the capital city of Peru, which has been built by migrants who have arrived from rural areas. About 35 per cent of Peru's 10 million people live in its capital city, but the population has not always been distributed like this. In 1940, Lima's population was 600 000, or 10 per cent of the country's total, and most of the population lived in rural areas, mainly in the Andes mountains. As Peru's population has grown, more people chose to move away from their villages and small towns to the capital city, where they hoped for a better life for themselves and their children.

Cusipata is a typical village in the Peruvian Andes. Its population is about 500 people who live by combining agriculture with paid work outside the village. The main crops grown are potatoes, maize, barley and beans, and most families keep some sheep, a pig and some llamas. Due to steep slopes and the unpredictable climate, farming is a difficult job and yields are often low. So, traditionally, family members have worked for part of the year in the large town of Cuzco, which is one hour away by bus. However, increasing numbers of young men and women are leaving Cusipata to migrate permanently to Lima to find work in the capital city.

Task 3

Study **Source C**.

How and why does migration affect the population structure of rural Peru and Lima?

C Population pyramids for rural Peru and Lima

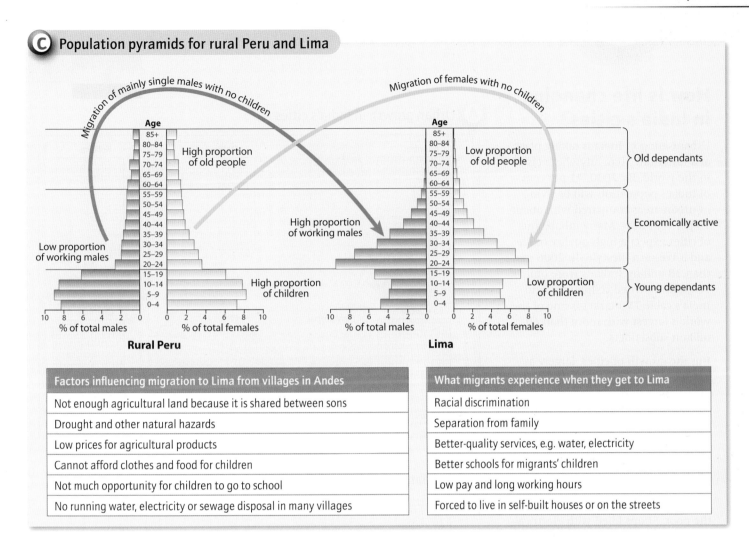

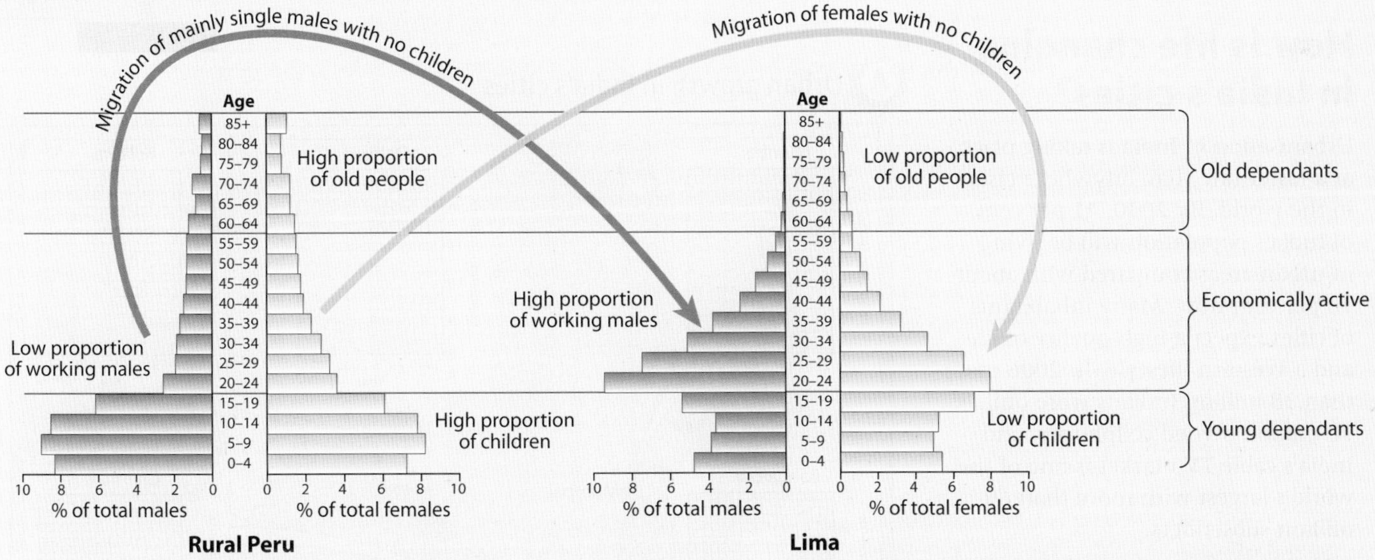

Factors influencing migration to Lima from villages in Andes
Not enough agricultural land because it is shared between sons
Drought and other natural hazards
Low prices for agricultural products
Cannot afford clothes and food for children
Not much opportunity for children to go to school
No running water, electricity or sewage disposal in many villages

What migrants experience when they get to Lima
Racial discrimination
Separation from family
Better-quality services, e.g. water, electricity
Better schools for migrants' children
Low pay and long working hours
Forced to live in self-built houses or on the streets

D A village in the Peruvian Andes

Task 4

Imagine you have migrated from Cusipata to Lima. Write a letter to your parents who still live in Cusipata, telling them about your new life and experiences in the capital city.

Urbanisation in India – Mumbai

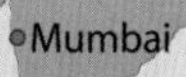

How is life changing in India's cities?

Urbanisation in India is taking place at a faster rate than anywhere else in the world. By 2030, 41 per cent of India's population will be living in urban areas compared with about 28 per cent now. Many inhabitants of cities expect a high quality of life and a Western lifestyle. In 2006 more than 38 million Indians were online, 70 million owned cellphones, and India's cable TV market is one of the world's largest with more than 60 million subscribers.

But the growth of cities, largely as a result of rural to urban migration, puts a great strain on urban infrastructure, such as road networks and public transport, power and water supplies, along with pressure on health care and education services. There are great contrasts between rich and poor. The well-built homes of the rich contrast with the huts of the poor. Shops filled with electrical goods and air-conditioned restaurants cater to the privileged, while children with outstretched hands wait outside in the hope of receiving a few coins.

A Urban growth in India's cities

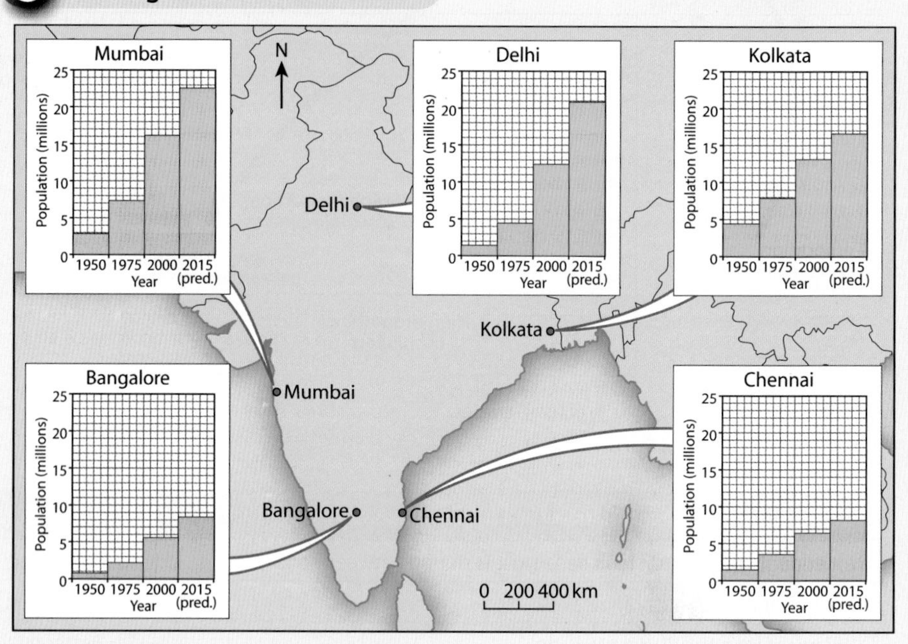

B Population growth of Mumbai

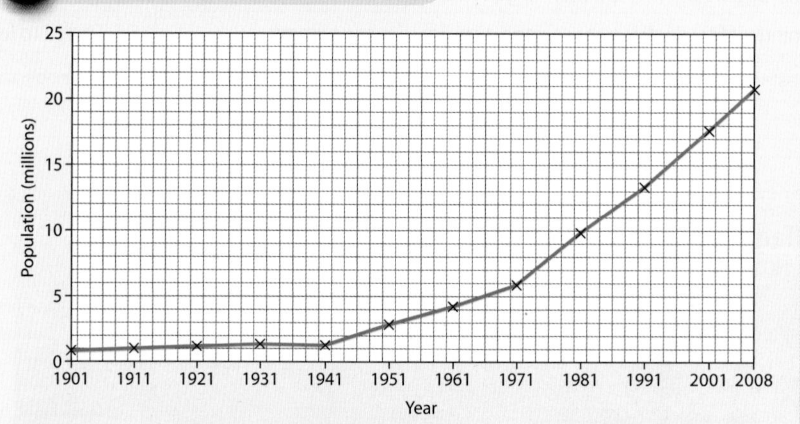

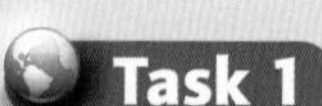

Task 1

Study **Source A**.

a Which city in India had the largest population in 1950?

b By how much did Kolkata's population increase between 1975 and 2000?

c What is Mumbai's expected population in 2015?

Task 2

Study **Source B**.

Compare the growth of Mumbai's population between 1901 and 1941 with its growth between 1951 and 2008. Use figures in your answer.

C Dharavi – Asia's largest slum

Dharavi, the largest slum in Asia, houses more than a million slum dwellers in cramped homes, close to the centre of India's financial capital, Mumbai.

The migrants who originally made Dharavi their home are the Maharashtrians from the Konkan coast, the Gujarati community, the Muslim tanners from Tamil Nadu and artisans from Uttar Pradesh.

In present-day Dharavi there are poor standards of sanitation and health care. But there is a silver lining as well, as Dharavi provides a cheap home to people who move to Mumbai to earn their living. Even in the smallest of rooms, there is usually a cooking gas stove and continuous electricity.

It has a thriving leather trade and garment industry and there are many small-scale industries that produce clothes, leather goods, pottery and plastic.

D Images of Mumbai

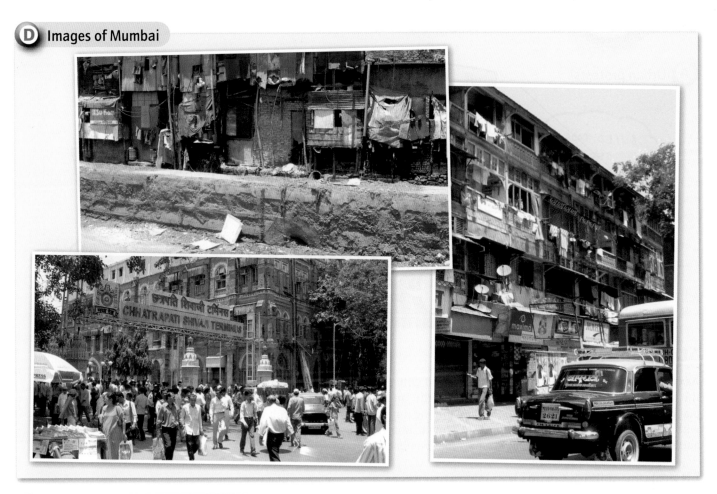

E The layout of the Dharavi slums

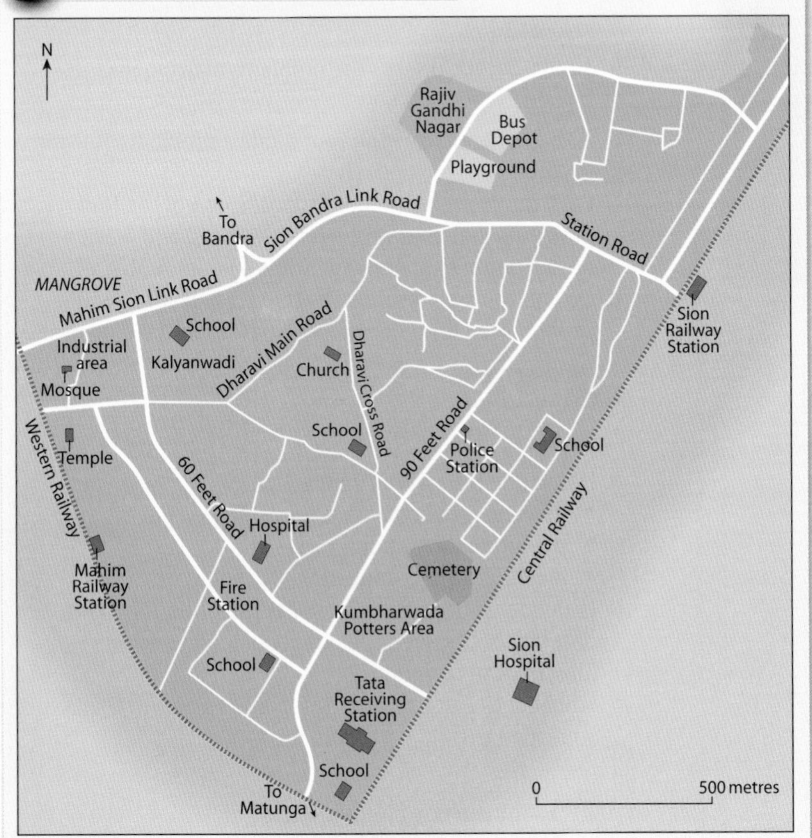

Task 3

Study **Sources C and D.**

Make a list of the advantages and problems of living in Mumbai for people who have migrated from rural areas.

Task 4

Study **Source E.**

a Identify:
- **three** services in Dharavi
- **two** areas where employment is available
- **two** methods by which people could travel to other parts of Mumbai to work.

b Use the scale to estimate the area of Dharavi.

Sample case study question

For a named city in an LEDC, explain how the living conditions have been improved.

TOPIC 9 Urban problems

A Urban protests!

Stress in the cities

As cities increase in size they become stressful and difficult places to live in. Parts of the cities become run-down and undesirable. As the land use of many cities was not planned for the current population, they are finding it more and more difficult to cope with the large numbers of people. Efforts to provide homes, services, transportation and jobs are already losing the race against rapid population growth.

B Quality of life indicators for eight urban areas

Urban area	Average number of people per room	% of homes with water and electricity	Murders per 100 000 people	Levels of noise (1–10) 1 = low 10 = high	Mean traffic speed (km/hr in rush hour)	Levels of air pollution (1–10) 1 = low 10 = high
Cairo (Egypt)	1.5	94	56.4	7	12.4	10
Jakarta (Indonesia)	3.4	85	5.3	6	16.3	10
London (UK)	0.6	100	2.5	8	10.4	3
Melbourne (Australia)	0.5	100	2.0	3	20.3	1
Moscow (Russia)	1.3	100	7.0	6	31.5	7
San Francisco (USA)	0.6	98	5.8	3	16.0	3
Seoul (South Korea)	2.0	100	1.2	7	13.8	7
Shanghai (China)	2.0	95	2.5	5	15.3	3

Task 1

Study **Source A**.

In groups of four, discuss the problems of living in cities as follows.

a As a group, identify the **four** biggest problems of living in cities.

b Each group member should choose **one** of the four problems that your group has identified and make a presentation explaining why it is a major problem.

c Do you think all residents of the city will agree with your choice of problems? Give reasons for your answer.

Task 2

Study **Source B**.

a Name **one** urban area where:
- housing is overcrowded
- the air quality is poor
- levels of traffic congestion are high.

b Using only information from the table, identify the differences between the quality of life of people in Moscow and Shanghai.

c Which of the cities would you prefer to live in? Explain your choice using data from the table.

C Solving problems in LEDCs

The Shanghai Metro

Pedestrian street in Shanghai

Solving Shanghai's traffic congestion

The Shanghai Metro is an urban rapid transit system which is used daily by an average of 2.18 million people. The system incorporates both subways and elevated light railways. Shanghai is the third city in China to build a subway system after Beijing and Tianjin. Whilst traffic congestion is still a problem in some parts of Shanghai, the metro system provides people with a cheap, efficient public transport service to most parts of the city, including traffic-free parts of the Central Business District.

Task 3

Study **Source C**.

a Explain how Shanghai has attempted to solve the traffic problem.

b Suggest the advantages and disadvantages to residents of Shanghai of using a public transport system such as this.

Task 4

Study **Source D**.

With a partner discuss the advantages and disadvantages of comprehensive development and urban regeneration as methods of solving problems of urban decay.

D Solving problems in MEDCs

Urban decay

Urban decay occurs when parts of the city become run-down and undesirable to live in. Examples of urban decay are:

- slum housing, with outside toilets, overcrowding, no hot water or central heating
- buildings in disrepair with leaking roofs, draughty windows and crumbling brickwork
- empty buildings boarded up or vandalised
- areas where buildings have been knocked down and which turn into derelict land.

There have been a number of schemes to reduce the problems of urban decay. Comprehensive redevelopment occurs when all the buildings are knocked down and the area is completely rebuilt, for example old housing and factories demolished and replaced by new flats and multi-storey high-rise buildings. This approach has been criticised as people have to move from their established communities and workplaces – they no longer know their neighbours and they are moved away from their friends and relations.

Urban regeneration is the renovation of existing housing and improvement of the environment and economy including:

- rewiring the houses and fitting central heating
- fitting double glazing
- cleaning the outsides of old buildings by sand-blasting
- improving the environment by landscaping
- building or improving the social facilities such as clubs and medical centres
- encouraging new businesses and industry to set up in the areas with grants and loans.

This has proved more popular as people have been able to stay in their own area.

Comprehensive redevelopment

Urban regeneration

Urban problems and solutions – Cairo

A Cairo – a city in Egypt

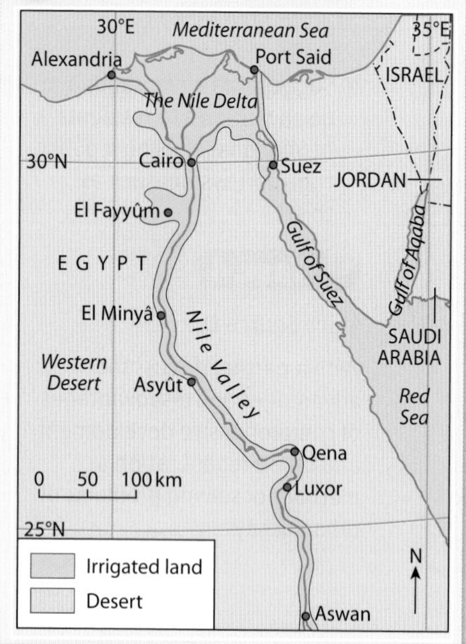

Cairo – a city with problems!

Cairo is located around the banks and islands of the river Nile in the north of Egypt, immediately south of the point where the river leaves its valley and enters the Nile delta. Since the 1950s the city's growth has been rapid, rising from 2 million to 18 million by 2000, as a result of natural increase and rural to urban migration. The growth has been too rapid for the city to cope, with increasing demands for services such as piped water, sewers, schools, paved roads and electricity. Traffic congestion, along with noise, air and water pollution, add to the problems.

Task 1

Study **Source A**.

a Give a reference, using latitude and longitude, for Cairo.

b Using evidence from the map, suggest reasons for the location and growth of Cairo.

Task 2

Study **Source B**.

a List the **four** main problems faced by Cairo. Use examples in your answer.

b Put the problems in a rank order 1–4 depending on which you would want to solve first. Do your classmates agree? Justify your order.

Task 3

Study **Source C**.

Describe the pattern of migration to Cairo. Refer to named places or areas and use statistics in your answer.

B Planning problems

Lack of housing	• Self-built brick houses are built illegally on farmlands by the river Nile. These 'informal' houses cover 80% of Cairo.
	• In the Cities of the Dead, 2–3 million people have set up homes amongst the tombs of Old Cairo.
	• Half a million people live in homemade huts on roof spaces of office blocks and flats in the city centre.
Traffic congestion	• Between 1970 and 2000 the number of cars in Cairo rose from 100 000 to over a million.
	• Travel to work times can be very slow.
	• Many drivers are aggressive and do not keep to the rules of the road, causing danger for road users and pedestrians.
Lack of jobs	• Jobs for unskilled workers are hard to find.
	• Whilst many university graduates get jobs with the government, salaries are low.
	• Many poor people are forced to work in the informal sector, selling things on the streets to earn a meagre living.
Pollution	• The air is heavily polluted by a cocktail of vehicle exhausts and fumes from fuels used in homes and workplaces.
	• Groundwater is polluted by waste illegally dumped by factories and workshops.
	• Leaking and inadequate sewers pollute water courses.

C Migration to Cairo

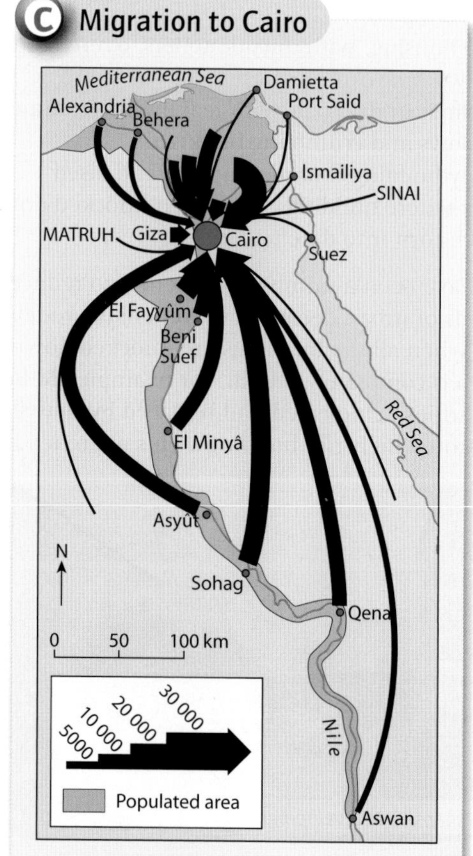

D Six solutions?

E New towns – another solution?

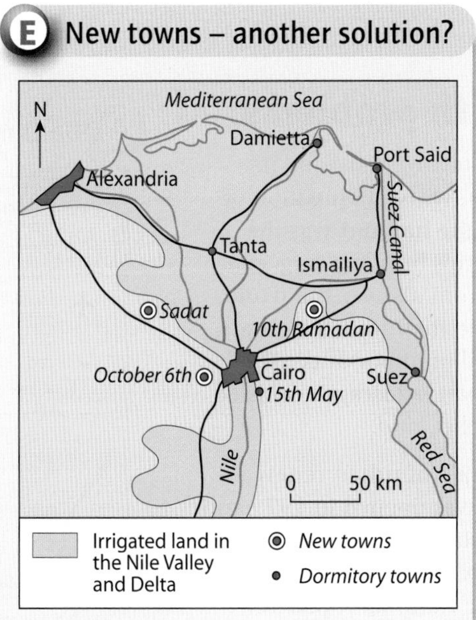

Task 4

Study **Source D**.

a How might each solution help to solve Cairo's problems?

b Suggest **two** problems that will not be solved by these solutions.

Task 5

Study **Source E**.

a Name **two** new towns and **two** dormitory towns.

b Explain how the building of new towns and dormitory towns will help to solve Cairo's problems.

F The Cairo metro

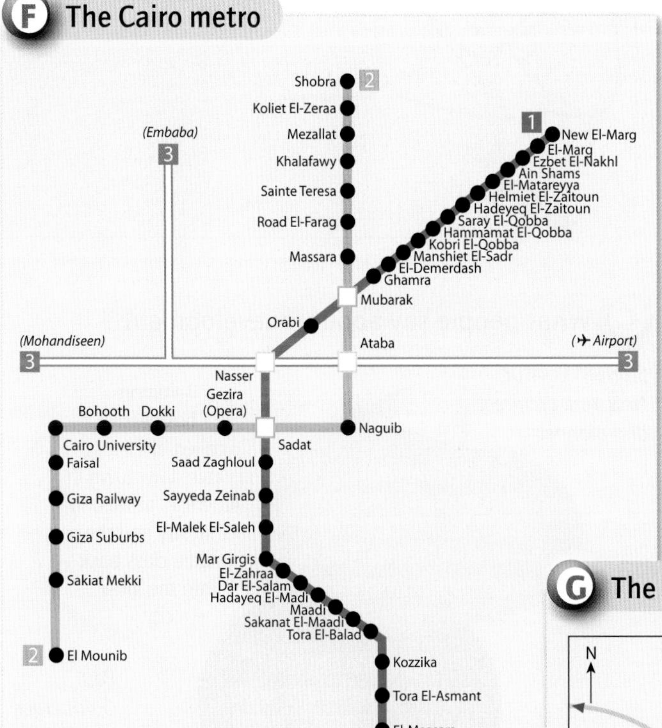

Task 6

Study **Sources F and G**.

Two groups of international tourists are visiting Cairo. They will land at the international airport. Produce an annotated (fully labelled) map to show:

a the directions to drive from the airport to the Giza pyramids

b the directions to use the metro from the airport to Cairo University.

G The Cairo ring-road

N
To Alexandria
To Ismailiya
Bahtim
Usim
Heliopolis
Cairo International Airport
To 6 October City
To Suez
Kardasa
Bulaq al-Dakrur
City Centre
Abbasiya
Nasr City
The Fifth Aggregation
Muqattam Hills
Old Cairo
Giza Pyramids
To Fayoum
Nile
To Upper Egypt
0 5 km
Ring road
Highway
Main road
Bridge

CASE STUDY 9b Urban problems and solutions – Baltimore

Baltimore – a city with problems!

Baltimore is the largest city in the state of Maryland in the United States of America (USA), with a population of 650 000. In Baltimore's early days, the harbour was the landing destination for boats and ships bringing cargoes such as bananas, sugar and cocoa from all over the world. By the 1970s the port and associated manufacturing and shipbuilding industries had declined in importance. The inner harbour and surrounding urban landscape consisted of abandoned warehouses and derelict land.

Today the area is a successful example of urban renewal. The Baltimore Convention Center was opened in 1979 and renovated and expanded in 1996. Harborplace, a modern urban retail and restaurant complex, was opened on the waterfront in 1980, followed by the National Aquarium and the Baltimore Museum of Industry in 1981. Over 100 hectares of previously derelict industrial buildings and wasteland have been transformed into a mix of businesses, housing, recreation and tourist attractions.

A Baltimore – a city in the USA

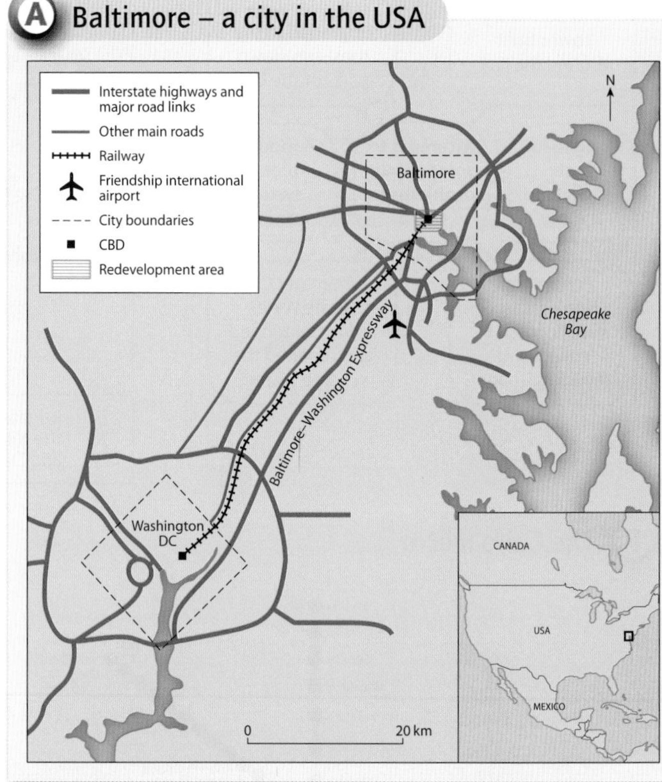

B Baltimore's inner harbour

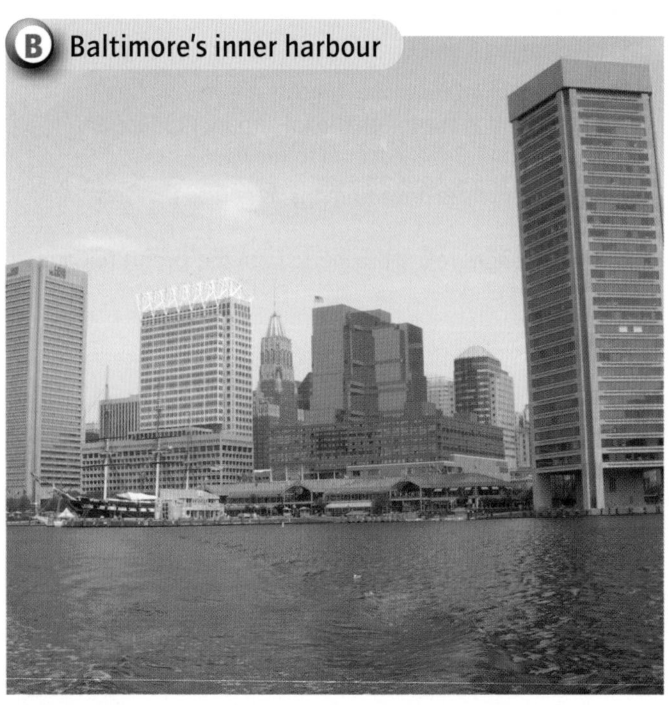

C What people say about redevelopment

Stanton Eckstut, New York architect and planner: The downtown has to be one of the most diverse, comfortable and convenient in America. Cars do not dominate, people do.

Paul Goldberger, New York Times: Baltimore has been called 'the most livable downtown in America', attracting industry and the middle class back into the inner city.

Richard Rogers, British architect: Today the city, and especially the harbour area, is one of the most beautiful modern places I have ever visited.

Task 1

Study **Source A**.

a Describe the location of Baltimore in the USA.
b Give **three** reasons why Baltimore is in a good position to attract businesses and tourists to the new inner harbour development.

Task 2

Study **Sources B, C, D and E.**

a Describe the main features of the urban landscape shown in the photographs.
b Using the evidence in the photographs, do you agree with the quotations in **Source C**? Give reasons for your views.

D Baltimore's 'Power Plant' development

The Power Plant is a mixed-use project developed in the late 1990s in a historic power station, built in 1900. The $30 million project includes loft offices on the upper floors, a bookstore, Hard Rock Café, a gym, nightclubs and entertainment.

E Redeveloped housing in Baltimore

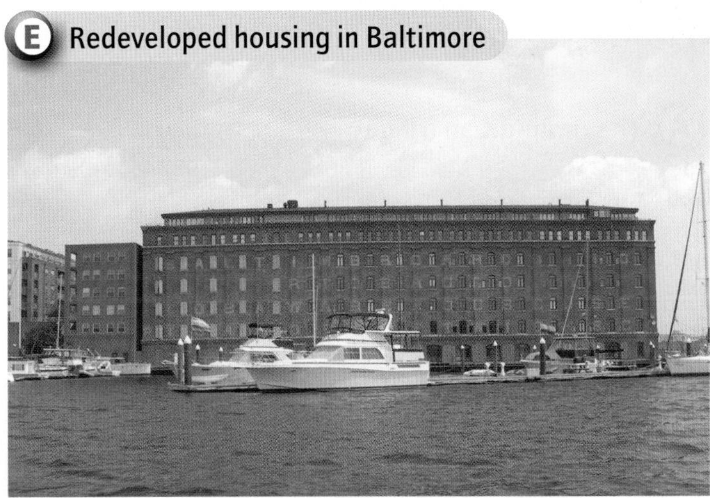

F How do you feel ...?

Retired dock worker

Banker who works in Washington DC and lives in a new inner-harbour apartment

16-year-old school leaver with no qualifications

Owner of construction firm in Baltimore

Why has this scheme succeeded?

This urban redevelopment scheme has been very successful in that it has created both jobs and housing, and changed the economic base of the city. The mixture of business, residential, recreational and cultural developments has made it attractive to different groups of people.

Baltimore's proximity to Washington DC has been crucial. Investors, including large businesses such as IBM and Lazard Freres, liked this. Costs were lower than in Washington DC, but the standard of living was as high. It is only 45 minutes between the centres of Washington DC and Baltimore. There are over 30 trains a day linking the two cities and the Baltimore/Washington international airport is located between them. Within the city commuting is highly efficient: from suburbs like Guilford and Ashburton it takes no more than 10 minutes to the harbour area using public transport.

Task 3

For each of the four people shown in **Source F**, decide what they will feel about the redevelopment of Baltimore's inner harbour. Give reasons for their views.

Sample case study question

In all large urban areas there have been changes in land use. These include the development of:

- road networks
- industrial areas
- residential areas
- leisure and shopping facilities.

For a named urban area, identify a recent change in land use. Describe the advantages and disadvantages of this development for people who live in the urban area that you have named.

Urban sprawl

A The rural–urban fringe

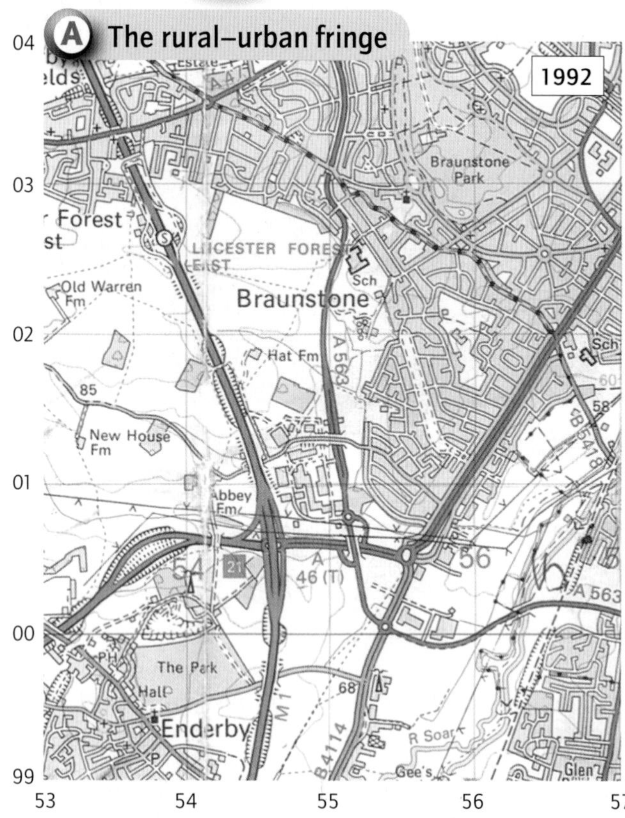

Map 1 shows the rural–urban fringe to the south-west of Leicester, a city in the United Kingdom (UK), in 1992.

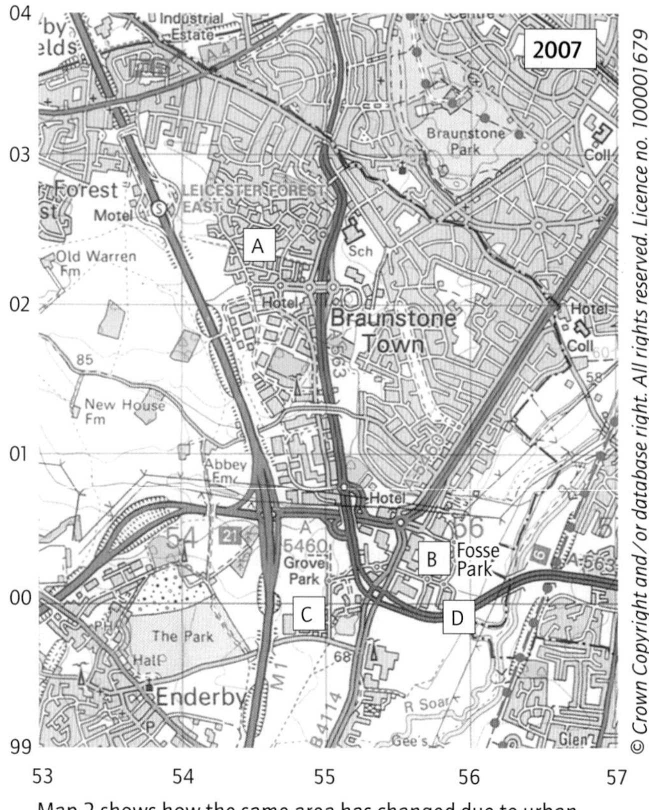

Map 2 shows how the same area has changed due to urban sprawl over the 15-year period 1992–2007.

B Changing views

Sprawl – different causes, same result!

A century ago, nine in every ten people lived in villages and the countryside. Now almost 50 per cent of the planet's population jostles for space in fast-growing congested cities. By 2050 the figure is expected to reach 75 per cent. All these people will hope for or expect housing, work, services and a high quality of life.

As population increases in towns and cities, urban sprawl takes place. This happens in both MEDCs and LEDCs but the causes are different. Urban sprawl tends to be unplanned in LEDC cities and planned in MEDC cities – but the outcome is similar. In both cases the urban area expands into the countryside, affecting people and changing the environment at the rural–urban fringe. Land use changes around the urban area for the benefit of some and to the disadvantage of others.

Task 1

Study **Source A**.

- **a** Estimate the land use in km² that was built on in 1992. How had this changed by 2007? (Note: The scale is 1:50 000 or 2 cm = 1 km.)
- **b** Use 4- or 6-figure grid-references to identify **two** different types of land use that have been built on since 1992.
- **c** In which direction do you think sprawl will take place in the next 15 years? Justify your decision.

Task 2

Study **Sources A and B**.

- **a** Match photos 1–4 with locations A–D on Map 2.
- **b** List the **four** different land uses shown.
- **c** Suggest why these have been located in the rural–urban fringe.
- **d** Suggest groups of people who will benefit from or be disadvantaged by this sprawl. Explain your choices.

C Urban sprawl in MEDCs

In MEDCs the building of houses and services on the edge of existing towns and cities is planned. A decision is made by the local government that it is necessary to expand into rural areas and the countryside. Although there may be objections, once a decision is made to expand into the countryside then the urban sprawl will happen in an organised way.

Housing developments on the edge of Sacramento, California, USA

Little Boxes
Little boxes on the hillside,
Little boxes made of ticky-tacky,
Little boxes, little boxes,
Little boxes, all the same.
There's a green one and a pink one
And a blue one and a yellow one
And they're all made out of ticky-tacky
And they all look just the same.

Written by Malvina Reynolds

D Urban sprawl in LEDCs

Squatter settlements (favelas) *on the edge of São Paulo, Brazil*

In LEDCs urban sprawl is often unplanned. The urbanisation of cities in LEDCs has been so rapid that planners rarely have time to organise and build the infrastructure to cope with the newcomers. This means that many unplanned squatter settlements develop around the edge of the city without permission from the authorities.

E Waiting for the city

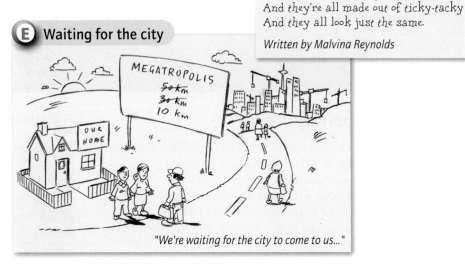

"We're waiting for the city to come to us..."

Task 3

a On an outline sketch of **Source C** shade in:
- housing
- roads
- trees
- fields.

b How can you tell that this urban sprawl is 'planned?

c Read 'Little Boxes'. How well do you think this describes urban sprawl in MEDCs?

Task 4

Study **Source D**.

a How might the materials used to build these houses differ from the houses shown in **Source C**?

b How 'planned' does this urban sprawl appear to be?

c Suggest **three** problems that residents here may experience that would not be found in **Source C**. Explain your choices.

Task 5

Study **Source E**.

Draw a cartoon or write a short poem or a song that puts across the message related to urban sprawl in either an LEDC city or an MEDC city.

CASE STUDY 10 Urban sprawl in Atlanta

Atlanta

A Sprawl at night – growth since 1993

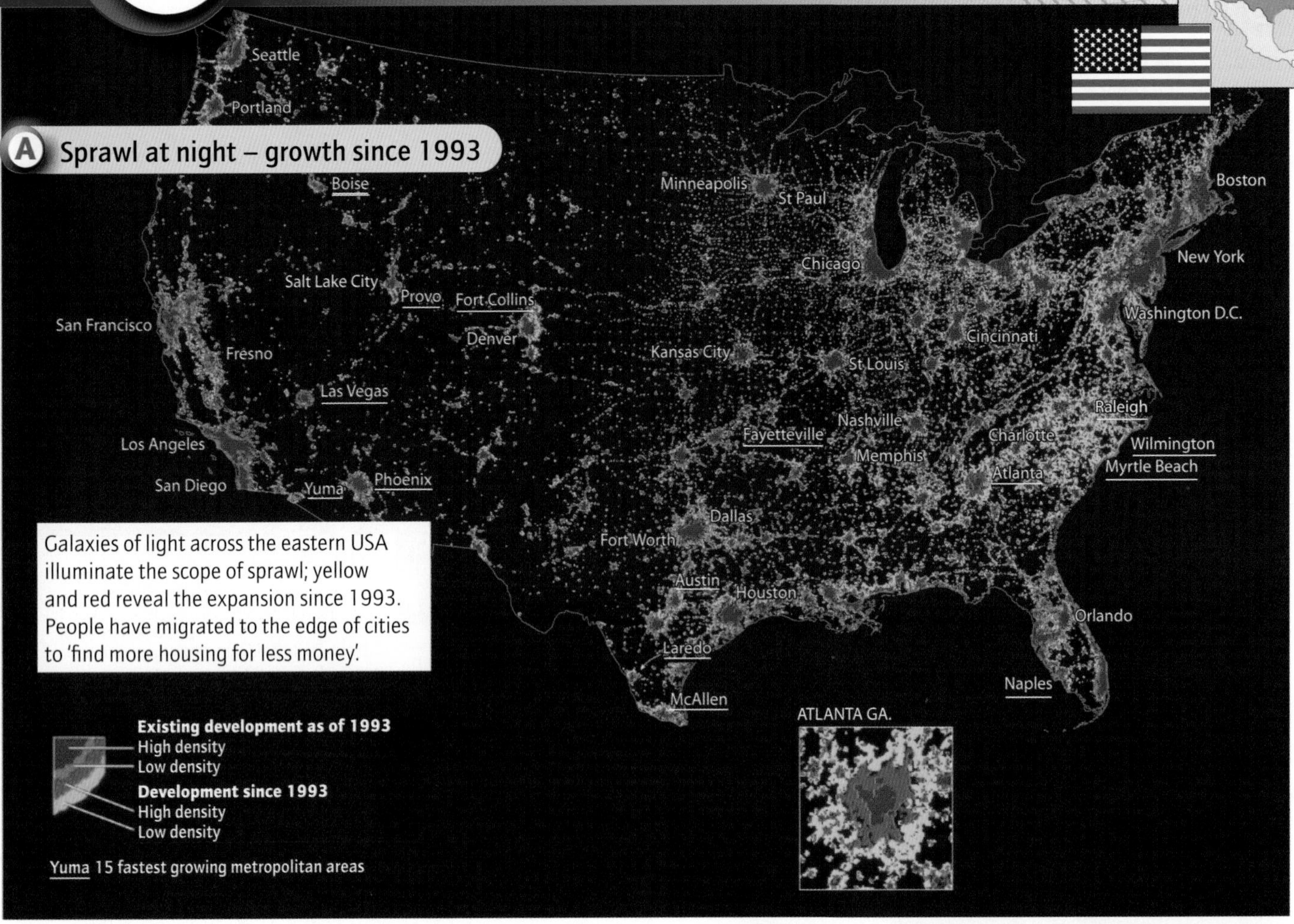

Seattle
Portland
Boise
Salt Lake City
Provo
Fort Collins
Denver
San Francisco
Fresno
Las Vegas
Los Angeles
San Diego
Yuma
Phoenix
Minneapolis
St Paul
Chicago
Kansas City
St Louis
Cincinnati
Boston
New York
Washington D.C.
Nashville
Fayetteville
Memphis
Charlotte
Raleigh
Wilmington
Myrtle Beach
Atlanta
Dallas
Fort Worth
Austin
Houston
Laredo
McAllen
Orlando
Naples
ATLANTA GA.

Galaxies of light across the eastern USA illuminate the scope of sprawl; yellow and red reveal the expansion since 1993. People have migrated to the edge of cities to 'find more housing for less money'.

Existing development as of 1993
High density
Low density
Development since 1993
High density
Low density

Yuma 15 fastest growing metropolitan areas

A rapidly growing city

Atlanta is the capital city of Georgia state. Its population has grown from 1.4 million in 1970 to a figure of 5 138 000 in the US 2006 census. Between 2000 and 2006 Atlanta added almost 1 million residents to its total – the fastest-growing metropolitan city in the USA. One-third of the increase was by births, the rest from newcomers. Inevitably this growth, over 40 years, has resulted in urban sprawl.

Task 1

Study **Source A** and an atlas.

a List the five fastest-growing cities in the eastern USA.
b Which parts of the USA have seen most growth since 1993?
c Describe the location of Atlanta.
d Estimate by how much the city has grown since 1993. Why has this growth continued into the 21st century?

Task 2

Study **Source B**.

a Give **two** reasons why Atlanta became an important city.
b Why has recent growth taken place?
c What problems has rapid population growth created? What are the planners aiming to do?

B Atlanta, a City in the Forest – once!

The city was established in the 1840s in woodland near the junction of railway lines. It was called the 'City in the Forest'. Its location was ideal to link the north-east with south-east USA. An airport was built and it became a financial centre. Atlanta has attracted migrants for over 150 years. Recent population growth has been caused by newcomers from cities around the Great Lakes where unemployment is high. Others have moved from expensive housing in the north-east to Atlanta's relatively cheap housing. The city now has a reputation of wall-to-wall offices, shopping centres and suburbs. The Atlanta of today is traffic-choked, overdeveloped, polluted and has a major water supply crisis. Today's planners are trying to give the city an environmental makeover and economic boost. Martin Luther King (1929–68), the civil rights activist, was born in Atlanta and the 1996 summer Olympic Games was held here.

C Growth creates problems

Population growth – Atlanta is the largest metropolitan area in south-east USA. With 5.1 million people in 2006 (up from 1.4 million in 1970) urban sprawl was inevitable.

Traffic congestion – plus air and noise pollution is the fourth worst in the USA. There are 50 000 km of roads in Atlanta. 90% of residents drive to work experiencing 68 hours of delays per year.

Air quality – traffic congestion causes increases in respiratory illnesses such as emphysema, bronchitis and asthma. Air stagnates here so fumes from vehicles are rarely blown away.

Water quality and quantity – suburbs along the Chattahoochee river increase run-off and contaminate drinking water with pollutants. Sanitation systems cannot cope. Over 1 million Atlantans use septic tanks, which often leak. Increased water demand for industry and irrigation uses up supplies, affecting fishing habitats.

Agricultural land – expansion has meant that farmland has been bought and covered with shopping malls and other developments.

Cherokee
Forsyth
N
Gwinnett
Cobb
Norcross
Marietta
Dekalb
Fulton
Conyers
Douglas
Rockdale
Clayton
Henry
Coweta
Fayette
0 16 km

Urbanised areas
Edge of Atlanta metropolitan area 1973
Edge of Atlanta metropolitan area 2008

Loss of green space/ecosystems – between 1982 and 2002 over 38% of green space within Atlanta's city boundary was built on. The city loses an average of 125 hectares of trees per day by deforestation. Ecosystems suffer as wildlife dies or migrates away.

Impermeable surfaces – more concrete and asphalt replacing soil and trees means surface water cannot drain away, causing flash floods and water contamination.

Cultural loss – civil war battlefields surrounding Atlanta, such as the Kennesaw Mountain National Battlefield to the north, are under threat from suburban homes.

Socio-economic division – most sprawl is to the north where white middle-class suburbs have developed. The inner city has had less investment; this is where the poorer black population has stayed.

Hotlanta – the removal of trees such as maple, oak and elm and the addition of concrete encourages more heat build-up and a 'heat island' over the city. Temperatures can be up to 10°C higher than in the countryside.

There are no large bodies of water, mountains or other obstacles to limit the city's outward growth. Atlanta's urban area has more than doubled since 1973.

D Reversing sprawl

Outer Limits

Sprawling Atlanta seeks new route to the future

May 2008

The city's new plan is focused in the city rather than on the edge. It includes public transport with a 35-mile Beltline project that combines light rail with new pedestrian and bike links. There is also a heavy investment in 'green' buildings such as the university campus setting new standards for sustainable construction. Brownfield sites are also being regenerated with 'green' buildings rather than extending the city's edge.

Atlantic Station is being built on a former steel mill site. When completed this will provide office space plus 5000 high-rise loft units, town-houses and single-family homes. Cars can be left here as there are dedicated lanes for walking or biking to work. This is part of Atlanta's 'smart growth' project where homes and businesses are easily linked by transport routes. Reversing sprawl by infilling the centre with sustainable high-rise buildings linked to transport routes is a key part of the new plan. 'Trees Atlanta' is also using volunteers to plant maple, oak and holly trees. Residents are now starting to move back inside the city limits.

Task 3

Study **Source C**.

a Describe how Atlanta has expanded since 1973.

b Identify **two** problems that affect people and **two** problems affecting the environment. For each one suggest a strategy to deal with it.

c Discuss with your classmates how you would solve the problems they chose.

Task 4

Study **Source D**.

a List **three** ways in which Atlanta is trying to solve its sprawl problems.

b In which part of the city are these ideas taking place? Why?

c Is there any evidence of success with this plan? Give examples to explain your answer.

d What other plans do you think are needed? What should be the priorities for Atlanta?

Sample case study question

Name an example of a town or city you have studied where urban sprawl has taken place. Describe its impacts on local people.

GLOBAL ISSUE

1 HIV/AIDS

A What is HIV/AIDS?

The **Human Immunodeficiency Virus (HIV)** is a sexually transmitted infection (STI) – a virus that attacks the body's immune system. The virus attacks special cells found in blood which help immunity. Once these cells stop working the immune system stops working. With no immunity a person can develop a serious infection. Once diagnosed the virus will stay with the person for life. **Acquired Immune Deficiency Syndrome (AIDS)** is a term used to describe later stages of HIV when the immune system has stopped working. At the moment there is no cure.

Task 1

Study **Source A**.

a Write down what the initials HIV, STI and AIDS mean.

b How is the body's immune system affected by HIV/AIDS?

B Adult rate of HIV/AIDS infection

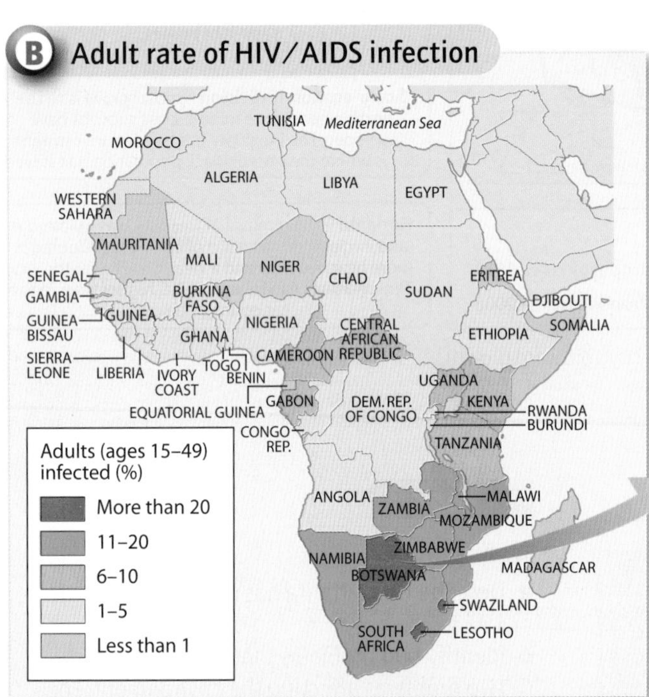

C HIV/AIDS and population structure in Botswana

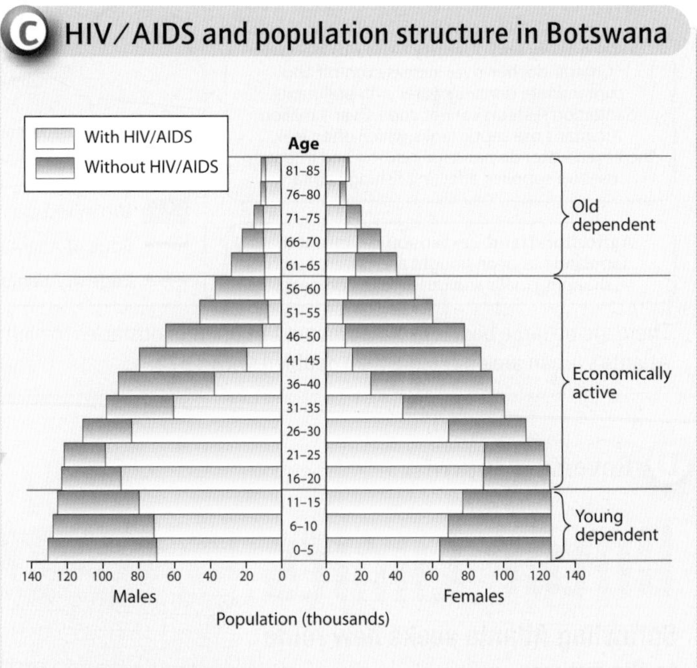

D Tackling HIV/AIDS

HIV can be transmitted in several ways: through unprotected sex, from mother to baby during pregnancy or in breast milk, or from blood-to-blood contact through sharing needles.

AIDS
We are all at risk
TALK ABOUT AIDS
So....
• Stay faithful to your partner
• Use a condom properly everytime

HIV/AIDS – Progress in Africa Threatened

Together with conflict, HIV/AIDS poses the greatest threat to development in Africa. It has the potential to change population structures, damage economies and undermine political stability. Any progress made in recent years could be reversed.

Task 2

Study **Source B**.

a Name **two** countries where over 20% of the adult population are infected by HIV/AIDS and **two** countries where 5% or less are infected.

b Compare the pattern for southern Africa with that in the rest of Africa.

Task 3

Study **Source C**.

a Describe the likely impacts of HIV/AIDS on the size and structure of Botswana's population.

b Suggest how HIV/AIDS could affect the economic development of Botswana.

Task 4

Design a poster similar to the one in **Source D** to advertise to people in Botswana ways to reduce the spread of HIV/AIDS.

Theme 2
The Natural Environment

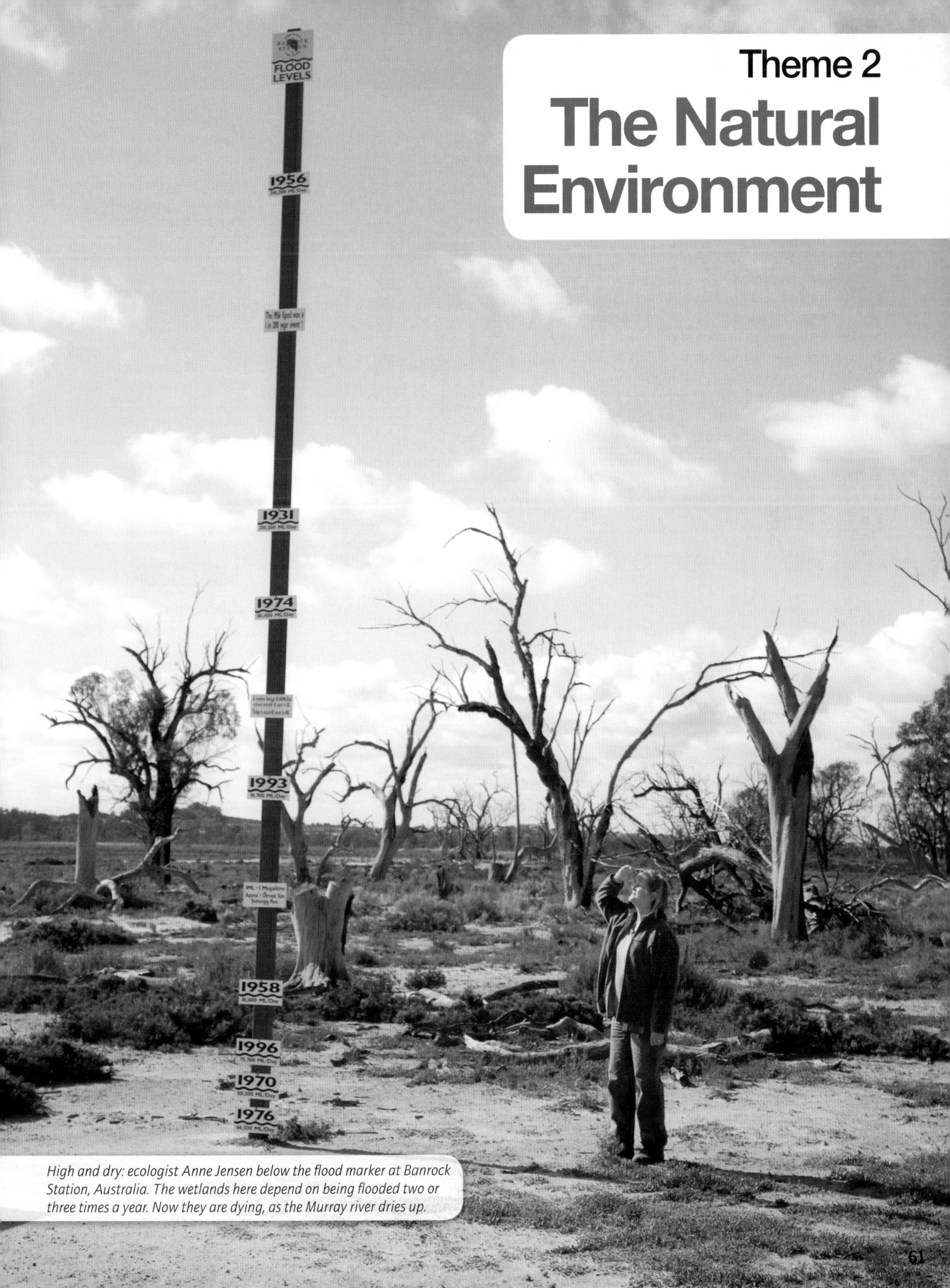

High and dry: ecologist Anne Jensen below the flood marker at Banrock Station, Australia. The wetlands here depend on being flooded two or three times a year. Now they are dying, as the Murray river dries up.

TOPIC 11 Plate tectonics

Under and at the Earth's surface

- Have you experienced an earthquake?
- Do you live near a volcano?
- Do tourists visit your country for the mountain scenery?

For millions of years powerful forces have been at work creating these features. Today scientists know a great deal about the Earth's structure. This is because they study earthquakes, volcanoes and fold mountains. These give clues to what is happening beneath the Earth's crust. Although it is difficult to predict when they will take place, we do know they only occur in certain parts of the world.

A Like biting an apple

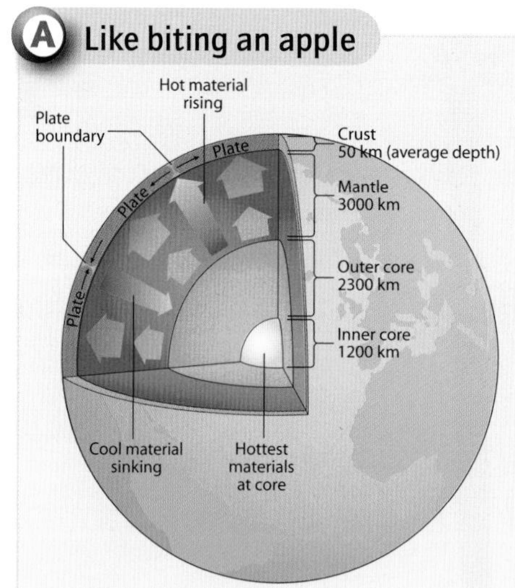

The surface of the Earth is known as the crust. This is a collection of solid **tectonic plates** that join together like a jigsaw puzzle. Around the solid core at the centre of the Earth is a layer of molten **magma**. This is called the mantle. Through this layer flow convection currents. The plates float on the mantle. The **convection currents** move these plates away from or towards or alongside each other. These movements along plate boundaries give rise to earthquakes, volcanoes and fold mountains.

B We all live on a plate …

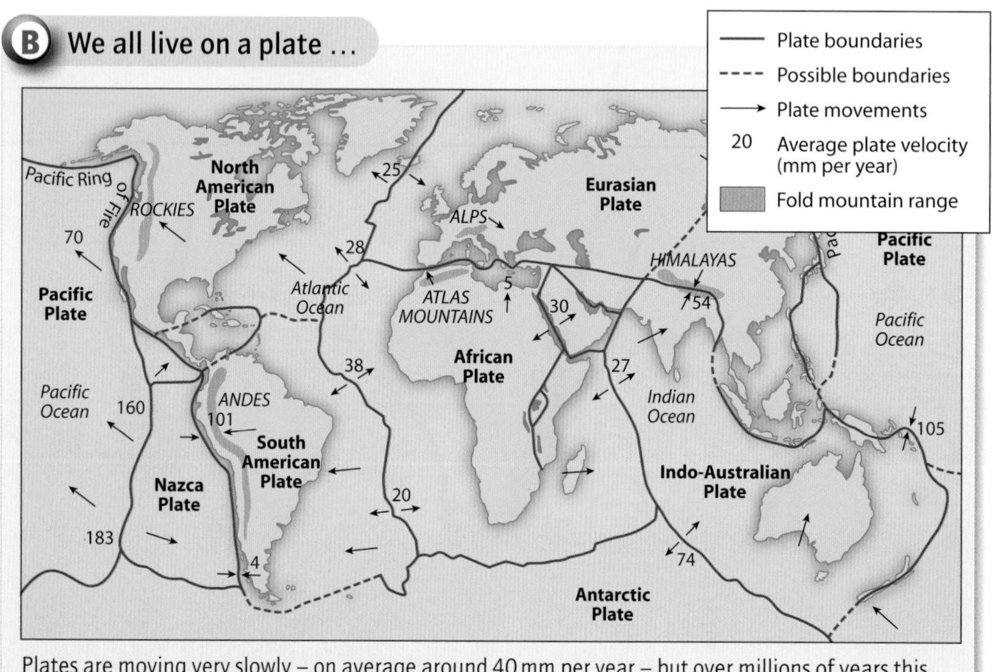

Plates are moving very slowly – on average around 40 mm per year – but over millions of years this can amount to great distances in kilometres.

C The plates are still moving!

A satellite image of the Red Sea

Force of nature parts Red Sea

The Red Sea is parting and creating a new ocean basin. The African and Arabian tectonic plates that meet near the Afar Desert in Ethiopia are pulling apart, creating cracks in the Earth's crust. In six weeks an 8 metre crack appeared along a 60 km stretch of desert. The cracks are being filled with molten magma from the mantle below which then cools to form new crust. The plates are being pushed apart, or **diverging**, by the rising magma. The widening is usually about 30 mm per year but the rate of sea-floor spreading below the Red Sea is more rapid than that.

Task 1

Study **Source A**.

a Make your own labelled drawing of the Earth's structure.

b Why is the structure 'like an apple'?

Task 2

Study **Source B**.

a On which plate do you live?

b List the plates that form boundaries with the plate you live on.

c How close are you to a plate boundary?

d Are these plates moving towards or away from each other?

Task 3

Study **Source C**.

What evidence suggests that the plates are moving apart?

D Converging and diverging plates

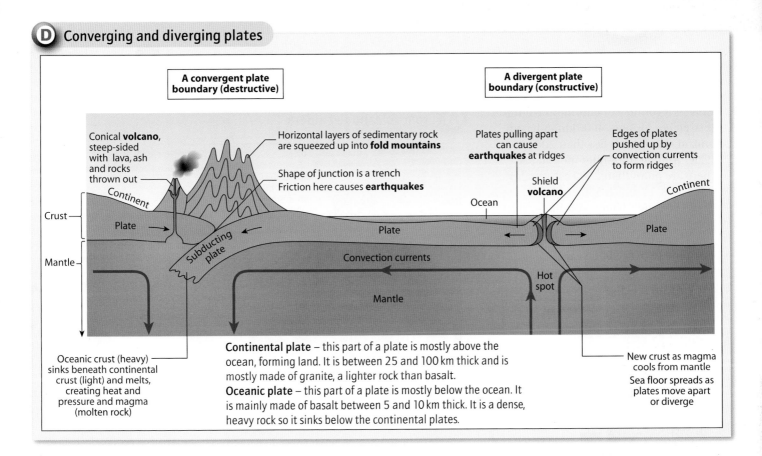

A convergent plate boundary (destructive)

A divergent plate boundary (constructive)

Conical **volcano**, steep-sided with lava, ash and rocks thrown out

Horizontal layers of sedimentary rock are squeezed up into **fold mountains**

Shape of junction is a trench
Friction here causes **earthquakes**

Plates pulling apart can cause **earthquakes** at ridges

Edges of plates pushed up by convection currents to form ridges

Shield **volcano**

Ocean

Continent

Continent

Crust

Mantle

Plate

Subducting plate

Plate

Plate

Convection currents

Hot spot

Mantle

Oceanic crust (heavy) sinks beneath continental crust (light) and melts, creating heat and pressure and magma (molten rock)

Continental plate – this part of a plate is mostly above the ocean, forming land. It is between 25 and 100 km thick and is mostly made of granite, a lighter rock than basalt.
Oceanic plate – this part of a plate is mostly below the ocean. It is mainly made of basalt between 5 and 10 km thick. It is a dense, heavy rock so it sinks below the continental plates.

New crust as magma cools from mantle
Sea floor spreads as plates move apart or diverge

Earthquakes, volcanoes and fold mountains

All recent earthquakes, volcanoes and fold mountains are found along plate boundaries. However, as these plates have been moved around for millions of years, it is possible to find ancient volcanoes and fold mountains some distance from current boundaries. You may live near ancient volcanoes and fold mountains that are now a long way from activity at plate boundaries.

E Fold mountains

Task 4

Study **Source D**.

a Make your own copy of the diagram including all labels.
b Write down the meaning of the following terms:
- *convergent* • *divergent* • *subducting plate.*

c Compare the features found at a destructive plate boundary with those found at a constructive plate boundary.
d What role do convection currents play in plate movement?

Task 5

Study **Sources D and E**.

a Explain where and how fold mountains are formed.
b Why is Mt Everest still rising?

Mount Everest is named after George Everest (Surveyor-General of India who surveyed it in 1865). Locally (in Nepal) it is called Sagermartha, 'Goddess of the Sky' or (in Tibet) Chomolunga, 'Mother Goddess of the Universe'. Fold mountains consist of folded sedimentary rock which can be up to 12 000 metres thick. Originally the rocks were deposited beneath a sea or lake in horizontal layers. Converging plates squeezed together and raised these beds up to form fold mountains. Mt Everest, in the Himalayas, is the highest mountain above sea level at 8848 metres. It was formed about 60 million years ago. It is still rising by a few millimetres each year as the Indian plate continues to move towards the Eurasian plate.

CASE STUDY **11a**

A volcano in Chile

A country of contrasts

Chile is a country of enormous contrasts. It stretches for over 4000 km in length and, at the most, is less than 200 km wide. Among the Andes mountains there are more than 2000 ash and lava volcanoes, of which 500 are active. On 2 May 2008 the Chaiten volcano – which was thought to be dormant – surprised everybody by suddenly erupting for the first time in over 9000 years.

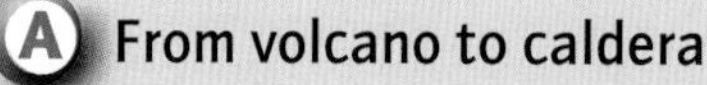

A From volcano to caldera

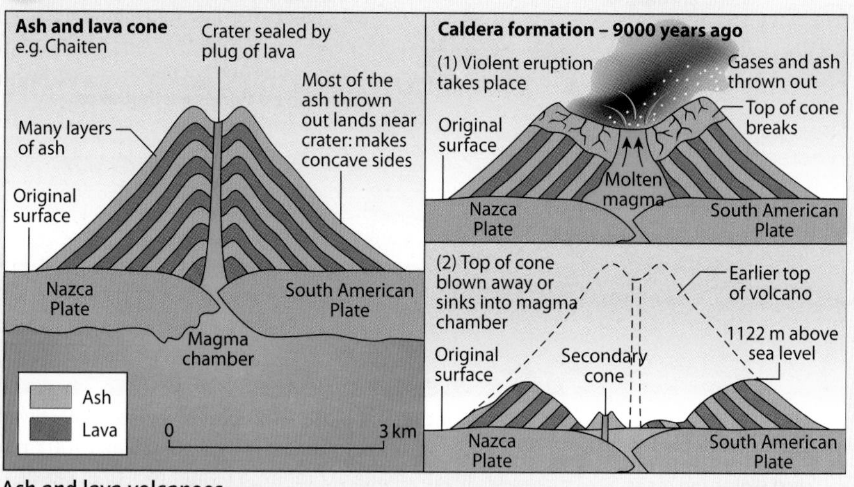

Ash and lava volcanoes

These form at convergent plate boundaries. The subducting plate melts and heat and pressure build up due to friction between the plates. The eruption is explosive. Hot lava flows out and lighter ash clouds settle on the lava in layers. The volcanoes have steep sides because the material under pressure contains acid. The lava does not flow far before cooling quickly to form solid rock. A caldera is usually formed when the top of a volcano is blown off. It sometimes contains a crater lake.

B Chile – relief

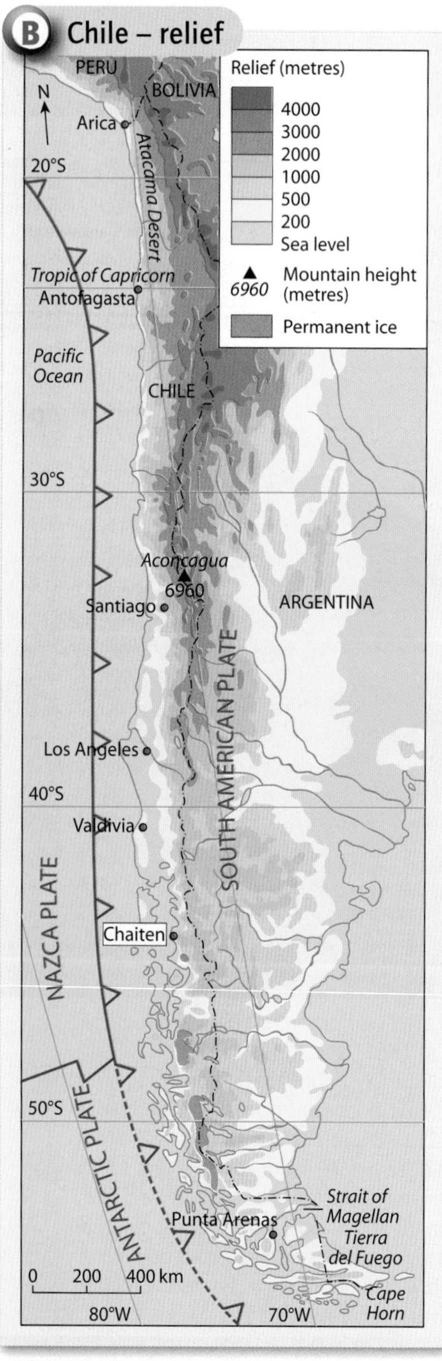

C Notes for a press briefing

NOTES FOR PRESS BRIEFING RE. CHAITEN VOLCANO

Last erupted 9000 years ago – created a crater 3Km wide

Chaiten is a caldera volcano – top of previous volcano blown off in last eruption ...

Dormant status – was not monitored by scientists

Chile very active volcano region – sits on edge of South American plate which forces Nazca plate beneath it

Magma trickled through plate boundary and built up huge chamber beneath crater ...

Task 1

Study **Source A**.

a Describe Chile's location. Refer to:
- a continent
- lines of latitude and longitude.

b Describe Chaiten's location in relation to Santiago and two tectonic plates. Refer to distances and directions.

Task 2

Study **Source B**.

a Make your own drawing of an ash and lava volcano.

b Explain how this volcano is formed – refer to **Source D** on page 63 to help you.

c The Chaiten volcano is a caldera. When and how was this formed?

Task 3

Imagine you are a government scientist who has been asked to brief journalists about the eruption. Write out your briefing using **Source C** as an outline of the key points to expand upon.

D Chaiten – a tourist destination

Chaiten (which means 'basket of water'), on Chile's jagged coastline, has a population of 4500. It is developing as a tourist centre because of the towering snow-capped mountains, glaciers, lakes and valleys of the Andes. Hiking, climbing and rafting are popular. Sea fishing is also offered between inlets and islands. The Chaiten volcano, which overshadows the town, is a particular attraction. Today it has a small airport (only local flights), a ferry service and a narrow dirt road from the south.

E Hot in Chile!

CHILEAN VILLAGERS FLEE AS 'DORMANT' VOLCANO ERUPTS

More than 4000 people had to flee their homes after a huge cloud of ash and lava was thrown into the sky by a long-dormant volcano in southern Chile. Some residents had never travelled beyond Chaiten until the volcano forced them to go. Terrified citizens of the fishing village, 10 km west of the volcano, spoke of a series of tremors lasting hours. Getting people out has been difficult due to the terrain. Because the mountains rise immediately from the coast, people had to queue to be evacuated by naval ships. The ash rose to a height of 20 km and was still settling in Chile and Argentina five days later. Cars, houses and trees were coated with ash up to 15 cm thick. Forests were set on fire by hot rocks thrown out in the explosion. Schools have been turned into makeshift shelters and people provided with bottled water after the ash contaminated the groundwater. People were advised to avoid rubbing their eyes and to wear glasses and long sleeves to avoid contact with ash.

May 2008

Task 4

Study **Source D**.

a Design a poster to attract more tourists to Chaiten.

b Why might tourists have difficulty accessing Chaiten? Use an atlas to help you.

Task 5

Study **Source E**.

a Why was it difficult to evacuate people from Chaiten?

b List the damage caused by the volcano.

c How did the authorities respond to the effects of the ash?

Task 6

Use **Source F** to help you explain why some people live close to a volcano.

F Why live here? – village voices

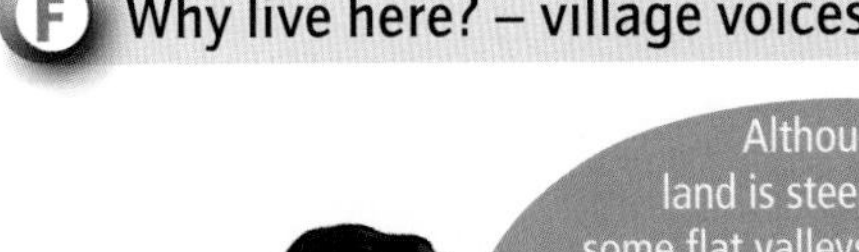

Although the land is steep there are some flat valleys where the soil is fertile from the volcanic deposits. We can grow wheat and grapes and it is wet enough for good pasture land for cattle and pigs.

My grandparents and parents were born here. Our history is here. We have never lived anywhere else – nor do we want to.

This is not the easiest place to move away from or to get to. I have no car, the bus services are poor and ferries are slow. It is easier to stay.

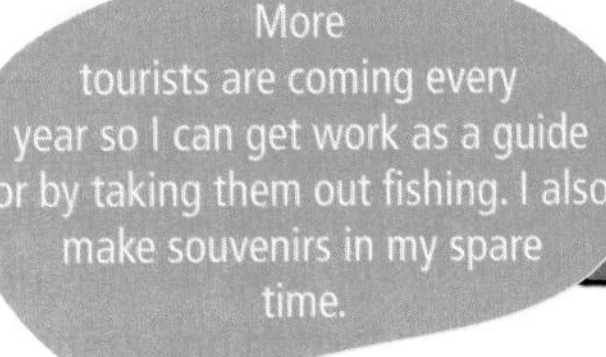

More tourists are coming every year so I can get work as a guide or by taking them out fishing. I also make souvenirs in my spare time.

We were told that the volcano had not erupted for over 9000 years so there was a good chance that it would not erupt in our lifetimes. We know differently now!

An earthquake in China

A Sichuan – no stranger to earthquakes

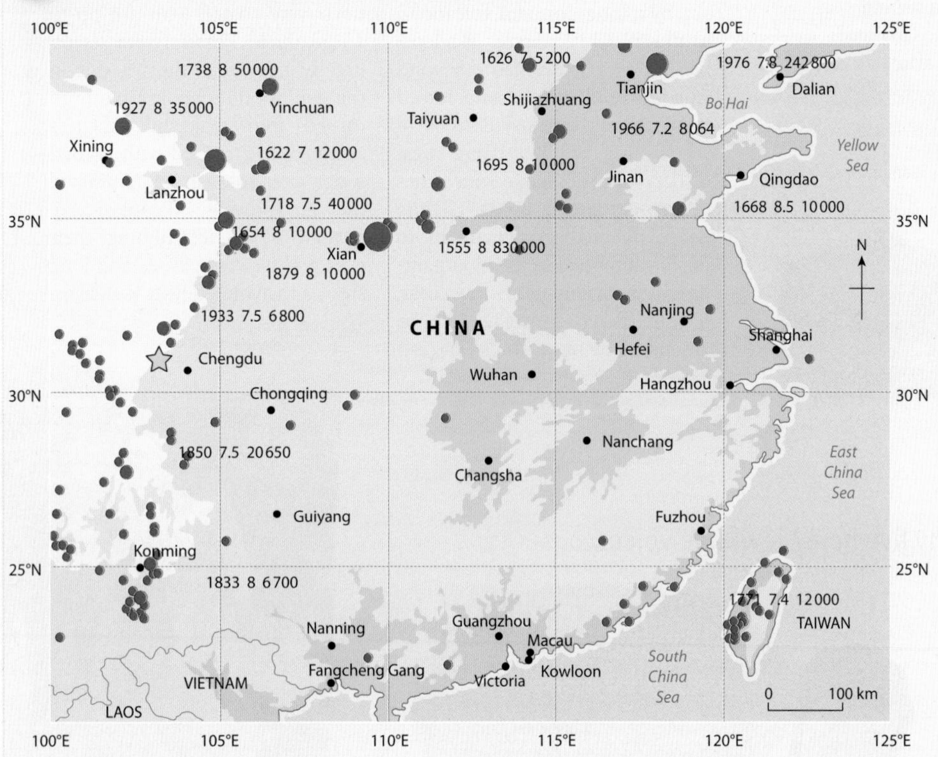

Earthquake energy is measured on the Richter scale. Most are felt between 3.5 and 8 magnitude. The higher the number the more energy is released and more damage caused. The Great Chilean earthquake of 22 May 1960 was measured at 9.5. The Sichuan area is vulnerable to earthquakes because it is close to the boundary of two converging plates. These have also created many surface cracks or faults.

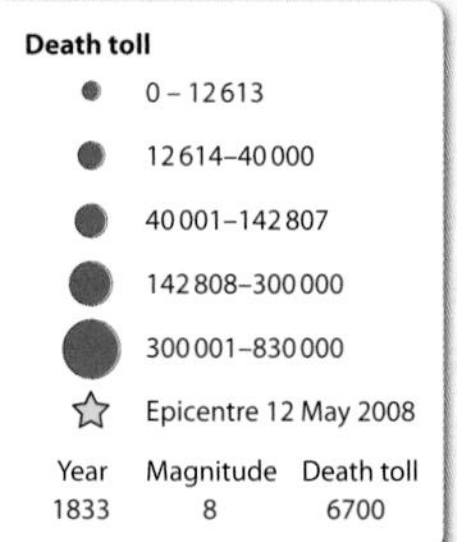

CHINA'S ONE-CHILD FAMILIES OFFER HOME TO ORPHANS

Almost 2000 children have been made orphans by the earthquake. The Chinese authorities have relaxed their one-child policy and are allowing childless and one-child families to adopt some of the orphans over the next 6 months. Some one-child families also lost their only child in the disaster. Over 68 000 people are estimated to have died since the earthquake hit Sichuan 3 weeks ago; 10 000 were school children. Over 18 000 are still missing.

2 June 2008

From Chaiten (Chile) to Chengdu (China)!

No country has suffered natural disasters on the scale of China. Tens of millions died from famine, floods and earthquakes in the 20th century alone. Just ten days after the Chaiten volcano erupted, on Monday 12 May 2008 China's most devastating earthquake in 30 years took place. The epicentre of the 7.9 magnitude earthquake was in a mountainous region of Sichuan province. This was about 100 km north-west of Chengdu, a bustling city of 10 million people.

Task 1

Study **Source A**.

a How many earthquakes have been recorded in this area of China with a magnitude of more than 7?

b Describe the distribution of the earthquakes with a magnitude larger than 7.

c Describe the location of the epicentre of the 2008 earthquake. Refer to latitude and longitude in your answer.

d The 2008 earthquake killed over 87 000 people. How many earthquakes listed on the map caused a higher death toll? When did these earthquakes occur and what was their magnitude?

e How can you tell that the area west of Chengdu is vulnerable to earthquakes? Give evidence.

B The first day: what happened, where and why?

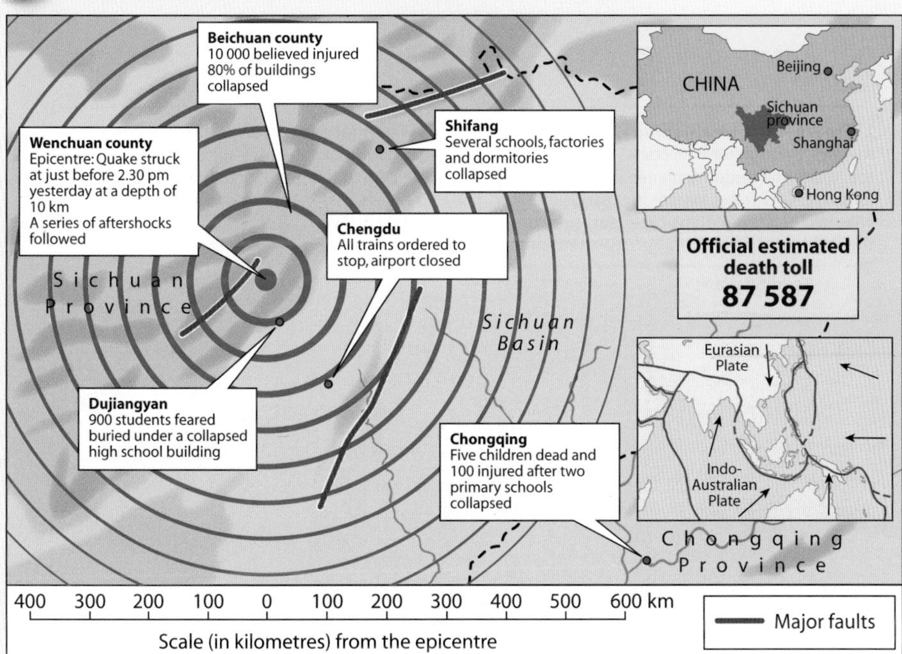
Beichuan county
10 000 believed injured
80% of buildings collapsed
Wenchuan county
Epicentre: Quake struck at just before 2.30 pm yesterday at a depth of 10 km
A series of aftershocks followed
Shifang
Several schools, factories and dormitories collapsed
Chengdu
All trains ordered to stop, airport closed
Sichuan Province
Sichuan Basin
Dujiangyan
900 students feared buried under a collapsed high school building
Chongqing
Five children dead and 100 injured after two primary schools collapsed
Chongqing Province
CHINA
Beijing
Sichuan province
Shanghai
Hong Kong
Official estimated death toll
87 587
Eurasian Plate
Indo-Australian Plate
400 300 200 100 0 100 200 300 400 500 600 km
Scale (in kilometres) from the epicentre
Major faults

The earthquakes in this region are caused by the Indo-Australian plate subducting beneath the Eurasian plate at a rate of 50 mm per year. Occasionally the plate slips as it overcomes friction, causing earthquakes. The focus (directly below the epicentre) where the plate 'slipped' was only 10 km beneath the surface which increased the area affected by the shocks. They were felt in Beijing, Hong Kong and Shanghai – nearly 1500 km away.

C 13 May onwards – after-effects

'JUST 10 SECONDS. ONE MOMENT THE SCHOOL WAS THERE, THEN IT WAS GONE'

A primary school of 900 pupils in Dujiangyan was amongst thousands of buildings that collapsed on Monday. There were also reports of 1000 students and teachers killed or missing after a six-storey school in Beichuan county crumbled into a pile of rubble. Rescuers pulled out bodies while, with no power, survivors ate bread and biscuits, unable to light a fire or boil water. Soldiers were drafted in to repair roads and restore electricity.

14 May 2008

600 000 AT RISK FROM DAMAGED DAM

Two thousand soldiers have been sent to plug cracks in a dam upriver from the earthquake-stricken town of Dujiangyan. The Zipingpu dam is one of the most modern in China but was built, against experts' advice, close to a significant fault line. Two HEP stations have been seriously damaged.

15 May 2008

LANDSLIDES BLOCK RIVER VALLEYS AS RAIN THREATENS FLOODS

Heavy rain and landslides have added to the earthquake effects. Almost 200 000 survivors have been evacuated as lakes and reservoirs fill up. They may burst their banks and flood towns and villages downstream. 1.3 million people have been moved to higher ground.

18 May 2008

Task 2

Study **Source B**.

a Why did this earthquake take place in Sichuan?

b List the damage caused at **two** places on the map and estimate the distance of these places from the epicentre.

Task 3

It is 12 May 2013 – the fifth anniversary of the Sichuan earthquake. You are a journalist who has been asked to write an article about the earthquake for a magazine. The audience is 14–16-year-old teenagers who remember little about this earthquake.

Your article should contain one headline, one illustration and one map, and have a maximum word-count of 250 words. You should cover causes and effects. (Use **Sources A–C** and the Internet to help you.)

Sample case study question

Name an area you have studied and state whether it has been affected by an earthquake or a volcanic eruption. Describe how the earthquake or eruption affected people and the environment in the area.

Weathering

A A landscape decays

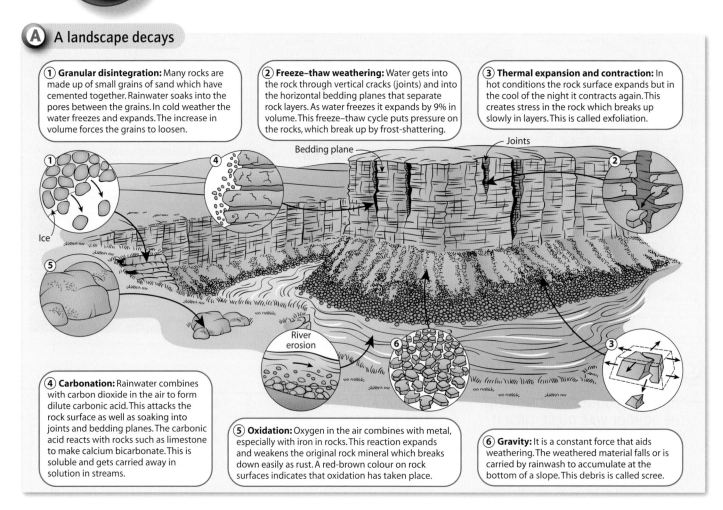

(1) **Granular disintegration:** Many rocks are made up of small grains of sand which have cemented together. Rainwater soaks into the pores between the grains. In cold weather the water freezes and expands. The increase in volume forces the grains to loosen.

(2) **Freeze–thaw weathering:** Water gets into the rock through vertical cracks (joints) and into the horizontal bedding planes that separate rock layers. As water freezes it expands by 9% in volume. This freeze–thaw cycle puts pressure on the rocks, which break up by frost-shattering.

(3) **Thermal expansion and contraction:** In hot conditions the rock surface expands but in the cool of the night it contracts again. This creates stress in the rock which breaks up slowly in layers. This is called exfoliation.

Bedding plane

Joints

Ice

River erosion

(4) **Carbonation:** Rainwater combines with carbon dioxide in the air to form dilute carbonic acid. This attacks the rock surface as well as soaking into joints and bedding planes. The carbonic acid reacts with rocks such as limestone to make calcium bicarbonate. This is soluble and gets carried away in solution in streams.

(5) **Oxidation:** Oxygen in the air combines with metal, especially with iron in rocks. This reaction expands and weakens the original rock mineral which breaks down easily as rust. A red-brown colour on rock surfaces indicates that oxidation has taken place.

(6) **Gravity:** It is a constant force that aids weathering. The weathered material falls or is carried by rainwash to accumulate at the bottom of a slope. This debris is called scree.

Two types of weathering

Weathering is the breakdown of rock by mechanical, physical and biological forces that do not remove it. No transport of material is involved apart from the weathered material slipping or falling downwards under the influence of gravity. Erosion is the breakdown of rocks by moving water, ice and, to a small extent, wind which then transport the eroded material away.

There are two main types of weathering:

- Mechanical (physical) weathering – this involves disintegration or breaking of rocks into smaller pieces with no chemical change in their composition. It takes place in all regions where there are changes in temperature and is seen in hot tropical desert areas where there is a large daily (diurnal) temperature range.
- Chemical weathering – this involves the decomposition of rocks by changing their chemical composition. It takes place in all regions where there is rain but is seen mostly in humid tropical areas with high temperatures.

Most landscapes experience both types working together at the same time. Some climates favour more mechanical weathering; others favour greater chemical weathering.

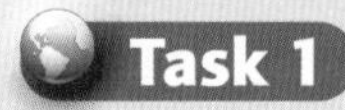

Study **Source A**.

a How is *weathering* different from *erosion*?

b What is the difference between *mechanical weathering* and *chemical weathering*?

c Draw six boxes around a copy of **Source A**. Summarise captions 1–6 in the boxes. Draw arrows from each box to the matching circular diagram. Shade mechanical and chemical weathering boxes in different colours.

B Biological weathering

Rabbit burrows, UK

Tree roots, Cuba

Plants contribute to mechanical weathering by using their roots to force apart rocks along bedding planes, joints or cracks. Burrowing animals contribute to the breaking up and loosening of rocks. Both plants and animals contribute to chemical weathering by releasing acids and other chemicals in their life-cycle, including during their own decomposition. They are especially important in soil formation which continues the weathering process further.

C Tenerife, one of the Canary Islands

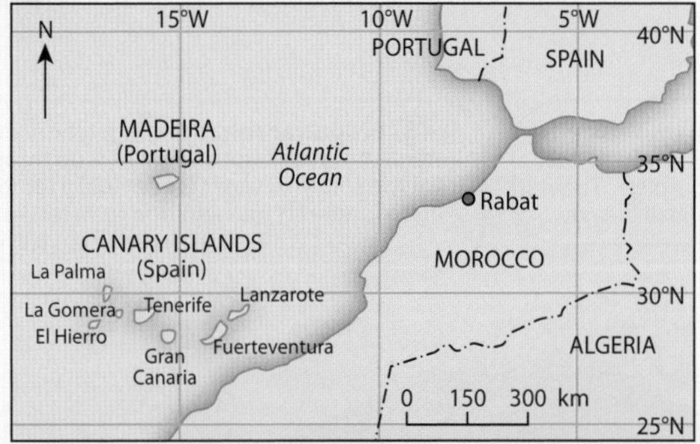

Tenerife is the largest of the Canary Islands, which are formed from volcanoes sticking out above the sea. It lies off the west coast of Africa north of the Tropic of Cancer. It has a climate that is hot all year with a dry season in the summer months.

	J	F	M	A	M	J	J	A	S	O	N	D
Temperature (°C)	15	15	17	16	18	20	24	23	22	21	19	17
Rainfall (mm)	45	66	55	37	6	1	1	10	2	55	72	76

Average annual temperature = 18.9 °C Average annual rainfall = 426 mm

Task 2

Study **Source B**.

In what ways do plants and animals contribute to mechanical and chemical weathering?

Task 3

Study **Source C**.

- **a** Describe Tenerife's location. Refer to hemisphere, latitude and longitude.
- **b** Describe the average climate of Tenerife. Can 'average' figures be misleading? Use evidence from the data to support your view.
- **c** Suggest how and why the type of weathering affecting the rocks of Tenerife might change during the year based on this climate data.

Task 4

Study **Sources C and D**. The rate at which temperature decreases with altitude is known as the lapse rate. An average figure for this in dry conditions is about 0.6 °C for every 100 metres height.

- **a** Use the height of El Teide to calculate the difference between average temperatures at the peak and sea level on a dry, cloudless day.
- **b** What advice would you give to a person who wanted to climb El Teide in July? Explain your advice.
- **c** What evidence supports the fact that postcard 1 was taken in July? What type of weathering might be taking place here?
- **d** How and why has the scene changed in postcard 2? How might the type of weathering taking place here have changed?

D Postcards from Tenerife

These postcards show the scenery close to El Teide – the peak of a volcano 3718 metres above sea level. One photo was taken in July and the other in December.

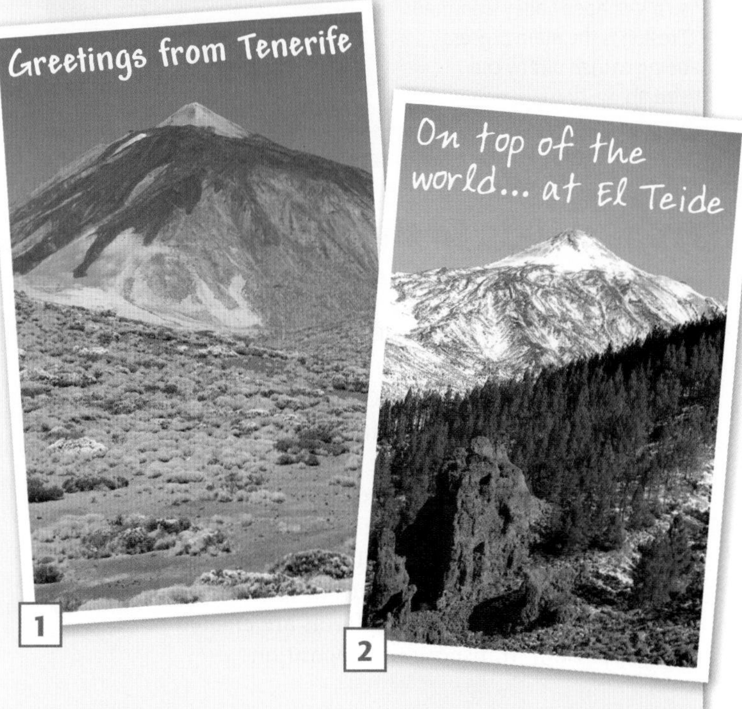

Greetings from Tenerife
1
On top of the world... at El Teide
2

TOPIC 13 Rivers – from source to mouth

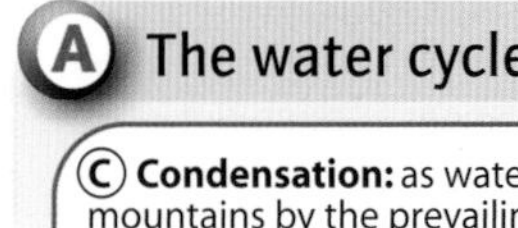

A The water cycle

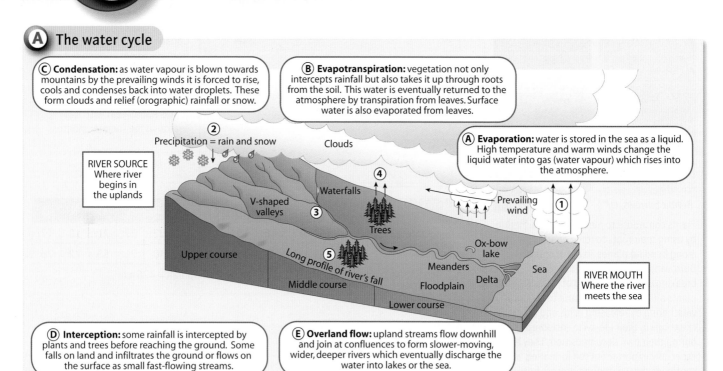

Ⓒ **Condensation:** as water vapour is blown towards mountains by the prevailing winds it is forced to rise, cools and condenses back into water droplets. These form clouds and relief (orographic) rainfall or snow.

Ⓑ **Evapotranspiration:** vegetation not only intercepts rainfall but also takes it up through roots from the soil. This water is eventually returned to the atmosphere by transpiration from leaves. Surface water is also evaporated from leaves.

Ⓐ **Evaporation:** water is stored in the sea as a liquid. High temperature and warm winds change the liquid water into gas (water vapour) which rises into the atmosphere.

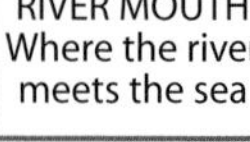

Ⓓ **Interception:** some rainfall is intercepted by plants and trees before reaching the ground. Some falls on land and infiltrates the ground or flows on the surface as small fast-flowing streams.

Ⓔ **Overland flow:** upland streams flow downhill and join at confluences to form slower-moving, wider, deeper rivers which eventually discharge the water into lakes or the sea.

B Upland and lowland valleys

In the upper course the stream flows over steep ground. The main process is **vertical erosion**. It flows around obstacles creating interlocking spurs. Weathering processes wear back the valley sides as the stream erodes vertically, so a V-shaped valley is formed. Erosion is the main process being carried out by the stream.

1

In the lower course the river flows over flatter ground. It often meanders on a wide floodplain. The valley is wide due to **lateral erosion** of the valley sides. Deposition is a major process, especially at times of flooding.

2

From clouds to the sea and back

Only about 3 per cent of the Earth's water is fresh. Most of that is stored in the ice-caps of the Arctic and Antarctic. The Great Lakes of North America contain one-fifth of the Earth's fresh water. The small amount left is spread out unevenly across the surface of the globe in rivers and lakes. When water falls from clouds as rain, a small amount falls directly into streams and rivers and flows back to the sea. During this journey many landforms are created by river erosion, transport and deposition.

Task 1

Study **Source A**.

a On an outline copy of the diagram match captions A–E to locations 1–5.

b Explain how the water cycle works.

c How does the long profile of a river change as it moves from uplands to lowlands?

Task 2

Study **Source B**.

a Label the following on a sketch of photo 1.
- interlocking spurs
- steep slopes
- the stream
- poor-quality grass

b Annotate your sketch to show where processes of erosion and weathering are taking place.

c How and why are the cross-profiles of the valley and river different in the two photographs?

C Erosion, transport and deposition

River erosion	River transport	River deposition
A river erodes in four main ways: • hydraulic action • corrasion (abrasion) • attrition • solution (corrosion). These processes can take place at the same time. Erosion creates material ranging in size from heavy boulders to silt. Waterfalls and rapids, V-shaped valleys and potholes in river beds are landforms of erosion.	Once eroded, material is transported by the river. There are four types of load: • solution load – minerals such as limestone are dissolved and carried in solution • suspension load – very light materials are carried near the surface giving the river its colour, e.g. the Blue Nile • saltation load – large particles are bounced along the river bed. • traction load – the heaviest rocks are rolled along the river bed.	Once the river slows down and loses energy, it deposits material. Three main landforms are formed: • meanders and ox-bow lakes – erosion on the outside of bends and deposition on the inside of bends leads to the river 'swinging' along the valley; ox-bow lakes form when a meander is cut off from the main river • floodplains – when the river floods it deposits material forming a wide, flat valley floor • deltas – when the river slows on entering a sea or a lake it deposits more material than can be removed.

Task 3

Study **Source C**.

a In which type of load would you expect to find the following:
- a heavy lump of granite
- dissolved chalk
- blue clay?

b Give **two** reasons why there is less vertical erosion in the lower course of a river than in the upper course. Refer to the long profile and the load in your answer.

Task 4

Source D illustrates how a river creates different landforms. (Waterfalls and deltas are not included here – see case studies on pages 72–75.)

a For each landform, state whether you would expect to find it in the upper or lower course of the river. Explain your choice.

b Choose **one** of these landforms. Copy the diagram of your choice or use other sources to find other diagrams. Write a paragraph describing the landform and explaining how it was formed.

Types of river erosion

Hydraulic action: the impact of moving water.
Corrasion (abrasion): the wearing away of the bed and banks of a river by the load being carried.
Attrition: the wearing away of the load as the particles bump against each other while being carried in the river.
Solution (corrosion): the dissolving of material by the river water.

D River landforms

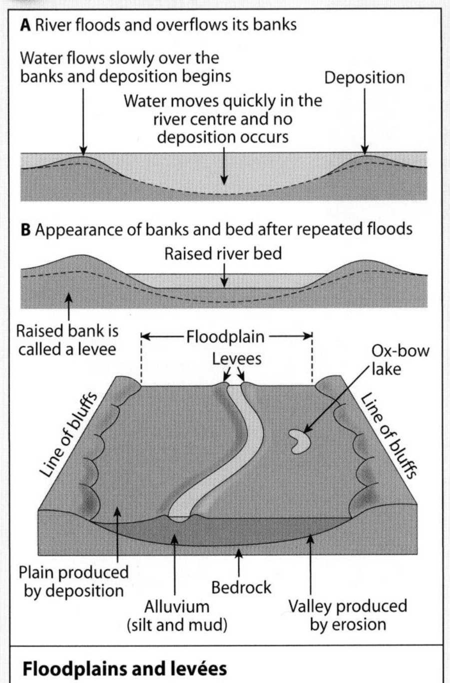

Floodplains and levées

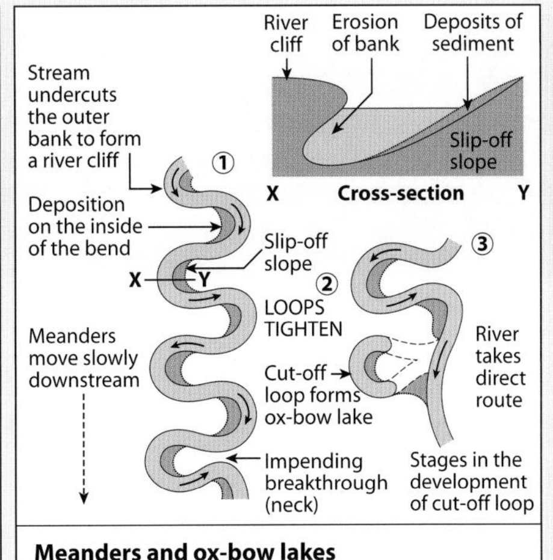

Meanders and ox-bow lakes

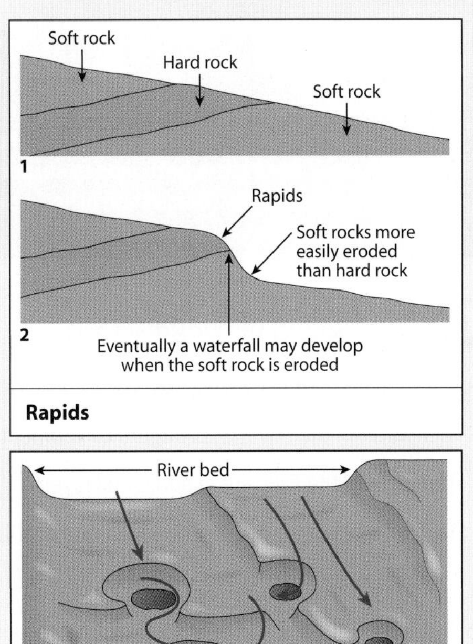

Rapids

Potholes

CASE STUDY 13a River erosion – Niagara Falls

The formation of Niagara Falls

Niagara Falls consists of two waterfalls on the Niagara river which marks the border between New York State, USA (the American Falls) and Ontario, Canada (the Canadian or Horseshoe Falls).

In terms of geology Niagara Falls is quite young. The formation of the falls began at the end of the Ice Age in North America around 18 000 years ago when the area was covered in ice sheets 3 metres thick. Torrents of water were released into the Great Lakes as ice melted into what is now the Niagara river. About 12 300 years ago this water, travelling north from Lake Erie to Lake Ontario, plunged over the edge of the north-facing Niagara Escarpment. The force of the water gradually wore away the rock layers and Niagara Falls 'retreated' as it moved upstream back towards Lake Erie.

A Where is Niagara Falls?

B Aerial view of the Falls

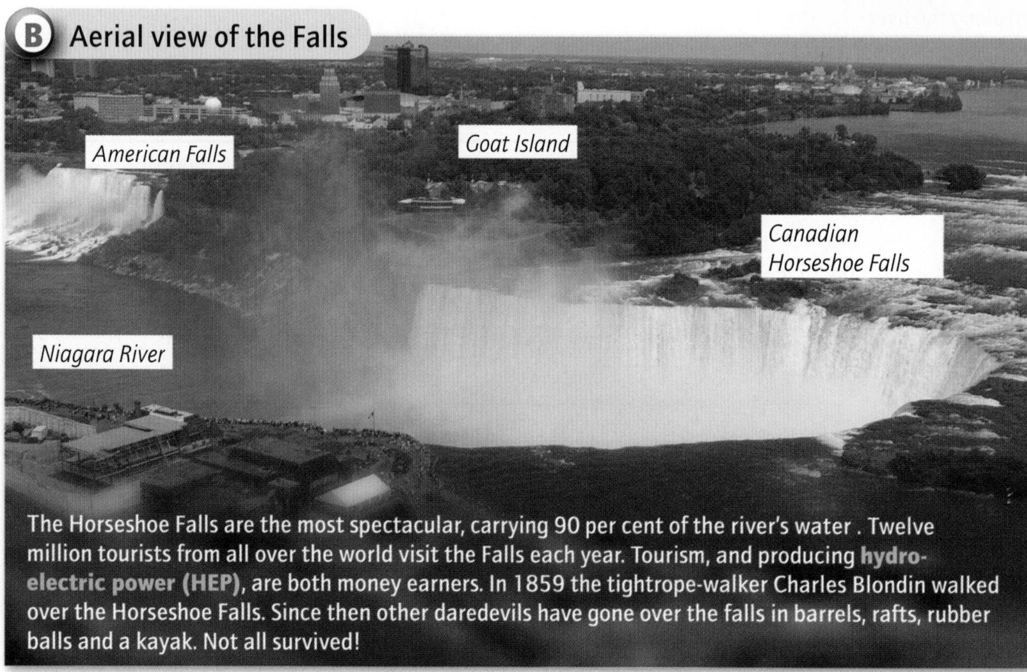

The Horseshoe Falls are the most spectacular, carrying 90 per cent of the river's water . Twelve million tourists from all over the world visit the Falls each year. Tourism, and producing **hydro-electric power (HEP)**, are both money earners. In 1859 the tightrope-walker Charles Blondin walked over the Horseshoe Falls. Since then other daredevils have gone over the falls in barrels, rafts, rubber balls and a kayak. Not all survived!

Task 1

Study **Source A**.

- **a** Use an atlas to name the five Great Lakes of North America.
- **b** Which international boundary is shown on **Source A**?
- **c** Describe the location of Niagara Falls.

C The making of Niagara Falls

The glaciers melted over 12 000 years ago.

Meltwater poured over the Niagara Escarpment.

The rocks of the Falls are in horizontal layers.

The top layer of hard dolomite sandstone overlies softer rocks.

Splashback also erodes the soft rock, undermining the hard rock above.

Today the Falls has moved back or 'retreated' over 10 km to the south of the escarpment.

Without this support below, the top layer continually collapses under its own weight to fall into the plunge pool below.

This movement back has eroded the narrow Niagara Gorge or canyon.

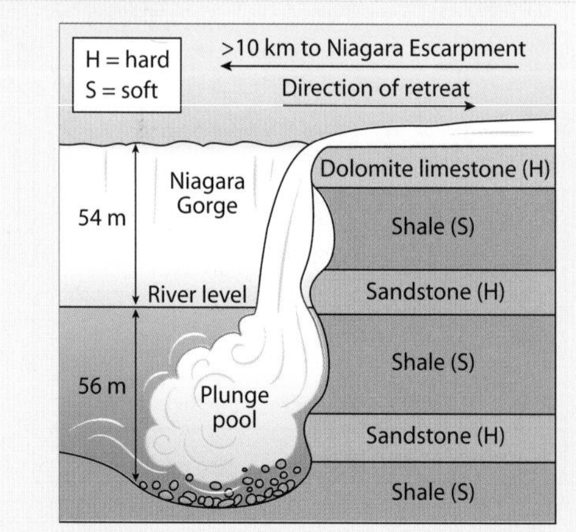

D A slow retreat – 10 km in 12 000 years!

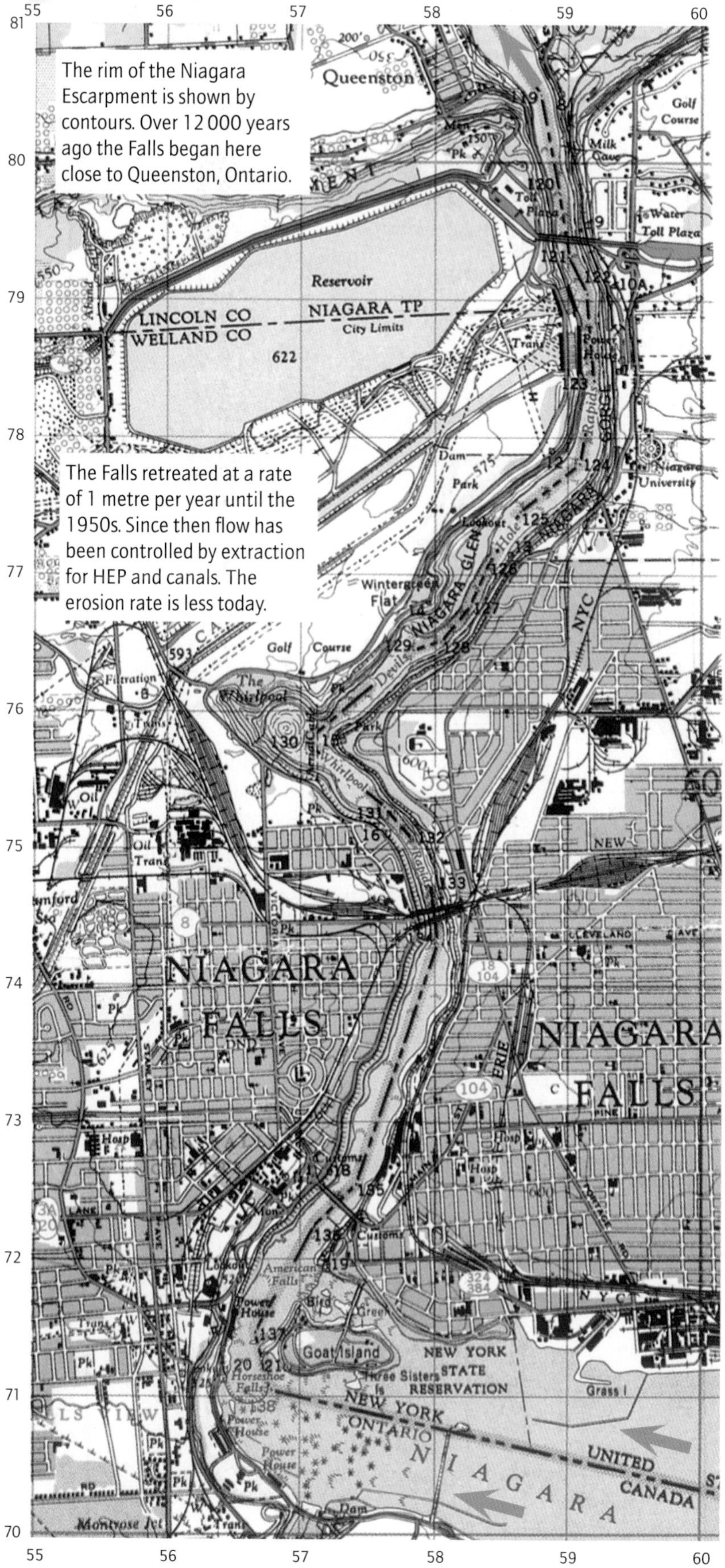

The rim of the Niagara Escarpment is shown by contours. Over 12 000 years ago the Falls began here close to Queenston, Ontario.

The Falls retreated at a rate of 1 metre per year until the 1950s. Since then flow has been controlled by extraction for HEP and canals. The erosion rate is less today.

Scale 1: 50 000
(2 cm = 1 km)

Task 2

Study **Sources B and D**.

a Use **Source D** (grid squares 5671 and 5771) to help you decide from which direction the camera was pointing to take this photograph.

b Draw a labelled sketch of the photograph.

c In what ways are people benefiting from the Niagara river and Falls?

Task 3

Use the captions beside **Source C** to annotate a copy of the sketch to show how the Falls was formed.

Task 4

Study **Source D**.

a Measure the length of the gorge from the scarp slopes of Niagara Escarpment (5880) to the Falls (5671). Use this measurement to calculate the average annual rate of retreat (metres per year) of the Falls since they were created over 12 000 years ago.

b Estimate the maximum and minimum width of the gorge in metres.

c Draw a large sketch map of the Niagara Gorge and Falls. Label the following:

- Niagara Escarpment
- American and Canadian Falls
- US/Canadian border
- canals and power stations
- Niagara Gorge, river and rapids
- Niagara Falls town.

d Annotate your sketch with captions of key facts from these pages. The captions on **Source D** are examples of some annotations you could use.

CASE STUDY

13b River deposition – the Ganges delta

Bangladesh – a 'floating' country

Bangladesh lies north of the Bay of Bengal and shares borders with India and Myanmar (Burma). Over 120 million people live here. It is one of the most densely populated countries in the world, yet most of the country is part of a huge low-lying delta. This has been formed by deposition from some of the longest rivers in the world – the Ganges and its tributary, the Brahmaputra – and the Meghna river. Although the delta deposits are continually shifting, large numbers of people prefer to live here than in crowded city slums. Flooding and irrigation allow all-year cropping of rice and vegetables. Jute is a major crop and fish are plentiful. The price of living here can be high – monsoon rains, cyclones and floods regularly cause natural disasters.

A Bangladesh – the 'drain of the Himalayas'

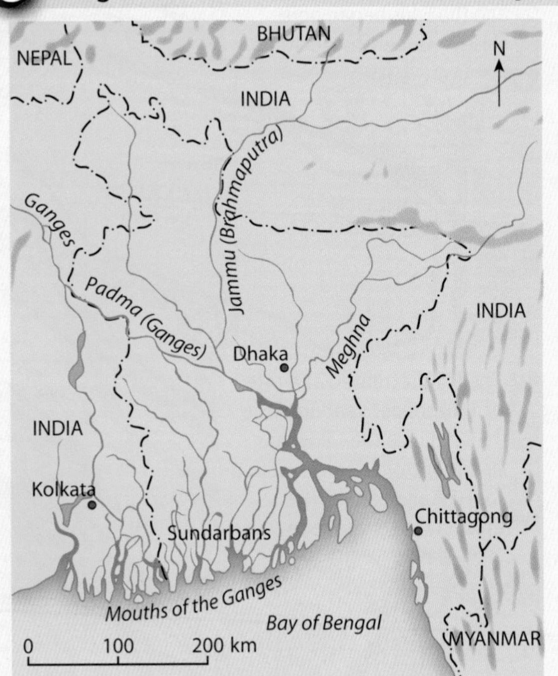

Bangladesh (formerly East Pakistan until 1971) is an LEDC. Over two-thirds of the country is made up of the Ganges delta. The Ganges river is over 2500 km long, having its source in snowmelt and rainfall in the Himalayan mountains north of India. It flows eastwards and empties into the Bay of Bengal after being joined by the Brahmaputra and Meghna rivers from the east.

B Making the Ganges delta

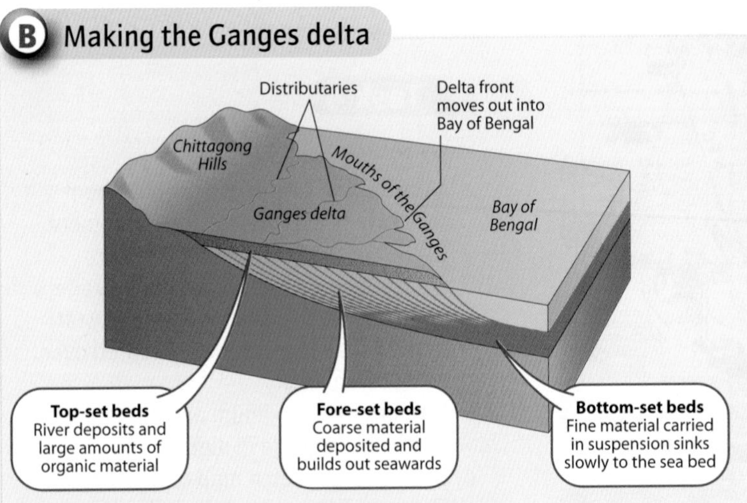

Most of the load carried by a river eventually deposited in a lake or the sea. If the river's journey is not too long or there is a small load then the freshwater merges into the saltwater quite easily in an estuary. Large rivers, however, often form deltas.

Stage 1	Stage 2	Stage 3
The lower course of the slow-moving Ganges river carries a large quantity of fine silt as suspension load. The river's energy is used in transporting it. As it enters the Bay of Bengal its speed reduces and deposition takes place. The heaviest material is dropped first and builds up to form islands.	Over time more sediment is deposited as the waves are too weak to remove it quickly. The river channel becomes blocked by the silt. More flooding also takes place. The river finds its way to the sea by winding itself around the islands. These channels are **distributaries**. Swamps and brackish water are found here.	The sediment continues to be added to the delta. Islands of dry land emerge and vegetation grows. The delta is continually moved by currents and floods.

Task 1

Study **Source A** and an atlas.

a Which **two** countries on the map are close to Bangladesh but do not share borders?

b What do the map and atlas tell you about the relief of Bangladesh compared with countries around it? What problems might this cause?

c Why is Bangladesh called 'the drain of the Himalayas'?

Task 2

Study **Source B**.

a Make your own copy of the diagram.

b Explain in your own words how the delta has formed.

C The delta – a 'true colour' satellite image

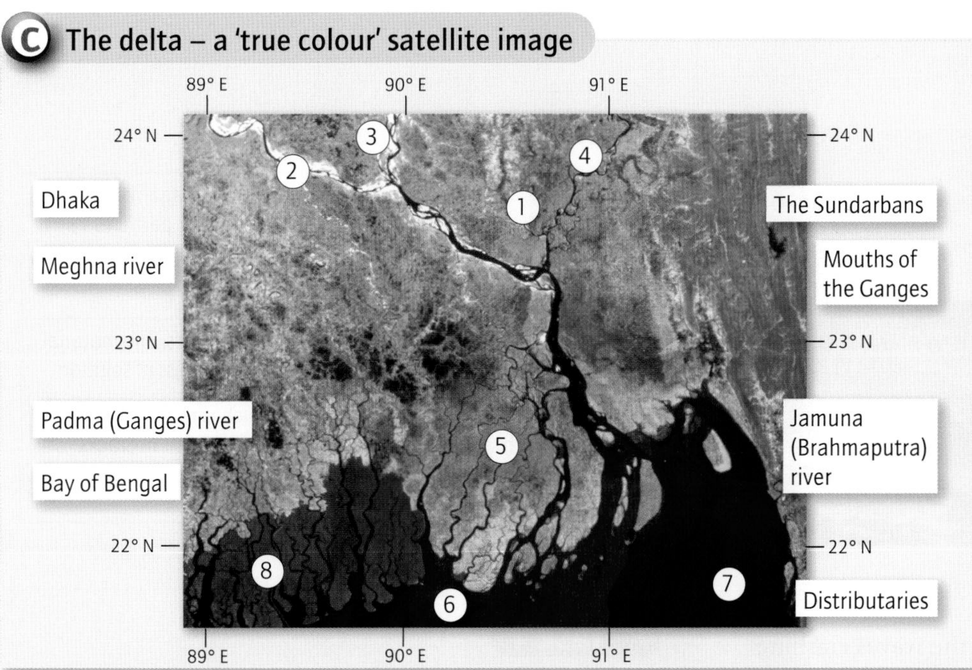

Task 3

Study **Sources A and C**.

On an outline sketch of **Source C**, use the captions to label the city at 1, the three rivers at 2, 3 and 4 and the delta/water features 5–8.

The Ganges river of India becomes the Padma in Bangladesh.

The Brahmaputra river of India becomes the Jamuna in Bangladesh.

The Sundarbans is the largest single area of mangrove forest in the world.

Task 4

Study **Source D**.

a Draw a bar graph to show the distribution of rainfall in Dhaka. Identify the dry and wet seasons on your graph.

b Describe the distribution of rainfall. Refer to data and months.

c For Bangladesh to suffer a disastrous flood, what factors need to occur at the same time? Which months pose the highest risk? Why?

Task 5

Study **Source E**.

a When did this cyclone take place? If it had struck earlier in the year it could have caused more damage – why?

b How did Cyclone Sidr affect people and the environment?

c Suggest reasons why so many people still live on the Ganges delta despite the dangers.

D And then the monsoon arrives at Dhaka …

	J	F	M	A	M	J	J	A	S	O	N	D
Rainfall (mm)	18	31	58	103	194	321	437	305	254	169	28	2

Average annual rainfall = 1920 mm

Bangladesh has a sub-tropical monsoon climate. It is one of the warmest and wettest places in the world. Average temperatures range from 10 °C in January to 35 °C in August. The monsoon rainfall adds to the water flowing in the rivers. If the monsoon rains fall when the rivers are full and summer high tides up to 6 metres are present in the Bay of Bengal, disastrous floods occur. Tropical cyclones between May and November can make matters worse!

E … followed by Cyclone Sidr!

CYCLONE DEATH TOLL MAY RISE TO 8000

The death toll from Cyclone Sidr, which devastated the south coast of Bangladesh, could reach 8000. The cyclone generated waves up to 8 metres high that surged almost 50 km inland in some low-lying areas. Nearly 2 million flimsy bamboo and tin homes were swept away, leaving at least 3 million people homeless and damage to property and crops. Roads were blocked by fallen trees and untreated sewage from rivers is creating a health risk. Sattar Gazi, a 55-year-old farmer, said 'I lost six of my family members in the cyclone. I am afraid the rest of us will die of hunger'. Vast areas of farmland were under saltwater so it will be several months before farmers can work again. The storm struck at the end of the cyclone season just before the harvest.

18 November 2007

Sample case study question

Describe and explain the formation of an ox-bow lake. You should use labelled diagrams.

TOPIC 14 Coasts

A Coastal erosion

Cliffs on the Algarve, Portugal

Changing coastlines

If you sit on a beach, you can watch the waves crashing against the shore. After each wave, the water runs quickly back into the sea, carrying and moving fine grains of sand and pebbles. If you stand in the sea, you can sometimes feel the pebbles move under your feet. In storms, large waves can move huge boulders. The waves, with their load of sand, pebbles and rocks, batter the cliffs and dislodge big pieces of rock, which fall into the sea. Coasts are always changing. Erosion occurs when the sea is wearing away the land. Deposition occurs when the sea piles up sand and pebbles to form new land.

C Coastal deposition

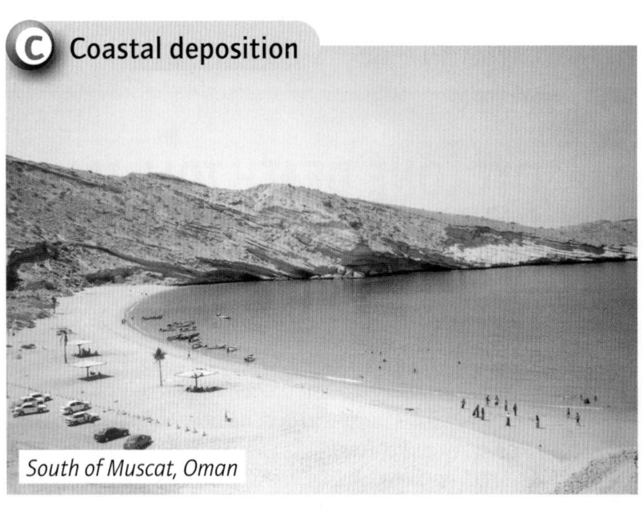
South of Muscat, Oman

B Processes of coastal erosion

Attrition	Particles carried by the waves crash against each other and are broken up into smaller particles
Corrasion (abrasion)	Particles carried by the waves crash against the cliffs, eroding the cliffs
Solution (corrosion)	The seawater slowly dissolves the cliffs. The material produced is carried away by the process of solution
Hydraulic action	Waves have great energy which is released as they break against the cliffs. Waves trap air in cracks in the rock. This air is compressed by the waves, eventually causing them to crack

Task 1

Study **Source A**.

Write a paragraph describing the main features which can be seen in the foreground (at the front) and in the background (at the back) of the photograph.

Task 2

Study **Source B**.

Copy these sentences. Complete each one by writing the name of one type of erosion.

- The force of waves crashing on the cliffs is called ....
- Waves carry bits of rock and sand which help to grind down cliffs. This is called ....
- Waves cause rocks and pebbles on the shore to hit each other and become smaller which is called ....
- Seawater will slowly dissolve certain types of rock by the process of ....

Task 3

Study **Sources C and D**.

a Describe the differences between constructive and destructive waves.

b Which type of waves do you think are shown in **Source C**? Give reasons for your answer.

D Different types of waves

Source C shows an area of coastline where deposition is taking place. When an area is sheltered, sand and pebbles may be deposited by constructive waves to build up wide, gently sloping beaches.

Constructive waves:	Destructive waves create a steep, narrow beach and they:
• have a stronger swash than backwash, causing the beach to be built up with sand and pebbles • are less frequent than destructive waves, breaking on the shore between 6 and 9 times per minute • are low, with a long wavelength so they roll onto the beach rather than crashing onto it.	• have a stronger backwash than swash, removing material from a beach • are frequent, breaking on the shore between 10 and 15 times per minute • are tall waves with a greater distance to fall when they break and with a short wavelength.

E Bays and headlands

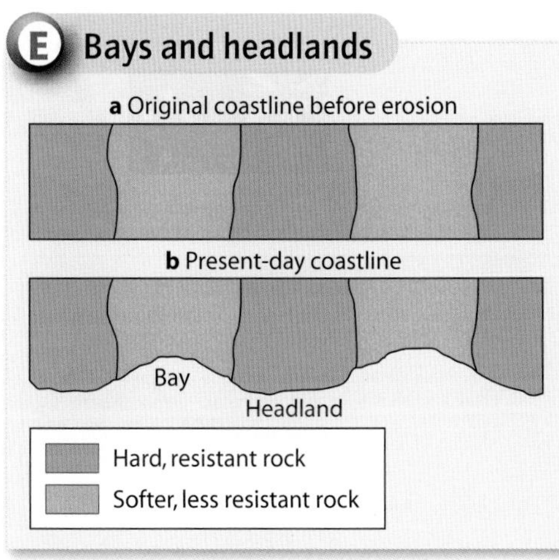

Erosional features

In areas where soft rock reaches the coast this is easily eroded to form a bay. More resistant rocks form headlands. On the headlands waves attack the rock face along lines of weakness between the high and low water marks. Eventually:

- a notch is created
- overhanging rock above the notch collapses and falls as the notch is cut deeper into the rock
- as the cliff is eroded backwards it leaves behind a wave-cut platform at the low water mark
- a line of weakness, such as a fault or joint, is increased in size until it becomes a cave
- the waves continue to erode the back of the cave until an arch is formed
- when the arch roof falls into the sea it leaves behind a stack
- after more erosion it is reduced in size to form a stump.

F Features of headlands

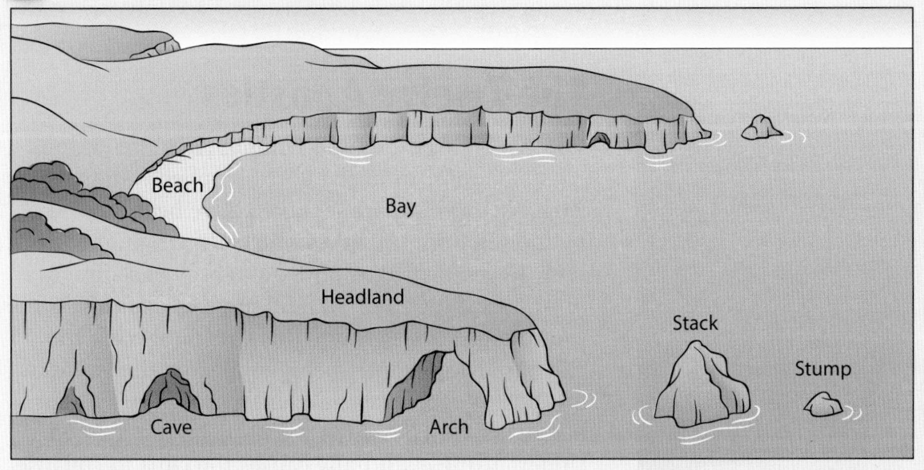

Task 4

Study **Sources E and F**. Make a copy of **Source F**.

a Label your diagram fully to explain the formation of the features that are shown.

b If an examination question asks you to explain how a stack is formed, why do you need to explain how caves and arches are formed?

G Depositional features

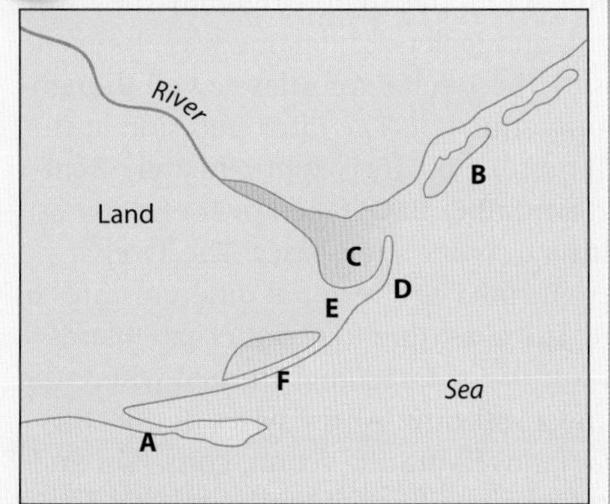

Task 5

Study **Source G**.

Name the features A–F which are formed by coastal deposition.

Depositional features

The depositional features shown in **Source G** are formed as a result of longshore drift.

- Sand spit: a long, narrow stretch of sand and/or shingle, with one end attached to the mainland.
- Sand bar: develops when a spit stretches across a bay linking two headlands.
- Tombolo: forms when a beach or sand spit joins up with an offshore island.
- Barrier islands: sandy islands that run parallel to the coastline forming a tidal lagoon between them and the shore.
- Sand dunes: formed by winds blowing dry sand from the beach inland and depositing it there to form mounds of sand on which marram grass and other plants grow.
- Saltmarsh: a sheltered area, flooded at high tide, where silt collects behind a sand spit or sand bar.

CASE STUDY 14a Coastal erosion – The Twelve Apostles

A Where is Port Campbell National Park?

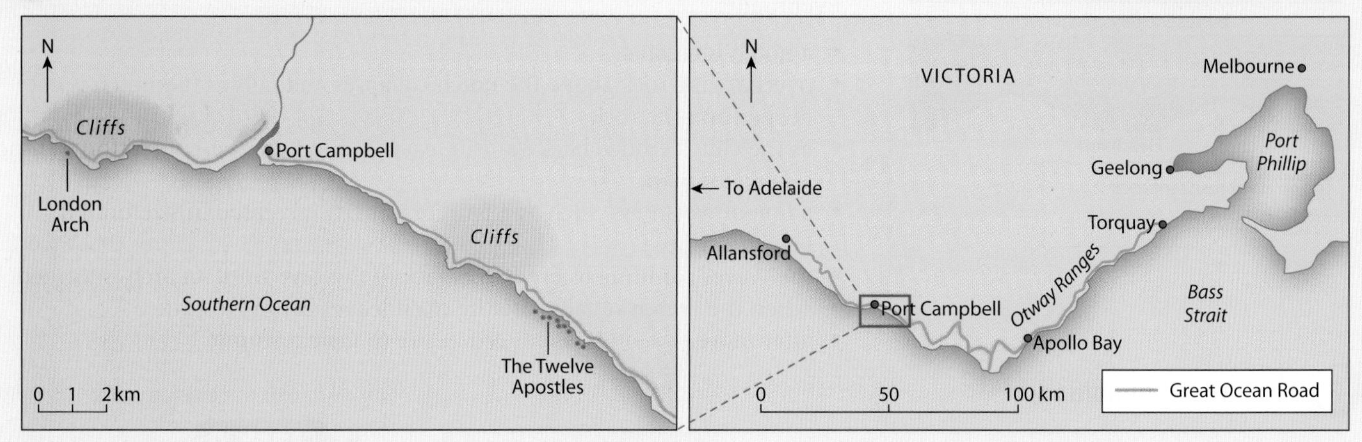

B The Twelve Apostles

Task 1

Study **Source A**.

Describe the location of The Twelve Apostles and London Arch.

Task 2

Study **Source B** and the text.

Design a tourist information leaflet about The Twelve Apostles. Your leaflet should include a description and a clear explanation of their formation. Use a sequence of labelled diagrams to help your explanation.

The Twelve Apostles

The Twelve Apostles and London Arch are famous coastal landforms in the Port Campbell National Park, Victoria, Australia which have been carved by the sea from the limestone cliffs. Originally the rock layers formed as horizontal beds of sediment on the sea floor over 10 million years ago to become sedimentary rock. Along this stretch of coast the cliff base is constantly being eroded by the waves. Steep cliffs which reach 70 metres high, wave-cut platforms, notches, arches and stacks are formed. Undercutting eventually causes the cliffs to collapse along vertical joints, keeping the slopes steep.

The Twelve Apostles is a collection of stacks, the tallest reaching 45 metres high. Originally they were called the Sow and Piglets. The name was changed in the 1950s to The Twelve Apostles – even though there were only nine left. The rate of erosion at the base of the limestone pillars is approximately 2 cm per year and a number have fallen over entirely as waves continue to erode their bases. The Twelve Apostles were formed as a result of different rates of erosion along the coast due to the alternate bands of hard and soft rocks. Headlands formed where the rocks were most resistant. At the bases of the cliffs on these headlands hydraulic action, corrasion and corrosion eroded along lines of weakness (e.g. joints, faults and bedding planes). Back-to-back caves first formed on each side of the headlands. Continuous erosion caused these caves to extend backward until the caves met and natural arches were formed, linking the tip of the headland with the mainland. When the arches collapsed, the pillars were left standing and became stacks.

C London Arch

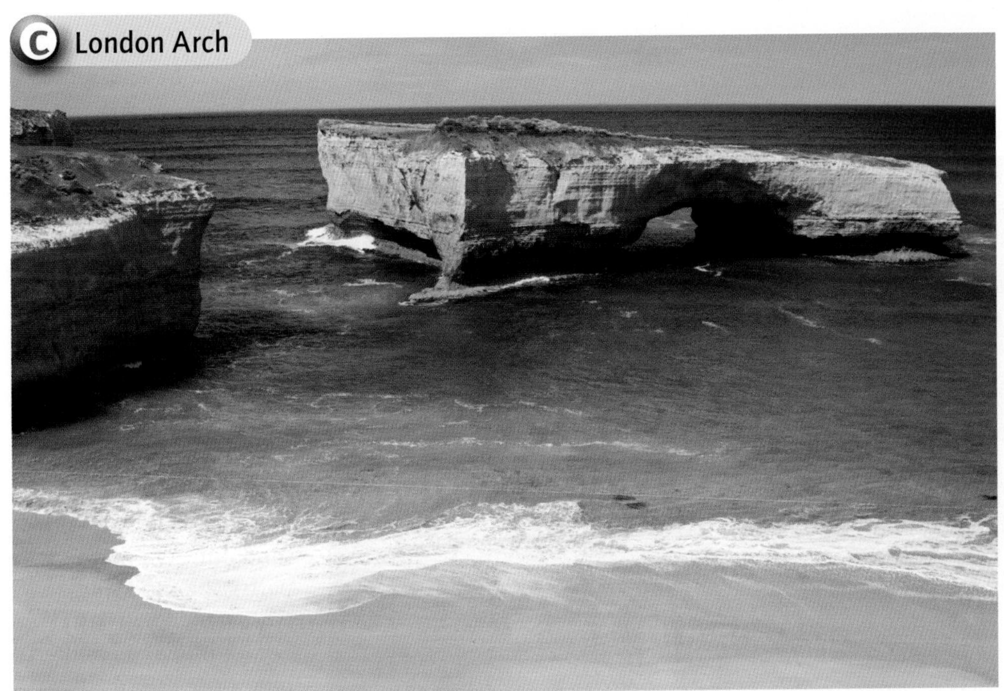

London Arch

London Arch is a natural arch which is one of the main tourist attractions in the Port Campbell National Park. It was formed by the processes of coastal erosion, and until 1990 formed a complete double-span natural bridge. The arch closest to the shoreline collapsed unexpectedly on 15 January 1990, leaving two tourists stranded on the outer part. They had to be rescued by helicopter. Before the collapse, the arch was known as London Bridge because of its similarity to the bridge over the river Thames in London, UK.

D Collapsing stacks

Stack Collapse Leaves Eight Apostles Standing

A pile of rubble is all that remains after the collapse of one of the sea stacks at the '12 Apostles' off Victoria's south-west coast.

Around 9:00am the 50 metre limestone pillar that stood off Victoria's south-west coast crumbled into the water. In a matter of seconds, all that remained was rubble.

Stunned tourists took photos of the dramatic change in the landscape.

'Reports were it sort of shimmied or shuddered a bit, it fractured and sort of imploded in on itself and pretty much slid straight into the ocean,' Alex Green from Parks Victoria said. 'So we've gone from a 50-metre sea stack down to a ten metre pile of rubble. 'We expect from reports of previous collapses like this that that pile of rubble will very quickly be eroded away by the ocean.'

The collapse was part of the natural process that has shaped the popular tourist attraction for centuries.

But it leaves only 8 of the 12 apostles still standing.

Just 15 years ago another of the site's main attractions, London Bridge, fell into the sea. Tourists trapped on what was left of the bridge had to be rescued.

But experts are confident the disappearance of the apostle will not detract from the popularity of the area.

Before and after photos of London Bridge already generate much discussion about the constant changes to the coastline and the latest collapse is another talking point.

Victorian Tourism Minister John Pandazopoulos says he does not expect the latest collapse will have an effect on tourism. 'Since London Bridge fell down tourism has grown in the region,' he said.

Numerous ads and promotions featuring the 12 apostles may now have to be re-shot.

20 May 2007

STOP PRESS Only 7 stacks left ... September 2009

Task 3

Study **Sources C and D**.

a The photograph shows what London Arch now looks like. Draw a labelled sketch to show what you think the feature was like before the collapse.

b Use geographical terminology to explain why one of The Twelve Apostles collapsed.

Task 4

There are many other famous arches and stacks. Here are some examples.

Stacks:	Arches:
Goat Rock, USA Old Harry Rocks, England The Needles, England Old Man of Hoy, Scotland Hopewell Rocks, Canada Po Pin Chau, Hong Kong Needle of Arsene Lupin, France Lange Anna, Germany	Percé Rock, Canada Holei Arch, Hawaii Durdle Door, England Porte d'Amante, France Great Pollet Arch, Ireland

Carry out research in groups and prepare a presentation, perhaps using PowerPoint. In your presentation you need to choose **one** stack and **one** arch from the list, or an example from your own country.

a Describe the precise location of your chosen stack and arch and show them on a map.

b Find photographs to show your chosen stack and arch and describe their main features (e.g. shape, size, rock type).

c Explain clearly how each of the features was formed.

CASE STUDY 14b

Coastal deposition – the Hel spit

Hel Spit

A The Hel spit, Poland

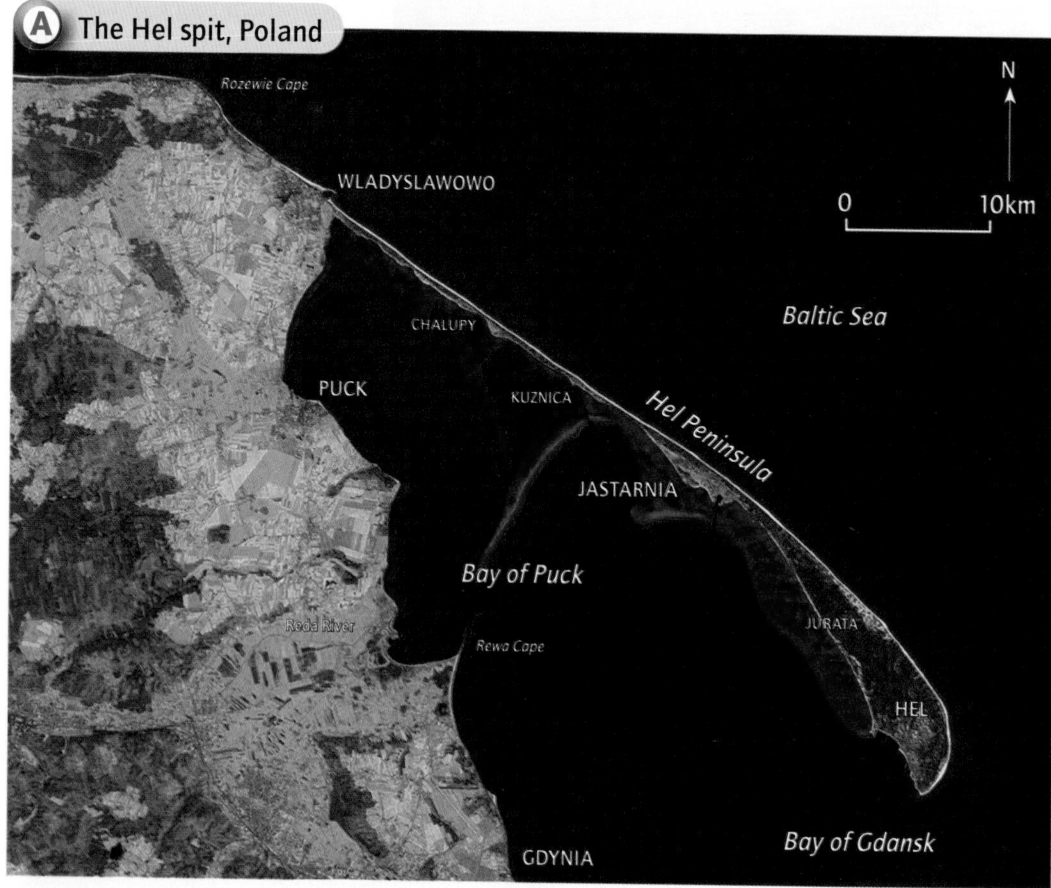

The Hel spit, Poland

The Hel peninsula is a long sand spit situated at the western end of Gdansk Bay of the Baltic Sea in northern Poland. It is long, narrow, low and relatively flat, with sand dunes in many parts. The sand spit was formed by coastal deposition, as a result of longshore drift from west to east. The predominant winds are from the west and north-west and this transports sediments from the west of the spit, where it is subject to erosion, to its eastern end where sediment is still building up. The beach material is sorted by the waves, resulting in large sediments (e.g. pebbles) at the top of the beach and smaller ones (e.g. sand and shingle) close to the sea.

B The process of longshore drift

Waves approach beach at angle controlled by prevailing winds

Material moved up the beach at an angle in the swash

Material carried directly down the beach in the backwash under gravity

Direction of longshore drift

Task 1

Study **Source A**.

a Measure the length of the Hel peninsula in kilometres.
b Measure the width of the Hel peninsula between Chalupy and Wladyslawowo.
c How does the width of the sand spit change between Jastarnia and Hel? Suggest a reason for this change.

Task 2

Study **Sources A and B**.

Explain in detail how the Hel sand spit was formed. Refer to:

- prevailing winds
- swash and backwash
- direction of longshore drift.

C Cross-section of Hel spit

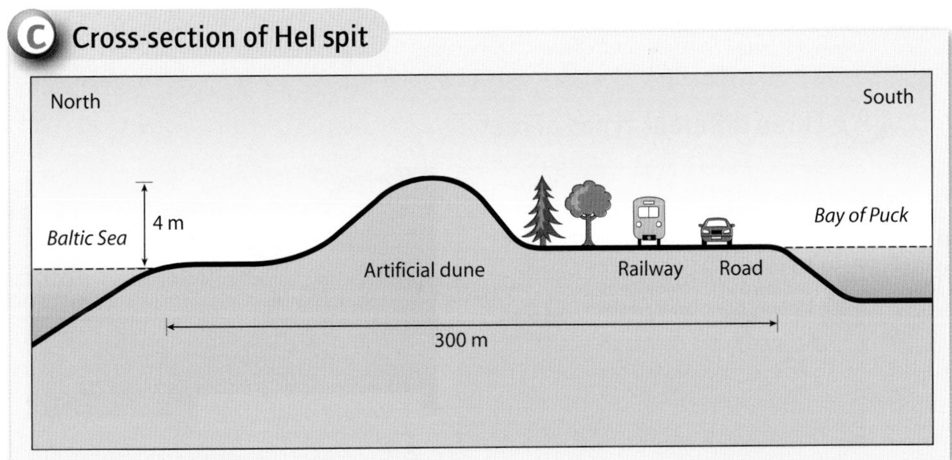

Task 3

Study **Source C**.

The highest waves which have been observed in the area were 8 metres high when a strong wind was blowing from a northerly direction for more than two days. Explain why it is necessary to protect the sand spit from coastal erosion.

D Coastal protection

Sea wall and rock armour

Groyne

Beach replenishment

Task 4

Study **Source D**.

The three photographs show methods used to protect Hel peninsula from coastal erosion. Carry out your own research so that you can explain how each method works.

Sample case study question

For a stretch of coastline where coastal deposition has occurred, describe the coastal landforms and explain their formation. You may use labelled diagrams in your answer.

Coral reefs

Landforms beneath the sea

The river and marine landforms studied so far have been created above sea level. Coral reefs, however, are landforms created beneath the sea.

Reefs are established when a large continuous mass of coral builds upwards and outwards from a rock base. Scientists know the conditions needed for corals to grow but the development of different types of reef over thousands of years is less well known.

A Three different types of reef

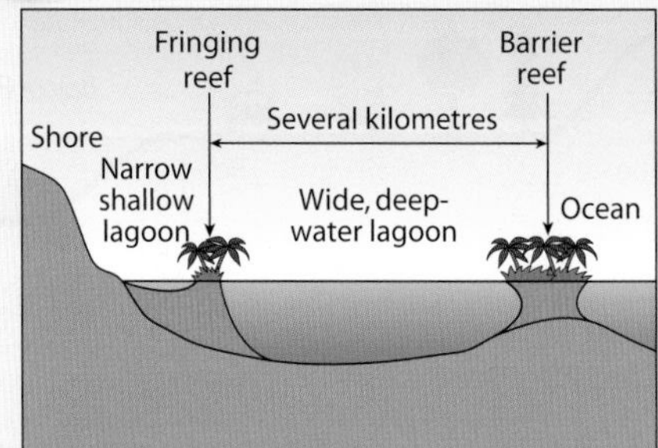

1 Monuriki Island, Fiji

1 **Fringing reef** Coral platforms grow out to sea attached to the mainland. A shallow lagoon lies above them.
2 **Barrier reef** Coral grows in a shallower area away from the mainland. The water between is too deep for coral to grow and forms a lagoon. These reefs form off-shore barriers along coastlines.
3 **Atoll** These develop around islands. Fringing reefs grow in a circle attached to the land. Sea-level rise or subsidence of the land causes the coral to grow at the height of the rising sea level to reach the light. This eventually forms a ring of coral reefs with a lagoon replacing the island in the centre.

2 Great Barrier Reef, Queensland, Australia

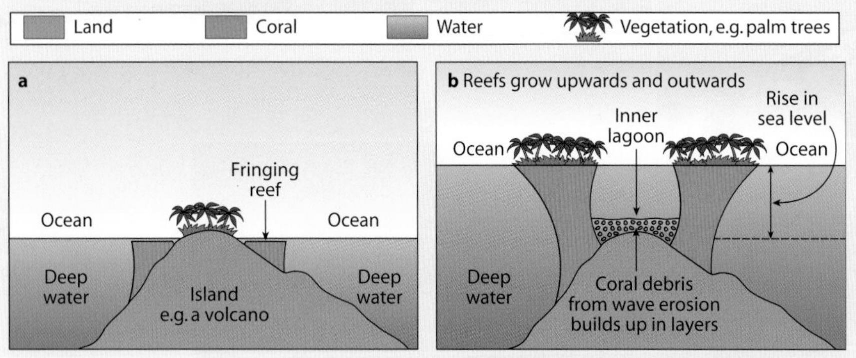

3 Blue Hole Lighthouse Reef Atoll, Belize

Task 1

Study **Source A**.

a Name the **three** different types of coral reef.
b Name a place where an example of each can be found.
c Describe how a fringing reef differs from a barrier reef.
d Explain how an island with fringing reefs can become an atoll.

Task 2

Study **Source B**.

a List the factors needed for coral to grow.
b Name **two** situations in which coral cannot grow. Suggest why.
c What material from coral produces the reef?
d How much would a coral reef grow in:
- 1 year
- 10 years
- 1000 years?

e What evidence is there of a high biodiversity in the photograph?

B Coral reefs – a delicate and diverse ecosystem

Biodiversity = The variety of plants and animals and other living things in a place.

Coral has a solid skeleton of limestone, and forms reefs at a rate of 2.5 cm a year. Coral needs three main factors for growth:

- warm water – between 23 and 25 °C is best
- clear, shallow saltwater, no deeper than 50 metres
- plenty of sunlight to aid photosynthesis.

Coral cannot grow in freshwater, and cannot tolerate silt nor water high in nutrients that allow plants to use the oxygen that the coral needs. Many countries in the tropics have the right climatic conditions but do not always have a large area of shallow water to absorb sunlight.

C Coral reef regions of the world

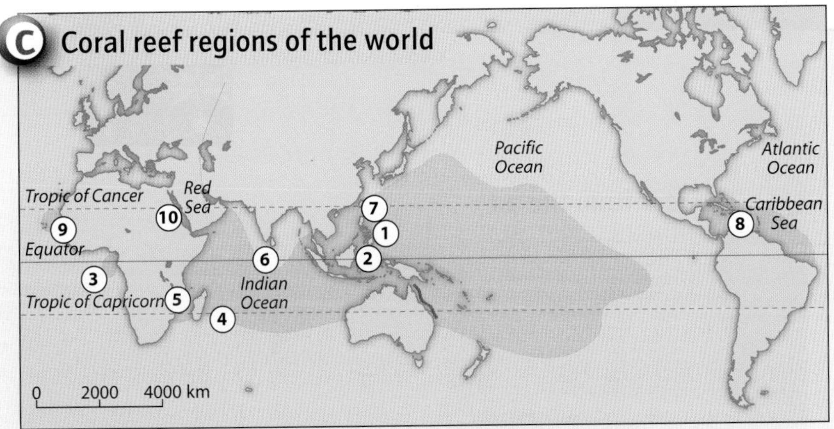

Corals can grow in temperate regions but are usually found in tropical and sub-tropical waters between 30°N and 30°S. Fifty per cent are found in the Indian Ocean and Red Sea, 35 per cent in the Pacific Ocean and 15 per cent in the Caribbean.

Biodiversity 'hotspots' – regions that contain a great diversity of species and have been significantly affected by human activity.	**Endangered species** – plants or animals that face a high risk of extinction in the near future due to human activity.

D Reefs at risk from human activity

These are the top 10 coral 'hot spots' ranked according to threat from human activity.

- Philippines
- West of central Africa, e.g. Gulf of Guinea
- East of Madagascar, e.g. Mauritius
- Indonesia, e.g. Sunda Islands
- Eastern South Africa
- Northern Indian Ocean, e.g. Maldives
- Southern Japan, Taiwan and south China
- West of Africa, e.g. Cape Verde Islands
- Western Caribbean, e.g. Jamaica
- Red Sea and Gulf of Oman

United Coral Reef Action Network

Coral reefs – an ecosystem under threat

Coral reefs provide habitats for a marine ecosystem full of colour, pattern and bizarre lifeforms. Some 3000 species have been recorded on a single reef. For these reasons they have an irresistible appeal to tourists. The visitors can have positive and negative effects:

- **Positive**, e.g. they create employment and income in some of the world's poorest regions.
- **Negative**, e.g. they damage coral while swimming beneath the sea.

Other human activities such as farming, fishing and water pollution also affect the coral reefs. Already 25 per cent of reefs have been damaged or lost. Some scientists estimate that, by 2020, 70 per cent might be permanently lost.

Task 3

Study **Sources C and D**.

a On an outline map of the world, shade and name the major coral reef regions.
b Name **two** oceans where coral can be found.
c Describe where coral reefs are **not** found between the tropics. Suggest why.
d Match the numbers on **Source C** to the places listed in **Source D**.
e Mark and name these places on your map.
f Name the top **three** coral reef 'hot spots' under the greatest threat.

Task 4

Study **Source E**.

a Why are coral reefs important to the economy of many countries?
b Identify which threats are due to natural causes and which may be because of human activity.
c Choose **one** article. Write a letter to your local newspaper outlining your concern about the threat.

E Coral grief – reefs under threat

Coral reefs are important. They provide employment for millions of people and supply seafood, building materials, medicines, and income from tourists. They also protect shorelines and communities from storms and erosion.

Earthquake Damages Coral in Indonesia

An earthquake measuring 8.7 on the Richter scale has lifted all the coral along a 190-mile coast a metre above sea level. All the coral have died.

LAWS PASSED TO PROTECT PHILIPPINES CORAL REEFS

Laws have been passed recently to prevent the use of 'blast-fishing'. Here cyanide bombs are used to stun fish on the coral reefs. Fisherman are also being encouraged to use fine-mesh barrier nets to drag over the reef, so only large fish are caught and smaller species are protected.

TOURISTS RUINING MALDIVE REEFS

Snorkelling and swimming out in hire boats to see the marine wildlife is damaging the reef. Coral is broken off by careless swimmers. Boats drop anchor onto coral or people just stand on it. Coral is also being sold as souvenirs.

Coral Reef Turns White in Tobago!

Beneath the blue Caribbean seas, the Buccoo coral reef, home to one of the richest marine ecosystems, has turned white. This 'bleaching' is due to global warming. The seas have risen by 3 °C above normal – even to 31 °C – which is above the coral's tolerance limit. Algae, which live in and provide the coral life-support system, die and are expelled from the coral leaving white skeletons. This is a tragedy for an island whose main industries are tourism and fishing.

The Great Barrier Reef, Australia

A The Great Barrier Reef, Australia

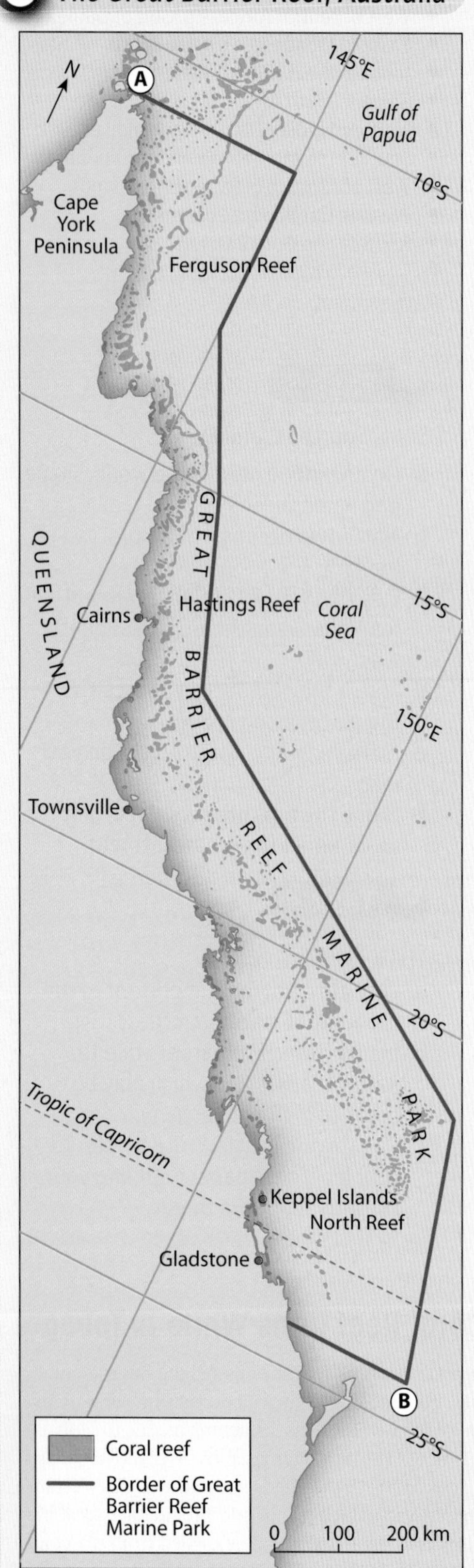

B The reef from the air …

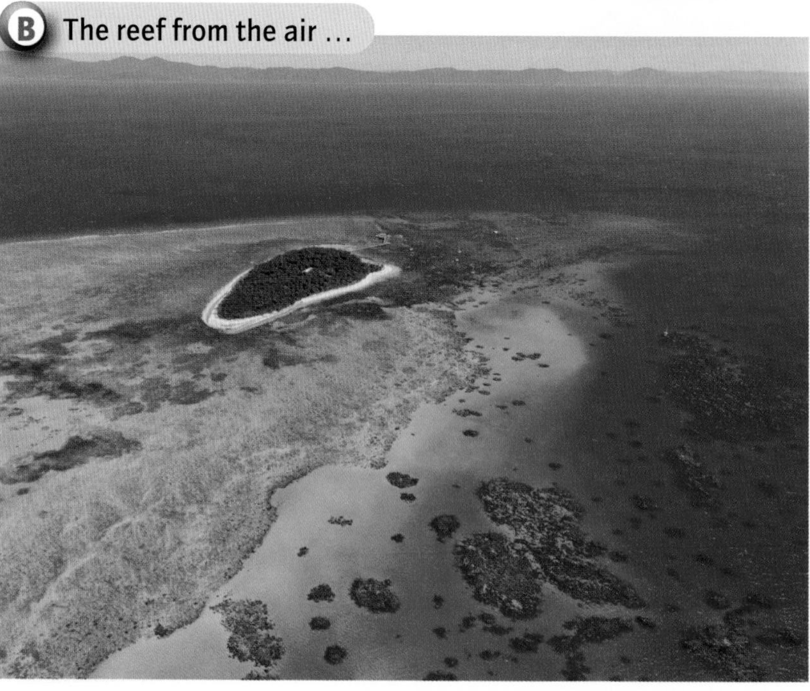

The Great Barrier Reef – important for Australia!

The Great Barrier Reef Marine Park was created a World Heritage Area in 1981. Since then human activity has been managed by the Marine Park Authority to protect the shallow lagoon waters between the Queensland coast and the reef from damage. The reef is important to the country's economy. It employs 6 per cent of the workforce and contributes 12 per cent of all exports.

Task 1

Study **Source A**.

- **a** Describe the location of the Great Barrier Reef. Refer to distances, directions, lines of latitude, Queensland and the Tropic of Capricorn in your answer.
- **b** A and B on the map mark the ends of the Great Barrier Reef Marine Park. Estimate the straight-line distance between A and B in kilometres.
- **c** Within what range of distances from the coast can the reef be found?

Task 2

Study **Source B**.

You have been asked to write a brief description of the reef aimed at attracting tourists. Imagine you are flying over the reef looking down at this area. Write down at least **four** key points you would mention in your article.

C The Barrier Reef under threat

Threats to the Great Barrier Reef

AUSTRALIA

Agriculture: The Queensland coast is sugarcane and cattle country, so pollutants arrive in the sea from rivers flowing into the reef areas. These are often nutrient-rich, so encourage plant growth which lowers oxygen levels for other coral wildlife. This is called eutrophication.

Industry and sewage: Rivers bring toxic and metal pollutants to the reef from industrial activities. Nitrates and phosphates are present in sewage. These lead to algal blooms and eutrophication.

Fishing: Over-fishing the reef affects the top layers of the ecosystem. Cyanide bombs have been used to stun fish so they can be collected easily. Fishermen are to be banned from one-third of the Barrier Reef.

Dredging: Taking out building materials such as sand and gravel from the sea bed causes mud to cloud the clear waters. Coral die through lack of sunlight.

Housing and shoreline development: On the Queensland coast more building and construction not only creates demand for materials from the sea bed but also creates sediment that flows into the sea. This muddies the waters.

Tourism: Nearly A$5 billion* is generated by tourists visiting the reef. Day-tour boats (up to 400 tourists), cruise ships, yachts and kayaks all use these waters. Most tourists stick to advice but some ignore it completely, often standing on live coral or bumping coral when snorkelling.

*A$1000 = US$800

Coral at the Keppel Islands is completely bleached due to starfish expansion. Global warming means that this natural predator has expanded into new areas, eating more **algae** and coral and leaving white coral skeletons. How this will develop across the Great Barrier Reef is the number one question right now.

Professor Ove Hoegh-Guldberg – marine biologist at the University of Queensland, 2006

Task 3

Study **Source C**.

a What do you understand by these terms: *natural predator, bleaching, eutrophication, sediment*?

b Choose **one** human activity that is causing a threat to the reef. Explain the damage it is causing.

Task 4

Study **Source D**.

a When was the GBRMPA established?

b What is meant by *sustainability*? How is the GBRMPA trying to manage the reef to achieve this?

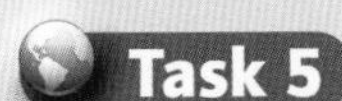

Task 5

Study **Source E**.

Read the advice given in the cruise company brochure. Devise a piece of illustrated media (e.g. a poster, video, interview) to support the list of suggestions for preventing damage to the reef.

D Managing the tourists

The Great Barrier Reef Marine Park Authority (GBRMPA)

The reef is a World Heritage Area which has been managed by the GBRMPA since 1981. The main aim of the managers is sustainability of the reef. To achieve this they are developing laws to protect the reef from oil pollution, over-fishing and tourist damage. Much of the reef is now zoned for particular activities. Managers are also required to maintain its outstanding natural beauty.

E Cruise company advice

HOW CAN YOU HELP PRESERVE THE GREAT BARRIER REEF ON YOUR TRIP?

The coral reef you will visit on this trip is a World Heritage Site. Its preservation is everybody's responsibility.

- Don't stand on the bottom while snorkelling, as the coral is alive.
- Snorkel in deep water along the edge of the coral reef.
- Only snorkel in shallow water if your fins will not bump corals.
- Don't throw food to the fish – we will hold fish-feeding sessions at the swim platform.
- Don't handle or harass marine animals.
- If smoking, use the ashtrays – do not throw butts overboard.

THIS IS A MARINE PARK. COLLECTING IS NOT ALLOWED.

TAKE AWAY ONLY PHOTOGRAPHS AND HAPPY MEMORIES.

PROTECT OUR CORAL FOR OUR CHILDREN.

Sample case study question

For a place you have studied, explain why an area of coral reef provides opportunities for people.

Weather and climate

A Weather and climate are different

Moscow, in Russia, can experience a cold and cloudy night with heavy snow, and temperatures in the morning of around minus 16 °C.

Weather: Short-term day-to-day changes in the atmosphere for a place. Rainfall, temperature, wind direction and strength, air pressure, sunshine, humidity and cloud cover are all studied as 'weather'.

Climate: The average weather conditions over a period of time – at least 30 years. Temperature and rainfall are shown on climate graphs. Climate regions cover large areas.

In Morocco, records show that desert winds from the Sahara can cause temperatures easily exceeding 40 °C on average during the summer months.

B How do we measure the weather?

Relative humidity – percentage moisture in air (%)

HEAD 1 Rain gauge

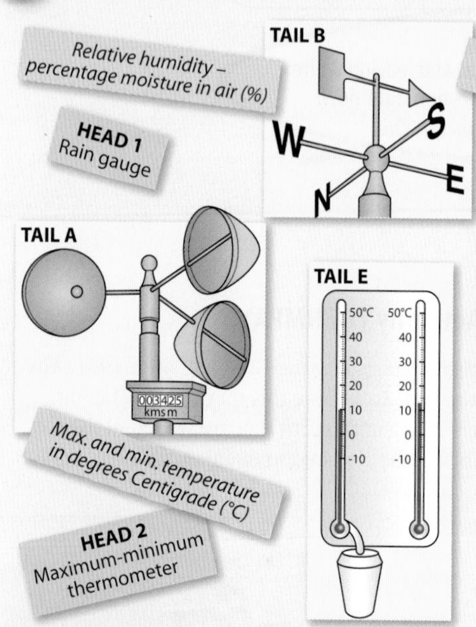

Max. and min. temperature in degrees Centigrade (°C)

HEAD 2 Maximum-minimum thermometer

Pressure in millibars (mb)

HEAD 3 Wet and dry bulb thermometer (hygrometer)

Weather station

A traditional weather station includes the instruments shown here. Computers and digital technology are making these instruments obsolete.

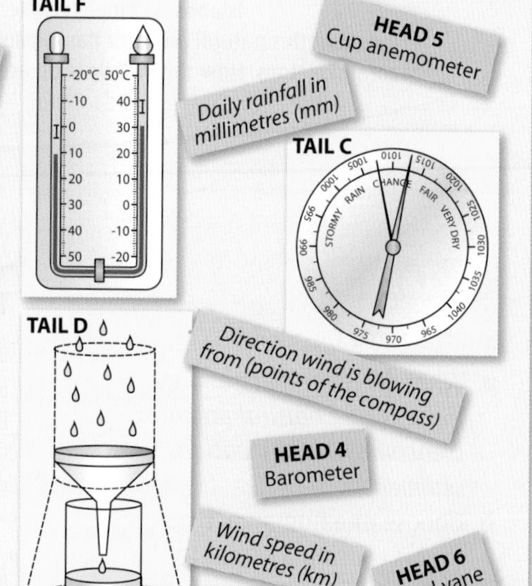

HEAD 5 Cup anemometer

Daily rainfall in millimetres (mm)

Direction wind is blowing from (points of the compass)

HEAD 4 Barometer

Wind speed in kilometres (km)

HEAD 6 Wind vane

The Stevenson screen

A traditional weather station has a Stevenson screen. It is built so that the shade temperature of the air can be measured. It consists of a square wooden box on a stand. The box has louvred sides to allow the entry of air. The roof is made of double boarding to prevent the sun's heat from reaching the inside of the screen. Insulation is further improved by painting the outside white to reflect the sun's rays. It is placed on a stand 110 cm above ground level to avoid any effects of concrete or grass at the surface. It is sited in open space, clear of trees and buildings to avoid any obstacles affecting the readings. In this way instruments inside the screen avoid external influences.

Studying the weather

What is the weather like today? Has it changed since you came to school this morning? Weather affects so many of our daily activities. We rely on weather forecasts to plan what we are going to do and when. But how is the weather measured and how can we predict what is going to happen from these measurements?

Task 1

Read **Source A**.

a How is **weather** different from **climate**?

b Study the statement with each photograph. Decide which one is about the weather and which is about climate.

Task 2

Study **Source B**.

Make a three-column table. In the first two columns match the instruments labelled 1–6 with the drawings A–F. In the final column use the other captions to state what each instrument measures and the units being measured.

C World climates

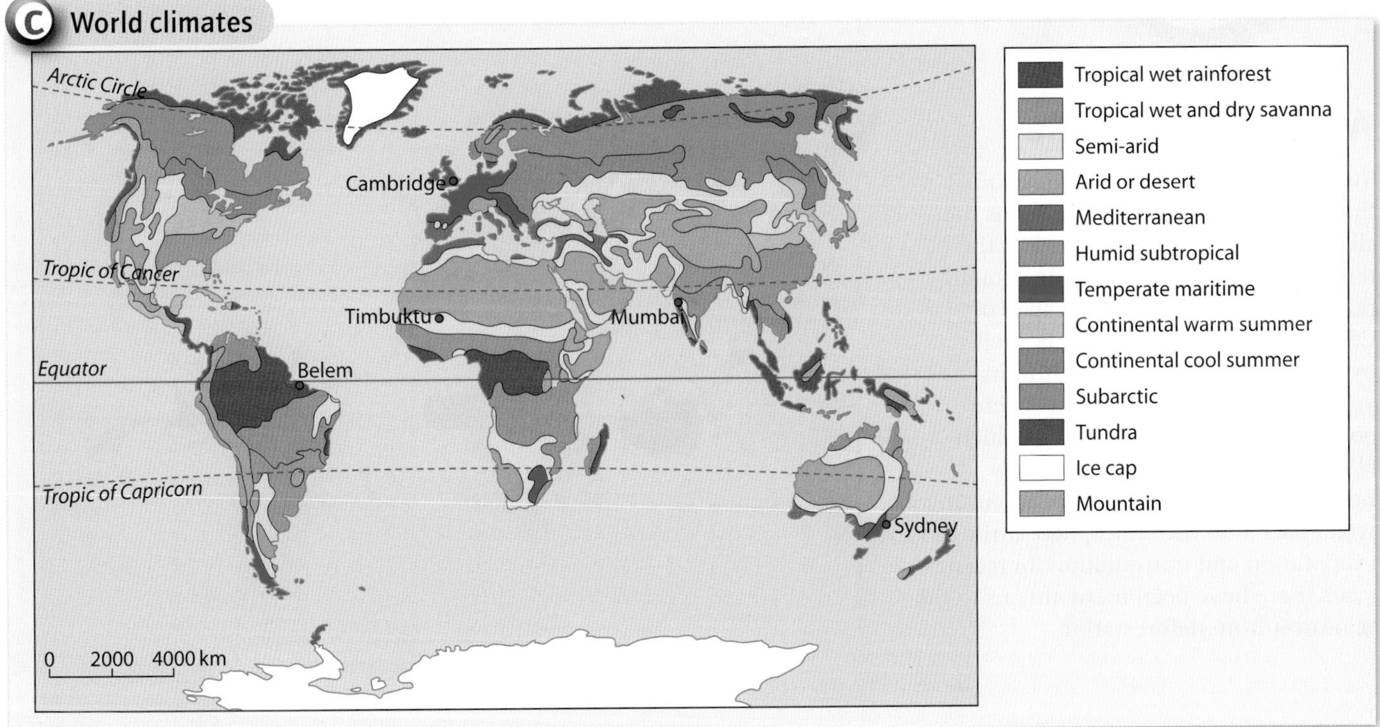

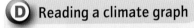

World climates … and Cambridge!

Many people mix up the weather and climate. Climate is more related to what we can expect to happen over a large area based on the records of at least 30 years of weather. A world map of climate types helps us find out the type of climate we live in. These vary from extremely cold, dry climates to extremely hot, wet climates.

To decide how the climate we live in compares with others we must have an idea of what one average climate is like. We need a place where it is neither too hot nor too cold, too wet nor too dry, as a reference point. The United Kingdom (UK) has a climate without extremes. It is between the cold Arctic region (north of 66½°N) and the hot Tropic of Cancer (23½°N). Cambridge (52°N), in the UK, is a good reference point for a climate between the two.

D Reading a climate graph

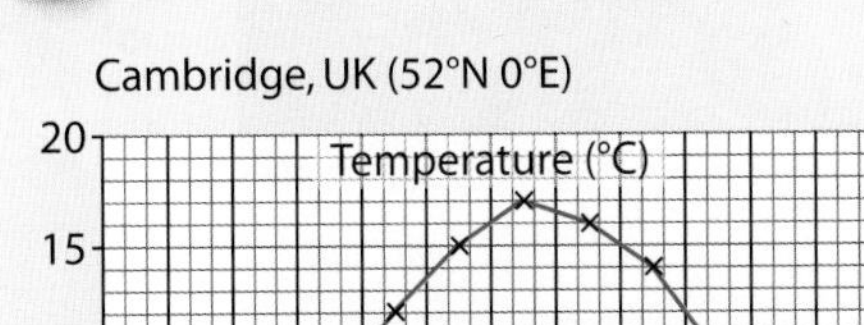

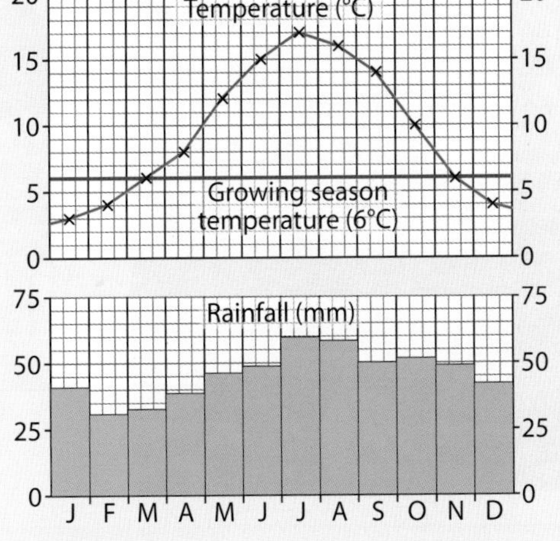

	J	F	M	A	M	J	J	A	S	O	N	D
Temperature (°C)	3	4	6	8	12	15	17	16	14	10	6	4
Rainfall (mm)	41	31	35	38	46	48	60	57	50	53	49	44

Average annual rainfall = 552 millimetres Temperatures are average (mean) for each month

Task 3

Read **Sources C and D**.

a Work out where you live on this map.

b Which climate type do you experience?

c What type of climate does Cambridge, in the UK, experience?

d From the graph describe the climate of Cambridge. Refer to:
- average monthly temperatures
- annual temperature range
- average annual rainfall
- rainfall distribution.

Task 4

Find climate data for where you live. Draw a climate graph and compare your graph with that of Cambridge. (Use the same scales for comparison.)

TOPIC 17 Tropical rainforests

At the global scale

Moving towards tropical regions and the equator from temperate regions the climate changes. It gets hotter and the temperatures stay high all year, though rainfall varies between the Tropics of Cancer and Capricorn. It can be well over 1500 mm or less than 250 mm a year. Tropical rainforests grow where both rainfall and temperature are high all year. Ten per cent of the world's rainfall depends on the rainforest putting water back into the atmosphere through evaporation and transpiration. In recent years there have been many threats to the rainforest from deforestation.

A Where are the rainforests?

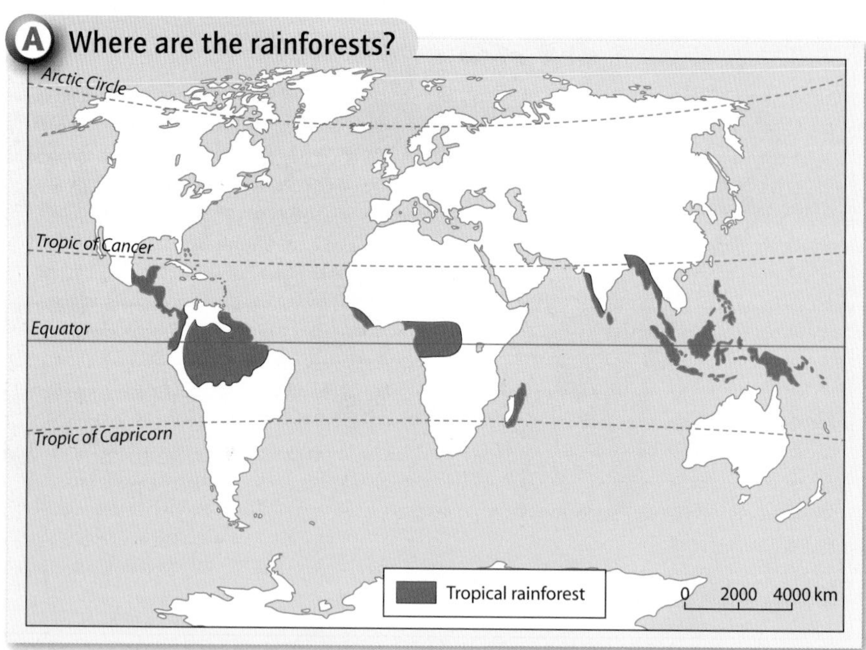

B Structure of rainforest vegetation

Rainforest in Langkawi, Malaysia

These broad-leaved evergreen forests show dense growth and extremely diverse fauna and flora, forming unique ecosystems. There can be 40–100 tree species per hectare. Large amounts of shade prevent much growth at low levels so most plant and animal species are in the canopy where there is light. All the plants compete for light to photosynthesise – this causes vegetation to grow in layers. Those that reach the sky – the emergents – form islands of green above the main forest. Rainforests are called the 'lungs of the Earth' due to the oxygen they produce.

Lianas creep up from the floor to the canopy

Metres: 0, 5, 10, 15, 20, 25, 30, 35, 40, 45

Metres: 0, 10, 20, 30, 40, 50

Emergent trees The tallest trees emerge through the main canopy layer.

Main canopy layer This is the true jungle. Most animals live here.

Lower canopy layer Small trees and saplings grow in shady, humid conditions.

Shrub layer Smaller trees and ferns grown in deep shade

Ground layer Leaf and animal remains cover the ground. Not much can grow here.

Task 1

Study **Source A**.

a On an outline map of the world, shade and label regions that have tropical rainforest.

b Use an atlas to help you label **three** countries from **three** different continents that have rainforests.

c Describe the global distribution of rainforests.

Task 2

Study **Source B**.

a Make your own labelled copy of the vertical structure of a rainforest.

b Are there any forests near where you live? If so, how does their structure compare with that of the rainforest?

c Why does so little rainfall and light reach the ground in the rainforest? How does this affect the growth of vegetation in the lower levels shown in the photo?

d Explain how competition for light leads to layers of vegetation in the rainforest.

C A rainforest climate graph

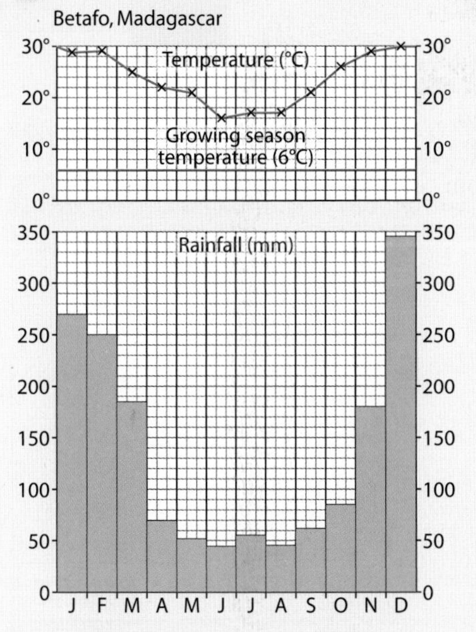
Betafo, Madagascar
30° 20° 10° 0°
Temperature (°C)
Growing season temperature (6°C)
350 300 250 200 150 100 50 0
Rainfall (mm)
J F M A M J J A S O N D

Betafo	J	F	M	A	M	J	J	A	S	O	N	D
Temperature (°C)	29	29	25	22	21	16	17	17	21	26	29	30
Rainfall (mm)	270	251	183	71	52	46	54	48	62	87	171	345

Average annual rainfall = 1640 mm   Temperatures are average (mean) for each month

Although it is hot and wet for most of the year, temperature and rainfall are not evenly distributed. The sun is over the Tropic of Capricorn in December, giving maximum **insolation**, but is over the Tropic of Cancer in June so temperatures fall. All year the warm moist air rises to give low pressure and clouds over Madagascar. The prevailing trade wind from the south-east also brings rain from the Indian Ocean but from May to October it is weaker so less rain falls.

D Does Madagascar tick the boxes?

Heads	Tails
Temperatures over 20 °C for most months of the year …	… so photosynthesis can take place all year.
High rainfall in each month of the year …	… result in the rapid recycling of nutrients.
Long hours of daylight and sunshine …	… so there is water available for growth all year.
High temperatures and high rainfall …	… so plant growth is not limited by low temperatures.

E Nutrient recycling

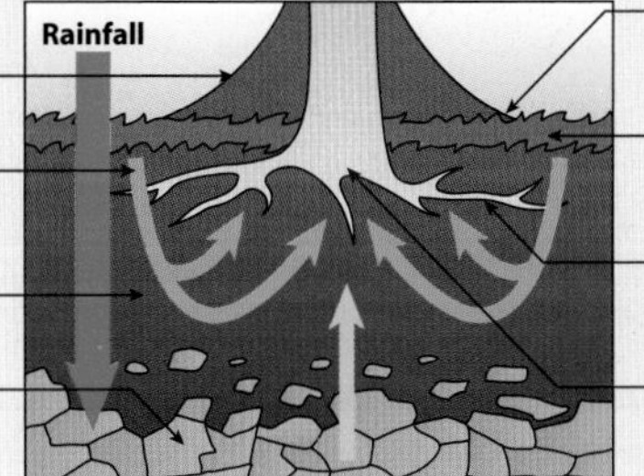
The trees grow buttresses to hold them up because their roots are shallow and do not give support.
Recycling of nutrients back into trees is rapid because it is so hot and wet.
Nutrients only stay in the soil for a short time.
Rocks provide trees with some minerals and nutrients.
Rainfall
Leaves, dead branches and twigs fall from trees all year.
Decomposers quickly break down dead plants and animals.
Roots search for nutrients and water near the soil surface.
Water, nutrients and gases return quickly into the trees through their roots.

Task 3

Study **Source C**.

- **a** Which month has the highest mean temperature?
- **b** Which month has the lowest mean temperature?
- **c** Work out the mean annual temperature range.
- **d** How can you tell this place is in the southern hemisphere?
- **e** Explain why rainfall and temperature are not evenly spread during the year.

Task 4

Study **Sources C and D**.

- **a** Match the 'Heads' to the 'Tails'.
- **b** Look back at the climate data for Cambridge on page 87. Explain why the climate at Betafo is better for rapid plant growth than the climate at Cambridge.

Task 5

Study **Source E**.

Imagine trees have been logged and removed. Redraw the main diagram, changing or adding new labels to show the effects of deforestation.

Task 6

Study the articles in **Source F**.

- **a** Label each of the countries named on your world map (see Task 1). Annotate the country to show how the rainforest is being affected.
- **b** Design a poster to show why tropical rainforest is being removed across the world.

F Rainforest issues

Cups of Coffee Spell Doom for the Hairy Rhino

20% of the rainforest in the Bukit Barisan Selatan National Park of Sumatra has been hacked down for illegal coffee plantations due to a boom in export demand. Tigers, elephants, orang-utans and the hairy rhino are all at risk …

January 2007

LOGGERS GO DEEPER INTO THE AMAZON JUNGLE IN BRAZIL

Illegal logging for mahogany is pushing loggers further into the Amazon rainforest. One mahogany tree will make furniture, veneers and floors worth US$200,000 …

November 2002

Rainforests Felled to Feed Demand for Lipstick

Go into any shop and the chances are that palm oil could be in a tenth of your purchases. Palm oil can be found in everything from margarine and ice cream to soap, shampoo and lipstick. Benin, in West Africa, has cleared forest for palm plantations.

March 2004

Madagascar's rainforest

Madagascar – a world apart

Madagascar is the world's fourth largest island. Before people arrived here years ago, nearly all of the island was forested. Since then local people have gradually cleared the land for farming which has led to deforestation. Today there are also threats from mining companies, and tourism is growing. The rainforest here is disappearing fast.

A Where is Madagascar?

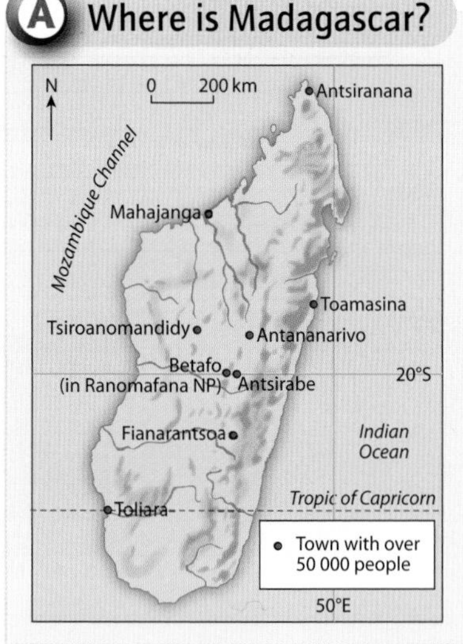

B Rainforest and rainfall

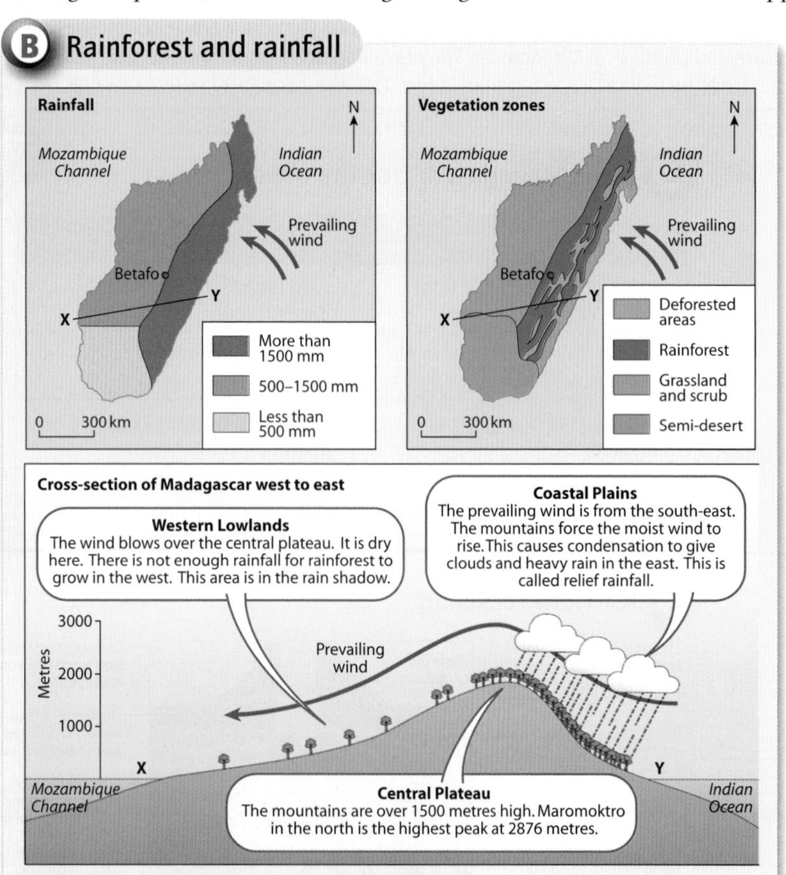

Task 1

Study **Source A**.

a Estimate the greatest length (north–south) and greatest width (west–east) of the island in kilometres. Use a world map to find one other island that is larger.

b Describe the location of Madagascar in relation to Mozambique and the Tropic of Capricorn.

Task 2

Study **Source B**.

a Where does it rain most and least in Madagascar?

b Use the cross-section to explain the rainfall pattern.

Task 3

Study **Source C**.

a What is the difference between a producer, a herbivore and a carnivore? Give **one** example of each.

b Using examples of food chains, suggest what would happen to the food web if:
- all the producers were removed
- the fosa (a large cat) became extinct.

Explain your answer.

C All these are under threat

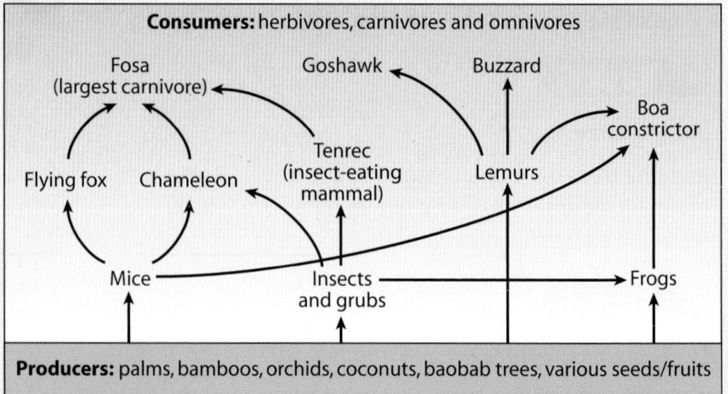

The rainforest ecosystem on Madagascar is unique. Over 90 per cent of the animals living here only exist on this island. Over 50 million years ago the continents of India and Africa separated when two plates drifted apart. Madagascar was left as an island between two continents. This meant that the ecosystem evolved in a different way from those in India and Africa.

Why has the forest gone?

Madagascar is an LEDC – it is the ninth poorest country in the world. The people have relied on subsistence farming for many years. Early settlers lived on the east coast at first but, as population grew, they moved inland and removed more forest from mountain slopes for farmland. In most rainforest areas this shifting cultivation allowed rainforests to recover. Now, however, more is being removed to plant cash crops such as rice, coffee and tobacco. These provide 70 per cent of overseas earnings from exports; this is the main reason why the forest is being removed so quickly – 90 per cent of the original forest has already been destroyed. Recovery of the ecosystem is impossible.

D Difficult choices

Rainforest cover is decreasing. What do you expect us to do? We have to live. We need land to grow crops. We need meat and skins so we have to hunt animals. Other countries want our rice and coffee. We grow it to earn money from abroad. This will help our economy develop. You may care about the lemurs. I care about my family.

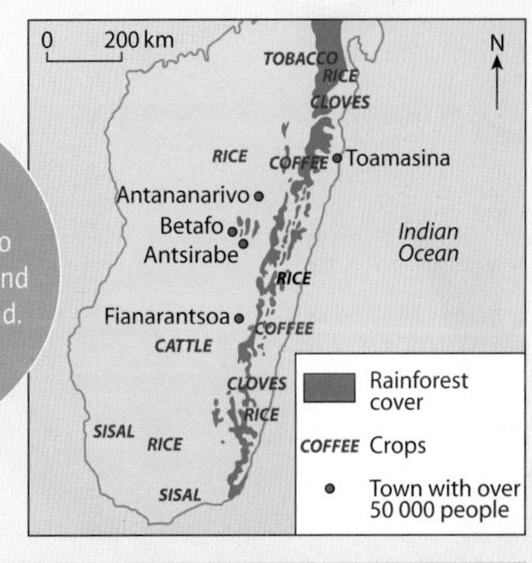

Madagascar factfile	
Population	15.5 million
Infant mortality rate	95 per 1000
Urban/rural %	28/72
Children per woman	5.4
Doctors	1 per 4000
Access to safe water	40%
Average income	US$ 260
Life expectancy	56M/59F
Employment structure (%)	
Primary	78
Secondary	7
Tertiary	15

Task 4

Study **Source D**.

- **a** Why are the farmers removing trees?
- **b** List the crops being grown in Madagascar. How are other countries causing the removal of forest?
- **c** Select **three** indicators which suggest that Madagascar is an LEDC. Justify your choices.
- **d** Suggest how developing the tourist industry could help or harm the country.

Task 5

Study **Source E**.

- **a** Describe the scenes in the photographs.
- **b** What is:
  - slash-and-burn farming
  - shifting cultivation?
- **c** Put the eight captions in the correct time order. Use them to produce your own storyboard.
- **d** Some people say that Madagascar is 'bleeding from the heart'. Why?

Sample case study question

Describe and explain how human activity is changing an area of tropical rainforest you have studied.

E Removing trees creates space … but bleeds away the soil

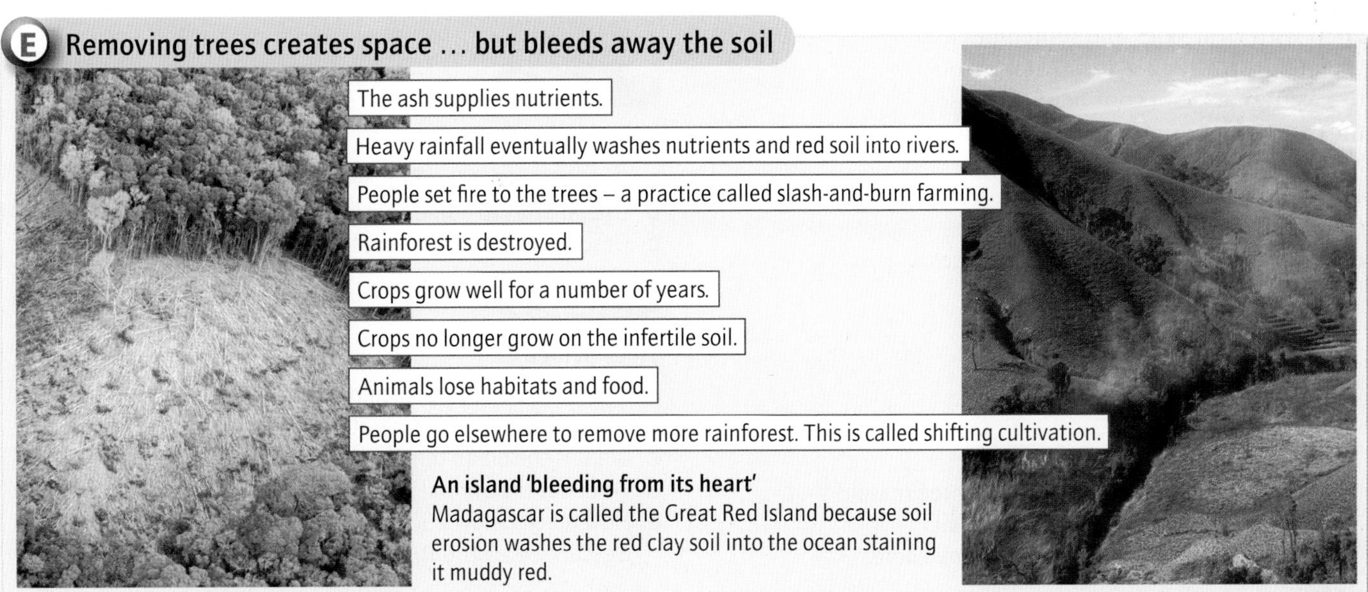

The ash supplies nutrients.
Heavy rainfall eventually washes nutrients and red soil into rivers.
People set fire to the trees – a practice called slash-and-burn farming.
Rainforest is destroyed.
Crops grow well for a number of years.
Crops no longer grow on the infertile soil.
Animals lose habitats and food.
People go elsewhere to remove more rainforest. This is called shifting cultivation.

An island 'bleeding from its heart'
Madagascar is called the Great Red Island because soil erosion washes the red clay soil into the ocean staining it muddy red.

TOPIC 18 Hot deserts

A A desert scene

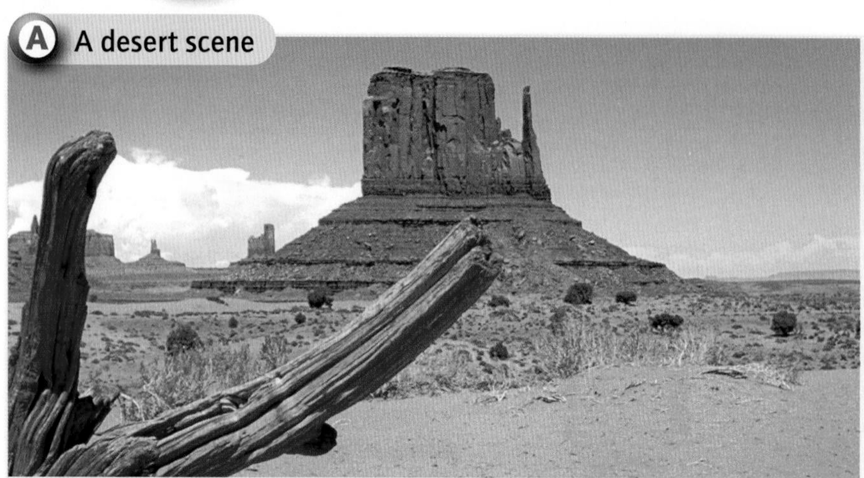

Monument Valley, the Mojave Desert, USA
The Mojave Desert is a dry, barren desert. The Monument Valley area was originally a basin of sandstone and limestone layers. It has slowly been uplifted to become a flat plateau up to 3 km above sea level. Heat, wind and water have eroded the land for over 50 million years, cutting it up and peeling away the rock layers. Hard horizontal rocks have been left as isolated caps above softer sandstone. These are called 'mesas'. Due to low rainfall the features are not rounded.

B The world's hot deserts

NORTH AMERICA
Californian current
23½°N
0°
SOUTH AMERICA
Peruvian current
Fog
23½°S
Hot desert climate
Semi-arid climates
Cold ocean currents
ASIA
Canaries current
Fog
23½°N
AFRICA
0°
Benguela current
Fog
23½°S
West Australia current
AUSTRALIA
23½°S

Deserts – challenging places

A desert is an area that receives less than 250 mm precipitation in a year. Arid (dry) deserts can be hot, for example the Sahara Desert in Africa; or cold, as found in the northern tundra regions of North America and Eurasia. These pages are about hot deserts that are found in sub-tropical and tropical latitudes. They have very high daytime temperatures, often over 50 °C, and low night-time temperatures, below 20 °C with clear skies and sometimes a ground frost. They are mostly found on the western edge of continents because the prevailing winds in tropical regions are off-shore blowing from the east across land, so cannot pick up moisture from the sea. Hot deserts are extreme environments which present challenges for people who live or visit there.

C A hot desert climate

Monument Valley, the Mojave Desert, USA	J	F	M	A	M	J	J	A	S	O	N	D
Temperature (°C)	10	13	15	19	20	23	28	36	30	24	19	14
Rainfall (mm)	25	30	34	37	4	6	3	12	22	18	15	13

Average annual rainfall = 219 mm
Temperatures are average (mean) for each month

Task 1

Study **Source A**.

a Describe the scene. Give at least **three** reasons that suggest this is an area of low rainfall.
b Explain how mesas have been formed here.

Task 2

Study **Source B**.

a On an outline map of the world, shade the deserts shown.
b Use an atlas to name these deserts.
c Describe the distribution of hot deserts.

Task 3

Study **Source C**.

a Draw a climate graph using this data.
b What is the mean temperature of the hottest month?
c What is the mean temperature of the coldest month?
d Work out the annual mean temperature range.
e How much below 250 mm is the average annual rainfall? Describe its distribution.

D Creating hot deserts

The **tropopause** is the boundary between the atmosphere and space. Rising air cannot penetrate it so it is diverted towards the tropics.

N. Pole
Tropopause
$23\frac{1}{2}$°N Tropic of Cancer HIGH PRESSURE
0° Equator LOW PRESSURE
$23\frac{1}{2}$°S Tropic of Capricorn HIGH PRESSURE
S. Pole

The air movement from ① to ④ is called a Hadley cell after George Hadley who put forward this idea in the 18th century.

Key to diagram (left)

1. Due to the heat of the sun, which is overhead at the equator, the land surfaces are warmed up and air rises. This gives low pressure at the surface along the equator. This rising air cools and condenses to give thunder clouds and heavy rainfall in equatorial regions.
2. Once this rising air reaches the tropopause it then travels to the north and south towards each Tropic.
3. As it moves away from the equator at high altitude it cools. Between 20° and 35° north and south of the equator the air begins to sink or subside towards the surface.
4. This gives permanent sub-tropical high-pressure systems (anticyclones) in these areas. Rainfall cannot occur where air sinks. These areas of aridity are the hot deserts of the world.

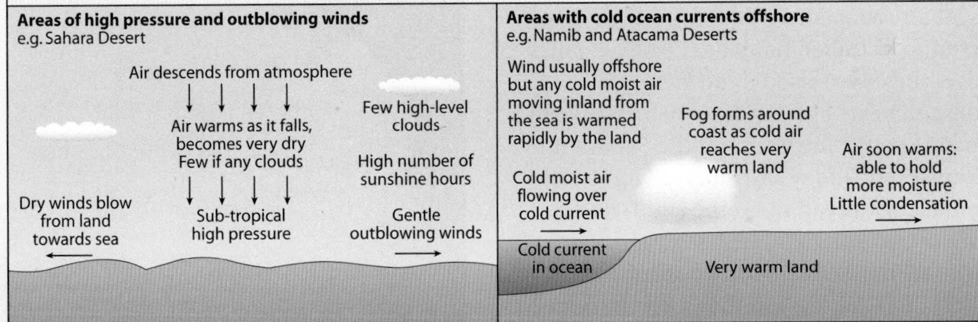

Areas of high pressure and outblowing winds
e.g. Sahara Desert
Air descends from atmosphere
Air warms as it falls, becomes very dry
Few if any clouds
Few high-level clouds
High number of sunshine hours
Dry winds blow from land towards sea
Sub-tropical high pressure
Gentle outblowing winds
Areas with cold ocean currents offshore
e.g. Namib and Atacama Deserts
Wind usually offshore but any cold moist air moving inland from the sea is warmed rapidly by the land
Fog forms around coast as cold air reaches very warm land
Air soon warms: able to hold more moisture
Little condensation
Cold moist air flowing over cold current
Cold current in ocean
Very warm land

E Living in hot deserts

Camels are called 'ships of the desert' because they can cross the desert better than any other animal. They have bushy eyebrows and two pairs of eyelashes to keep sand out of their eyes. They only have two toes and thick padded feet so they can walk easily across sand. The hump stores fat reserves that can be used as food as the animals travel. If the hump shrinks the camel's reserves are low.

The Saguaro cactus is the state flower of Arizona, USA. The blossoms open during desert nights and close in the day. It has a tall, thick stem with smooth waxy skin and 20 mm spines. The stem can expand to store water.

Heads …	… Tails
Plants are low-growing …	… to avoid water loss by strong winds.
Some animals can store food and water for days …	… to prevent water loss by evapotranspiration.
Animals are often small …	… to reach underground water supplies.
Plants store water in thick stems …	…to use in dry periods.
Small animals can hide in burrows or under stones …	… to reach the maximum area for water and to find any surface moisture.
Some rodents are nocturnal …	… so there is less water loss from a small surface area.
Plants have roots that travel horizontally …	… so they can avoid intense daytime heat.
Insects and reptiles have waterproof skins …	… so they can hunt in cooler nights.
Plants have long roots …	… so they can retain water in their bodies.
Plants have small, thick leaves or needles …	… so they can travel far without the need for daily supplies.

Task 4

Study **Source D**.

a Explain how sub-tropical high pressure zones are created.
b Why is it difficult for rain to form in these areas?
c Name **two** hot deserts in each of:
- areas of sub-tropical high pressure
- the western side of continents close to cold ocean currents.

d How can cold ocean currents help create fog but also cause a lack of rainfall in some deserts?

Task 5

Study **Source E**.

a Match the 'Heads' and 'Tails' in **two** different tables: one for plants and one for animals.
b Draw an annotated sketch showing your design for a plant or animal that would survive desert life.

Task 6

List some opportunities that deserts present for making a living.

The Sahara Desert and Mali

The Sahara and the Sahel

The Sahara, sprawling across north Africa, is the world's largest and hottest desert – it covers roughly the same area as the USA. About one-quarter is covered by sand desert – known as ergs. The rest consists of gravel-strewn plains called reg and areas of barren rocks called hamada. Fossil evidence shows the desert used to be wetter a thousand years ago but human activity and climate change have turned the Sahara into a true desert. Today the Sahara is growing even larger, spreading to the south due to more overgrazing and deforestation. This moving edge of the desert is called the Sahel – an Arabic word that means 'fringe'.

A The desert moves south

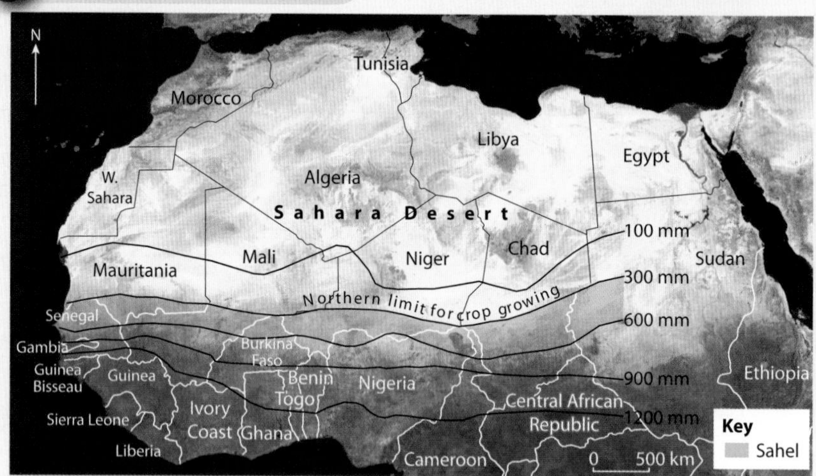

The Sahel is a semi-arid belt of poor, dry soil 300–500 km wide from north to south. It stretches from west to east across north Africa between the Sahara Desert and savanna grasslands. Here average rainfall ranges from 300 to 600 mm per year. When – and if – it rains, up to 90 per cent of the moisture evaporates. Drought is natural to the Sahel but desertification and land degradation by people have moved the limit for growing crops and grazing animals further south each year. Countries like Mali now have even less inhabitable land to survive on.

A camel train travelling from Timbuktu to Taoudenni to exchange goods for salt

Task 1

Study **Source A**.

a Describe the distribution of rainfall from north to south. Use figures in your answer.

b List all the countries in which the Sahel can be found.

c How will desertification affect these countries if the 300 mm isoline moves further south?

Task 2

Study **Source B**.

a What are the causes of desertification?

b How is this different from land degradation?

c Explain how:

- the lack of rain since 1969 has led to the Sahel extending south
- population pressure has led to the Sahel extending south.

Task 3

Study **Source C**.

a Describe the location of Mali. Refer to lines of latitude, neighbouring countries, the Sahara Desert and the Sahel in your answer.

b In what ways is the Niger river important to Mali?

c Suggest reasons why the population of Mali is not evenly distributed.

B The changing Sahel

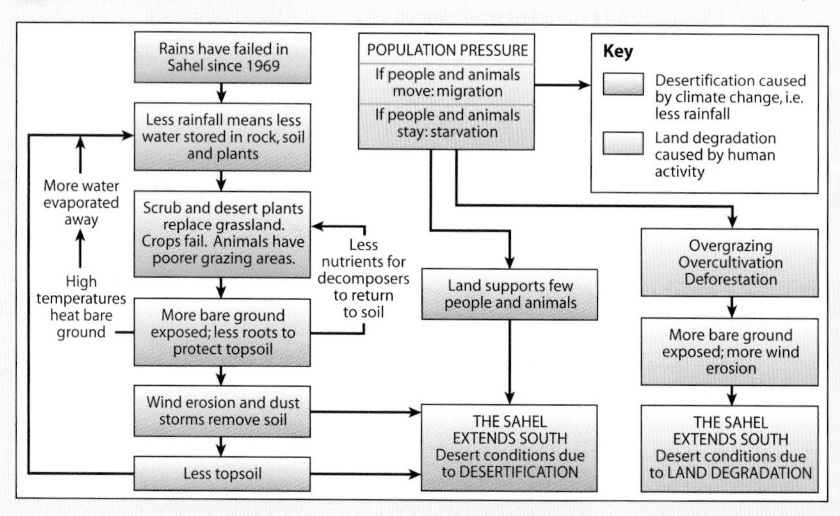

Mali – a land-locked country

Once home to one of Africa's greatest empires, Mali is a vast land-locked country nestled between the Sahara Desert and six neighbouring countries in West Africa. It is the largest country in West Africa but one of the poorest countries in the world. Bordering the Sahel region of West Africa in the north, 65 per cent of Mali's land is desert or semi-desert. In these areas Malians suffer from periods of drought and widespread food shortages. Population density is only 5 per km². It is an extreme environment for plants, wildlife and people to survive in.

C Where is Mali?

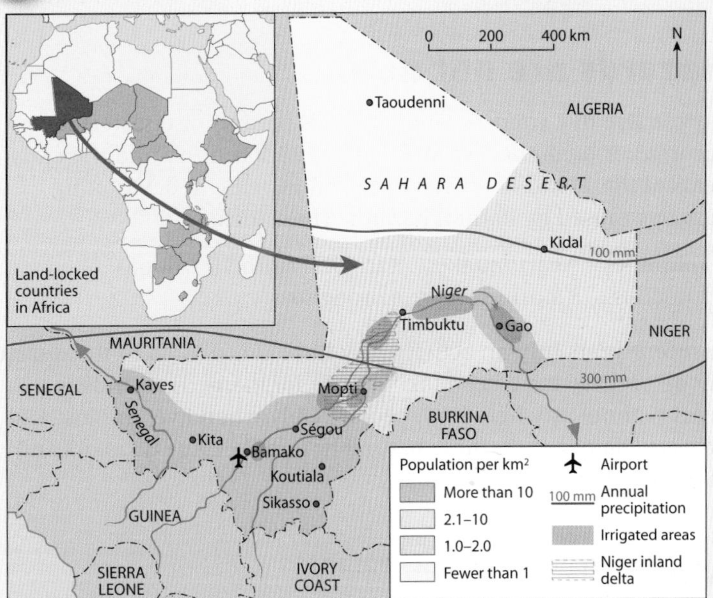

The Niger river is the most important feature in Mali. It provides a reliable water supply and is a vital transport route for goods and people. The Niger's high-water flood season is from August to December.

D Surviving the desert climate

The fennec fox

The fennec fox is a mammal and is the world's smallest fox. It has enormous ears to help radiate heat to help it stay cool. It lives deep in the ground in long, cool burrows and emerges around dusk to hunt when the day is less hot. Most of northern Mali has less than 100 mm of rainfall a year – sometimes none. In most places the main source of moisture for animals is dew. The desert is fiercely hot by day but can freeze at night. Most animals are small so they can lose heat more easily, as their surface area is large compared with their size.

The acacia tree

The acacia tree has developed a long shallow root system which enables it to find moisture. It has thorny leaves to prevent water loss and its crown is wide so the foliage can absorb the maximum amount of sunlight. Smaller shrubs and cacti have little foliage above ground but rely on long or deep roots and fleshy stems for water storage. The best-known desert plant is the date palm which grows only around waterholes or oases.

Timbuktu, Mali	J	F	M	A	M	J	J	A	S	O	N	D
Temperature (°C)	23	24	26	31	35	34	34	33	33	32	27	23
Rainfall (mm)	0	0	10	0	14	30	77	50	20	17	0	0

Average annual rainfall = 218 mm
Temperatures are average (mean) for each month

Signs like this, found all over West Africa, indicate the remoteness of Timbuktu from other places. It was founded as a trading post in the 11th century midway between the north and south of West Africa.

Task 4

Study **Source D**.

a Draw a climate graph for Timbuktu. Use the same scales on the axes as you did for Monument Valley on page 92.

b Compare and contrast the two hot desert climates.

c How have the fennec fox and the acacia tree adapted to survive in northern Mali?

Task 5

Study **Source D**.

Imagine you are to lead a camel train from Timbuktu to Taoudenni. The round trip will take four weeks.

a At what time of year would you **not** go? Why?

b Discuss and list the equipment and supplies you would need.

c How would you ensure the health and safety of the people and the camels?

Sample case study question

For a named hot desert you have studied, describe and explain how plants have adapted to the climate.

TOPIC 19 Natural hazards

Hazards are not new

Do you live in a country where natural hazards or disasters have occurred or might occur? Much of the 20th century and the early years of the 21st century have seen an increase in devastating disasters caused by natural hazards. These include:

- volcanoes
- earthquakes
- tropical storms
- floods
- tsunamis
- storm surges
- droughts.

In recent years human activity may have contributed to the disasters but all of these have been taking place for many thousands of years without any help from people! Only when lives are lost and property damaged do these natural hazards become disasters and make the news.

A Deaths from natural disasters

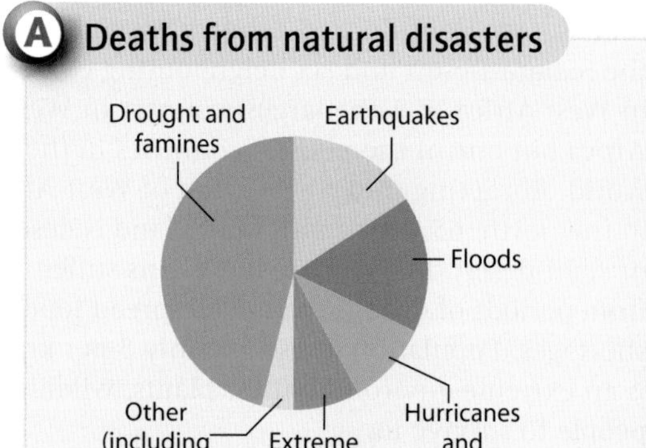

B Disasters of the 21st century

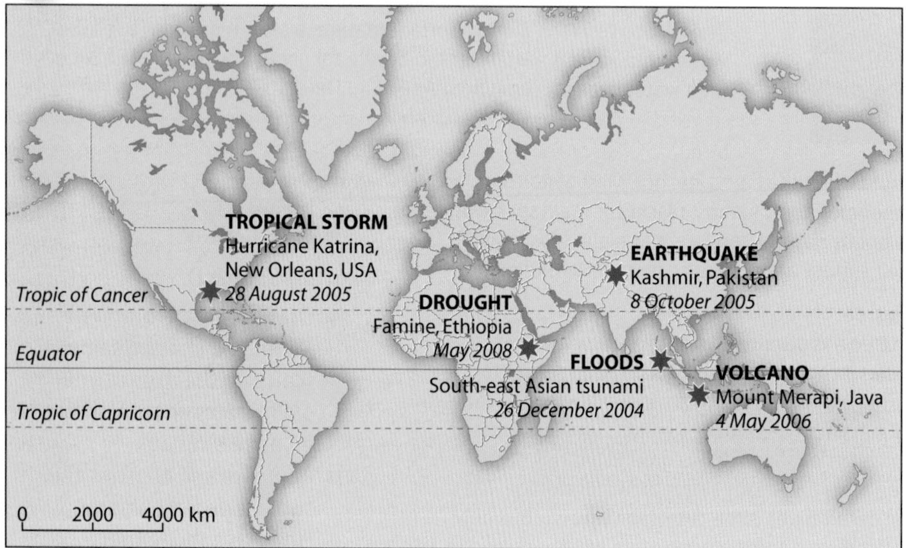

C

MEGA-CITIES ADD TO PERILS

A survey by insurance companies has shown that about 250 great natural disasters have hit the planet in the past 50 years killing at least 1.4 million people. The late 20th century was especially dangerous with a level of disasters four times higher than in the 1950s. Most of these were related to floods, hurricanes and windstorms. Experts say these will continue to increase as people move from the countryside into urban areas on or near the coast. In 1950 only New York had more than 10 million people; today there are 20 mega-cities of which 16 are in the developing world. Floods, earthquakes and cyclones easily devastate shanty towns. Thunderstorms also increase over large urban areas due to their 'heat island' effect. Global warming will add to the problem due to high wind speeds, rising sea levels and more storm surges. While the number of volcanoes and earthquakes remains constant, climate-related disasters are increasing. Landslides, forest fires, heat waves and periods of extreme cold are far more common now.

Task 1

Study **Source A**.

a Which natural disaster causes the highest percentage of deaths? Suggest how human activity might have caused this figure to be so high.

b Why do we not find out about some of the natural hazards that take place globally?

Task 2

a On an outline world map, locate and label the **five** examples given.

b In boxed captions around your map, add a brief summary about each natural disaster based on **Sources D–H** on page 97.

c Add other disasters to your map. Keep it up to date.

Task 3

Study **Source C**.

a What did the insurance survey find out about the frequency of natural disasters?

b Why do the numbers of volcanoes and earthquakes stay fairly constant compared with climate-related disasters?

c How and why can urbanisation increase climate-related disasters?

D Volcanoes – Mount Merapi, Java

In the news … 4 May 2006

MERAPI SHUDDERS BACK TO LIFE

Indonesia's Mount Merapi, the most feared volcano in the Pacific 'Ring of Fire' stretching from Japan to South-east Asia, has rumbled back to life. Lava, ash and gases have erupted from the cone forcing evacuation of villagers living on its slopes. It last erupted in 1964 killing 60 people.

E Earthquakes – Kashmir, Pakistan

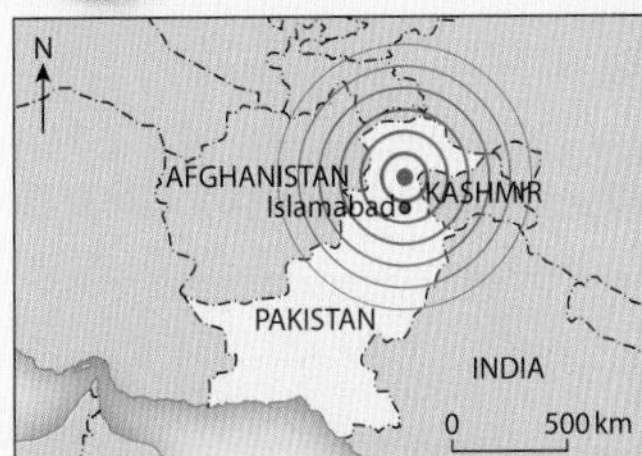

In the news … 8 October 2005

Worst Natural Disaster in Pakistan's History

An earthquake measuring 7.6 on the Richter scale struck an area 100 km north of Islamabad. The Kashmir and North-West Frontier Region have seen hospitals and homes flattened, roads, bridges and power destroyed, families separated and all hope lost. In addition to 79 000 killed, 120 000 were injured and 3 million made homeless.

F Tropical storms – Hurricane Katrina, New Orleans, USA

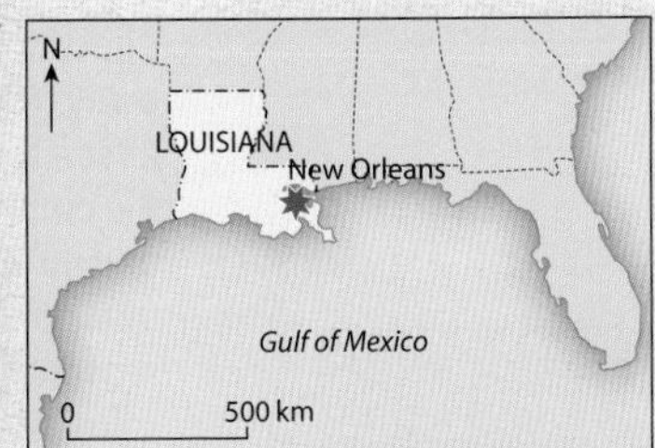

In the news … 28 August 2005

DEADLY KATRINA

Hurricane Katrina hit the low-lying coast of New Orleans causing damage costing $81 billion to fix and killing up to 1900 people. This was the deadliest Category 5 hurricane since 1928. All of the city's flood defences and levées were breached. Most damage was caused by storm surges from the Gulf of Mexico.

G Flooding – South-east Asian tsunami

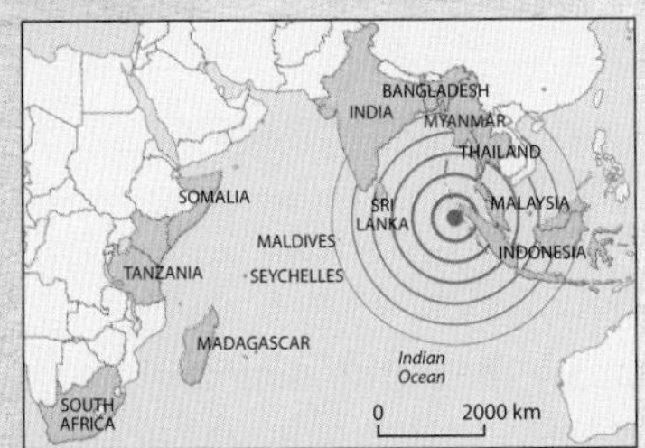

In the news … 26 December 2004

Tsunami Devastates South-East Asia

Up to 350 000 people were killed by the tsunami, which mostly affected coastlines bordering the Indian Ocean in Sri Lanka, Indonesia, Thailand and India. The undersea earthquake measured 9.3 on the Richter scale – the second highest ever recorded. Its epicentre was west of Sumatra and the quake lasted over 8 minutes. Tsunami waves were up to 30 metres high.

H Drought – famine in Ethiopia

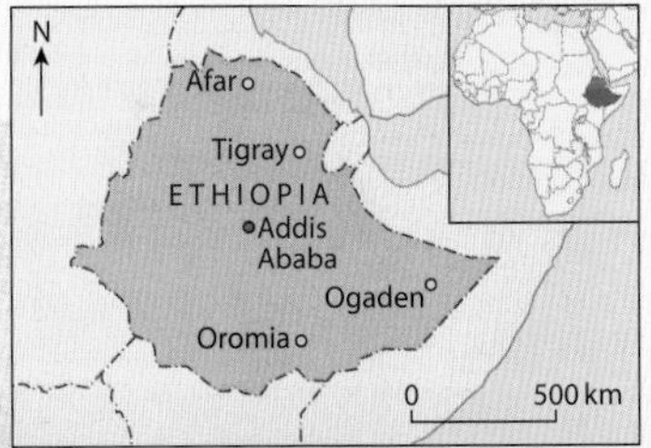

In the news … May 2008

DROUGHT CONTINUES IN ETHIOPIA

By the end of May 2008, millions faced hunger in eastern Ethiopia as the drought caused crops to fail and food prices to rise, said UNICEF. Successive seasons with no rain left the east of the country in drought. Afar, Tigray, Ogaden and Oromia are the worst-affected regions. Estimates suggest 3.4 million people will need food aid this year as crops continue to fail.

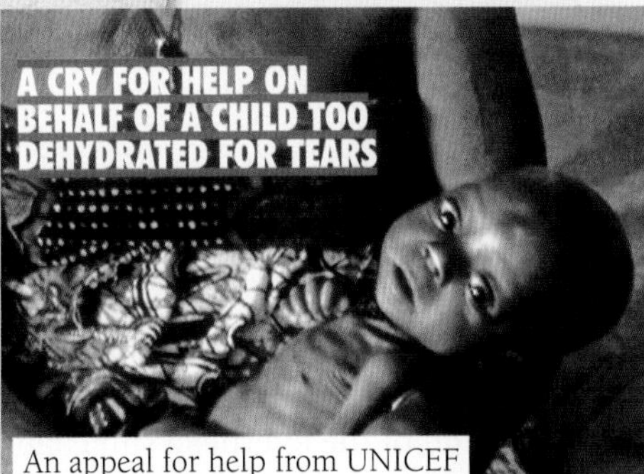

An appeal for help from UNICEF

Task 4

Study **Sources D–H**.

Choose **one** of the disasters mentioned or another you know of or have experienced.

a Find out additional information about the disaster of your choice.

b Produce a front-page report on this disaster for your local newspaper. You should include a headline, a location map, an illustration, a report and an appeal asking for help to be sent.

CASE STUDY 19a
Cyclone Nargis – Myanmar

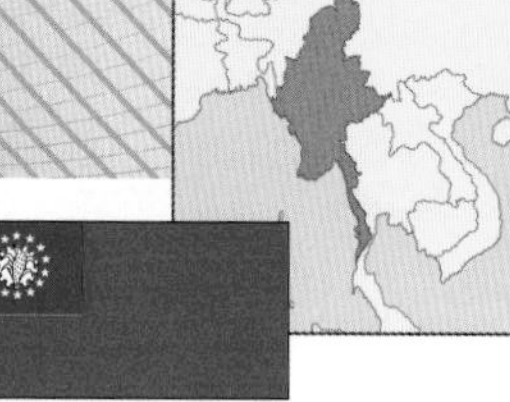

A When, where and why do tropical storms take place?

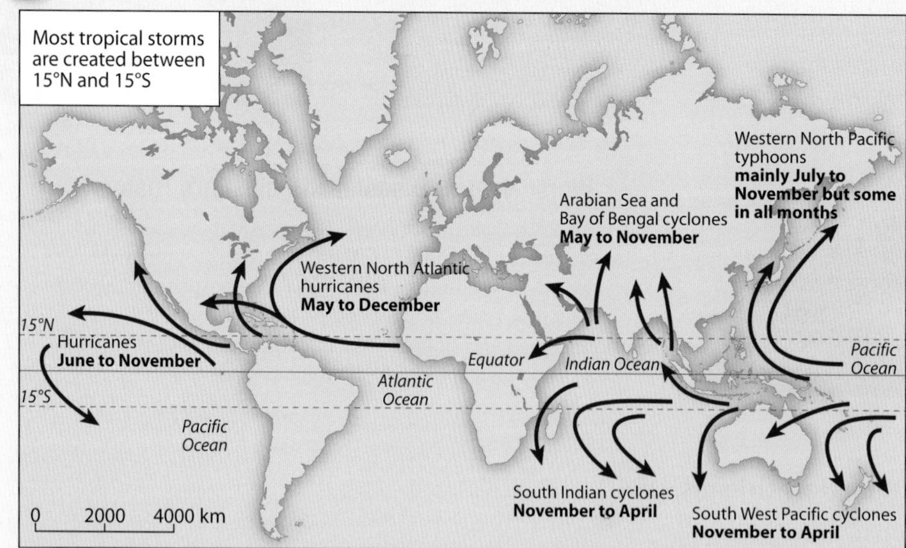

Between the Tropic of Cancer and the Tropic of Capricorn, warm air from the north meets warm air from the south. Over large oceans, where the sea temperature reaches 27 °C and the water is at least 60 metres deep, the winds begin to circulate in an anticlockwise fashion in the northern hemisphere due to the Earth's rotation. These forces create the eye of the storm, an area of intense low pressure, as the spiralling air rises to create low pressure along and close to the equator. Hurricanes and cyclones develop from tropical depressions and storms as the wind speeds increase. The easterly winds at high level (jet streams) move the tropical storms from east to west to begin with; other high-level winds then carry them in other directions. As they move north or south away from the equator they lose strength as sea temperatures fall. Eventually they die out over land where there is less heat and no water to keep them going. Each hemisphere has its hurricane or cyclone season. In the northern hemisphere this is from May to November; in the southern hemisphere it is from November to April.

B A section through a typical cyclone or hurricane

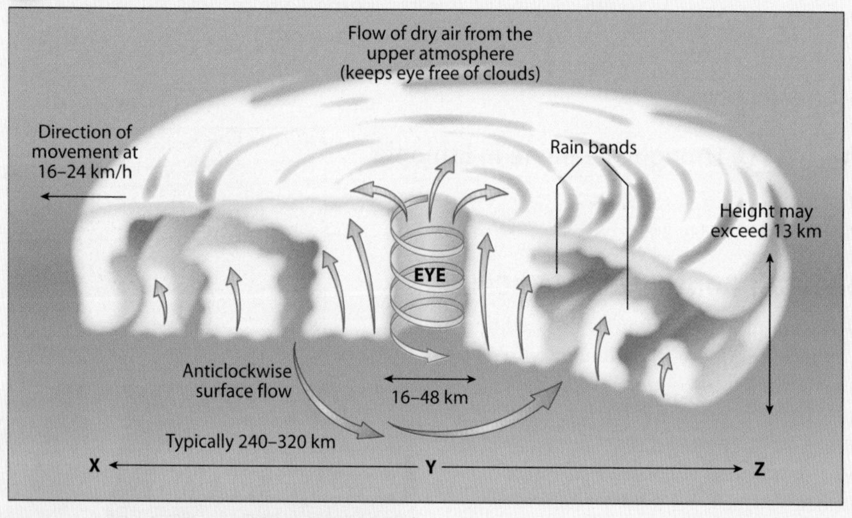

Depressions, storms and cyclones

In tropical regions the temperature is always high although it does change as the position of the overhead sun changes during the year. Rainfall, however, can be more variable. Much rain comes during the wet season of monsoon climates but intense rain is also brought by low-pressure weather systems created by high sea temperatures. These systems are divided into three types:

- tropical depressions (winds at 60 km/h or less)
- tropical storms (winds from 61 to 120 km/h)
- tropical cyclones or hurricanes (winds over 120 km/h).

In May 2008 Cyclone Nargis caused devastation and death in Myanmar (formerly Burma).

Task 1

Study **Source A**.

a Compare the distribution of cyclones with that of hurricanes.
b What conditions are required for a cyclone or hurricane to develop?
c Explain how the position of the sun during the year affects when tropical storms develop. Refer to the equator and the Tropics.

Task 2

Make your own copy of **Source B**. Carry out research and add labels to show:

- places with relatively high and low wind speeds
- places with relatively high and low pressures
- a place of calm.

C Satellite image of Cyclone Nargis

D An early report, 5 May 2008

Tropical Cyclone Nargis hit the south-east Asian country of Myanmar on Saturday 3 May 2008. It blew roofs off homes, hospitals and schools and cut electricity in Myanmar's largest city of Rangoon where 6.5 million people live. In Bogale, a town on the Irrawaddy delta, almost 3000 people are reported dead or missing. Blocked roads, broken telephone wires and poor communications mean rural casualties are unknown. Residents and Buddhist monks were clearing roads of trees with axes.

'What is clear is that thousands of people are in need of shelter and clean drinking water,' said a United Nations official. 'Roofing materials, plastic sheets, temporary tents, medicine, water-purifying tablets, blankets and mosquito nets are essential.'

With Rangoon's already unstable electricity supply not working, citizens lined up to buy candles and water since lack of electricity to drive pumps left households dry. Some walked to local lakes to wash. Traffic lights did not work and public transport stopped.

Cyclone Nargis made landfall on the southern coast of Myanmar on 3 May 2008. Wind speeds varied from 200 to 300 km/h. Very strong winds were responsible for much of the damage. Flooding and mudslides were the result of heavy rainfall. A 3.6 metre storm surge caused death and destruction by flooding the low-lying Irrawaddy delta where most people live. An estimated 2.4 million people were severely affected including over 140 000 killed or missing.

E The coast of Myanmar suffered long-term and short-term damage

Myanmar is one of Asia's poorest countries. The cyclone disaster was not reported in the local press and overseas aid was not allowed in until 24 May 2008. The military claimed it could deal with the disaster without outside help. South of Rangoon 75 per cent of houses were destroyed by wind, rain and flooding on the delta of the Irrawaddy river. This area provides rich fishing and supports the most fertile rice fields in Myanmar. The country will be unable to export rice overseas or feed its people. Rangoon airport was closed for four days. Thousands of cars formed queues waiting up to six hours for their ration of 3 litres of petrol. Every road in the city was blocked by trees.

Shanty towns in Rangoon suffered most. The wood and corrugated-iron houses blew away first; heavier ones lost roof tiles and had broken windows. Many slum dwellers work as labourers across the city; now the cost of fuel means that bus fares cost more than the daily wages. The flooding of sanitation systems increases the risk of epidemics, for example of malaria and typhoid.

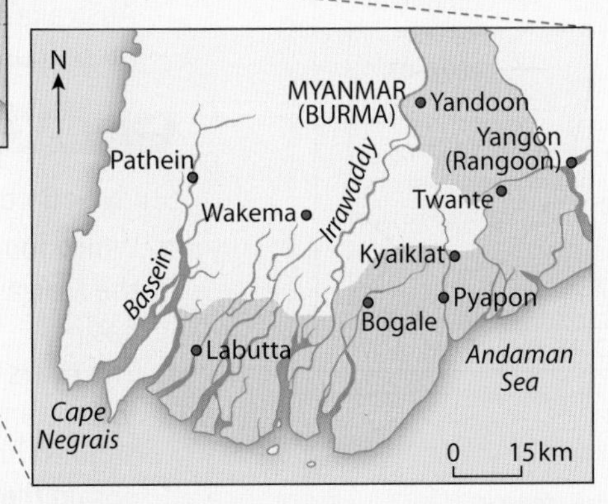

Task 3

a When did Cyclone Nargis hit Myanmar?

b Draw a labelled diagram of Cyclone Nargis shown in **Source C**. Label:
- the countries on the image
- the outline of the cyclone
- the clouds and the eye of the storm
- the wind direction around the cyclone.

c What factors caused most of the damage?

Task 4

Study **Sources D and E**.

a Make **two** lists: one of short-term damage and one of long-term damage.

b Discuss how Myanmar could start to recover from the cyclone damage. Decide on an action plan stating what you would do in the first two weeks and then over five years. Explain your choice of activities.

Task 5

Myanmar is a less economically developed country (LEDC). Suggest why countries such as Myanmar find it difficult to prepare for, and recover from, disasters such as this cyclone.

CASE STUDY 19b Drought in Australia

A Australia – the world's driest continent?

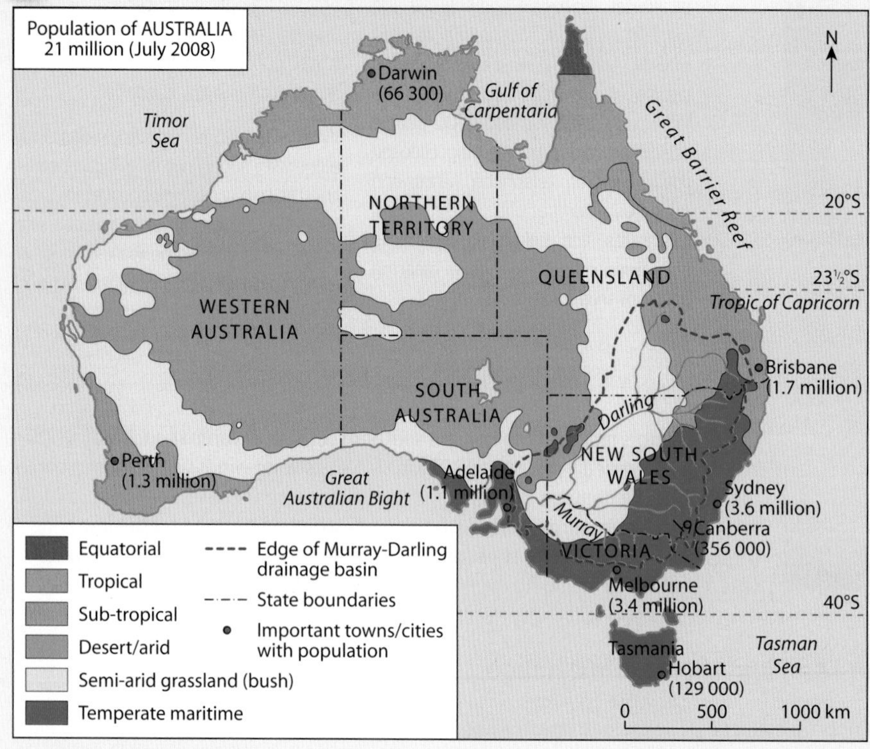

The Murray-Darling rivers flow west from the Snowy Mountains towards Adelaide. These flat plains have fertile soil and high temperatures but rainfall is low. The river water is used to provide over 70 per cent of irrigation to the farming areas which produce 40 per cent of Australia's food. Since 2002, rainfall has been well below average and river flows and reservoirs are too low to provide enough water for crops and livestock to survive. This period of drought has been called 'The Big Dry'. Coastal cities have rainfall but need extra water from reservoirs to meet the demand from the urban populations.

B The Murray-Darling Basin dries up

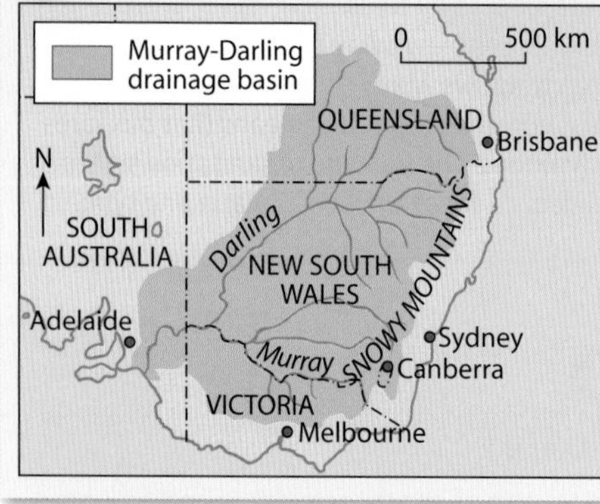

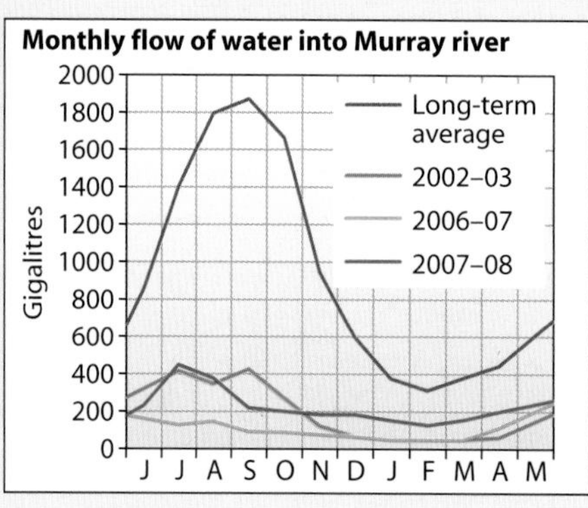

Australia runs out of water

Australia is a country in the southern hemisphere. It is so large that it experiences several climate types. The daily weather can vary enormously depending on which climate zone you are in. There are monsoon rains in the north near Darwin, desert temperatures up to 50°C in the centre of the Northern Territory, and much of the west and south are also dry. Only within 400 km of the coast in the south-east is the temperate maritime climate not too hot nor too cold and wet enough for people to farm and live in. Many Australians live in the two states that cover this area: New South Wales and Victoria. Any failure in rainfall or river flow will cause a drought. Australia is the world's driest continent but, since 2002, this area has experienced its worst drought in over 100 years.

Task 1

Study **Source A**.

a How many climate types can be found in Australia?

b Estimate the percentage of Australia that is arid (desert) and semi-arid (grassland).

c Describe the location of the temperate maritime climate.

d Add up the population of the four cities that are found in this climate type.

e What percentage of Australia's population live in these four cities?

Task 2

Study **Source B**.

a Which **four** states contain the Murray-Darling drainage basin?

b The rivers do not flow towards Sydney and Melbourne. Suggest how these cities obtain their freshwater supplies.

c Compare the Murray river flows since 2002 with the long-term average. Refer to data in your answer.

d How does the photograph on page 61 illustrate the drought?

'The Big Dry' hits Bourke

Bourke, in New South Wales, is one of Australia's most famous Outback towns. Known as the 'Real Gateway to the Outback', which lies at the 'back of Bourke', tourists flock here on their way to the desert. But, since 2002, while tourists come and go, the population of 3500 has fallen. Five years of drought have left the land dying of thirst; the town faces social and economic ruin. Bourke is not alone. Other settlements that exist on the margins of cultivation in the Murray-Darling drainage basin are also seeing communities decline. People cannot see a future in crop and livestock farming any longer. They are moving out or staying to make a living from tourists.

C Bourke – close to the Outback

'The Outback' refers to the remote and arid areas of Australia. It is where farming ends and desert begins.

Bourke (30°S 145°E)

	J	F	M	A	M	J	J	A	S	O	N	D
Temperature (°C)	29	28	25	20	15	12	11	13	17	21	25	27
Rainfall (mm)	36	38	28	28	25	28	23	20	20	23	31	36

Average annual rainfall = 336 mm Temperatures are average (mean) for each month

Task 3

Study **Source C.**

a What is the Outback?
b Draw a climate graph using the data for Bourke.
c Give **one** disadvantage of this climate for growing crops and keeping livestock.

D Urban and rural areas have been affected since 2002 ...

Here in Bourke the temperatures have exceeded 50°C. The bone-dry heat is oppressive and the ground parched. This is the last town before the outback – this is where pubs, post offices and shops stop. In the primary school children have not seen a downpour for half their lives. Shop fronts are boarded up as people move away. Crime is up, and so is unemployment. The local Aborigines are struggling as they rely on farm work but do not wish to move. In good times anything can be grown in Bourke, from cotton to citrus fruit, but the Darling river, which provides water for irrigation, has stopped flowing. Their best hope is to make a living from the tourists.

I own a 1200-hectare farm just south of Deniliquin. In the last 4 years I haven't made a cent. I've suffered depression and spoken to a counsellor. Farmers' children are leaving the land now. I know the town's population of 4000 is falling fast.
Wayne Cockayne aged 44 – cereal farmer

DROUGHT NOT ONLY AFFECTS THE SMALL TOWNS INLAND ...

GOULBURN – pop. 22 000

- Once it was Australia's best grazing area for merino sheep.
- Farmers cannot keep livestock in the hills as the Pejar reservoir has run dry.
- Abattoirs and wool plants have cut consumption by 30%.
- Tap water unfit for human consumption. Bottled water must be bought.

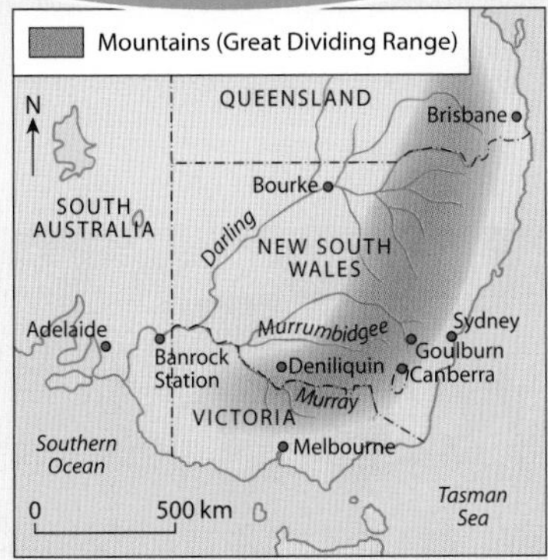

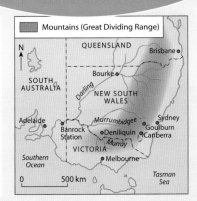

... BUT ALSO THE CITIES ON THE COAST

MELBOURNE – pop. 3.2 million

- The worst drought in a hundred years led to water restrictions.
- Residents to be fined or imprisoned if they wash their cars, fill swimming pools or sprinkle gardens.

SYDNEY – pop. 3.5 million

- Water-rationing after 4 years of drought reduces main reservoir to 40% of capacity.
- Bush fires ring the city of 4 million people, destroying homes due to the dry weather.

Task 4

Study **Sources C and D.**

a On an outline map of this area, draw in the rivers, the Great Dividing Range and the towns mentioned on this page.
b Label each town with **two** impacts that the drought has had.
c List **five** impacts that the drought has had on Bourke.
d Suggest how people who want to stay in Bourke could make a living out of tourism.

Sample case study question

Choose a hazard you have studied, in a named area, which was caused by the weather or climate. Choose from:

- a tropical storm (cyclone, typhoon or hurricane)
- a flood
- a drought.

Describe the causes of the hazard.

TOPIC 20 Human activity has impacts

A Natural environments

A flood plain

A coastal area

A mountain area

Managing environments

Different types of environment offer different opportunities for people to live, work and spend their leisure time, but in some areas the natural environment causes problems for people. The use of environments by people may be a threat to the natural landscape and its flora and fauna, as in many areas human activity has been destructive. People are now more aware of the importance of conservation of the natural environment. The management of environments needs to be sustainable so that it can offer opportunities for people both now and in the future.

Task 1

Study **Source A.**

For each of the photographs identify **two** opportunities for people in the area shown and **two** problems which the natural environment could cause for people.

Task 2

Study **Source B.**

a What is a conurbation?
b Which **three** settlements make up the Trojmiasto conurbation?

B The Trojmiasto conurbation

0 10 km
Baltic Sea
N
Hel Peninsula
Gdynia
Sopot
Gdansk Bay
Gdansk
Vistula River

C Opportunities in Trojmiasto

The Trojmiasto conurbation

Trojmiasto, with a population of over 800 000, is a conurbation on the northern coast of Poland (**Source B**). It lies on the edge of Gdansk Bay (near the Baltic Sea), and consists of the shipbuilding centre of Gdansk, the resort town of Sopot, and the port of Gdynia. Gdansk is situated at the mouth of the Motlawa river, which is connected by the nearby Vistula river to the national capital, Warsaw.

D The Baltic Sea

E Polluting the Baltic Sea

CONCERN FOR A PRECIOUS SEA

In late summer the water lapping the shores of the Baltic is warm. Children would like to go swimming but their mothers often have to stop them. The reason for this is easy to see. The water is cloudy and greyish-green, and there are great rafts of blue-green algae floating on top. Many types of blue-green algae are dangerous to humans, as the toxins they give out damage the nervous system and liver. Many of the fish species in the Baltic are at risk, and pregnant Swedish women are being warned not to eat herring because of the chemicals in it.

In the Gulf of Finland, the seabed is in many places completely dead. There is no oxygen in the water and no living organisms of any kind at the bottom of the sea. In fact the Baltic is the most polluted sea in the world. Nine industrialised nations border on it. Some 85–90 million people live in the catchment area, and there is a lot of heavy industry and intensive agriculture. The Baltic also carries a large amount of shipping.

In 1974 the Helsinki Convention to protect the Baltic Sea was signed by all the countries around the Baltic Sea (HELCOM countries).

In 1992, the HELCOM countries identified the worst sources of pollution, and devised a 20-year programme for cleaning them up and in 2007 an ambitious new Baltic Sea Action Plan was drafted to dramatically reduce the Baltic's pollution level by 2021.

Task 3

Study **Source C**.

Using the evidence in the photographs, make a list of opportunities for employment in the Trojmiasto area.

Task 4

Study **Sources D and E** and refer to an atlas.

The Baltic Sea is one of the most polluted seas in the world. Explain the reasons for this, using the following headings:

- Shape
- Rivers
- Currents
- Surrounding land uses.

Task 5

Study **Source E**.

Draw a table like the one below and fill in the two columns with impacts of pollution of the Baltic Sea on people and the natural environment.

Impacts on people	Impacts on the natural environment

Task 6

In groups, discuss what the HELCOM countries can do to reduce pollution levels in the Baltic Sea by 2021.

Floods in Mozambique

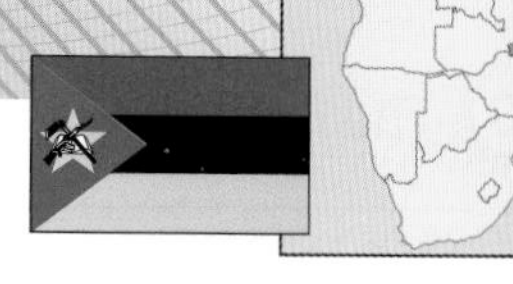

A Flooding in Mozambique

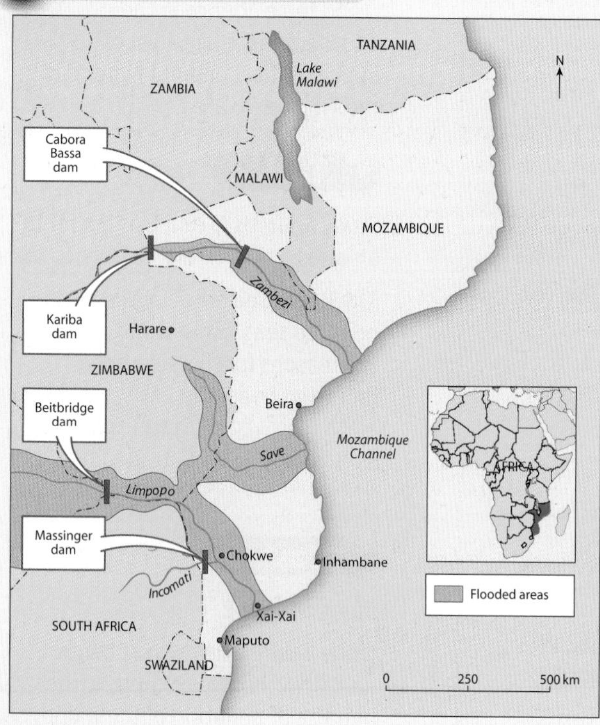

B Living on the floodplain

FLOODS DISPLACE THOUSANDS IN MOZAMBIQUE

More than 180 000 people have fled from floods in Mozambique and are living in temporary accommodation centres. The Zambezi river has been over two-and-a-half metres above flood level for more than five weeks. Rain is continuing upstream in Malawi and Zambia and floodwaters are expected to remain at this level for at least a fortnight. So far 81 people have died. Most people who live in Mozambique work in agriculture, and they live in the most fertile areas along the country's rivers. Now these rivers are creating death and destruction to people who usually depend on them. Planning to move communities away from the river valleys, to prevent future disasters, will not work. In countries as poor as this, people have no choice but to live where they can make a living.

The navy began evacuating people from low ground in January using rubber boats. At first many people refused to leave their homes but with their fields still under water and their food stocks exhausted, thousands are now making their way daily by foot or canoe to accommodation centres.

The authorities were well prepared, but Mozambique is one of the world's poorest countries and it does not have the resources to cope with the growing number of evacuees. There are few paved roads and heavy rains have turned dirt roads to mud. It takes two days for a food lorry to travel the 200 miles from the port of Beira to Caia, the town used as a food distribution centre. It takes another day to reach the three accommodation centres further downstream, near Marromeu, which now contain 24 000 people.

February 2000

C Flood damage in Mozambique

A flood in Mozambique

Mozambique is one of the poorest countries in southern Africa with a GDP per capita of US $800. Many of its 19 million people live on the floodplains of the Limpopo, Zambezi and Save rivers. In 2000 floods occurred on 9 February with high levels of rainfall across southern Africa. Mozambique received the most rainfall, and the capital Maputo was flooded, as was the road between the capital and the second largest city, Beira. Torrential rain continued until 11 February, and the banks of the Limpopo river burst, causing severe flood damage. On 22 February, tropical cyclone Eline hit the Mozambique coast near Beira, north of the areas already affected by flooding. On 27 February, after further heavy rainfall, flash floods inundated low farmlands around Chokwe and Xai-Xai.

Task 1

Study **Source A**.

a Describe the location of the areas of land in Mozambique that were flooded.
b Use the scale of the map to estimate the total area of land affected by the floods.

Task 2

Study **Sources B and C**.

In pairs, prepare a script for a short news item about the floods in Mozambique. It should describe the cause and the effects of the flooding.

 Opportunities and problems of living on a floodplain

Opportunities

- Fertile soils for farming
- Water for irrigation
- Can travel by boat along river
- Flat land for building roads and railways
- River is source of fish for food
- Flat land for building

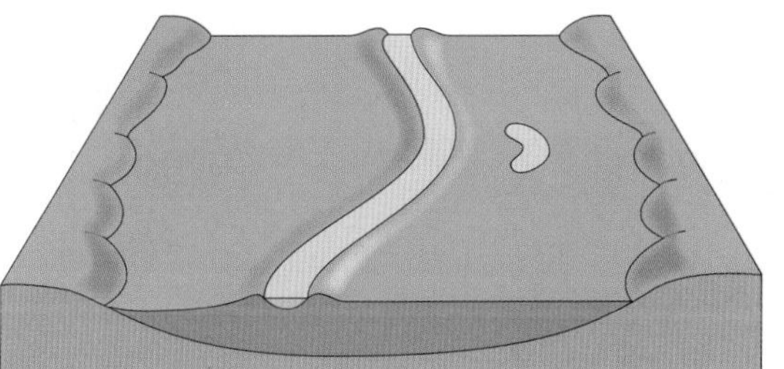

Problems

- Farmland can be flooded
- Stores of food can be damaged by floods
- Foundations of homes are unstable
- To travel people may need to bridge the river
- Flooding makes travelling impossible
- Danger from crocodiles

 Aid for flood victims – short-term and long-term

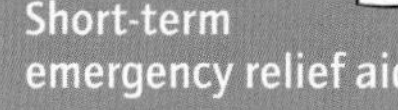

Short-term emergency relief aid

Aid from governments, organisations and charities to help people survive straight after a flood. This is sometimes called humanitarian aid.

Long-term development aid

Aid from governments, organisations and charities to enable countries and communities to ensure people have access to basic needs so they can improve their living conditions in the months and years after a flood.

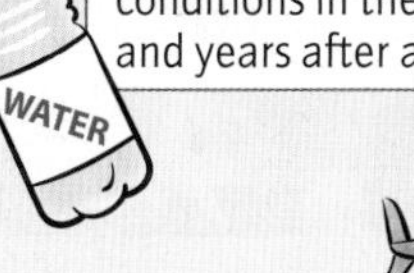

 Task 3

Study **Sources B and D**.

Explain the comment 'Planning to move communities away from the river valleys, to prevent future disasters, will not work'.

In your answer you should write about the opportunities and problems for poor people in Mozambique of living on the floodplains.

 Task 4

Study **Source E**.

On a copy of the following table, shade the short-term and long-term aid boxes in two different colours. Don't forget to include the key.

Key

Short-term aid 
Long-term aid ☐

Helicopter rescue	Seeds for crops	Building a well	Clothing	Training a teacher
Blankets	Buying crops at a fair price	Lending money to a small business	Tents	Setting up a refugee camp
Building a dam	Giving out food parcels	Vaccinating babies and children	Water pumps	Tablets for malaria

CASE STUDY 20b

National Parks in Costa Rica

A National Parks in Costa Rica

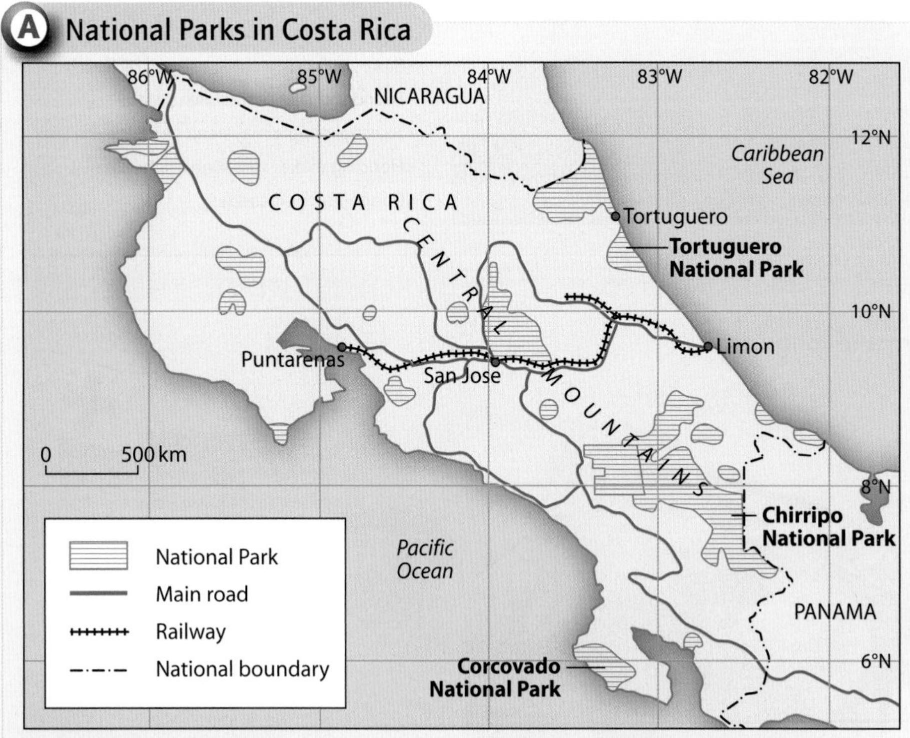

B Comparing three National Parks in Costa Rica

Tortuguero National Park
The area was a group of volcanic islands until sediments filled in the spaces and formed a network of marshy islands. Sand piled up where the river met the sea, and the turtle-nesting beaches of Tortuguero were formed. The beaches, canals, lagoons and wetlands of Tortuguero are areas of great biodiversity and opportunity for nature lovers. The marked trail along the beach is used mostly for observing turtles nesting, but the best way to see most of the park is from a boat. There are plenty of places to rent canoes and kayaks.

Chirripo National Park
Chirripo means 'Land of the Eternal Waters'. In the rainy season there are many streams and brooks. On the top of Cerro Chirripo Grande the participant has a view of more than 30 lakes and lagoons. Many large rivers have their source in the valleys of the Talamanca Mountain Range, such as Rio Chirripo Atlantico, Rio Telire, Rio Chirripo Pacifico and the Rio Ceibo. This is one of Costa Rica's wilder parks, but it is relatively accessible by foot. Much of the rugged terrain has been protected from development and exploitation by its inaccessibility. Besides the challenge of climbing Costa Rica's highest peak (Cerro Chirripo) there are miles of trails that wind through more ecologically rich zones than you will find in most entire countries.

Corcovado National Park
If you want to swim up to a deserted golden sand beach lined with coconut palms, then bathe under a rainforest waterfall, you'll find Corcovado's 39 km of beaches appealing. Corcovado National Park is the backpacking experience of a lifetime. It comprises 13 major ecosystems, including lowland rainforest, highland cloud forest, jolillo palm forest, and mangrove swamps, as well as coastal marine and beach habitats. There is a good chance of spotting some of Costa Rica's shyest and most endangered inhabitants here: Baird's tapirs, jaguars, scarlet macaws, harpy eagles, red-backed squirrel monkeys and white-lipped peccaries.

Task 1

Study **Source A**.

Describe the location of the following National Parks in Costa Rica:

- Chirripo
- Corcovado
- Tortuguero.

Managing the National Parks

Costa Rica has 29 National Parks, which cover 12.5 per cent of the total land area. The National Parks help to protect many of the country's 208 species of mammals, 850 species of birds, 220 species of reptiles and 132 species of amphibians, as well as over 9000 species of plants. The Parks also contain volcanoes, caves, tropical forests and beaches. The varied natural environments of the National Parks offer many opportunities for tourists, scientists and naturalists who visit them. The National Parks are carefully managed so that the natural environment is not threatened by human activity, and any developments are sustainable.

Task 2

Study **Source B**.

a For each of the National Parks, list **three** different opportunities that are offered to people.

b Which National Park would you recommend to someone who:
- is interested in trekking
- enjoys observing plants and animals
- wants to spend time on attractive sandy beaches?

Give reasons for your answers.

C Tortuguero National Park

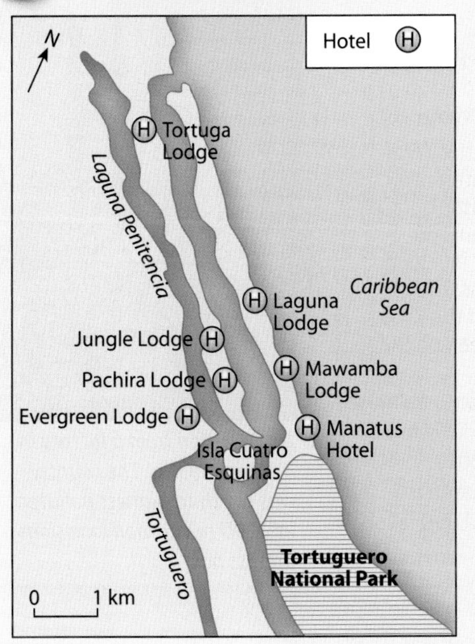

D Overseas visitors to Tortuguero National Park

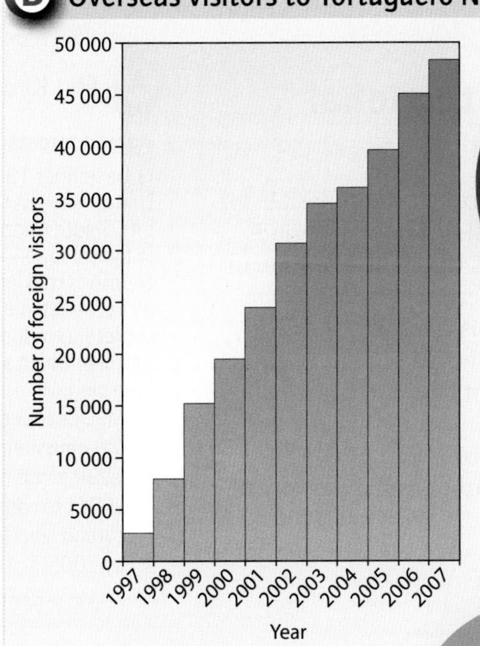

There are just too many people wanting to use the park. We should limit the number of visitors. At the moment, anyone can visit – we have no control. We must make sure the environment is not over-used.

National Parks – for people or nature? We could leave things as they are, and do nothing.

Task 3

Study **Source C**.

Describe the distribution of hotels shown on the map.

Task 4

Study **Source D**.

Describe how the number of overseas visitors to Tortuguero National Park has changed since 1997. Give dates and figures in your answer.

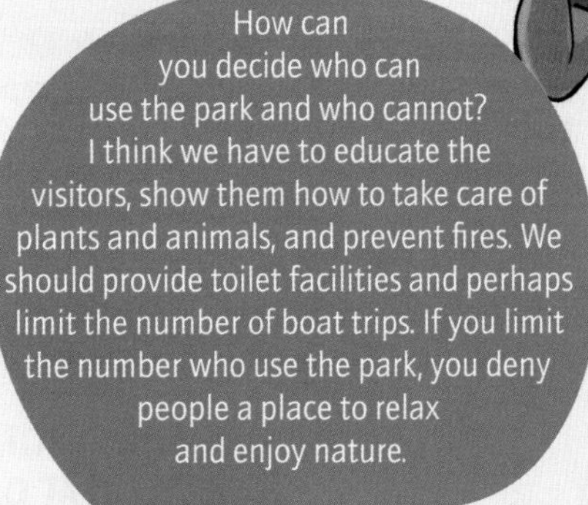

How can you decide who can use the park and who cannot? I think we have to educate the visitors, show them how to take care of plants and animals, and prevent fires. We should provide toilet facilities and perhaps limit the number of boat trips. If you limit the number who use the park, you deny people a place to relax and enjoy nature.

Task 5

The Tortuguero National Park is an important wildlife sanctuary. Since the 1980s the government has encouraged tourism as a way of bringing money to the country. This has led to the environment of the park being threatened.

The government of Costa Rica has to consider how to:

- protect wildlife and its habitats
- improve living standards of the people of Costa Rica
- cater for an increasing number of visitors to the area.

Below are three possible plans:

Plan A Make the whole area a wildlife sanctuary. No further building or development will be allowed.

Plan B Build trails and campsites through the forest and along the coast.

Plan C Develop a small tourist resort with hotels, shops and an airstrip, and offer guided tours of the forest and beaches.

In a group, discuss the advantages and disadvantages of each plan and decide which you feel will be the best one. Prepare a presentation giving reasons for your choice.

Sample case study question

Flooding sometimes causes difficulties for people who live on floodplains and deltas.
For a river which you have studied, explain what has been done to reduce flooding.

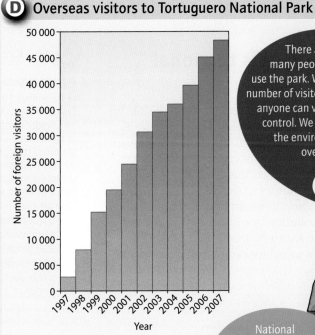

GLOBAL ISSUE

2 Reducing carbon emissions

Human activity adds to global warming

Nobody is sure how much human activity is responsible for global warming. There have been cold and warm periods before in the Earth's history. What is certain is that human activity is increasing the amount of carbon dioxide in the atmosphere. As a greenhouse gas this traps heat leaving the Earth, causing temperatures to rise. Many international conferences have been held in recent years to agree on policies to reduce air pollution. A conference held in Japan in 1997 established the Kyoto Protocol – part of which included a requirement to reduce carbon emissions by 2012 and beyond.

A The Kyoto Protocol

Agreed targets at Kyoto

In December 1997 the Third United Nations Conference on Climate Change took place in Kyoto, Japan. Over 160 countries took part, including all European nations. The conference adopted the Kyoto Protocol which agreed on the following:

- MEDCs to reduce greenhouse gas emissions by 5% below 1990 levels by 2012.
- LEDCs to continue to reduce carbon levels to 1990 levels by 2005.

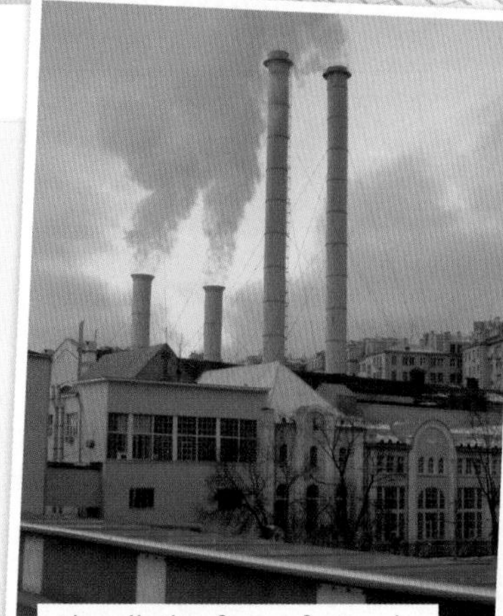

Air pollution from a factory in Moscow, Russia. The country was the third highest polluter in 1990 but carbon emissions are less now.

Task 1

Study **Sources A and B**.

- **a** Why is it important to reduce carbon emissions?
- **b** How were targets set at Kyoto different for MEDCs and LEDCs? Suggest why.
- **c** Draw a bar graph to show the total carbon emissions produced by these countries in 1990.
- **d** On the graph rank the countries from 1 (most carbon emitted per person) to 6 (least carbon emitted per person).
- **e** Comment on your findings.
- **f** Comment on changes in carbon emissions between 1990 and 2007.

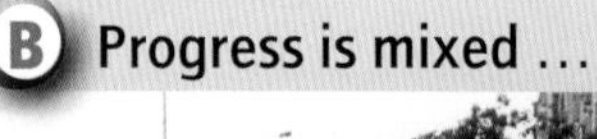

B Progress is mixed …

Here's one way of keeping carbon emissions per person low – in Ahmadabad, India!

Carbon emissions, 1990 –2007

Country	Total emissions (million metric tonnes)	Emissions per person (tonnes)	% change 1990–2007
USA	1392	5.35	+20
China	848	0.76	+150
Russia	462	3.22	−20
Japan	303	2.53	+11
Germany	237	2.96	−18
India	225	0.31	+103
World	–	–	**+38**

Task 2

Study **Source C**.

- **a** Describe the project.
- **b** How and why will this benefit:
  - Hawaii
  - the world in general?
- **c** How does 'offsetting carbon' help?

Task 3

Design a poster to encourage people to walk or cycle or use transport that does not use fuel derived from carbon products.

C Transport is a key issue

ALOHA TO ELECTRIC CARS AS HAWAII TRIES TO BEAT OIL ADDICTION

Hawaii is to become the first US state to create a transport infrastructure that will allow cars to run almost entirely on electricity. The plan involves building 100 000 charging stations in car parks and streets by 2012 and importing electric vehicles made by Nissan and Renault. 'This will help us meet our goal of reducing fossil fuel use by 70% within the next 30 years', said the Governor of Hawaii, Linda Lingle. At present the island imports 90% of its oil from Saudi Arabia, costing $7 million. The electricity for the charging stations will be generated by renewable resources – mostly wind power. With 5 million tourists the project should help educate them, too.

I'm returning from London to Honolulu in Hawaii. My one-way flight is over 23 000 km. On average I will generate just under 3 metric tonnes of carbon dioxide. To offset this I will donate $100 to a tree-planting scheme in Nepal which will use up the same amount of carbon produced. It's not much, but imagine if everybody who flew did this …!

Easing a guilty conscience – offsetting carbon

Theme 3

Economic Development and the Use of Resources

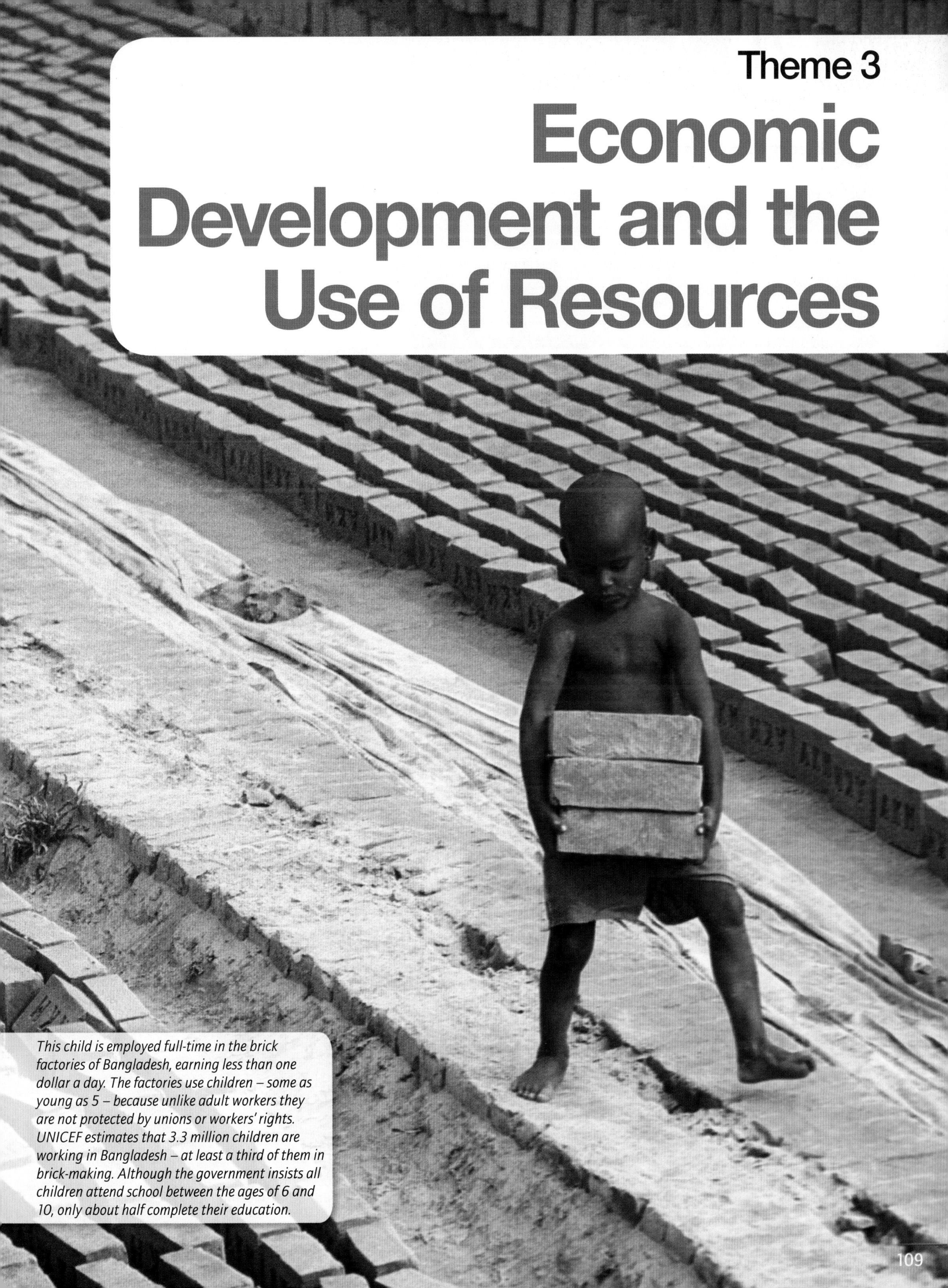

This child is employed full-time in the brick factories of Bangladesh, earning less than one dollar a day. The factories use children – some as young as 5 – because unlike adult workers they are not protected by unions or workers' rights. UNICEF estimates that 3.3 million children are working in Bangladesh – at least a third of them in brick-making. Although the government insists all children attend school between the ages of 6 and 10, only about half complete their education.

TOPIC 21 Agriculture

A Different types of farming

B Intensive or extensive?

Extensive ⟷ Intensive

Dairying
Factory farming
Nomadic herding
Ranching
Commercial livestock
Commercial mixed
Commercial grains
Shifting cultivation
Subsistence crops
Market gardening
Plantations

Profits per hectare increase →
Average yields per hectare increase →
Number of workers per hectare increases →
← Average size of farms increases

C An agricultural systems diagram

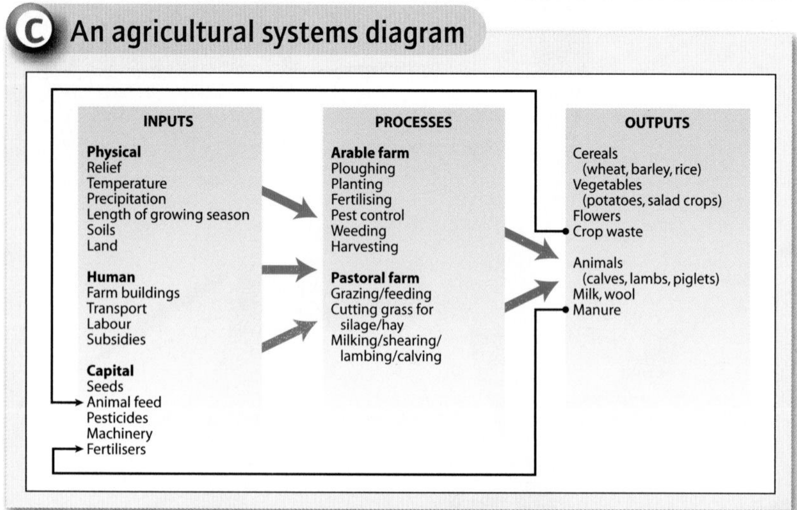

Types of farming

Agriculture (or farming) is the production of food and other resources through the growing of plants and the raising of domesticated animals. About 35 per cent of the world's population makes their living through agriculture. The proportion of the population involved in agriculture varies from about 2 per cent in the USA to about 80 per cent in some parts of Asia and Africa.

Task 1

Study **Source A**.

Suggest **three** differences between the two types of farming shown in the photographs.

Classification of farming types

Subsistence farmers produce only enough crops (or animal produce) to feed their families. Commercial farmers, however, produce crops and/or animal products to sell at a market in order to make their living.

Arable farmers grow crops whilst pastoral farmers keep animals.

Sedentary farmers farm the same land all the time whilst nomadic farmers move from place to place, often with herds of animals, in search of water or the best grazing land.

Intensive farming is characterised by the high inputs of capital, fertilisers, labour, or labour-saving technologies such as pesticides or machinery relative to the area of land. Extensive farming involves a low input of materials and labour, with the crop yield depending largely on the naturally available inputs.

Task 2

Study **Source B**.

a Find out the meanings of the following farming types:
- market gardening
- plantation
- dairying
- factory farming.

b Give **two** examples of extensive farming.

c Use the ideas in the diagram to compare nomadic herding with commercial livestock farming.

Task 3

Study **Source C**.

a Give **one** example of a physical input to a farm and **one** example of a human input.

b Give **one** example of a process that takes place on an arable farm and **one** example of a process that takes place on a pastoral farm.

c Give **one** example of an output of an arable farm and **one** example of an output of a pastoral farm.

Task 4

Study **Source D**.

Map 1 shows the main types of farming in a part of an MEDC in Europe. Maps 2 to 6 show some of the factors that influence the land use.

Describe and explain the location of market gardening and beef cattle farming.

D Commercial farming in an MEDC

Map 1 Distribution of agriculture

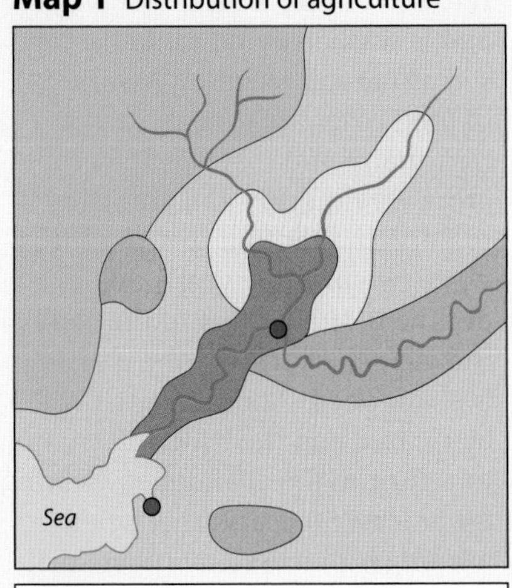

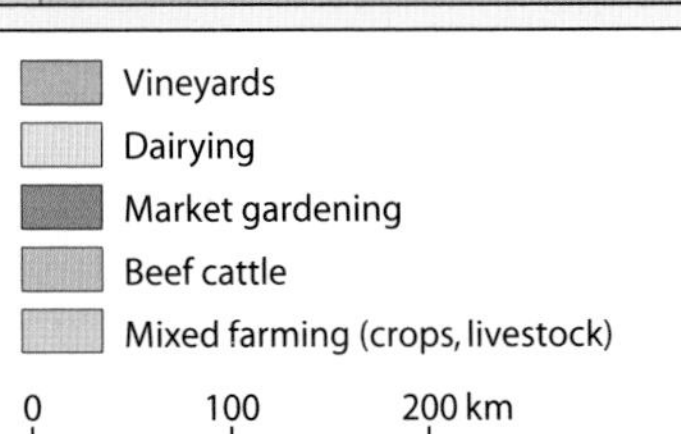

Map 2 Population density

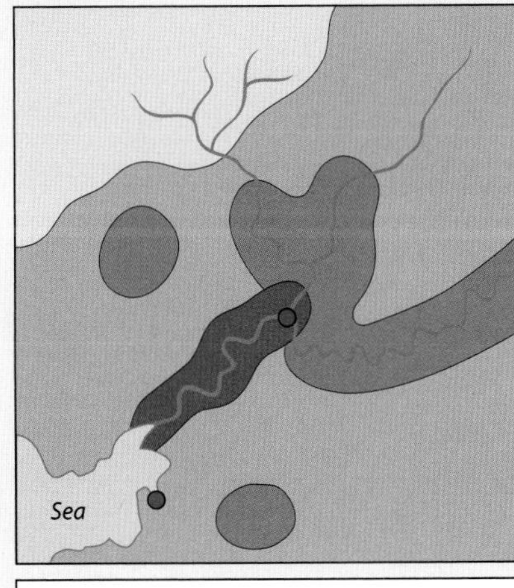

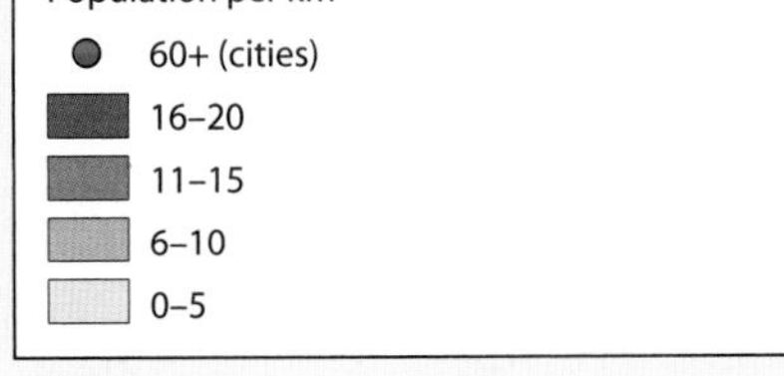

Map 3 Communications

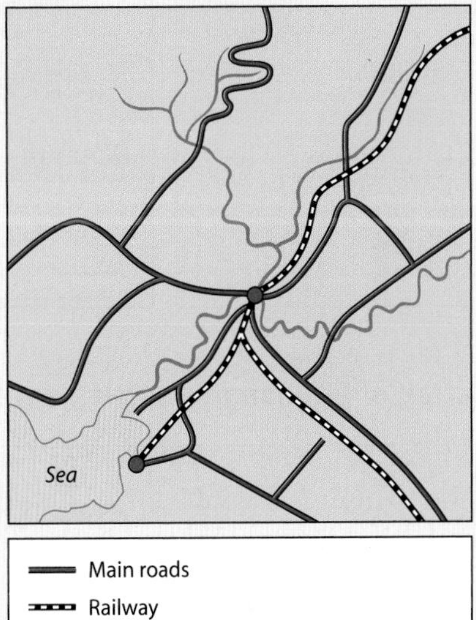

Map 4 Topography

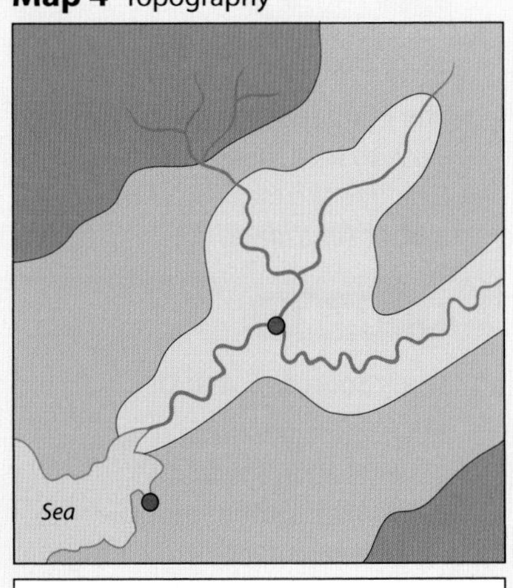

Map 5 Soil composition

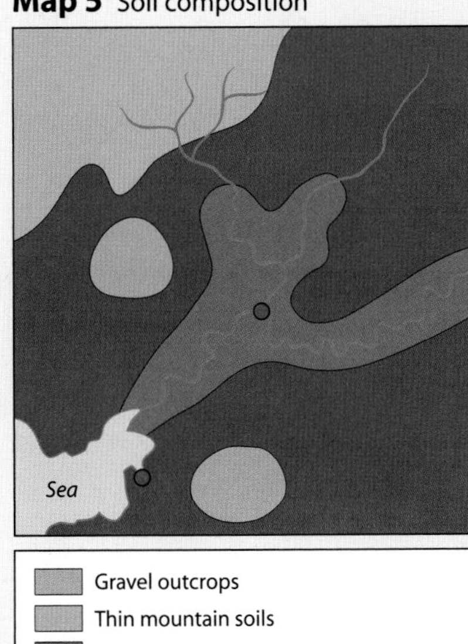

Map 6 Frost risk

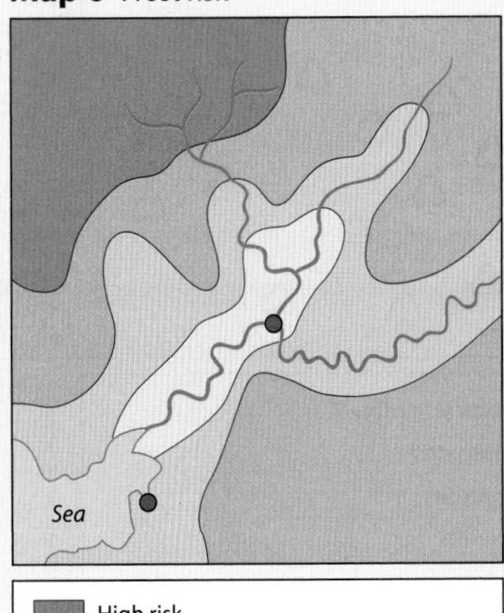

Subsistence agriculture in Brazil

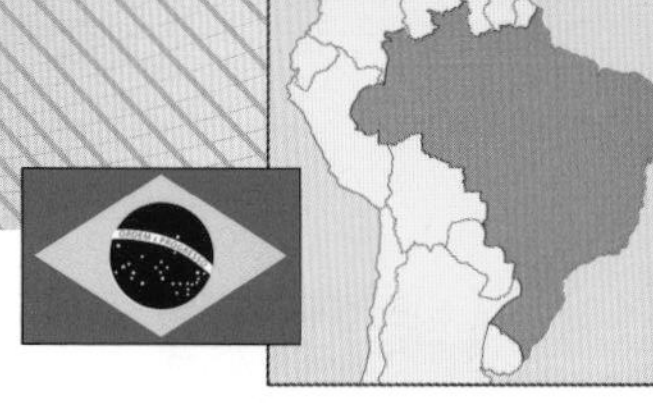

A Part of Amazonia, Brazil

B Location of Erigbaagtsa settlement

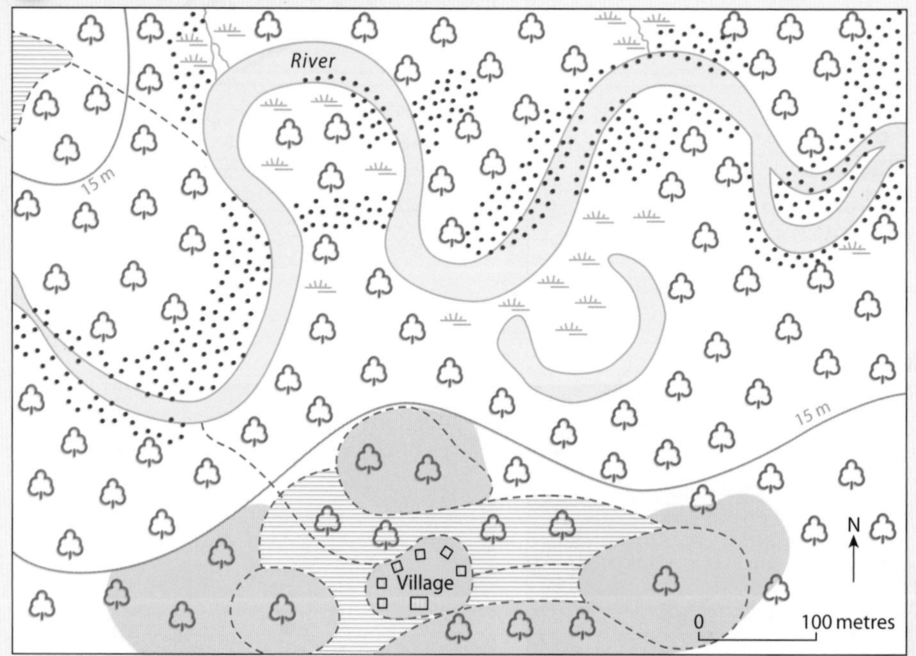

Shifting cultivation

Shifting cultivation is still practised by some tribes in the remote, forested areas of the Amazon Basin, in Brazil. The tribe first selects a small patch of rainforest. To create a clearing in the forest, the people cut down the natural vegetation using simple tools, and burn the logs. The nutrients are released as ash, which dissolves and is washed by rain into the soil as natural fertiliser. A variety of food crops are grown, such as rice, maize and cassava. The crops grow very quickly and are ready to harvest after four to six months. After two or three years, due to a decline in the fertility of the soil, the yield declines and the clearing is abandoned. Another patch will be cleared and the tribe will try not to return to the abandoned clearing for at least 50 years. This type of farming is practised by tribes such as the Erigbaagtsa, who also obtain food and other useful materials by hunting and gathering in the rainforest. However, deforestation now threatens the continuation of this lifestyle.

Task 1

Study **Source A**.

The Erigbaagtsa tribe lives close to the Upper Juruena river. Describe the location of this part of Amazonia.

Task 2

Study **Sources C and D**.

a Describe the natural vegetation shown.

b What difficulties may the tribe experience in clearing the land for agriculture?

C Natural vegetation of the rainforest

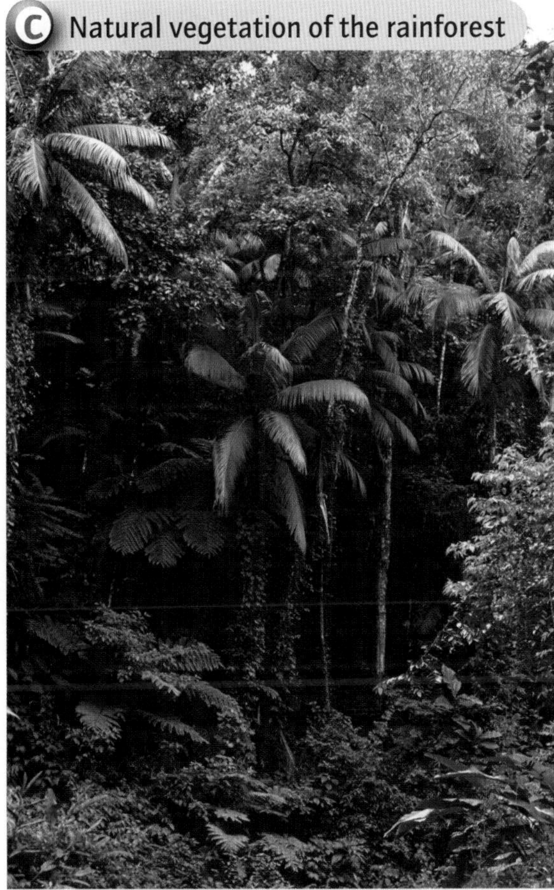

Task 3

Study **Sources C and D**.

From the following list choose **three** statements that are true about the land cultivated by the Erigbaagtsa tribe:

- It is above the floodplain of the river.
- It is less than half a kilometre from the huts where the tribe live.
- It is used to graze cattle.
- It is on the banks of the river.
- It is cultivated using traditional methods.
- It is abandoned after being used for a few years.
- It has very fertile soils.
- It is marshy land.

Task 4

Study **Sources D, E and F.**

a Draw a systems diagram (see **Source C** on page 110 for this technique) to show the inputs, processes and outputs of shifting cultivation by the Erigbaagtsa tribe.

b Explain why the areas cultivated by the Erigbaagtsa tribe have to be abandoned after a few years.

D Clearing the land

Like all the tribe, I cultivate my 'garden' by shifting cultivation.
Using an axe and a bushknife, I clear away all but the largest trees. The branches are left on the ground to dry. I pile all these branches around the tree stumps and burn them. The fire clears the ground, kills off some weeds and pests and the ash fertilises the ground. I plant the crops in holes made with a digging stick. After that I go to the garden from time to time to weed and harvest the crops. After two or three years we just leave the garden so that the forest can re-grow.

E Shifting cultivation

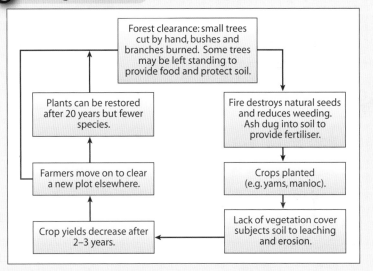

Forest clearance: small trees cut by hand, bushes and branches burned. Some trees may be left standing to provide food and protect soil.

→ Fire destroys natural seeds and reduces weeding. Ash dug into soil to provide fertiliser.

→ Crops planted (e.g. yams, manioc).

→ Lack of vegetation cover subjects soil to leaching and erosion.

→ Crop yields decrease after 2–3 years.

→ Farmers move on to clear a new plot elsewhere.

→ Plants can be restored after 20 years but fewer species.

→ Forest clearance (Farmers move on to clear a new plot elsewhere → Forest clearance)

F An Erigbaagtsa tribe settlement

Commercial agriculture in New Zealand

A Physical features

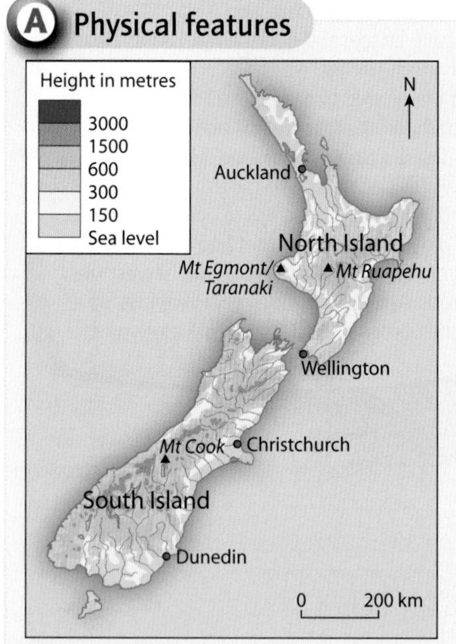

B Climate data for New Zealand

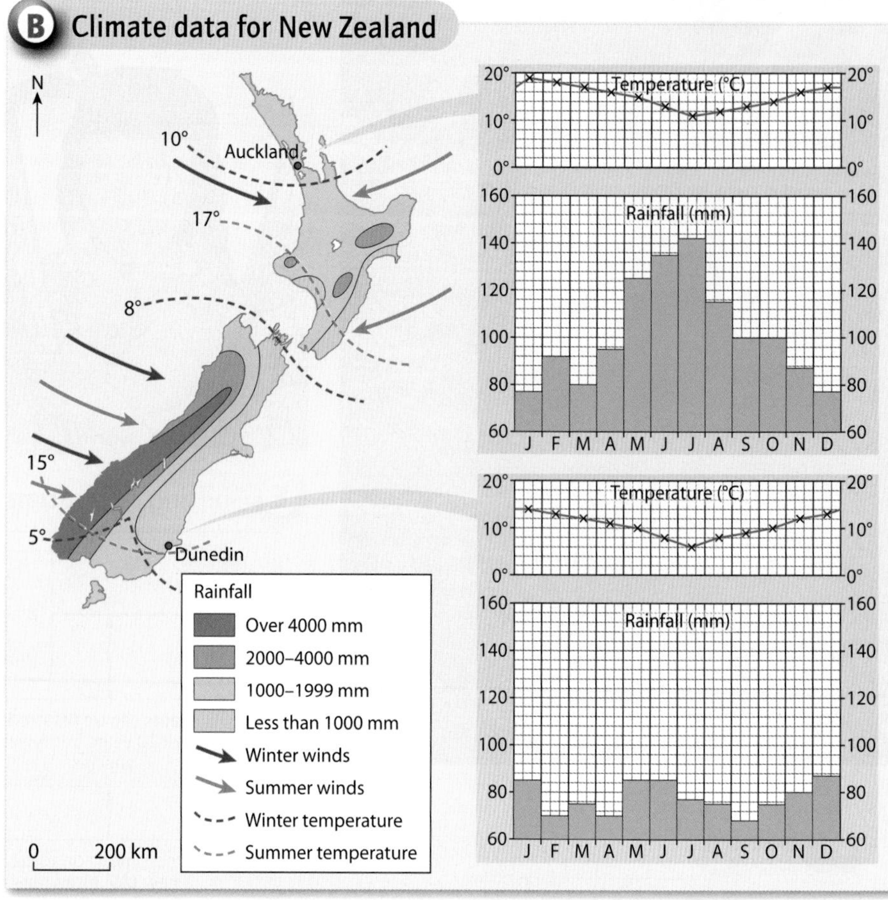

C Land use in New Zealand

Pastoral farming in New Zealand

Many of New Zealand's farms rear animals – mainly sheep, dairy cattle and beef cattle. Pastoral farming is a successful land use in many parts of the country because the warm, wet climate is ideal for growing grass. Grass grows well where the annual rainfall is between 1000 and 1500 mm and when the temperature is above 6°C. The type of pastoral farming varies from one area to another. In North Island beef cattle are most important in the far north, with dairying in the western part. Sheep and beef cattle are reared on the higher land and in the southern part of the island. In South Island merino sheep are reared extensively for their wool on the higher land where the grass is poor. On the lower land farming is more intensive, with sheep and some cattle being grazed there for meat and milk.

Task 1

Study **Sources A, B and C.**

Make a copy of the table below and fill in the information about North and South Island.

	Relief	Rainfall	Temperatures	Farming
North Island				
South Island				

D Map of Harwood's Farm

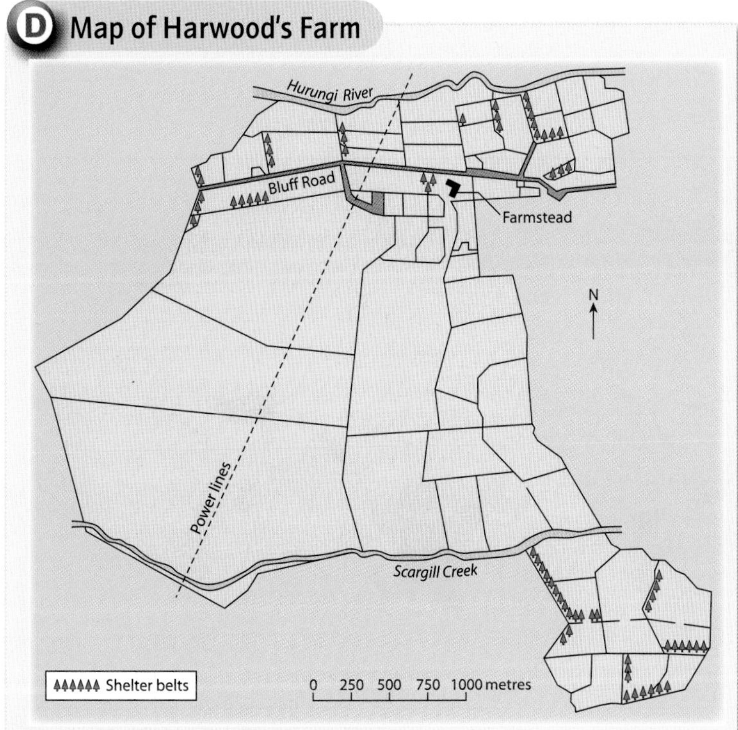

Harwood's Farm

Harwood's Farm, in North Canterbury, is over 1500 hectares in size, most of which is hill country or rolling downs, but there are 270 hectares of irrigated flat land. Each year large quantities of fertiliser are used on some of this land, which is planted with special grasses to provide high-quality feed for the large herds of sheep and cattle through the winter. Whilst the animals can graze outdoors for much of the winter, they have to be fed on hay and silage when snow covers the grass.

The sheep bred on the farm are Corriedales, which give a good quantity of both meat and wool. The lambs are born in the hills, and after six months they are brought down onto the lower land, where the grass is richer, and fattened before they are taken to be sold for their meat. The cattle kept on the farm are Herefords, and these are sold for meat in October to save the cost of feeding them through the winter. Rabbits can be a problem on the farm, as they eat large amounts of grass, so they are regularly culled which means more grass is available for the sheep and cattle to graze on.

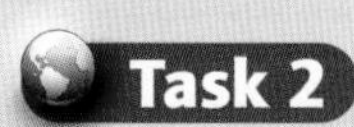

Task 2

Study **Sources D and E**.

- **a** Draw a pie chart to show the proportion of each type of land on Harwood's Farm.
- **b** Which type of land will be used for:
  - extensive farming
  - intensive farming?
- **c** Where on the farm would you expect to find the flat, irrigated land?
- **d** Draw bar graphs to show the numbers of sheep and cattle on Harwood's Farm.
- **e** Calculate the overall profit made by the farmer.

E Harwood's Farm

Land use	
Hill country	936 hectares (60%)
Rolling downs	351 hectares (23%)
Flat land (irrigated)	270 hectares (17%)

Stock

Sheep (Corriedales)		
Breeding ewes	3549	Ewes are female sheep.
Ewe hoggets	1200	Hoggets are young sheep over 1 year old.
Rams	55	Rams are older male sheep.
Lambs	2000	
Total	*6804*	

Cattle (Herefords)		
Breeding cows	287	
Heifers	252	Heifers are young female cattle.
Steers	145	Steers are castrated male cattle.
Bulls	10	
Calves	690	
Total	*1384*	

Budget summary (NZ$)

Income		Expenses	
Sheep	89500	Wages	35000
Wool	75600	Shearing	11500
Cattle	204000	Animal health	21000
Other	5300	Fertiliser	40000
		Purchase of stock	18600
		Seeds	8200
		Other	95060

Sample case study question

For a named area of small-scale subsistence farming, describe the inputs, processes and outputs.

TOPIC 22 Food shortages

A Where are food shortages?

The 25 hungriest countries

% of population undernourished

1	Somalia	75
2	Burundi	66
3	Congo	64
4	Afghanistan	58
5	Eritrea	57
6	Haiti	56
7	Mozambique	54
8	Angola	51
9	Ethiopia	49
10	Tajikistan	47
11	Zambia	47
12	Kenya	46
13	Tanzania	46
14	Central African Rep.	43
15	Mongolia	42
16	Liberia	42
17	Nigeria	42
18	Sierra Leone	41
19	North Korea	40
20	Madagascar	40
21	Rwanda	40
22	Zimbabwe	39
23	Azerbaijan	37
24	Cambodia	37
25	Sudan	36

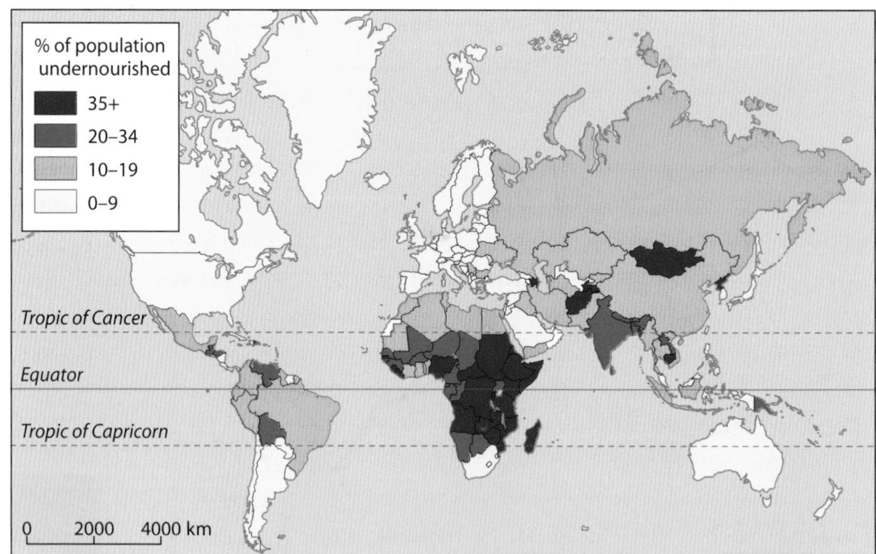

The Hungry Planet

Some 815 million people in the world suffer from hunger – about 15 per cent of the world's population. Yet, according to the Food and Agricultural Organisation (FAO), with record grain harvests in 2007 there is more than enough food in the world to feed everybody – at least 1.5 times the current demand. Over the last 20 years food production has risen steadily at over 2 per cent per year while the rate of population growth has fallen to 1.1 per cent a year. Population is not outstripping food supply.

Why is there hunger in the world? The World Bank has estimated that over 100 million more people have been driven into hunger by rising food prices. In some countries this has caused riots; in Haiti the Prime Minister was forced from office as food prices rose by 50–100 per cent. World prices have risen by 83 per cent in the last three years.

Add to this the difficult issue of transporting food from areas of surplus to areas of need and it is clear why many LEDCs cannot access the food that is available internationally – it is too expensive and it is mostly in the wealthy MEDCs where obesity rather than hunger is a problem. While the MEDCs enjoy plenty of food, LEDCs cannot produce enough for their own needs for a variety of reasons.

Task 1

Study **Source A**.

a List **four** areas of the world where 9 per cent or less of the population are undernourished.

b Describe the distribution of countries where 35 per cent or more of their population are undernourished.

c On an outline map create your own choropleth map using the data in the table 'The 25 hungriest countries'. Use a different key and group interval to that used in **Source A**.

Task 2

Study **Source B**.

a Copy and complete the following table by naming a country, or countries, with a food shortage for the reason given.

b Which of the seven reasons for food shortages listed do you think people can influence either for better or worse? Explain your choices.

Reason	Named country/ies
Drought	
Soil erosion	
Locusts	
Tropical cyclones	
Severe winter weather	
Economic and political factors	
Transport/ access issues	

B Food shortages – different causes

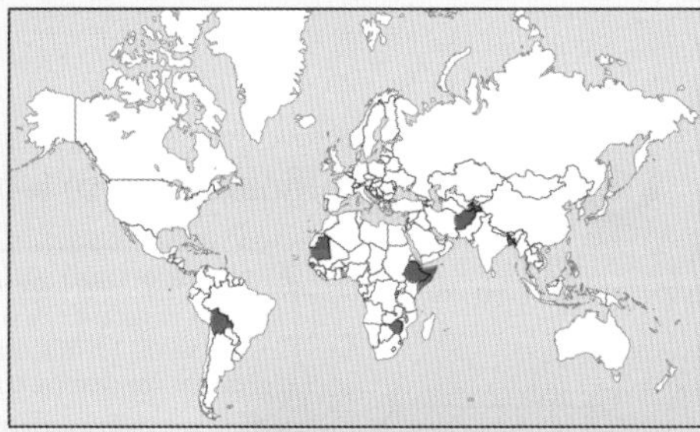

Desert locusts affect many African countries. They eat their own weight in vegetation every day.

Bolivia Struggling to Feed its People

Bolivia, situated in the heart of South America, is a mosaic of high mountains, valleys and extensive tropical rainforest. One result of the steep slopes of the Andes is soil erosion. Farming, deforestation and grazing livestock have all increased soil loss and erosion at rates that prevent replacement. Massive amounts of topsoil have been lost as vegetation cover is removed. Population density is increasing with over 7 million living on the marginal farming lands, using wood for cooking and clearing land for food.

Tajikistan Faces Food Shortages

The central Asian country of Tajikistan, the poorest in the region, is experiencing its coldest winter for decades. As it depends so much on HEP, people have to spend money on fuelwood as many rivers are frozen. Roads are blocked with snow and electricity is limited to two hours per day. Two-thirds of the people live below the poverty line so, after buying fuel, not much is left to buy food. The severe weather has destroyed the potato harvest and over half a million local people are unable to afford minimum food needs.

Food Shortage Threatens Millions in Bangladesh

With aid teams still trying to get emergency supplies into the areas affected by Cyclone Sidr – a massive storm that struck 10 days ago killing 3200 people – officials estimate that up to 3 million people will be short of food in the next 6 months. The storm destroyed 50–90% of the region's rice crop. Every year thousands are killed in floods and storms in this low-lying region of the Ganges delta. These also cause a lack of clean water, food and shelter.

ACCESS A PROBLEM IN AFGHANISTAN

Afghanistan faces a deficit of 2 million tonnes of wheat flour and rice to feed over 6 million people in the next six months, claimed a Minister. 'Drought has led to failure of 90% of the crops and high prices have affected imports. Our biggest problem is transport – we need the food convoys to reach the mountain areas quickly as heavy snow will block roads and make them inaccessible in winter. Some people may have to move to towns if they want food.'

Starvation Grips East Africa

Rapidly rising food prices and drought have contributed to the worst hunger crisis seen in Ethiopia and Somalia this century. At least 14 million people are at risk of malnutrition, aid agencies claim. Ethiopian farmers blame the lack of rain. 'We haven't had rain for 8 months now,' said a tribal chief. 'We have to buy water to save our lives but now we have nothing.'

Carpet of Jaws Devouring West Africa

As the swarm descended on Nouakchott, it was so thick it blotted out the sun. The locusts settled and began to eat every bit of greenery in sight. 'They just strip every plant and leave it looking like a telephone wire,' said a resident of the Mauritanian capital. The worst plague for 15 years has affected much of West Africa. As the Sahel moves south the locusts seek greener pastures. 'The country is short of spraying planes,' said an FAO spokesperson.

Task 3

A Chinese man, Lao Tzu, once wrote: 'Give a man a fish and you feed him for a day. Teach him how to fish and you feed him for a lifetime.'

a What did he mean by this?

b How does this relate to providing food aid to LEDCs with food shortages?

POLITICAL UNREST CAUSING FOOD SHORTAGE

Since President Mugabe decided to seize land in Zimbabwe in 2003, commercial farming has collapsed. Prices of basic foods have rocketed and six million people – 49% of the population – are in need of food aid. With internal conflict continuing, little food is being produced. Severe drought also plagues the country, making access to food almost impossible.

CASE STUDY 22

Famine in Darfur, Sudan

A Where is Darfur?

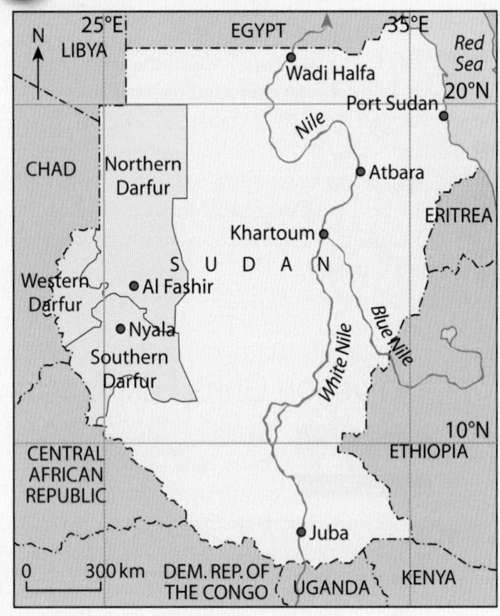

B Darfur – a difficult area to work and live in

The northern Libyan desert is hot with almost constant dry winds. Rain may not fall for years. 1.5 million people live here in drought conditions. Locusts are a threat, too.

In western and central Darfur there is a short wet season where, for a few months of the year, the dusty brown environment changes to a lush green. In normal years pearl millet can be harvested by November and the dry stalks fed to livestock during the long dry season.

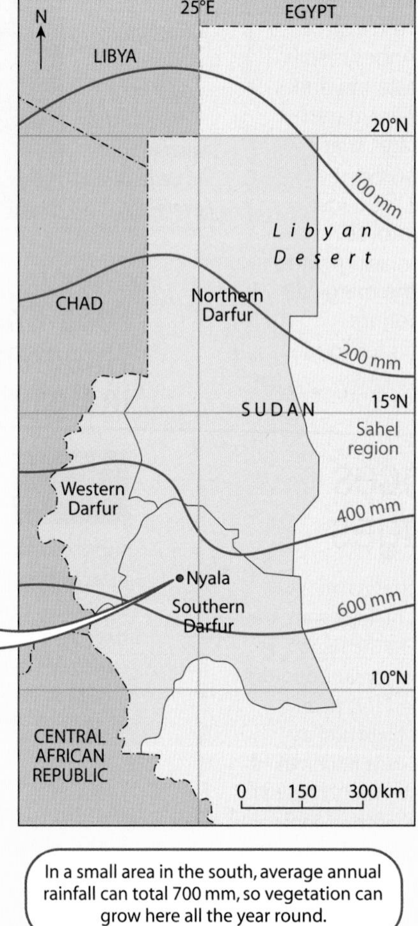

The river Nile flows in the east so agriculture can be developed there using irrigation even with low amounts of rainfall.

Nyala is the capital of southern Darfur. It is a town full of government officials, with food in the market and cafés. Yet, close by, the needs of 40 000 refugees in tented camps are ignored.

In a small area in the south, average annual rainfall can total 700 mm, so vegetation can grow here all the year round.

— Isohyets

A region of drought and conflict

Bordering the Red Sea, Sudan is the largest country in Africa. It is a country of contrasts – both physical and human. Its landscape changes from desert in the north to forests in the south and grassy plains and swamps in the centre. The river Nile provides water to the east but many areas receive no rainfall. The country also contains two different groups of people: the Arabs in the north and Africans in the south. Tension between these groups has led to two civil wars since independence in 1956; the second of these began in 2003.

In 2009 periodic droughts and civil war meant that parts of Sudan required large amounts of food aid. Most of these people are concentrated in Darfur, a region in the west of Sudan. Since 2003 the region has seen one of the world's largest concentrations of human suffering.

Task 1

Study **Source A**.

a Describe the location of Sudan. Refer to a continent, lines of latitude and longitude, the Red Sea and neighbouring countries.

b Suggest **three** reasons why it has been easier to develop the country east of, and around, the capital Khartoum.

Task 2

Study **Sources B**.

a Write a heading 'Why I would not want to live in northern or western Darfur'. List **five** reasons.

b Compare your lists with those of your classmates. How many different reasons have you suggested?

C Diary of a disaster

1956 Independence granted to Sudan from Egypt and the UK. Leaders begin to develop areas that could sustain rain-fed agriculture along the Nile river valley. Muslim leaders try to impose language, religion, and sharia law on Christian and other communities in the south and west.

1980s/1990s Civil war between the Arab Muslims of the north and the black African Christians and other faiths in the south costs 2 million lives through fighting and famine.

2003 Rebels in Darfur, a western region of Sudan that is predominantly African, rise up against the government, claiming that they have been neglected while the rest of Sudan and the capital Khartoum – mostly Arab – have been favoured. The violence on both sides has led to many atrocities. Many villages have been burned to the ground and around 200 000 people have died. More than 2 million people (1 in 3 from Darfur) have been forced to flee their homes because of the violence. They are known as internally displaced people (IDPs) who live in vast and crowded refugee camps – tented villages on the edge of towns – in Darfur and Chad. The camps hold about 130 000 people with 200 000 refugees in Chad. Most have been there since 2003. There are no toilets, medical facilities, food or water supplies. Many have died of disease, water shortage, heat and malnutrition in overcrowded conditions. Up to 4.5 million depend on international aid.

Refugee camp, Darfur

2007 In an attempt to protect people the United Nations and African Union have provided a joint UN–AU peace-keeping force of 26 000 soldiers but only one-third had arrived by October 2008.

D Life is a tent and little else ...

Hawa Abdraman (20) who crept past army forces after they attacked her village so she could retrieve a bowl with which to feed her 1-year-old son Mahamat Youssour

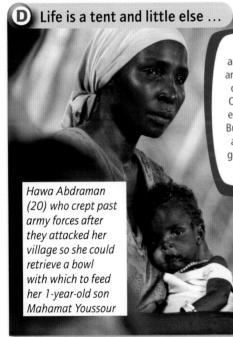

Just a short distance from Nyala, the capital of south Darfur, thousands of men, women and children have been abandoned – ignored by those who are supposed to help them. There is no food, toilets, drainage or medical facilities, and little water. These illegal camps at Otis and Siref hold 40 000 people between them and are on either side of the road to the airport where relief aid arrives. But the government does not distribute the food or allow aid agencies to operate there. It wants the displaced people to go back to their villages. But the refugees will not go back – they say the government military forces have destroyed their villages and will destroy them too.

Task 3

Study **Source C**.

a What part have religious differences played in causing civil conflict in Sudan since 1956?

b What caused rebels in Darfur to rise up against the government in 2003?

c What is an IDP? How many people have become IDPs since 2003?

d List other ways in which people have suffered due to the war.

Task 4

Study **Source D**.

a What basic services are missing in the camps? How will this affect the displaced people living here?

b Why does the government not distribute international aid?

c Why won't the people return to the villages?

Task 5

The Darfur crisis continued through 2009. Find out from the media and/or the Internet if the situation is any better now.

Sample case study question

For a named country or region where a food shortage has taken place, describe what caused the shortage.

TOPIC 23 Work and employment

A Types of employment

Shepherd herding goats, Gujarat, India

WORK ON OIL RIGS 5

No qualifications required. For a complete list of jobs available, send 4 loose stamps and your name and address to: Universal Jobs Oil Rigs Department, PO Box 55102, Eerstemyn 9466.
PLEASE DON'T SEND ANY CV'S!

Jobmail, *Johannesburg, South Africa*

2 *School transport, Miami, Florida, USA*

NAVAJO TIMES 6

News Reporter

The Navajo Times is currently seeking a qualified, educated and experienced journalist to fill the position of temporary News Reporter.

From The Navajo Times, *Arizona, USA*

ENGINEERING TECHNICIAN 4

(REF: RWT 340)

Reporting to the Engineering Supervisor, your role will be to manufacture and assemble precision tools and assemblies to quality standards, and ensure the continuous improvement of manufactured equipment.

From The Leicester Mercury, *UK*

Employment is classified into three sectors:

Primary: the sector of a country's economy that grows or extracts raw materials. It includes fishing, agriculture, forestry, and mining.

Secondary: the sector of a country's economy that is concerned with the manufacturing and processing of goods. It uses the products of primary industry either directly or indirectly. For example coal, iron ore and limestone are used **directly** to make steel. They are used **indirectly** when steel is used in manufacturing industries to make other goods such as cars.

Tertiary: the sector of a country's economy that provides services. People may pay directly for a private service, e.g. paying for a taxi. The government, using money taken indirectly through taxes, may provide public services such as schools and hospitals.

3

Weaving carpets, Sousse, Tunisia

We are all working ...

In more economically developed countries (MEDCs) most people of working age are in formal employment. In many less economically developed countries (LEDCs) much work is informal employment.

B Employment structures change over time

	Primary		Secondary		Tertiary	
	1990	2007	1990	2007	1990	2007
USA	3	2	26	21	71	77
UK	2	2	29	18	69	80
Russia	14	11	42	29	44	60
Tunisia	28	20	33	30	39	50
China*	72	43	15	25	12	32
India*	54	28	16	29	30	43
South Africa*	13	9	26	24	61	68

* Regarded as a newly industrialised country (NIC).

By 2050 China, USA, India, Japan, Brazil and Mexico are expected to be the most economically developed countries in the world.
As a country develops its economy, the proportion of its workforce in the different employment sectors changes. Using more machinery in farming, for example, releases people from working the land so they can work in the other sectors. Using more machinery and IT in the secondary sector releases people to move into the services sector. These changes can be shown on graphs or charts.

Task 1

Study **Source A**.

a Describe the work shown on page 109 and in each photo on this page numbered **1–3**.
b Describe the work being offered by adverts **4–6**.
c Decide which of the photos and adverts show primary, secondary and tertiary employment. Explain your choices.
d Give **three** examples of unpaid work in your country. Why do people do this?

Task 2

Study **Source B**.

a Place the countries in rank order for 2007, using employment structure as an indicator of economic development.
b Decide which country has made most progress with economic development since 1990. Give reasons for your choice.
c Which **three** countries in the table are regarded as NICs? What evidence supports this?

C Representing employment structures

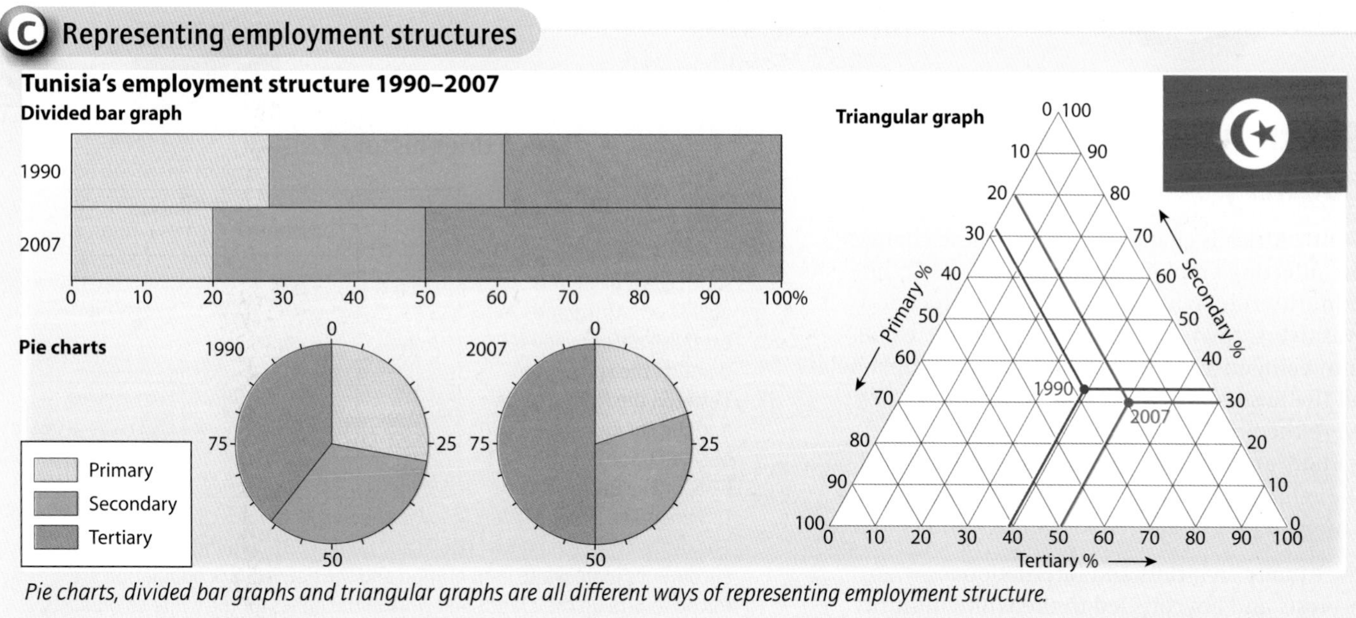

Pie charts, divided bar graphs and triangular graphs are all different ways of representing employment structure.

Task 3

Source C shows how employment data for Tunisia would look for the years 1990 and 2007 using all three graph techniques.

a Describe how Tunisia's employment structure has changed since 1990.

b Choose **one** other country from **Source B** or find data for the country you live in. Draw similar graphs and compare the changes in employment structure with Tunisia and **two** other countries in **Source B**.

Task 4

Study **Source D**.

a Give **two** advantages and **two** disadvantages of formal and informal employment.
Which would you prefer? Why?

b Look back at **Source A**. Choose **one** job that is formal and **one** that is informal. Explain your choices.

c What issues are raised by the photograph shown on page 109? Discuss these with your classmates.

Task 5

Collect at least **five** advertisements for different jobs from the media. In a group decide whether the jobs are for the primary, secondary or tertiary sectors of the economy. These could be mounted on a wall display.

D Formal and informal employment

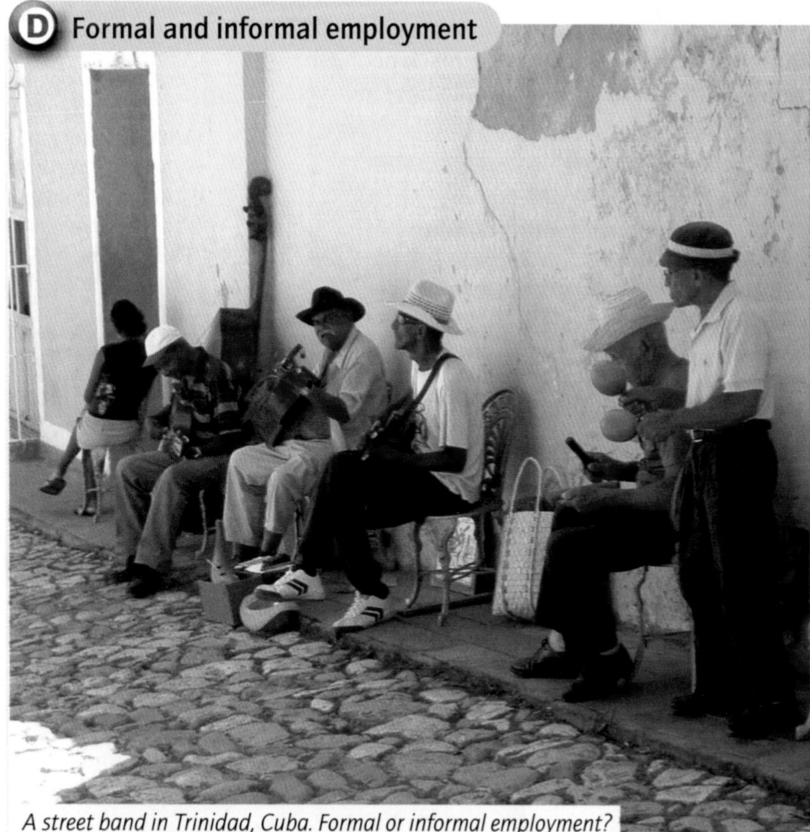

A street band in Trinidad, Cuba. Formal or informal employment?

Formal employment: a person who is formally employed receives a wage or salary from their employer. They usually have a contract that gives them certain rights, e.g. paid holidays, maternity leave. They are also responsible for attending work every day during set hours. A formally employed person has taxes deducted from their pay before they receive it. In MEDCs most people have a formal job.

Informal employment: a person who is informally employed does not receive a regular wage. They work when they need to or when they feel like it. They often avoid paying tax this way but, if they do not work, they get no benefits or sick pay. In LEDCs most people have an informal job; often children work informally instead of attending school.

CASE STUDY 23a Changing employment – South Africa

South Africa – a changing country

South Africa is changing rapidly. These changes are affecting employment opportunities. White minority rule, which began in the 17th century, was overthrown and black majority rule came into being in 1994. Before then white people held all the positions of power and influence – they were the politicians, factory managers, land-owners and farmers. The black majority relied on the white minority for employment, usually in low-paid jobs as farmhands, miners and labourers.

Eventually civil riots and international protests and boycotts led to the white minority government relinquishing power, abandoning apartheid, and allowing each person a vote. Since the election of a black president in 1994 the employment situation for some black people has improved. However, many people have not yet seen progress.

A South Africa – a brief history

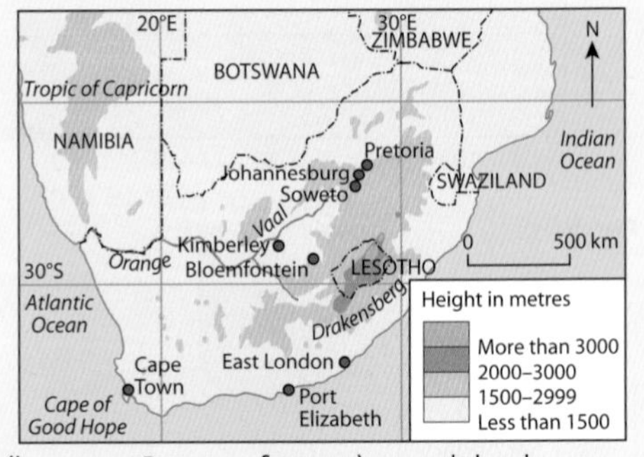

1652 White Dutch traders from the Netherlands land on the south coast of what is now South Africa and establish a stopover point on the spice route between the Netherlands and the Far East. This became Cape Town.

1806 The British seize this area. The Dutch settlers (known as Boers, or farmers) move inland. The discovery of diamonds (**1867**) and gold (**1886**) around Johannesburg encourages more white immigration and the native black population are forced to give up their lands and work in the mines for the white colonialists.

1899–1902 The British and the Boers fight the Boer War which the British win. The British and Afrikaners, as the Boers became known, rule the black majority under the Union of South Africa.

1948 The National Party (mostly Afrikaners) is voted into power and institutes a policy of apartheid – the segregation of the population into white, black, coloured* and Indian 'races'.

1990 After much internal conflict, and pressure from other countries, the white government agrees to end apartheid and to legalise the African National Congress Party (ANC). For four years white and black leaders work together running the country.

1994 The first non-racial elections took place. This brings in black majority rule for the first time. Nelson Mandela is elected President.

[The term 'coloured' is still used today in South Africa and is not deemed to be offensive there.]*

B Apartheid and employment

Apartheid can be traced back to the use of black slave labour by white settlers in the 1650s. However, it was in the 1950s that an organised separation of 'races' took place. The National Party developed laws based on white supremacy. Different 'races' could only live and work in set areas, had to travel on separate buses and stand in their own queues. Many black Africans were moved to townships like Soweto on the south-west fringe of Johannesburg. Pass laws were brought in restricting movement. Townships only existed as dormitory towns for black Africans to work in white houses, factories and industry. Within the township they could only operate shops, butchers, food shops, sell milk or vegetables or hawk goods. No other businesses were allowed although many informal illegal activities developed as people struggled to survive in a place where basic services like running water were rare.

Entrance to the Apartheid Museum, Johannesburg, South Africa

Task 1

Study **Source A**.

a Describe the location of Cape Town. Why did the Dutch traders settle here?
b How did the influx of white people affect the employment of black people between 1652 and 1948?
c When and why was apartheid introduced? How long did this policy stay in place? Why did the government abandon apartheid in 1990?

Task 2

Study **Source B**.

a Describe the entrance to the Apartheid Museum. Why was it designed like this?
b How did the National Party restrict the type of work black people could do?
c What was the purpose of townships like Soweto? How was employment restricted here?

C Employment changes

Workforce %	1980	1990	2000	2007
Primary	15	13	11	9
Secondary	28	26	24	24
Tertiary	57	61	65	68

Ethnic groups	
Black African	79%
White	9%
Coloured*	9%
Indian/Asian	3%

- In 2007 unemployment was 24% with one-third aged 15–35.
- More women are unemployed than men.
- In 2007 white unemployment was 4.5%, African 31%.

[*See note on page 122.]

Soweto

Black Economic Empowerment

A policy of Black Economic Empowerment (BEE) was adopted in 1995. This provides for measures to prevent discrimination against the black majority when applying for work and employment. These rules should enable more black people to gain jobs but, although this has helped skilled workers and educated in-migrants, most adult black Africans could not access school so have no qualifications or transport to get these new jobs. With unemployment at 24 per cent, limited progress has been made since 1994. Many white people have left the country, leaving behind a skills shortage. The poorest people – both black and white poor – feel let down by ANC promises.

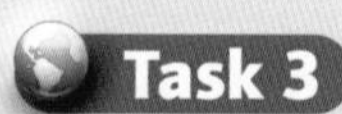
Task 3

Study **Source C**.

a Draw a graph to show the changes in employment structure between 1980 and 2007.
b Describe the unemployment situation in 2007.
c Suggest why BEE has had little effect on black Africans living in townships like Soweto.

D New opportunities for some ... but not for all

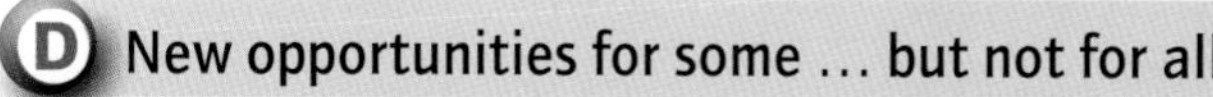

South Africa's Widening Divide

Brian Mdluli is living the African dream. At 33, he is the chief executive in the marketing world with a lifestyle to match – his and her BMWs parked in the driveway, a swimming pool, and a boat. Mr Mdluli is part of South Africa's small but rapidly growing black middle-class – the so-called 'Black Diamonds'. They are benefiting due to the policy of black economic empowerment (BEE). The current leadership has delivered opportunities for people like Mr Mdluli but many others have been left behind. The old division between black and white has given way to a yawning gap between rich and poor black people.

Mr Mdluli knows both sides of the story as he stays close to his birthplace in Soweto. From his spacious home in Johannesburg's leafy suburbs it is a half-hour drive back to the narrow streets and modest homes of Soweto. Here families still live in shacks. The numbers living in severe poverty have doubled in the country in a decade. In 1996 there were nearly 2 million living on less than $1 a day; by 2005 it was over 4 million.

Jacqueline Rosetta is one of those trapped in poverty. An articulate, lone parent aged 40 she has been looking for a job for five years and waiting for a house for twice that long. She lives in a one-room tin shack in a rough area of Soweto where crime rates are high. There is no heating, no running water, no fridge and no cooker – just a hotplate. 'The people we voted for in the ANC are living in mansions and driving smart cars. The poor are getting poorer and the rich richer.'

E What the tourist saw ...

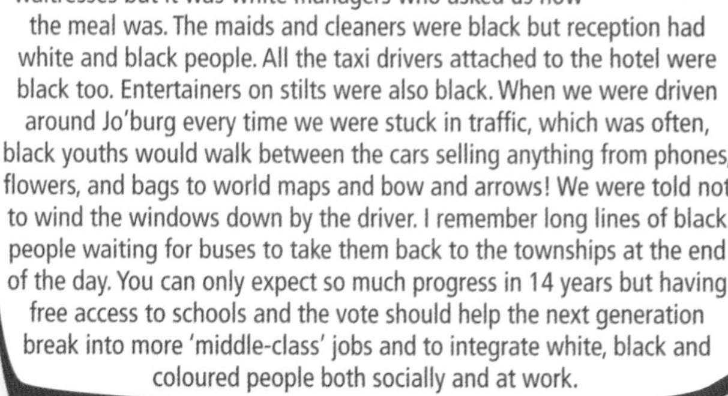
I visited Jo'burg for three days in 2008. We stayed at the Montecasino complex in Fourways which contained a hotel, restaurants and shops aimed at tourists. Security was high with guards screening entrances so it was difficult to get to see the 'real' Jo'burg or its people. We were served by black waiters and waitresses but it was white managers who asked us how the meal was. The maids and cleaners were black but reception had white and black people. All the taxi drivers attached to the hotel were black too. Entertainers on stilts were also black. When we were driven around Jo'burg every time we were stuck in traffic, which was often, black youths would walk between the cars selling anything from phones, flowers, and bags to world maps and bow and arrows! We were told not to wind the windows down by the driver. I remember long lines of black people waiting for buses to take them back to the townships at the end of the day. You can only expect so much progress in 14 years but having free access to schools and the vote should help the next generation break into more 'middle-class' jobs and to integrate white, black and coloured people both socially and at work.

Task 4

Study **Source D**.

a Why is Brian Mdluli a 'Black Diamond'?
b Why is a new 'gap' being created by BEE?
c Why does Jacqueline Rosetta feel let down by the government?

Task 5

Study **Source E**.

a What evidence is there of a race 'divide'?
b Why might the tourist's description be unreliable?

CASE STUDY 

23b Changing employment – Russia

A Russia – a large, cold country

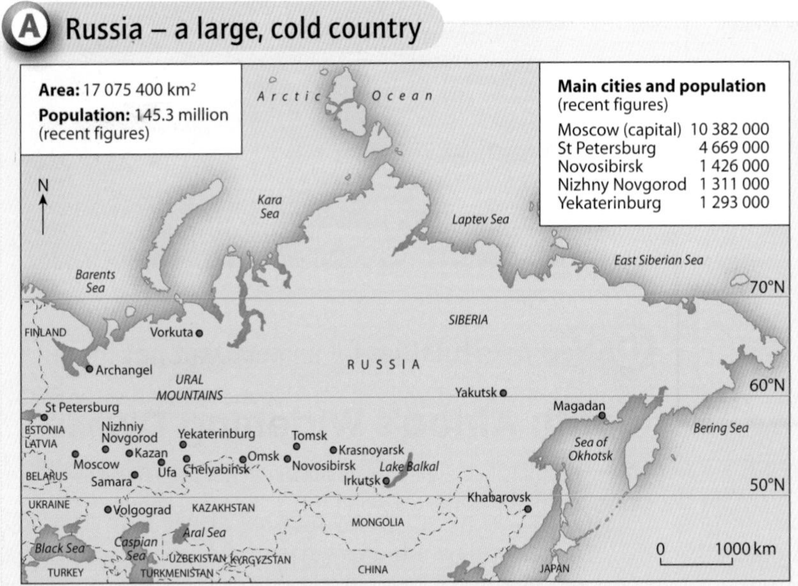

From communism to capitalism

Covering an area of 17 million km², Russia is the world's largest country – almost twice as big as either the USA or China. On the north and east coasts are the Arctic and Pacific Oceans and it has land boundaries with 13 countries. Until 1989 the economy of the USSR (Union of Soviet Socialist Republics), which included Russia and many other countries, was based on communism. For much of the 20th century it competed with the USA, whose economy was based on capitalism, to be the world's largest superpower.

By 1989 it was clear that Soviet communism was not working. Many republics chose to become independent and a new Russia, reduced in size and influence but still large in area, was founded. In the past 20 years Russia has moved towards a more capitalist economy. This has created new employment opportunities although at present most change is within the two major cities of Moscow and St Petersburg.

B Two different systems

Communism	Capitalism
• All land and resources are owned by the state representing the people.	• Some land and resources are owned by the state – the rest by private organisations and individuals.
• People are educated for the benefit of the state and are allocated jobs in the best interests of the country, not by choice.	• People are educated and can then seek jobs in any activity or place they choose.
• Fixed wages are paid by the state and housing and jobs are provided for all. Unemployment is not allowed without a genuine reason, e.g. disability.	• Wages vary with no upper limit. Unemployment is allowed though discouraged.
• All industry and services are owned by the state as public ownership. The state uses all profits to spend on services such as schools, hospitals, and the armed forces.	• Some industry and services are owned by the state; others by private ownership through individuals and organisations who can keep profits for themselves.
• Individuals are not allowed to 'make money' for themselves.	
• Elections are allowed but only communist party candidates can stand.	• Elections are allowed and any person can stand, representing different views for the people to vote upon.

C Employment starts to change …

Workforce (%)	1990	2007
Primary	14	11
Secondary	42	29
Tertiary	44	60

Age group (%)	2007
0–14	14.6
15–64	71.2
65+	14.2

Tourists crowd around a street stall in Moscow. Service employment has increased partly due to tourists coming in large numbers since 1989.

Task 1

Study **Source A**.

a Estimate the maximum width and length of Russia in kilometres. How does this size compare with the country you live in?

b Why is the size of a country not always a good indicator of how easy it is to live and work in, or as a guide to its resources?

Task 2

Study **Source B**.

a Give **one** advantage and **one** disadvantage of living in:
- a communist system
- a capitalist system.

b How and why do employment opportunities vary between the two systems?

c Make a list of the points from **Source B** that match the country you live in. What would you like to change about the way your country is run? Why?

Task 3

Study **Source C**.

a Draw a graph to show the changes in employment structure from 1990 to 2007.

b Describe how this structure has changed. What impact have tourists had?

D Employment – legacies from the past

1 *Using natural resources:* lack of investment, poor management and the flight of young people to the cities have left the villages with old machinery and a tired workforce trying to feed the country.

2 *Making goods:* the Krasny Oktyabr (Red October) chocolate-making factory was established in Moscow beside the Moskva river in 1889. Much of its chocolate is bought by tourists.

3 *Providing a service:* the Metro underground in Moscow was opened in 1935. It is the second busiest in the world and provides a fast service out of the city centre to the huge tower-block estates where most workers live.

Task 4

Study **Source D**.

a Each of the photos **1–3** shows an example of primary, secondary and tertiary employment. Which shows which? Explain your choice.

b Write down at least **two** examples of each type of employment in your home area.

Task 5

Study **Source E**.

a What is a multinational company?

b Do any multinational companies provide employment in the country where you live? Name them, and describe what they do and the types of job they create.

c Are there any disadvantages in relying on work from companies based in other countries? Explain your answer.

E Multinationals create new jobs

McDonald's is a multinational fast-food provider based in the USA. This shop opened in Moscow in 1990.

Multinational companies (MNCs) are those with branches in more than one country. Since 1989 Russia has allowed companies from overseas to build factories and provide shops and services especially in Moscow and St Petersburg. These provide new opportunities for employment as well as more choice for consumers, but it is only the wealthier middle-class urban people who can benefit from these new opportunities.

F Events bring more employment

Winners, Winners Everywhere on European Football's Biggest Night

The winners of the European Champions League Final, Chelsea or Manchester United, will not only be on the field in the Luzhniki stadium in Moscow. For businesses, big and small, this is all about cashing in on the biggest night of televised European sport. With a global audience of 112 million, the six main sponsors, including Heineken, Sony, and MasterCard, have paid £20 million a year each for their adverts and logos to be used during the Championship. Not all businesses involved are large. Red Square will be full of stalls with baseball caps, bags and other souvenirs for supporters of both teams. They will also need food, accommodation, transport and flights into and out of Moscow. Security issues too will create an increase in policing at airports and in the city itself.

May 2008

Task 6

Many countries gain global prestige as well as work and employment by holding major sporting events such as the Olympic Games or the Rugby and Soccer World Cups. In 2008 Moscow was the venue for the European Champions Soccer Final.

Study **Source F**.

a Working in a group, list the types of short-term employment that were likely to be created by the European Champions Final in Moscow, both within the city and outside of Russia.

b Name **two** multinational companies sponsoring this competition. How can they benefit from this?

Sample case study question

For a named country or region you have studied, describe how and why employment structure has changed or is changing.

TOPIC 24 Manufacturing industry

A Decisions, decisions ...

	Location factor	Questions to ask
PHYSICAL	Site requirement	Is there cheap land available of the correct size, level and well-drained?
	Natural routes	Is there a natural land or sea route, which provides speedy and cheap transportation for raw materials and industrial goods?
HUMAN	Access to market	What is the distance between the site and the market?
		What is the cheapest form of transport available?
	Availability of raw materials	Are sufficient raw materials available at an affordable price?
		Will the supply of raw materials be reliable?
	Skilled labour	Is the required number of workers with necessary skills available?
	Power supply	What sources of power are available and at what cost?
	Industrial linkage	Are there any industries in the area that we can benefit from?
	Capital	Is capital available for developmental purposes?
	Government policies	Does the government offer any incentives to develop a new industry?

Secondary industry

Manufacturing involves making things. It is the production of goods by industrial processes. It is classified as secondary industry and is an important economic sector in all countries. Secondary industries take raw materials produced by the primary sector and process them into manufactured goods and products.

The Industrial Revolution began in the UK in the 18th century, and affected most of western Europe and the USA. The development of large manufacturing industries caused them to become MEDCs. Since then many other countries have developed a secondary industrial sector and have moved towards becoming MEDCs from LEDC status.

B Secondary industry as a system

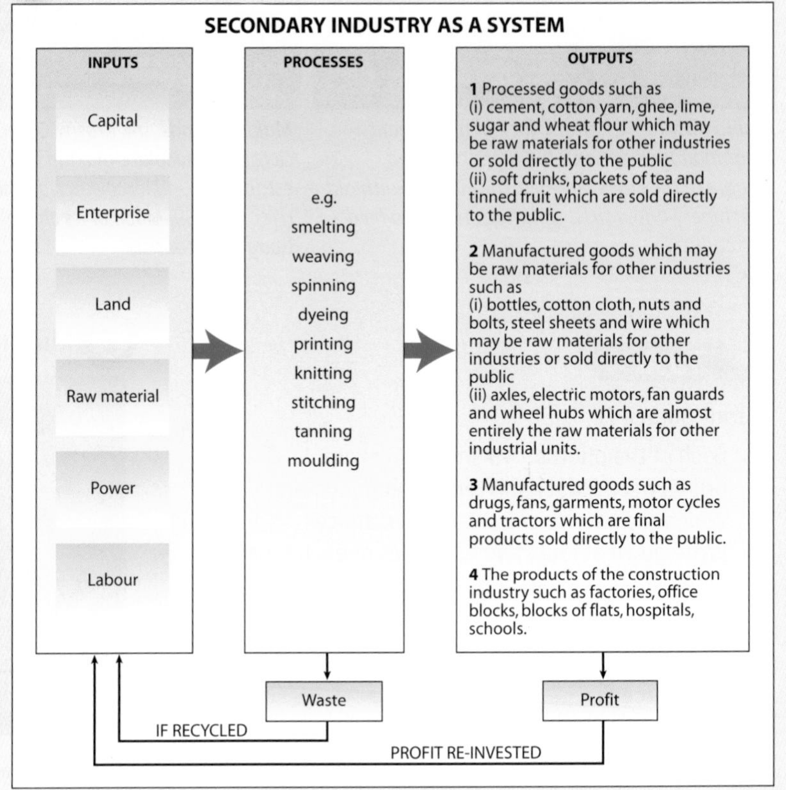

SECONDARY INDUSTRY AS A SYSTEM
INPUTS
Capital
Enterprise
Land
Raw material
Power
Labour
PROCESSES
e.g.
smelting
weaving
spinning
dyeing
printing
knitting
stitching
tanning
moulding
OUTPUTS
1 Processed goods such as (i) cement, cotton yarn, ghee, lime, sugar and wheat flour which may be raw materials for other industries or sold directly to the public (ii) soft drinks, packets of tea and tinned fruit which are sold directly to the public.
2 Manufactured goods which may be raw materials for other industries such as (i) bottles, cotton cloth, nuts and bolts, steel sheets and wire which may be raw materials for other industries or sold directly to the public (ii) axles, electric motors, fan guards and wheel hubs which are almost entirely the raw materials for other industrial units.
3 Manufactured goods such as drugs, fans, garments, motor cycles and tractors which are final products sold directly to the public.
4 The products of the construction industry such as factories, office blocks, blocks of flats, hospitals, schools.
Waste
Profit
IF RECYCLED
PROFIT RE-INVESTED

Study **Source A**.

a Make a copy of the table. Leave space in column two to add one other question you could ask about each factor. Discuss these with your classmates.

b Choose **two** physical factors and **two** human factors from the table. Suggest how each could influence the location of a factory.

Study **Source B**.

a List **one** example for each input stated, e.g. capital = a bank loan.

b Suggest **one** manufacturing industry for each of the listed processes, e.g. smelting = iron and steel industry.

c Give **one** example of:
- an output that is a final product sold directly to the general public
- an output that becomes a raw material for another industry.

d What happens to the outputs 'Waste' and 'Profit'?

C Small-scale manufacturing industry – Tamegroute, Morocco

Mohammed's story

"I have been here for over 10 years as a potter. I pay rent on the land but for that I can use the shed and kilns. I use red clay from the bank of a nearby river but buy some in if I get short. We use donkeys to bring clay and water here in plastic bottles and use dung and local wood for fuel. To get the clay ready, three large holes are dug in the ground and filled with water. The raw clay is mixed in to create a wet, slushy material. We then shovel out the wet clay into a large puddle on the ground and walk on it to flatten it and squeeze out surplus water. The clay is cut into large chunks and stored in a cool place in plastic bags. I have a wheel where I throw the clay into pots, plates and bowls; I use my feet to drive the wheel. Most of my day is spent throwing pots using water and fingers to create the shape I want. Once there are enough pots made, they are left to dry in the sun, then they are stacked in the kilns which are sealed. Dung or firewood is lit to fire the pottery. We are hoping to get gas bottles here soon. The fired pottery is left for a day to cool. The unglazed pots are then removed for decorating. There are three of us working here – one to prepare the clay, one to throw it and another to glaze and sell the pottery. Tourists buy a great deal but some villagers come here too. Any profit goes back into the pottery after paying rent. There is no waste unless a pot breaks before it is fired; the clay can then be re-used. One day we hope to buy the pottery from the landlord."

Throwing – pedal power is used to turn the wheel.

D Large-scale manufacturing industry – Karachi, Pakistan

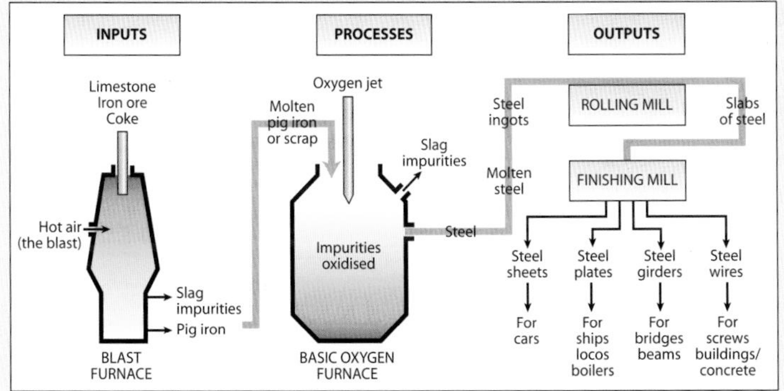

Task 3

Study **Sources B and C**.

a Read Mohammed's story and then copy and complete this table based on what he says about his work.

Inputs	Processes	Outputs

b Suggest some social, economic and environmental consequences of making pottery in this area.

Task 4

Study **Source D**.

a List the main raw material inputs from the diagram. List **three** other inputs – use **Source A** to help you.

b Explain the processes that turn these raw materials into molten steel.

c List **three** different outputs from the steel mill.

d How might the social, economic and environmental consequences of making steel in Pakistan be similar and different to making pottery in Morocco?

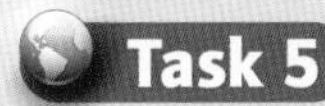

Task 5

Is there a factory near you or that you could study? If so:

a Find out what it manufactures.

b Suggest why the factory was located there. Refer to factors from **Source A**.

c Draw an inputs–process–outputs diagram based on **Source B**.

d What are the factory's social, economic and environmental influences on the local community? Decide if they are positive or negative.

Manufacturing at different scales

People or organisations can make products at different scales. These can vary from small-scale craft industries (e.g. making pottery) to huge large-scale industries (e.g. steel or car-making). All have:

- social effects, by affecting the quality of life and standard of living of employees and the community
- economic effects, by providing employment, developing trade and creating wealth
- environmental effects, by using raw materials, taking up land and producing waste products.

Manufacturing steel – Pakistan

A slow start

After independence from India in 1947, it did not take long for Pakistan to realise that in order to develop the industrial sector of its economy, it needed an iron and steelmaking plant. Otherwise the country would be paying huge import bills and relying on other countries. After much debate lasting many years, the first steel factories for Pakistan Steel were built in 1973. The project was so large it took another 12 years before the plant was completed and formally opened.

A The history of Pakistan Steel, 1947–85

1947	Partition and the creation of West Pakistan (Pakistan since 1971).
1955–60	Idea of an iron and steel plant put forward in the first five-year plan.
1968	Government decides the steel plant should be funded from public money. This would allow control over the future development and integration across the country. Karachi Steel Project created.
2 July 1968	Pakistan Steel Mills Corporation set up as a private limited company controlled by the government with the objective of establishing and running steel mills at Karachi and other places in Pakistan. Russian finance and expertise sought as Pakistan does not have the capital or skilled labour to build the steel mills.
1971	Pakistan and the USSR (now Russia) sign an agreement for the construction of a coastal-based integrated steel mill at Karachi.
1973–81	Construction of over 20 steel plants and associated infrastructure took place at Pipri, about 40 km east of Karachi using Pakistani construction companies managed by Russian experts.
15 Jan 1985	Steel mill completed and formally opened. Pakistan Steel remains the largest industrial complex in Pakistan.

B Why choose Karachi?

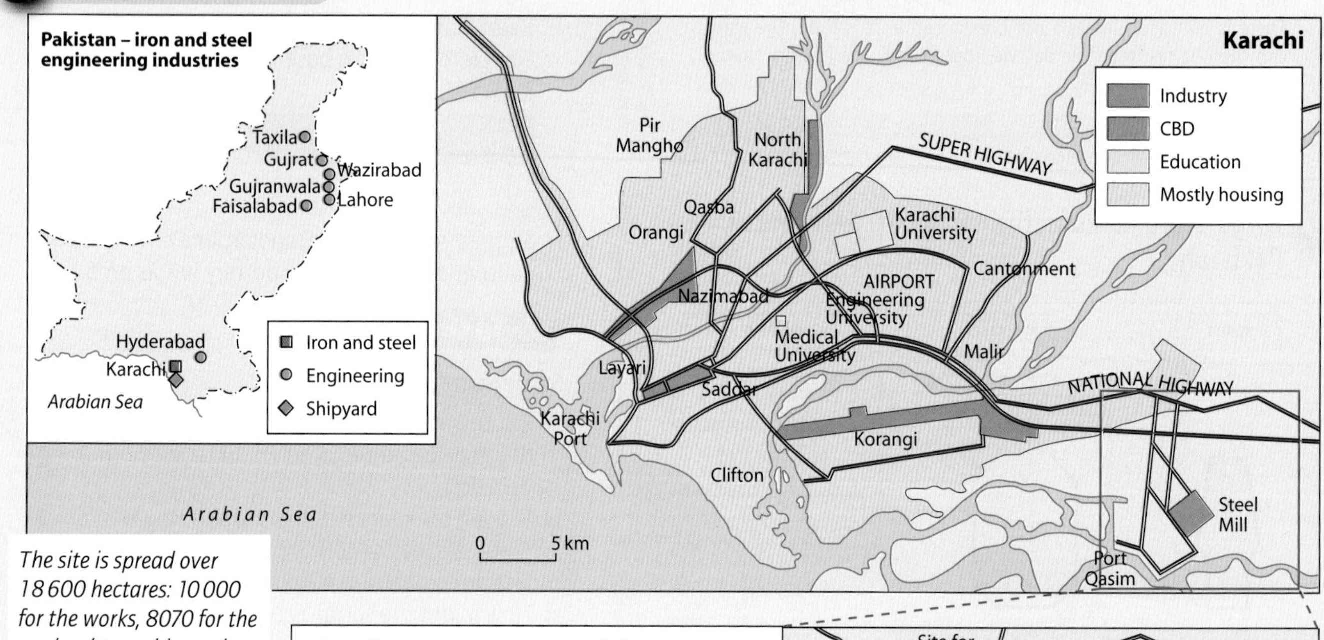

The site is spread over 18 600 hectares: 10 000 for the works, 8070 for the workers' township, and 200 for the water reservoir.

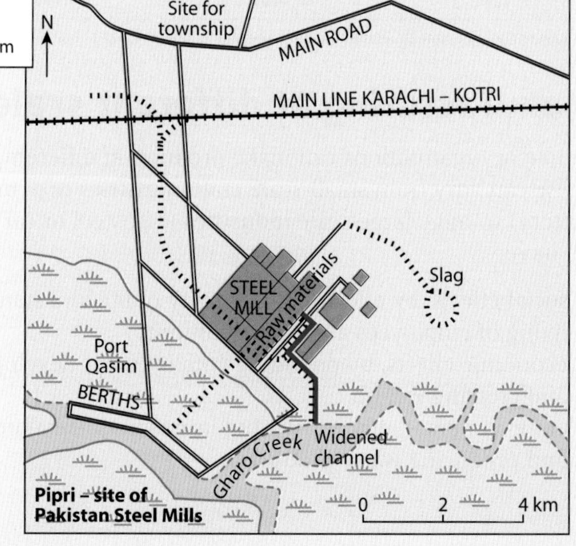

Task 1

Study **Source A**.

a Why did Pakistan need an iron and steel plant of its own after 1947?

b Why did the government decide to pay for building the steelworks?

c What outside help was needed? Why?

Task 2

Study **Source B**.

a State **one** advantage of Karachi's location for building a steelworks.

b Describe the situation of the steel mill in relation to Karachi. Refer to distances and directions.

c Describe the site of the steel mill. What advantages does this site have for moving raw materials and products around?

C Why choose Pipri?

Factors influencing location	Reason
PHYSICAL	
Site	
Natural routes	
HUMAN	
Capital	
Raw materials	
Energy	
Labour	
Markets	
Transport	

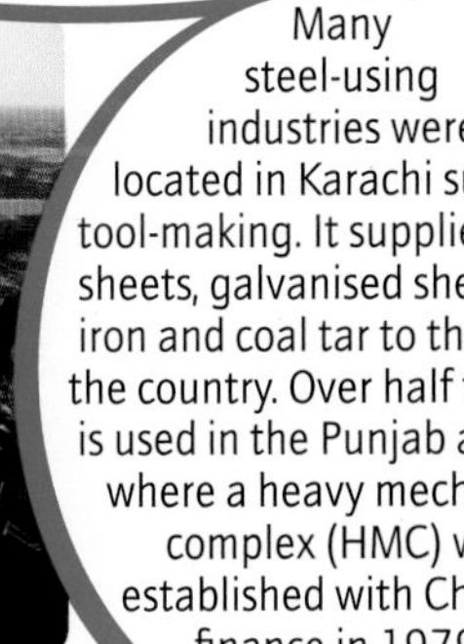

Iron ore, manganese and most of the coking coal can be imported through Port Qasim. Limestone, needed as a flux, can be brought by road from the nearby Makli Hills near Thatta. Large quantities of water required for making steel can be brought from Lake Haleji, 50 km to the east (saltwater is not suitable).
Flat, cheap unused land was available at Pipri near Gharo Creek.
Port Qasim has a natural harbour that can deal with imports of materials and exports of steel to the countries neighbouring the Arabian Sea and east and west of the Indian Ocean. The 2.5 km long seawater channel is kept navigable for ships.
The former USSR (now Russia) provided economic assistance in the form of technical expertise, finance and capital.
Many steel-using industries were located in Karachi such as tool-making. It supplies rolled sheets, galvanised sheets, pig iron and coal tar to the rest of the country. Over half the steel is used in the Punjab at Taxila where a heavy mechanical complex (HMC) was established with Chinese finance in 1979.
Pipri was connected to the main Karachi–Kotri railway. Metalled roads also connected this area to the main road system
Plenty of skilled and unskilled cheap labour was available locally from Karachi.
Port Qasim and Karachi had the highest electricity-generating capacity in the country. Pipri thermal power station produced 21% and Koranga thermal power station produced 15% of the total. Karachi also has a nuclear power station.

D Pakistan Steel – environmentally responsible?

Pakistan Steel has always been environmentally responsible and this is built into our business and process activities. Our original location was deliberately chosen to be out of the way on marshy land near a tidal creek that nobody else wanted. The steelworks may not be the prettiest place but only the workers see it! We also built the plant 40 km downwind of Karachi so that any pollution – air and noise – would not blow over areas where people live.

Pakistan Steel has invested in making the environment green and beautiful. In the past two years we have reforested the area around the factories and set new targets for waste and pollution reduction. Extensive work has been carried out on water treatment, especially of freshwater supplies that feed lakes and reservoirs for the local community. We have also created a landscaped cricket ground, lakes, bird sanctuaries and a running track for employees. Given what was here before, nobody can argue that we have not improved the environment.

Task 3

Study **Source C**.

On a copy of the table, write in the 'Reason' column the matching label.

Task 4

Study **Source D**.

a List environmental factors that influenced the location of Pakistan Steel.

b List **four** different ways that show the company has tried to improve the environment since it began producing steel here.

Task 5

Study **Source E**.

a What did the government decide to do with its 75 per cent stake in Pakistan Steel in 2006? Give **two** reasons for this decision.

b Who opposed the sale and why?

c Suggest some risks of selling a state-owned activity to overseas buyers.

E The Russians return …

Pakistan Steel to be privatised

Pakistan Steel, the only steel company in the country, has been sold to a Russian-led consortium backed by Saudi money. It was only 20 years ago that the steel company was created with Russian technical expertise and financial help. The sale was controversial, with union opposition and long debates in parliament. The main objection was that, at US $362 million, the 75% stake of the Pakistan government was sold too cheaply. Although the company had not performed well between 1985 and 2003, since then it has achieved record production levels, sales and profits as steel prices soared. The firm also increased capital equipment and cut the workforce by 35%, making it less labour-intensive. Today it produces one-quarter of Pakistan's steel with the rest being imported. The advantage of the company going into the private sector is that the sales bring in foreign currency to the private company which funds the steelworks instead of government money which can be spent on public services. Although job losses through restructuring and retraining will take place, more people can be channelled into areas of job shortages such as IT, banking and education.

June 2006

Sample case study question

Name an area you have studied where manufacturing industry is carried out. Describe the impacts of this industry on the natural environment.

Hi-tech industry

A Products of hi-tech industry

Hi-tech – a growing industry

Hi-tech industries involve making and using silicon chips, computers, semi-conductor devices and computer-controlled machinery. They use micro-electronics to make computers, pharmaceuticals, communications equipment and equipment for the aerospace industries. Hi-tech industries have been growing rapidly. Although hi-tech industries are 'footloose' they do cluster together in some areas. One of the earliest concentrations of hi-tech industry was in 'Silicon Valley', near San Francisco, in the USA, and this is still one of the most important locations. In many other areas science parks, with purpose-built factory units, have been set up to attract new developments.

Task 1

Study **Source A**.

a Identify the products of hi-tech industry that are shown in the photographs.

b Explain why industries manufacturing products such as those shown in the photographs are growing rapidly.

B Location of hi-tech industry

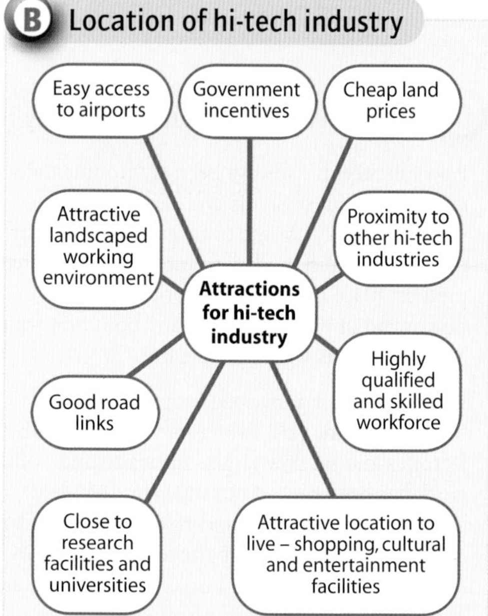

Task 2

Study **Source B**.

Working in pairs, discuss the **nine** attractions for hi-tech industries.

Select the **five** that you think are the most important and explain why you have chosen them.

Task 3

Study **Source C**.

a Describe the main features of the buildings and environment shown in the photograph.

b Do you think this is a good area for hi-tech industry? Give reasons for your answer.

C An area of hi-tech industry

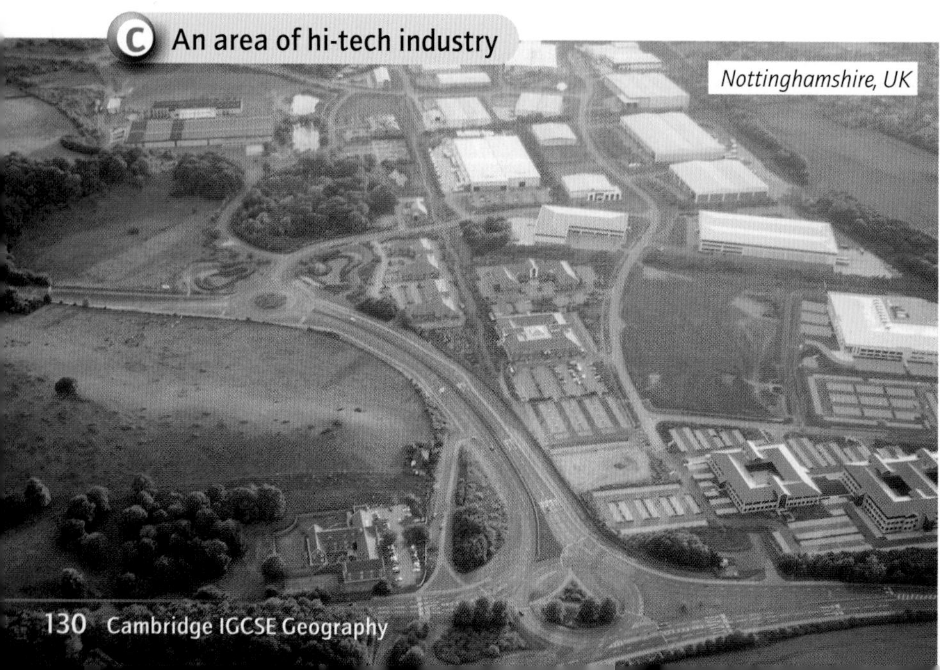

Silicon Valley, California

Source D shows 'Silicon Valley' in the USA where hi-tech industry has grown along a 50 km stretch of California. Silicon Valley lies along the south side of San Francisco Bay, from Palo Alto in the west to San Jose in the east. Companies involved in the research, development and manufacturing of micro-electronics have been present in the region since the last half of the 20th century. Many software companies, internet-related businesses and companies in the fields of biotechnology and aerospace are also here. In this area average incomes are amongst the highest in the USA – but so are property prices. The roads are often very busy and congested, with fumes from exhaust emissions being a major problem.

D Silicon Valley

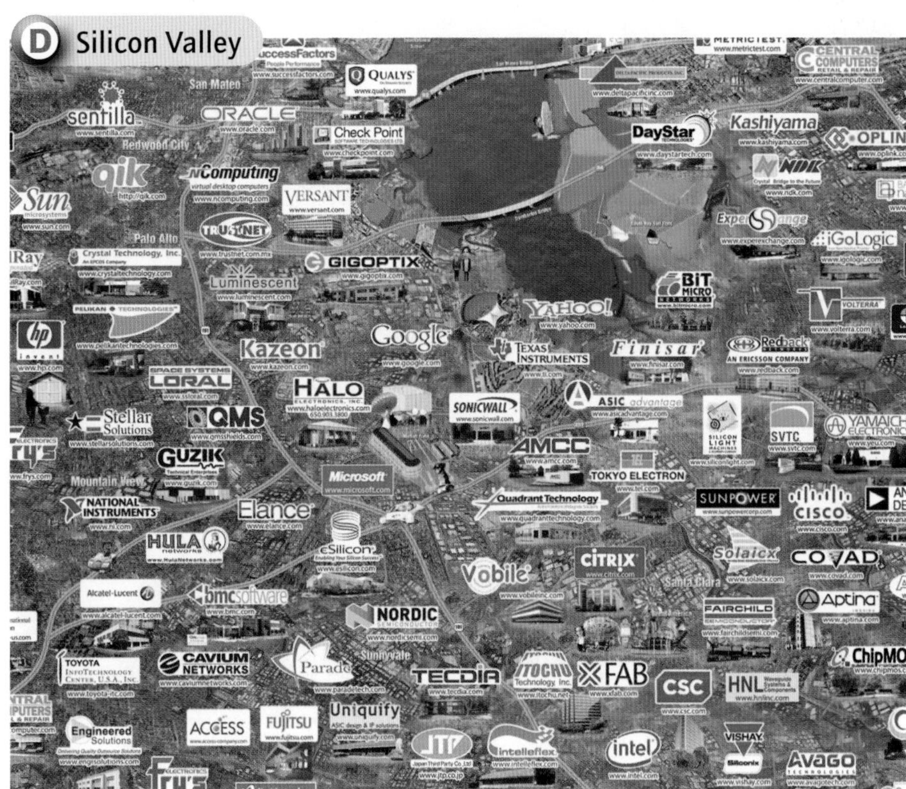

E Share of information technology (IT) employment in USA

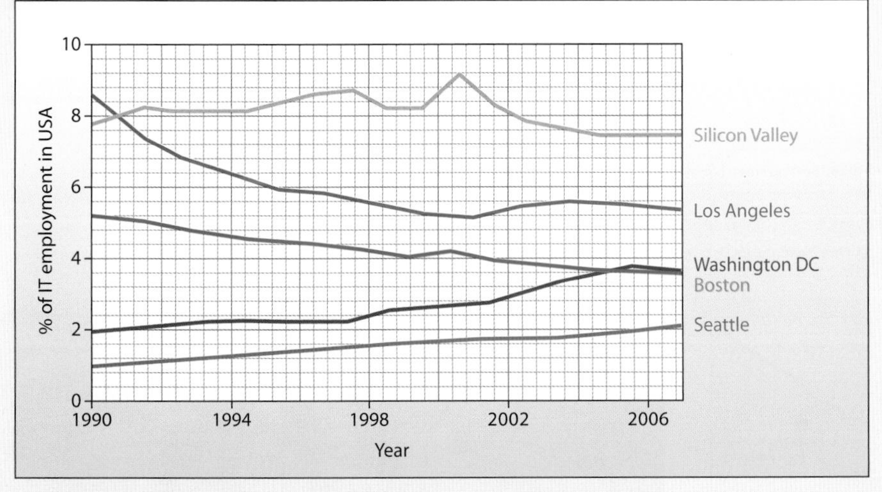

Task 4

Study **Source D**.

Choose a major hi-tech company that is located in Silicon Valley.

a Use the internet to carry out research about the company and write a short paragraph describing the business in which it is involved.

b Describe the exact location of the company.

c Explain the advantages and disadvantages of the location in Silicon Valley for this company.

Task 5

Study **Source E**.

a Copy and complete the following sentences. Choose from the words below.

Between 1990 and 2006 Silicon Valley has had the ____ share of IT employment in the USA. Its highest percentage share was in ____ and since then the importance of the IT industry in Silicon Valley has been ____ slightly. Areas of the USA where the percentage of IT employment in the USA has increased are ____ and ____.

increasing Los Angeles largest 1997 declining smallest Washington DC Seattle 2001 Boston 1991

b On an outline map of the USA mark and label Silicon Valley, Los Angeles, Boston, Washington DC and Seattle. Next to each location draw a bar to represent its percentage of IT employment in the USA in 2006.
Use a scale of 5 mm = 2%.
Don't forget to include a title and a key.

CASE STUDY 25

Hi-tech industry in Bangalore

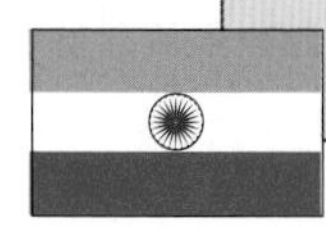

The Silicon Valley of India

Bangalore, in the Indian state of Karnataka, is one of India's largest industrial cities. Many industrial products are manufactured here, including aircraft, batteries, paper, cement, watches and railway wagons. However, since the 1970s the IT (information technology) industry has become important. In 1991 a Software Technology Park was created and since then a number of multinational IT companies have set up their offices in Bangalore. It is the most important hardware and software centre of India and is known as the 'IT capital of India' or 'Silicon Valley of India'. The reasons for the growth of the industry in Bangalore are:

- pleasant climate conditions
- good transport facilities
- highly trained and qualified workers
- government policies
- establishment of science and technology parks.

A Location map of Bangalore

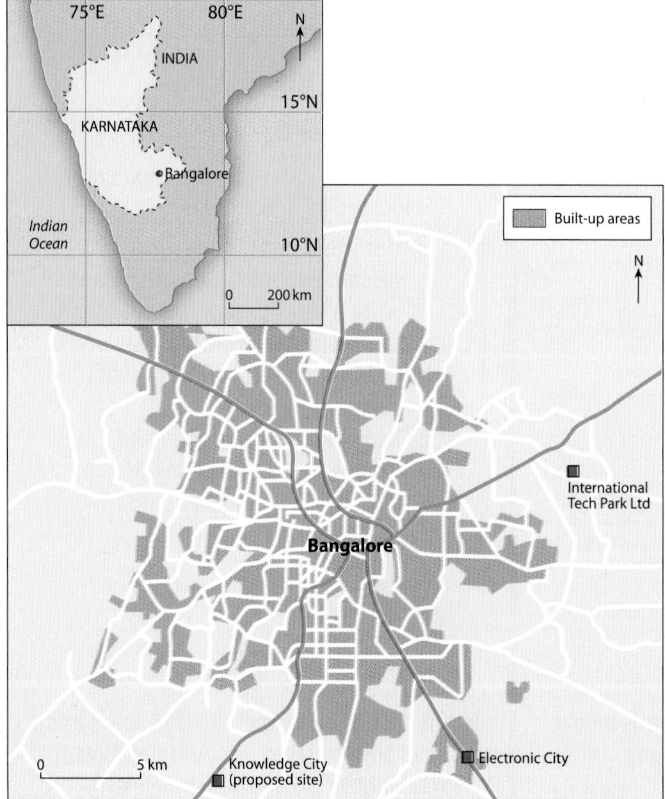

B Bangalore International Technology Park

- Area of the property: 28 hectares
- Located 18 km from city, 12 km from international airport
- 1.5 million m^2 of office, production, commercial and retail space
- Residential block of 51 apartments
- Dedicated power plant, water supply and centrally controlled and monitored air-conditioning
- Reliable access to voice and data communication
- Parking space with multi-parking levels for about 950 four-wheelers and 400 two-wheelers

C UBINETICS – coming to a phone near you ...

Ubinetics is a hi-tech company involved in wireless telecommunications. They develop the advanced technology used in mobile phones. Ubinetics sells its products to mobile phone manufacturers such as Nokia, Ericsson and Motorola. Ubinetics has units in Cambridgeshire and Swindon in the UK, but their largest unit is in Bangalore. It is an important unit as there are a large number of highly qualified people, especially computer programmers, in the area. It currently employs 150 people whose salaries are less than 25% of those of similar British workers.

D Constructing Bangalore's hi-tech industry

Study **Source A**.

Describe the location of:

a Bangalore
b Bangalore International Technology Park.

Study **Sources B and C**.

Describe the attractions of Bangalore for hi-tech industries.

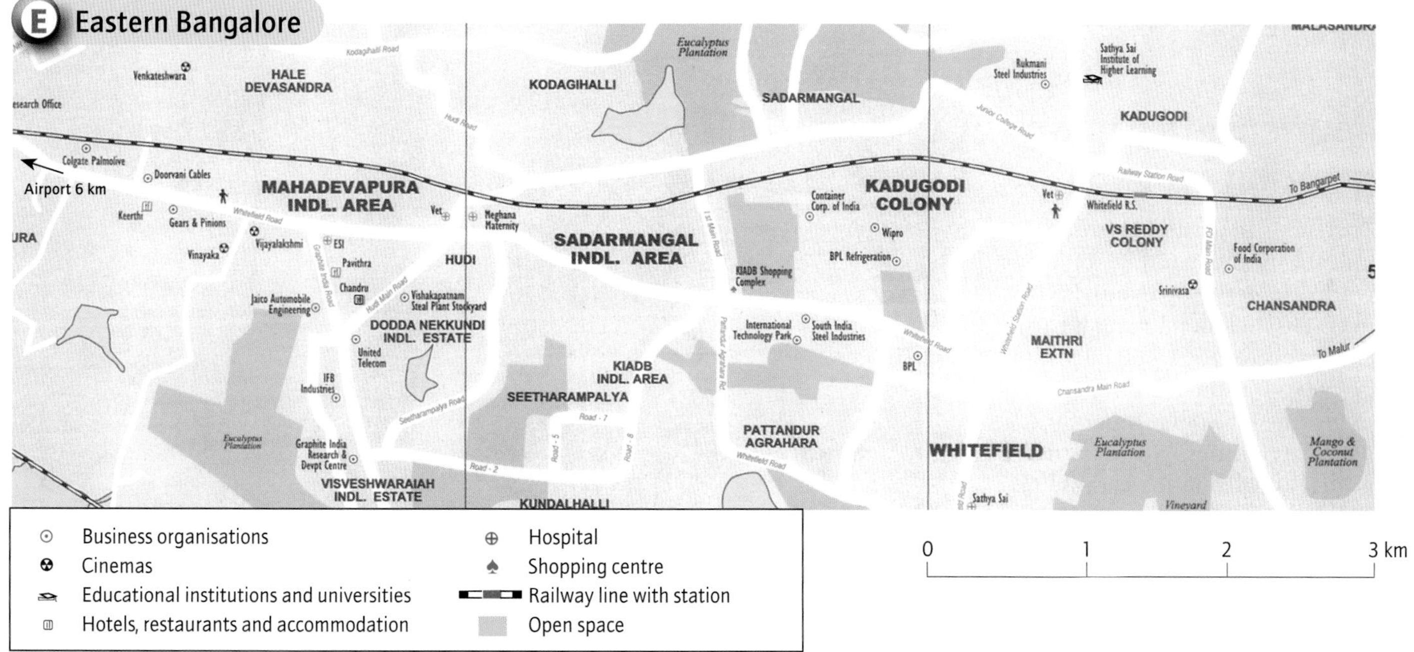

Task 3

Study **Sources D and E**.

The buildings shown in **Source D** are being constructed for Accenture, a global company involved in hi-tech industries. The location of the construction site is close to the International Technology Park near Pattandur Agrahara, which is shown in **Source E**.

How might each of the following three people benefit from the building of new hi-tech industries in the area? Give reasons for their views.

- A school leaver with no qualifications
- A young university graduate
- The owner of a food store at the local KIAOB shopping complex

Task 4

Study **Source E**.

a Name **two** industrial areas shown on the map.

b Name **three** examples of hi-tech industries shown on the map.

c Use map evidence to suggest why industries have been developed in the area.

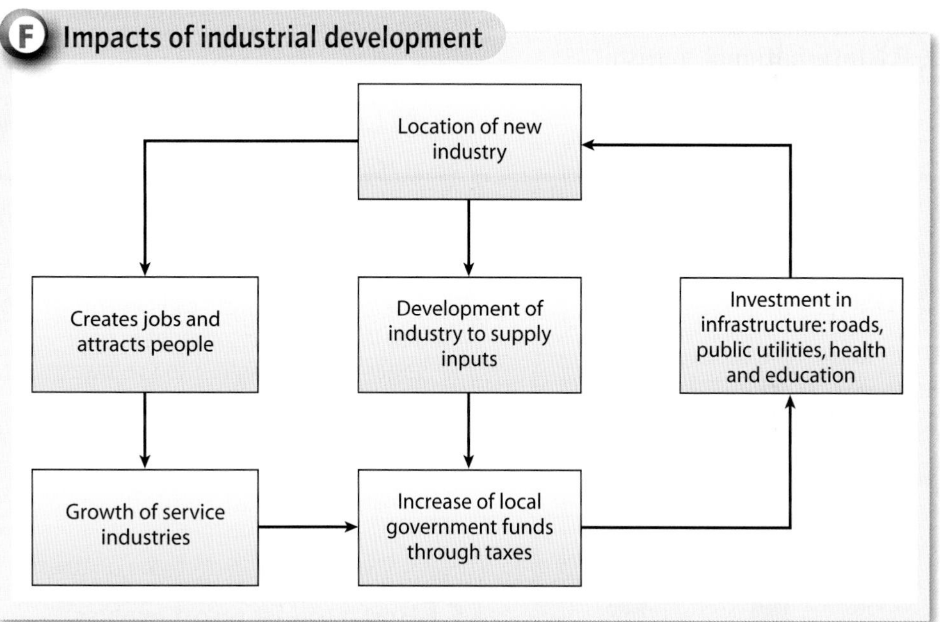

Task 5

Study **Source F**.

Even though Bangalore is important for hi-tech industry there are still many people living in poverty here. There are great inequalities between rich and poor.

Use the ideas shown in **Source F** to explain how poor people in Bangalore may benefit from hi-tech industry.

Sample case study question

For a country or area you have studied, explain the factors that have encouraged the growth of hi-tech industries.

Tourism

Tourism – a rapidly growing industry

Tourism is the fastest-growing industry in the world. It is the world's largest employer with over 250 million jobs and it earns countries over US$ 600 billion per year. It is the main source of income for 80 per cent of the world's countries. World tourism is increasing so much because of:

- rising incomes
- improved transport
- escapism/adventure
- education
- advertising.

A International tourism

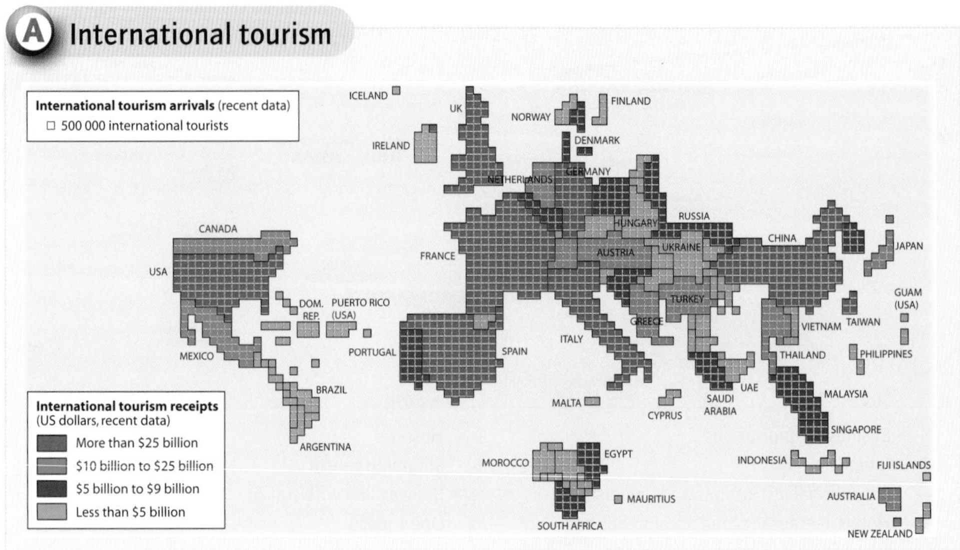

B International tourism is growing ...

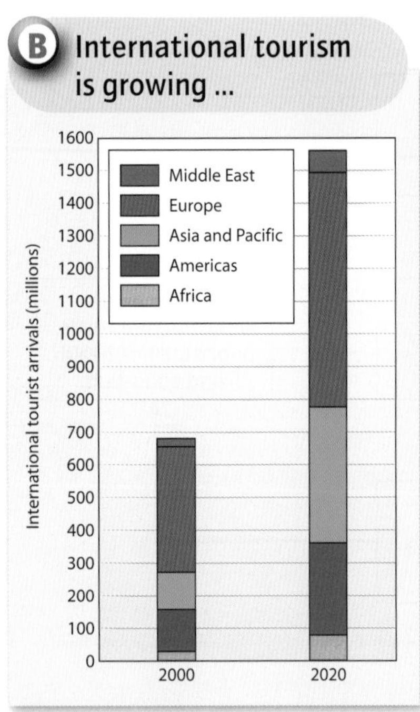

Task 1

Study **Source A**.

a How many international tourists visited Portugal?

b How much income was earned from international tourism by Egypt?

c Put the following countries in rank order from the highest to the lowest number of international tourist arrivals.
- China
- France
- Italy
- Spain
- USA

Task 2

Study **Source B**.

a By how much was the total number of international tourists expected to increase between 2000 and 2020?

b Identify the part of the world that:
- had over 50 per cent of the world's international tourists in 2000
- is likely to increase its number of international tourists from 115 million in 2000 to over 400 million in 2020.

C How a tourist resort evolves

In 1980 this model was developed to show the evolution of a tourist resort.

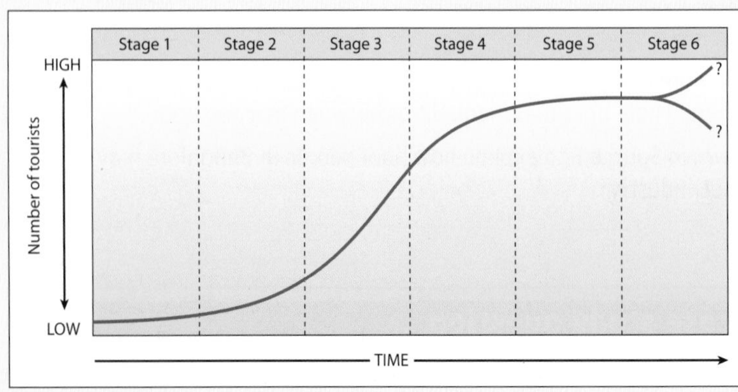

Stage 1
A secret spot is discovered and visitors come in small numbers. There are no amenities.

Stage 2
More visitors arrive and local people set up amenities.

Stage 3
A well-defined tourism industry is developed with the destination being advertised.

Stage 4
Tourism becomes a dominant feature of the local economy.

Stage 5
Tourism growth slows as the resort becomes too built up and overcrowded, or polluted.

Stage 6
- Decline may result as tourists choose other destinations.
- Rejuvenation can take place, sometimes by attracting a different kind of tourist.

D Different tourist destinations

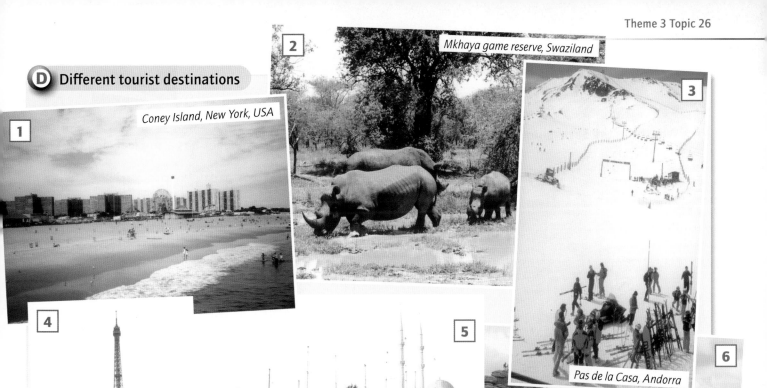

1 Coney Island, New York, USA

2 Mkhaya game reserve, Swaziland

3 Pas de la Casa, Andorra

4 Paris, France

5 Turgutreis, Turkey

6 Dartmoor National Park, UK

Task 3

Study **Source C**.

Choose a tourist resort that you know – it may be one where you have been for a vacation. Which stage of the model do you think it is in? Give reasons for your answer.

Task 4

Study **Source D**.

a In pairs look at each photograph and make a list of the different types of tourist destination they show.

b For each photograph make a list of the attractions of that area. For each attraction identify whether it is a natural (physical) or human (built) attraction.

Task 5

Study **Source E**.

Explain why the author of the article thinks that tourism is having a greater impact than the tsunami in Thailand. Do you agree with him? Give reasons for your views.

E The impact of tourism

The tsunami was nothing compared to the impact of tourism in Thailand. It is a much larger, long-term problem … I was born in 1972 and when I was eight or nine it was still largely virgin rainforest here on the island. By the late 1980s, though, it was mostly developed. We have now lost so much of the biodiversity and primary forest and the soil is destabilising in many places. The construction of hotels upstream is creating a lot of sediment in the water and this causes damage to the coral reefs when it washes out to sea. It also affects the mangroves on the east coast. A lot of our waste water – about 40 per cent – is still being pumped out to sea on the west coast where all the resort areas are. Land is now so expensive here due to tourism; the cost of living is even higher than Bangkok – it has meant that many local people have been forced to sell off their ancestral home and have now lost their only real asset. There is even competition for schools here for the first time. And there is a lot of overfishing here; this is for export rather than for the tourists, but lobsters are now being brought in from Burma to meet the tourists' appetite for these vulnerable creatures. The corals are also damaged by tourism. Snorkellers actually cause more damage than divers because they touch the coral more often …

Leo Hickman, The Final Call – In Search of the True Cost of our Holidays, *2007*

CASE STUDY 26a Tourism in the Seychelles

A Where are the Seychelles?

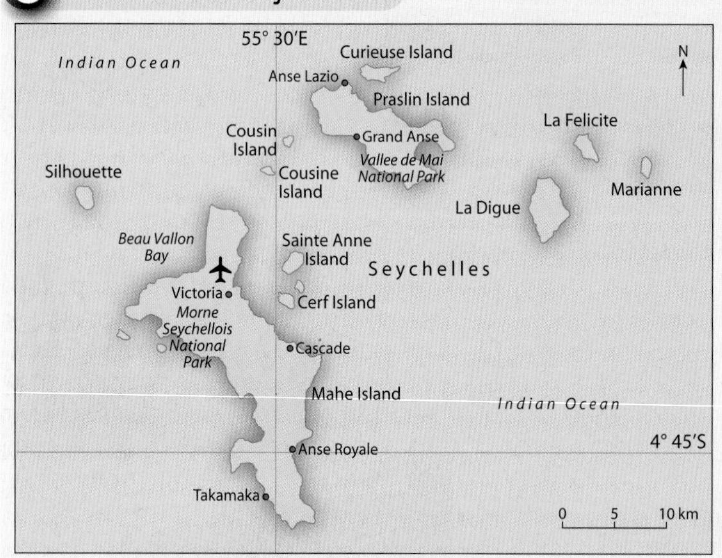

C The Seychelles has a tropical climate

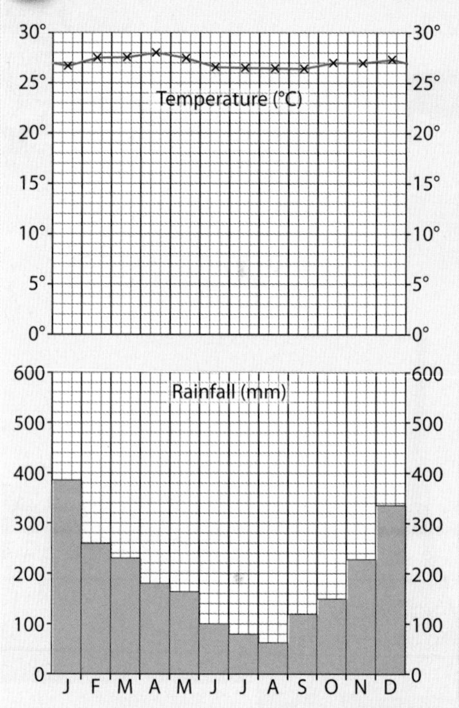

B Tourist attractions on Mahe Island

The Seychelles relies on tourists

The Seychelles is made up of 115 islands in the Indian Ocean, 1500 km east of mainland Africa, north-east of the island of Madagascar.

The traditional economy was the growing of coconut palms and tea on plantations and the cultivation of spices such as cinnamon and vanilla on small farms. There are also craft industries, and some fishing, especially for tuna, takes place around the coast.

Since independence in 1976 the government has encouraged foreign investment in order to build hotels and other tourist amenities. Now the tourist industry provides the islands with 70 per cent of their income and it employs about 30 per cent of the labour force.

Task 1

Study **Sources A and B**.

Describe the different natural attractions of the Seychelles.

Task 2

Study **Source C**.

a Which months do you think will be the most popular for tourism in the Seychelles? Give a reason for your answer.

b Explain the disadvantages of tourist activity being concentrated into a few months of the year.

D Weddings in Paradise

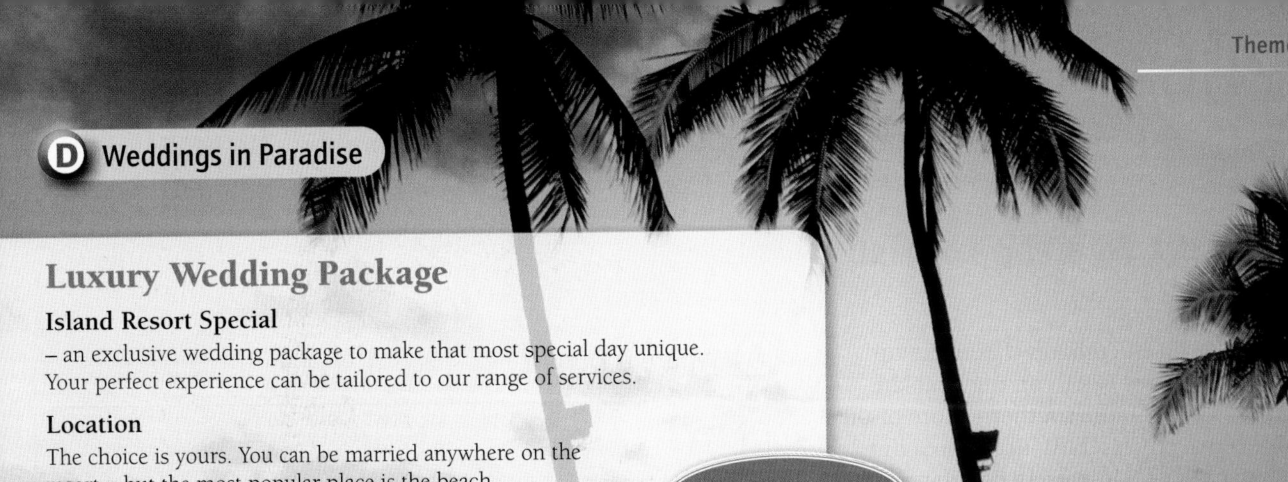

Luxury Wedding Package

Island Resort Special

– an exclusive wedding package to make that most special day unique. Your perfect experience can be tailored to our range of services.

Location

The choice is yours. You can be married anywhere on the resort – but the most popular place is the beach.

EXCLUSIVE!

What's included (for the bride and groom)

- Registrar services and costs
- Natural tropical decorations at the chosen location
- Wedding cake
- A bottle of champagne on arrival, and one bottle of champagne during the ceremony
- Romantic cocktail with snacks on board a private boat at sunset
- Romantic candlelit dinner at the resort – meet the chef to choose the theme of your dinner (e.g. seafood, sushi, fish or game)
- Breakfast next day in your villa

Price: From €800 per couple. Minimum 4 nights stay

E

Water Shortages May Affect Tourism in Seychelles

The reality of water shortages in Seychelles became all too apparent this week. In a chic restaurant in town some tourists were heard complaining about the filthy toilet without a drop of water next to the restaurant. The poor owner was trying to explain to the tourists that around this time of the year there is a drought in Seychelles and everywhere they go they will encounter the same problem.

The government took out a loan of US$ 25 million not so long ago to invest in a desalination plant but there are still water restrictions and water shortages. We lose 75% of our water because of old and leaking water pipes.

One wonders if the money could have been better spent building reservoirs everywhere around our islands similar to the one being built at upper Anse La Mouche, especially since there is an abundance of water during the rainy season which ends up in the sea. Better still, why was the money not used to purchase and install new water pipes? One also questions the wisdom of taking such a large foreign exchange loan to invest in a desalination plant.

August 2006

F Where does the money go?

Foreign developers and hotel owners take out their profits
Foreign workers send money to their own countries
Travel costs taken out by foreign airlines, cruise ship companies, etc.
Payments for goods imported for tourists
Local business people invest their tourism earnings abroad
Governments and local investors repay loans and interest to international banks

Task 3

Study **Source D**.

Make a list of all the jobs that you think can be created for people in the Seychelles by attracting international tourists to get married there.

Task 4

Study **Source E**.

In what ways does the tourist industry contribute to water shortages in LEDCs such as the Seychelles?

Task 5

Study **Source F**. The Minister of Tourism of the Seychelles wants to limit tourist numbers to 200 000 per year by 2010 to ensure that the industry is sustainable. In groups, discuss other ways by which the government could make sure that the tourist industry is sustainable.

From a desert to a top tourist destination

Dubai is one of the seven emirates that make up the United Arab Emirates (UAE) on the Arabian Peninsula. It is located on the southern shore of the Arabian Gulf. Dubai city is a busy urban area but, outside the city itself, it is a sparsely populated desert area.

Dubai has a sub-tropical, arid climate. Rainfall is infrequent and irregular, falling only on about five days per year. The mean daily temperature maximum is 30°C in January rising to over 40°C in July.

Dubai's growing tourist industry now makes up more than 30 per cent of Dubai's GDP. Hotels and apartments recorded 6.5 million guests in 2006, generating revenues of more than US$ 3 billion. In a short period of time tourism has transformed an area of desert into one of the world's top tourist destinations of the 21st century.

A Where is Dubai?

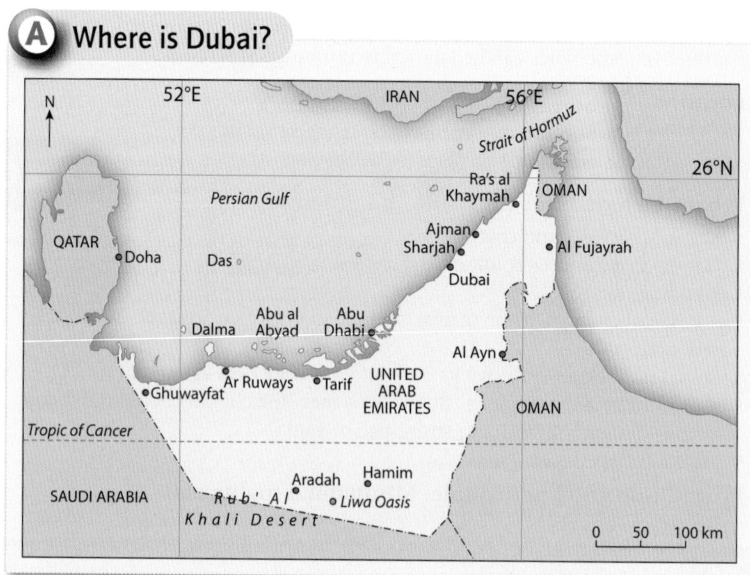

Task 1

Study **Source A** and an atlas.

a Describe the location of Dubai.

b Explain why Dubai is perfectly positioned to attract tourists from all parts of the world.

B Dubai – a growing destination for tourists

C What the brochure says ...

Wild Wadi Waterpark is a water theme park that covers an area of 5 hectares and comprises 24 adrenaline-pumping state-of-the-art rides and slides.

This water park was designed like an Arabian wadi (oasis) with characters from Arabian folklore. Once you enter the Wild Wadi water theme park, you will be given access to all the water rides, as well as the use of rubber rings, lifejackets and body boards. The water park has 90 lifeguards on duty, keeping you safe while you are having fun. Wild Wadi's rides suit people of all ages, making it a favourite water sports area in Dubai.

Dubai Desert Safari is the most exciting and most popular tour in Dubai. You will experience a thrilling drive in the sand dunes and enjoy a great dinner and live belly dance in a desert camp outside Dubai. Desert Safari in Dubai begins with a drive in a 4 by 4 vehicle driven by an expert driver. Once in the desert, enjoy the ride on a camel and go wadi-bashing or sand-skiing. Take a trip to the local Bedouin village to look at the traditional desert life.

Ski Dubai is the first indoor ski resort in the Middle East and offers an amazing snow setting to enjoy skiing, snowboarding and tobogganing or just playing in the snow. Young or old, there is something for everyone, from the beginner to the snow sport enthusiast.

Ski Dubai is a unique mountain-themed attraction that offers you the opportunity to enjoy real snow in Dubai all year round, bringing an Alpine experience to the middle of Dubai's desert. This monumental indoor snowdome has a capacity of 1500 guests and is one of the largest in the world.

D Ship of the Dubai desert

E Dubai skyline

F Comparing satellite images of Dubai

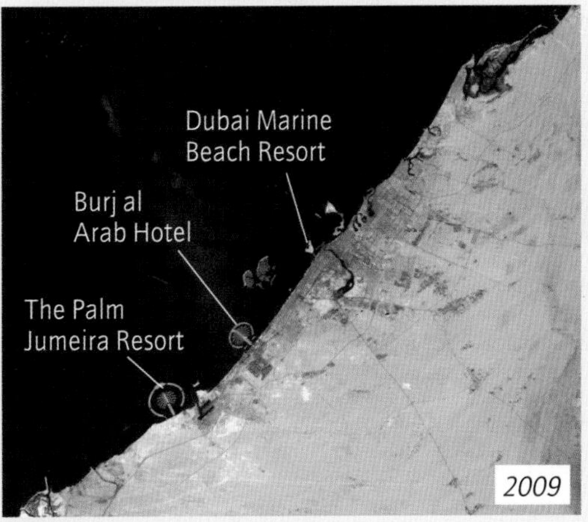

Sample case study question

Explain why the tourist industry has developed at a named location which you have studied.

Task 2

Study **Sources B–F**.

The growth of Dubai into one of the top tourist destinations in the world has been rapid and spectacular.

a In groups, prepare a presentation about the attractions for tourists in Dubai.

b Suggest the impacts on people and the natural environment. Further information and images can be obtained by carrying out research on the internet.

Energy supply and demand

A Energy resources – what's being used?

Oil provides 37% of the world's energy.

Coal provides 25% of the world's energy.

Natural gas provides 23% of the world's energy.

Nuclear power provides 6% of the world's energy.

Non-renewable resources	Renewable resources
The most important of these are oil, coal and natural gas. These are also **fossil fuels** as they are derived from the remains of plants and animals that have been buried and fossilised over thousands of years. They are **non-renewable** resources as there is a limited amount, so they are not sustainable. Nuclear power is also non-renewable. It uses plutonium or uranium – both fixed resources.	These can be used continuously and will not run out unless people interfere with nature – they are sustainable. They include geothermal supplies, wind, HEP, solar energy, bio-fuels, wave and tidal energy. Removing trees for fuelwood can be **renewable** if reforestation restores the forests; if this does not happen they become non-renewable sources.

Using fossil fuels ...

People's use of energy resources has changed over time. Up to the 18th century wood-burning provided most of the world's energy. With the Industrial Revolution affecting western Europe and the USA in the 19th century, coal became the most used energy source. The 20th century saw the rise of transport and industry, which required large amounts of fuel, usually oil. In the 21st century oil is the most sought-after source. Because only a few countries have oil supplies, and so dictate who gets it at what price, many countries are searching for oil reserves of their own or looking at alternative ways of meeting their energy demand.

B World fossil fuel energy producers, 2007

Top 6 oil producers	Million tonnes	Top 6 coal producers	Million tonnes	Top 6 gas producers	Million m^3
Russia	487	China	2 549	Russia	650 993
Saudi Arabia	483	USA	981	USA	546 140
USA	310	India	452	Canada	183 395
Iran	218	Australia	323	Iran	106 693
China	188	South Africa	244	Norway	90 839
Mexico	173	Russia	241	Algeria	89 970

C World energy use, 2007

Energy resource	% global use
Oil	37.0
Coal	25.0
Natural gas	23.0
Nuclear	6.0
Fuelwood	4.0
HEP	3.0
Solar	0.5
Wind	0.3
Geothermal	0.2
Waves/Tides	0.1
Others	0.9

Task 1

Study **Source A**.

a Name **three** non-renewable sources of energy. Why are they non-renewable?
b Name **three** renewable sources of energy. Why are they renewable?
c Suggest why many countries are developing renewable energy resources.

Task 2

Study **Source B**.

a Represent this data on an outline world map. Add a title and key.
b Describe the global distribution of fossil fuel energy production.
c List countries that are in the top six for all four types of energy production.
d Suggest why environmentalists are concerned about China's energy production.

Task 3

Study **Source C**.

a Draw a graph to represent this data.
b What percentage of the world's energy use was accounted for by non-renewable resources in 2007?
c Which **two** renewable energy resources are used the most?
d Find out how the types of energy used in your country compare with the world pattern. Explain any similarities and any differences.

More renewables needed ...

Renewable energy resources provide less than 10 per cent of the energy used in the world. Responsible governments have been pursuing policies to increase the use of renewable energy resources for a number of reasons.

- High carbon emissions from non-renewable sources are thought to be causing global warming.
- Oil prices are rising and countries with little oil are dependent on the few that have it.
- Renewable resources are cost-effective and have low carbon emissions.

European Union (EU) leaders agreed in March 2007 that 20 per cent of the Union's energy should come from renewable fuels by 2020.

D One alternative: geothermal energy

Australia Looks for Power from Hot Rocks

A small bleak township in Australia's outback is sitting on a source of energy that could power the nation for thousands of years. Deep beneath the tiny community of Innamincka lie the world's hottest rocks which could provide geothermal energy.

'Hot rocks' are created in granite that is heated naturally by decay of its elements. Water will be pumped down 4 km to rocks that are 300 °C. The hot water recovered can be used for heating or steam can generate electricity. The energy providers expect to produce 10 000 megawatts – the equivalent of up to 15 coal-fired power stations – from this area. While there are few carbon emissions and the power plant has little impact on the environment, there is one problem. The national electricity grid is 450 km away!

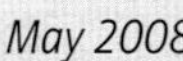

May 2008

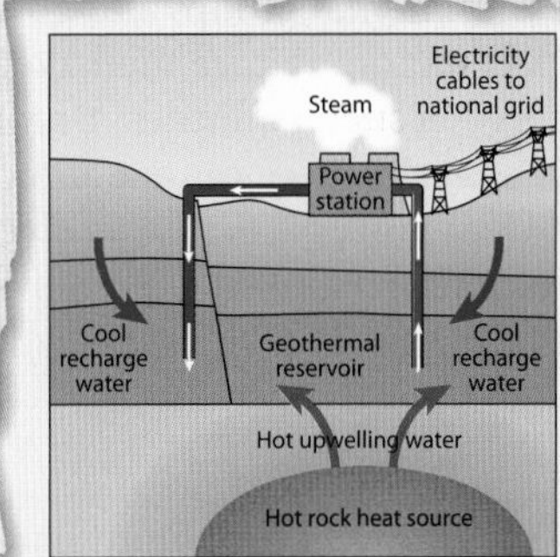
Electricity cables to national grid
Steam
Power station
Cool recharge water
Geothermal reservoir
Cool recharge water
Hot upwelling water
Hot rock heat source

E Another alternative – biogas

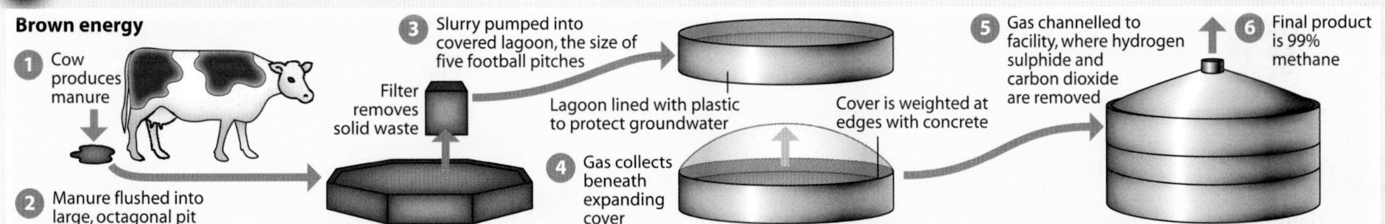
Brown energy
1 Cow produces manure
2 Manure flushed into large, octagonal pit
Filter removes solid waste
3 Slurry pumped into covered lagoon, the size of five football pitches
Lagoon lined with plastic to protect groundwater
Cover is weighted at edges with concrete
4 Gas collects beneath expanding cover
5 Gas channelled to facility, where hydrogen sulphide and carbon dioxide are removed
6 Final product is 99% methane

Cattle Have Power Too!

It's not so much green energy as brown power: a dairy farm in Fresno, California has found a new way to generate electricity for houses. It uses a vat of liquid cow dung, 10 metres deep and as large as five football pitches. As cow dung decomposes it produces methane, a greenhouse gas more damaging than carbon dioxide. Scientists say that, if treated, it can produce renewable natural gas. This could be used instead of coal to power electricity plants. One single cow's dung can produce about 100 watts of power. California's government has ordered energy companies to make renewable energy at least 20 per cent of their electricity supplies by 2010.

March 2008

Task 4

Choose **Source D or E**. For the source you choose:

- name the place and type of renewable energy resource in the article
- explain how energy can be created from this resource
- suggest **one** advantage and **one** disadvantage of using this renewable energy resource.

Task 5

Study **Source F**.

a List the different types of renewable energy resource being used in the Navarre region of Spain.

b 'I think the model we have here in Navarre is perfectly transferable to other countries.' Jose Javier Armendariz, Industry Minister

To what extent might this be true for the country you live in?

F Several alternatives – wind, solar and hydro-power

Renewable Energy – An Environmentalist's Dream

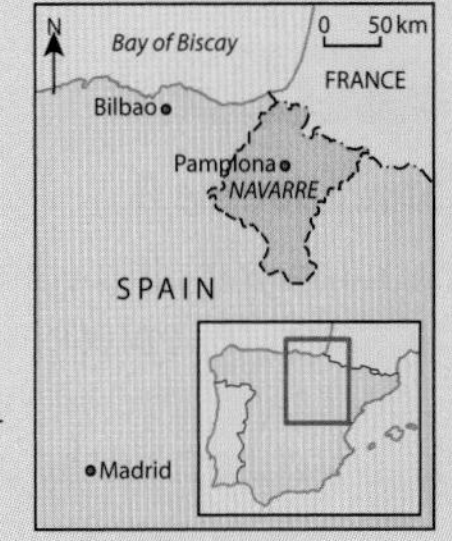
N
Bay of Biscay
0 50 km
FRANCE
Bilbao
Pamplona
NAVARRE
SPAIN
Madrid

It sounds like an environmentalist's dream: a rural area that generates its electricity from nothing more polluting than sun, wind and hay. But that is exactly what the Spanish region of Navarre hopes to achieve within a few years. The region gets almost 70% of its electricity from renewable resources; by 2010 this should rise to 75%. Navarre is a sparsely populated region of fewer than 600 000 people but is connected to the Spanish national grid. It can draw on gas, coal and nuclear power through the grid when the wind does not blow or the sun shine. There are 1100 wind turbines in the region. More than 55% of the region's electricity comes from wind power. Navarre has also built several solar farms which turn sunlight into electricity. It also has a biomass plant that generates power from straw and mini hydro-electric plants that generate electricity using local river flow. Spain is a world leader in renewables – it produces more than 21% of its electricity from these resources and plans to reach 30% by 2010.

June 2007

Fuelwood in D.R. Congo

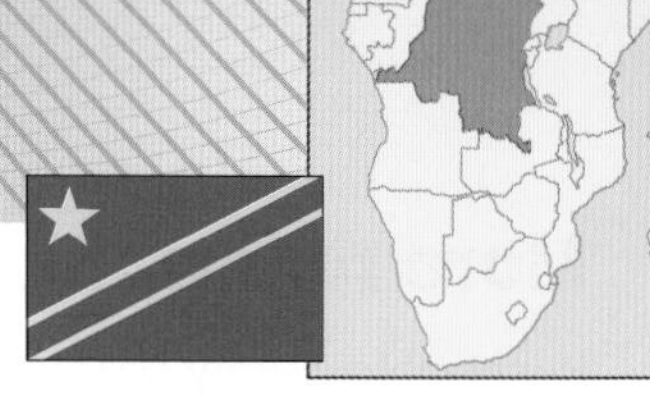

A fuelwood crisis

At least 2.6 million people in LEDCs – 40 per cent of the world's population – rely on fuelwood to cook and heat their homes. While much of this is fallen branches and dead wood, demand exceeds supply in many countries so people cut down trees to survive. The consequences of continued deforestation are major. Many environmental groups and governments are looking for ways to slow down deforestation, reduce fuelwood demand and provide alternative sources of energy in such countries. Unfortunately many have little choice. If fossil fuels are available they cannot afford to mine them, or they lack the technology. Nuclear power is too expensive. HEP is only possible if there are large amounts of precipitation and suitable geology. Fuelwood is the only choice for many people in LEDCs such as the Democratic Republic of Congo (D.R. Congo).

A Where is fuelwood used?

% of total fuelwood used

Asia and Pacific | Africa | North America | South America | Europe

0 10 20 30 40 50 60 70 80 90 100

B Will demand go down?

Projections of fuelwood consumption in developing regions, 2000–30

	2000	2010	2020	2030
South-east Asia	762	697	620	546
Africa	440	485	526	545
South America	100	107	115	122
World	*1302*	*1289*	*1261*	*1213*

Figures in million cubic metres of wood

Task 1

Study **Source A**.

a How dependent are LEDCs on fuelwood for cooking and heating?

b What percentage of the world's fuelwood is used in:
- Asia and the Pacific
- Africa?

c Suggest reasons why the type of energy used varies globally.

Task 2

Study **Source B**.

a Draw a multiple line graph to represent this data.

b Describe how the overall fuelwood consumption is expected to change between 2000 and 2030. Suggest reasons for this change.

c Which developing areas are expected to increase fuelwood consumption? Suggest reasons for this.

Task 3

Study **Source C**.

a Describe how the system works when it is in balance.

b What other sources of fuel are used once the fuelwood has gone?

c How do these uses affect the soil and nutrient cycle?

d How are people affected when fuelwood supplies are used up?

C Environmental issues

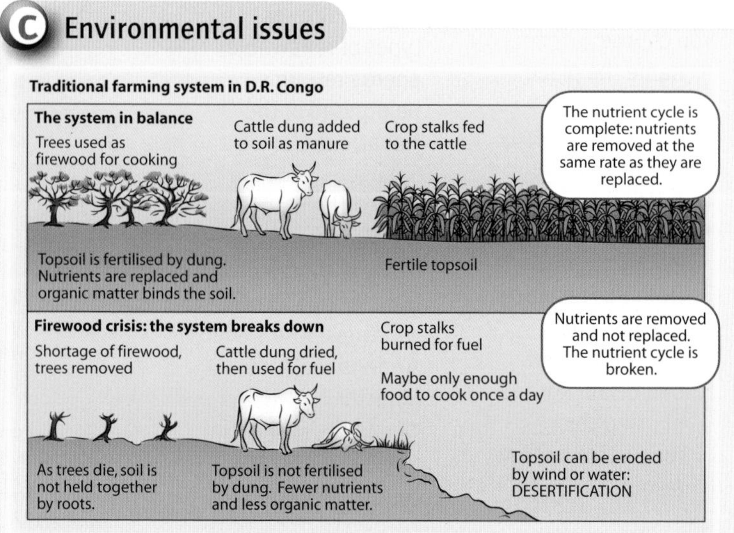
Traditional farming system in D.R. Congo
The system in balance
Trees used as firewood for cooking
Cattle dung added to soil as manure
Crop stalks fed to the cattle
The nutrient cycle is complete: nutrients are removed at the same rate as they are replaced.
Topsoil is fertilised by dung. Nutrients are replaced and organic matter binds the soil.
Fertile topsoil
Firewood crisis: the system breaks down
Shortage of firewood, trees removed
Cattle dung dried, then used for fuel
Crop stalks burned for fuel
Maybe only enough food to cook once a day
Nutrients are removed and not replaced. The nutrient cycle is broken.
As trees die, soil is not held together by roots.
Topsoil is not fertilised by dung. Fewer nutrients and less organic matter.
Topsoil can be eroded by wind or water: DESERTIFICATION

Fuel and fighting means deforestation

D.R. Congo has suffered decades of economic mismanagement and 80 per cent of the people live in poverty. Commercial logging by foreign companies had already removed much forest before a civil war began in 1998, when they left. However, deforestation continues as many villagers have been made landless and, along with refugees, have been forced into the forests to survive. Seventy per cent of the population rely on subsistence farming and on collecting fuelwood and charcoal from the forest. Clearance for agriculture and hunting bush meat has also contributed to forest loss. The country has many rare species of wildlife, most living in the 18 protected rainforest areas, one of which is the Virunga National Park close to the Ugandan border where the endangered mountain gorilla lives. Unfortunately the government cannot monitor the forest as the rebels holding it are supported by Uganda.

D Africa's fuelwood crisis

Fuelwood consumption as a percentage of total energy use

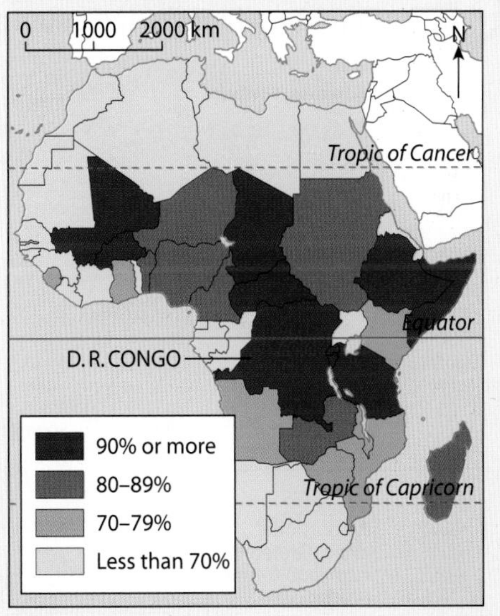

Task 4

Study **Source D** and an atlas.

a Use an atlas to name the countries that rely on fuelwood for 90 per cent or more of their total energy use.
b Describe and explain the distribution of countries where 70 per cent or more of their total energy use depends on fuelwood.
c What percentage of D.R. Congo's energy use depends on fuelwood?
d Why does the location of D.R. Congo make it difficult to change from fuelwood to other types of energy use?

E The supply chain for fuelwood

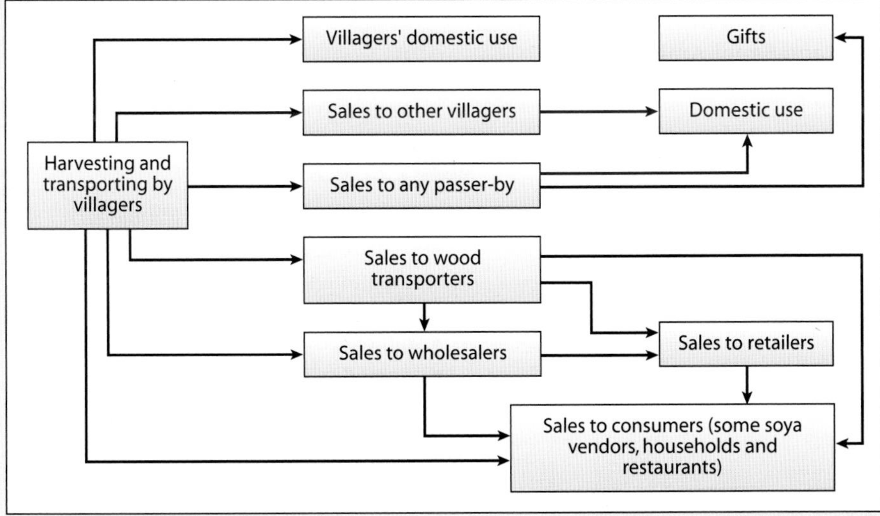

A family needs about 3 kg of firewood – a few sticks – per day to provide cooking and heat. As there is less wood now, villagers have to walk up to 7 km to find it. Around 70 per cent of wood is generally transported by cart and 30 per cent on people's heads – usually women's. The wood is tied in bundles of round branches or split logs with branches. The smallest bundles weigh 6 kg and the largest 19 kg. What is left over is sold locally or taken to towns like Kinshasa. There it is used for heating, cooking and in small enterprises, e.g. brick kilns, bakeries and food processing. Buying fuelwood can use up 30 per cent of family income. An alternative fuel is dung but that deprives the fields of fertiliser, reducing crop yields.

Task 5

Study **Source E**.

a How is fuelwood transported by villagers?
b List **three** different groups of people who buy fuelwood from the villagers.
c Apart from heating and cooking, how else can fuelwood be of use?

Task 6

a How has the civil war caused the rainforest and its wildlife to be under threat?
b Discuss why it is difficult to balance the fuelwood needs of people with conservation in D.R. Congo.

Oil in Saudi Arabia

A The top ten oil producing countries, 2007

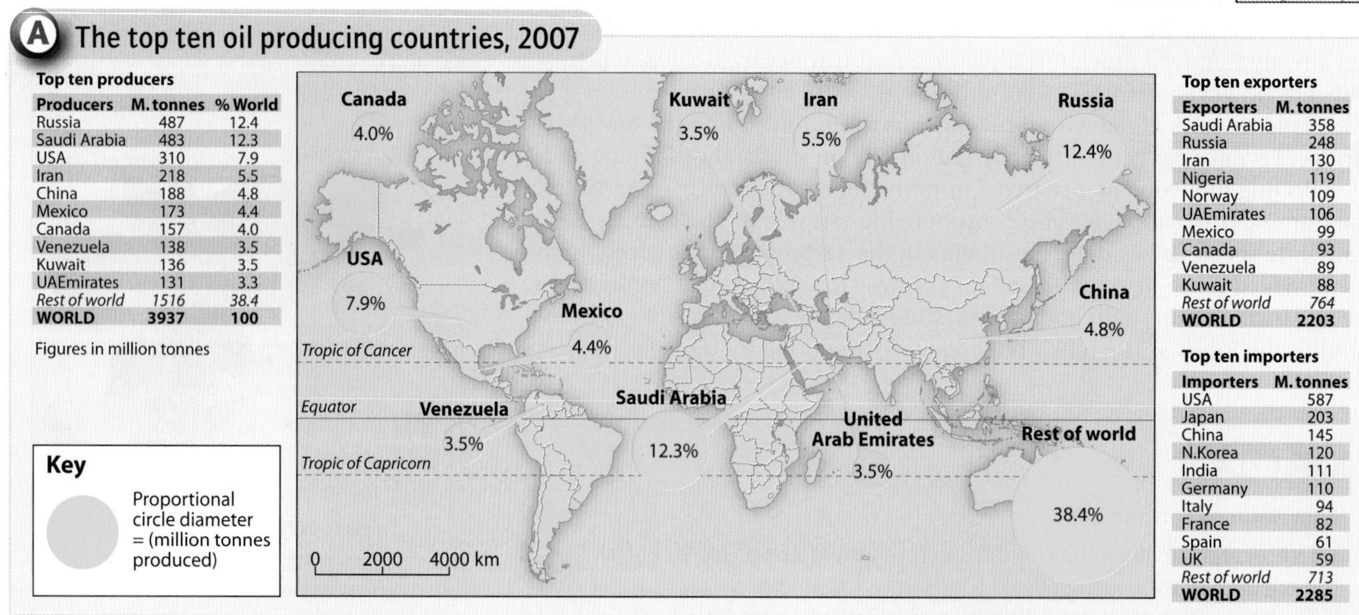

Top ten producers

Producers	M. tonnes	% World
Russia	487	12.4
Saudi Arabia	483	12.3
USA	310	7.9
Iran	218	5.5
China	188	4.8
Mexico	173	4.4
Canada	157	4.0
Venezuela	138	3.5
Kuwait	136	3.5
UAEmirates	131	3.3
Rest of world	*1516*	*38.4*
WORLD	**3937**	**100**

Figures in million tonnes

Top ten exporters

Exporters	M. tonnes
Saudi Arabia	358
Russia	248
Iran	130
Nigeria	119
Norway	109
UAEmirates	106
Mexico	99
Canada	93
Venezuela	89
Kuwait	88
Rest of world	*764*
WORLD	**2203**

Top ten importers

Importers	M. tonnes
USA	587
Japan	203
China	145
N.Korea	120
India	111
Germany	110
Italy	94
France	82
Spain	61
UK	59
Rest of world	*713*
WORLD	**2285**

Oil – a prized possession

Before the late 19th century there was little demand for oil. The first oil well was dug in 1859 in Pennsylvania in the USA; since then oil has become the most desired energy resource of the 21st century, mostly due to developments in industry and transport that need oil or oil products.

Since 1973 oil prices have risen rapidly as the oil-producing countries, many of which were LEDCs, realised the value of the product to MEDCs. Some individuals, and countries such as Kuwait and Saudi Arabia have become very rich by exporting oil. These countries do not need to develop their economy further.

B The Middle East – a global oil power

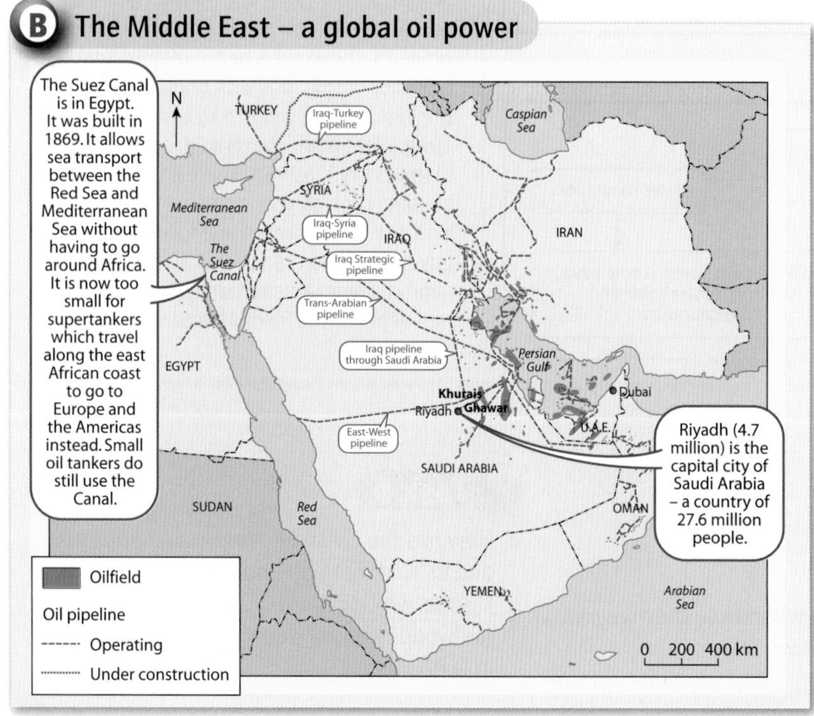

Task 1

Study **Source A**.

a Describe the distribution of the top ten oil producers.

b Which countries export more than 50 per cent of their production? Suggest why.

c Which countries in the top ten producers also need to import oil? Suggest why.

Task 2

a On an outline map of the Middle East add the following from **Source B**:
- the names of all countries and sea areas
- oilfields
- named oil pipelines
- the Suez Canal.

b For all the Middle East countries named in **Source A**, add divided bar graphs to your outline to show how much oil they produce and how much they export.

c From **Source A** calculate the percentage of oil produced that is exported by **each** of:
- Saudi Arabia
- UAE
- Kuwait
- Iran.

d 'All four of these countries (see **c**) export more than 59 per cent of oil produced.' 'None of these countries imports oil.' Suggest reasons for these facts.

Saudi Arabia – supplying oil to the world

In 2007 the countries of the Persian Gulf (Bahrain, Iran, Iraq, Kuwait, Qatar, Saudi Arabia and the United Arab Emirates) produced about 30 per cent of the world's oil. Saudi Arabia is the world's most important oil producer. It contains over 20 per cent of known oil reserves and has a central strategic location near to international shipping lanes to distribute oil around the world. It controls international oil prices simply by balancing international oil demand with supply.

C Saudi Aramco – a responsible company?

Saudi Arabia's oil production and refining are dominated by the state-owned company Saudi Aramco. It is the world's largest oil company in terms of oil produced and known reserves that are under its control. Consequently it has a major responsibility for showing environmental awareness in its operations.

Saudi Aramco's Environmental Policies

1 Preventing water pollution
- All tanker movements are handled by trained harbour pilots with powerful tugboats to safeguard terminal facilities.
- Extensive measures are taken to avoid oil spills. Aramco has never had one but regular drills take place so staff are ready.
- Control centres with emergency equipment, dedicated airplanes and surveillance are ready to provide instant responses to spillages.
- Strict loading procedures are followed.
- Water quality is assessed through sampling.

2 Preventing land pollution
- On-shore landfills are used for disposing of solid waste.
- Industrial waste is separated depending on its hazard risk.
- Medical waste is sterilized before disposal.
- A waste minimisation programme reduces emissions and lowers costs.

3 Preventing air pollution
- Air monitoring stations measure sulphur dioxide, carbon monoxide and other parameters.

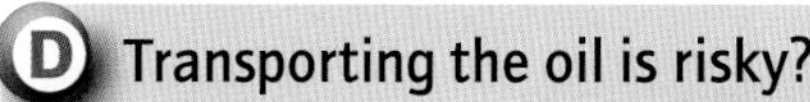

D Transporting the oil is risky?

High Price of Oil Leads to Piracy on the High Seas

Somali pirates hijacked a Saudi Arabian-owned supertanker off the east coast of Africa at around 07.15 on 10 November 2008. The tanker, *Sirius Star*, was carrying crude oil worth at least $100 million when pirates scaled the 10-metre side of the ship. There have been at least 60 incidents in 2008 in the Gulf of Aden between Yemen and Somalia. About 11% of the world's oil carried at sea travels through the Gulf. It is thought the rising crude oil price is responsible for the pirates' action as they can ransom the tanker back for a higher price from its owners. At worst they could threaten to create a disastrous oil spillage or accidentally run aground in coastal waters far too shallow for the supertanker. Ransoms paid for the return of ships average about $1 million.

November 2008

E An expensive solution?

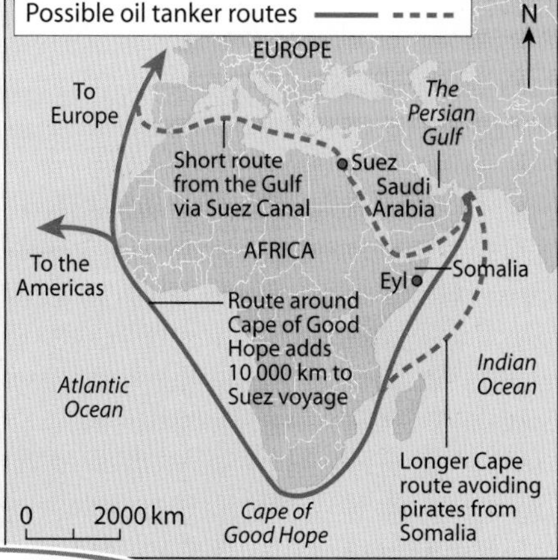

With over 60 hijacks a year taking place, we have decided to take the longer, wider route away from Africa and the Somali coast to deliver oil to Europe and the Americas. This route around the Cape of Good Hope will increase fuel costs and delay delivery by at least three weeks as well as increase any risk of a spillage at sea but it will ensure supplies do arrive. Unfortunately this will raise the price of oil. We cannot continue to pay ransoms to these pirates as insurance companies are raising the premiums we pay because of the increased risk of losing a load.

Task 3

Study **Source C**.

a How large is Saudi Aramco?

b Give **one** example of how the company tries to prevent each of the following:
- water pollution
- land pollution
- air pollution.

Task 4

Study **Sources D and E**.

a Suggest how rising oil prices are linked to the hijacking of supertankers by Somali pirates.

b What problems might this create for:
- the environment
- the owners of supertankers?

c Discuss how you would resolve the problem of Somali pirates hijacking oil supertankers for a ransom.

Renewable energy in Iceland

Iceland – a model for the world?

Renewable energy, while supported by many nations at international conferences, still plays only a small part in the global energy mix. However, Iceland has reached the stage where 70 per cent of its energy needs are met by its own sustainable energy resources. The remaining 30 per cent consists of imported fossil fuels for motor vehicles and ships. It is the only western country that produces all its electricity from emission-free and sustainable natural resources in the form of geothermal power and HEP.

A Iceland sits on a 'hotspot'!

Iceland, a country of just 300 000 people, is located on the Mid-Atlantic Ridge. This is a constructive plate boundary between the North American and Eurasian plates. These are moving apart at about 2 cm a year, creating volcanic activity and rising heat in the gap. Precipitation here is also high with over 800 mm per year. Consequently Iceland has a wealth of geothermal sources and water for HEP. Three-quarters of its population live in the south-west (with 60 per cent in the capital Reykjavik) where most geothermal sources are found.

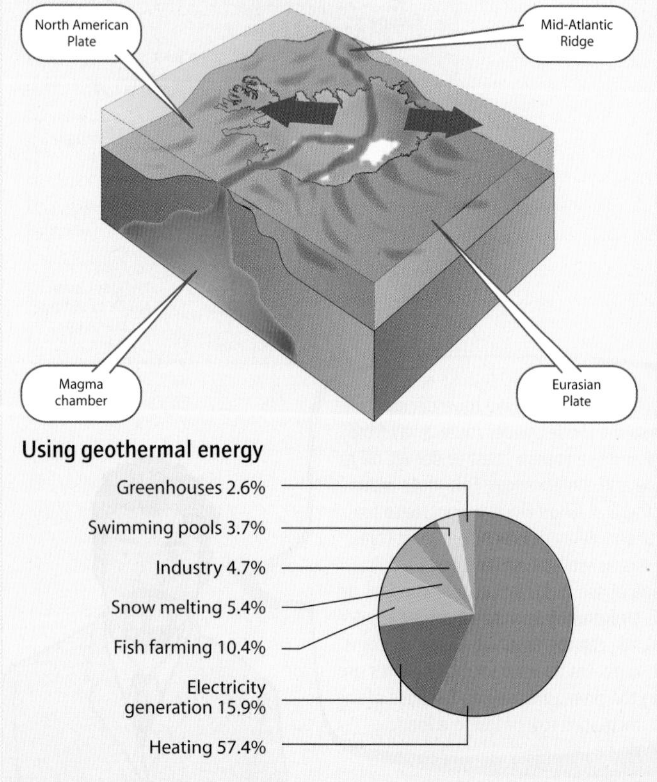

B Volcanic zones and geothermal areas

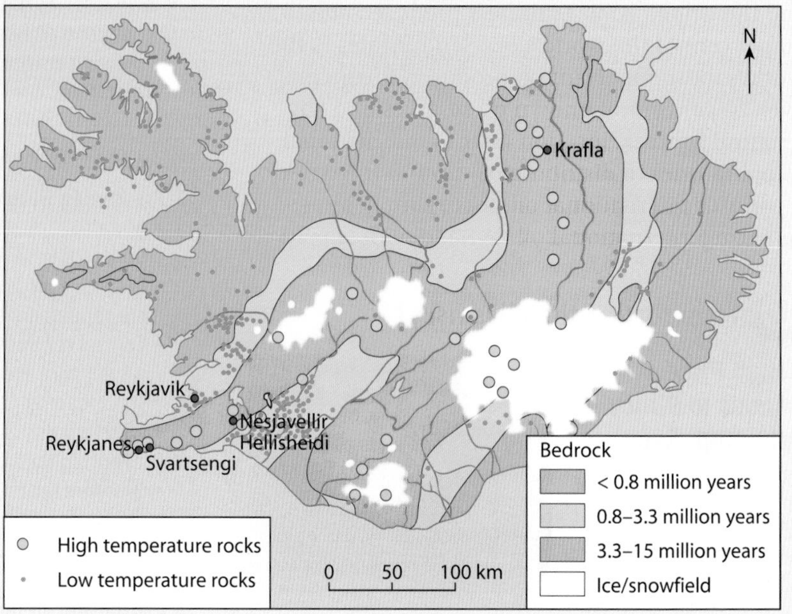

Low temperature activity – located away from the main volcanic zone close to the surface at about 1 km depth. Rock temperature varies from 50° to 150°C. Water from precipitation is heated by the rock to create hot, boiling springs at the surface.
High temperature activity – located within the active volcanic zones at a depth below 1 km where temperatures are at least 200°C. Here groundwater exists in deep reservoirs so hot water is not seen at the surface but steam is.

Task 1

Study **Source A**.

a With the help of an atlas and the diagram, describe the location of Iceland. Refer to lines of latitude and longitude, the Mid-Atlantic Ridge and diverging plates.

b Explain why Iceland can create energy from geothermal and water sources but is not able to create energy using fossil fuels of its own, or solar power.

c List in order (by percentage) the different uses of geothermal energy.

d What is the major use of geothermal energy? Suggest why it is used to melt snow.

Task 2

Study **Source B**.

a Describe the location of Reykjavik. How does the city get most of its energy?

b Where are most of the high-temperature geothermal sites?

c How does this compare with the distribution of low-temperature geothermal sites?

Hydro-electric power (HEP)

HEP is the source of 60 per cent of Iceland's electricity, with geothermal sources producing 40 per cent. Landsvirkjun is the company responsible for producing HEP in Iceland. It was founded in 1965 and is now run as a state-owned national energy provider. Six HEP stations have been constructed since 1965. Today the company not only produces electricity for Iceland but has a surplus that is exported to earn foreign currency. The reservoirs and HEP stations are built on glacial rivers which are largely fed by snowmelt. Some of the snowmelt is activated by using geothermal energy.

C Where are Iceland's HEP stations?

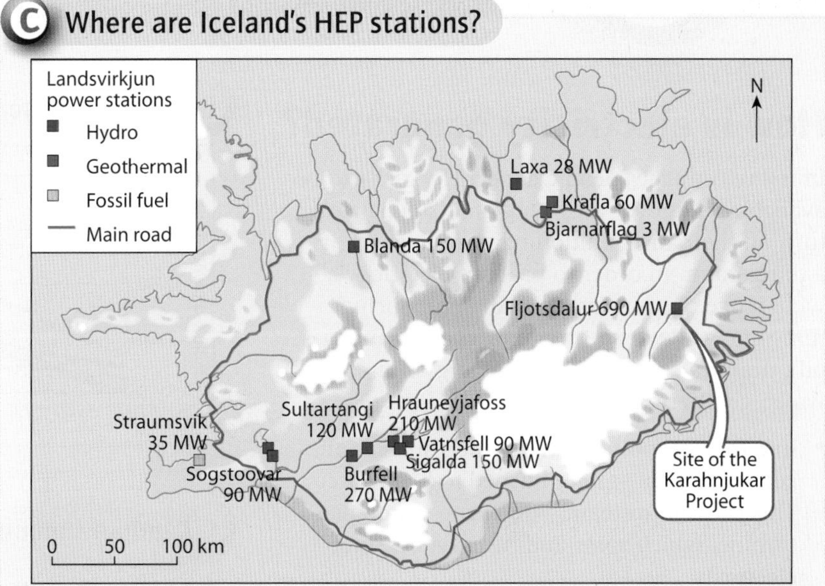

D The Karahnjukar project

The largest HEP station was completed in 2009 in the north-east of Iceland at Fijotsdalur away from the populated south-west. The Karahnjukar project is the largest construction project ever built in the country. It involves damming two glacial rivers that flow from the Vatnajökull glacier then creating the Hálslón reservoir covering 57 km² behind the dams. The project created controversy because it is in one of Europe's largest wilderness areas with 2000 reindeer grazing here. The diversion of water plus submergence of land would also remove habitats for birds such as the pink-footed goose and harbour seals which breed on the river deltas. The government built it for Alcoa (Aluminium Company of America) which wanted to move here because of pollution problems created by its US plant. Iceland offered cheap electricity and a clean environment. It will provide 750 jobs plus foreign currency for Iceland, which has little industry.

The greenhouse effect of producing 1 kg of aluminium

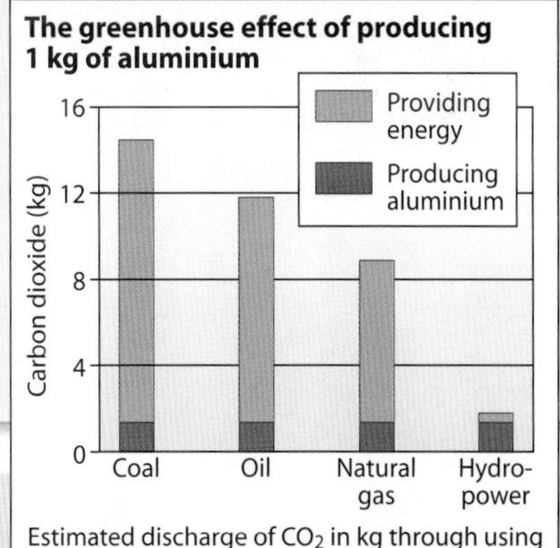

Estimated discharge of CO_2 in kg through using varying energy sources for energy production, calculated per kg of processed aluminium

Task 4

Study **Source C**.

a What is the range of capacities (in megawatts) of Landsvirkjun's HEP stations? Describe and explain their distribution. Explain why many are close to ice caps.

b Why are reservoirs needed as part of HEP stations?

Sample case study question

For a named country you have studied, describe the main types of energy resources used.

Task 5

Study **Source D**.

a Draw an outline labelled sketch of the photograph.

b Give **two** advantages and **two** disadvantages of the Karahnjukar project for Iceland.

c Compare the amount of carbon dioxide produced in making 1 kg of aluminium using coal, oil or natural gas, and using HEP. Why is Iceland an attractive place for Alcoa to move to from the USA?

d Why is it important to reduce the amount of carbon dioxide in the atmosphere?

TOPIC 28 Generating electricity

How is electricity generated?

In many countries people expect electricity to be available whenever they plug in an appliance, turn on their air-conditioning system, or open a refrigerator. In order to produce electricity a wide range of sources are used. These include non-renewable fossil fuels (e.g. coal, natural gas, oil), uranium, and renewable energy sources (e.g. water, geothermal, solar, wind).

- In a thermal power station, fuels such as oil, coal or natural gas are burned to heat water. This turns into steam, which goes through a turbine, which spins and turns, generating electricity.
- In a nuclear power station, nuclear reactions using uranium heat water, which turns into steam to spin the turbine.
- In a geothermal power station water is pumped down into hot volcanic rocks. Steam comes out and spins the turbine.
- When electricity is generated by wind, the wind pushes against the turbine blades, causing the rotor to spin.
- In a hydro-electric power station the turbines are turned by fast-flowing water.

B Electricity generation by fuel worldwide

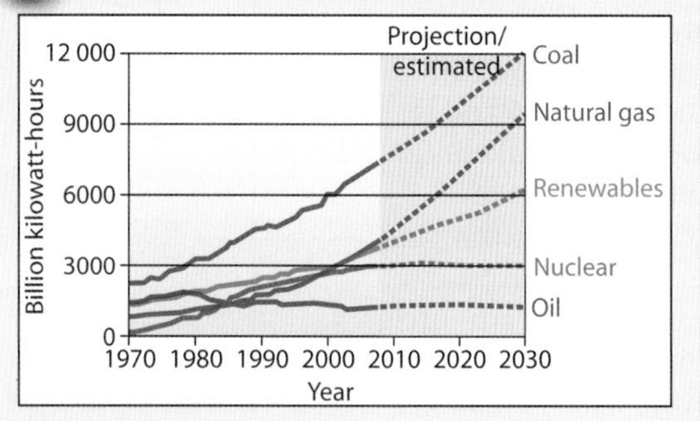

C Indian summer!

India Swelters as More Power Cuts Loom

DELHI – As Indians swelter in the first big power cuts of summer, they know that it is only going to get worse in the hot months ahead. Already India's capital has called on residents to run just one air-conditioner as temperatures soar. The appeal comes as residents endure cuts lasting up to 10 hours in parts of Delhi. Over the last decade, power generation has increased by 5 but demand has risen by around 12 per cent. Businesses have worked around the shortfall by building their own generating plants. Tempers, meanwhile, are already fraying over the latest outages. In Uttar Pradesh, people went on the rampage on Friday over power cuts and at least 18 were arrested as protesters stormed electricity stations and government offices. Adding to the nation's woes is the fact that as many as 47 new power plants are behind schedule.

May 2006

A Different uses of electricity

Task 1

Study **Source A**.

Give **four** examples of ways in which electricity is used.

Task 2

Study **Source B**.

a How much electricity was generated in total by thermal power stations in 2010?

b By how much did the amount of electricity generated by coal increase between 1970 and 2010?

c Identify **three** changes that are likely to occur in the generation of electricity by 2030.

Task 3

Study **Source C**.

a Make a list of **five** different problems that the people in Delhi are likely to face as a result of power cuts.

b Explain why there are power blackouts in many cities in LEDCs.

Locating thermal power stations

Thermal power stations are generally located close to their source of fuel. For example, coal-fired power stations may be located on or near coalfields as coal is bulky, heavy and expensive to transport. Many have their own railway lines linked to mines in order to transport the coal. Power stations that are fired by oil or natural gas are located close to oil refineries or oil and gas pipelines. In some countries fossil fuels are imported so power stations are built close to major ports. The areas of flat land required for building thermal power stations may be found close to rivers, where the large quantities of water needed for cooling can be extracted from the river and waste water returned to it.

D A coal-fired thermal power station

Eggborough, UK

E Thermal power stations – advantages and disadvantages

Advantages	Disadvantages
Large amounts of electricity can be produced in one place.	Burning any fossil fuel produces carbon dioxide and sulphur dioxide, which contribute to the greenhouse effect and acid rain.
Transporting oil and gas to power stations is easy and cheap.	Mining, and the use of large areas of land for power stations, destroys natural vegetation and scars the landscape.
Gas-fired power stations are very efficient and can generate electricity at low cost.	Pollution of rivers may occur as a result of using large amounts of water for cooling.
A thermal power station can be built almost anywhere, so long as you can get large quantities of fuel to it.	Oil and gas stocks are running low. Their 'ownership' often leads to argument by the leading countries of the world.
They are less expensive to build than nuclear power stations.	Fossil fuels are non-renewable and increasing in cost.
They do not produce dangerous waste.	Transporting coal by lorry and train from the mine to the power station causes atmospheric pollution.

More coal-fired power stations in China

In the last six years the Chinese coal industry, with reserves put at more than 1 trillion tonnes, has doubled production to more than 1.2 billion tonnes a year. The country is now building 550 coal-fired power stations – opening at the equivalent of two a week. Between 2000 and 2005, electricity generation rose 150%.

Task 4

Study **Sources D and E**.

Draw a fully labelled sketch to show how a coal-fired power station may cause problems for local people and the natural environment.

Task 5

Study **Sources D–F.**

Working in groups, use the sources on these pages and carry out research to prepare a report on electricity generation in China. In your report you should:

- give the reasons why so many new coal-fired power stations have been built
- explain why many people in China and in other parts of the world are concerned about the increase in thermal power stations
- consider the advantages and disadvantages for China of using renewable energy sources (e.g. wind, solar and hydro-electric power) instead of building so many coal-fired power stations.

Electricity generation in France

How is electricity generated in France?

In 2006 France generated 574.5 billion kWh of electricity and used 482 billion kWh (6700 kWh per person), leaving a surplus for export.

France has 59 nuclear reactors operated by Electricité de France (EdF), which supply over 430 billion kWh per year of electricity – 78 per cent of the total generated there.

The present situation is due to the French government deciding in 1974, just after the first oil crisis, to expand the country's nuclear power capacity. This decision was taken because France had few energy resources and nuclear energy, with the fuel cost being a relatively small part of the overall cost, made good sense in reducing imports and achieving energy security.

The cost of electricity in France is low when compared with that in many other European countries. It also has an extremely low level of carbon dioxide emissions from electricity generation, as over 90 per cent of its electricity is generated in nuclear or hydro-electric power stations.

A Generating electricity in France

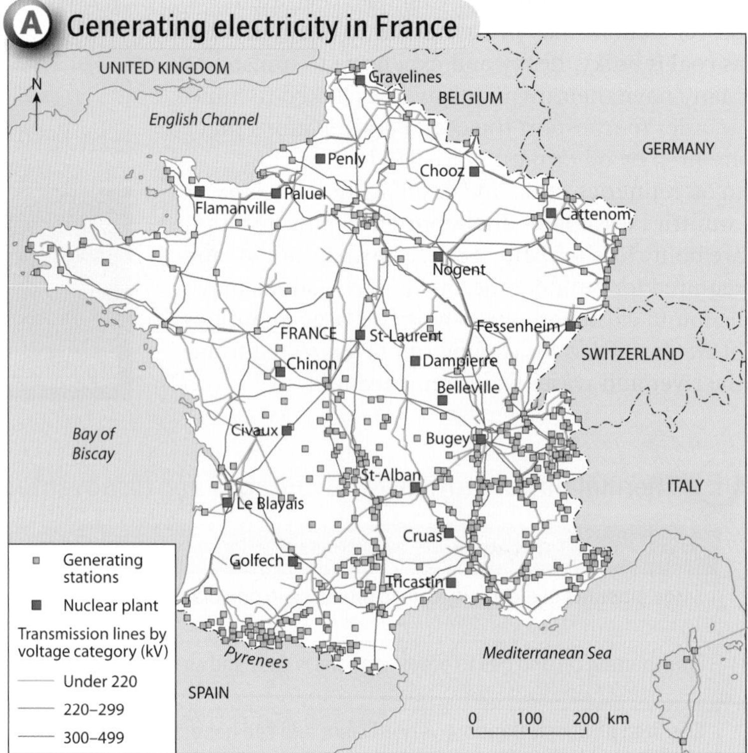

B Nuclear power in France

France Presses Ahead with Nuclear Power

1 May 2006 After the energy crisis of the 1970s, France invested heavily in nuclear facilities, and today the country is much less dependent on foreign oil.

On the coast of Normandy overlooking the English Channel, is the nuclear power plant at Flamanville. Its two reactors generate enough electricity for the entire regions of Normandy and Brittany. France's nuclear plants meet almost 80 per cent of its total electricity needs – and allow it to export power to Britain, Germany and Italy.

'France chose nuclear because we have no oil, gas or coal resources, and recent events have only reinforced the wisdom of our choice,' says Laurent Striker, senior vice-president at Electricité de France, the world's largest power company.

French environmentalists say the economic benefits of nuclear energy are far outweighed by its dangers and they say nuclear facilities are potential targets for terrorists.

Greenpeace activists recently surrounded and chained themselves to a truck transporting plutonium from the La Hague nuclear recycling facility to a burial site, as it stopped in the middle of a French town.

But the French government is determined to press on towards its goal of using nuclear power to achieve energy independence for France.

French President Jacques Chirac recently announced plans for yet another generation of nuclear power stations, which would come on line by 2020. Areva, the government-owned builder of nuclear power stations, and the French government are also selling French nuclear know-how to other countries, especially China.

Task 1

Study **Source A** and an atlas.

a Describe the distribution of power stations in France.

b Name a nuclear power station in France that is located:
- near to the Mediterranean coast
- close to the border with Belgium
- 160 km to the north of the Pyrenees.

c Explain why there are many hydro-electric power stations in south-east France.

Task 2

Study **Source B**.

a Explain why France produces most of its electricity from nuclear power stations.

b Carry out your own research to find out why some people protest against the use of nuclear power. Write a paragraph which a protestor against nuclear power might use to convince other people about its dangers.

La Rance tidal power station

La Rance tidal power station, opened in 1967, was the world's first tidal power station. It is located south of Dinard and Saint Malo, on the estuary of the river Rance, in Brittany. In spite of the high cost of the project, the plant's costs have now been recovered, and electricity production costs are lower than for nuclear power generation. There have been some environmental impacts. The barrage has caused silting of the estuary and affected the ecosystem. Sand-eels and plaice have disappeared, though sea bass and cuttlefish have returned to the river. The tidal power plant is now a tourist attraction which draws 200 000 visitors per year.

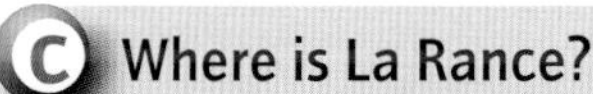

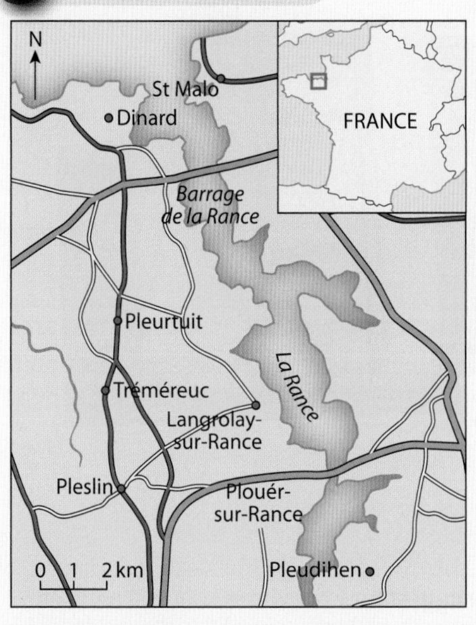

To create the power station a **barrage** was built across the estuary 750 metres long, from Brebis Point in the west to Briantais Point in the east. The tidal area of water behind the dam measures 22.5 km^2. The tidal range (the difference between high and low tides) averages 8 metres and reaches up to 13.5 metres. The plant consists of 24 large turbines which generate electricity whether the tide is going in or out. The power station generates enough energy to power 4 per cent of the homes in Brittany – equivalent to the consumption of a town the size of Rennes. A canal lock in the west end of the dam allows boats to pass through. A main road crosses the dam and allows vehicles to travel between Dinard and Saint-Malo. There is a bridge which may be raised to allow larger vessels to pass through.

E Tidal power – how does it work?

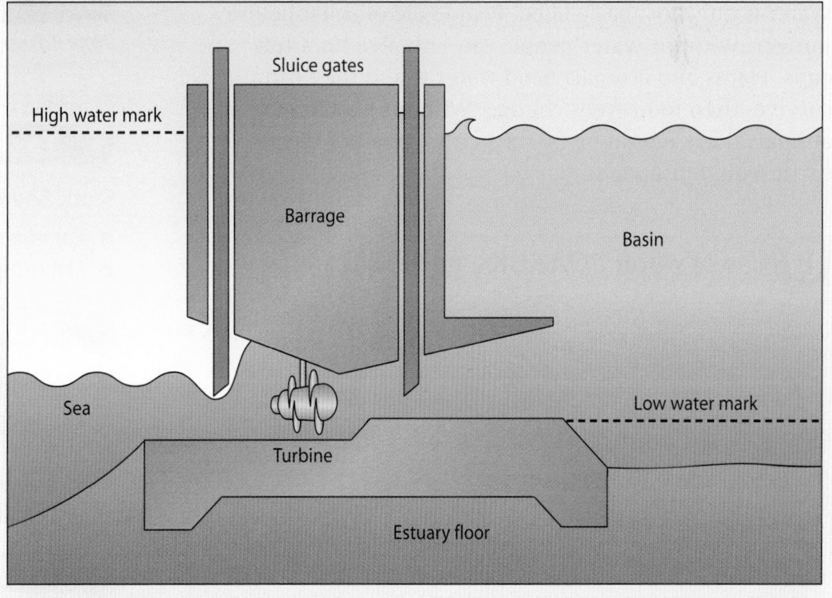

Study **Sources C, D and E**.

a Describe the location of La Rance tidal power station.

b Explain how electricity is generated at La Rance.

c When the power station was built in the 1960s it caused conflict in the area. Give **three** arguments which would have been used for building the power station and **three** against it.

Sample case study question

For a named power station you have studied, describe and explain its location.

TOPIC 29 Water

A Different uses of water

Sichuan Province, China

Water is important for plants and animals in ecosystems.

Ntalikwa village, Tanzania

Water is important for drinking and staying clean and healthy.

Lake Powell and Glen Canyon Dam, USA

Water power is important to generate energy.

Water is important for waste disposal.

Near Tozear, Tunisia

No water ... no life

Water is our most basic need. People die of thirst before hunger. Without water people can only live for a few days. Plants and animals need water too. If they cannot survive, then food webs change. Without plants and animals there would be no oxygen to breathe. Life on earth would disappear.

B Use of water in the UK – an MEDC

Where the water goes	Amount consumed (litres)
Flushing toilets / waste disposal	40
Washing and showers	36
Washing machines / dishwashers	32
Dripping taps / leakage	14
Drinking / cooking	6
Gardening / outside use	4
Car washing	2

Average daily consumption per person = 134 litres
This nearly equals 400 cans of cola!

Task 1

Study **Source A**.

a For each photo suggest how the water is, or will be, used.
b List other uses of water not shown in the photographs.

Task 2

Study **Source B**.

a Draw a graph to illustrate this data.
b How would the water use change in an LEDC?
c The average daily consumption per person in Ethiopia is only 4 litres. Suggest some problems this might cause.

Task 3

Look back through your day so far.

a Write a diary showing when and how you used water.
b Compare your diary with uses shown in **Source B**. List similarities and differences.

Water supply varies

The distribution of global rainfall varies. Countries that receive heavy rainfall may have a water surplus but suffer from floods. Countries that receive low amounts of rainfall may have a water deficit and suffer from drought. They may have to rely on a river flowing from an area of heavy rainfall through their dry country, for example the Nile as it flows through Egypt.

It is very difficult for people to influence their natural water supplies. However, now there is the technology to redistribute water surpluses to areas of water deficit – though this depends on having the money and expertise to do it. Large dams can store water in reservoirs and this can be transferred by lorry, pipeline or rivers to areas where demand is high. Large dams, however, are often controversial schemes.

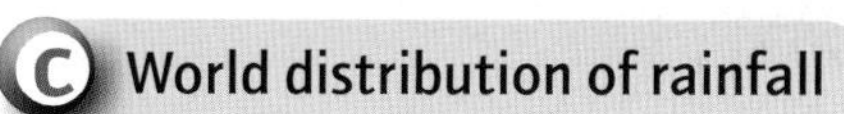

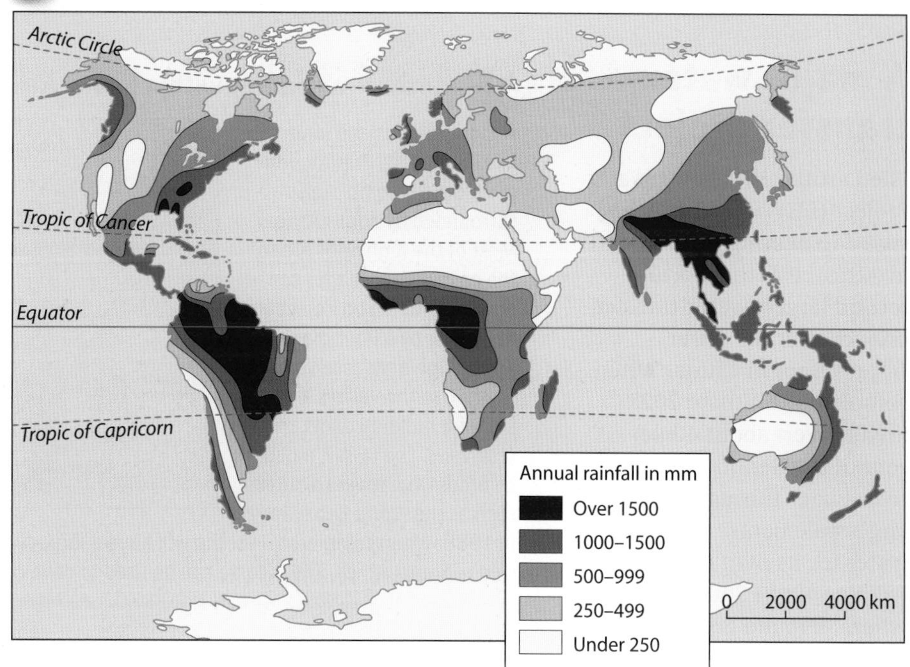

D Issues in transferring water

Spain Accused of Diverting Water Supplies from Rivers

Drought in Spain has forced some farmers to use sewage water to keep their crops alive in the worst drought in 60 years. The government has transferred clean water by pipeline from one of its largest rivers, the Tagus, to the Segura in Murcia to help farmers there. This has upset other provinces in Spain, such as Castilla La Mancha which now receives less. Portugal is also accusing Spain of transferring water from the river Douro which means they receive less. This action breaks an agreement between the countries signed in 1998.

June 2005

Burmese Dam Will Displace Thousands

Thousands of villagers could be displaced and a fragile ecosystem be destroyed by the Ta Sang hydro-electric power (HEP) project being built on the Salween river in Burma, claims the World Wildlife Fund (WWF). 'It is the only free-flowing river linking the Himalayan glaciers to the Andaman Sea,' a spokesman said. A Burmese official said the dam was in a remote area and few people would need relocating. The country needs water and electricity to meet growing demand.

April 2007

Water shortages likely to trigger wars

A struggle by nations to secure clean water sources could lead to water wars, the first Asia-Pacific Water Summit heard yesterday. This was especially true in Asia where high population growth, pollution and poor water management pose significant threats. If global warming continues, water shortages could trigger more wars. The Asia Development Bank (ADB) promised to double investment in Asian water projects to $2 billion per year to increase supply and encourage co-operation between countries instead of conflict.

December 2007

Task 4

Study **Source C**.

a Describe the distribution of areas with more than 1500 mm of rainfall per year. Refer to continents in your answer.

b Use an atlas to help you name **two** countries that may experience a water surplus. Explain your choices.

c Name **two** countries that may experience a water deficit. Why did you choose these?

Task 5

Choose **one** water transfer issue from **Source D**. For the issue you have chosen:

a Use an atlas to describe its location.

b Explain how and why the government is dealing with this water issue.

c Provide some arguments against the government's action.

d Why might water shortages trigger 'water wars' between neighbouring countries?

CASE STUDY 29 The Lesotho Highlands Water Project

A major water-transfer project

The Lesotho Highlands Water Project (LHWP) is the largest civil engineering project in Africa. It is the world's second largest water-transfer project after the Three Gorges Dam in China. When completed (estimate 2027), it will divert about 40 per cent of the Senqu/Orange river water through five large-scale dams. After taking water for its own use, much will be sold to South Africa where demand is greater than supply.

A Lesotho – a country within South Africa

A mountainous and land-locked country, the kingdom of Lesotho is completely surrounded by South Africa. Most of the highlands are to the east where villages can only be reached on horseback, on foot or by a light plane. These highlands receive heavy rainfall, so the valleys are ideal for building dams and reservoirs. The LHWP, aided by funds from several sources such as the World Bank, began in 1988. When completed, Lesotho will have a larger water supply than it needs. Surplus water can be sold to South Africa. The income can be used to develop its infrastructure and its economy.

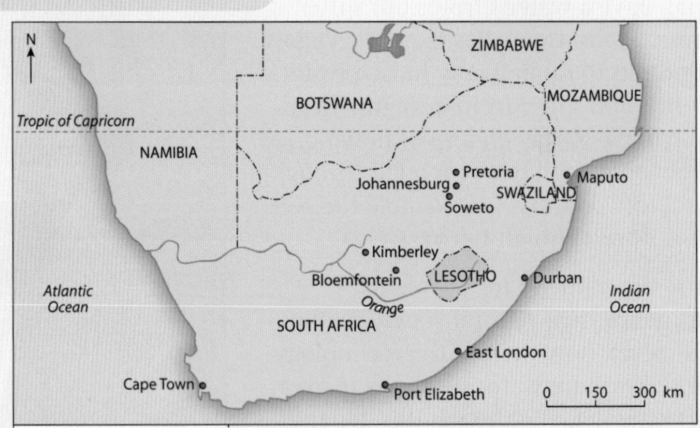

Task 1

Study **Source A**.

a Describe the location of Lesotho. Use distances and directions in your answer.

b Give **one** advantage and **one** disadvantage of the relief of Lesotho for development. Explain your choices.

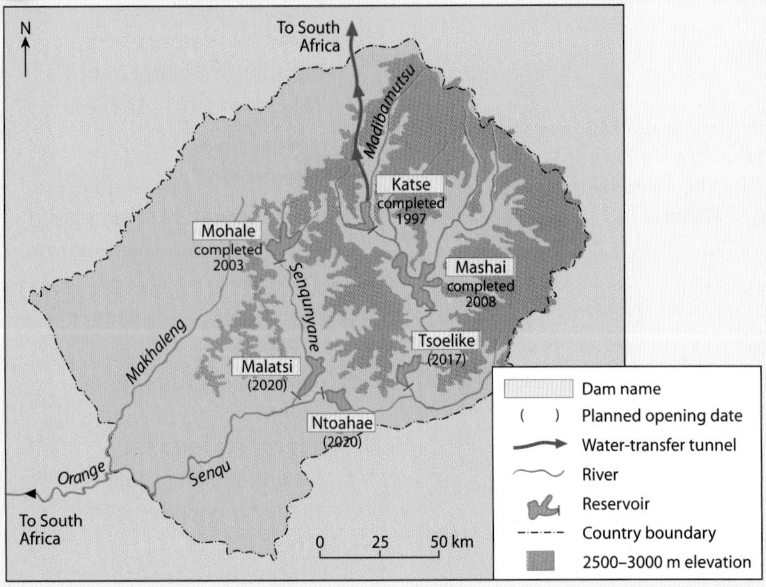

B Climate graph for the highlands of Lesotho

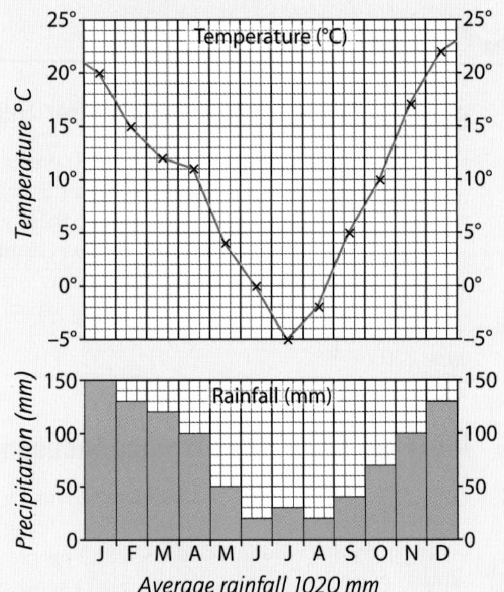

Average rainfall 1020 mm

The average annual temperature range is between 3°C and 15°C, but temperatures can reach 35°C in January. Snow falls from May to September in the highlands.

C The water transfer scheme

N
To South Africa
Madibamatsu
Katse completed 1997
Mohale completed 2003
Senqunyane
Mashai completed 2008
Makhaleng
Tsoelike (2017)
Malatsi (2020)
Ntoahae (2020)
Orange
Senqu
To South Africa
0 25 50 km

Dam name
( ) Planned opening date
Water-transfer tunnel
River
Reservoir
Country boundary
2500–3000 m elevation

Task 2

Study **Source B**.

a In what ways is the climate suitable for building dams and reservoirs?

b Give **two** disadvantages of this climate for the LHWP.

Study **Source C**.

a Which three dams will be completed by 2009? When should others be finished?
b Give **two** different ways by which water will be transferred from the reservoirs.
c Describe the location of the Katse dam.

D The Katse Dam

E Different views!

The case for... ▶

We are a poor country. We only grow a little corn and wheat. Farming is subsistence and heavy rainfall in the mountains causes soil erosion. But we do have water and good sites for reservoirs, so why not sell our water to South Africa? We can also use the dams to generate hydro-electric power (HEP) and large reservoirs will attract tourists. We will develop transport routes and there will be better jobs than subsistence farming. We are being paid US$20 million a year for 50 years. A poor country can do a lot for its people with this money.
Minister of Natural Resources, Lesotho

... and against! ▼

Over 30 000 of us were moved. Our farms are now under water. Some villagers were relocated onto steeper slopes where nothing can grow and
it gets cold in winter.
Villager who used to farm in the valley now covered by the Katse reservoir

Our culture and way of life will be changed for ever by tourism.
Village community leader

Lesotho will now be dependent on South Africa for future income. If South Africa wants more water than we can supply, we could have a water war here.
Opposition politician in Lesotho parliament

As reservoirs have filled, the extra pressure has caused earth tremors. This has damaged villages close to the lake shorelines.
Australian geologist and water engineer

F Factfile on Lesotho

	Lesotho	UK
Population (millions)	1.8	60.1
Life expectancy (M/F)	34/34	77/81
Average annual income (US$)	730	33 630
Size of classes in primary schools	44	17
Infant mortality rate (number dying per 1000 born)	61	5
Lesotho employment structure: Primary 40% Secondary 28% Tertiary 32%		

a On a sketch of **Source D**, label the following:
- the Katse dam
- steep valley sides
- the reservoir
- the river outflow
- an area of overland flow
- an area of evaporation.

b Suggest **two** reasons why this site was chosen for the reservoir. Explain your reasons.
c Suggest **two** reasons why this was **not** the ideal site for a new reservoir.

Study **Source E**.

a Read the different views. Make a table with two columns: one for reasons in favour of the LHWP and one for reasons against it.
b Briefly summarise your own views on whether the LHWP scheme should continue to be built. Do others agree with you?

Study **Source F**. Lesotho is a land-locked LEDC. Suggest how it could use the water income to help improve the quality of life for its own people.

Sample case study question

Choose a country where a water transfer scheme or a large dam has been (or is being) created. Explain the advantages and disadvantages the scheme has brought, or will bring, to the country.

Damaging the environment

The natural environment

This includes the Earth's:

- physical landscape
- rivers, seas and lakes
- soils
- atmosphere
- natural vegetation
- wildlife.

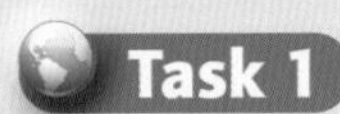

Task 1

Study **Source A**.

Explain how this quarry might affect each part of the natural environment.

A A sandstone quarry in Dorset, UK

B A river in Shanghai, China

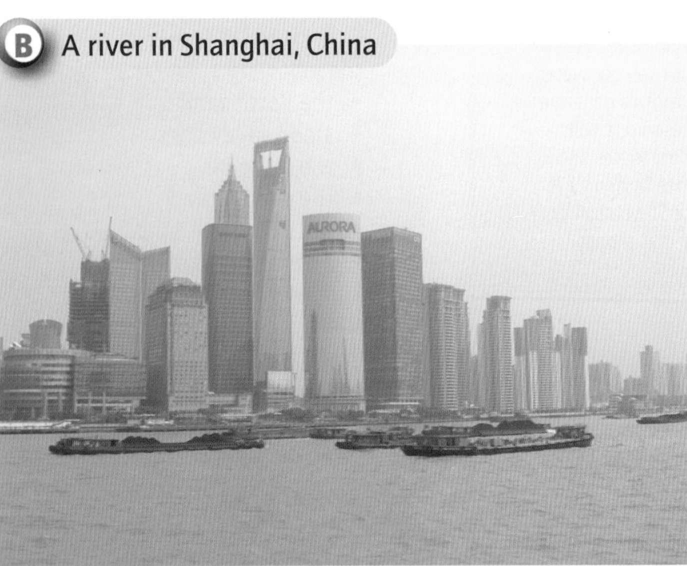

Human impact

Human beings affect the natural environment by using the Earth for:

- farming
- fishing
- building places to live
- mining and quarrying
- industry
- transport
- throwing away rubbish
- tourism.

Task 2

Study **Source B**.

Explain how any of the different human activities listed might affect the natural environment of this river.

Problems caused...

Human activity causes problems such as:

- the loss of vegetation
- loss of habitats
- threats to wildlife
- soil erosion
- air and water pollution
- global warming
- acid rain.

Task 3

Study **Source C**.

The factory shown in the photograph is processing sugar beet which has been grown on nearby farms. Explain how the growing of the sugar beet and processing it into sugar might affect the natural environment in the ways listed.

C A sugar-beet processing factory in Newark, UK

D Industrial and mining pollution in Albania

MONTENEGRO
SERBIA
N
Shkoder
Fusche-Arrez
Rubik
Adriatic Sea
Furshe-Kruje
MACEDONIA
Durres
Sharra
Tirana
Elbasan
ALBANIA
Fier
Ballash
Vlore
Palos
GREECE
0 50 100 km

Hazardous industrial site
Mining site
Waste disposal site
Mining industry hotspots
Serious water pollution

E Air pollution in Albania

Albania at Risk of Disaster from Pollution

According to experts Albania is facing disaster due to growing pollution caused by poisonous gases.

'We are concerned about growing numbers of people suffering from cancer, cardiovascular and pneumonia diseases due to various poisonous gases', said Environment Minister Ethem Ruka.

Tirana, Albania's capital city, is one of the most polluted cities in the world. Experts said that deaths due to illnesses caused by pollution have increased by 20% in Tirana in the past two years.

'90% of the vehicles are too old, 70% use diesel and 30% petrol, but mostly petrol with lead and a huge quantity of sulphur, banned in the European Union countries,' Ruka said.

Until recently the worst air pollution was in Elbasan, the centre of heavy industry, where pollution from dust and sulphur gas was 15 times above acceptable levels.

Here there has been an increase in the number of babies born with deformities. There have also been reported cases of deformed animals being born: four-legged roosters and two-headed calves and rabbits. The soil is so contaminated that in some places planting food crops is banned.

F Elbasan – a heavily polluted industrial centre

Task 4

Study **Source D**.

Albania is one of the most polluted countries in Europe. Write a paragraph, including named examples, to describe the location of areas where mining and industry are causing pollution in Albania.

Task 5

Study **Sources E and F**.

a Draw a labelled sketch to show how the natural environment has been affected by people in the area shown in the photograph.

b Explain how and why people in Albania are being affected by air pollution.

Soil erosion in Nepal

A Nepal – physically challenging

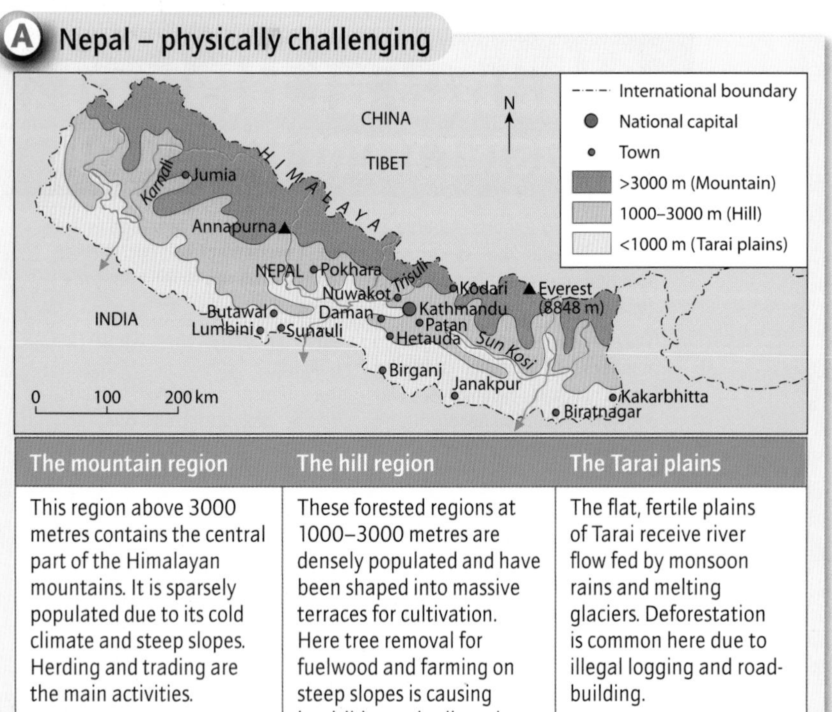

The mountain region	The hill region	The Tarai plains
This region above 3000 metres contains the central part of the Himalayan mountains. It is sparsely populated due to its cold climate and steep slopes. Herding and trading are the main activities.	These forested regions at 1000–3000 metres are densely populated and have been shaped into massive terraces for cultivation. Here tree removal for fuelwood and farming on steep slopes is causing landslides and soil erosion.	The flat, fertile plains of Tarai receive river flow fed by monsoon rains and melting glaciers. Deforestation is common here due to illegal logging and road-building.

Steep terraced land in Nepal is vulnerable to landslides and soil erosion.

Heading for disaster?

In the last 25 years there has been growing global concern about the effects of removing forests for fuelwood. Around 18 per cent of Nepal is forested but deforestation is taking place at an alarming rate – 25 per cent of its forest was removed between 1990 and 2005. This continues at a rate of 3 per cent a year. Nepal is famous for its mountains, but removing trees on steep slopes leads to soil erosion and land degradation. The effect of heavy monsoon rains, and the fact that the country's population has grown (from 12.8 to 28.9 million between 1997 and 2007) means that more land has been cleared to grow food crops. All may contribute to an environmental disaster.

B Climate data for Kathmandu

	J	F	M	A	M	J	J	A	S	O	N	D
Temperature (°C)	10	12	16	20	23	24	25	24	23	20	15	11
Precipitation (mm)	15	41	23	58	122	246	373	345	155	38	8	3

Average annual precipitation = 1427 mm Temperatures average (mean) for each month.

C Causes of land degradation

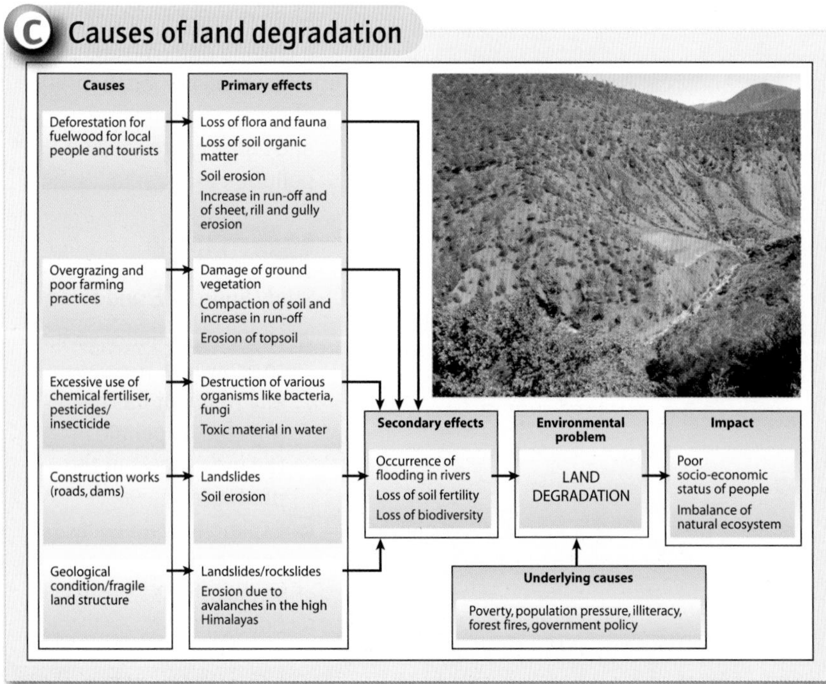

Task 1

Study **Source A**.

a Describe how the relief of the land changes as you travel from south-west to north-east across Nepal. Refer to the **three** named regions.

b How does the relief cause problems for people?

c Nepal is land-locked and cannot easily import fossil fuels. What do people use for cooking and heating?

Task 2

Study **Source B**.

a Nepal has a monsoon climate. How does this cause soil erosion?

b How might population change 1977–2007 have contributed to soil erosion?

D Forest removal – for local people and tourists!

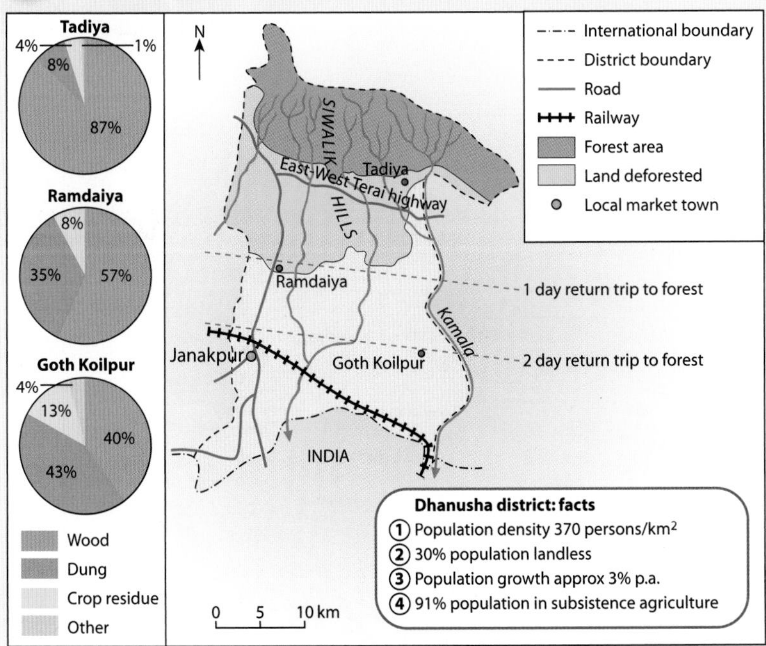

Sources of fuel in three villages in the Dhanusha district of Nepal

Villagers in Tadiya have easy access to the forest and wood is the main source of fuel. Many families now have to go further into the forest to collect fuel and fodder as nearby areas are deforested. Women here spend one-third of their day collecting firewood for fuel. One reason for the removal of wood is to sell it at the nearby market of Janakpur, the main town in Dhanusha district. Demand has increased as rural dwellers migrate into the urban area.

Tourist revenue is important to Nepal; over 70 000 trekkers arrive each year, creating many jobs. Many expect cooked food, heating and hot water for showers. It is estimated that using fuelwood for tourists has increased deforestation and soil erosion by 10 per cent. The temporary wealth obtained from tourist payments must be set against the long-term damage to the environment, as it is often spent on new hotels encouraging more tourism.

Task 3

Study **Source C**.

a List the **five** main causes of land degradation. Which are related to human activity?

b Explain how each cause contributes to soil erosion.

Task 4

Study **Source D**.

a Describe the differences in fuel use between the three villages.

b Suggest how these energy uses might affect:
- the natural environment
- the lives of the people.

c Why is tourism important to Nepal? How does it contribute to soil erosion?

Task 5

In 1987 the Annapurna Conservation Area Project (ACAP) was set up to attempt to conserve the environment in Nepal. **Source E** shows some solutions that have been tried in the last 20 years.

You are a member of the village council for the village of Tadiya. Study **Source E** and other sources on these two pages. There is a growing problem of soil erosion in your local area. Write a report that:

- explains why there is a problem
- suggests some solutions that could help reduce the problem.

E Some solutions …

Community development
Educate farmers to contour plough instead of ploughing up and down the slopes, to prevent rapid run-off, loss of soil and the development of gullies.

Alternative energy sources
Only 10% of Nepal is connected to the national electricity grid. Invest in micro-HEP schemes using fast-flowing streams to generate electricity. Increase use of yak dung for fires and as a building material.

Environmental education
Restrict tourist visits and demand a larger fee for use of facilities involving heating and cooking. Enforce a minimum impact guide for all trekking groups. Develop environmental education in schools.

Fuelwood conservation
Provide grants to replant trees where any deforestation has taken place or is going to take place. Fund forest guards and fence off protected areas. Develop solar and HEP alternatives.

Organic fertilisers
Reduce use of inorganic chemicals, pesticides and insecticides. Increase use of animal manure, green manure and compost to help soil recover and to reduce toxic chemicals in the soil and in the food chain.

CASE STUDY 30b

Global warming – the Maldives

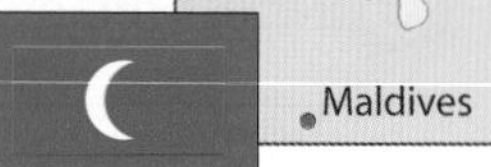

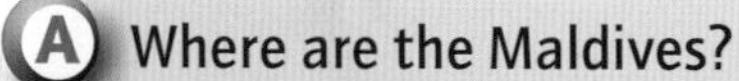

A Where are the Maldives?

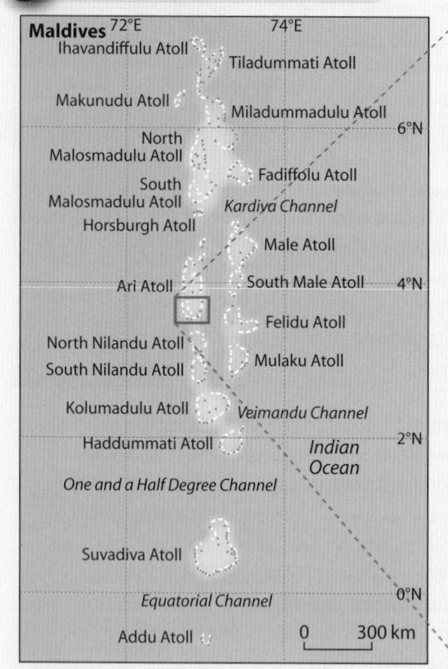

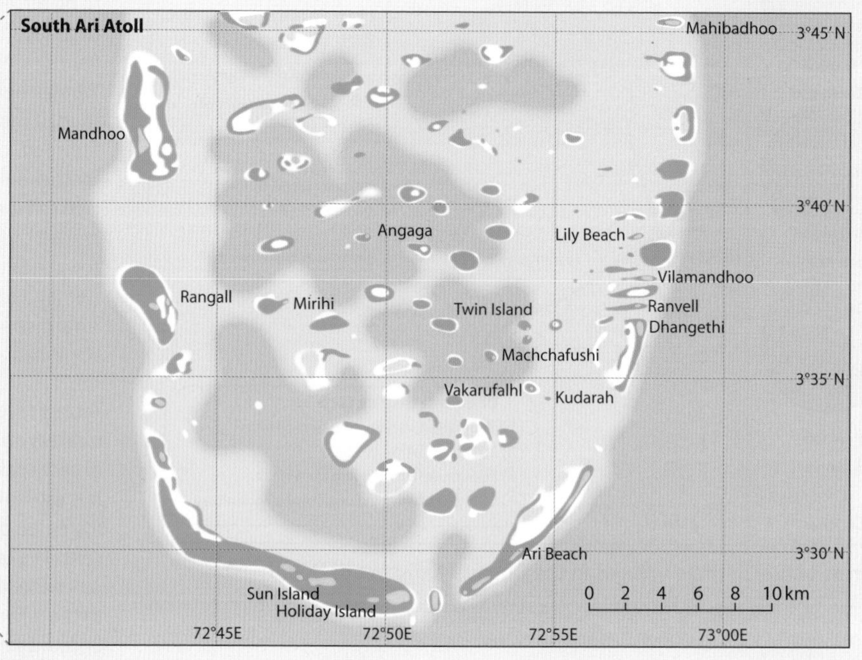

Paradise (soon to be) Lost

The Maldives is made up of 1200 tiny islands. This area is known to most of the world as a paradise tourist destination – but it is at risk. The highest point on any of its islands is only 2.4 metres above sea level, and 80 per cent of its islands are no more than 1 metre above sea level. This makes them especially threatened by rising sea levels caused by global warming. Unless the world reduces its carbon dioxide emissions, the little island paradise may soon be lost.

The Maldives is doing everything it can to avoid that. Male, the capital, is surrounded by a 3 metre-high wall, which took 14 years to build, at a cost of US$63 million. The government has identified five 'safe' islands which will be designed to resist the rising sea. If necessary, the government has even proposed artificially raising the height of some islands to keep them above water. Near the capital city a land reclamation project is making a new island, which could eventually be home for 50 000 people – most of the nation's population.

B A holiday island – South Ari Atoll

Task 1

Study **Source A**.

a Describe the location of the Maldives.

b What is the distance from Ihavandiffulu Atoll, in the north of the Maldives, to Addu Atoll in the south?

Task 2

Source B shows the eastern end of Holiday Island on South Ari Atoll.

a Give a latitude and longitude reference for the area shown.

b Explain why the area shown in the photograph is attractive to tourists.

c Tourists visiting Holiday Island will fly in to the international airport on Male Atoll. How far will they have to travel to the resort? What method of travel do you think they are likely to use?

d Explain why rising sea levels are likely to threaten the Maldives.

C The greenhouse effect

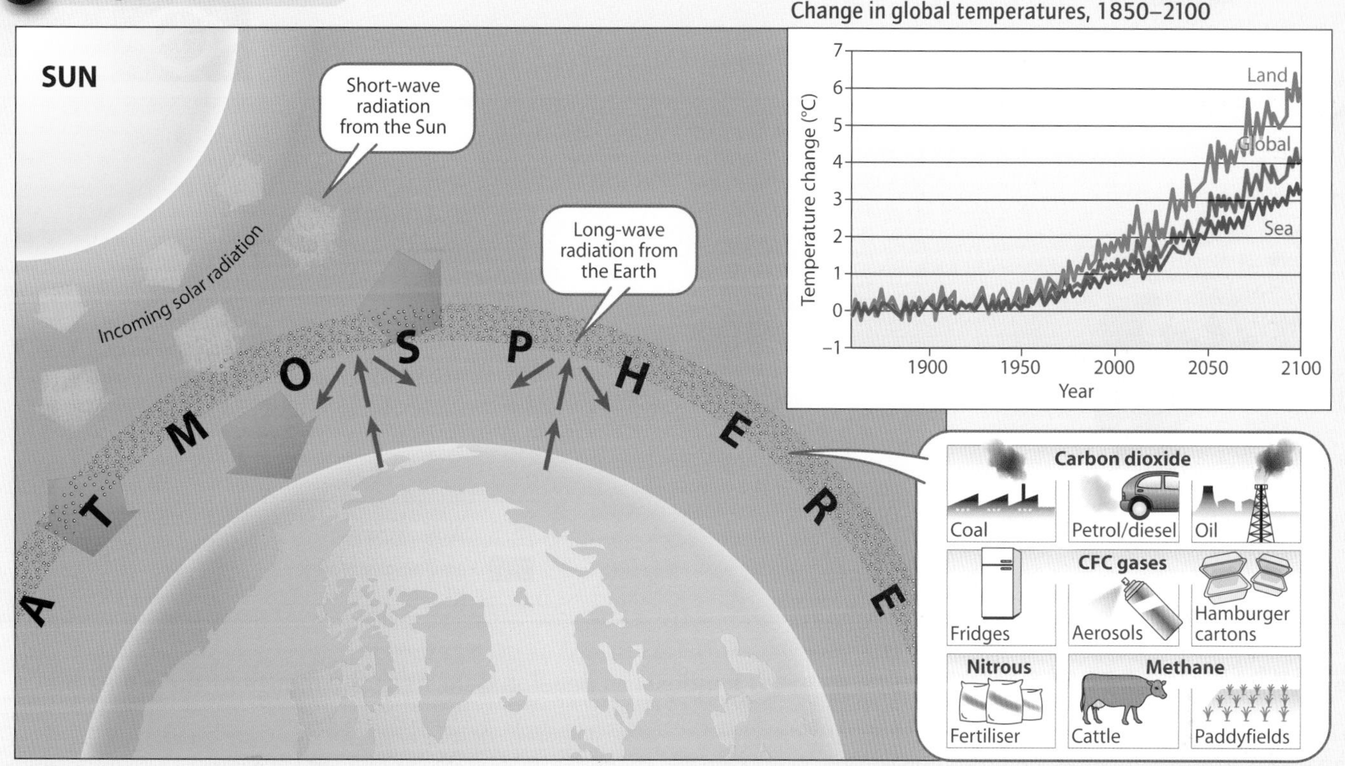

D Population and global warming

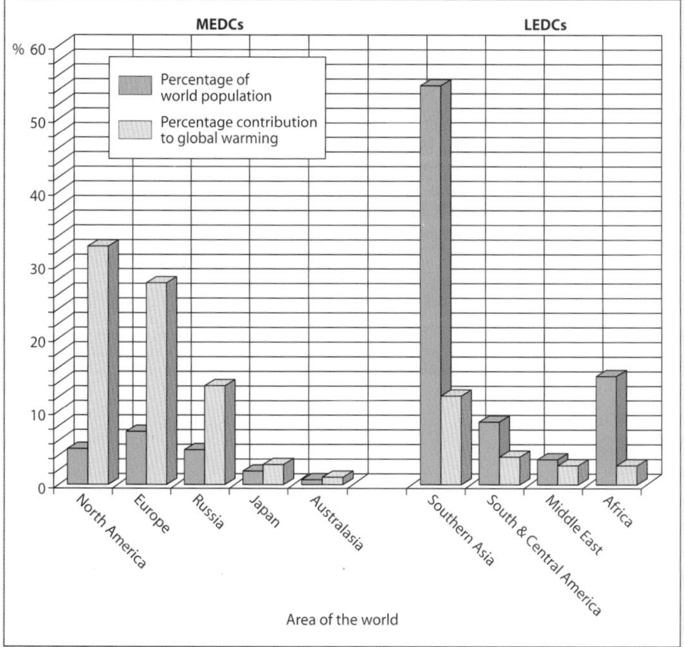

E Producing carbon dioxide – two nations compared

The average British citizen produces 26 kg of carbon dioxide in a day made up from:

• electricity	7.4 kg
• fuel production	1.6 kg
• manufacturing	3.8 kg
• transport	7.4 kg
• offices	1.0 kg
• heating	3.8 kg
• agriculture	1.0 kg

The average Nigerian citizen produces 0.7 kg of carbon dioxide in a day made up from:

• electricity	0.08 kg
• fuel production	0.08 kg
• manufacturing	0.16 kg
• transport	0.31 kg
• heating	0.07 kg

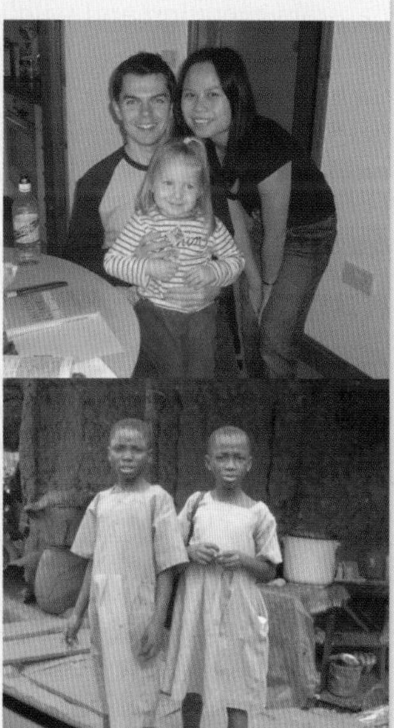

Task 3

Study **Source C**.

a Describe how global temperatures are expected to change during this century.

b Explain the causes of these temperature changes.

Task 4

Study **Sources D and E**.

a Compare the percentage share of the world population and contribution to global warming between North America and Southern Asia.

b Give reasons why the contributions of MEDCs (e.g. the UK) to global warming are different from that of LEDCs (e.g. Nigeria).

Deforestation in Amazonia, Brazil

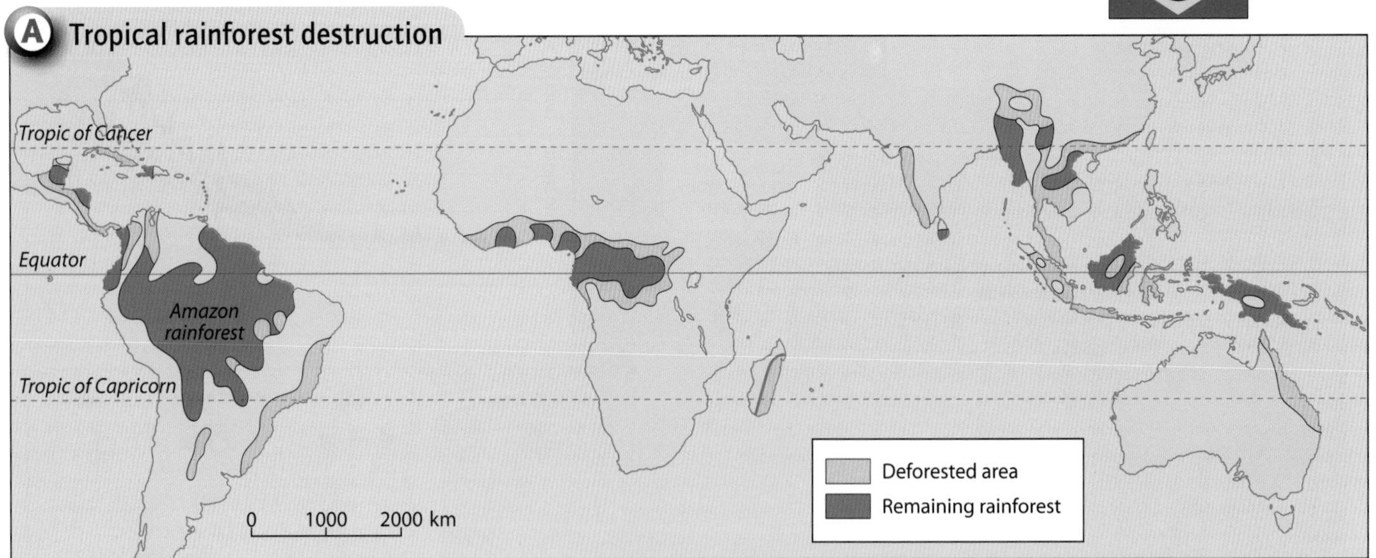

A Tropical rainforest destruction

What is deforestation?

Throughout the tropics, rainforests are being cut down. This is known as 'deforestation'. Many people are worried about the destruction of tropical rainforests. Beautiful areas of natural vegetation and wildlife are being lost. Deforestation is also causing the extinction of many species and affects the global climate. If deforestation continues at the current rate, the world's rainforests will be gone within 100 years.

Why does deforestation happen?

Commercial logging – the cutting of trees for sale for timber or pulp – is the most common reason for deforestation. Commercial logging uses heavy machinery, such as bulldozers, road graders, and log skidders, to remove cut trees and build roads.

Large areas of rainforest are also cleared for agricultural use such as grazing animals and planting crops. Poor subsistence farmers chop down a small area and burn the tree trunks, a process called 'slash and burn'. Commercial agriculture occurs on a much larger scale, for growing crops and grazing animals. Large cattle pastures often replace rainforests to raise beef for the world market, and food crops are grown on plantations.

There are other ways in which deforestation happens, e.g. building settlements and industries, the construction of dams and mining for natural resources.

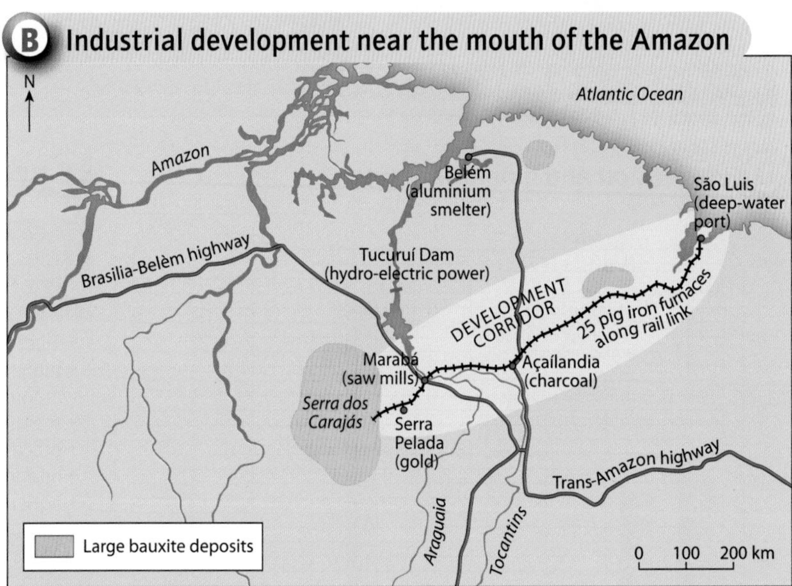

B Industrial development near the mouth of the Amazon

Task 1

Study **Sources A and B** and an atlas.

a Identify:
- the continent with the largest area of remaining rainforest
- a country in Africa where there are large areas of deforestation.

b Estimate the percentage of the world's rainforest that has already been deforested.

c Draw a spider diagram showing some causes of deforestation in Amazonia.

C Deforestation rates in Amazonia

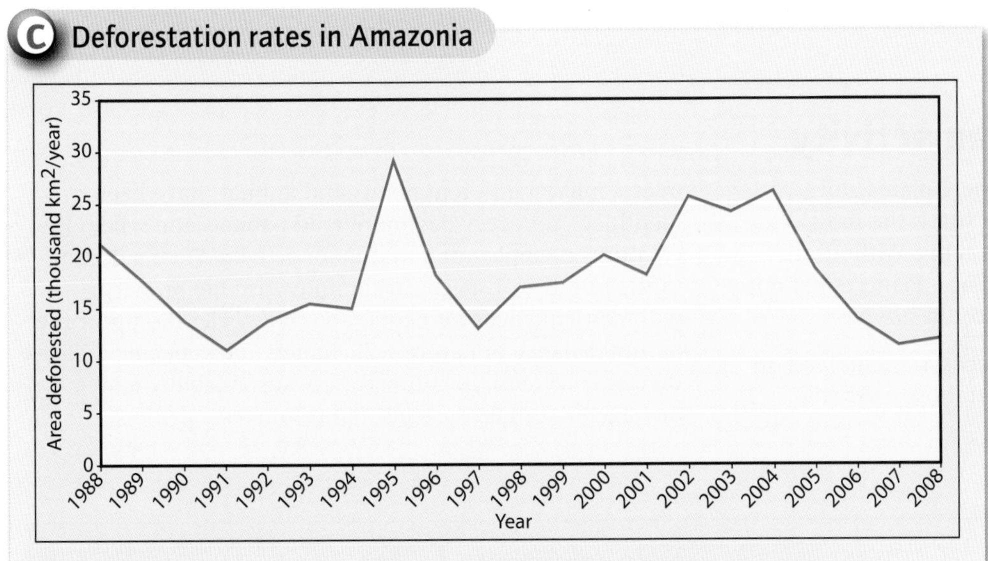

Study **Source D**.

Describe the impacts of deforestation on the natural environment. Use the Internet to find out more information to add.

D How deforestation affects the natural environment

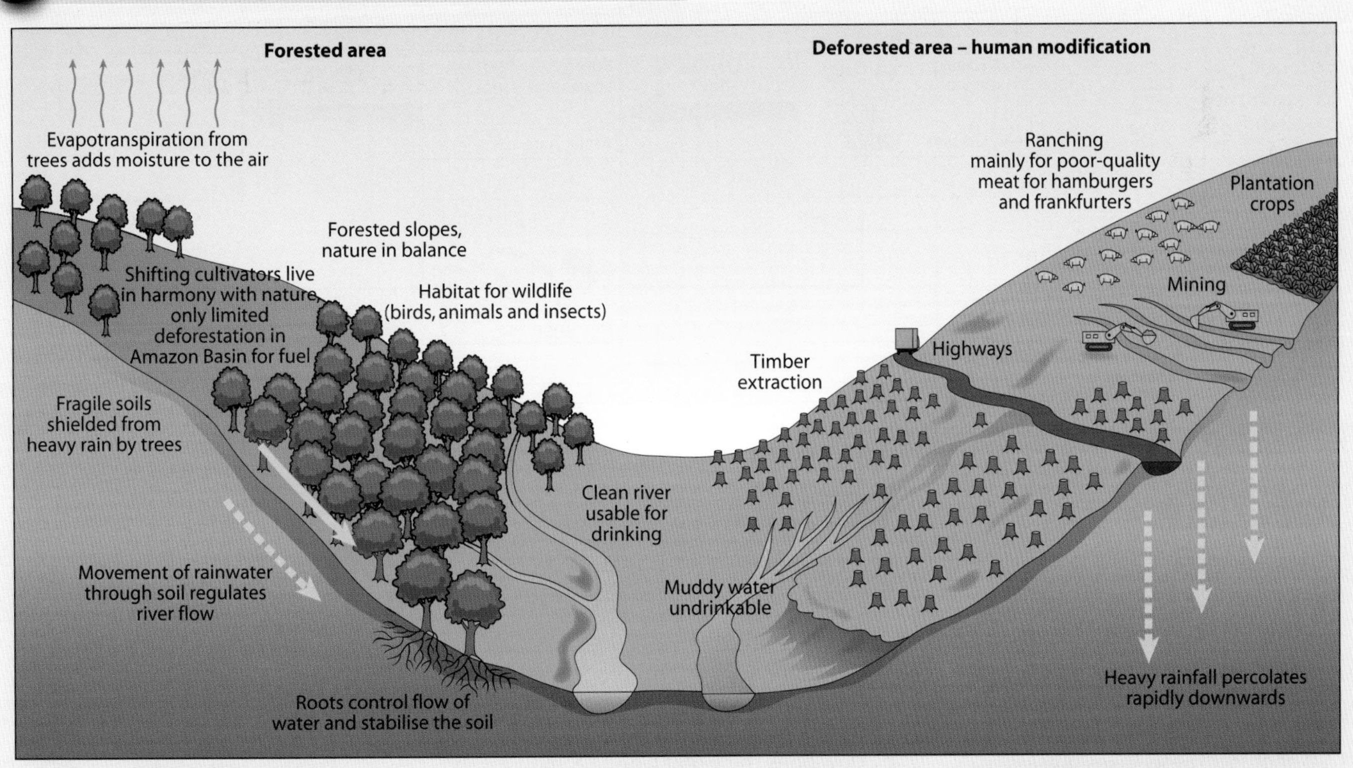

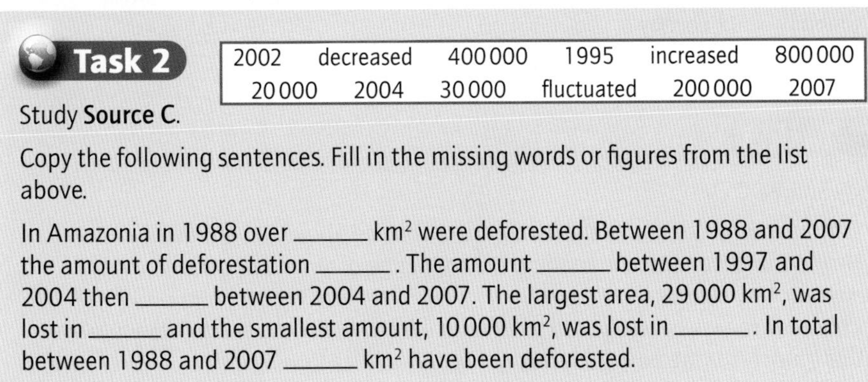

Task 2

2002	decreased	400 000	1995	increased	800 000
20 000	2004	30 000	fluctuated	200 000	2007

Study **Source C**.

Copy the following sentences. Fill in the missing words or figures from the list above.

In Amazonia in 1988 over ______ km^2 were deforested. Between 1988 and 2007 the amount of deforestation ______. The amount ______ between 1997 and 2004 then ______ between 2004 and 2007. The largest area, 29 000 km^2, was lost in ______ and the smallest amount, 10 000 km^2, was lost in ______. In total between 1988 and 2007 ______ km^2 have been deforested.

Sample case study question

Name an area you have studied where the environment is at risk from water pollution. Describe the human activities causing the risk and explain how they have affected the people and natural environment of your chosen area.

TOPIC 31 Conservation and management

Ecosystems and human activity

An ecosystem is an environment where plants and animals grow and live together. The sun is the most important influence for life in ecosystems. Without the sun photosynthesis could not take place. Plants could not produce food and oxygen. Nothing could survive.

There are several different types of ecosystem on land, in freshwater and in the oceans. Within those ecosystems over 3 million different plants and animals have been identified. Yet every day more wild habitats and wild creatures disappear due to human activity. Such a decline in the number of species will impoverish life on Earth with consequences for people too. As species disappear the natural balance of nature will change unless people increase their involvement in conservation, sustainability and management of ecosystems and resources.

A Life begins with the sun

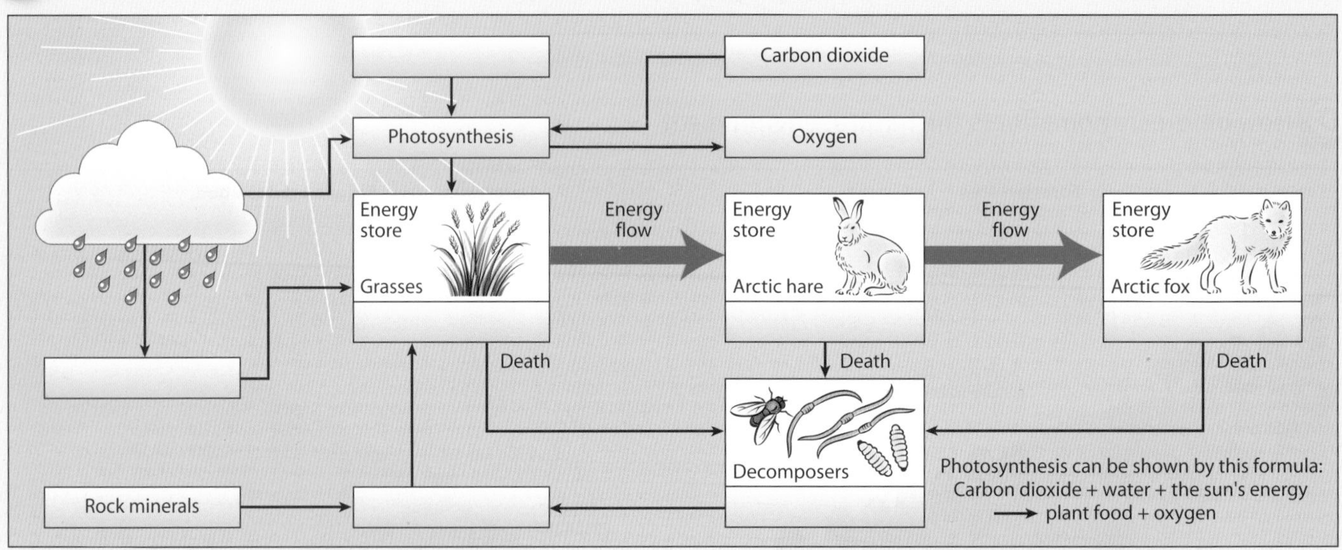

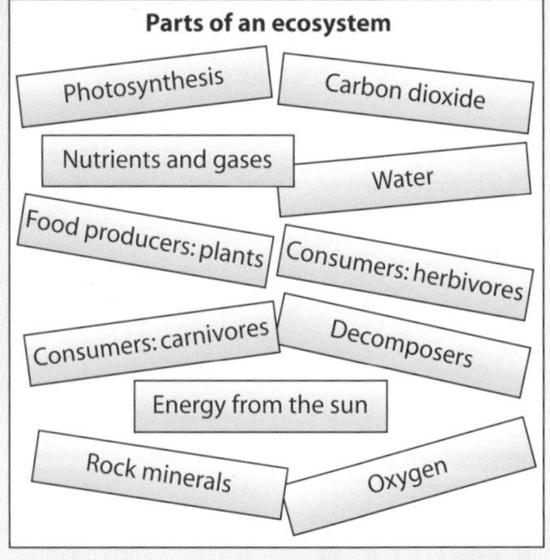

Parts of an ecosystem
Photosynthesis
Carbon dioxide
Nutrients and gases
Water
Food producers: plants
Consumers: herbivores
Consumers: carnivores
Decomposers
Energy from the sun
Rock minerals
Oxygen

Study **Source A**.

a On your copy of the diagram write the correct captions in the blank boxes. Four have been done for you.

b Explain what happens when photosynthesis takes place.

c What type of food producer is shown?

d Suggest what might happen in this tundra ecosystem if:

- arctic foxes increased because there were fewer polar bears to eat them
- grasses increased because of higher temperatures
- oil pollution destroyed most of the decomposers.

Study **Source B**.

a Why are mountain gorillas under threat in Rwanda?

b How does the Gorilla Organization prevent villagers using the gorilla's habitat?

c How does the Great Gorilla Run match up to the idea of 'Think Globally – Act Locally'?

Study **Source C**.

a Why are the government and Mr Lagware worried about soil fertility?

b How is the government managing the challenge of developing a sustainable approach by villagers?

c Choose **three** ways being used in Burkina Faso to provide a sustainable future in this country for the next generation. Explain how each will work.

B Conservation in action

Think Globally
Gorillas are only found in Central Africa but The Gorilla Organization in the UK and other environmental groups are concerned that they could become extinct without careful conservation and management.

The Gorilla Organization – Thinking Globally

The threats
Imagine that you're one of the poorest people on Earth. Now imagine your only chance to survive is by mining, farming and hunting in the rainforest next to your home. It's a no-brainer – right! Trouble is this land is home to some of the most endangered species in the world. Every time you enter the forest you are damaging the habitat of gorillas. And you're not alone –you live in one of the most densely populated areas of Africa.

How we help
The Gorilla Organization (based in London, UK) works with African NGOs (non-governmental organisations) to help people get what they need outside the forest. Everything the gorilla needs is in the forest so we work with local communities to make sure the forest stays as it is. For example, in a Rwandan village:

- we teach villagers how to grow crops so they do not need to take food from the forest
- we show villagers how to make a stove that uses 80% less fuelwood than old stoves
- we provide a new water cistern so they can just turn on a tap instead of spending half a day collecting water from the forest.

the gorilla organization

Act Locally
Each year the Great Gorilla Run takes place in London, UK. In September 2009 there were as many runners as there are mountain gorillas – 720 – each raising a minimum of £500 (US$1000) in sponsor money for the gorillas.

Conservation, sustainability and management

Conservation involves protecting natural resources as well as the biodiversity of plant and animals and their habitats. Today there are many global conservation movements such as Greenpeace and the WWF.

Sustainability involves fulfilling the requirements of the present generation without reducing the ability of future generations to do the same. To be sustainable the Earth's resources must be used at a rate that allows for replenishment.

Management involves putting into action policies to conserve resources for the future. Conferences take place at international level to agree on environmental policies but this is difficult as each country has its own agenda for economic development. Politicians are often interested in the short-term future of their own country rather than the long-term future of the planet.

C Sustainability and management in action

BURKINA FASO PROTECTS ITS FRAGILE SOILS

by Jean-Marie Sawadogo, Ouagadougou

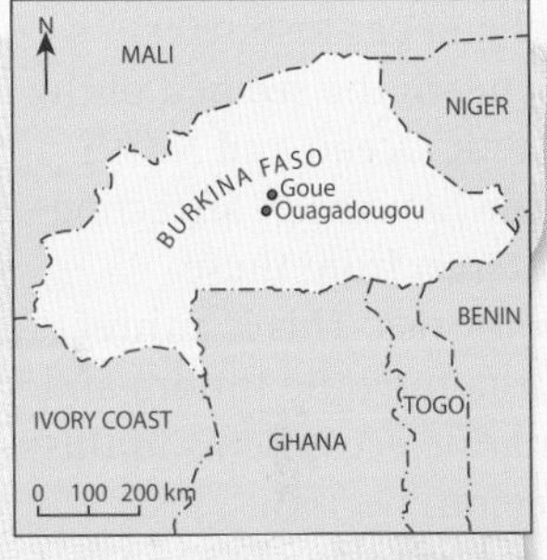

Like other farmers in the village of Goue, 30 km from Ouagadougou, Mr Pierre Lagware is worried about the fertility of his land which has been declining each year from overexploitation and poor farming practices. Here methods to combat soil erosion and restore fertility are not well known but, with agriculture employing 86% of the population, the government is just as concerned. It is in debt to the World Bank for loans and needs to produce more to improve its trade balance.

Local communities have been made responsible for managing their farmlands, pastures and forests to ensure environmental protection and sustainability. Several strategies are taking place.

- Overcultivation and overgrazing have reduced soil nutrients, so increased phosphate and organic fertilisers are being applied to overcome the deficiency.
- Many farmers are unaware that their soil fertility can be improved. Farmers now apply organic compost with mineral fertilisers to improve soil-water retention.
- Farmers are encouraged to grow fodder crops to avoid overgrazing.
- In the north farmers have been taught to build bunds with stones, earth and vegetation to allow water run-off and prevent topsoil erosion.
- Higher-yielding seeds for rice and grain and small-scale irrigation projects are being developed.
- The villagers are now involved in replanting seedlings, regulating tree cutting and increasing the use of domestic stoves. The Long Live The Farmer Association shows farmers how to cut fuelwood selectively while conserving vegetation that provides soil nutrients.

The Arctic – a challenging environment

The Arctic environment is defined by the Arctic Circle at 66½°N; anywhere north of here is part of the Arctic region which extends to the North Pole. Unlike its counterpart, the Antarctic continent, the Arctic region has a good deal of exposed land belonging to countries before the floating Arctic ice cap is reached. Bordering countries, such as Russia, Canada and the USA (Alaska), own land within the Arctic region that can be exploited for resources. More recently oil and gas resources beneath the sea bed of the Arctic Ocean and North Pole have been attracting interest from these countries. This is a threat to sustaining the tundra and marine ecosystems in this region.

A A difficult climate in the tundra

Climate data for Verkhoyansk, Russia (66°N 129°E)

	J	F	M	A	M	J	J	A	S	O	N	D
Temperature (°C)	−50	−45	−32	−15	0	12	14	9	2	−15	−38	−48
Precipitation (mm)	5	5	3	5	8	23	28	25	13	8	8	5

Average annual precipitation = 539 mm Temperatures are average (mean) for each month.

B The Arctic – land and sea

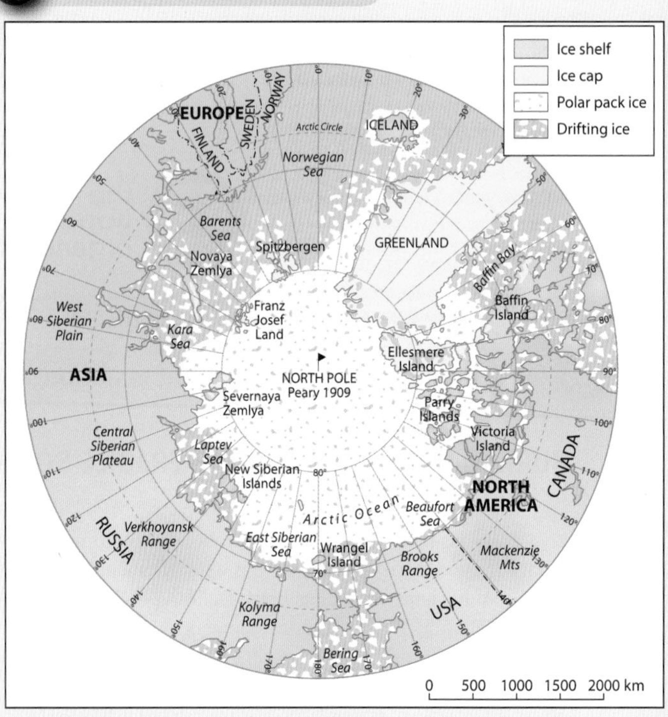

New shipping lane opens across the top of the world

'Waters in the Arctic Ocean linking the Barents Sea with the Bering Strait and the Pacific Ocean are now passable by modern cargo ships,' said a spokesman for the Scott Polar Institute in Cambridge, England. A 10% retreat of ice due to global warming has made this voyage possible. The route will soon become a commercial shipping lane, halving current costs using longer routes. Oil exploration and mining in Alaska and Siberia will be a lot easier for the USA and Russia. Japan may even be able to export cars to Europe by this route!

Battle for the final frontier

A mad scramble is under way for Arctic riches: fish, diamonds, oil and gas. America and Russia are quarrelling over rights to the Beaufort Sea while Norway and Russia argue over the Barents Sea. Underlying these disputes is the certain knowledge that oil and gas lie beneath the ice, as well as control over shipping routes across the 'top of the world'. The physical difficulties are great and the costs gigantic but, whatever the price, countries that need oil are pushing north. If Shell, BP and ExxonMobil are to stay in business, the Arctic is the only frontier left. This will create major challenges for conservation, sustainability and management.

Task 1

Study **Source A**.

a Draw a climate graph for Verkhoyansk.

b Describe the patterns shown by your graph. How can you tell it is in the northern hemisphere?

c To what extent would you agree that the Arctic region is 'a challenging environment to live and work in'? Support your view with evidence.

Task 2

Study **Source B**.

a List the countries that own land north of the Arctic Circle.

b Suggest how melting ice has affected shipping routes in this region.

c Use an atlas and **Source B** to describe a shipping route from Japan through the Bering Sea, past the north coast of Russia to Norway and the UK.

C An Arctic food web

The Inuit villagers of northern Alaska, USA, benefit from the oil companies' contribution to the local economy but the caribou and their tribal way of life are more important and are sustainable. The Inuit culture is dying and now only one-third of the people speak the native language; the rest speak English. They also rely on seals and whales for food and to sell. Once oil is being mined, carbon emissions will increase global warming. What ice is left will melt and the ecosystem will be destroyed for ever.

A spokesperson for WWF, the environmental group opposed to extracting more oil from Arctic regions

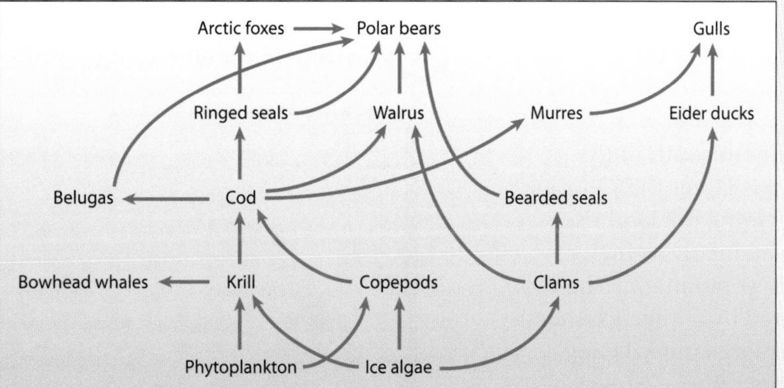

Polar bears are the top carnivores in the Arctic food web. They fear nothing. They live in dens on the ice and in the sea hunting seals from floating sea-ice platforms. As the ice thins and melts with global warming, the polar bear is affected in two ways. There is less ice to live on and hunt from, and algae cannot grow below the ice as it has disappeared. This affects krill which feed on the algae. Without krill many animals in the food web will struggle for food and migrate away or die. At the top of the web polar bears will lose both their habitat and food.

We are already extracting oil along the coast of Alaska but it is drying up. In north Alaska there are 16 billion barrels – that's 30 years' worth of imports from Saudi Arabia. Oil now accounts for 85% of the Alaskan economy, and has provided jobs, schools and houses. They would not be here without the mining. Almost 20% of the world's oil reserves are under the Arctic Ocean – there is no way that oil can stay in the ground.

A representative of Arctic Power, a BP-funded group that wants to mine more oil in Alaska and the Arctic Ocean

Task 3

Study **Source C**.

a Draw a simple food chain involving polar bears.

b Suggest how polar bears and their prey might be affected by:

- thinning ice and warmer seas
- more fishing and whaling ships
- oil mining beneath the sea
- tankers transporting oil.

c Give **two** reasons for and **two** reasons against allowing more oil mining in northern Alaska and the Arctic Ocean.

Task 4

Read **Source D**.

a What was the first manned journey to the North Pole's sea bed for?

b Why are four countries angry with Russia's actions? Justify their views.

Task 5

Produce **one** of the following, using IT if you can do so.

- An A4 illustrated leaflet that tries to persuade people to support environmentalists in conserving the Arctic region and its wildlife.
- An A4 illustrated leaflet that tries to persuade people that governments and oil companies are right to exploit the Arctic region.

D Threats from Russia

RUSSIA STAKES ITS CLAIM ON NORTH POLE IN UNDERWATER SEARCH FOR OIL

Russia is making a grab for the vast energy riches of the Arctic with an underwater mission to plant its flag beneath the North Pole. A team of explorers plans to descend 4300 metres to the sea bed in a miniature submarine to stake Russia's claim to an area the size of Western Europe. The expedition aims to prove that the Lomonosov Ridge is an extension of Russian territory. The trip is costing US$20 million and is the first manned journey to the sea bed of the North Pole. What's at stake is the right to over 10 billion tonnes of oil and gas. No country owns the Arctic Ocean or the North Pole but four nations oppose the claim – Canada, the USA, Norway and Denmark (Greenland). Under international law each country can control an area within 320 km of its coastline but these limits are disputed by Russia.

July 2007

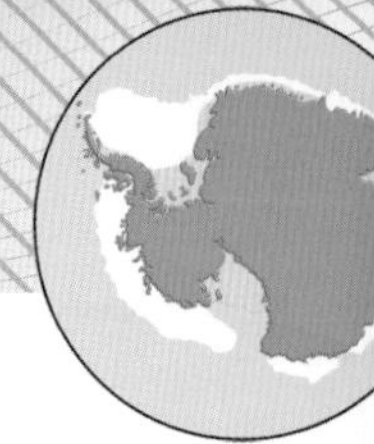

Antarctica – the White Continent

Antarctica is a frozen continent south of the Antarctic Circle (66½°S). It is larger than Europe, and higher. The ice cap covering the land rises to over 4 km above sea level, nearly as high as Mont Blanc, Europe's highest mountain. The continent used to be covered by a huge ice sheet; today there is less ice and more land is being exposed due to higher temperatures. However, it remains a challenging environment. Once it was only visited by explorers such as Amundsen, the first man to reach the South Pole in 1911. A hundred years later tourists take Antarctic cruises and many countries have bases there. As the continent becomes more accessible, more pressure is being created to allow ownership and mineral exploitation. Like the Arctic region, these threaten the sustainability of fragile ecosystems on land and in the sea.

A Antarctica – who wants a piece?

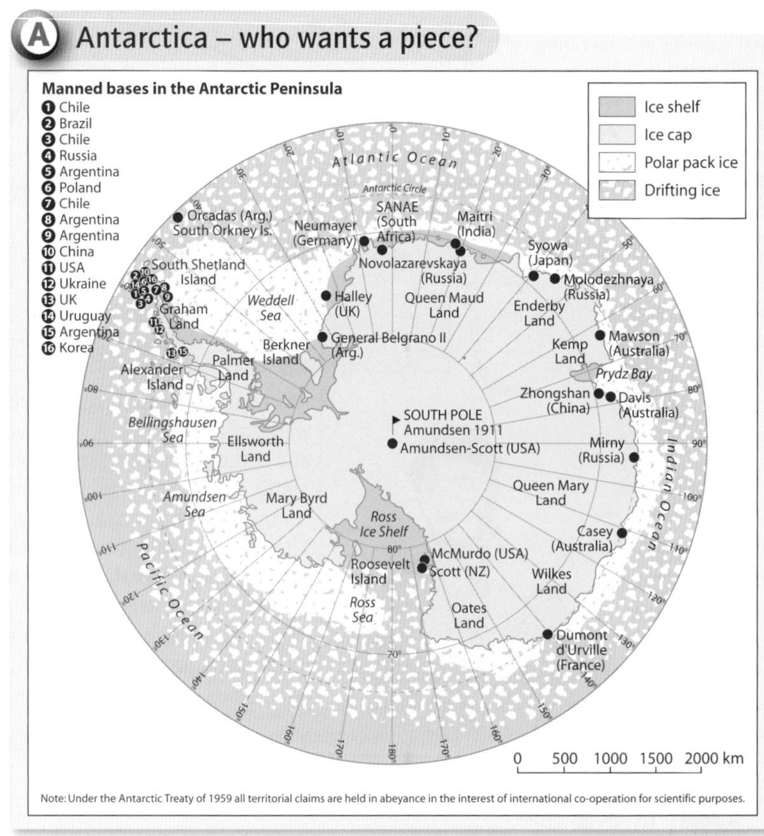

B Not an easy place to live and work …

Climate data for McMurdo, Ross Sea, Antarctica

	J	F	M	A	M	J	J	A	S	O	N	D
Temperature (°C)	–4	–15	–20	–29	–30	–30	–32	–37	–20	–20	–3	–4
Precipitation (mm)	almost no precipitation recorded											

Antarctica is the driest, windiest and most remote continent on Earth. Total precipitation is only 30–70 mm per year. Winds can reach 248 km per hour. It is so cold that air sinks to the surface giving permanent high pressure systems called anticyclones. These are called the polar highs.

C … but good for a holiday!

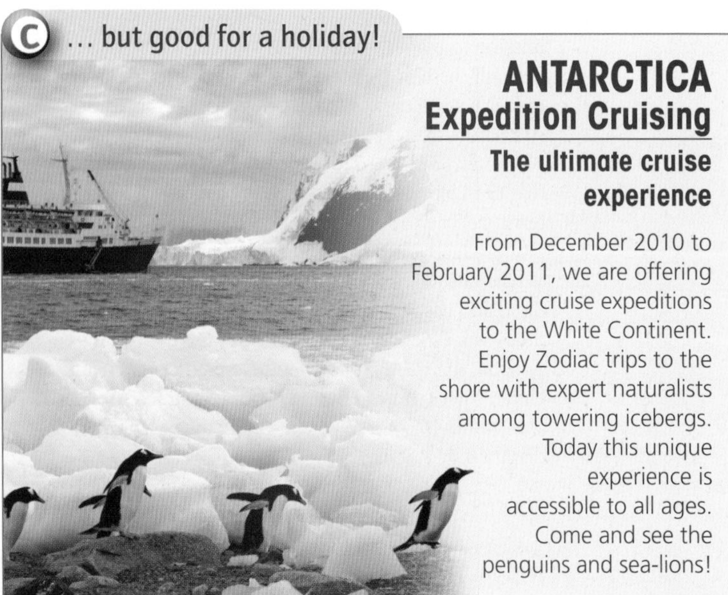

Task 1

Study **Sources A and B** and an atlas.

a List the countries that have managed bases in Antarctica. Suggest why most are located in a similar area.

b How can you tell that Antarctica is in the southern hemisphere?

c How would you describe the climate of Antarctica compared with where you live?

Task 2

Study **Sources B and C**.

a When do the cruise ships visit Antarctica? Why?

b Over 15 000 tourists visit the White Continent each year. Suggest why.

c In what ways might increasing tourism change Antarctica?

D The Antarctic food web

Krill feed on algae which live beneath the surface ice. They keep the Antarctic food web going. If the ice continues to melt, sea level will rise but more land will be exposed. The krill will lose their source of food. Along with the loss of their usual habitats and higher temperatures on land and sea, the effect on other wildlife in the marine ecosystem could be devastating.

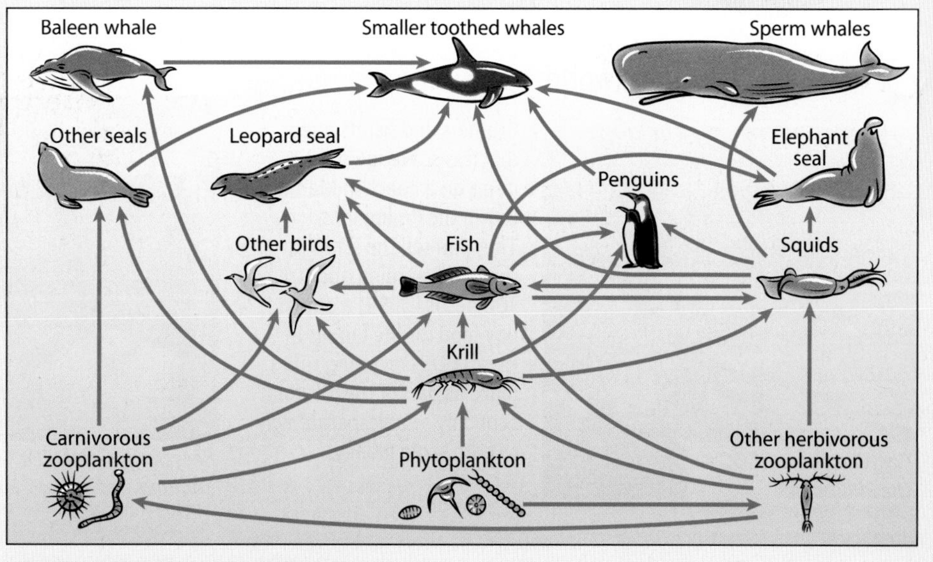

Task 3

Study **Source D**.

a Check the food chain for a baleen whale. How important is krill to the baleen whale?

b Describe how **two** other animals would be affected if krill was removed from this marine ecosystem.

Task 4

Study **Source E**.

a Give **three** reasons why countries want to own part of Antarctica.

b What prevents countries from exploiting these resources at present?

c Give examples of ways in which countries are trying to justify their ownership.

d List the mineral resources that lie beneath the Antarctic ice cap. Which resources are in the area claimed by Britain, Argentina and Chile?

e Why might conflict occur in Antarctica before 2048?

Task 5

'Antarctica is a remote, isolated continent.' To what extent do you think this is now true? Use evidence from the sources to justify your views.

E Antarctica – safe for now?

The Power Games that Threaten World's Last Pristine Wilderness

by James Bone, Eduardo Frei Montavo Base, Antarctica

Antarctica, once the torment of explorers such as Scott and Shackleton, is slowly being settled by mankind. Global warming, shrinking ice and soaring oil prices have forced countries to compete for the world's final frontier.

The Frei base sits on King George Island off the tip of the Antarctic Peninsula, a territory claimed by Britain and Argentina as well as Chile. Once a remote whaling station, the island is now known as the unofficial 'capital of the Antarctic'. The first surprise on landing in a Chilean C130 transport airplane is that my Blackberry works. I check my email and call my wife in New York to tell her I am surrounded by turquoise-tinted icebergs. As well as a mobile phone signal Frei base has a bank, post office, hospital, supermarket, bar, chapel, a school and an FM radio station called Sovereignty.

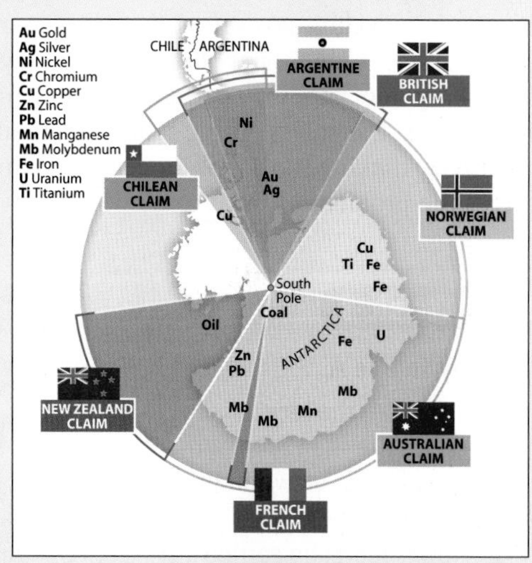

Flying over Antarctica we see colonies of sea-lions and penguins among corrugated shelters that are the international bases. However, despite all the overlapping territory claims, there is no conflict between countries yet. All the countries with bases are signed up to the 1959 Antarctic Treaty, which prevents exploitation and territorial claims. The 1991 Madrid Protocol to the Antarctic Treaty declares the icy continent 'a natural reserve devoted to peace and science' and outlaws mining or oil-drilling for 50 years. Despite this each country carries out administrative duties as if it owned that part of their claim. The British Antarctic Territory issues its own postage stamps, visitors' passports get stamped, and Chile and Argentina fly out pregnant mothers to have Antarctic-born children. However, polar scientists fear conflict is inevitable as global warming and deglaciation make it tempting to exploit the exposed land for oil and gas. 2009 was the deadline for lodging claims to the sea bed around Antarctica. In 2049 the unanimous ban on exploitation of Antarctica's resources will expire.

November 2007

Sample case study question

For a named area of natural environment that is threatened by human activity, describe how it is being conserved and managed.

GLOBAL ISSUE

3 Reduce, reuse, recycle

A Recycling across the world

Recycling in an LEDC – the Philippines

Brothers and sisters aged 9 or less scavenge plastic items on a beach in Manila Bay in the Philippines. They can sell the scrap for recycling, earning about 100 pesos (US$2) a day to buy food for the family. In most LEDCs recycling takes place as part of the informal economy as a desperate way to earn some money.

Recycling in an MEDC – England

Most houses are provided with green bins (garden waste) and black bins (non-recyclable waste) for collection by the council each week. Boxes for newspapers and for glass and cans are also provided. Each town has a council tip where people can take other items for recycling, e.g. computers, plastic bottles, wood and furniture. These services are funded by householders who have to pay council tax.

A waste of resources

Many goods that we buy, from drinking bottles to newspapers, are disposable: we throw them into a bin as soon as we have finished with them. But much of this waste is not useless: glass, plastic, metal and paper are valuable materials that can be recycled. Recycling saves energy. Making new paper from old uses only 50 per cent of the energy used in making new paper, so conserving trees and their ecosystems. Using less plastic reduces demand for oil resources, making them last longer. Recycling also solves the problem of what to do with the waste.

B What makes up the waste?

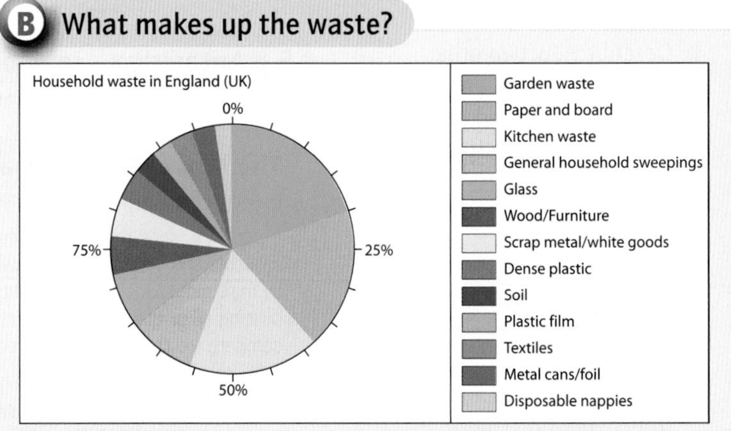

Task 1

Study **Source A**.

a Who does the recycling in LEDCs like the Philippines? Discuss your views on this with your classmates.

b How is recycling carried out in an MEDC like the UK?

c Why is it important to increase the amount of recycling in the world?

Task 2

Study **Source B**.

a Which **three** types of waste make up over 50 per cent of the household waste in England?

b How do the different types of waste and their amounts compare to waste in your home?

C Meet Sustainable Dave …

A rubbish life for LA marathon recycler

Dave Chameides has spent almost an entire year living a life full of utter garbage. The Los Angeles cameraman has lived in his Hollywood home without throwing away a single piece of trash. Instead the 39-year-old – nicknamed 'Sustainable Dave' – recycles his garbage or stores it in his basement. Instead of the usual 725 kg of trash the average American family produces each year, Dave, his wife and two daughters have amassed only 15 kg. This has been done by:

- drinking filter tap water instead of bottled water
- buying rice and pulses loose by the kilo in bulk and putting them in containers instead of cardboard packaging
- buying fresh fruit and vegetables loose from a weekly farmers' market instead of using paper bags or plastic wrapping
- using worms to mince up organic waste such as banana skins and eggshells to create a compost
- fitting his Californian home with solar panels
- using cooking oil to fuel his car
- wrapping presents in comics or other existing paper sources.

Task 3

Study **Source C**.

a What is Dave Chameides' nickname? Why?

b What difference has recycling made to the amount of waste his family now produce compared with the average American family?

Part B Geographical Skills

Preparing for Paper 2

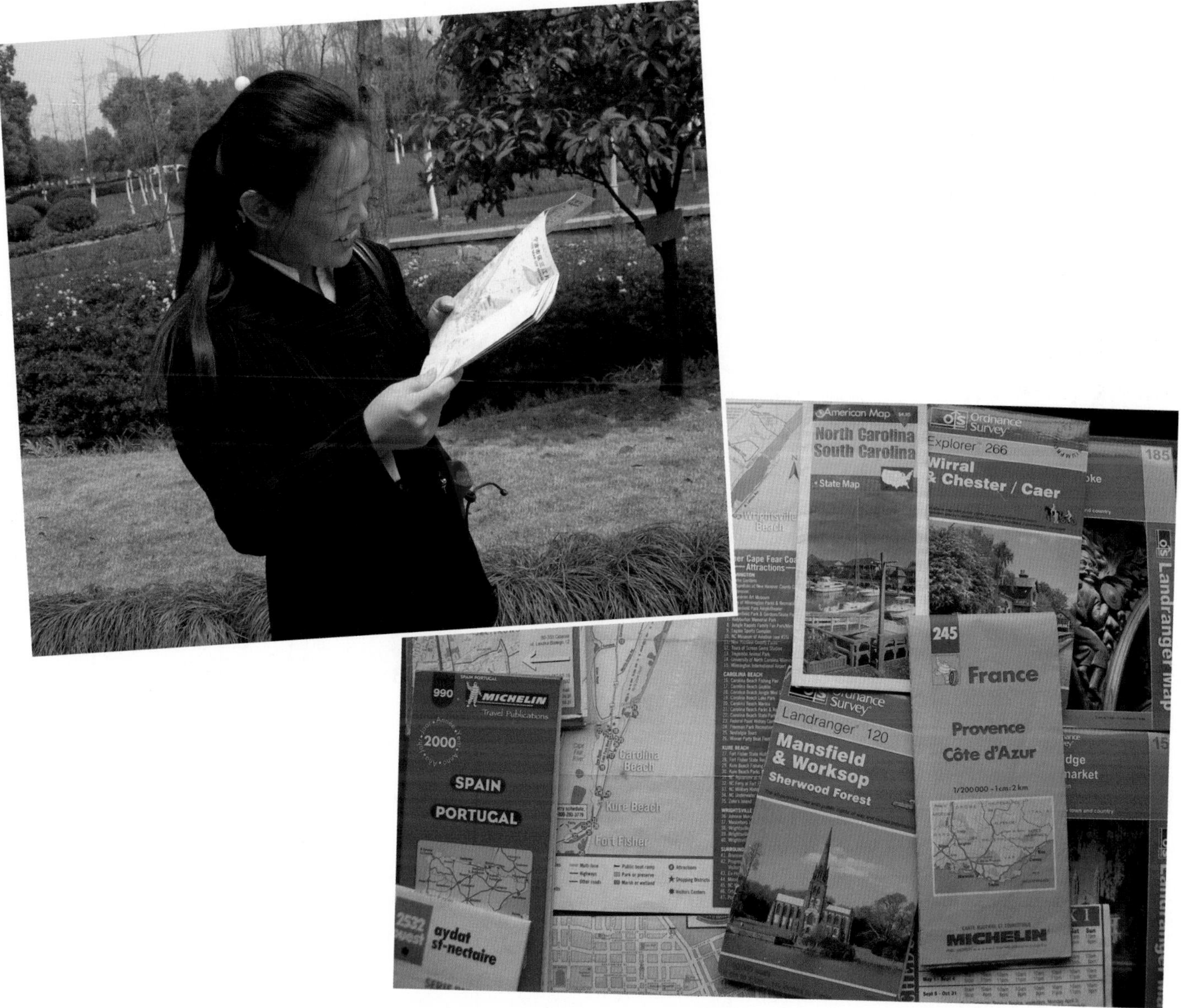

Paper 2 tests the interpretation and analysis of geographical information. Candidates need to be able to demonstrate skills of using topographical and other types of maps, diagrams, tables of data, written text and photographs. As one question will be based on a large-scale (1:25 000 or 1:50 000) topographical map of a tropical area, this part of the textbook provides six examples of these maps, from Peru, Zimbabwe, Kenya, Jamaica, Indonesia and Reunion Island. For each country an extract of a map is provided with guidance on the main map skills required for Paper 2, along with examples of map skills questions to practise. Further tasks develop these map skills. Additional relevant data on issues relating to the areas shown by the maps is also provided, along with tasks that enable candidates to practise skills in the interpretation and analysis of geographical information.

From June 2010 there will be three different versions of Paper 2, numbered 21, 22 or 23. The Paper the centre receives will depend on which of the three international time zone groups it is allocated to. A recent past paper and mark scheme for Paper 2 is available for reference at www.cie.org.uk

MAP WORK 1 Monsefu, Peru

Monsefu

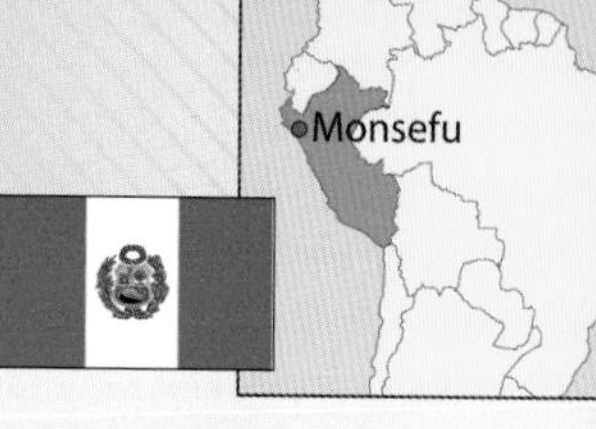

Peru – a country of varied relief

Peru, in western South America, covers almost 1.3 million km². The country borders Ecuador and Colombia to the north, Brazil to the east, Bolivia to the south-east and Chile to the south. The Andes mountains run parallel to the Pacific Ocean, dividing the country into three regions:

- The Costa (coast), in the west, is a narrow plain.
- The Sierra (highlands) is in the Andes mountains. It includes the Altiplano plateau as well as the highest peak of the country – Huascarán at 6768 m.
- The selva is a wide expanse of flat terrain covered by the Amazon rainforest in the east.

The 1:50 000 map extract below shows the area around Monsefu and Puerto Eten, in the northern part of the Costa region.

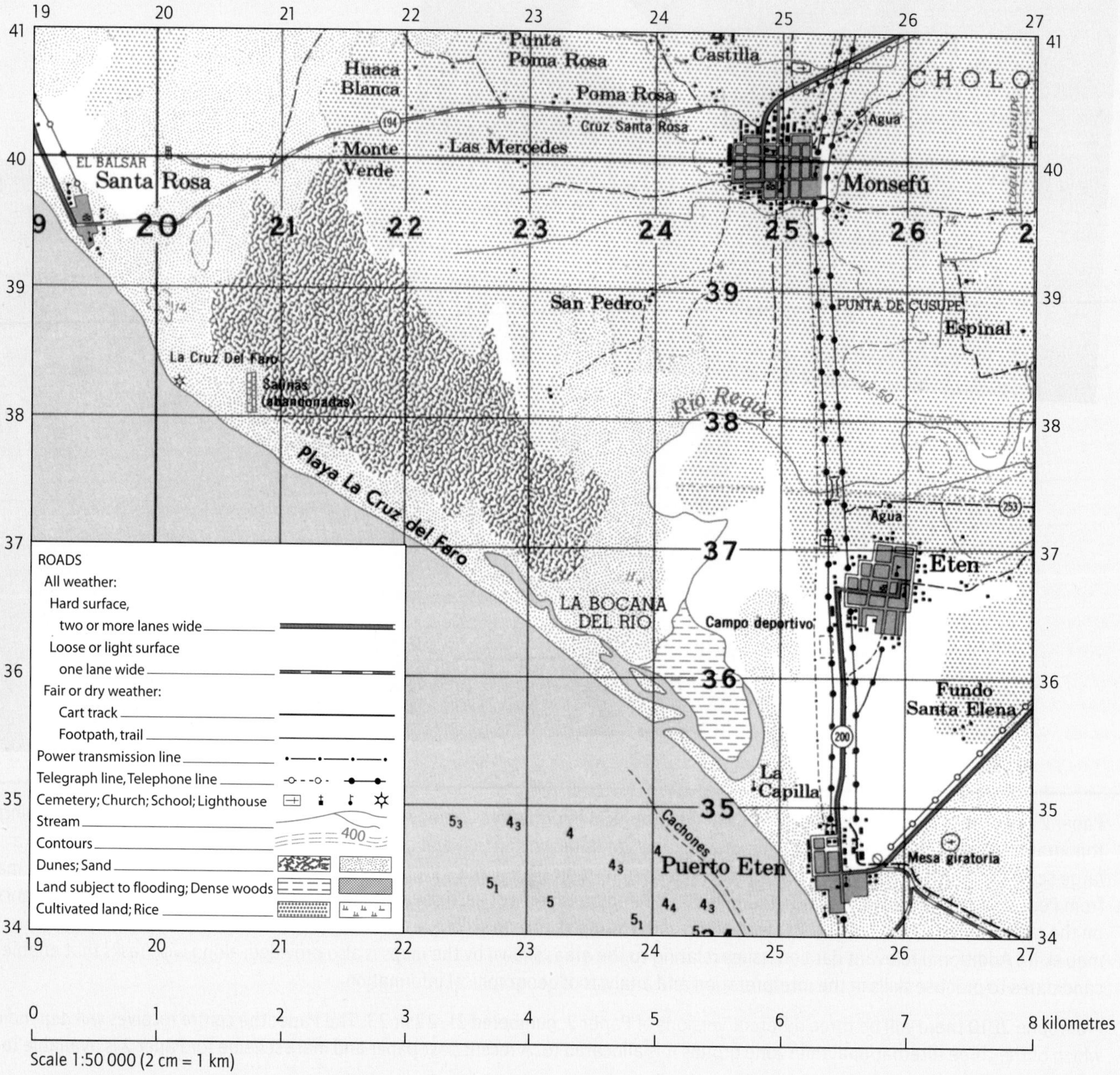

Punta Poma Rosa
Castilla
Huaca Blanca
Poma Rosa
Cruz Santa Rosa
Agua
CHOLO
Monte Verde
Las Mercedes
EL BALSAR
Santa Rosa
Monsefú
Acequia Cusupe
San Pedro
PUNTA DE CUSUPE
Espinal
La Cruz Del Faro
Salinas (abandonadas)
Rio Reque
Playa La Cruz del Faro
Agua
Eten
LA BOCANA DEL RIO
Campo deportivo
Fundo Santa Elena
La Capilla
Cachones
Puerto Eten
Mesa giratoria
ROADS
All weather:
Hard surface, two or more lanes wide
Loose or light surface one lane wide
Fair or dry weather:
Cart track
Footpath, trail
Power transmission line
Telegraph line, Telephone line
Cemetery; Church; School; Lighthouse
Stream
Contours
Dunes; Sand
Land subject to flooding; Dense woods
Cultivated land; Rice
0 1 2 3 4 5 6 7 8 kilometres
Scale 1:50 000 (2 cm = 1 km)

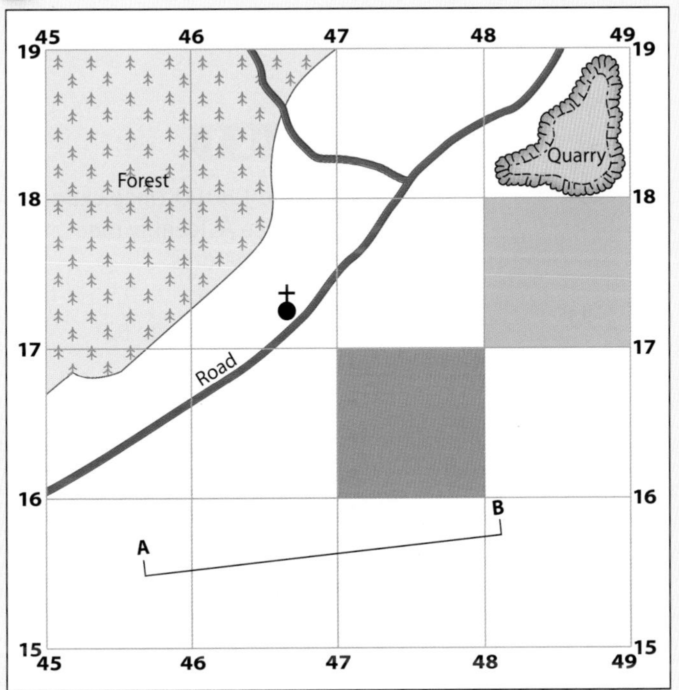

SKILLS Giving 4-figure and 6-figure references

1:25 000 and 1:50 000 maps have a grid of numbered squares on them. To see how a 4-figure grid reference is given, look at the grid in **Source A** and follow these instructions to give the reference for the red shaded square.

- 47 is the line left of the square.
- 16 is the line below the square.

Put these two numbers together and you have a 4-figure grid reference: 4716.

The 4-figure grid reference of the green shaded square is 4817 because the line on the left is line 48 and the line at the bottom is 17.

6-figure grid references are used to identify a location within a square. To see how a 6-figure reference is given, follow this example using **Source A**.

- For the church symbol 467 is the easting. 46 is the grid line to the left and 7 is the number of tenths along towards the next grid line.
- 173 is the northing. 17 is the grid line below and 3 is the number of tenths up towards the next grid line.
- The 6-figure reference is 467173.
- The 6-figure reference of the road junction is 475182. This point is halfway (five-tenths) between eastings 47 and 48 and two-tenths of the way between northings 18 and 19.

Task 1

Study the 1:50 000 map extract of Monsefu.

a Name the small settlements in the following squares: 2338 2635 2638

b What is at the following 6-figure references? 248352 195396 202383

SKILLS Working out distance and area

The scale of the Monsefu map is 1:50 000. This means that every centimetre on the map represents 50 000 centimetres (0.5 kilometres) in reality. Therefore the map has a scale of 2 cm = 1 km. This scale is shown by the line below the map.

To work out a **distance**, place a piece of paper with a straight edge between the two points you are measuring. Mark off these points, then transfer the piece of paper to the line below the map. Make sure that the first point marked on the paper is level with zero, then read off the distance between the two points. If you do this on the grid in **Source A** to measure line A–B you should get 2.5 km as your answer.

Each grid square on the map measures 2 cm x 2 cm and therefore it represents 1 square kilometre of land. To work out an **area**, count the total number of grid squares, or estimate areas that are smaller than a grid square, giving your answer in square kilometres. In **Source A**, the forest occupies a total of three grid squares so it is 3 km^2. The quarry takes up about half a grid square so this is an area of 0.5 km^2.

Task 2

Study the 1:50 000 map extract.

a What is the distance :
- along the telephone line from Puerto Eten to where it crosses the road north-east of Monsefu
- along the road from Monsefu to Santa Rosa?

b Estimate the area:
- of sand dunes between Santa Rosa and La Bocana del Rio
- of land subject to flooding at La Bocana del Rio.

Task 3

Study the 1:50 000 map extract. Find the following settlements:

- Eten (in and around grid square 2536)
- Monsefu (in and around grid square 2539)
- Puerto Eten (in grid square 2534)
- Santa Rosa (in grid square 1939).

The built-up area in each settlement is shown in pink.

Estimate the area of land covered by each settlement and then write the names of the four settlements in a list, from the largest one to the smallest.

Monsefu – some physical features

A Part of the 1:50 000 map

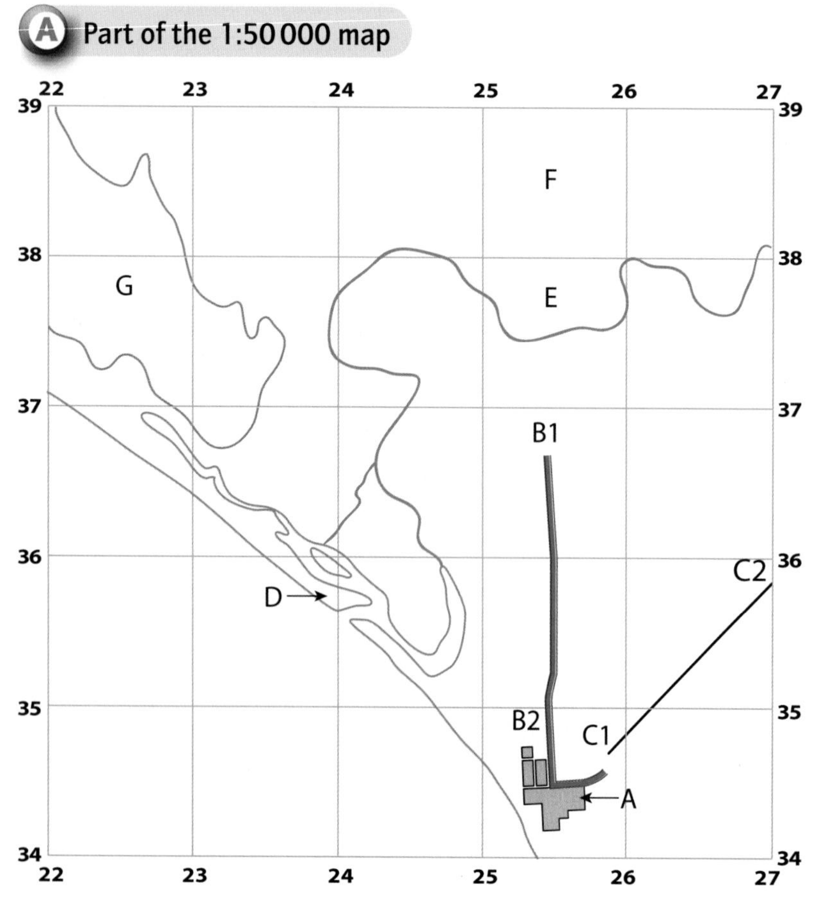

Study the 1:50 000 map extract and **Source A**. Identify the following features:

- settlement A
- road number B1 to B2
- line C1 to C2
- coastal landform D
- river E
- land use at F
- landform G.

Study **Source B**.

a Identify **two** similarities and **two** differences between the weather at Monsefu at 13.00 on 18 February and 07.00 on 20 February 2009.

b Describe how the weather changed between 01.00 and 19.00 on 19 February.

B Weather at Monsefu, 18–21 February 2009

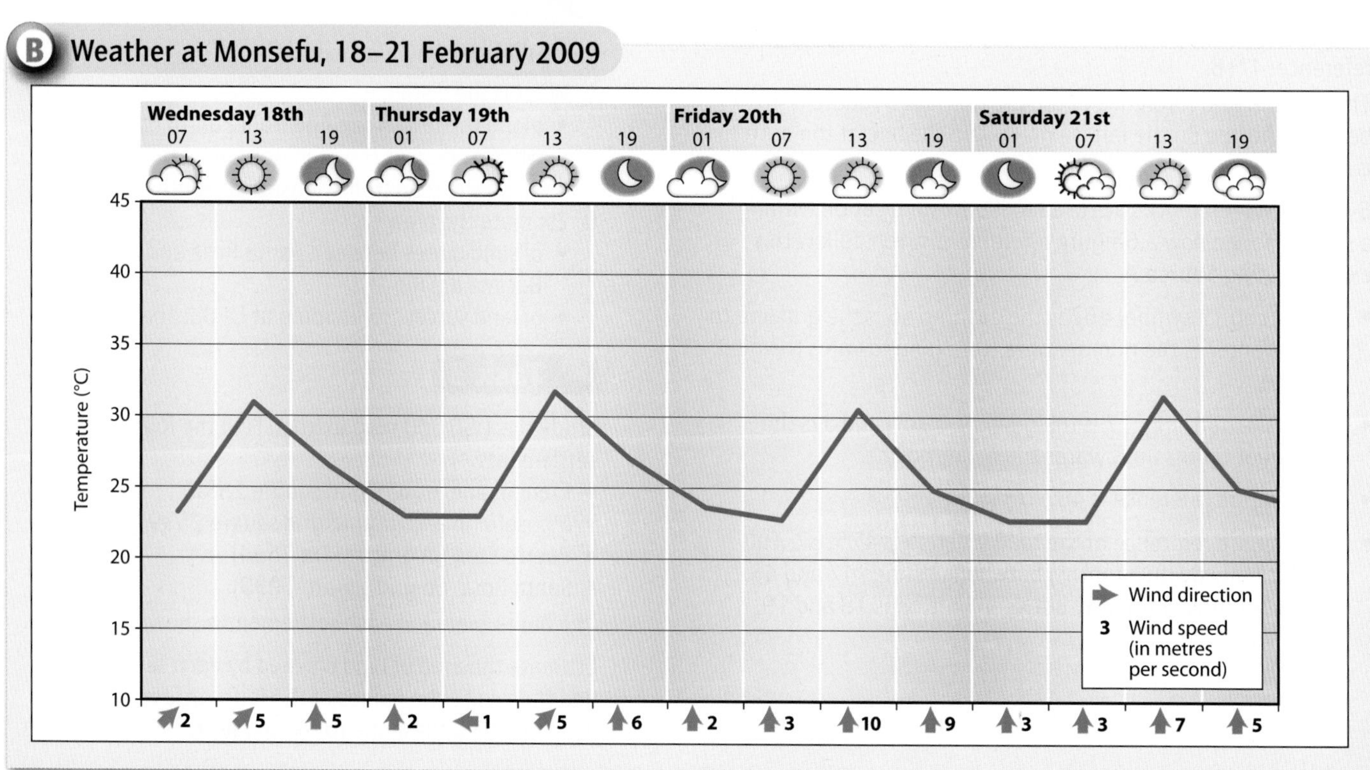

C Climate graphs for Lima and Cajamarca

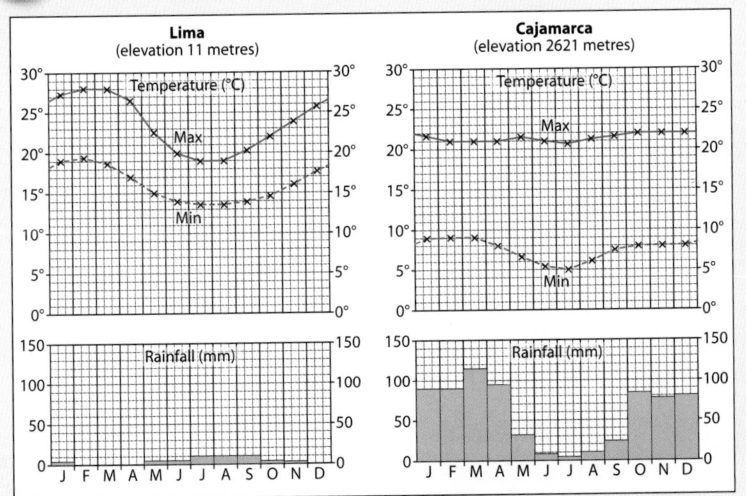

Task 3

Study **Sources C and D.**

a What is the average maximum temperature in Lima in April?
b Which month in Cajamarca has the highest rainfall?
c What is the average range of temperature in Lima in January?
d What is the average annual rainfall in Lima?
e Suggest reasons why there is more rainfall in Cajamarca than in Lima.
f Suggest reasons why January temperatures are higher in Lima than in Cajamarca.

D Regions of Peru

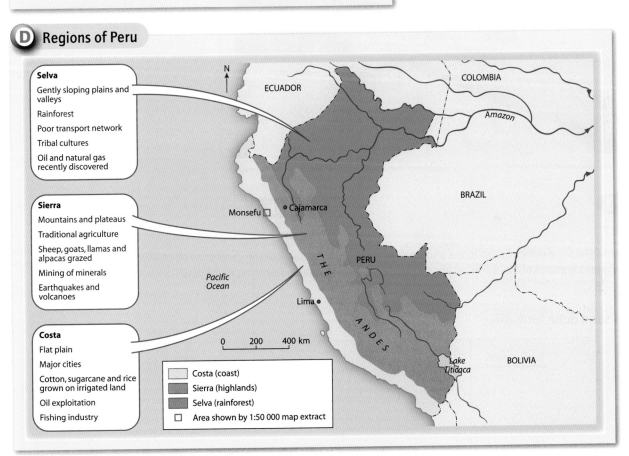

Selva
- Gently sloping plains and valleys
- Rainforest
- Poor transport network
- Tribal cultures
- Oil and natural gas recently discovered

Sierra
- Mountains and plateaus
- Traditional agriculture
- Sheep, goats, llamas and alpacas grazed
- Mining of minerals
- Earthquakes and volcanoes

Costa
- Flat plain
- Major cities
- Cotton, sugarcane and rice grown on irrigated land
- Oil exploitation
- Fishing industry

N
ECUADOR
COLOMBIA
Amazon
BRAZIL
Monsefu
Cajamarca
PERU
THE ANDES
Pacific Ocean
Lima
BOLIVIA
Lake Titicaca
0 200 400 km

Costa (coast)
Sierra (highlands)
Selva (rainforest)
Area shown by 1:50 000 map extract

Task 4

Study **Sources C and D.**

a Compare the relief of the three regions in Peru.
b Suggest reasons why over 40 per cent of the population of Peru live in the Costa region.
c Give **two** advantages and **two** difficulties of living in the Sierra region.
d Oil and natural gas have recently been discovered in the Selva region. Explain why it is difficult to exploit these resources.

Task 5

In recent years the tourist industry has become important in parts of Peru. In groups, carry out research and prepare a presentation that identifies, locates and describes the attractions of Peru as a tourist destination.

Sand dunes on the coast of Peru

A Coastal sand dunes

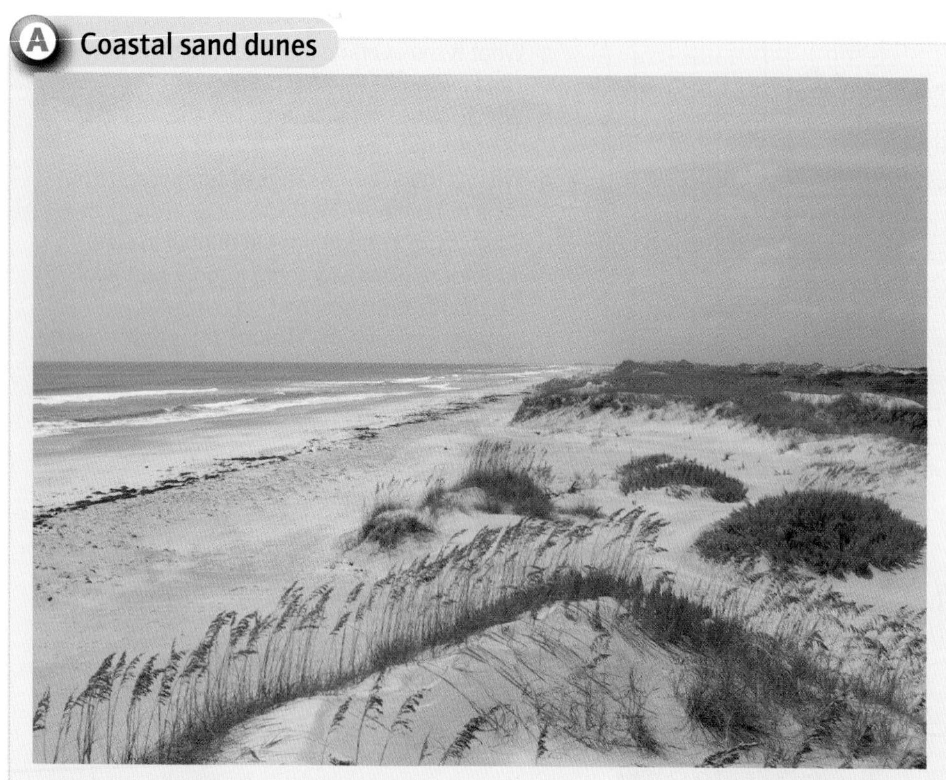

The 1:50 000 map on page 172 shows an area of sand dunes between Santa Rosa and La Bocana del Rio. Coastal sand dunes form where constructive waves encourage the deposition of sand on a beach, and where prevailing onshore winds blow this sand inland. An obstacle, such as a plant or a pebble, traps the sand and as the particles get trapped they start to accumulate to create a mound of sand. The wind then erodes particles from the windward side and deposits them on the leeward side. Gradually this action causes the dune to move inland. As it does so it accumulates more and more sand.

Task 1

Study **Source A**.

Draw a sketch of the sand dunes shown in the photograph. Label **four** different features of the dunes on your sketch.

Task 2

Study the 1:50 000 map on page 172 and **Source B**.

Explain how the sand dunes between Santa Rosa and La Bocana del Rio were formed.

B Coastal sand dune formation

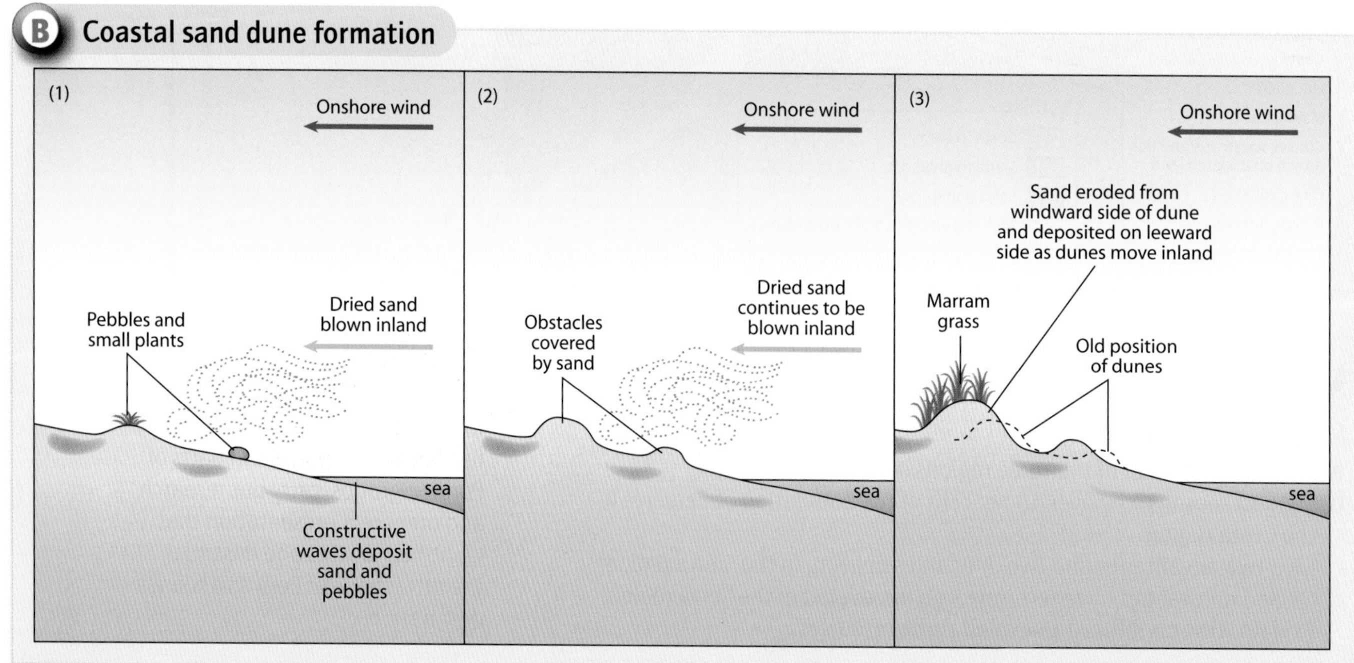

C How sand dunes are used

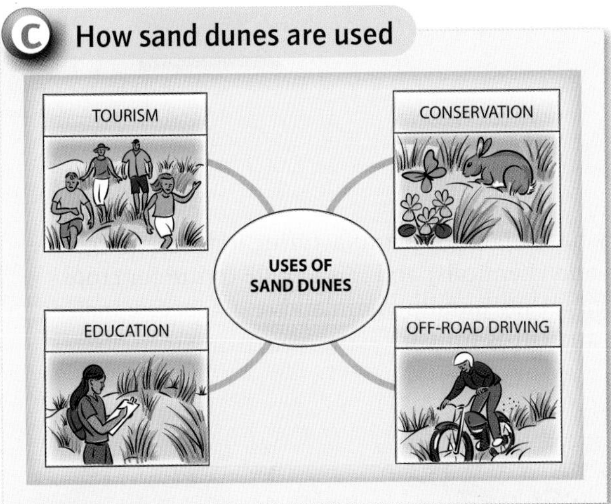

E Schools use sand dunes

D Tourists using sand dunes

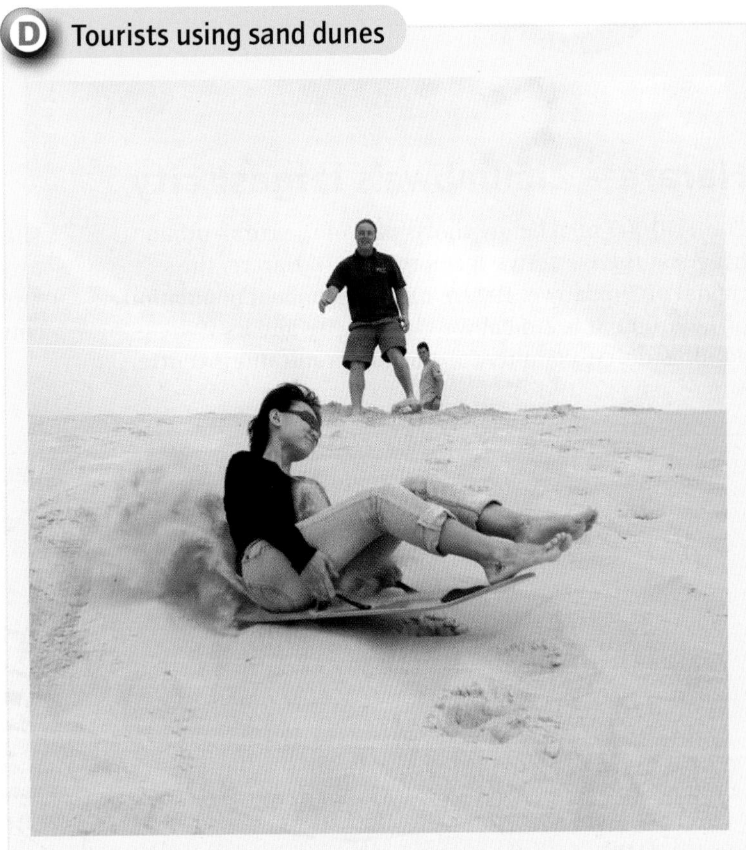

F A conflict matrix

	TOURISM	EDUCATION	CONSERVATION	OFF-ROAD DRIVING
TOURISM	—	?	?	?
EDUCATION	?	—	✓	✗
CONSERVATION	?	✓	—	✗
OFF-ROAD DRIVING	?	✗	✗	—

✗ Conflict
? Possible conflict
✓ No conflict

G Dune management

Task 3

There are conflicts arising over the use of the sand dunes between Santa Rosa and La Bocana del Rio. They are being used for many different purposes and the dunes and ecosystems are being damaged.

Study **Sources C to G**.

The table shows information about four possible schemes being considered to manage the dunes.

In groups, choose the scheme that you think will be most useful to manage the dunes. Explain your reasons for choosing this scheme. You should do this by describing the advantages of the scheme you have chosen and the disadvantages of the schemes you have rejected.

Scheme 1	Scheme 2
Ban all human activities on the dunes, and use 24-hour security patrols and CCTV.	Fence off areas of the dunes so that different activities can take place in each.
Scheme 3	**Scheme 4**
Provide a free information centre and guides for students and visitors.	Allow unlimited use and charge an entrance fee to all users of the dunes.

Harare, Zimbabwe

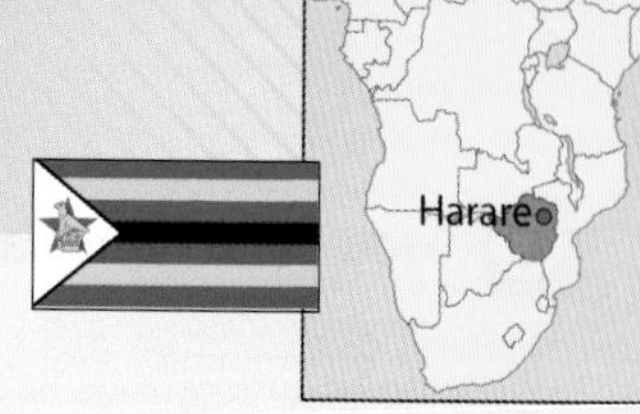

Harare – Zimbabwe's largest city

The 1:50 000 map below shows part of the rural–urban fringe on the western edge of the city of Harare, the capital of Zimbabwe. Harare has an estimated population of 1 600 000. It is Zimbabwe's largest city and its administrative, commercial and communications centre.

The city has important manufacturing industries (e.g. steel, textiles and chemicals) and it is a trade centre for crops produced on surrounding farmland (e.g. tobacco, maize, cotton, and citrus fruits).

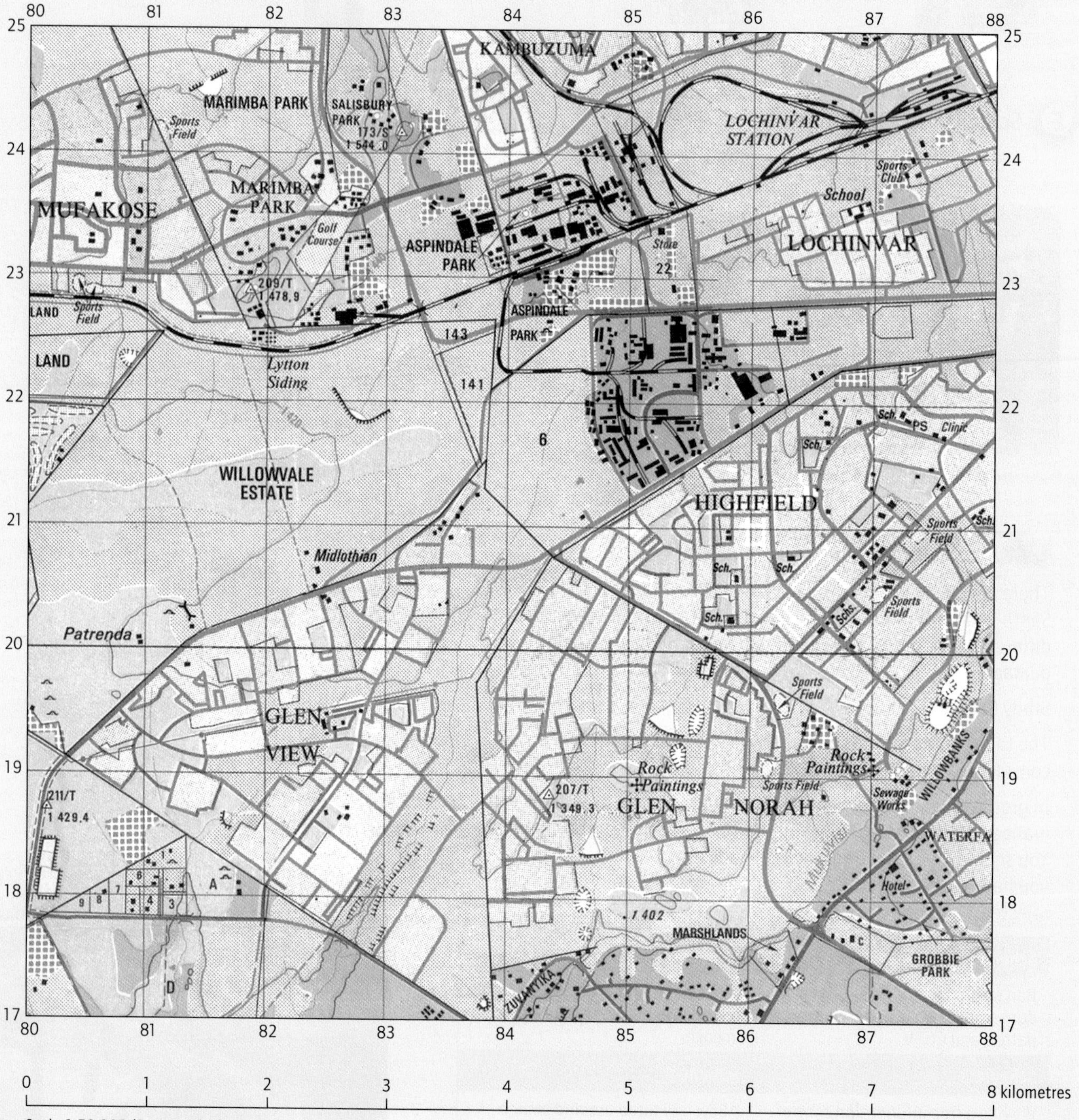

SKILLS Giving a compass bearing

A bearing is a numerical measurement of direction between two points. Bearings use all 360° of a compass to indicate direction. The bearings on a compass are numbered clockwise with north as 0°, east 90°, south 180°, and west 270°. So a bearing of 135° would be south-east and a bearing of 315° would be north-west. A protractor can be used to measure the bearing.

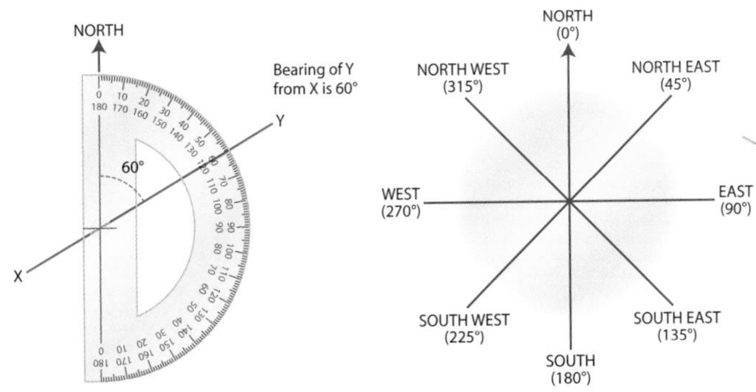

Key for 1:50 000 map

- Road, Wide tarred
- Road, Narrow tarred
- Road, Gravel or earth, Bridge
- Railway, with embankment, Cutting, Tunnel
- Built-up area, Buildings
- Church
- Dip tank
- River, Watercourse
- Dam
- Contours at 20 metre vertical interval, with Cliff feature (1 000, 900)
- Cultivation
- Medium bush
- Sparse bush
- Orchard or plantation

Task 1

Study the 1:50 000 map extract. Find where the railway line crosses the road at 832228. Imagine that a train is travelling along this railway to the eastern edge of the map.

- **a** Use the scale of the map to work out the distance of this journey.
- **b** Work out the compass direction in which the train will be travelling.
- **c** What is the compass bearing from where the railway crosses the road to the eastern edge of the map?
- **d** Imagine you are sitting on this train, looking out of the window on your right-hand side (i.e. to the south of the railway line).
  Write a paragraph to describe what you would see from the window on this part of your journey. You will need to use the map key.

Task 2

Study the 1:50 000 map extract.

- **a** Give evidence from the map which shows that Highfield (in and around grid square 8621) is a densely populated area.
- **b** Suggest reasons why the land around the Mukuvisi river (in and around grid square 8618) does not have many people living on it.

Task 3

Study the 1:50 000 map extract. Much of the land in grid square 8423 is used for manufacturing industries.

- **a** Use map evidence to suggest the advantages of the site for manufacturing industries.
- **b** Suggest benefits and problems of this manufacturing industry for local people and the natural environment.

Urban farming in Harare

A Land use in Harare

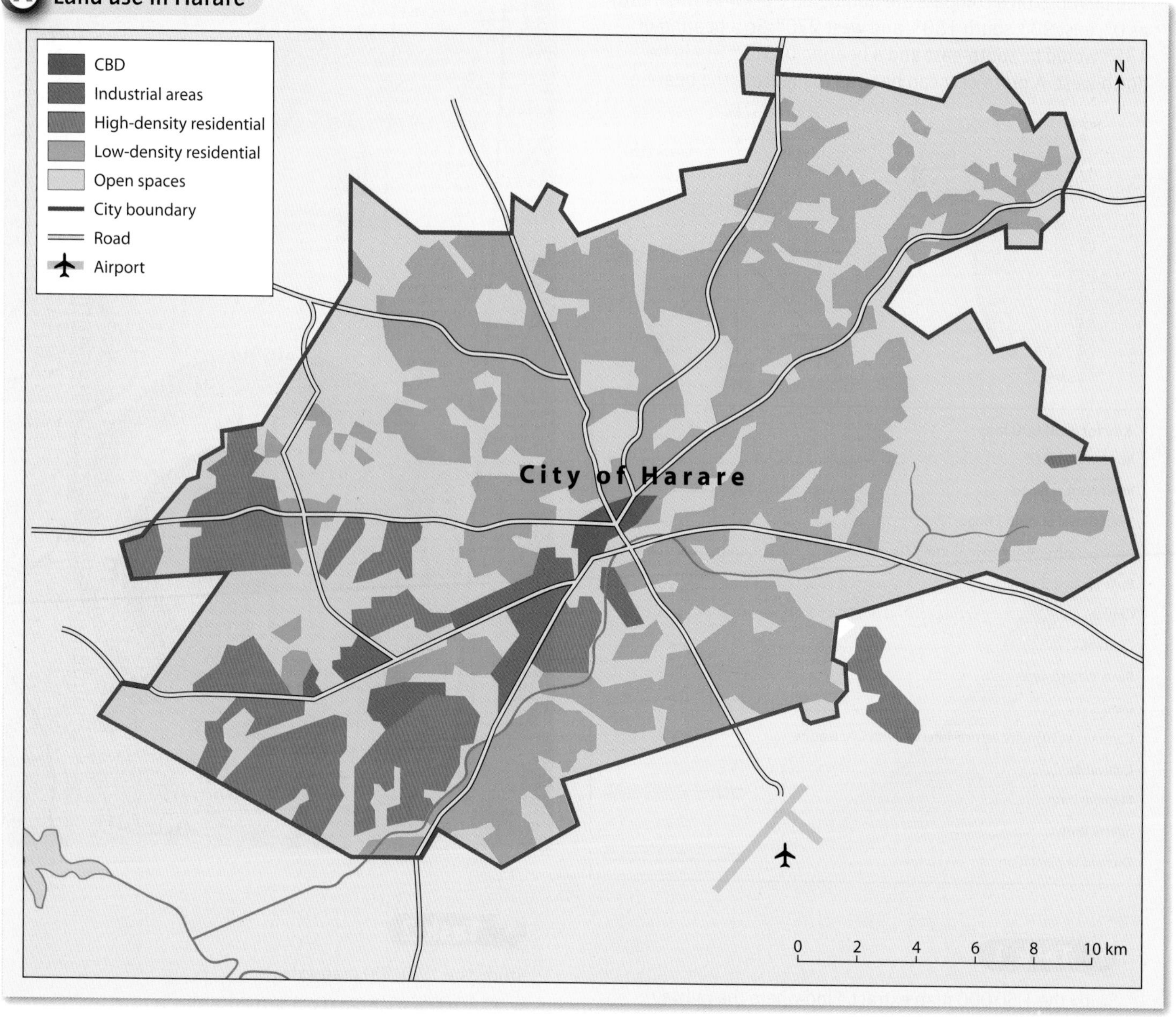

Whilst farming is often thought of as a rural activity, many poor families who live in cities in LEDCs would not have food to eat without growing crops in their backyards, on roadside verges or allotments, and any other areas of open space. Harare has a warm, wet climate and there are large open spaces in and around the city. River floods in the long, wet season prevent building on low land, but provide water for irrigation for farmers. Tomatoes, green vegetables and maize are the main crops. Urban farmers, mainly women, grow the crops to eat, or to sell at market to earn money to buy meat and pay for their children's education. In some parts of the city more than two-thirds of households carry out some farming, either around their homes or on public land such as roadside verges.

Task 1

Study **Source A**.

- **a** What is the distance and direction from the airport to the CBD?
- **b** Estimate the percentage of land within the boundary of Harare that is open space.
- **c** Suggest reasons why large areas of land are likely to be used for farming within the city boundary to the south-west of the CBD of Harare.

B What do the farmers grow?

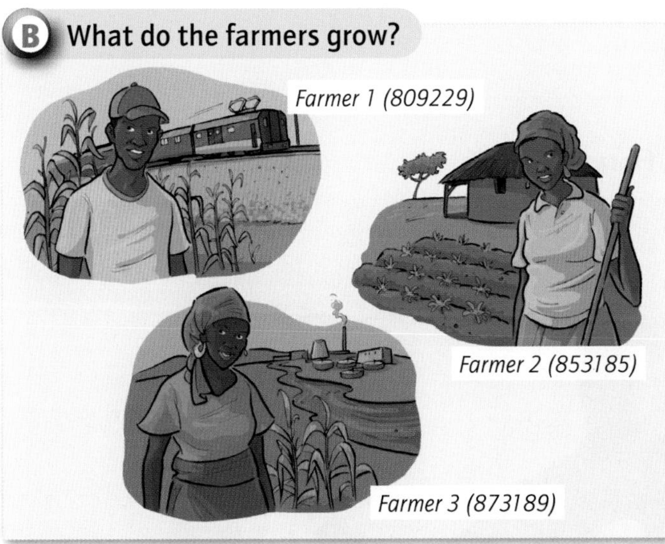

Task 2

Study the 1:50 000 map extract on page 178 and **Source B**.

a Use the 6-figure reference to name the suburb and describe the characteristics of the area where each of the urban farmers grows crops.

b Suggest a different difficulty faced by each of farmers 1, 2 and 3 when growing their crops.

C Benefits and problems of urban farming in LEDCs

BENEFITS

- Food is produced for poor families
- Surplus food sold on local markets for income to reduce poverty
- Use made of land that may otherwise be wasted
- Plants grown help reduce atmospheric pollution
- Producing food locally saves transport and storage costs
- Waste water and organic solid waste can be used on the farms

PROBLEMS

- Chemicals used may pollute local drinking water supplies
- Farmers will be at risk from mosquitoes when farming near rivers
- Conflict occurs over the use of land and farmers can lose their land at any time
- Crops grown close to roads and railways could be contaminated by fumes
- The use of land for farming competes with other urban land uses, especially public open spaces
- Use of water for crops reduces scarce supplies and increases cost

D The growth of urban farming

Harare's middle-class residents take up urban farming to counter food shortages

January 2007

Urban farming, widely practised by the poor and lower-income groups in the Zimbabwean capital, Harare, is becoming popular among the city's wealthy people. In rich suburbs like Avondale and Mabelreign, maize and vegetable plots are being cultivated to counter expected food shortages brought on by an economic crisis that has seen the inflation rate remaining well above 1000 per cent, the highest in the world.

With unemployment estimated at above 80 per cent and basic foodstuffs becoming unaffordable, even for those who have jobs, vacant land is being turned into agricultural land. Tatenda Muzenda, a domestic helper in Cotswold Hills, a middle-class suburb, said: 'I was so desperate to grow maize that I went and planted some maize seeds on the only available open field that I could identify, and that was next to the local police station.'

In the past, police have uprooted crops being grown on vacant land in the city, but they now seem to be turning a blind eye as the capital goes green.

Suppliers of agricultural inputs in Harare said that most of their clients were now urban farmers. 'We have noticed that now most of the people buying maize seed and fertiliser are urban farmers, because they are buying in smaller quantities, an indication that they will only apply it on smaller pieces of land,' said an employee at one supplier.

Although the Harare Municipality has officially banned urban farming, it appears to be ignoring it. However, Harare municipality spokesman Percy Toriro said: 'We will not allow people to plant maize anywhere they want. Residents should find out from their local district offices if there is any piece of land where they can practise urban farming. We want to ensure that the environment is well looked after.'

Task 3

Study the 1:50 000 map extract on page 178 and **Sources C and D**.

Imagine you are an adviser to the Harare Municipality. Consider the arguments for and against allowing urban land to be used for farming and decide whether urban agriculture should be allowed to continue in suburbs such as Glen Norah and Glen View. Prepare a report to justify your decision.

Quality of life

A Children collect stagnant water for use in Glen View, Harare

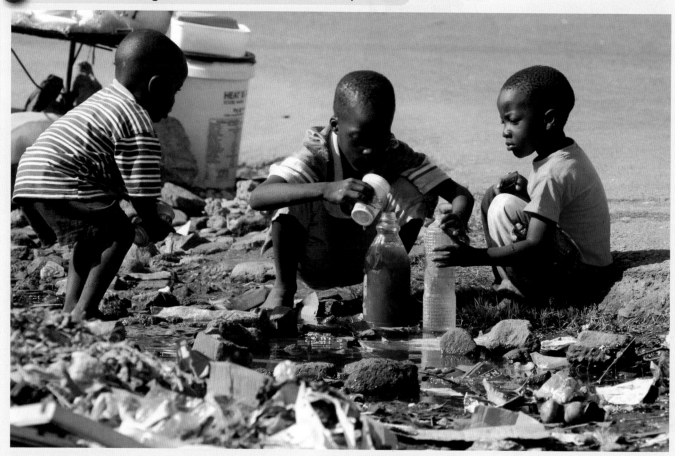

B Access to clean water in Africa

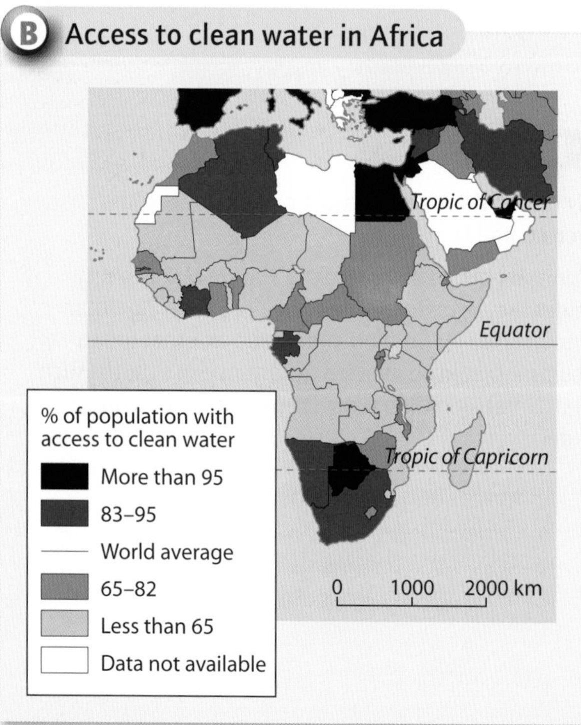

Task 1

Study **Source A** and the 1:50 000 map on page 178.

a Give a 4-figure reference for the grid square in which the photograph could have been taken.

b Suggest what the quality of life will be like for the children shown in the photograph.

Task 2

Study **Source B** and an atlas.

a Put the following countries in rank order according to the percentage of their population that has access to clean water. Rank from high to low.
- Algeria
- Egypt
- Mali
- Zimbabwe

b Name **three** countries where between 83 and 95 per cent have access to clean water.

c Describe the distribution of those countries where less than 65 per cent of the population have access to clean water.

d Suggest reasons why the access of the population to clean water varies from country to country.

C Quality of life indicators for selected LEDCs

Country	GDP per person (US$)	Energy use per person (kg oil equivalent)	Number of doctors (per 100 000 people)	Adult literacy (percentages)
Algeria	6603	1036	85	70
Bangladesh	1870	158	23	41
Egypt	4211	708	212	56
Ethiopia	756	299	3	42
India	3139	519	51	61
Mexico	9803	1563	171	85
South Africa	11 192	1093	69	81
Zimbabwe	2100	752	6	90

Source: The World, 11th edition, published 2008 (Amnesty International)

Task 3

Study **Source C**.

a 'People in Zimbabwe have a lower quality of life than people in Egypt.' Give **two** pieces of evidence from the table to support this statement.

b Which country in the table do you think has the highest quality of life? Give reasons for your answer.

E Assessing quality of life 1

F Assessing quality of life 2

D GDP and energy use

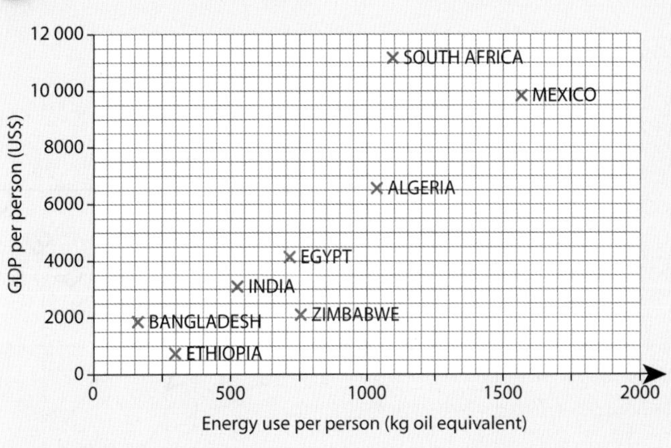

Task 4

Study **Sources C and D**.

a To what extent is there a relationship between GDP per person and the use of energy? Use examples of countries and give figures in your answer.

b Draw a scatter graph showing the relationship between GDP per person and adult literacy.

c Explain why there is a positive relationship between GDP per person and adult literacy.

d Suggest reasons why Zimbabwe does not fit into the pattern shown by the scatter graph.

G A bi-polar chart for quality of life

Clean	+3	+2	+1	0	−1	−2	−3	Dirty
Healthy	+3	+2	+1	0	−1	−2	−3	Unhealthy
Quiet	+3	+2	+1	0	−1	−2	−3	Noisy
Safe	+3	+2	+1	0	−1	−2	−3	Dangerous
Empty	+3	+2	+1	0	−1	−2	−3	Crowded
Permanent	+3	+2	+1	0	−1	−2	−3	Temporary

Task 5

Study **Sources E, F and G. Source G** is a chart which can be used to assess the quality of life in an urban area.

a The photographs in **Sources E and F** show areas where people live in the same city. Use **Source G** to compare the quality of life in the two areas. To do this you will need to give each of the areas a score between +3 and −3 on each line. When you have done this you can work out an overall score for each area.

b Use a suitable method to graph your figures.

c Which area would you want to live in: the one shown in **Source E or Source F**? Give reasons for your answer.

MAP WORK 3 Ewaso Kedong, Kenya

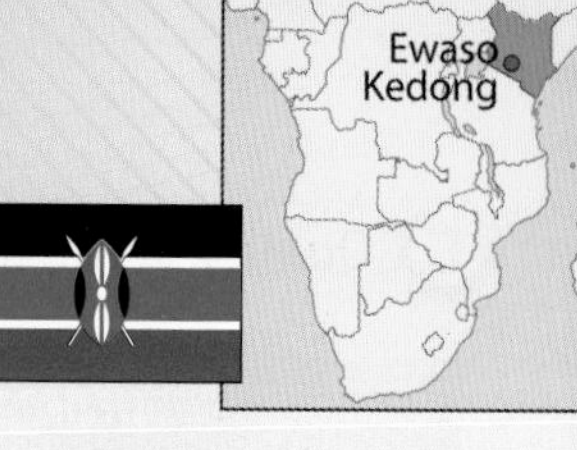

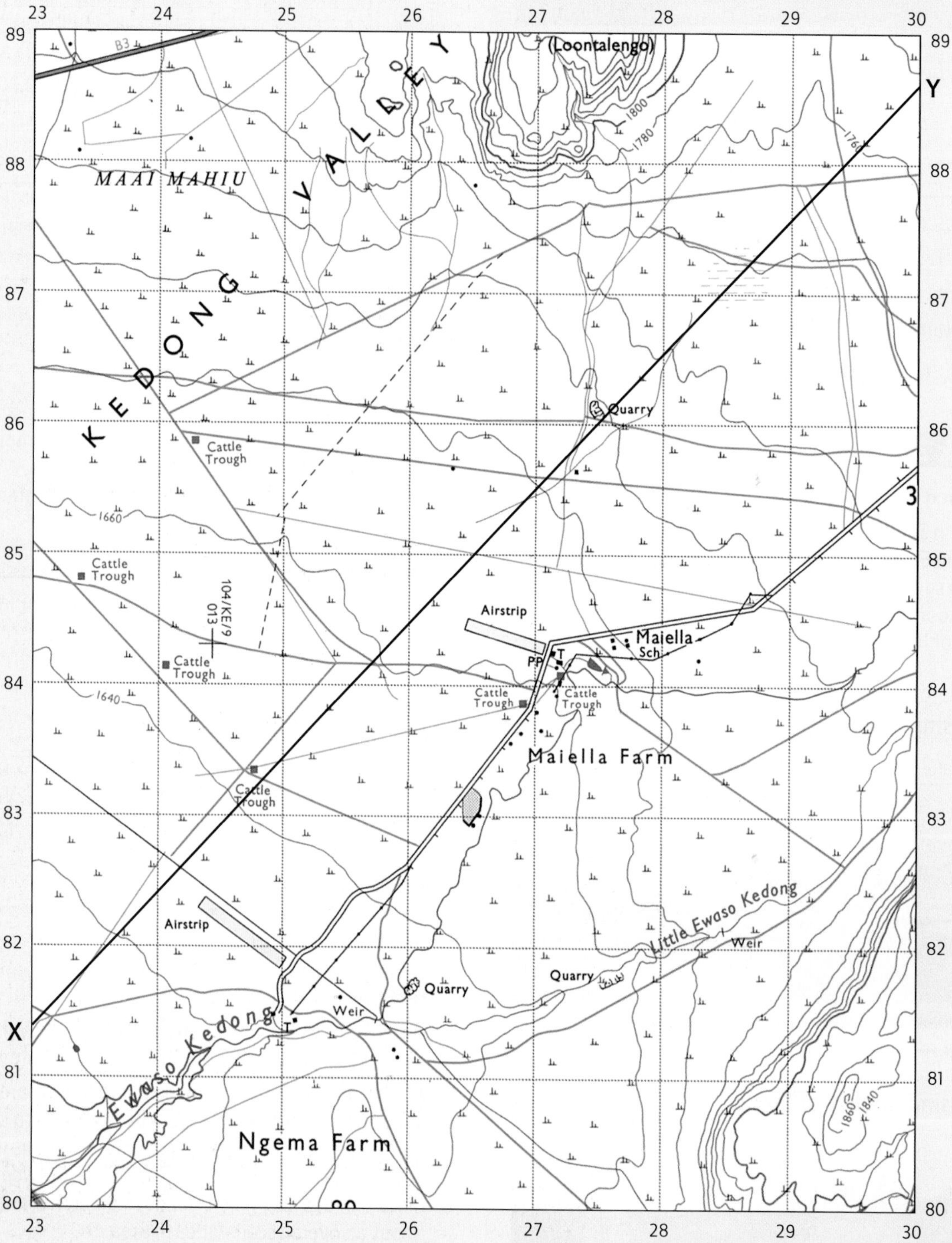

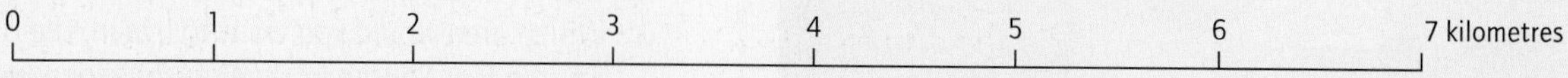

(Loontalengo)

MAAI MAHIU

KEDONG VALLEY

B3

1800

1780

1760

1660

1640

1860

1840

Quarry

Cattle Trough

Cattle Trough

Cattle Trough

Cattle Trough

Cattle Trough

Cattle Trough

104/KE/9 013

Airstrip

Airstrip

Maiella

Sch

PP

T

Maiella Farm

Little Ewaso Kedong

Weir

Quarry

Quarry

Weir

Ewaso Kedong

Ngema Farm

X

Y

Grid eastings: 23, 24, 25, 26, 27, 28, 29, 30

Grid northings: 89, 88, 87, 86, 85, 84, 83, 82, 81, 80

0 1 2 3 4 5 6 7 kilometres

Scale 1:50 000 (2 cm = 1 km)

Key to 1:50 000 map

Populated area, Houses		Contours (V.I. 20m) Depression	2000 1980 1960
All weather road: Bound surface	A12 Road Number	Watercourse, Waterfall, Rapids, Dam	
Dry weather road	Culvert Bridge	Water tank	■
Main track (motorable)		Scrub	
Other track and footpath		Police post	PP
Spot height (in metres)	• 2256	School	Sch
		Telephone	T

Representing height

To represent height on a map, spot heights and contours are used.

Spot heights are dots placed anywhere on the map with a number next to them. This tells us the exact height of that spot in metres above sea level. Sometimes spot heights show the highest part of a hill, but they can show any height, anywhere on the map.

Contours are brown lines on a map that join together places of equal height. These can be used to work out what the relief of the land is like (its height and shape).

Conflict over water in Kenya

Kenya is a country in East Africa which, in many regions, relies on agriculture. Most of the land in the valley of the Ewaso Kedong river is used for grazing cattle, but like many other parts of the country there is not enough water available.

Water shortages have resulted in conflict in various parts of the country as people fight over this scarce commodity. The amount of water in the Ewaso Kedong river has been reduced because of drought. The Maasai, who live downstream, claim that farmers upstream are using the river water for irrigation, thereby reducing the supply for themselves and their animals.

Task 1

Study the 1:50 000 map extract and **Source A**.

Give a 4-figure reference for a grid square for each of the following.

a Steep slopes between 1700 and 1800 metres above sea level

b A plateau above 1800 metres high

c A gentle slope between 1640 and 1660 metres above sea level

A A landscape in Kenya

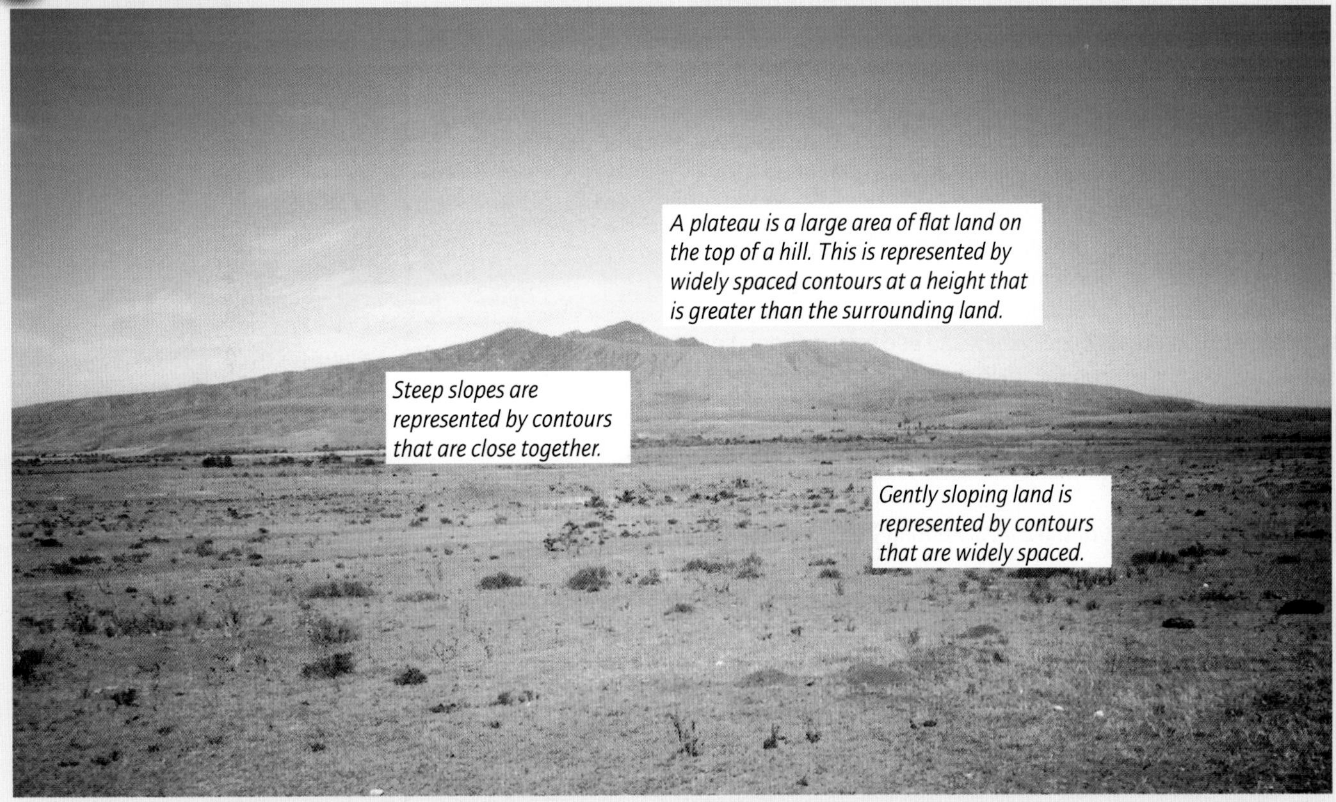

A plateau is a large area of flat land on the top of a hill. This is represented by widely spaced contours at a height that is greater than the surrounding land.

Steep slopes are represented by contours that are close together.

Gently sloping land is represented by contours that are widely spaced.

Describing the physical landscape

SKILLS Describing relief and drainage

When you are describing the **relief** of an area you should begin by referring to the main relief features, e.g. glaciated upland, coastal plain or escarpment etc. Name any such feature and describe it if possible, e.g. 'This map area forms part of a coastal plain with gentle slopes.'

Then refer to relief features within the area, e.g. valleys, spurs, ridges, plateaus, stating where they are (possibly by the use of grid references), and describe them. It is useful to describe slopes on the map, e.g. flat, gently sloping, steep, and to add some references to height. You can get this information from contour lines or spot heights, e.g. 'The river, which flows around interlocking spurs through grid square 3498, has steep valley sides which lie between 240 and 475 metres and its source is on the ridge at 337976 at 512 metres above sea level. The ridge has steep north-facing slopes, although those that face south are gentler.'

When you are describing the **drainage** of an area you should note the following:

- Name the main rivers and state the direction(s) of flow.
- Density of surface drainage. This can be judged by the number of rivers and streams shown and how close together they are, e.g. 'There are many rivers in the east of the map but very few in the west.'
- Width of rivers, e.g. 'The wide river that flows through grid square 9811 is joined by many narrow tributaries.'
- Long profile of rivers: this can be judged by how close together the contours are where a river crosses, e.g. 'The river has a steep and irregular long profile and there is a waterfall at grid reference 348512.'
- The course of the rivers, e.g. are they meandering or straight? Perfectly straight drainage is usually artificial, and used for drainage or irrigation.

When you have described the relief and drainage it should be possible to summarise your comments on a sketch map to show the main aspects of the physical landscape. Label significant features in each region, e.g. plateau, ridge, valley, and add information about the drainage by marking on the main rivers and their valleys.

Task 1

Study the map extract of the Ewaso Kedong valley on page 184.

Also use **Sources A and B** which show how to use contour patterns to identify types of slope and relief features.

a Describe the relief and drainage of the area shown on the map.

b Draw a labelled sketch map to show the relief and drainage of the area.

A Contour patterns and slopes

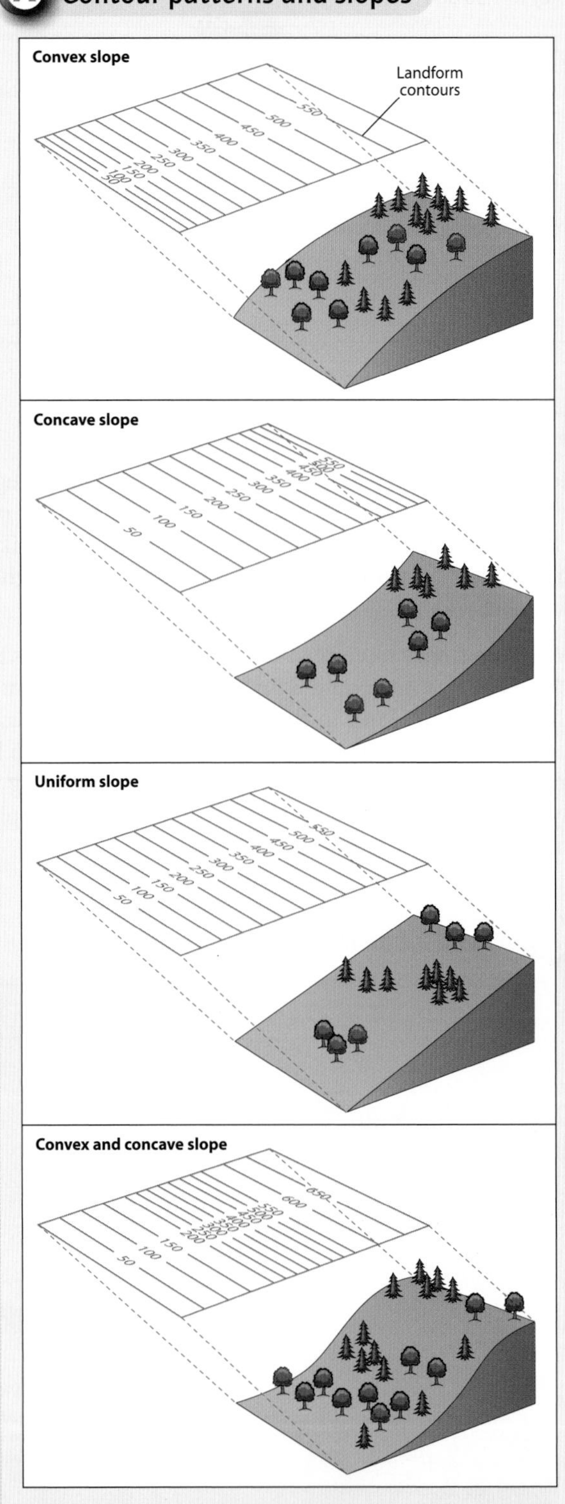

Task 2

Study the map extract again.

Give evidence from the map to identify **three** ways in which the area is used by people. For each piece of evidence you should give a grid reference.

B Contour patterns and landforms

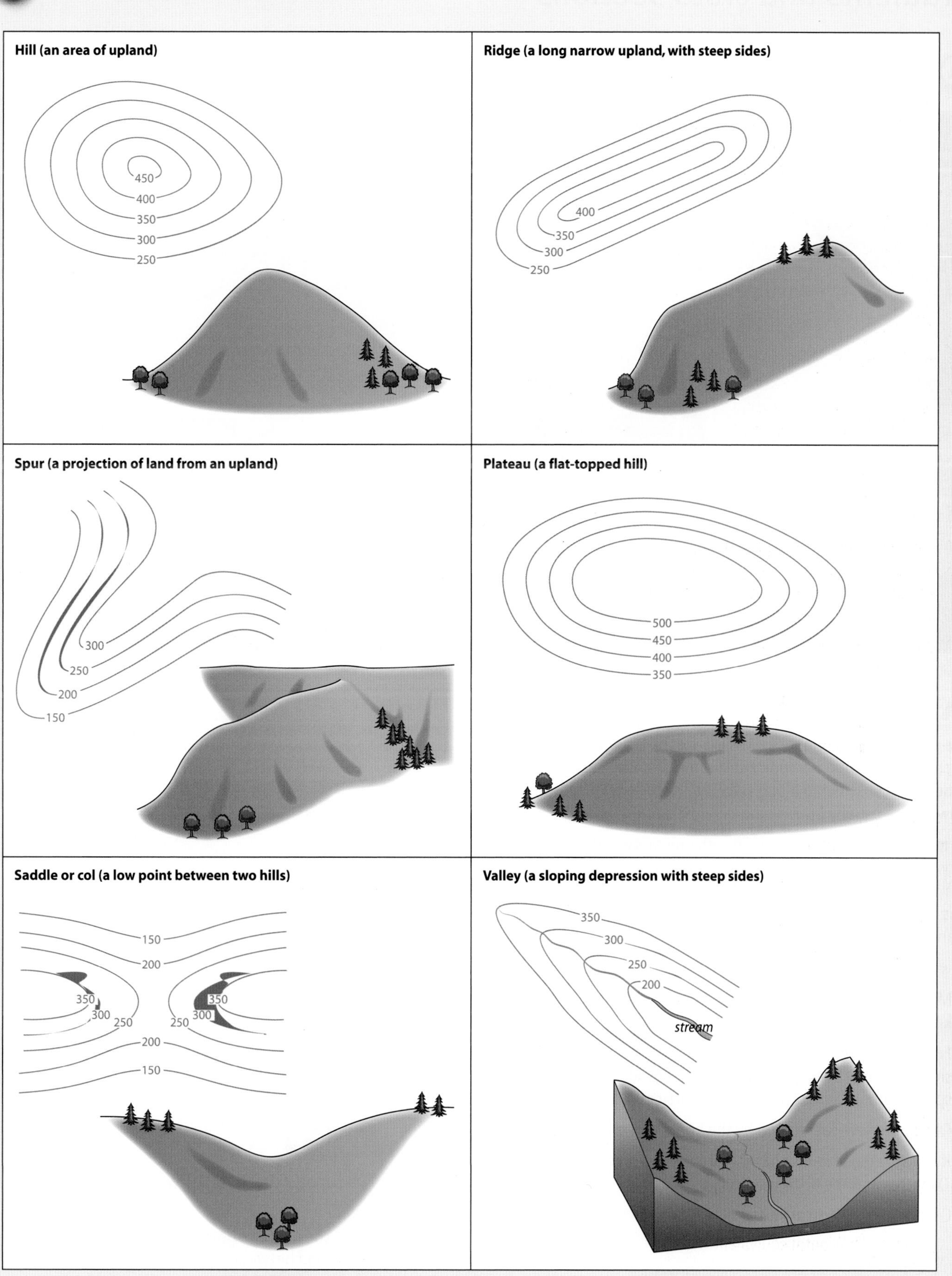

Gradients and cross-sections

A Gradients

SKILLS How to calculate a gradient

The gradient of a slope measures the steepness of the slope. The steepness of a slope is important to walkers and cyclists. Roads are sometimes constructed along slopes with steep gradients, although railways are usually built on more gentle slopes.

On many maps roads are marked with one arrow if the gradient is between 1 in 7 and 1 in 5, and with two arrows if it is steeper than 1 in 5. A gradient of 1 in 5 can also be expressed as a 20% gradient. This means that for every 5 metres of horizontal distance there is a change in height of 1 metre. This is shown in **Source B**.

To work out the average gradient of a slope on a map:

- Measure the horizontal distance along the slope in metres. This is known as the **horizontal equivalent**.
- Find the difference in height between the two end points of the slope (this can be worked out in metres by looking at contours or spot heights). This is known as the **vertical interval.**
- Divide the vertical interval by the horizontal equivalent.

So if the difference in height between the top and bottom of a slope is 10 metres and the distance along the slope is 100 metres:

$$\text{Gradient} = \frac{\text{Vertical interval}}{\text{Horizontal equivalent}} = \frac{10}{100} \text{ or 1 in 10 or 10\%}$$

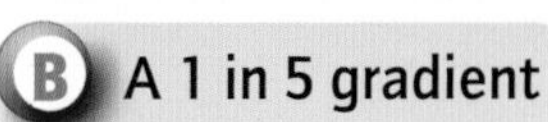

B A 1 in 5 gradient

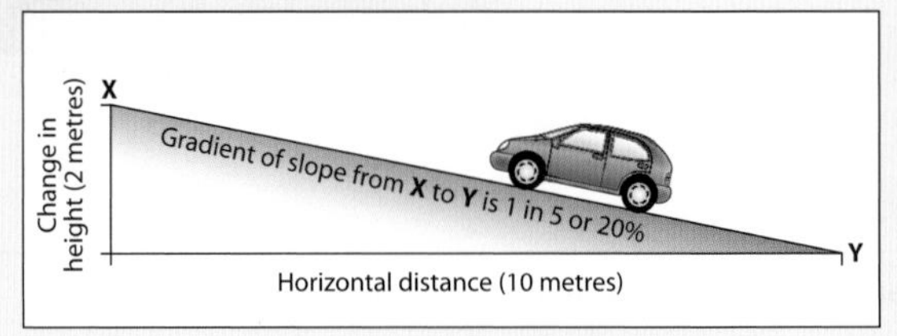

Task 1

a Why can roads be constructed on steeper gradients than railway lines?

b Which gradient is steeper?
- 1 in 3 or 1 in 10
- 10% or 20%

Task 2

Study the map extract of the Ewaso Kedong valley on page 184.

Calculate the average gradient along the Dry Weather Road between 256824 and 288847.

SKILLS How to draw a cross-section

A cross-section is a diagram showing variations in height and slope along a line drawn on a map. To draw a cross-section:

- Place a piece of paper with a straight edge along the cross-section line on your map. Mark the beginning and ending of the line with the letters X and Y.
- Along the straight edge of your paper mark the point where each contour crosses it, labelling the height of each contour. You will need to estimate the heights at the end of the line. Also mark the points where features such as rivers, roads and railway lines cross the line of the cross-section (see **Source C** Stage 1).
- Draw a frame for your cross-section on graph paper. The base of the frame should be the same length as your cross-section line. Use a vertical scale that shows the height in metres.
- Put the straight edge of your piece of paper along the base of the frame and mark a small cross at the correct height, using the vertical scale, where each contour line is marked on the straight edge (see **Source C** Stage 2).
- Join the dots with a smooth line and shade the land. Draw arrows and label the position of rivers, roads, railway lines and any other features (see **Source C** Stage 3).

Task 3

Study the map extract of the Ewaso Kedong valley on page 184.

a Draw a cross-section along the line from X to Y.

b On the cross-section you have drawn, mark the positions of a main track, a cattle trough and a quarry.

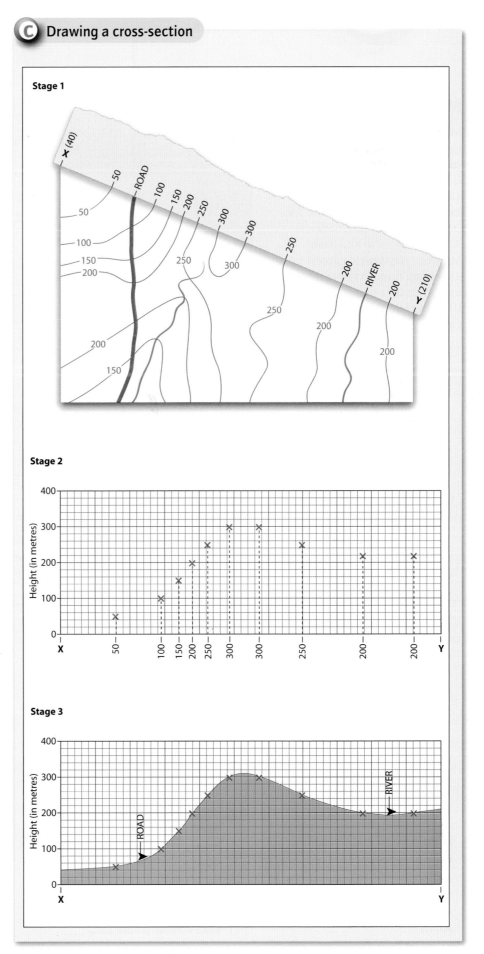

C Drawing a cross-section

Stage 1

Stage 2

Stage 3

Montego Bay, Jamaica

Montego Bay

Montego Bay is an important tourist resort on the north-west coast of the island of Jamaica. It has a population of about 120 000 people and close by is Jamaica's largest airport, the Sir Donald Sangster International Airport. Flights to and from Montego Bay provide access for increasing numbers of tourists from countries such as the USA, the UK, Germany and Canada.

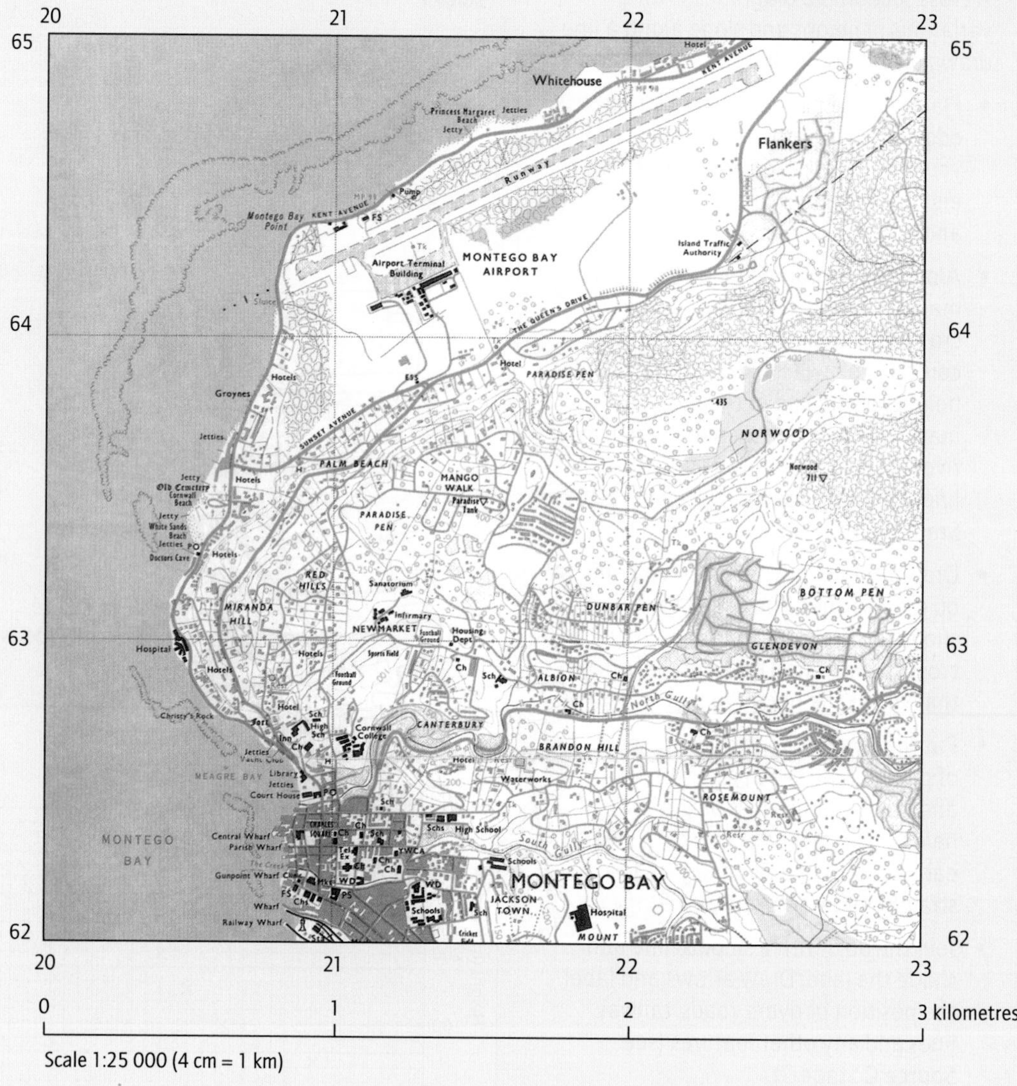

Key

- Road - 1st Class (Mile Post) — MP 6
- Road - Other
- Track or Footpath
- Railway
- Railway - Light or Siding
- Railway - Disused
- Power Line
- Telephone Line
- Telephone Line along Road
- Contours (V I 50 feet) — 550, 500, 450
- Contour showing Depression
- Antiquity — Fort
- Cemetery
- Ruin
- Mangrove

- Swamp or Marsh
- Line of Small Trees, Palms
- Bamboo
- Well, Waterhole, Spring — W, WH, S
- Reservoir, Tank — Resr, Tk

Church	Ch	Police Station	PS
Electricity Sub Station	ESS	Post Agency	PA
Fire Station	FS	Post Office	PO
Hospital	Hosp	Pump House	Pump
Hotel	H	School	Sch
Market	Mkt	Wireless Station	WS
Mission	M	Works Department	WD

- Town
- Building-Public, Other
- Areas of small or semi-permanent buildings

- Boundary - County
- Boundary - Parish
- Trigonometrical Station - Primary
- Trigonometrical Station - Secondary
- Trigonometrical Station - Tertiary
- Spot Height (Photogrammetric) — 646
- Dense Woodland
- Trees and Bushes
- Forest Plantation
- Plantation - Banana
- Plantation - Citrus
- Plantation - Coconut
- Plantation - Sugar
- Unclassified Plantation or Pasture
- Mixed or Scattered Cultivation

SKILLS Describing site and situation

Site is a description of the actual land on which a feature is built. This includes the relief of the land (its height above sea level, its slope and its aspect) and the size of the area of land.

Situation is a description of where the feature is built in relation to other features around it. This includes natural features such as rivers or the coast, and built features such as settlements. Distance and direction from these features should be used to describe the situation accurately.

A Montego Bay airport

Task 1

Study the map opposite.

a In which grid square is the airport terminal building? You will need to give a 4-figure reference.
b Use the scale to work out the length of the runway. Give your answer in kilometres and metres.
c Look at the symbol used to show the vegetation between the runway and the coast. Use the key to identify this vegetation.
d Find the symbol at 211644. Use the key to identify this building. Why do all airports need this type of building?

Task 2

Look at the photograph of the airport in **Source A**. In which direction do you think the camera was pointing? Give reasons for your answer.

Task 3

a In the box below, there are eleven statements about Montego Bay Airport. You will find **three** correct statements about the site of the airport and **three** about its situation.

- It is on low land, less than 50 feet above sea level.
- It is 4 km north of the resort of Montego Bay.
- It is in the Montego Hills.
- It is within 1 km of the coast.
- It is on a gentle, south facing slope.
- It is built on flat land.
- It is about 1.5 km^2 in size.
- It is the largest airport on Jamaica.
- It is called the Sir Donald Sangster International Airport.
- It is between Kent Avenue, Sunset Avenue and Queens Drive.
- It is 2 km east of Flankers.

Draw a table like the one below and fill in the columns with the correct statements:

Site of Montego Bay Airport	Situation of Montego Bay Airport

b Think about why the airport was built there. Use map evidence to explain why the site and situation of Montego Bay Airport are good ones.
c Choose **two** other features shown on the map. For each feature:
- give a grid reference
- describe its site and situation.

Using Montego Bay Airport

A Destinations served by direct flights from Montego Bay

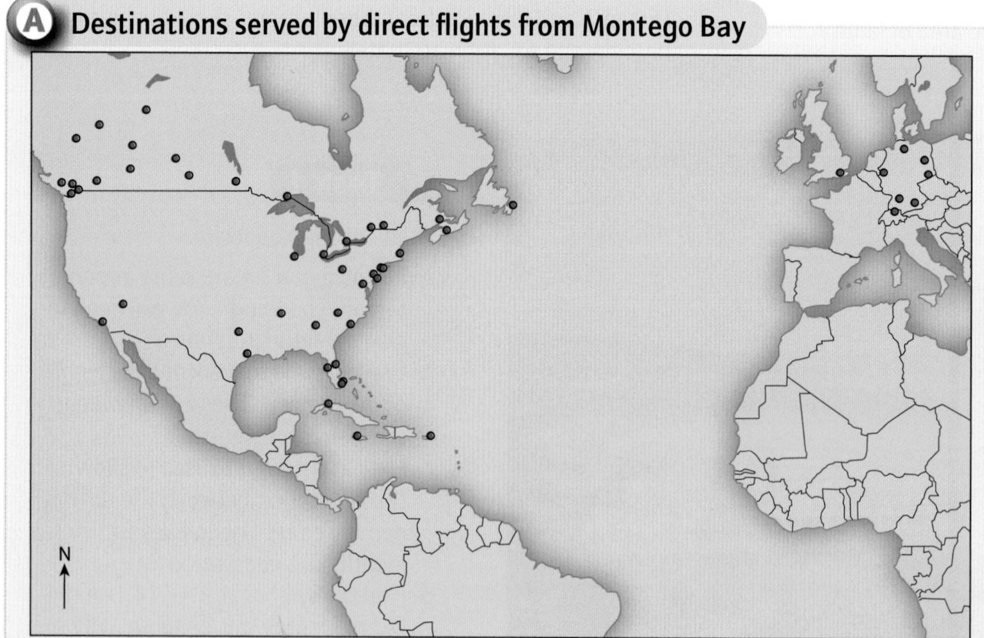

B Passenger arrivals to Montego Bay Airport

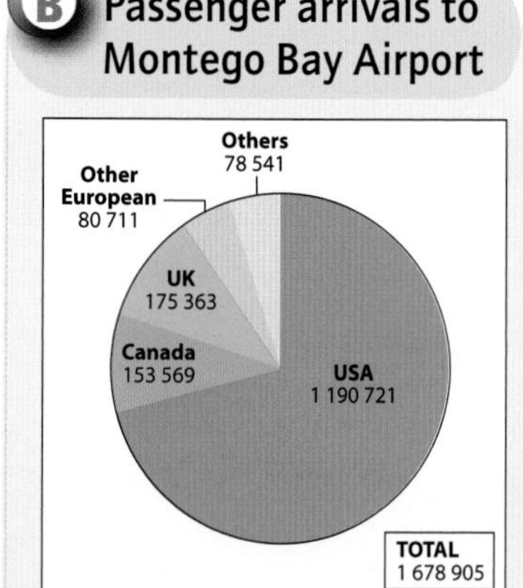

Task 1

Using **Source A** and an atlas, identify the following places to which there are direct flights from Montego Bay.

- One city in the UK.
- Two cities in Germany.
- Two cities in Canada.
- Two cities in the west of the USA.
- Two cities in the centre of the USA.
- Three cities near or on the east coast of the USA.

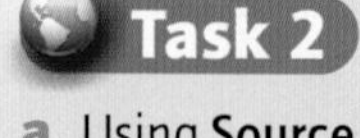

Task 2

a Using **Source B**, work out the percentage of the passenger arrivals at Montego Bay Airport from the USA.

b Suggest reasons why more passengers arrive at Montego Bay from the USA than from any other part of the world.

C Annual passenger arrivals at Montego Bay Airport, 1992–2006

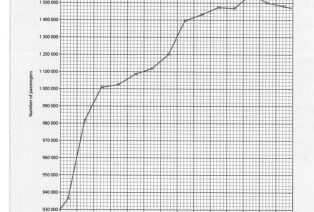

SKILLS How to describe a trend

Look for any overall changes shown by the graph between the first and last dates. For example, you may be able to use descriptive words like 'increased', 'decreased' or 'stayed the same'. Possibly the first and last years will have similar figures, but in between they might have gone up or down.

Write about the rate of change – was it large or small? Did it differ during the time period shown? Perhaps there was a time when it increased or decreased very rapidly.

Always use figures from the graph to support your comments, and remember to give the units, e.g. millions.

Task 3

Use **Source C** to describe the trends in passenger arrivals at Montego Bay Airport.

Make sure you use descriptive words and figures in your answer.

D Benefits and problems of an airport for local people

Benefits

- Jobs are created in building and operating the airport.
- Local businesses grow (the multiplier effect).
- People will be attracted to the area and extra houses will be built.
- More services will be opened, such as shops, schools and hospitals.
- New railway lines and roads will be built.
- More flight destinations may be available from the airport.

Problems

- Farmland and historic buildings may be lost for runways and new houses.
- Natural countryside and wildlife habitats may be destroyed.
- There will be more demand for water from the terminal and from new houses.
- More flights will create more noise and atmospheric pollution.
- Homes and listed buildings may be destroyed.
- Jobs may be seasonal.

Task 4

Study the map on page 190.

For each of the three individuals and one couple shown here, decide what they will feel about the continued growth in the number of flights using Montego Bay Airport. Give reasons for their views.

Owner of construction firm in Montego Bay at 212621

Plantation worker living in Flankers at 225645

Retired couple living in Canterbury at 213627

Owner of hotel on Kent Avenue at 223649

Tourism in Jamaica

A Money earned from tourism as a percentage of exports

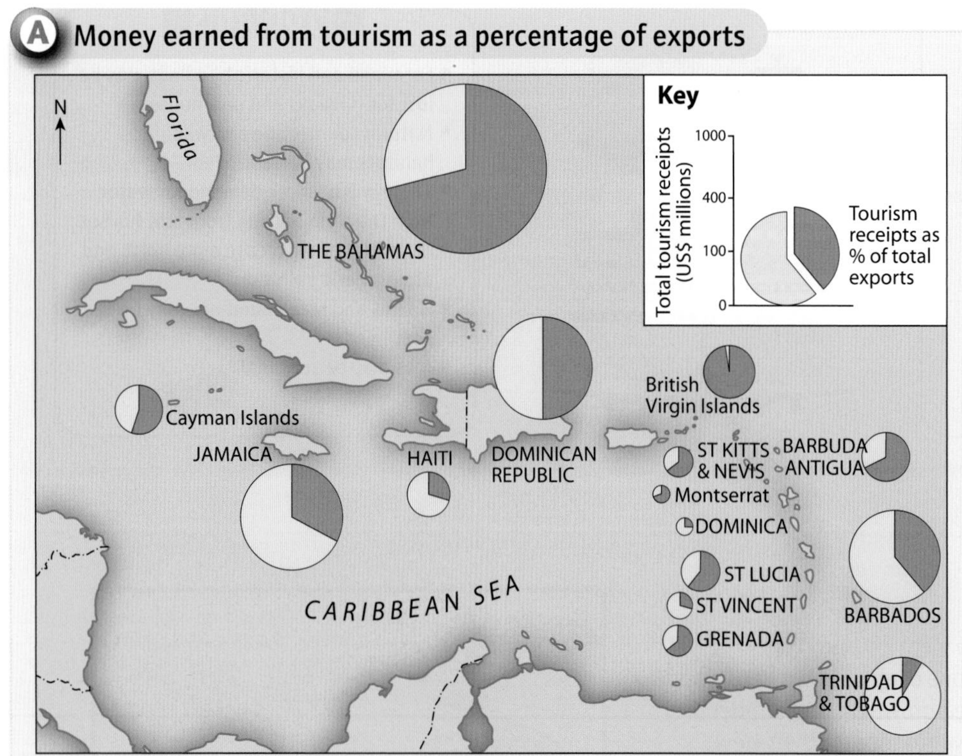

Using **Source A**, list the islands named below in rank order based on:

a their total tourism receipts

b the money they earn from tourism as a percentage of total exports.

In each list, you should arrange the countries from the highest to the lowest amount.

- Jamaica
- Dominican Republic
- Barbados
- Bahamas
- Cayman Islands
- Trinidad and Tobago
- Grenada
- Haiti

B Temperature and rainfall in Montego Bay

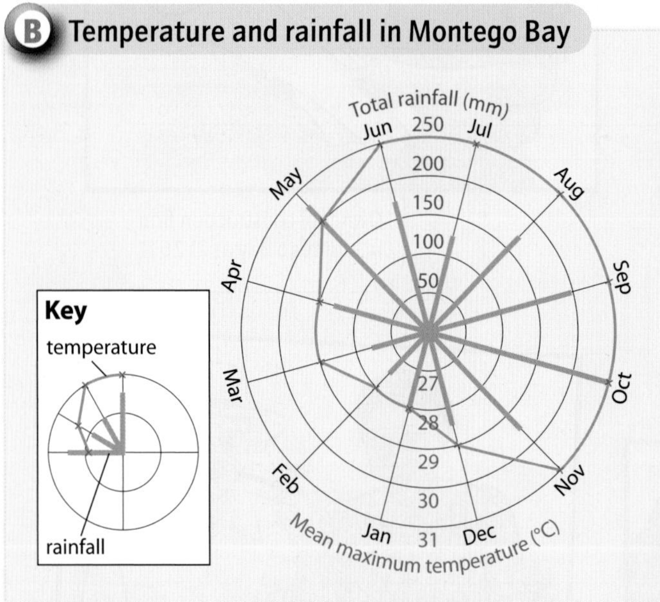

C Average number of tourists visiting Montego Bay, per month

January	61 800	July	46 800
February	53 300	August	59 800
March	63 100	September	36 100
April	51 000	October	32 100
May	41 100	November	39 200
June	44 100	December	43 400

a Using **Sources B and C**, explain how the climate of Montego Bay influences the number of tourists.

b Suggest what factors, other than the local climate, may help explain the variation in visitor numbers throughout the year.

D Doctor's Cave Beach

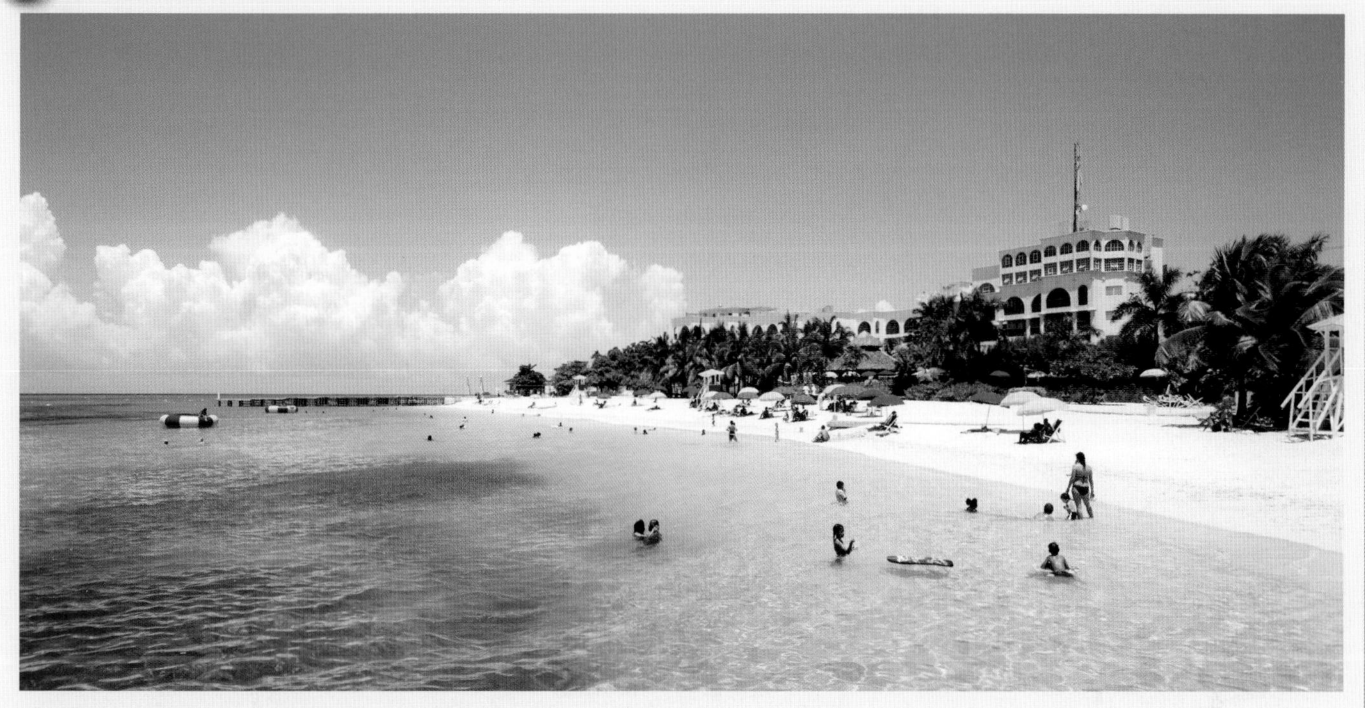

Montego Bay Marine Park

In 1992, Jamaica's first National Park, the Montego Bay Marine Park, was established. It is 15.3 km² in area. It begins at the high-tide mark on land, and extends to the 100-metre depth at sea. It stretches from Sangster International Airport to Rum Bottle Bay, 9 km west of Montego Bay. It includes mangrove forests and islands, white sand beaches, river estuaries, seagrass beds and corals. However, years of overfishing, of mangrove destruction, and of sewage disposal had almost destroyed the rich underwater life in the area. Now fishing, shell collecting, and all activities that can have a negative impact on the coral reefs, are forbidden. Watersports are regulated and park patrols keep a careful watch over the area.

Source D shows Doctor's Cave Beach. You will find this at grid reference 205632 on the map on page 190.

Task 3

a Using **Source D**, explain why Doctor's Cave Beach is attractive to tourists.

b The Montego Bay Marine Park was established to protect the coastal area around Montego Bay. Explain **three** different ways in which tourists in and around Doctor's Cave Beach may damage the natural environment.

Task 4

Using the map on page 190, match the features labelled 1 to 6 on **Source E** with the following:

- Montego Bay Airport
- Marine National Park boundary
- Main town of Montego Bay
- Coral reef
- Main area of hotels
- Doctor's Cave Beach

E Aerial photograph of Montego Bay Marine Park

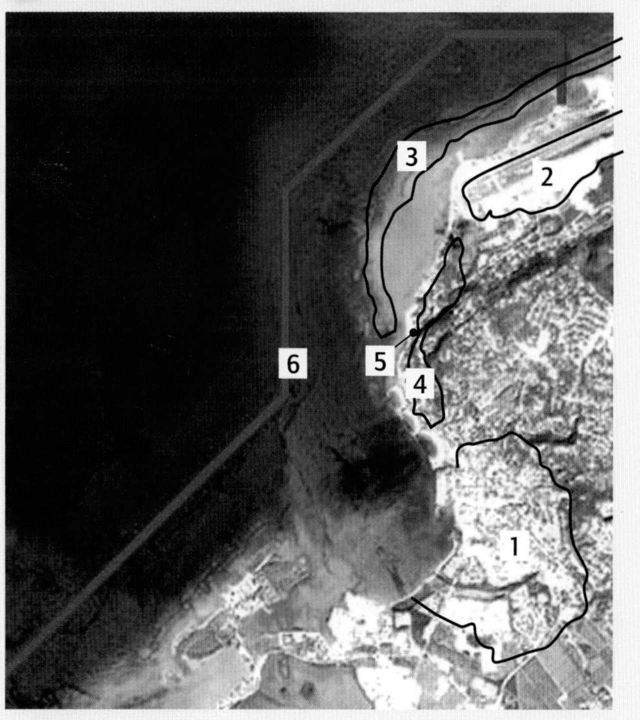

Negara, Indonesia

38'00 38'30 39'00 39'30 40'00

20'30 21'00 21'30 22'00 22'30

NEGARA
Br. Petanahan
Br. Yehmekecir
DESA
Br. Taman
Br. Anyar
Br. Yehmekecir
Br. Tegalasih
Br. Munduk
Batuagung
Br. Keladian
DESA DANGINTUKADAYA
Dangintukadaya
Br. Dauhwaru
Pamedilan
Br. Menega
Br. Sebual
Br. Tengah
Br. Delodbaleagung
Br. Panggunggondang
DESA BUDENG
KELURAHAN SANGKARAGUNG
Br. Sangkaragung
DESA
Pangkub Sebual
Tukad
N1.3082
12

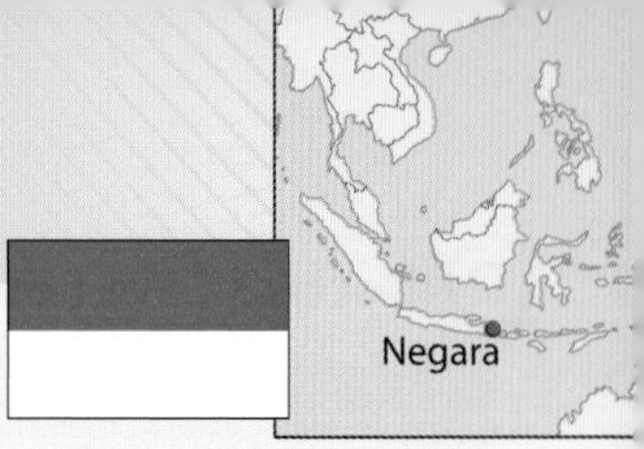

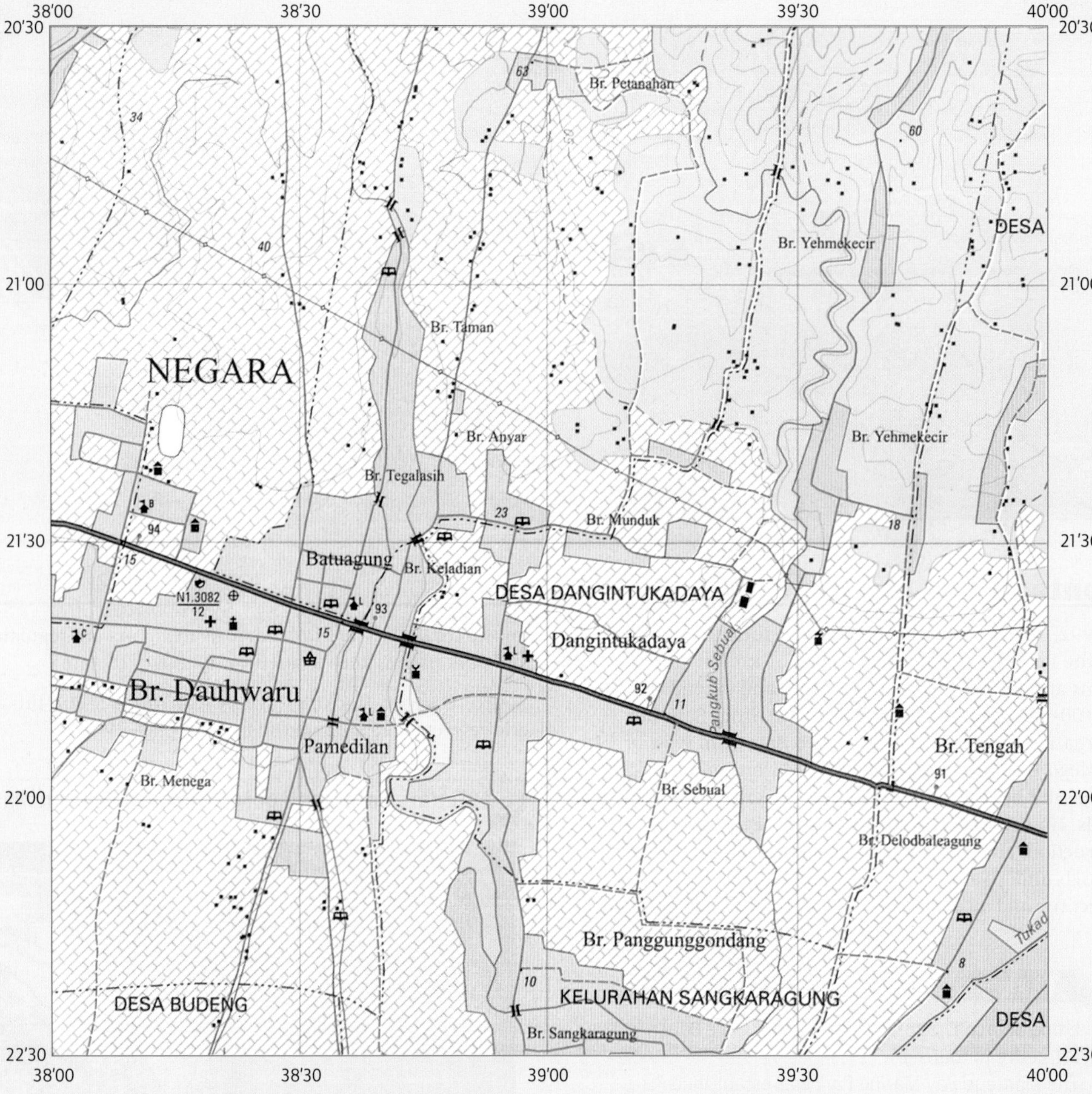

0 1 2 3 4 kilometres

Scale 1:25 000 (4 cm = 1 km)

Legend		Legend	
Built-up area		Telephone lines	
Building		Main road	
Mosque		Local road	
Temple		Track	
Church		Irrigated rice fields	
Market		Plantation	
School		Garden	

Indonesia – a country of islands

The country of Indonesia, in south-east Asia, covers an area of 2 million km^2. With over 237 million people, it has the world's fourth largest population. It consists of more than 17 500 islands, 6000 of which are inhabited. The largest islands are Java, Sumatra, Kalimantan and Sulawesi. The capital city of Jakarta lies on the island of Java. The map shows part of the town of Negara in West Bali. It is surrounded by agricultural land.

Task 1

Study the 1:25 000 map extract on page 196.

a Give examples of **three** different places of worship.

b Count the number of schools in the built-up area of Negara.

Task 2

Study the 1:25 000 map extract and **Source A**. Identify the following features:

- building A
- line B1 to B2
- type of road C1 to C2
- land use D
- spot height E.

A Part of the 1:25 000 map

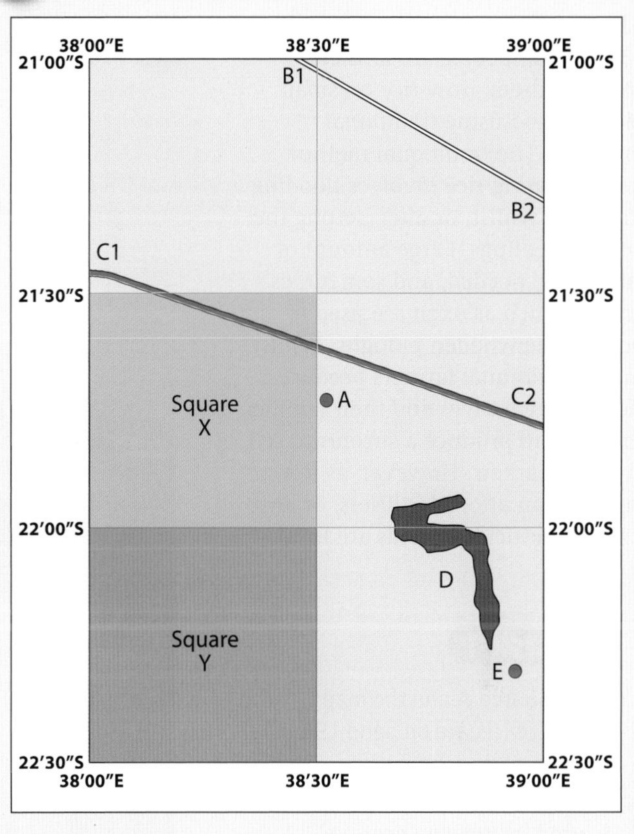

Task 3

Study the 1:25 000 map extract and **Sources A, B and C.**

Compare the land use in squares X and Y.

B Photograph taken in square X

C Photograph taken in square Y

Farming in Indonesia

Almost 70 per cent of Indonesia's 237 million people are farmers. Many of them grow rice on small plots of land using traditional methods. The traditional method for cultivating rice involves flooding the fields whilst, or after, setting the young seedlings. Large amount of labour are needed, and sometimes animals such as oxen are used to pull simple wooden ploughs. Whilst many traditional farmers produce rice for themselves and their families, they aim to produce a surplus to sell at local markets. However, as few farmers can afford fertilisers, or any form of pesticides, yields are low.

Study **Source A** and the map extract of Negara on page 196.

a Describe the relief (height and slope) of the land that is used for growing rice.

b Explain why relief of this type is needed by traditional rice farmers.

Carry out your own research using reference books or the internet to find out the climatic conditions that are needed for rice growing.

Study **Source B**.

Use your own words to explain why it is difficult for many traditional rice farmers in Indonesia to escape from poverty.

A Traditional rice farming

B The circle of poverty

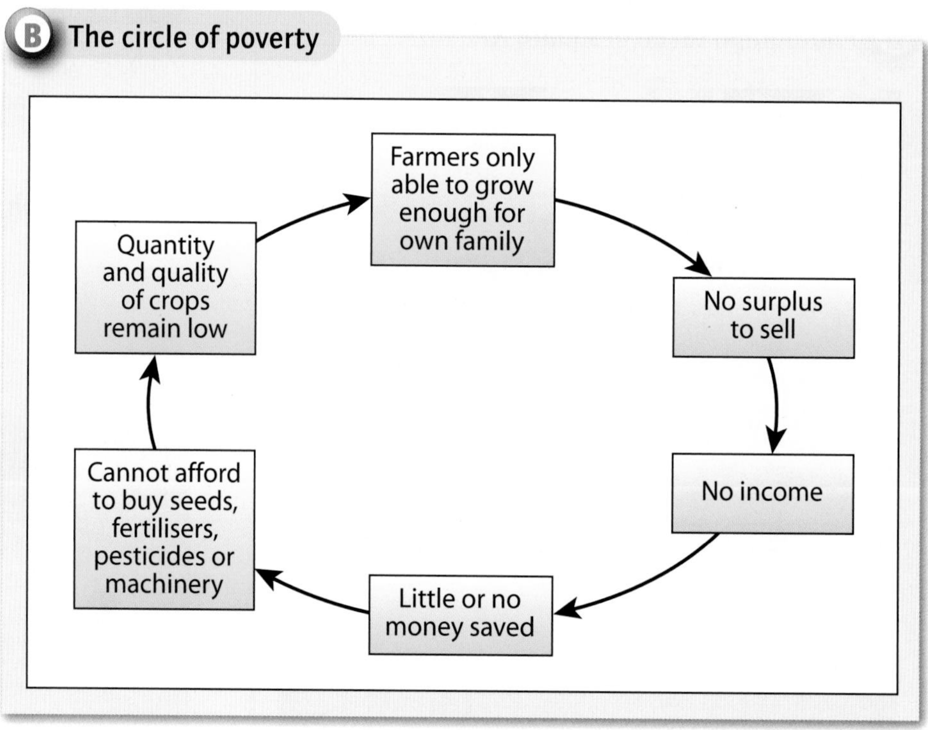
Farmers only able to grow enough for own family
No surplus to sell
No income
Little or no money saved
Cannot afford to buy seeds, fertilisers, pesticides or machinery
Quantity and quality of crops remain low

C Production and trade in rice

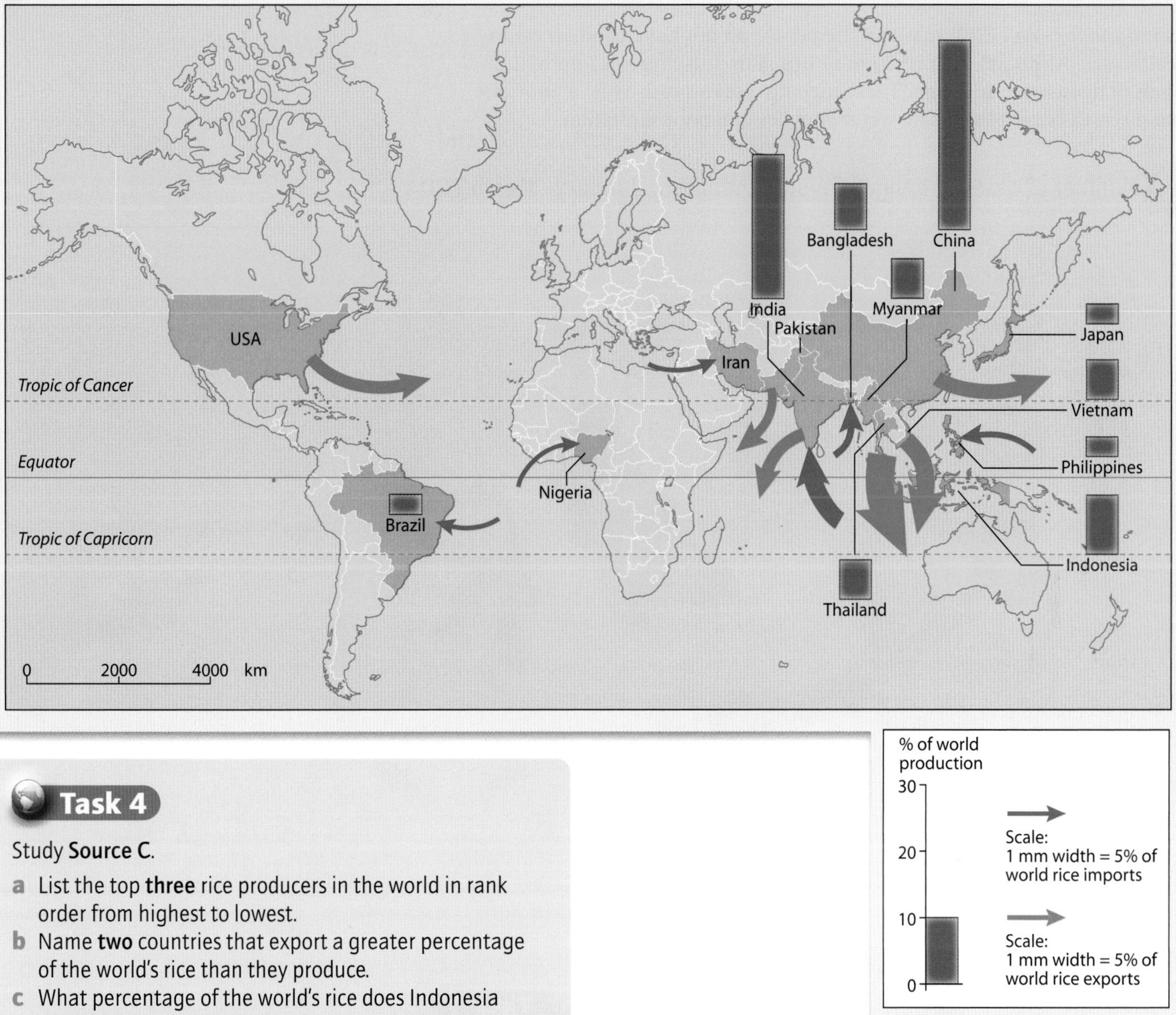

USA
Tropic of Cancer
Equator
Tropic of Capricorn
Brazil
Nigeria
Iran
India
Pakistan
Bangladesh
China
Myanmar
Japan
Vietnam
Philippines
Indonesia
Thailand
0 2000 4000 km

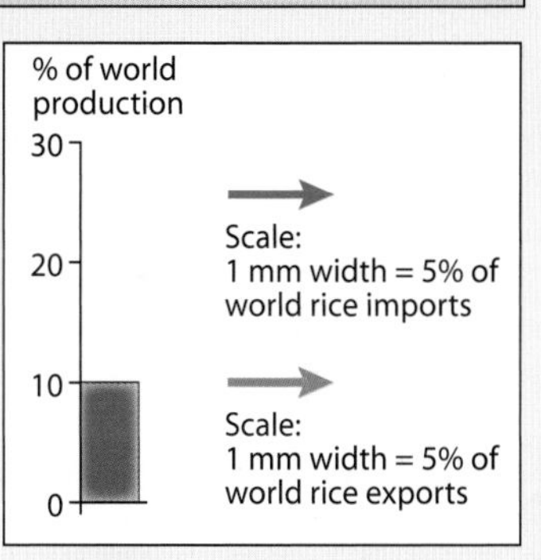

Task 4

Study **Source C**.

a List the top **three** rice producers in the world in rank order from highest to lowest.

b Name **two** countries that export a greater percentage of the world's rice than they produce.

c What percentage of the world's rice does Indonesia produce?

d Suggest reasons why Indonesia has to import rice even though rice farming is an important agricultural activity.

Task 5

Study **Source D**.

a Use suitable graphs to plot the statistics in the table. Remember to use titles for your graphs and label their axes.

b Suggest reasons for the increase in total production of rice in Indonesia between 1990 and 2005.

D Rice production in Indonesia, 1990–2005

	1990	1995	2000	2005
Area harvested (million hectares)	9.9	10.5	11.4	11.7
Yield (tonnes/hectare)	3.9	4.3	4.3	4.2
Total production (million tonnes)	39.1	45.2	49.7	49.2
Total fertiliser consumption (million tonnes)	1.9	2.4	2.5	2.8
Tractors used in agriculture (nearest thousand)	12	28	60	70

Disease in Indonesia

As Indonesia is an LEDC, many of the people do not have good access to health care. Although the provision of hospitals and clinics is improving, levels of disease are still high. These include diseases caused by a poor diet, and diseases caused by unsafe water supplies and poor sanitation.

A Number of cases of dengue fever in Indonesia, January–March 2004

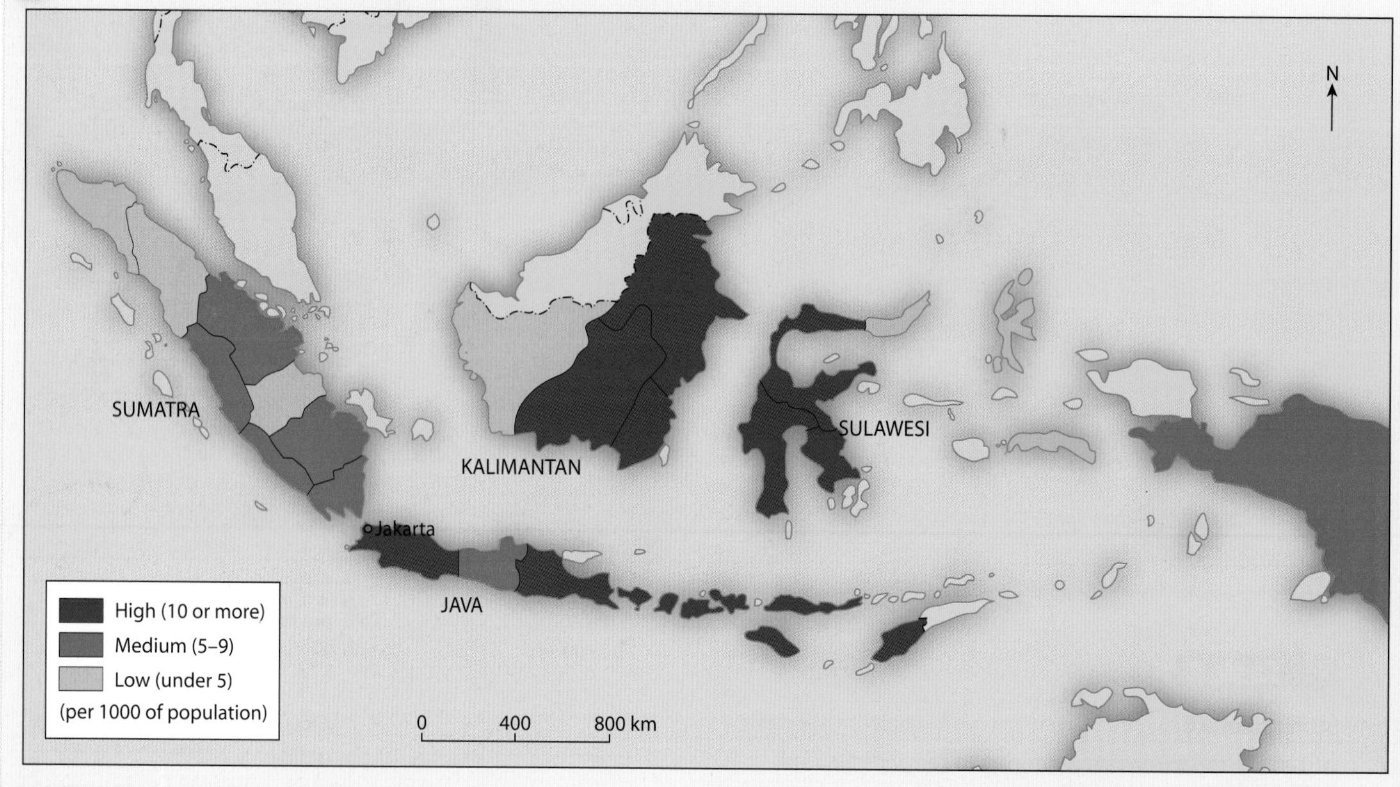

B Indonesia fights dengue fever

Indonesia is trying to contain an outbreak of dengue fever which has killed 91 people in six provinces since the start of the year. Health officials say around 4500 people have been taken to hospital with the disease – twice as many as in last year's outbreak.

Dengue fever is carried by mosquitoes which bite and infect about 100 million people worldwide each year. Java island has been the worst hit, with at least 38 people reported dead in East Java province and 17 others in the capital Jakarta. Symptoms of the disease include fever, body ache and, in the most serious cases, internal bleeding.

Officials in Jakarta have said that the increased number of cases could be to do with heavy rains and pools of stagnant water in the city which serve as a breeding ground for mosquitoes.

Workers in Jakarta have been spraying neighbourhoods with insecticide to try and prevent the disease from spreading.

Task 1

Study **Sources A and B.**

a Use your own words to describe the causes and effects of dengue fever.

b Describe how the numbers of people (per 1000) with dengue fever in Kalimantan differ from those in Sumatra.

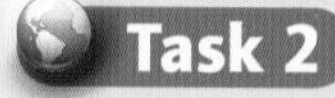

Task 2

You should work in pairs on this task.

a Think of **four** indicators that can be used to compare levels of health care between countries.

b Use the internet to find out recent statistics for the four indicators you have chosen. You will need to find statistics for Indonesia and **three** other countries of your choice.

c Explain what the indicators tell you about levels of health in Indonesia compared with the other three countries you have chosen.

C Dengue fever in Indonesia, 2001–07

Year	Number of cases (to nearest thousand)
2001	18 000
2002	22 000
2003	28 000
2004	36 000
2005	49 000
2006	114 000
2007	92 000

Task 3

Study **Source C**.

a Draw a pictograph to show the number of cases of dengue fever in Indonesia between 2001 and 2007. The statistics need to be plotted on your pictograph using coffins as symbols – use a scale of 1 coffin = 10 000 cases of dengue fever.

b Describe the changes in the number of cases of dengue fever in Indonesia between 2001 and 2007.

c Suggest reasons for the changes in the number of cases of dengue fever:
- from 2005 to 2006
- from 2006 to 2007.

D Interviews with health professionals

In the first three days of March there were 71 cases of dengue fever, compared with 50 cases for all of January. The hospital is like a war zone with patients sleeping in camp beds in any available space – corridors, hospital mosques and maternity wards. The health system was unprepared for the outbreak. The problem is that the number of cases is increasing – it is very high. So our staff are tired, but they are still working very hard. Some of the nurses, they should be home at 4 pm but they go home at 10 pm. We are asking the government to give us more nurses and doctors. Anyway, we can still handle the situation.

Extract from an interview with the nursing director at the Persahabatan Hospital

The hospitals are well equipped and staffed. The main problem is the increase in the number of mosquito breeding sites. A large number of construction projects came to a halt in Jakarta after the Asian financial crisis. The unfinished buildings collected pools of water where the mosquitoes bred. The people living in slums make the problems worse by dumping increased amounts of rubbish in urban slum areas.

Extract from an interview with Indonesia's Health Minister

Task 4

Study **Sources D and E** and the 1:25 000 map of Negara on page 196.

a The Health Agency is planning a campaign, using posters, to advise the local people how to prevent the spread of dengue fever. Produce a poster that could be displayed in the local clinic in Negara. Your poster should inform people what they can do around their homes to prevent dengue fever.

b To what extent do you think people in Negara are at risk from dengue fever? Give reasons for your opinions.

E Controlling dengue fever

PLANS TO STOP THE SPREAD OF DENGUE FEVER

To stop the spread of the disease the Health Agency will run a campaign on the prevention of dengue fever in February and March. The campaign will stress that the best way of preventing the disease, which is spread by the *Aedes aegypti* mosquito, is to make sure that pools of still water around houses are drained or covered so that mosquitoes cannot lay their eggs there. The Agency also plans to use groups of local people, working together, to spray the streets with insecticides.

MAP WORK 6 Le Port, Reunion Island

Reunion Island – a French territory!

Reunion is an island of 2512 km^2 located in the Indian Ocean, to the east of Madagascar. It is mainly mountainous although there are some lowlands along the coast. It is a French overseas territory with a population of 763 000 people, which is expected to rise above a million by 2030. The 1:25 000 map extract shows Le Port, the main port on the island.

Tourism is one of the most important economic activities on the island. Sugarcane is the main crop and sugar and rum are important exports. Reunion Island has an active volcano, La Piton de la Fournaise, which last erupted in 2007.

A A satellite image of Le Port, Reunion Island

Imagery ©2009 TerraMetrics

Task 1

Study the 1:25 000 map extract on page 202.

a Identify **six** services in Le Port.

b What type of road lies between the roundabouts at 223843 and 229847?

c What is the distance in metres between these two roundabouts?

d What is the compass bearing along the road from 229847 to 223943?

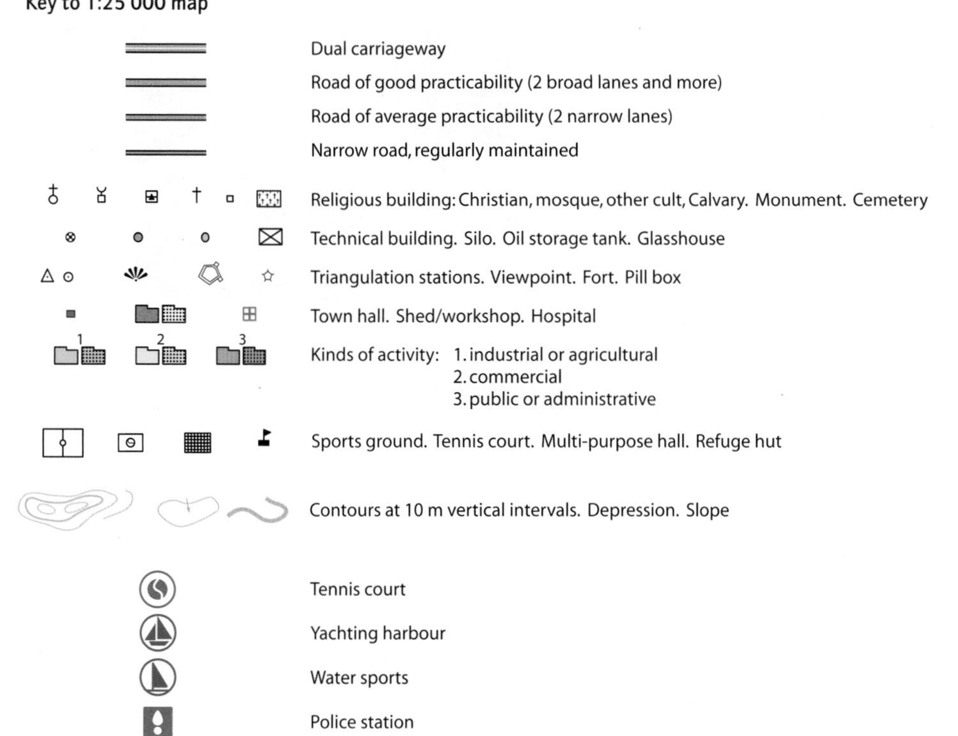

Task 2

Study the 1:25 000 map extract and **Source A** which is a satellite image showing part of the area in the map extract.

a Identify the main land use in each of areas A, B, C and D.

b Suggest a possible use of the circular buildings in area E. Give a reason for your answer.

c Draw a labelled sketch map to show the layout of Le Port. You should show the main roads and different types of land use.

Industry in Reunion

A The sugar industry in Reunion

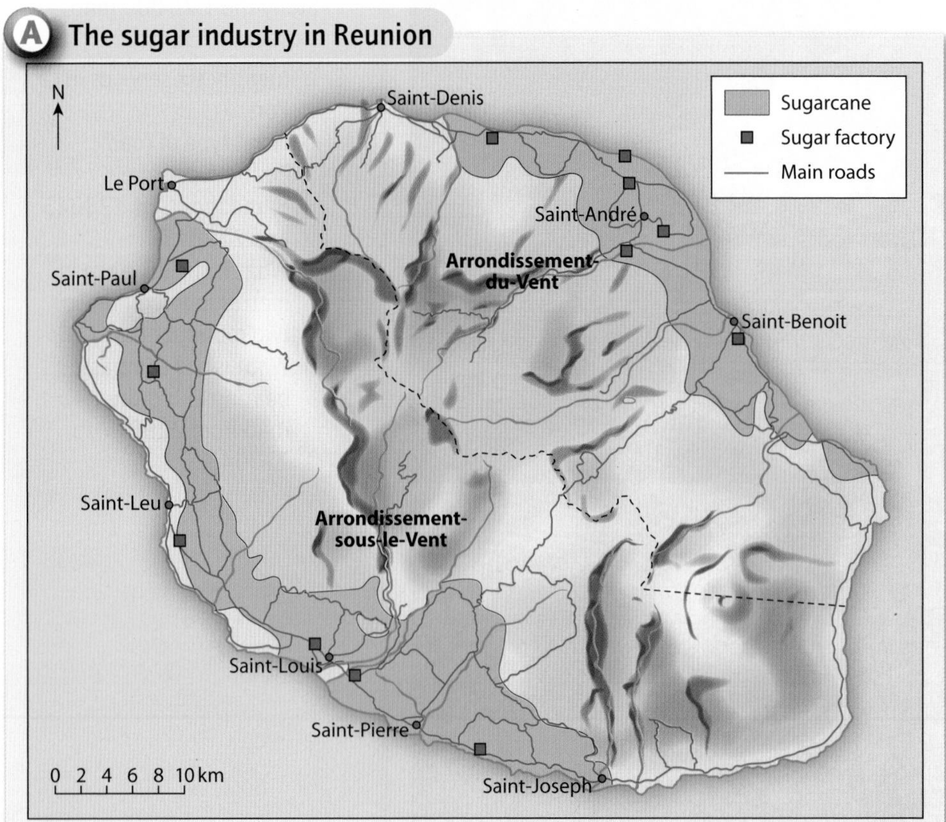

Task 1

Study **Source A.**

a Describe the distribution of the areas where sugarcane is grown in Reunion.

b Explain the location of the sugar factories.

Task 2

Study **Sources B, C and D.**

a What percentage of Reunion's exports are to France?

b What percentage of Reunion's imports are from Italy?

c What percentage of Reunion's total exports is sugar?

d In which employment sector is 30 per cent of the workforce of Reunion employed?

e In which sector would the following people be employed?

B Reunion's trade partners

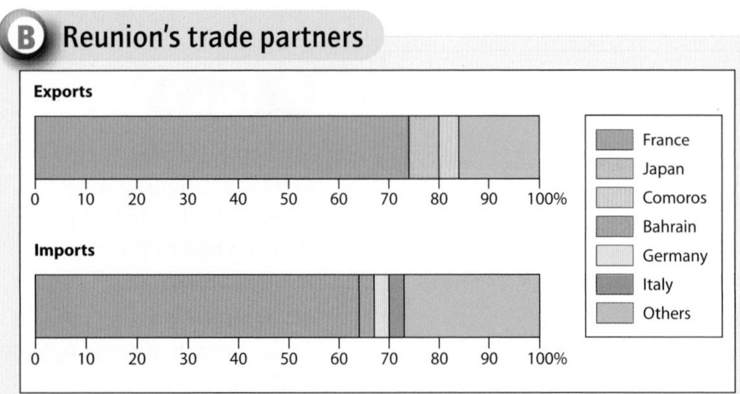

C Exports from Reunion

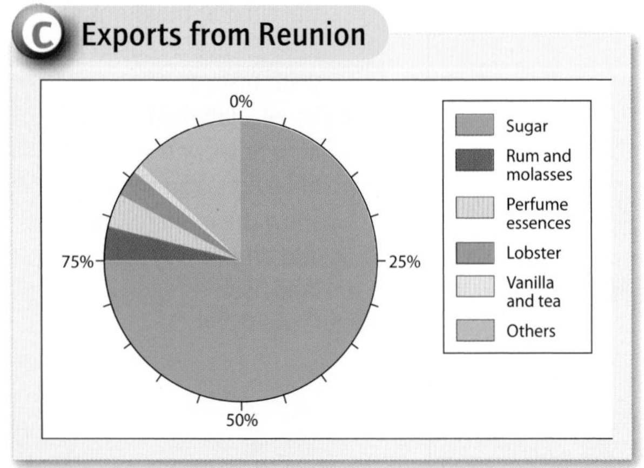

D Reunion's employment structure

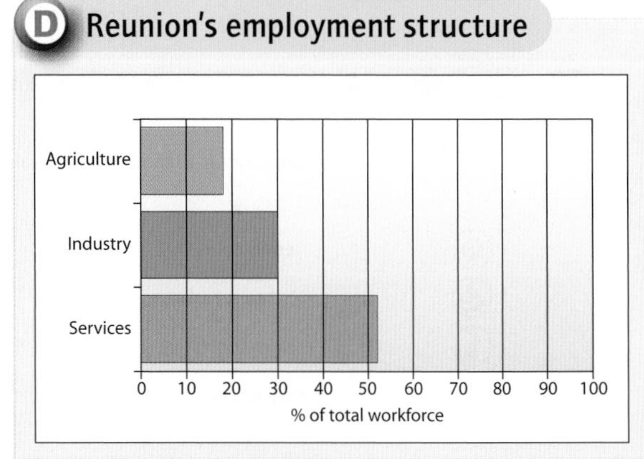

E Reunion looks to renewable energy

Reunion Island aims for zero CO_2

Surrounded by volcanic rock, sandy beaches and the Indian Ocean, Reunion Island is hardly a major polluter. But hit by rising fuel costs and worried about the impact of global warming, particularly on its delicate flora and fauna, the small island nation has set itself the ambitious goal of cutting its greenhouse gas emissions to zero.

By 2025 it wants to use renewable energy sources to produce 100% of its electricity, and to power all of its transport by 2050. 'We have water, sunshine, and even an active volcano. We have more energy than we need for our development,' Paul Verges, president of Reunion's regional council, said.

Thirty-six per cent of Reunion's electricity already comes from renewable energy, mostly hydro-electric power and electricity generated from sugarcane fibre (bagasse) and Reunion is expanding its solar and wind energy projects. But, as in other countries, the island's rapidly growing energy demands threaten to delay the targets. Living mostly along the coastline, Reunion's population is set to grow by more than 20% to over 1 million people by 2030 from about 800 000 at present. Reunion's average energy consumption per person is growing at 5% per year.

August 2008

F Manufacturing soft drinks

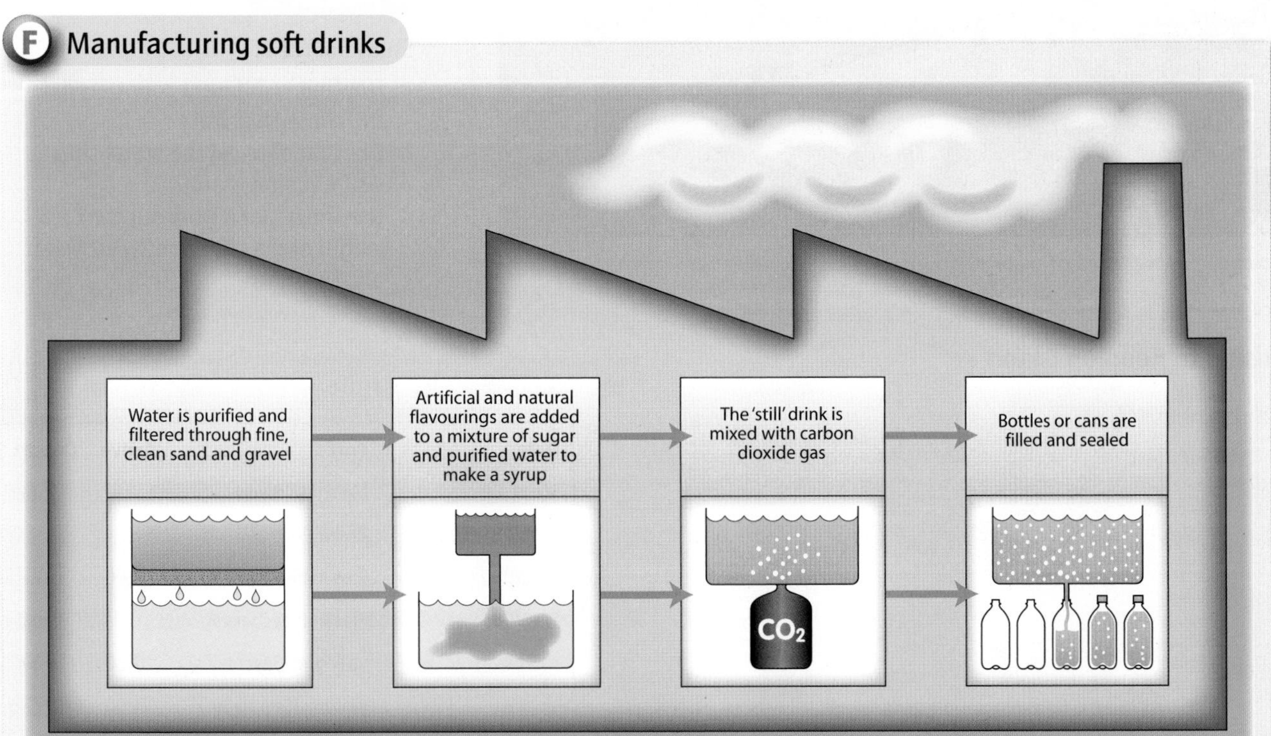

Water is purified and filtered through fine, clean sand and gravel
Artificial and natural flavourings are added to a mixture of sugar and purified water to make a syrup
The 'still' drink is mixed with carbon dioxide gas
Bottles or cans are filled and sealed
CO2

Task 3

Study **Source E**.

Use your own words to explain how Reunion is aiming to increase its use of renewable energy.

Task 4

Study the 1:25 000 map extract of Le Port on page 202, and **Source F**.

A multinational company is planning to open a factory making soft drinks in the 'Zone Industrielle' at grid reference 222849.

- **a** Use map evidence to explain why this is a suitable site.
- **b** Suggest reasons why the multinational company is planning to manufacture soft drinks in Reunion.
- **c** Explain the advantages and disadvantages of this factory for the local people and for the natural environment.

Impacts of cruise holidays

A A cruise ship

Task 1

Study **Source A** and the 1:25 000 map extract on page 202.

a Estimate the number of people that this cruise ship will accommodate.
b Suggest reasons why cruises are a popular type of holiday.
c Use map evidence to explain why cruise ships are able to stop at Le Port in Reunion.

Task 2

Study **Source B**.

a How many different countries did the cruise ship visit?
b On what date did the cruise ship visit Reunion Island?
c Use the scale to work out the total length of the cruise between Malé and Mauritius.

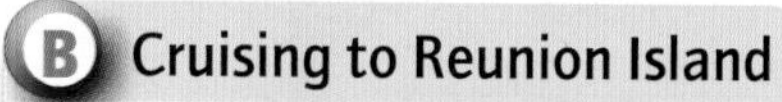

B Cruising to Reunion Island

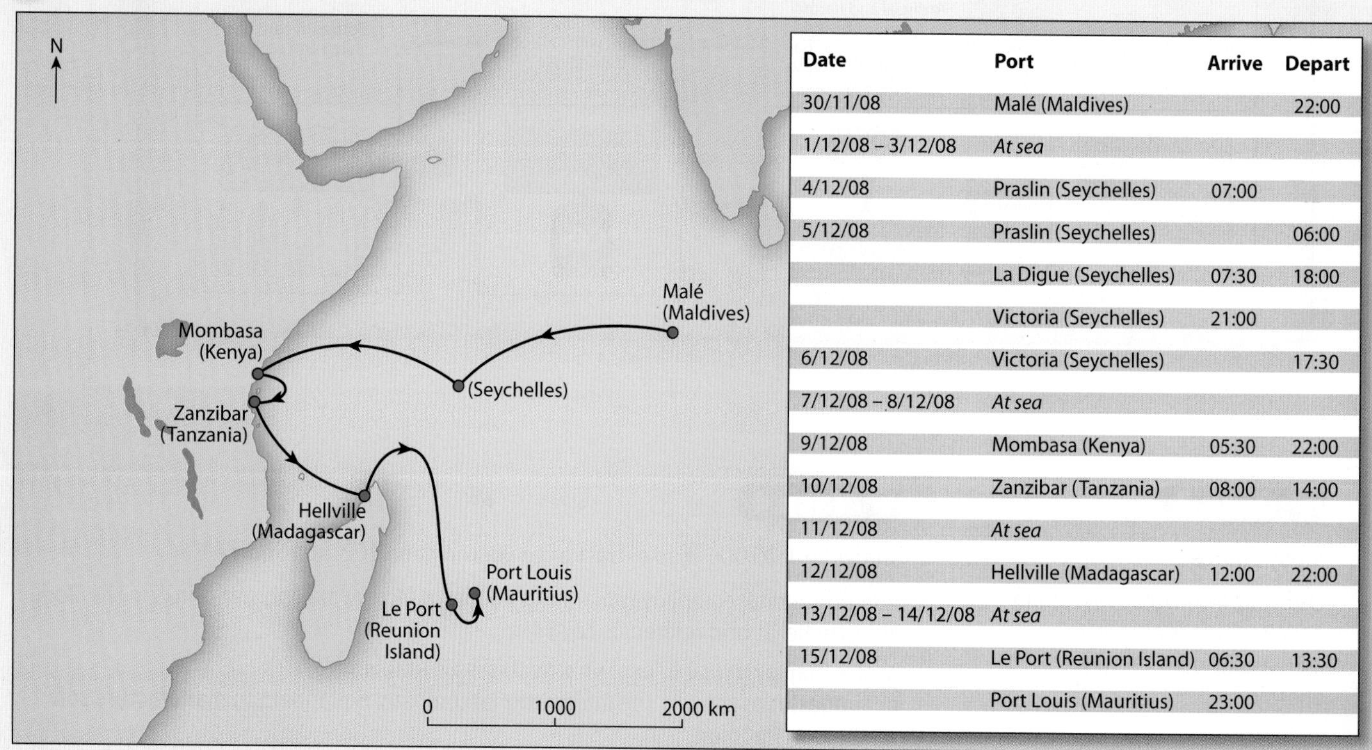

Date	Port	Arrive	Depart
30/11/08	Malé (Maldives)		22:00
1/12/08 – 3/12/08	*At sea*		
4/12/08	Praslin (Seychelles)	07:00	
5/12/08	Praslin (Seychelles)		06:00
	La Digue (Seychelles)	07:30	18:00
	Victoria (Seychelles)	21:00	
6/12/08	Victoria (Seychelles)		17:30
7/12/08 – 8/12/08	*At sea*		
9/12/08	Mombasa (Kenya)	05:30	22:00
10/12/08	Zanzibar (Tanzania)	08:00	14:00
11/12/08	*At sea*		
12/12/08	Hellville (Madagascar)	12:00	22:00
13/12/08 – 14/12/08	*At sea*		
15/12/08	Le Port (Reunion Island)	06:30	13:30
	Port Louis (Mauritius)	23:00	

C Comparing carbon dioxide emissions

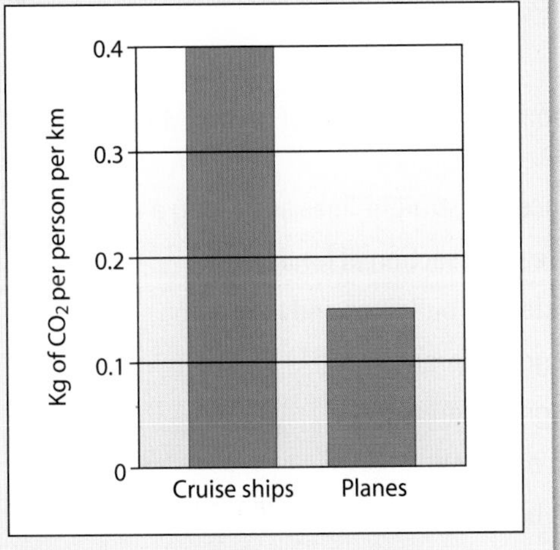

D One week's waste from a cruise ship

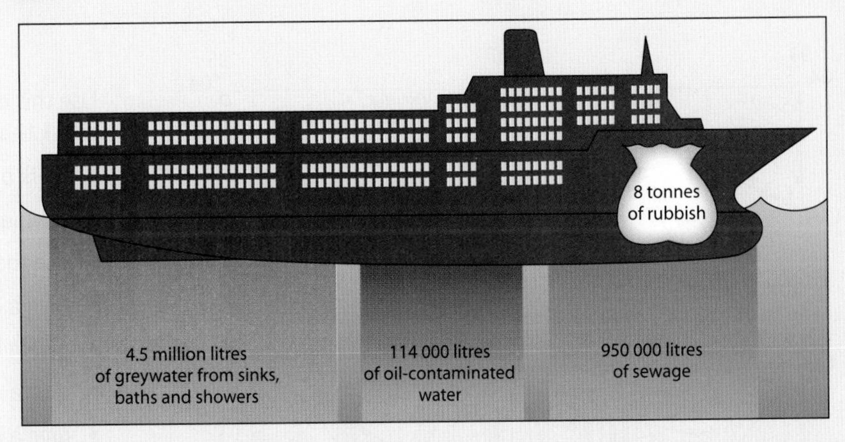

E The impact of cruising

As you prepare for your next cruise, consider this: Your destinations are someone else's home, and your trip can have impacts on the people who live there. Just ask Larry Spencer from Juneau, Alaska. Spencer recalls how before the current Alaska cruise boom, parts of the town were run down. That was 1984, when Spencer bought a historic but dilapidated building on Juneau's main commercial street. Today, the building is a successful retail mini-mall, one of many shops that line South Franklin Street.

Virtually everywhere it goes, cruising encourages economic growth. The cruise industry has turned the Mexican island of Cozumel into a major hub in the western Caribbean. Once known mainly to divers for its coral reefs, Cozumel has become the rival of Cancun as a tourist attraction. Last year it attracted more than 1.3 million cruise passengers who use local shops, restaurants and bars.

Competition is fierce among islands to attract cruises and the revenue that comes with them. In St Maarten the government is spending $65 million on improvements which include a new pier capable of handling 8000 to 10 000 passengers at a time, and a new waterfront complex with shops, restaurants, and a casino. In return for its investment, the government expects 500 new jobs to be created for island residents, and to generate revenue for the government, which will be channelled back into future development projects. Curaçao, meanwhile, recently opened a new 'mega-pier' to handle big ships. The result was a record season for cruise calls. Curaçao estimates that every cruise passenger who comes ashore spends about $75 on the island.

However, not every destination welcomes cruise ships. Grand Cayman has now banned cruise ships from visiting on Sundays. Also many people in Juneau are worried about the increase in cruise visitors, which has created congestion downtown and noise pollution from the buzz of sightseeing helicopters.

Task 3

Study **Sources C, D, E and F.**

Prepare a report for the government of Reunion Island which consider the advantages and disadvantages of allowing an increase in the number of cruise ships visiting Le Port. You should write a conclusion to your report which recommends and justifies a strategy that will be sustainable.

F Is it sustainable?

Sustainability is defined as progress that meets the needs of the present without making it impossible for future generations to meet their needs.

Development is considered to be sustainable if economic, social and environmental benefits are achieved in both the short term and the long term.

Map skills checklist

Use this extract from a 1:25 000 map of part of Mauritius to check that you can:

- work out distances (in straight lines and along a road)
- estimate the area of a section of land
- use the key to identify buildings and land use
- give a 4-figure grid reference
- give a 6-figure grid reference
- give a compass direction
- give a compass bearing
- describe relief and drainage
- interpret a cross-section
- mark features on a cross-section
- calculate a gradient
- describe patterns of settlement
- describe and suggest reasons for transport routes.

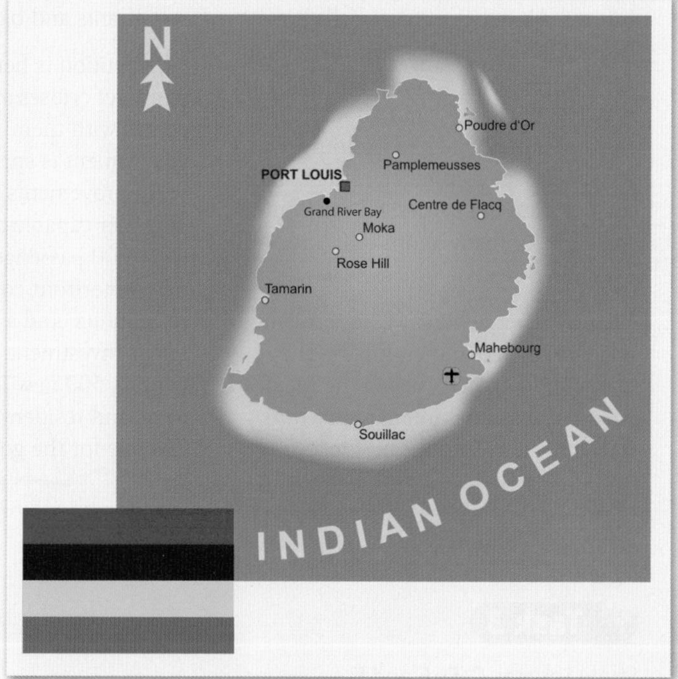

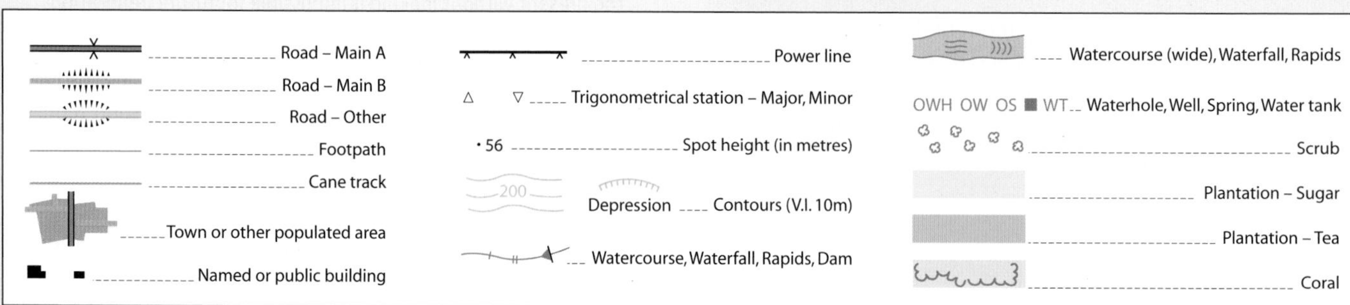

Part C
The Alternative to Coursework
Preparing for Paper 4

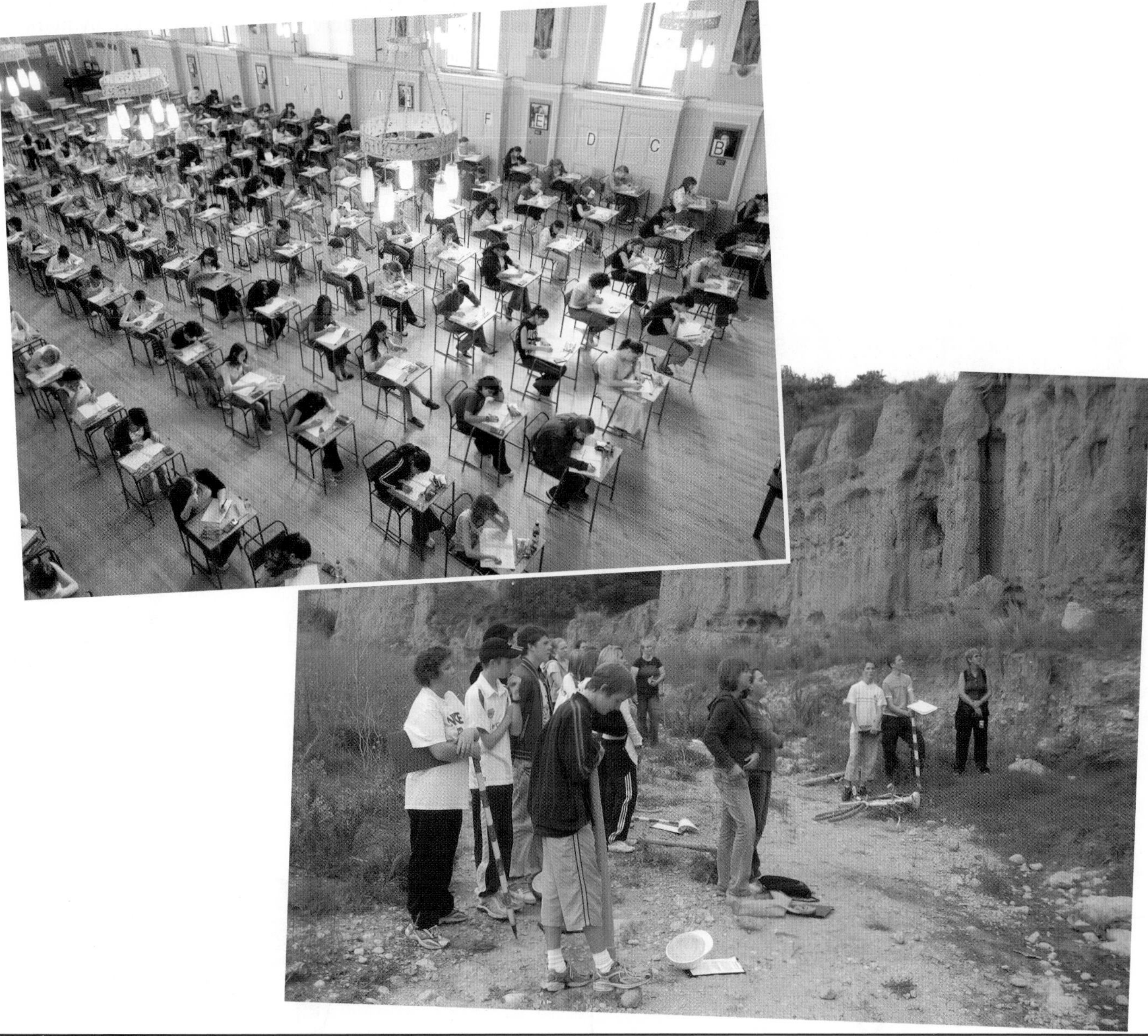

Part C covers four topics that are useful for either Paper 3 coursework investigations or Paper 4 examinations: the CBD (Central Business District), Rivers, Tourism and Weather. Each topic begins with an introductory double-page spread suggesting how these topics could be investigated through fieldwork and giving ideas that could be developed into coursework. The pages that follow contain Paper 4 exam questions related to the four topics, selected from examinations set between May 2007 and November 2008. Each question is provided in full (although lines for writing on have been removed) with analyses of the strengths and weaknesses of real candidate answers seen by examiners. Relevant exam tips are provided. Part C is best studied with the original papers that many centres will have. A recent past paper and mark scheme for Paper 4 is available for reference from www.cie.org.uk

Paper 4 can be taken by candidates as an Alternative to Coursework examination. From June 2010 there will be three different versions of Paper 4, numbered 41, 42 and 43. The Paper the centre receives will depend on which of the three international time zone groups the centre is allocated to.

TOPIC 1 Investigating the CBD

Ⓐ Part of the CBD of New York, USA

The Central Business District (CBD)

All urban areas, whether in an MEDC or an LEDC, will have a central area. The CBD has usually developed at the most accessible point for people surrounding the urban area to travel to. In some LEDC cities it is characterised by market functions; in MEDC cities markets may exist but there are mainly shops and offices at the centre.

There is a high demand for land in the CBD so the land is too expensive for housing. Instead commercial activities buy or rent a small area of land and build upwards to save space and money. Consequently, over time, a feature of all CBDs is the presence of tall buildings. Another feature is the large amount of traffic and number of people. There are many opportunities here for fieldwork investigations.

Task 1

Study **Source A**.

a Describe the main features of the scene.

b Where is your closest CBD? List any similarities and differences between it and the CBD of New York.

c To what extent is this photograph useful for describing New York's CBD?

Ⓑ In the CBD we could investigate …

Your enquiry can start as a hypotheses or a question. A hypothesis is a statement which your fieldwork may prove to be true, partially true, or false. A question needs an answer from your fieldwork.

Where does the CBD start and end?

The function of buildings changes with height.

To what extent are pavements congested during the day?

Route to Geographical Enquiry

Identify an enquiry question, issue or hypothesis

Decide what data is required and how it should be collected

Collect and record data

Present the data

Analyse and interpret the data

Report the conclusions and evaluate the investigation

Task 2

Study **Source B**.

a Suggest **one** other topic that could be investigated in the CBD.

b Choose **one** topic from those suggested in **Source B** or use your suggestion. Using the 'Route to Geographical Enquiry', plan how you would carry out an investigation into this topic.

C Investigating traffic flow in New York

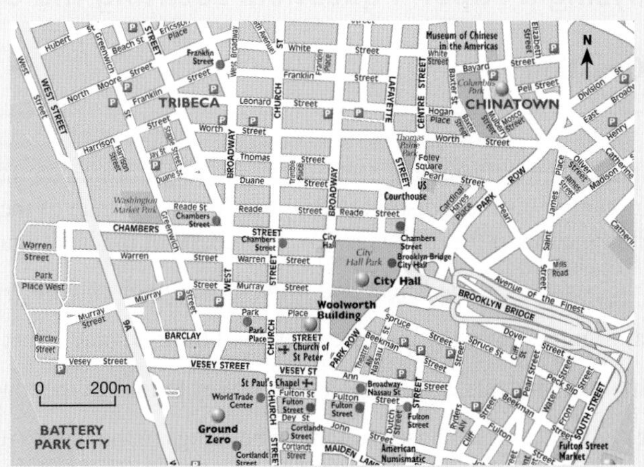

New York is a busy city. Vehicles travelling into the CBD have increased by 7 per cent per year since 1995. If that trend continues until 2035, over 1 million vehicles per day will be entering the CBD. In some places the average speed will drop to less than 22 km (14 miles) per hour. At present drivers spend more than the equivalent of a working week each year stuck in New York's traffic. As vehicle emissions can cause cancer and asthma as well as noise, monitoring traffic flow is an important part of identifying problems and proposing solutions to the traffic issue.

Our Route to Enquiry

Enquiry question: *How does traffic flow vary at a major junction in New York during the day?*

Equipment needed: *Clipboard, watch, recording sheet, pens/pencils, camera, 16 students making 8 pairs.*

Method: *At 09.00, 12.00 and 15.00 (equal three-hour intervals) 8 pairs of students will carry out a traffic count for 10 minutes. Two pairs of students will be responsible for one of the four roads merging at the junction. Each pair will stand on opposite sides of the road and record the numbers of different vehicles using a tally system on a recording sheet.*

Safety issues: *Clothing, ID, money, check if permission needed, stay in pairs, cell phone / school or teacher contact location, choose a safe position.*

D The traffic survey recording sheet

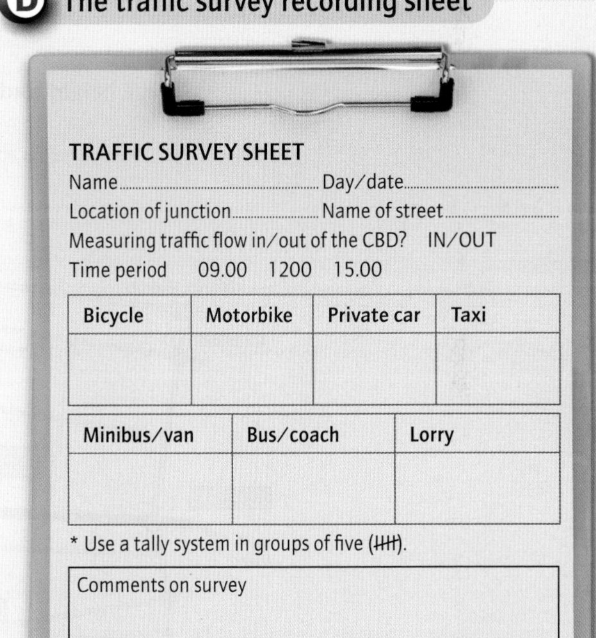

TRAFFIC SURVEY SHEET

Name........................ Day/date........................

Location of junction........................ Name of street........................

Measuring traffic flow in/out of the CBD? IN/OUT

Time period 09.00 1200 15.00

Bicycle	Motorbike	Private car	Taxi

Minibus/van	Bus/coach	Lorry

* Use a tally system in groups of five (~~||||~~).

Comments on survey

Task 3

A group of students in a New York school decided to study traffic flow at the junction of Broadway and Chambers Street. Study **Source C**.

a Describe the location of the junction. Refer to distances and directions.
b Do you think this is a good choice of location for this enquiry? Explain your views.
c Read the group's plan. Comment on its strengths and any weaknesses. What would you do differently?

Task 4

Study **Source D**.

a Comment on the layout and content of the traffic survey sheet. Could it be improved?
b Consider how the group might present the results of the survey.
c Suggest what conclusions the group might expect to draw from their fieldwork before they carry it out. Explain your views.

Analysing a Paper 4 question: Locating the CBD – May 2007

The Question

Students investigated the central area of a town located on the coast. They surveyed the buildings of the town to identify where the central business district (CBD) was located. A map of the town is shown on Fig. 1. The students recorded the height, width and function of the buildings. The hypothesis of the investigation was:

'the height and width of buildings and the price of the land increase towards the centre of the town'.

(a) Suggest why the increase in price of the land may affect the height and width of buildings. **[3]**

(b) The students carried out a pilot survey to look at the town. State **two** reasons for a pilot survey. **[2]**

(c) 10 sites were chosen to sample buildings in the town. At each site, the 10 closest buildings were observed. The height of each building was measured by counting storeys and the width of each building was measured in paces. An average height and width was calculated for each site. These are shown in Table 1.

(i) Use the results in Table 1 to plot the average building height and width at site C and site F onto Fig. 1. **[3]**

Site	A	B	C	D	E	F	G	H	I	J
Average height (storeys)	3	3	2	1	2	1	3	1	2	2
Average width (paces)	12	7	7	7	8	8	8	5	4	5

Table 1

Average height and width of buildings at each site

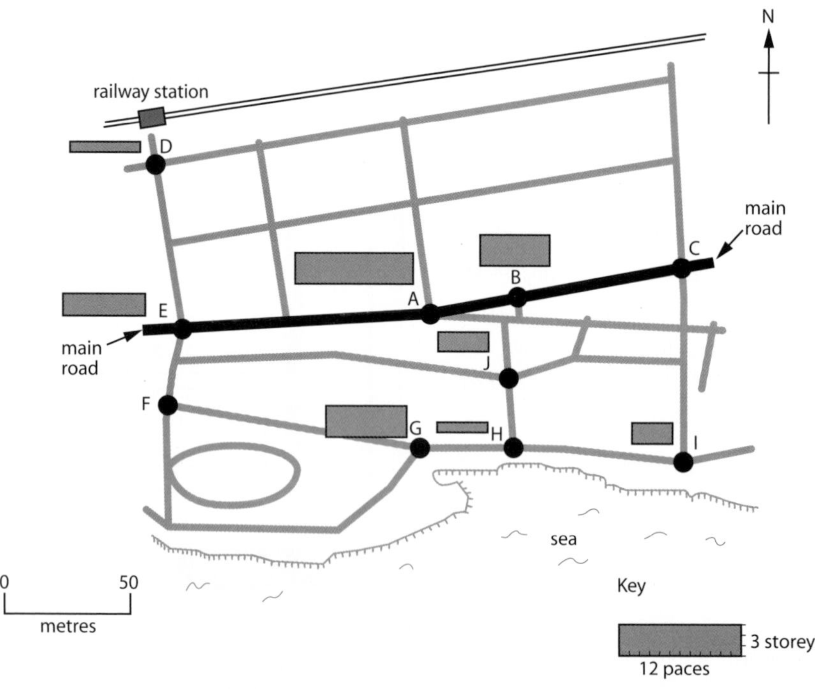

Fig. 1

Average height and width of buildings at each site

(ii) Study the completed map (Fig. 1) and describe the pattern of building heights and widths shown in the town. **[3]**

Source: IGCSE Geography (0460/04) May 2007 Question 1

Getting it right

(a) This was not well done. Candidates could relate the increased cost of land as a reason for why there were tall buildings in the CBD to 'save money' but did not relate this to a reason why width or ground cover was minimised to save rent.

(b) Answers were generally vague. Too many wrongly understood a 'pilot' survey to involve flying over the CBD and taking photographs of the location! Answers such as 'to be more accurate' were not sufficient – why would this make the fieldwork more accurate? It may be that centres that have not carried out fieldwork felt it unnecessary to deal with the reason for a preliminary survey before the real thing. However, it is an important part of preparation and planning for any investigation.

(c) (i) Below are two maps with Sites C and F plotted by two candidates. They should have plotted the average building height and width of Site C and Site F using the key. One gained 3 marks; the other 0. There was 1 mark per correct shaded bar then a 3rd mark if the location was close to the sites and shading used the key provided.

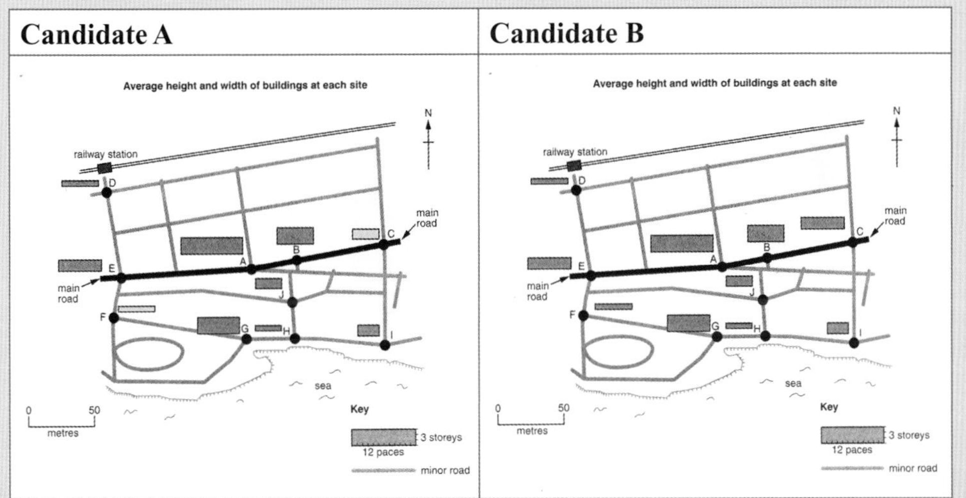

- Which map was awarded the full 3 marks?
- Why did the other map gain 0 marks?

(ii) The shading/drawing of bars was more successful than describing the pattern. Here are two candidate answers to the question on pattern. Note, again, the question says height and width. Candidates who described general patterns scored well; the only specific site reference that was allowed was the anomaly of Site G near the coast. Only the most able recognised that width had no clear pattern.

Candidate A	Candidate B
Site A is a tall building on the map. Site D is a wide building near the railway station. There are no sites near the top of the map.	*The narrow buildings are close to the sea. The tallest buildings, especially Site A, are along the main road. However Site G, which is as tall as Site A, is near the coast and not along the main road.*

- Which scored 3 marks?
- Which scored no marks?
- Can you understand why?

Exam tip

Read the question carefully. Many candidates only wrote about height – the question said '... and width'.

Exam tip

Bars have already been plotted for other sites on this map so, when adding Site C and Site F to the map, the examiner will expect a similar shading and use of the key provided. They should also be as close to the letter as possible. Some were drawn almost on other sites!

Exam tip

The word '...pattern...' in a question involves broad statements about the plots, not a description of each separate site or plot.

Analysing a Paper 4 question: Locating the CBD – May 2007

The Question (continued)

(d) (i) The ground floor function of the 10 buildings at each site was recorded. Why did the students only record the ground floor function of the buildings? **[1]**

(ii) In the boxes below, write 'CBD' next to two functions which are found in the CBD of a town. **[2]**

BANK		MAIN POST OFFICE	
DEPARTMENT STORE		GENERAL STORES	
LOW COST HOUSING		TOURIST OFFICE	

(iii) Tick the hypothesis which would be the best to use to investigate the functions of the CBD. **[1]**

A *'Buildings closer to the CBD have a mainly residential function.'*
B *'Buildings closer to the CBD have a mainly commercial function.'*
C *'Buildings closer to the CBD have a mainly tourist function.'*

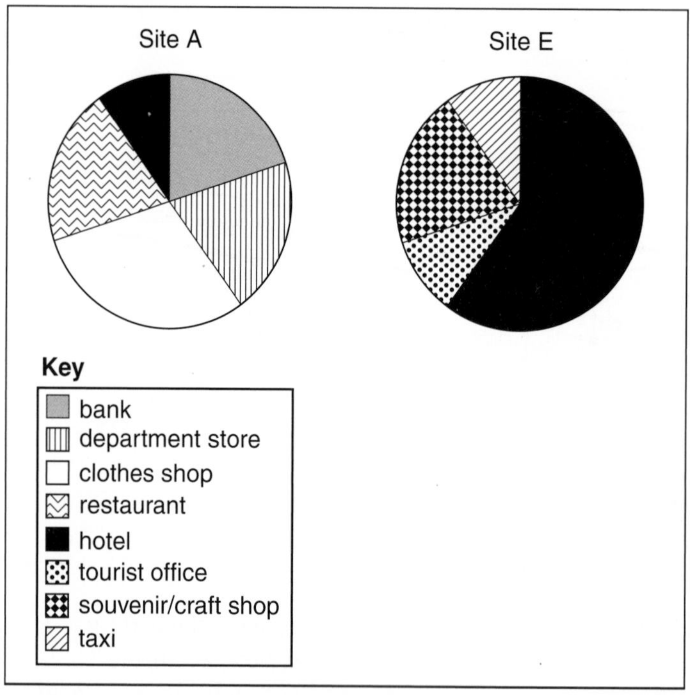

Fig. 2

Functions of buildings

(iv) The functions of the 10 buildings at Site A and Site E are shown in Fig. 2. Compare the functions of the two sites. **[3]**

(e) The teacher encouraged a group of students to organise their own pedestrian or traffic count. Describe in detail how and where the students could do this in the town. **[3]**

Source: IGCSE Geography (0460/04) May 2007 Question 1

Getting it right (continued)

(d) (i) Many candidates recognised that it was simpler and more practical to record the ground floor function but a large number regarded this as representing the function of all the floors of the building. Some suggested that they would need 'a ladder' to record the functions above ground floor, which was not accepted!

(ii)/(iii) This was well done. Virtually all candidates recognised two relevant CBD functions; a few wrongly suggested 'general store' and 'low cost housing' though. Almost all recognised the commercial function in the choices given.

(iv) The command word 'Compare…' was missed by too many candidates. Below are three very different responses to this question. A 'compare' response will describe one site in relation to another site, e.g. 'Site A is commercial but Site E is more for tourists' not 'Site A is commercial. Site E is for tourists.' 'Site A has a small number/ 1 of hotels but Site E has over half / 7 / more hotels.' The use of 'but…', 'whereas…' 'on the other hand…' or words ending in '…er' e.g. *longer*, indicate to examiners that a comparison is being made.

Candidate A	Candidate B	Candidate C
Site A has more clothes shops whereas in Site E there are none. Site E has much more hotels than in Site A; more than 50%.	Site A is for shopping or using the bank. Site E is for tourists to sleep and rest.	Site E is a tourist site but Site A is commercial. Site E offers more hotels, taxis, souvenirs and tourist offices than Site A. On the other hand Site A mainly has shops and some public services which Site E does not offer.

- Suggest which candidate was awarded 0, 2 or 3 marks for their response.
- Explain your decisions.

(e) The better candidates appeared to be from centres that had undertaken some fieldwork and had carried out such counts ('This is how we carried out…') even though the centres opted for the Alternative to Coursework paper. Good answers were precise and specific and included suggestions such as students in pairs, location of count, what would be counted, how it would be recorded and the time involved.

Candidate A
Traffic Count: in pairs use a tally system along the main road to count the cars passing in one direction in a 5-minute period.
Candidate B
Candidate B: Traffic Count: count the number of vehicles along the road and then write down how many there were.
Candidate C
Candidate C: Pedestrian Count: this could be done along the coast (Site G), on the main road (Site A) and near the railway station (Site D). One student stands on one side of the road and another one on the other side. 3 times a weekday (morning, lunch and rush-hour) for half an hour students tally pedestrians. Tallies are then added up to give a pedestrian count.

- Discuss the differences between the answers.
- How many marks would you give each response out of the 3 marks available?

Exam tip

It is vital to prepare for and identify command words in any question. The command word in (d) (iv) was 'Compare'. A number missed this and gave two entirely separate descriptions of the functions of the two sites.

Analysing a Paper 4 question: Locating the CBD – May 2007

The Question (continued)

(f) Land values for each site were collected from the municipal town hall. The value is measured in thousand US dollars for each square metre. The results are shown on Table 2 and plotted on Fig. 3.

(i) Draw the isoline for 50 thousand US$/m². **[2]**

(ii) Colour in the land valued above 60 thousand US$/m². **[1]**

Site	A	B	C	D	E	F	G	H	I	J
Land value thousand US$/m²	65	53	50	36	61	28	22	25	20	22

Table 2

Land values at each site (thousand US$/m²)

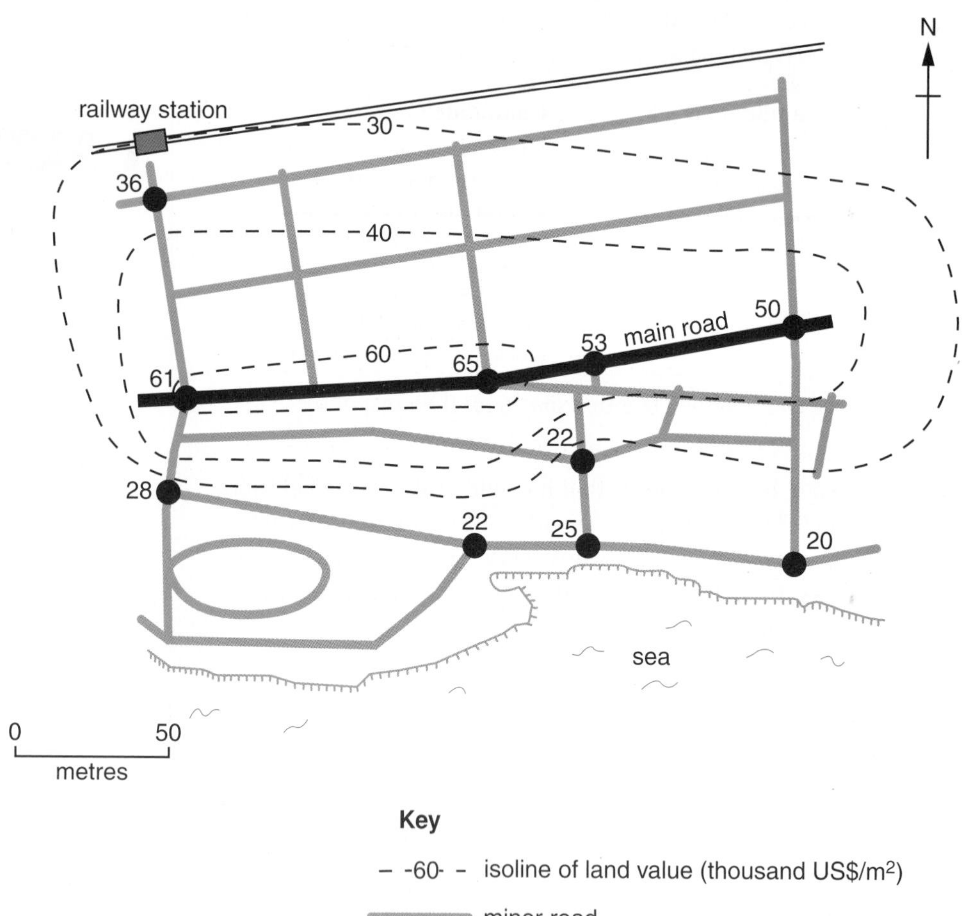

Fig. 3

(g) Look again at Table 1 and Figs 1, 2 and 3. Write a conclusion to this investigation. You should comment on the original hypothesis suggesting where the centre of the town is located. Give reasons for your decision, stating data from Table 1 and Figs 1, 2 and 3. You should mention building height, building width and the value of the land.

Comment on the original hypothesis. **[6]**

[Total: 30 marks]

Source: IGCSE Geography (0460/04) May 2007 Question 1

Getting it right (continued)

f Drawing the isoline proved too difficult for many candidates. Some partly drew it accurately but missed the significance of putting it through the 50 value at Site C. It needed to be drawn at the same distance from the 40 and 60 thousand US$/$m^2$ isolines and go through the 50 value (on the right at Location C) for both marks. Shading the land over 60 thousand US$/$m^2$ was completed more successfully for 1 mark.

Here are two candidates' attempts at drawing the isoline and shading the area required. Both candidates gained the mark for shading for (f) (ii) but one gained 2 marks for the isoline and the other just 1 mark.

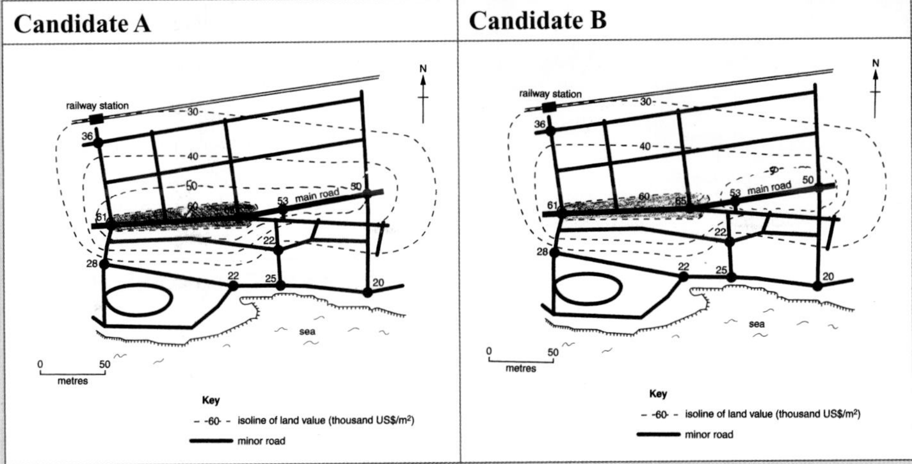

- Which isoline was awarded 1 mark and which 2 marks? Why?

g Read the two candidates' responses below. Now read the mark scheme and try and mark these. Note there were 3 marks for references to data!

Candidate A

The hypothesis was right. The height increased as we went towards the centre. As the centre of the city has a commercial function and has tall wide buildings, we decided that the CBD is located along the main road.

Candidate B

The height and width of the buildings increased towards the main road. Site A having 3 storey 12 pace buildings whilst Site H had 1-storey 5 pace buildings. The land value at Site A was also much higher than that of Site H (Site A = 65 thousand $US per m^2 and Site H = 25 thousand $US/$m^2$. We can see the centre of the town is around Site A on the main road. This hypothesis can be supported by Fig.3 which shows how land values decrease in rings around the centre of the town. Also Fig. 2 shows how site A is mainly commercial and buildings close to the CBD are mainly commercial.

Be a marker! Use the mark scheme below to decide how many marks each response should get and where the marks should be awarded. These answers were awarded 3 and 6 marks.

The hypotheses are correct/supported. The building heights generally increase towards the centre of the town; e.g. site A and B; but site G is a high building. Buildings are generally wider towards the centre or the town; site A and B. Site E is also a wide building but not in the town centre. The value of the land is higher along the main road and lower towards the south and the railway in the north. Above 60 thousand $ in the centre; below 30 thousand $ at the edge. (1 for Hypothesis decision, 1 for Location of centre, 1 for Reason, 3 for Data) = 6 @ 1 marks = 6

Exam tip

Drawing lines through the same point values is a technique seen on different types of maps. Contours (lines of equal height), isohyets (lines of equal rainfall), isotherms (lines of equal temperature), isobars (lines of equal pressure) are all examples. Some points will be exactly on the line required; others will mean that you have to judge where the isoline would come between the points given. This is a difficult skill well worth practising.

TOPIC 2 Investigating rivers

A Measuring rivers

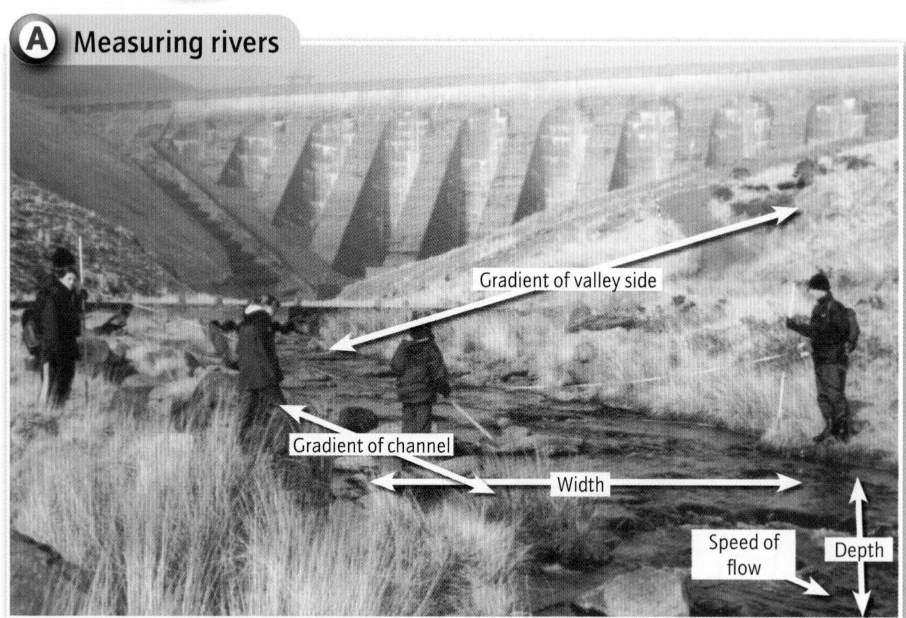

Measuring rivers

Measuring river features and processes is a popular fieldwork exercise. The students in **Source A** are measuring the width of a river in Wales, UK as part of their coursework investigation. They are working near to its source where, because the river is shallower and not too wide, measurements can be taken easily, quickly, safely and accurately. The labels show some of the measurements that can be recorded at any site. As the river gets wider and deeper, this becomes more difficult. Providing two or more sites are used, it is possible to describe and compare river features and processes along its length.

B Along a river we could also investigate …

SUGGESTION BOX

Enquiry questions and hypotheses to test

Channel size and shape
Does the river channel increase in width and depth as the river moves downstream away from its source?

Valley shape
How does the shape of the valley change as the river moves downstream from its source?

Load size and shape
The bedload of a river will be smaller and rounder as it moves away from its source.

Gradient
Does the river bed gradient decrease as the river moves downstream from the source to its mouth?

Speed of flow
The river does not increase its speed as it moves downstream towards its mouth.

Impact of human activity
People have changed some parts of the river and its valley.

Route to Geographical Enquiry

Identify an enquiry question, issue or hypothesis
⬇
Decide what data is required and how it should be collected
⬇
Collect and record data
⬇
Present the data
⬇
Analyse and interpret the data
⬇
Report the conclusions and evaluate the investigation

Task 1

Study **Source A**.

a Identify **three** different river characteristics that can be measured.
b Suggest how each could be measured accurately.
c Compare the health and safety issues that must be considered in river studies with those in the CBD (see pages 210–211).

Task 2

Every investigation needs a clear purpose. This can be written as a **hypothesis** to test or an **enquiry question** to be answered. Study **Source B**.

a Write down **one** investigation that is a hypothesis to test.
b Write down **one** investigation that is an enquiry question to answer.
c Suggest **one** other investigation that could be carried out on a river.

C Location of two sites for fieldwork

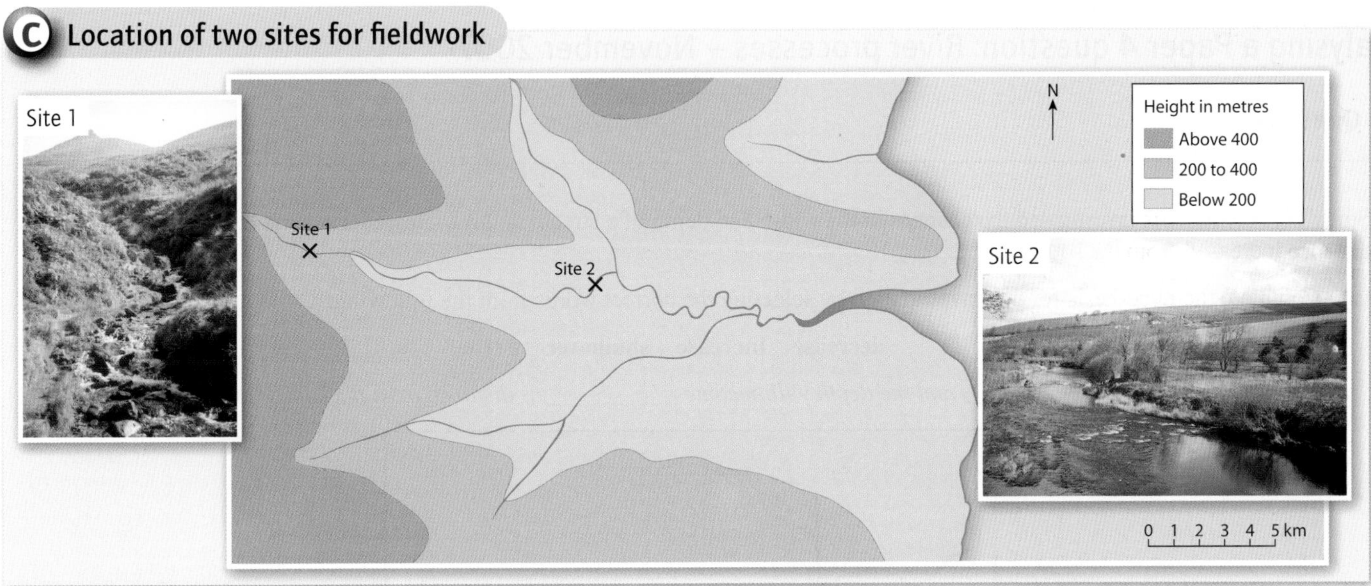

Comparing two sites

A group of students carried out an investigation comparing Sites 1 and 2 along a river. **Source C** shows a photograph taken at each site and also the location of each site on a map. The students chose this hypothesis from those suggested in **Source C**:

'The bedload of the river becomes smaller and more rounded as it moves away from its source.'

At each site they randomly selected 25 pebbles from the bed of the river and measured the long axis. They also used Powers' scale of roundness to make a judgement about how rounded each pebble was.

Task 3

Sources D and E show how to measure size and roundness. **Source F** is an extract from the group's results. Some preliminary conclusions can be drawn from these extracts.

a Draw graphs to present the data for the first 7 results at Sites 1 and 2.

b Describe any relationship that appears to exist between:
- size and roundness
- distance from the source and size
- distance from the source and roundness.

Task 4

Decide whether you think the hypothesis is true, partially true or false. Support your decision with evidence from the data and graphs you have drawn.

Task 5

Study **Source B** again and the 'Route to Geographical Enquiry'.

a Choose **one** other hypothesis or question or the one you suggested in Task 2c.

b Use the 'Route to Geographical Enquiry' to plan how you would investigate this topic.

D Measuring the long axis of a pebble

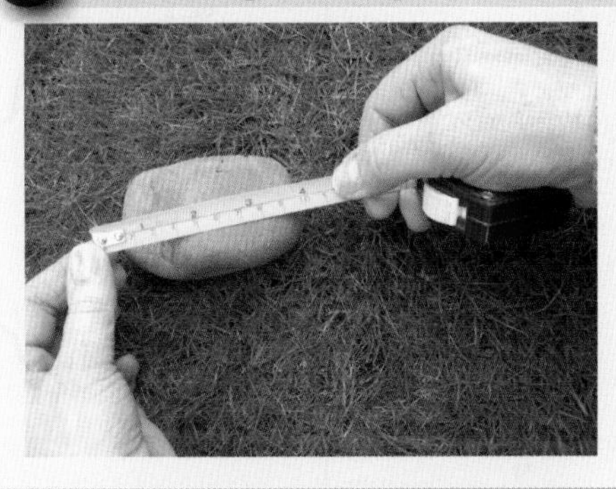

E Powers' scale of roundness

very angular	angular	sub-angular	sub-rounded	rounded	well rounded
1	2	3	4	5	6

F Recording the results

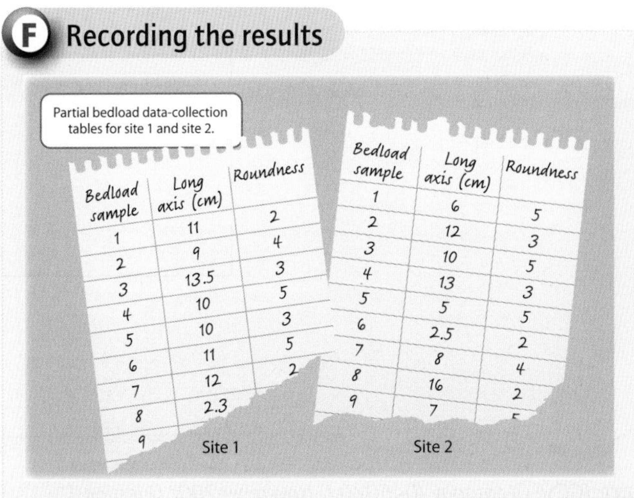

Partial bedload data-collection tables for site 1 and site 2.

Site 1

Bedload sample	Long axis (cm)	Roundness
1	11	2
2	9	4
3	13.5	3
4	10	5
5	10	3
6	11	5
7	12	2
8	2.3	
9		

Site 2

Bedload sample	Long axis (cm)	Roundness
1	6	5
2	12	3
3	10	5
4	13	3
5	5	5
6	2.5	2
7	8	4
8	16	2
9	7	5

Analysing a Paper 4 question: River processes – November 2007

The Question

Study Fig. 1. Students investigated the changes in the width and depth of a stream at three sites, Site A, Site B and Site C, as distance increased from the source.

(a) Complete the hypothesis for this investigation by selecting the correct words from the following:

decrease increase shallower deeper

'The width will ________ and the depth will become ________ as distance from the source increases.' **[1]**

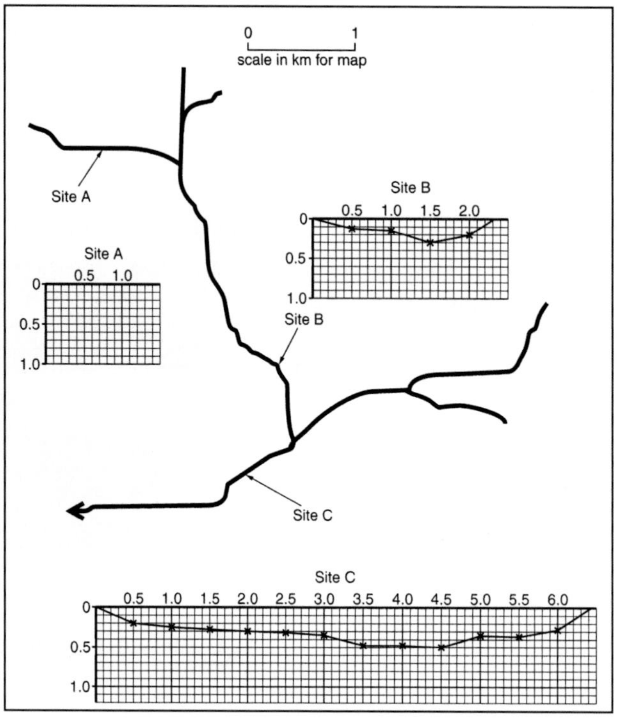

Fig. 1

(b) (i) How did the students measure the width of the stream at each site? Their equipment included two ranging poles and a measuring tape. Draw a labelled diagram, Fig. 2, for your answer. **[3]**

Fig.2

Source: *IGCSE Geography (0460/04) November 2007 Question 1*

Getting it right

(a) Almost 75% of candidates chose *decrease* and *shallower* to put in the blank spaces.

- Can you think why? What were the correct answers? Why did so many candidates get this wrong?

(b) (i) Below are two very different labelled diagrams answering this question. One gained the full 3 marks; the other was awarded just 1 mark.

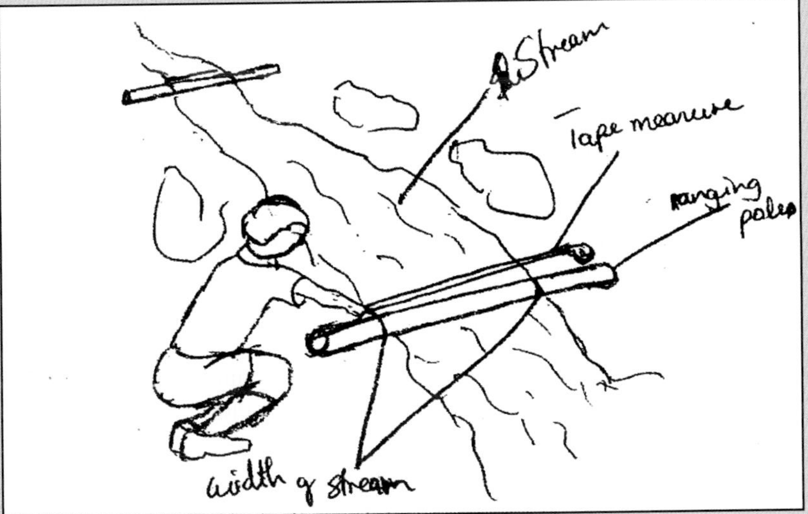

Candidate A

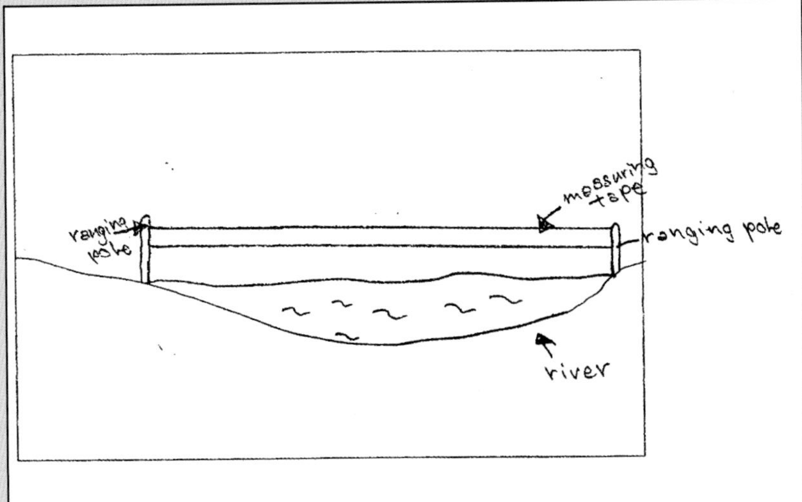

Candidate B

- Which sketch was awarded the full 3 marks? Why?
- Why did the other sketch gain 1 mark but not the other 2 marks?

Exam tip

Read the question carefully – the last part says '…as distance from the source increases.' Check the difference between the mouth and the source of a river. Many candidates did not know the difference and mixed them up!

Exam tip

The two ranging poles had to be located vertically at the edge of the river on both sides with the measuring tape between them. One sketch shows this. The other technique does use both poles and the tape but this isn't the correct way to measure these features of the stream. Both sketches are labelled; those that were not could only gain 1 mark.

Analysing a Paper 4 question: River processes – November 2007

The Question (continued)

(b) (continued)

(ii) At each site, the students also measured the depth of the stream systematically (every ½ metre). The results of the investigation are shown in Table 1.

Site	Total width (m)	Depth in metres at distances from left bank												Wetted perimeter (m)	Discharge (m/sec)
		0.5 m	1.0 m	1.5 m	2.0 m	2.5 m	3.0 m	3.5 m	4.0 m	4.5 m	5.0 m	5.5 m	6.0 m		
A	1.40	0.15	0.10											1.50	0.01
B	2.31	0.12	0.15	0.30	0.20									2.50	0.09
C	6.42	0.20	0.25	0.28	0.30	0.32	0.35	0.48	0.48	0.50	0.35	0.36	0.28		1.25

Table 1

Draw a line graph for Site A on Fig. 1, to show the depth of the stream, using information from Table 1. **[3]**

(c) (i) The wetted perimeter is the amount of bank and bed which the stream water touches. Use Fig. 1 to calculate the length of the wetted perimeter at Site C. Write your answer in Table 1. **[2]**

(ii) Explain how the wetted perimeter can change the speed of the river. **[2]**

(d) (i) The students also measured the velocity of the stream at each site. A floating object was timed travelling over a distance of 10 metres. The recording sheet for Site B is shown in Fig.3. Fill in two other pieces of important information on the recording sheet. **[2]**

Location		Site B		
Time in seconds of floating object over 10 metres				
18.0	16.8	15.4	18.5	13.3

Fig. 3

Source: IGCSE Geography (0460/04) November 2007 Question 1

Getting it right (continued)

(b) (continued)

(ii) Look at the examples of line graphs drawn by three candidates below.

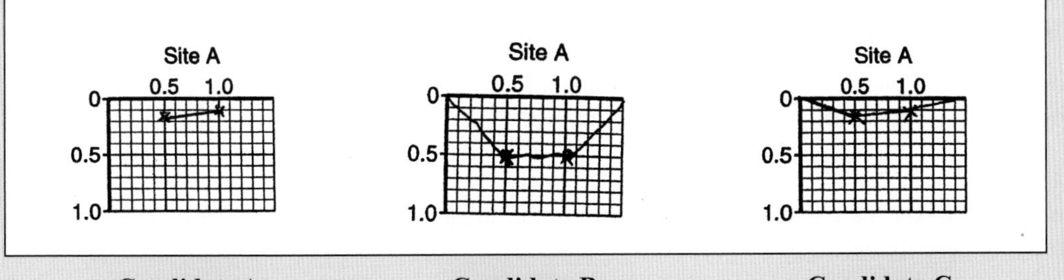

- Marks awarded were 0, 2 and 3 for these graphs. But which gained which mark? Explain your choices. Can you understand why the one awarded 0 was plotted like this?

Exam tip

Completing line graphs must be done accurately. Take a sharp pencil and ruler into the examination room. Plot the points as accurately as possible – don't forget to join them up carefully. Check you are using the correct axes too.

(c) (i) This question asked candidates to calculate the wetted perimeter from Fig. 1 and then write it on Table 1. Too many did not measure from Fig. 1. They used Table 1 instead. Some added up all the figures for row C giving 10.57; others added the two wetted perimeter figures for A and B giving 4. The range of answers acceptable for 2 marks was 6.5–6.7 metres.

Check it yourself.

(ii)
- Compare the two candidates' answers below.
- The first answer was awarded both marks, the second answer none? Why?

First answer:
The greater the wetted perimeter, the more friction the water encounters with the bed and sides. This reduces the speed of the river.

Second answer:
The wetted perimeter changes the speed of the river because more water can be held in the stream of the river.

(d) (i) This question was about extra pieces of information that students would add to the recording sheet. One example could be the date. The velocity measurements are given so the missing items are not to do with measuring anything . Some candidates listed what they were going to measure, such as width and depth, which is not relevant here.

- Can you think of two other important items that you could add to the recording sheet before you measured the velocity?

Exam tip

(i) You must know the meaning of terms such as *wetted perimeter*, *friction*, *discharge*, *source* and *mouth* before you take this examination. If a question refers you to a Figure you must use that Figure, not find another way to answer it!

(ii) The first answer gains 2 marks because it links an increase in wetted perimeter with an increase in friction. It then explains that this reduces speed. The second answer does not say how or why the speed changes and the increase in stream water is irrelevant so no marks.

Analysing a Paper 4 question: River processes – November 2007

The Question (continued)

(d) (continued)

(ii) State a reason why the timing of the floating object over 10 metres was repeated five times. **[1]**

(iii) The cross-sectional area is used to calculate the discharge. Look again at Fig. 1 and select the cross-sectional area most appropriate for Site B from the possibilities below. Underline your answer.

$3.29\,m^2$ $0.32\,m^2$ $0.09\,m^2$ **[1]**

(e) Study Table 1 and Fig. 1 again. Describe how the following characteristics of the stream change from Site A to Site C. You should state data to support your descriptions.

- Width
- Depth
- Discharge **[6]**

(f) The stream was measured again at the same sites after a storm, when 60 mm of rain fell in 48 hours. Describe how this storm would change the discharge and the processes of the stream.

- Discharge change
- Processes change **[3]**

(g) **(i)** Describe in detail how the investigation could be improved. Suggest reasons for these improvements. **[4]**

(ii) Write a brief conclusion to this investigation. **[2]**

[Total: 30 marks]

Source: IGCSE Geography (0460/04) November 2007 Question 1

Getting it right (continued)

(ii) 'To be more accurate' was an answer given by far too many candidates. It is much too vague. The velocity was measured five times to get an average velocity and to eliminate errors.

- Think of two experimental errors that justify carrying out the measuring of the velocity more than just once.

(iii) The correct answer is 0.32 m^2. Try to explain why many candidates circled 0.09 m^2 instead.

(e) Here are two candidate answers.

Candidate A	Candidate B
Width: *The width of the river increases from A to C as it was 1.4m at A and at C it is 6.42m.* Depth: *The depth of the river also increases as the river moves from A to C as the maximum depth at A is 0.15m and at C it is 0.5m.* Discharge: *The discharge of the river increases from A to C as the river moves downwards as it is 0.01m^3 at A while it is 1.25m^3 at C.*	Width: The width goes wider from A to C. Depth: The depth gets deeper as you go down the river from A to C Discharge: The level and amount of discharge goes up from A to C.

- Why did Candidate A get 6 marks but Candidate B only 3 marks?

Exam tip

Most candidates could identify that all three measurements increased from A to C. However, despite the question asking for it, Candidate B did not give any data to support the statements – consequently losing 3 marks. If the question asks for data or evidence you will be penalised for not providing it. Don't forget the units – m and m^3 here.

(f) Most students recognised that discharge would increase if more water entered the river after the storm. However, many did not understand what a river process was and wrote about width, depth or velocity changing. River processes include erosion (refer to types), transportation and deposition.

- Check the meaning of erosion, transportation and deposition. How do you think these would change in this river after the heavy storm?

(g) (i) An improvement means what could the students have done better or different in this investigation. Many candidates repeated what had already been done. The best answers suggested more sites, measuring at different times of the year or in different weather conditions. Some wrote 'improve equipment' – but what equipment and how would it be better than that used?

(ii) Here are two candidate answers.

Candidate A	Candidate B
Therefore the students can conclude from the measurements that the width and depth did increase as distance from the source increases. The hypothesis was correct.	So the conclusion is that more people are needed with more accurate instruments to get a more accurate result.

- Which candidate has met the criteria in the Exam Tip and was rewarded with 2 marks?
- Why did the other get 0 marks?

Exam tip

If you are asked to write a conclusion at the end of a question, always return to the hypothesis that has been stated at or near the start. The answer requires a conclusion to this fieldwork. It should include a judgement on whether it has been proved correct, partly correct or incorrect, with reasons for your decision.

Investigating tourism

A The City Palace, Jaipur, India

MAHARAJA SAWAI MANSINGH II MUSEUM TRUST
THE CITY PALACE, JAIPUR
BOOKING WINDOW UDAI POLE
TIMINGS-9.30 A.M. TO 5.00 P.M.
ENTRANC FEE FOR FOREIGN VISITORS
1. ADULT: Rs.180/EACH (NO EXTRA CHARGE FOR ORD. CAMERA)
2. CHILDREN: Rs.100/EACH (BETWEEN 5 TO 12 YEARS)
3. VIDEO CAMERA: Rs.200/ EACH.
1. PHOTOGRAPHY IS STRICTLY PROHIBITED INSIDE THE GALLERIES.
2. MUSEUM WILL CLOSE AT 4.00 P.M. ON GANGAUR (BOTH DAYS) AND TEEJ (BOTH DAYS)
MUSEUM REMAINS CLOSED ON DHULANDI (HOLI FESTIVAL)
4. IF FOUND FILMING WITHOUT VIDEO CAMERA TICKET Rs.600/ WILL BE CHARGED.
BY ORDER

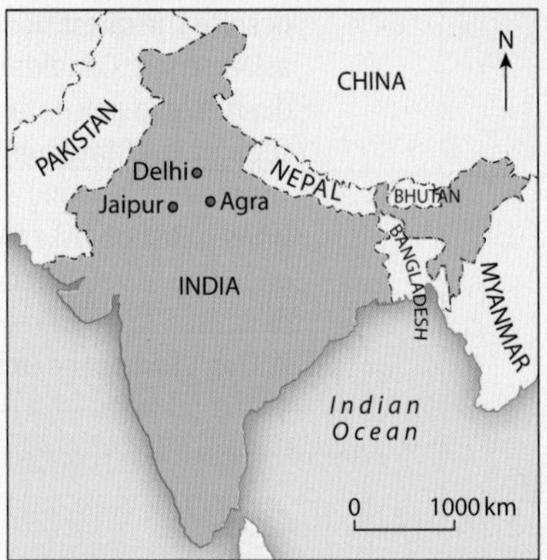

Jaipur is the capital city of Rajasthan, a state in the northern part of India. It is located in a very dry and sandy area but attracts tourists who usually visit the Delhi-Agra-Jaipur triangle of cities. Known as the 'pink' city, Jaipur has many historical buildings. One is the City Palace.

International tourism to India

Many countries rely on income from tourism. This is especially true of LEDCs such as India. Almost 3 million visitors travel from overseas countries to India, of which more than 83 per cent travel by air, with the majority landing at Delhi. Western Europe provides over one-third of these visitors, with more travelling from the UK (16 per cent) than any other country. The most popular period is October to December whereas the least visitors arrive between April and June. Carrying out fieldwork investigations of visitor patterns is a popular coursework topic in many countries.

B So what shall we investigate … and how?

Next month we are going to spend time at the City Palace in Jaipur. We will be carrying out a survey of visitors to the building. I want you to think about what hypothesis or question we could investigate using questionnaires. Also bear in mind that we cannot ask every visitor so we will have to take a sample. Think about the best way to do that too.

Task 1

Study **Source A** and an atlas.

a Describe the location of Jaipur in relation to:
- Delhi, Agra and other features on the map
- the country you live in.

b In what ways does the local economy benefit from tourists? Refer to evidence from the photograph and your own ideas.

Task 2

The teacher in an international school in Jaipur (**Source B**) decided to take a group of students to the City Palace to carry out a survey of tourists, using questionnaires. He obtained permission from the authorities to do this outside the main entrance for a period from 10 to 11 am on one day in June.

a Do you think this was a good time and month to carry out this work?

b Suggest how the results might differ at other times of day or in other months.

Route to Geographical Enquiry

Identify an enquiry question, issue or hypothesis

Decide what data is required and how it should be collected

Collect and record data

Present the data

Analyse and interpret the data

Report the conclusions and evaluate the investigation

Sampling and questionnaires

Sampling is a necessary and acceptable part of many geographical investigations. There is never enough time, money, energy, equipment or students to ask questions of every visitor to a tourist attraction. The larger the sample the more reliable the data. Group work is one way of obtaining more results in a fixed time. But how do we sample the 'population' of tourists?

Task 3

Study **Source C**.

- **a** Why is sampling necessary in many geographical investigations?
- **b** What is systematic sampling? How is it different from random sampling?
- **c** In what situations might you use stratified sampling?
- **d** Take a sample of six students from your class using systematic, random and stratified sampling methods. Comment on your findings.

C Random or systematic sampling?

Random sampling for questionnaires

There are several ways of using this method. It is best to use random number tables. Using the extract below (see shaded numbers) you could ask questions of the 61st, 2nd, 10th and 54th person you meet. It avoids bias and any subjectivity but does take time to set up.

Extract from a random numbers table

23	17	59	66	38	61	02	10	86	10	51	55
03	04	10	33	53	70	11	54	48	63	94	60
38	67	23	42	29	65	40	88	78	71	37	18

Systematic sampling for questionnaires

The people asked are chosen by a system that is evenly distributed, e.g. every 3rd person. This avoids bias such as only asking people who might appear to be cooperative or of a certain age-group. It is easy and simple to use.

Stratified sampling for questionnaires

This can be used when the proportions of people in a sample are very different, e.g. in a class of students two-thirds may be girls and one-third boys. In this case you could use either systematic or random sample methods to choose four girls and two boys. This would reflect the gender balance.

D Which is better: Questionnaire 1 or Questionnaire 2?

The hypothesis: 'The characteristics of visitor patterns to the City Palace in Jaipur show that they are mostly from overseas rather than from India.'

VISITOR QUESTIONNAIRE 1

1. Why have you come here? ____________
2. Have you been here before?
   Yes No Can't remember
3. How long do you intend to stay here?
   <4 hours >4 hours
4. Are you aware that by visiting this place you may cause damage? ____________
5. Where have you come from? ____________
6. How did you get here?
   Car Train Bus

VISITOR QUESTIONNAIRE 2

Good morning. I am carrying out a geography investigation for my IGCSE examination. Could I ask you a few questions please?

Time/date ________ Weather ________ Place ________

1. Have you ever visited this site before?
   Yes No
2. How did you get to hear about this place?
   Advert Television Friend Other
3. How far have you travelled to get here today?
   5 km <6–20 km >30 km
4. If you did not arrive by car, how did you travel to the site?
   Bus Walk Bike Motorbike Train Other
5. Why are you attracted to this site?
   ____
6. How long do you intend staying here?
   <2 hours 2–4 hours >4 hours Longer
7. In which country or place are you a permanent resident ?
   ____

Gender: *Male Female*
Age estimate: *<20 20–35 36–50 51–65 >65*

Task 4

Study **Source D** and note the hypothesis. The teacher divided the class into six groups of four students and set them each a task of devising a questionnaire. The questionnaires were shown to each group to vote on the best one to use. Questionnaire 1 received least votes and Questionnaire 2 received most votes.

- **a** List **three** differences between the two questionnaires.
- **b** Discuss in a group why Questionnaire 2 was judged to be the best one to use.
- **c** Following your discussion, write down **four** reasons why Questionnaire 2 would be more effective for this investigation than Questionnaire 1.

Task 5

When devising questionnaires it is useful to carry out a pilot survey.

- **a** Use a copy of Questionnaire 2 with friends or family to see if it could be improved. They will have to imagine they are visiting a tourist destination in your country.
- **b** Check the 'Route to Geographical Enquiry' opposite. Devise a plan for the investigation into visitor patterns at a tourist destination of your choice. Refer to the plan on page 211 if you need help.

Analysing a Paper 4 question: The impact of tourism – May 2008

This question relied on using questionnaires provided on an insert to the exam paper. The insert can be found on pages 232 and 233. As this was Question 2 on the exam paper, note that references to Figures begin at Fig. 5 (not Fig. 1).

The Question

Students investigated the impact of tourists on the settlement of Pescasseroli in the Abruzzi National Park in central Italy. The hypothesis for the investigation was *'The tourists who visit the National Park have a positive impact on the settlement of Pescasseroli'*. Information about the settlement of Pescasseroli is shown below.

Pescasseroli is a settlement of 2000 inhabitants. It is located on a wide plain surrounded by mountains, in the heart of the Abruzzi National Park. Activities in winter include downhill skiing and cross-country skiing. In the summer there are ample opportunities for a variety of trekking and outdoor activities. There are six hotels in the settlement and 11 restaurants for visitors and residents to use.

Fig. 5

(a) The students used the Internet to find out about the settlement. The information in Fig. 5 is from this secondary source of data. They also collected primary data.

(i) What is meant by a *primary* source of data? **[1]**

(ii) State **two** examples of a primary source of data. **[1]**

(b) The students designed questionnaires for the tourists and residents to assess the impact of tourists. Fig. 6 [see page 232] shows the questionnaires.
Question T1 (i) to the tourists was designed to investigate the method of transport used by tourists to reach the National Park. Fig. 7 is a pie chart of the results.

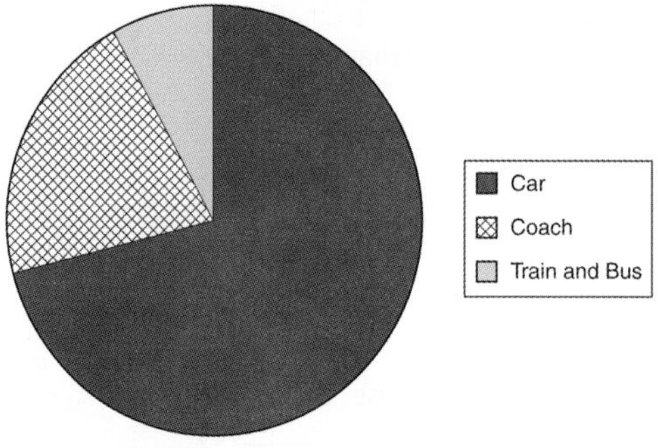

Fig. 7

Method of transport used by tourists

(i) Describe the pattern shown by these results. Suggest **one** reason for this pattern. **[3]**

(ii) Fig. 8 [see page 233] shows the results of the questionnaire for tourists. Use the results from question T1 (ii) to complete the pictograph on Fig. 9, to represent the tourists' opinions about parking problems in the settlement. **[2]**

☹ Very difficult	
😐 A little difficult	
☺ No problem	☺ ☺ ☺ ☺ ☺ ☺ ☺ ☺ ☺ ☺ ☺ ☺ ☺ ☺ ☺ ☺

☹ or 😐 or ☺ = 4 people

Fig. 9

Tourists' opinions about parking

Source: IGCSE Geography (0460/04) May 2008 Question 2

Getting it right

(a) (i) Examiners were looking for answers that made it clear the information was being collected for the first time by the person; not for examples of primary sources as that is needed in (ii). Here are three answers.

Candidate A	Candidate B	Candidate C
Collecting data using questionnaires and interviews from the general public.	*When they obtain the data first hand and it has not been collected before. Original data for a specific purpose.*	*The data is original.*

Only Candidate B was awarded the mark.

- Discuss why Candidates A and C did not gain a mark.

(ii) A number of candidates wrote 'farming' or 'fishing' or 'coal mining'.

- What mistake have they made?

Questionnaires and interviews were accepted here – the important thing was that candidates knew that a 'primary' source was information that they were collecting first; it had not been provided by other people such as in a newspaper or book which would be a secondary source.

(b) (i) The pie chart showed three different methods of transport to reach the National Park. Many answers were disappointing as candidates failed to understand the word 'pattern' and just listed the percentages for each transport type. Pattern requires a comparative answer as given by Candidate A below. Reasons were also surprisingly weak.

- Look at these answers; there is 1 mark for Description and 2 marks for Reasons.

Candidate A
Describe: *Most people came by car to Pescasseroli.* Reason: *Because most people that come there are wealthy.*
Candidate B
Describe: *We can see 65% travel by car, 25% by coach, 10% travel by train and bus.* Reason: *Travelling by car is more practical as you can take all your luggage and visit different parts whenever you want.*

Candidate A gained 1 mark for description – 'most' is a comparative word that describes a pattern, but the reason is poor.

Candidate B just listed percentages (see page 233) but there are two good reasons for using a car here. Can you spot them? The ideal answer would have combined Candidate A's description with Candidate B's reasons!

(ii) Most candidates used the key to draw in 3 faces (for 12 people) and 1 face (for 4 people) for 'Very difficult' and 'A little difficult'. Some however ignored the key and drew in all 12 faces and 4 faces which was wrong and wasted time.

Exam tip

In questions that require a specific number of responses, e.g. one, two, three ... the number will be emboldened. In (a) (ii) ...**two** examples... were needed yet some candidates just provided one. Read the instruction carefully!

Exam tip

If you are asked to 'Describe the pattern' do not just read off data. You can provide the data but also give an overall statement that shows you have looked at all the data and are making an overall judgement, e.g. *most, more, least*.

Analysing a Paper 4 question: The impact of tourism – May 2008

The Question (continued)

(c) Study question T2 and question T3 of the questionnaire for tourists, Fig. 6 [see page 232]. Explain why these are important questions for the investigation. **[3]**

(d) Study the results of question T4 of the questionnaire for tourists, Fig. 8 [see page 233]. Draw a bar graph on Fig. 10 to show the main reasons why visitors come to the Abruzzi National Park. **[4]**

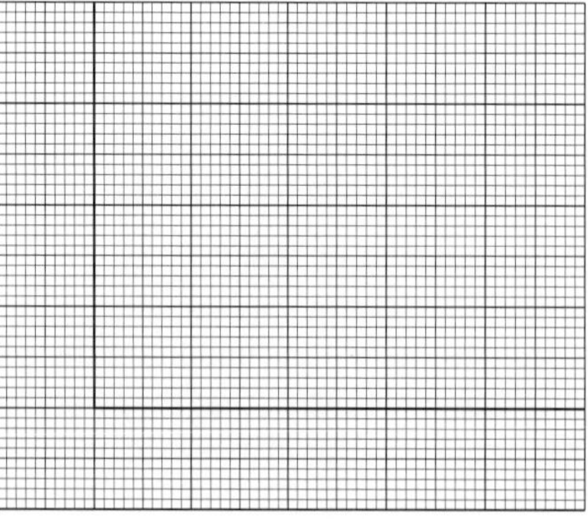

Fig. 10

Reasons for visiting the Abruzzi National Park

(e) (i) Use the age and gender information from Fig. 8 [see page 233] to explain whether the tourist questionnaire results in the sample are reliable and representative. **[2]**

(ii) Suggest how the main reason for visiting the National Park may change at a different time of the year or at a different time of the day. **[3]**

			Number	%
R1	Length of residency	Under 5 years	19	15
		5–10 years	22	18
		11–15 years	66	53
		Over 15 years	18	14
R2	Opinion of main problems	None	50	40
		Crowded	18	14
		Litter	15	12
		Traffic	26	21
		Noisy people	16	13

			Yes	No
R3	Residents' views on benefits of tourism	Tourism related job	66%	34%
		Adequate tourist facilities	72%	28%
		Adequate parking	69%	31%
		Improved facilities	83%	17%

Fig. 11

Results of questionnaire for residents (125 results)

(f) Study the results of the questionnaire for tourists, Fig. 8 [see page 233] again, together with the results of the questionnaire for residents, Fig. 11 [above].

Write a short conclusion to this investigation, ensuring that you state whether you agree with the original hypothesis, that *'the tourists who visit the National Park have a positive impact on the settlement of Pescasseroli'*. You must refer to data results from both questionnaires to support your comments. **[6]**

(g) Suggest, in detail, how the students could collect data to investigate the extent that tourists may increase the litter, noise and traffic in the settlement. **[5]**

[Total: 30 marks]

Source: IGCSE Geography (0460/04) May 2008 Question 2

Getting it right (continued)

(c) Question T2 on the questionnaire asked about the length of time tourists were staying in Pescasseroli; question T3 asked about the type of accommodation tourists were using. The exam question asked why these were important questions but most candidates just rewrote the question or gave vague responses and rarely achieved more than 1 mark out of 3. Here are three candidate answers.

Candidate A	Candidate B	Candidate C
To see if they are passing by or if they are here to see the city. To see if they are wealthy visitors and what type of accommodation they will be using.	To understand the impact tourists have on the settlement. They may contribute to pollution.	*It is important to know how long tourists stay to find out how much profit is being made. If tourists stay for long noise and litter may need managing. If more stay in hotels then more jobs are being created.*

Candidate A has re-written the question and does not explain why these questions are important.

Candidate B has a vague idea about some impact on pollution but does not say why or define the type of pollution.

Candidate C does attempt to go further with some reasons, e.g. 'how much profit', 'managing noise and litter' and 'job creation'. These three points are worth 3 marks; nothing in the other two answers deserves any credit.

(d) The bar graphs were generally completed well.

(e) (i) Most candidates judged that the gender balance percentages, while not equal, were close enough to be representative. Many, however, ignored the age issue completely. Too many failed to understand the term 'reliability'; some suggested young people may not tell the truth, which was not acceptable!

(ii) This was well done regarding variety of visitors during the year, e.g. skiing in winter, cycling/walking/trekking in summer. Less well done was the variety of visitors during the day which could be caused by e.g. school holidays, retired people or school parties in the day; workers visiting in the evening,

(f) Most candidates agreed with the hypothesis and supported it with valid statements taken from the questionnaire. Many, however, failed to gain the 6th mark, which was reserved for using both questionnaires, as asked in the question!

(g) The main problem here was that candidates wrote about the National Park not the settlement as asked. Failing to see the word 'settlement' in the question meant that the scale of the fieldwork became unrealistic, e.g. count the cars going into the National Park! The best answers referred to comparing litter, traffic and noise data in and out of the tourist season using small-group techniques at specific places.

Exam tip

Marks are not awarded for general terms, e.g. 'pollution', 'litter', 'money'. Always be more specific, for example pollution can be air, noise or visual; litter could be cans, paper, or plastic bags; money can be income, pay or profit.

Exam tip

Remember to state whether you agree, disagree or partially agree with the hypothesis if asked. Read the question too! The last sentence clearly said 'You must refer to … both questionnaires'; most candidates did not.

Analysing a Paper 4 question: The impact of tourism – May 2008

The Question (Insert)

Fig. 6 for Question 2

Questionnaire for tourists in Pescasseroli

Hello. Please could you give me a few minutes of your time? We are doing a survey about tourism for our Geography Investigation.

Are you a resident or a visitor to the settlement? (If resident use other questionnaire)

T1 (i) How did you get to the National Park today?

Car Coach Train and bus Bicycle Other ...

(ii) If by car then did you find parking difficult?

Very difficult A little difficult No problem

T2 How long are you staying in the area?

Only one day 2–3 days 4–7 days More than one week

T3 What type of accommodation are you using?

None Hotel in Pescasseroli Local hostel Campsite Private house

T4 What is the main reason for your visit?

Wildlife Scenery Trekking Cycling Other e.g. visiting friends

Thank you for your time

Age: Less than 20 years 20–40 years 41–60 years Over 60 years

Gender: Male Female

Questionnaire for residents in Pescasseroli

R1 How long have you lived in Pescasseroli?

Under 5 years 5–10 years 11–15 years Over 15 years

R2 In your opinion, what is the main problem with tourists visiting the settlement?

None Crowded Litter Traffic Noisy people

R3 Please answer YES or NO to the following questions.

- Is your job related to tourism? YES/NO
- Are the facilities for tourism adequate? YES/NO
- Is there adequate parking? YES/NO
- Has tourism improved facilities in the settlement? YES/NO

Thank you for your time

Source: IGCSE Geography (0460/04) May 2008 Question 2

Fig. 8 for Question 2

Results of questionnaire for tourists

			Number	%
T1(i)	Transport method	Car	56	71%
		Coach	17	21%
		Train and Bus	7	8%
		Bicycle	0	0%
		Other	0	0%
T1(ii)	Opinions about parking	Very difficult	12	15%
		A little difficult	4	5%
		No problem	64	80%
T2	Length of stay	Only 1 day	34	42%
		2–3 days	30	38%
		4–7 days	14	17%
		More than one week	2	3%
T3	Accommodation type	None	30	38%
		Hotel in settlement	10	12%
		Hostel in settlement	24	30%
		Campsite	6	8%
		Private house	10	12%
T4	Main reason for visit	Wildlife	20	25%
		Scenery	15	19%
		Trekking	17	21%
		Cycling	10	12%
		Other e.g. visiting friends/culture/relaxing	18	23%
		Skiing	0	0%
AGE		Less than 20 years	26	32%
		20–40	38	48%
		41–60	10	13%
		Over 60 years	6	7%
GENDER		Male	43	54%
		Female	37	46%

80 tourists interviewed

Measuring the weather

The weather refers to day-to-day changes in, for example, temperature, cloud cover, air pressure and rainfall. The teacher in **Source A** is reading and recording weather measurements in preparation for a coursework investigation.

A The Stevenson screen

Using appropriate instruments, it is possible to investigate many aspects of weather around a school:

- Cloud cover and type
- Maximum and minimum temperature
- Rainfall/precipitation
- Atmospheric pressure
- Relative humidity
- Wind speed and direction

B Heads … and tails

Tail F: Precipitation (rain, hail, sleet and snow) falls into the metal funnel and enters a glass container. At regular intervals the contents are tipped into a standard gauge and measured. Snow or hail must be melted first. This is measured in millimetres (mm).

Head 4: Barometer

Tail C: This instrument records the highest and lowest temperature over a period of time in degrees Centigrade (°C). There are two steel markers inside the tube. One marker stays at the maximum temperature; the other stays at the minimum temperature until they are reset. They are pushed into place by mercury which is affected by alcohol in the tube expanding or contracting as temperature changes. This instrument is known as the Six's thermometer after James Six who invented it.

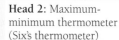

Head 2: Maximum-minimum thermometer (Six's thermometer)

Head 6: Wind vane

Tail A: The wind forces the cups to rotate. They are connected to a meter. The meter converts the rotations into windspeed. This is measured in kilometres per hour (km/hr).

Head 1: Rain gauge

Tail B: This measures air pressure in millibars (mb). The pressure of air moves a pointer around a dial. If pressure is high on the glass it moves the dial around to HIGH. If pressure is low on the glass the dial moves towards LOW.

Tail D: This consists of two thermometers. One records the air temperature; the other one is kept damp so it records the temperature as if the air was 100% saturated. The difference between the temperatures determines the relative humidity of the air which is read off a table which gives relative humidity as a percentage of 100%.

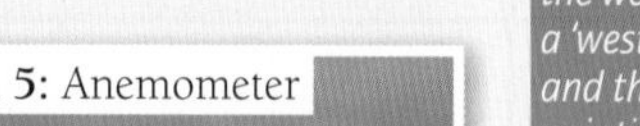

Head 5: Anemometer

Tail E: This shows wind direction. If the wind is from the west it is called a 'westerly wind' and the arrow is pointing from west to east.

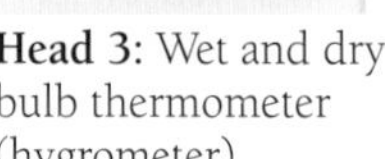

Head 3: Wet and dry bulb thermometer (hygrometer)

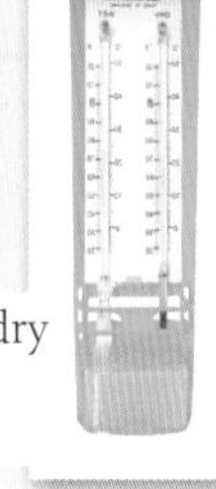

Task 1

Study **Source A**.

a List **three** factors that should decide where the Stevenson screen is sited. Explain why each factor is important. (Page 86 will help with this answer.)

b Answer the following:
- Why is it painted white?
- Why does it have slatted sides?
- Why is it mounted on legs?

Task 2

Study **Source B**.

a Create a two-column table. Match the Heads (instruments 1–6) with the Tails (labels A–F).

b Describe, after additional research, how **two** of these weather instruments work.

Task 3

Study **Sources C, D and E** and read the hypothesis on page 235.

a Look at the station circle describing the weather recorded by the students at 09.00 hours on Day 1. Check that this matches the weather shown in the table.

b In pairs, draw two weather station circles – one each. One of you should use the Day 2 data and the other the Day 3 data to add symbols to your station circle. When you have finished, check each other's station circle against the data.

c To what extent do you think the hypothesis is **true, partially true** or **false**? Support your views with evidence from the data.

C How to record the weather

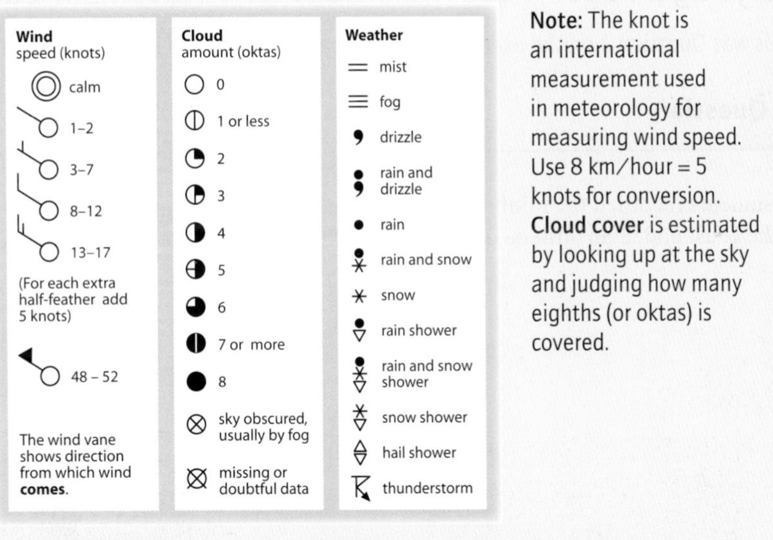

Note: The knot is an international measurement used in meteorology for measuring wind speed. Use 8 km/hour = 5 knots for conversion. **Cloud cover** is estimated by looking up at the sky and judging how many eighths (or oktas) is covered.

Recording the weather

Once measurements are taken, they need to be recorded. A common code of symbols is required so that weather can be compared between different regions. In the UK the Meteorological Office uses the system shown in **Source C**.

A geography class in the UK decided to investigate the hypothesis:

'The weather around the school shows little change on three consecutive days in March.'

The class carried out some fieldwork using the weather instruments they had in the school. They were divided into seven groups of four students. Each group was responsible for measuring or observing one aspect of the weather at the same time on three consecutive days. After taking their readings they presented these on weather station circles.

D Overall recording sheet – observations from 7 groups

	Time	Current temp. (°C)	Pressure (mb)	Direction wind from	Wind speed (knots or km/hour)	Cloud cover (oktas)	Cloud type	Current weather
Day 1 (17 March)	09.00	6	1010	South-west	10 kn (16 km/hr)	4	Stratus	Drizzle
Day 2 (18 March)	09.00	7	1015	West	14 kn (22 km/hr)	3	Cumulus	Mist
Day 3 (19 March)	09.00	9	1024	South	6 kn (10 km/hr)	1	Cirrus	Clear

E The weather station circle for 09.00 hours on Day 1

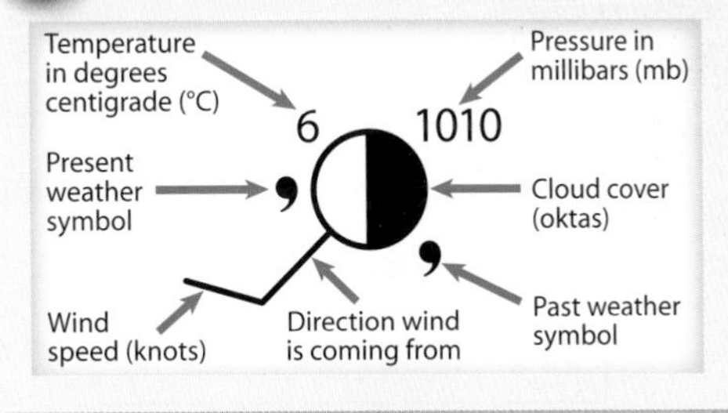

Task 4

Think of a suitable enquiry question or hypothesis for a weather investigation around your school.

a Work through the 'Route to Geographical Enquiry' and devise a plan to measure and record the relevant weather, then to present, analyse and evaluate the investigation.

b When measuring and recording weather, student errors often limit the value of the results. Why? How might such errors be overcome?

Route to Geographical Enquiry

Identify an enquiry question, issue or hypothesis

Decide what data is required and how it should be collected

Collect and record data

Present the data

Analyse and interpret the data

Report the conclusions and evaluate the investigation

Analysing a Paper 4 question: Weather – November 2008

As this was Question 2 on the exam paper, note that references to Figures begin at Fig. 6 (not Fig. 1).

The Question

Students recorded the rainfall and wind direction for 14 days at their school in September. The school is located to the east of the coast and at an altitude of 400 metres. The hypothesis for the investigation was:

'The school receives more rainfall when wind comes from the west'.

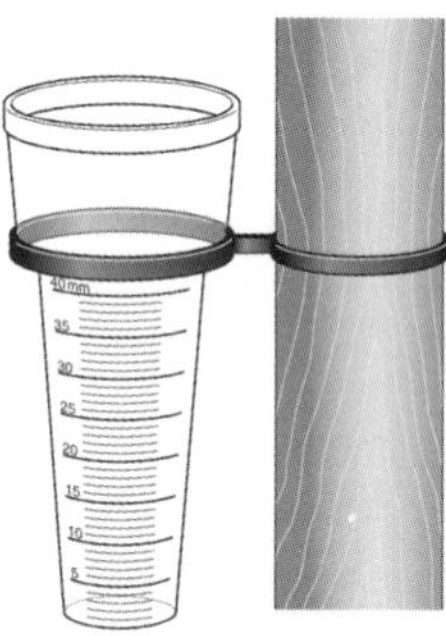

Fig. 6

(a) Study Fig. 6, which shows a low-cost rain gauge. The teacher fixed it to a fence post so that it was accessible for the students but secure.

(i) How is this instrument different from a traditional rain gauge? **[1]**

(ii) Explain how the rain gauge shown is used to measure the rain each day. Write the numbers 1–4 in the instruction box below to show the correct order for accurate measurements to be made. **[2]**

Instructions about how to measure rainfall each day:

Order:

.... Observe carefully how many mm of water in the cylinder

.... At 8.00 every day go to the rain gauge

.... Empty the cylinder of water

.... Record the amount of water on your recording sheet

Date September	1st	2nd	3rd	4th	5th	6th	7th	8th	9th	10th	11th	12th	13th	14th
Rainfall (mm)	0	0	0	3	4	1	0	0	5	13	10	4	0	6
Wind direction	E	SE	E	SW	W	SW	SE	S	SW	W	N	SW	S	W

Table 2

(iii) Table 2 shows the rainfall results. Describe the most appropriate graph type to use to represent this data. You should suggest labels for the axes of the graph. **[2]**

Source: IGCSE Geography (0460/04) November 2008 Question 2

Getting it right

(a) (i) Most candidates scored 1 mark here although a few thought the traditional rain gauge was placed 'underground' and gave the 'low-cost' as a difference. Examiners were looking for a physical difference in the instruments or in their siting. Some candidates listed many differences; only one was required for the mark. The use of 'It…' in answers should have been avoided as it was not clear which gauge was being referred to. Look at these three answers.

Candidate A
A traditional rain gauge is sunk into the ground and raised to at least 30 cm from the ground to prevent splash back from rain drops. In the rain gauge a measuring cylinder is placed. It is not hung on a fence post.
Candidate B
It does not contain a funnel and is not placed below the ground to improve accuracy of measurements.
Candidate C
It is placed in the ground and does not have measurements up the side.

- Are all these worth 1 mark?
- What confusion is caused by using 'It…' instead of the proper name?

(ii) The correct order 2, 1, 4, 3 was listed by almost all candidates. A few reversed the recording and the emptying of the cylinder.

(iii) A disappointing number of candidates failed to gain both marks for this answer; most gained 1 mark for the type of graph but failed to suggest appropriate labels. Examiners were looking for a bar graph (or histogram) with rainfall on the vertical axis and months/time on the horizontal axis. Too many candidates thought a scatter graph was appropriate or came up with complex graphs that also included wind direction. Read the three answers below.

Candidate A	Candidate B	Candidate C
The most appropriate graph type to represent this data would be a bar graph with the wind direction on the x-axis and the average rainfall (in millimetres) on the y-axis.	A Bar Graph is the most appropriate graph to represent the data. The X-axes of the graph is the Date of the days from 1st to 14th of September. The Y-axes is the amount or rainfall in millimetres.	Line Graph. y-axis Rainfall (mm) X-axis Wind direction

- Be a marker! Use the suggested mark scheme below to decide which of these candidates was awarded 0, 1 or 2 marks for their answers. Discuss your marking with your classmates.

(a) (iii) Mark as follows:
Bar graph or histogram [1] *Dates/month/time and rainfall [1]. Must refer to both axes for the mark. Each can be on either axis as bar chart could be horizontal or vertical.*

Exam tip

Many students referred to 'It…' in their answer but this could have meant the traditional rain gauge or the low-cost one. The candidate needs to name the instrument so that the examiner knows which one is being referred to.

Analysing a Paper 4 question: Weather – November 2008

The Question (continued)

(b) The wind direction was measured using a wind vane fixed to the school roof (Fig. 7). Complete the sentence in each box about the wind vane. **[4]**

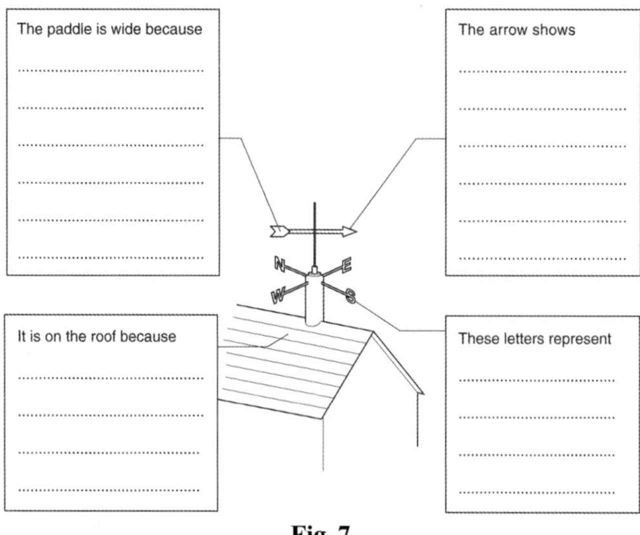

Fig. 7

(c) Re-read the hypothesis for the investigation:

'The school receives more rainfall when wind comes from the west'.

Study Fig. 8, which shows a sketch map of the location of the school.

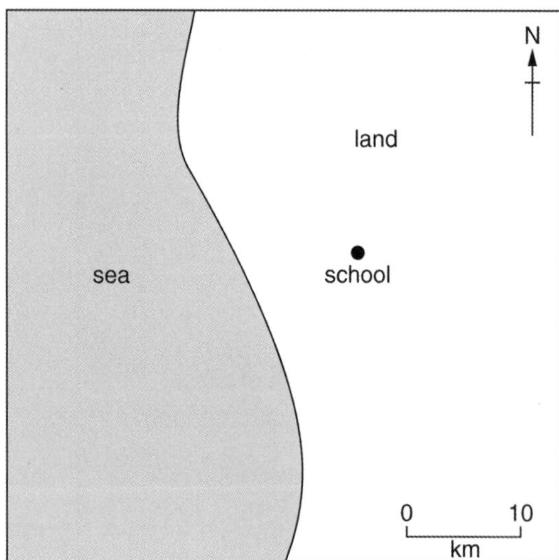

The school is located to the east of the coast and at an altitude of 400 m

Fig. 8

In detail, explain why wind from the west may bring rain to this school. **[4]**

Source: IGCSE Geography (0460/04) November 2008 Question 2

Getting it right (continued)

(b) Most candidates obtained 2 or 3 marks here. Here is the mark scheme for this sub-section.

> **(b) Mark scheme:**
> *The paddle is wide … – large surface area to allow wind to push it/catch the wind.* [1]
> *The arrow … – shows where wind direction is coming from.* [1]
> *The letters represent … – all 4 points/cardinal or compass points.* [1]
> *It is on the roof … – wind not obstructed/sheltered; so it is exposed.* [1]
> *Not more air/stronger winds.*

Candidate A

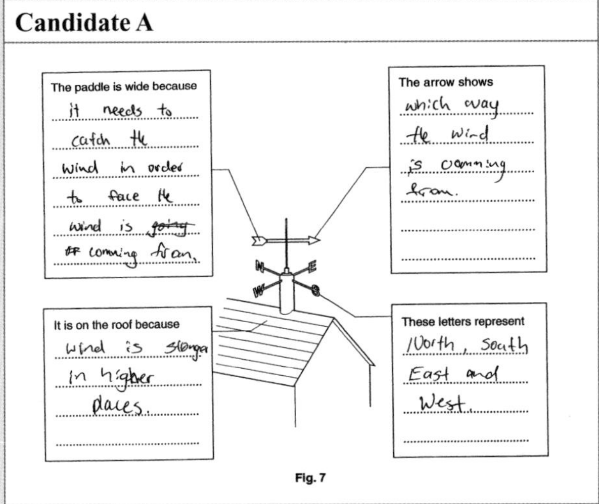

The paddle is wide because
it needs to catch the wind in order to face the wind is coming from.
The arrow shows
which way the wind is comming from.
It is on the roof because
wind is stonga in higher places.
These letters represent
North, South East and West.

Fig. 7

- Candidate A gained 3 marks – where?
- Why did this candidate not get the other mark?

(c) Most candidates recognised the sea to the west of the school (although some referred to it as the east!) and wrote that the wind from the west would pick up moisture or evaporate water to bring towards the school; this would gain 2 marks. However, too few noted the significance of the label to the map which stated that the school was at an altitude of 400 metres. Consequently, to get more than 2 marks out of 4, candidates had to refer to the process of relief rainfall. Those who did scored highly; some drew labelled diagrams to illustrate relief rainfall.

Read these two answers.

Candidate A	Candidate B
To the west of the school is the sea. Winds from the west bring rain to the school as the air is moist as it also carries moisture from evaporation. The moist wind flows to the east towards the school. Because the school is at an altitude of 400 metres above sea level, the moist air/wind is forced to rise. As it rises the air expands which causes it to cool. Water vapour in the air condenses to form clouds that bring precipitation.	Because the sea is close to the school on the west side the school gets more rain when the wind is coming from the west. This is because the wind brings all the water that has been evaporated from the sea and rains on the school.

- Candidate A gained 4 marks but Candidate B only gained 2 marks. Why?

Exam tip

Some people learn and explain more effectively by using pictures or diagrams. If you illustrate an answer with a labelled diagram, even if it not asked for, it will gain credit if it answers the question. If you do this there is no need to write an answer that says the same as the diagram. Only new material would gain extra marks.

Analysing a Paper 4 question: Weather – November 2008

The Question (continued)

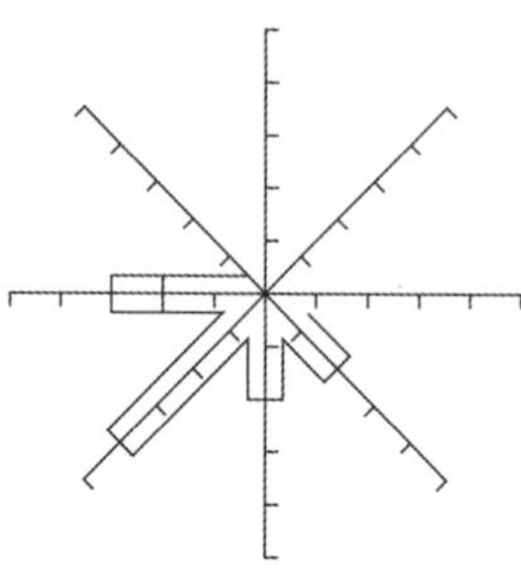

Fig. 9

Wind rose for September

(d) **(i)** Study Fig. 9, which shows a partly completed wind rose. Complete the wind rose for the east (E) and north (N) directions using the results shown in Table 2 [page 236]. **[2]**

(ii) The prevailing wind direction is south-west (SW). What is a prevailing wind? **[1]**

(iii) Describe the pattern of wind direction shown by the wind rose (Fig. 9). **[3]**

(e) The students linked the rainfall data and wind direction results by drawing a scatter graph (Fig. 10).

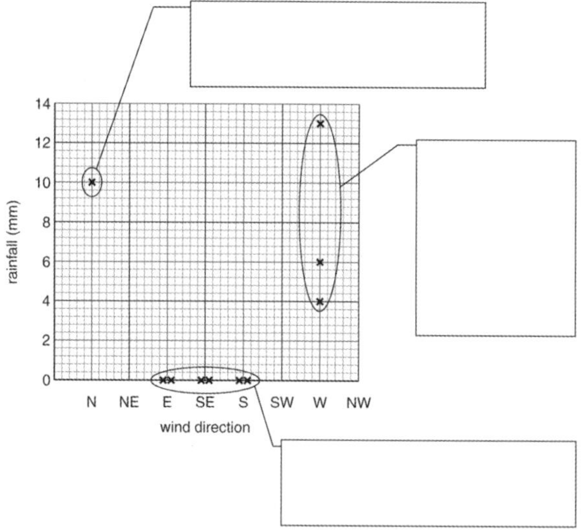

Fig. 10

(i) Complete the graph by adding the results for south-west (SW) winds from Table 2 [page 236]. **[2]**

(ii) Comment on the pattern of the results by completing the boxes on Fig. 10. **[3]**

(iii) The hypothesis for this investigation was: '*The school receives more rainfall when the wind comes from the west*'. Does this data support the hypothesis of the investigation? Circle your decision. **[1]**

YES TO SOME EXTENT NO

(f) In detail, suggest how this weather investigation could be improved and extended to make it more reliable and representative. **[5]**

[Total: 30 marks]

Source: IGCSE Geography (0460/04) November 2008 Question 2

Getting it right (continued)

(d) (i) The majority of candidates had no problem plotting the two results for east and north; a few drew them the wrong way round, though!

(ii) Understanding the definition of a prevailing wind is a basic requirement in studying weather. Read these three answers.

Candidate A
The direction the wind comes from most often
Candidate B
The wind that comes from the sea and is the strongest
Candidate C
The most frequently occurring wind direction

- Which two candidates gained the mark? Why?
- Why did the other candidate get the answer wrong?

(iii) Describing a pattern requires some overall comparison between data; no marks were awarded for just reading off data for individual directions on the wind rose. Some candidates described the winds blowing to areas when the wind rose shows where winds are coming from.

- Suggest why Candidate B was awarded all 3 marks but Candidate A gained none in the two answers below.

Candidate A	Candidate B
Wind blows to the west for three days. It blows for two days to the east and south-east and south. Most wind blows for 4 days to the south-west.	Most wind came from the west and south-west. There is no wind from the north-east or north-west. Wind came from the north for just one day whereas the next least wind (2 days each) came from the east, south-east and south.

(e) (i) Most candidates plotted the data correctly on the south-west line although a few just plotted three points correctly (the 4th being put at 11 or 13?); some put all four plots on the 0 line.

(ii)/(iii) Candidates were asked to comment on the 'pattern' of the results in the boxes. Pattern requires some overall judgement of these results, not a description of each plot. In (iii) most candidates agreed with the hypothesis although, given the data on the graph clearly supporting it, a number still suggested the hypothesis was wrong by circling NO. Only a few candidates recognised the anomaly and suggested it was unusual due to 'freak' conditions or student error.

(f) This was done well, with candidates suggesting extending the time, covering other seasons or using a traditional rain gauge – though not always stating how these would make this investigation more reliable and representative. Some suggested using other instruments but never explained how they would improve and extend this investigation as required. A few suggested the same techniques already covered in the question, which again is not improving or extending this investigation. Candidates must focus on what the question requires.

So what coursework could we do?

Fieldwork is vital ... even for an examination!

There are many varied reasons why centres choose the 'Alternative to Coursework' Paper rather than carrying out coursework. However, even with constraints preventing coursework, it is still important that candidates gain an understanding of the methods that could be used to do this. The world map below illustrates many different coursework titles that schools have used in various countries. All are either enquiry questions to answer or hypotheses to test. It should be possible in all centres to gain a basic understanding of fieldwork techniques, not only within the classroom, but also within the school grounds. Studies of vegetation, microclimates, and environmental issues are all feasible small-scale studies that, while not meeting the full coursework requirements, will give students vital experience of the 'real world outdoors'. Paper 4 may be an 'Alternative to Coursework' examination but the candidates who provide the best answers have clearly carried out some fieldwork activities in their school grounds or local area at least. This is to be encouraged.

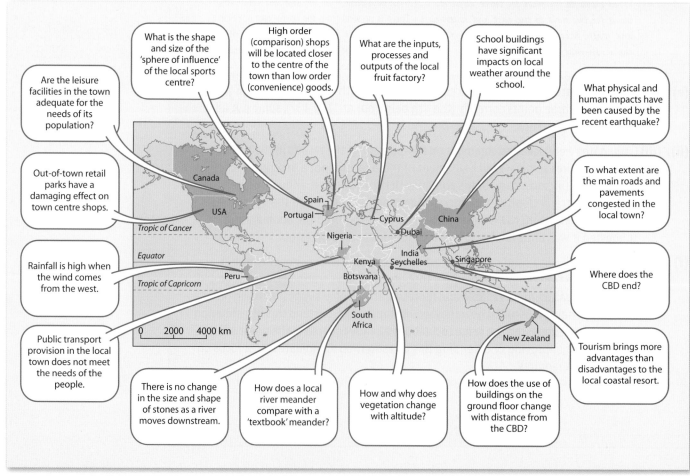

Are the leisure facilities in the town adequate for the needs of its population?

What is the shape and size of the 'sphere of influence' of the local sports centre?

High order (comparison) shops will be located closer to the centre of the town than low order (convenience) goods.

What are the inputs, processes and outputs of the local fruit factory?

School buildings have significant impacts on local weather around the school.

What physical and human impacts have been caused by the recent earthquake?

Out-of-town retail parks have a damaging effect on town centre shops.

To what extent are the main roads and pavements congested in the local town?

Rainfall is high when the wind comes from the west.

Where does the CBD end?

Public transport provision in the local town does not meet the needs of the people.

Tourism brings more advantages than disadvantages to the local coastal resort.

There is no change in the size and shape of stones as a river moves downstream.

How does a local river meander compare with a 'textbook' meander?

How and why does vegetation change with altitude?

How does the use of buildings on the ground floor change with distance from the CBD?

Canada
USA
Spain
Portugal
Cyprus
Dubai
China
Nigeria
India
Kenya
Seychelles
Singapore
Peru
Botswana
South Africa
New Zealand
Tropic of Cancer
Equator
Tropic of Capricorn
0 2000 4000 km

Resources

Abbreviations of Country Names

SOUTH AMERICA
FR.G. FRENCH GUIANA
GUY. GUYANA
SUR. SURINAME

AFRICA
B. BURUNDI
BE. BENIN
BUR. BURKINA
CAM. CAMEROON
C.D'I. CÔTE D'IVOIRE
EQ. G. EQUATORIAL GUINEA
GH. GHANA
R. RWANDA
T. TOGO

EUROPE
A. ANDORRA
ALB. ALBANIA
AUS. AUSTRIA
BEL. BELGIUM
BELA. BELARUS
B.H. BOSNIA-HERZEGOVINA
CR. CROATIA
CZ. CZECH REPUBLIC
DEN. DENMARK
EST. ESTONIA
GER. GERMANY
H. HUNGARY
K. KOSOVO
LAT. LATVIA
LITH. LITHUANIA
LUX. LUXEMBOURG
M. MONTENEGRO
MA. MACEDONIA
MO. MOLDOVA
NETH. NETHERLANDS
R.F. RUSSIAN FEDERATION
S. SLOVENIA
SER. SERBIA
SL. SLOVAKIA
SW. SWITZERLAND

ASIA
AR. ARMENIA
AZ. AZERBAIJAN
CYP. CYPRUS
GEO. GEORGIA
IS. ISRAEL
JOR. JORDAN
LEB. LEBANON
U.A.E. UNITED ARAB EMIRATES

Time Comparisons

Time varies around the world due to the earth's rotation causing different parts of the world to be in light or darkness at any one time. To account for this, the world is divided into twenty-four Standard Time Zones based on 15° intervals of longitude.

1:00am	2:00am	3:00am	4:00am	5:00am	6:00am	7:00am	8:00am	9:00am	10:00am	11:00am	noon
Samoa Tonga (next day)	Hawaiian Is Cook Is Tahiti	Anchorage	Vancouver Seattle Los Angeles	Edmonton Phoenix	Winnipeg Chicago Mexico City	New York Miami Lima	Puerto Rico La Paz Asunción	Nuuk Brasília Buenos Aires	South Georgia	Azores Cape Verde	Reykja[illegible] Londo[illegible] Freetow[illegible]

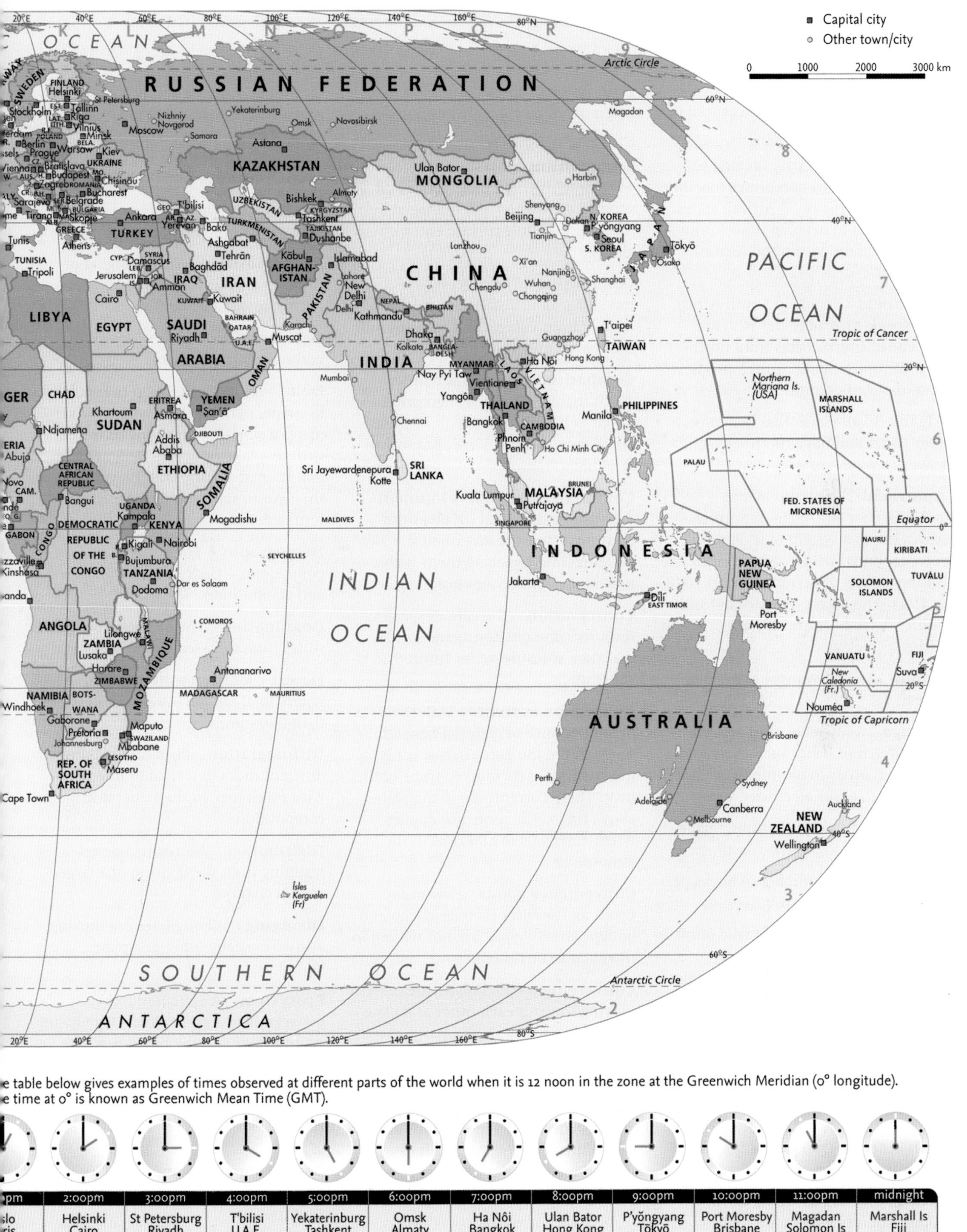

e table below gives examples of times observed at different parts of the world when it is 12 noon in the zone at the Greenwich Meridian (0° longitude).
e time at 0° is known as Greenwich Mean Time (GMT).

pm	2:00pm	3:00pm	4:00pm	5:00pm	6:00pm	7:00pm	8:00pm	9:00pm	10:00pm	11:00pm	midnight
slo ris hasa	Helsinki Cairo Cape Town	St Petersburg Riyadh Dodoma	T'bilisi U.A.E. Mauritius	Yekaterinburg Tashkent Karachi	Omsk Almaty Dhaka	Ha Nôi Bangkok Jakarta	Ulan Bator Hong Kong Perth	P'yŏngyang Tōkyō Palau	Port Moresby Brisbane Canberra	Magadan Solomon Is New Caledonia	Marshall Is Fiji Wellington

Access How easy it is to obtain a good or service. It can be measured in terms of cost, time or distance.

African Union (AU) Created in 2002, this organisation brings together the governments of 53 African states. The AU aims to develop peace, unity and integration within the African continent.

Afrikaners People in South Africa who speak Afrikaans and who are descended from settlers from north-west Europe – mainly Dutch people from the Netherlands.

Algae Small plants that live in or near water and have no true stem, leaves or roots.

Apartheid The word means 'separateness' in Dutch. In South Africa it was a system of legal racial segregation which was enforced by the National Party government from 1948 to 1994. The legacy of apartheid still influences politics and society in South Africa.

Arable The growing of crops, e.g. wheat.

Barrage A low dam built across a wide stretch of water such as a large estuary in order to use the water held behind it to make electricity.

Bay Part of the sea that fills a wide-mouthed opening in the coastline.

Birth rate The number of births per year per 1000 population.

Bush meat The meat of wild animals that are killed for subsistence or commercial reasons, mainly in tropical areas and LEDCs.

Capitalism An economic system in which the majority of goods and services are owned and managed by individuals and companies rather than by the state.

Cash crop A crop grown for sale rather than for subsistence.

Census An official count of the population carried out at regular intervals.

Colony A country that has been taken over and ruled by another country.

Communism A system of government where most goods and services are owned and managed by the state and little private enterprise is allowed.

Commuting The process of travelling some distance to work, usually from villages and suburbs into the central areas of a town or city.

Comparison goods High order goods that, due to their high price, purchasers wish to compare. People are willing to travel long distances to buy them.

Comprehensive redevelopment A housing policy that involves the clearing of areas of low-quality buildings and replacing them with a new higher-quality environment.

Conservation The care of species, resources and environments so that they will survive for future generations.

Convection currents Differences in temperature of material beneath the plates of the Earth's crust leads to the creation of currents to transfer the heat. These currents move the plates above them. The term also applies when air is heated and rises in the atmosphere.

Convenience goods Low order goods and services that are cheap and bought often. People are not willing to travel far to buy them.

Converging When plates are moving towards each other at a plate boundary.

Counter-urbanisation The process by which an increasing number of people within a country live in the countryside instead of in towns and cities. This could be the result of natural increase and/or migration.

Cyclone An area of low atmospheric pressure, e.g. below 980 mb. A tropical cyclone, with pressure often below 970 mb, is also known as a hurricane in North America and the Caribbean.

Death rate The number of deaths per year per 1000 population.

Decomposition The changing of rocks by chemical action causing a change in composition.

Deforestation Cutting down trees without replacing them.

Delta A landform, often triangular in shape, that develops where a river meets a slow-moving body of water such as a lake or ocean. Sediment builds up above the water level, forcing the river to split into distributaries to form a delta.

Demography The study of human populations – their size, distribution and composition.

Desalination The extraction of fresh water from salty sea water.

Desert A dry area, hot or cold, where total annual precipitation is less than 250 mm.

Disintegration Physical breaking down of rocks into smaller fragments with no change in their chemical composition.

Distributary A stream channel resulting from the division of a larger stream channel.

Diverging When plates are moving away from each other at a plate boundary.

Ecosystem A system of links between plants and animals (the living community) and the habitats where they live, including the non-living environment.

Emigrants People who permanently leave one country to live in another.

Emigration The permanent movement of people outward from a country.

Epicentre The point on the surface directly above where an earthquake has taken place.

Erosion The wearing away and removal of rocks by the action of the agents of erosion – wind, water, ice, gravity.

Escarpment A long ridge of high ground, often with a scarp (steep) and dip (gentle) slope.

Extensive farming Where there are small inputs of capital and labour compared with the large amount of land used, e.g. cattle-rearing. Yields per hectare are low.

Fauna Animals (including birds and insects) of an area.

Fertility rate In a country or region the average number of children a woman will have in her lifetime.

Flora Plants of an area.

Food & Agricultural Organisation (FAO) The FAO, based in Rome, Italy, is part of the United Nations. The organisation was created in 1945 to lead UN efforts to defeat hunger in both LEDCs and MEDCs.

Formal employment Official jobs with set hours and rates of pay. People who are formally employed pay direct taxes to the government.

Fossil fuel Any fuel found underground that is made up of the remains of plants and/or animals. Oil, natural gas, coal, brown coal and peat are all fossil fuels.

GDP (Gross Domestic Product) per person The total value of all the goods and services produced in a country in one year by all the people living in that country, divided by the population. It is used as a measure of wealth.

Geothermal power Energy gathered from the natural heat produced by rocks deep underground.

Glacial To do with ice, its movements and the features formed by it.

Headland A point of higher land jutting out into the sea, usually made of a resistant rock such as granite.

Hierarchy Any kind of organisation based on rank, class and order, e.g. a settlement hierarchy places cities, towns and villages in order of size or status.

High order Goods or services that are bought infrequently and are often expensive.

Hydro-electric power (HEP) Electricity generated by using moving water to turn turbines.

Immigration The permanent movement of people inward to a country.

Independence When a government takes on sole responsibility for making decisions about how to run the country it governs.

Industrial Revolution The period of time in a country or region's development when it changes from being mainly a rural agricultural society with small-scale cottage industries to one that is based on large-scale manufacturing industry in urban areas.

Informal employment Unofficial jobs that have no set hours or rates of pay. People who are informally employed may avoid paying tax and are usually self-employed.

Infrastructure The pattern of communication and transport links, power supplies, administrative, health, education and other services necessary for economic development.

Insolation The amount of sun's energy reaching the Earth's surface.

Intensive farming Where there are large inputs of capital and labour compared with the small amount of land used, e.g. battery hen farming. Yields per hectare are high.

Internally displaced people (IDPs) People who are forced to leave their homes but who are not refugees because they stay within the country's borders.

International migration The movement of people on a permanent basis between countries.

Irrigated Land that has water added to it for farming purposes. This can involve sprinklers, canals, lifting devices. It is usually required where rainfall is below 500 mm per year.

Lagoon A bay or sea inlet that is partly enclosed by a spit or wholly enclosed by a sand bar.

Lateral erosion Where a stream or river wears away the sides and banks on each side of the channel.

Lava Magma that has escaped from beneath the Earth's crust and has flowed onto the surface.

LEDC A less economically developed country as defined by the Brandt Report (1980).

Low order Goods or services that are bought frequently and which are usually cheap.

Magma Molten rock found beneath the Earth's crust.

Margin of cultivation Land towards the edge of a cultivable area on which it is just possible to farm economically.

MEDC A more economically developed country as defined by the Brandt Report (1980).

Metropolitan Refers to a single urban settlement of outstanding size and importance which has absorbed other urban areas. It is often the capital city of the country. The Greater Tokyo Metropolitan area is the largest, containing about 35 million people.

Migration The permanent, seasonal or temporary movement of people.

Monsoon Derived from the Arabic word *mawsam*, meaning season. It is a seasonal change of wind direction. The monsoon refers to both dry and wet seasons, although its common use refers to the wet season only.

National Park Area of such outstanding scenery that the government has put in place very strict checks on any new development.

Natural population change Change in population caused by birth and death rates only.

Newly industrialised countries (NICs) These countries, mostly based in south-east Asia, showed rapid growth in the late 20th century, largely through the creation and expansion of multinational companies based on modern technology and IT.

Nomadic People, usually farmers, who move from place to place seasonally to find good land or pasture.

Non-renewable Energy sources that are limited and finite. Once used up there are no future supplies available, e.g. oil, coal, natural gas.

Nutrients Proteins, carbohydrates, fats, vitamins and minerals provided by food and necessary for growth and the maintenance of life.

Overall population change Change in population caused by births, deaths and migration.

Overpopulated When a country or region does not have enough resources to keep its people at a reasonable standard of living.

Pass laws Introduced in 1923, the pass laws were designed by the South African government to prevent freedom of movement of non-whites who had to carry pass books at all times to prove they were authorised to live and work in 'white' South Africa.

Passport An official document that certifies a person's identity, nationality and citizenship of a country. It enables travel between countries and entitles the holder to protection overseas.

Pastoral The raising of animals on grass, e.g. cattle, sheep, goats.

Pastoralists Farmers whose main concern is the raising of animals using grass and pasture, e.g. cattle, sheep, goats.

Photosynthesis The process whereby plants take in the sun's energy with carbon dioxide and water to produce energy, oxygen and plant tissue.

Plateau Large area of relatively flat upland.

Population density The average number of people in a given area, e.g. per km^2.

Population pyramid A diagram showing the ages and gender of the population of an area.

Prevailing wind The direction from which the wind blows into an area for most of the year.

Range The distance people are prepared to travel to buy a good or a service, e.g. low order goods and services have a small range; high order goods and services have a large range.

Rapid transit system A railway system for passengers that is run by electricity both over- and underground and has high capacity and frequency. London's underground system was the first rapid-transit system, built in 1863. More than 160 cities now have them.

Reclamation To use or re-use resources that are serving no worthwhile purpose at present, e.g. derelict sites in inner-city areas, marshy land.

Renewable Resources that can be used without endangering future supplies, e.g. solar energy.

Rural To do with villages and the countryside.

Rural–urban fringe The area on the very edge of a town or city where it meets the countryside.

Savanna Tropical grasslands that lie between tropical rainforests where it is wetter and hot desert where it is drier.

Sedentary Farmers who are settled in one particular place.

Sedimentary rock Material that has been deposited by the force which originally carried it from elsewhere, e.g. wind, water or ice. It can also consist of the accumulated remains of dead sea animals, e.g. limestone.

Shifting cultivation A farming system often found in rainforests in LEDCs where a patch of land is cleared, crops are grown, then the patch is deserted until it regains its fertility.

Sphere of influence The area surrounding an activity that is influenced by it, e.g. a sports centre or a local park. It is also called the catchment area.

Spit A sand ridge, usually curving, that is joined to the land at one end and juts out into the sea at the other.

Standard of living The factors that affect a person's quality of life and which can be measured. Many measures to do with a person's standard of living are to do with material possessions.

Subsistence agriculture A means of supporting life by being able to meet one's own basic needs of food, water and shelter.

Sub-tropical Referring to those areas of the Earth that lie between the Tropic of Cancer (23½°N) and 40°N and the Tropic of Capricorn (23½°S) and 40°S.

Sustainable Capable, by careful use and management, of being maintained over time for future generations to use or enjoy whilst meeting the needs of the present.

Tectonic plates Rigid segments of rock that make up the Earth's crust. They meet at plate boundaries where earthquakes, volcanoes and fold mountains are created.

Temperate Areas that do not experience great extremes of heat or cold. They are in the mid-latitudes between the hot tropics and cold polar regions both in the northern and southern hemispheres.

Tenement A building that is split up into several apartments or flats.

Thermal power Energy generated by heating water to make steam which then turns turbines to create electricity. The heat source can be coal, oil, gas, geothermal or nuclear.

Threshold population The number of people needed to justify the provision of a good or service.

Tidal power Energy based on the movements of the tide. This works best where there is a large tidal range – that is, a large difference between the high-tide and low-tide levels.

Townships Urban living areas built on the edges of towns and cities that, under apartheid in South Africa, were reserved for non-whites (mainly black Africans, coloureds* and some working-class Indians). *[*See note on page 122]*

Transmigration The relocation of a large number of people as a result of a government plan.

Tropical Parts of the Earth that lie between the Tropic of Cancer ($23^1/_2$°N) and the Tropic of Capricorn ($23^1/_2$°S).

Tundra Areas in Alaska, northern Canada, northern Europe and Asia where the ground is permanently frozen for most of the year. Only lichen, moss, grasses and dwarf shrubs and trees can grow here.

Underpopulated When a country or region has more resources available than are being used by the people living there.

United Nations (UN) An organisation made up of delegates from almost all countries of the world, created in 1945. The UN headquarters are in New York. It deals with issues of global importance including those related to global development.

Urban To do with towns and cities.

Urbanisation The process by which an increasing proportion of people live in towns and cities instead of the countryside. This could be the result of natural increase and/or migration.

Urban regeneration The renewal of a declining part of a town or city by removing existing houses and buildings as well as redeveloping the area.

Urban renewal The process whereby the derelict areas of a town or city are improved by upgrading existing buildings. This process is sometimes known as gentrification.

Urban sprawl The expansion of the city into its surrounding rural area.

Vertical erosion Where a stream or river flowing quickly down a steep gradient in an upland area wears away the bed at a faster rate than the valley sides, leading to a narrow V-shaped valley.

Visa An additional requirement to a passport, usually given by endorsing the passport, allowing entry into some countries.

Weathering The breakdown of rocks by elements of the weather or biological influences but not their physical removal, e.g. frost, alternate heat and cold, tree roots, burrowing animals.

Workforce That part of the population of a country that is employed. In MEDCs this is usually those aged between 16 and 65; in LEDCs this often starts at a lower age.

World Bank An organisation set up by MEDCs in 1944 with its headquarters in Washington DC, USA. It contributes funds to be loaned to LEDCs for development projects.

INDEX

The author and publishers are grateful for the permissions granted to reproduce materials in either the original or adapted form. While every effort has been made, it has not always been possible to identify the sources of all the materials used, or to trace all copyright holders. If any omissions are brought to our notice, we will be happy to include the appropriate acknowledgements on reprinting.

Texts

p. 7 adapted from 'Population explosion' (2007); p.117 'Access a problem in Afghanistan' (2008); p.181 'Harare's middle-class residents': IRIN News Service.
p. 9 'A second baby?' by Fred Weir, excerpted with permission from 19 May 2006 issue of *The Christian Science Monitor* (www.CSMonitor.com): © 2006 *The Christian Science Monitor*.
p. 13 'Nigerian polls bring hope to chaotic Lagos' by Tume Ahemba and Daniel Flynn, April 2007: Reuters.
p. 28 adapted from 'Holiday island spoilt by seaborne immigrant invasion', *The Times*, August 2008; p. 31 adapted from 'The boomerang immigrants who chase their dreams to Britain' (Roger Boyes), *The Times*, April 2005; p. 62 adapted from 'Force of nature parts Red Sea' (Mark Henderson), *The Times*, July 2006; p. 75 adapted from 'Cyclone death toll may rise to 8000' (Dean Nelson), *The Times*, November 2007; p. 85 adapted from 'The Barrier reef under threat', *The Times*, February 2008; p. 89 adapted from 'Why a cup of coffee could spell doom for the last hairy rhino' (Nick Meo), *The Times*, January 2007; p. 89 adapted from 'Loggers go deeper into the Amazon jungle in Brazil', *The Times*, November 2002; p. 96 adapted from 'Mega cities add to perils' (Nick Nuttall), *The Times*, December 1999; p. 99 adapted from 'The coast of Myanmar suffered long term and short term damage' (Kenneth Denby), *The Times*, May 2008; p. 108 adapted from 'Electric cars put Hawaii on the road to independence' (Chris Ayres), *The Times*, December 2008; p. 117 adapted from 'The carpet of jaws that threatens to devour West Africa' (Jonathan Clayton), *The Times*, October 2004; p. 117 adapted from 'Starvation grips east Africa', *The Times*, August 2008; p. 125 adapted from 'Winners abound on football's big night' (Adam Sherwin), *The Times*, May 2008; p. 141 adapted from 'Australia looks for power from hot rocks' (Paul Larter), *The Times*, May 2008; p. 141 adapted from 'Cattle have power too', *The Times*, March 2008; p. 141 adapted from 'Solar city sets sights on ending pollution' (Thomas Catán), *The Times*, June 2007; p. 153 adapted from 'Disease and disputes spread as provinces start water fight' (Graham Keeley), *The Times*, July 2005; p. 153 adapted from 'Water shortages are likely to be trigger for wars' (Leo Lewis), *The Times*, December 2007; p. 167 adapted from 'Russia stakes its claim on the North Pole in underwater search for oil' (Tony Halpin), *The Times*, July 2007; p.168 adapted from 'The power games that threaten the world's last pristine wilderness' (James Bones), *The Times*, November 2007: © NI Syndication.
p. 30 adapted from 'Workers of the world' (2005); p. 89 'Forest felled to feed demand for lipstick' (Juliet Jowit, 2004); p. 104 'Living on the floodplain' (Joseph Hanlon, 2001): copyright Guardian News & Media Ltd 2005.
p. 35 information and map adapted from Ethiopian Village Studies document 'Korodegaga, Dodota, Arssi', June 1996: researched by Assefa Tolera and Mesfin Tadesse, designed and edited by Philippa Bevan and Alula Pankhurst.
p. 45 adapted from 'Slumdog Millionaire highlights impending global crisis': Indo Asian News Service.
p. 57 Lyrics of 'Little Boxes' – words and music by Malvina Reynolds, copyright 1962 Schroder Music Co. (ASCAP) renewed 1990, used by permission, all rights reserved.
p. 79 'Collapse of Apostle' published by the Australian Broadcasting Corporation (ABC), July 2005.
p. 103 'Polluting the Baltic Sea' Salla Korpela/thisisFINLAND.fi
pp. 114-115 data and information about New Zealand used by permission: Meat & Wool New Zealand.
p. 117 adapted from 'Food shortage threatens millions in Bangladesh', Andrew Buncombe, first published 25 November 2007: © Independent News & Media Limited.
p. 135 from 'The Final Call – In Search of the True Cost of our Holidays' by Leo Hickman: reprinted by permission of The Random House Group Ltd.
p. 137 adapted from 'Water shortages': Seychelles Weekly.
p. 148 adapted from 'India swelters as more power outages loom': Oman Daily Observer.
p. 150 'Nuclear power in France':NPR.org
p. 153 'Burmese dam will displace thousands': The Associated Press, 13 April 2007.
p. 165 'Burkina Faso protects its fragile soils': Africa Recovery, United Nations.
p. 205 Reunion looks to renewable energy' Ed Harris, August 2008: Reuters.
p. 207 'The impact of cruising' by M.T. Schwarzman.
Part C – examination questions reproduced by permission of the University of Cambridge Local Examinations Syndicate. The University of Cambridge Local Examinations Syndicate bears no responsibility for the example answers to questions taken from its past question papers which are contained in this publication.

Maps

p. 4 map created with data from the US Census Bureau; p. 37 extracts from maps 1710E Séries Bleue Etratat Cap d'Antifer, O818O Série Bleue Guémené-sue-Scoff © IGN – Paris – 2009 Authorisation no. 80-9047; p. 56 Leicester 1992 & 2007 reproduced by permission of Ordnance Survey on behalf of MHSO © Crown copyright 2009, all rights reserved, Ordnance Survey Licence No. 100001679; p. 58 map of the US – U.S. Gov'T Commerce Noaa Nat'L Geophysical Data Centre/National Geographic Image Collection; p. 66 map based on an original by the British Geographic Survey, reproduced by permission of the British Geological Survey © NERC 2008, all rights reserved, IPR/119-17CT; p. 73 © Department of Natural Resources Canada, all rights reserved; p. 133 TTK Healthcare Ltd India; p. 172 Monsferu, Peru 1:50000 (Chiclayo) prepared by Army Map Service (SX), Corps of Engineers, US Army, Washington DC 1967; p. 178 Harare, Zimbabwe 1:50000 (Lake Chivero) published by the Surveyor General, Zimbabwe 1994; p. 184 Ewaso Kedong, Kenya 1:50000 (Lumuru) published for the

Kenyan Government by the British Government's Ministry of Overseas Surveys, copyright 1976 Kenyan Government; p. 190 Montego Bay, Jamaica 1:25000 National Land Agency, Survey & Mapping Division, Jamaica; p. 196 Negara, Indonesia 1:25000 BAKOSURNATAL, the Indonesian National Coordinating Agency for Surveys and Mapping; p. 202 4401RT St-Paul le Port © IGN – Paris – 2009 Authorisation no. 80-9047; p. 208 Mauritius 1:25000 (Extract No 1220/Port Louis) map printed by Ordnance Survey 2000 © Government of Mauritius 1989; p. 211 © AA Media Limited 2009, cartographic data © Tele Atlas N.V. 2009; p. 244 map © Collins Bartholomew Ltd 2009

Images and photographs

(Key: *t* = top, *b* = bottom, *c* = centre, *l* = left, *r* = right, *(all)* = all photos on page)

pp. 1*l*, 3 James Marshall/Corbis; pp. 1*c*, 61 Michael Amendolia; pp.1*r*, 109 © G.M.B. Akash/Panos Pictures; p. 7 Boureima HAMA/AFP/Getty Images; p. 8 Hasan Doganturk/Alamy; p. 11 frans lemmens/Alamy; p. 16 UK Census form and logo source: National Statistics website www.statistics.gov.uk Crown copyright material is reproduced with the permission of the Controller Office of Public Sector Information (OPSI); p. 16 US Census logo from the US Census Bureau; p. 18*t* Keren Su/Getty Images; p. 18*b* EIGHTFISH/Getty Images; p. 26 Chad Ehlers/ Alamy; p. 27*t* Tohoku Color Agency/Getty Images; p. 27*c* DAJ/ Getty Images; p. 27*b* Shogoro/amana images/Getty Images; p. 28*b* Mauro Seminara/AFP/Getty Images; p. 30 Martin Godwin; p. 31 Profimedia International s.r.o./Alamy; p. 32 René Mansi/iStockphoto; p. 34 Adrian Arbib/Still Pictures; p. 35 Ariadne Van Zandbergen/Alamy; p. 36 Travel Ink/Alamy; p. 45 Film 4/Celador Films/Pathe International/The Kobal Collection; p. 46 Anja Kessler/Das Fotoarchiv/Still Pictures; p. 47 Arco Images GmbH/Alamy; p. 55 logo courtesy of Visit Baltimore; p. 57*t* Max Whittaker; p. 57*b* David R. Frazier/ Science Photo Library; p. 58 Bildarchiv Monheim GmbH/Alamy; p. 59 David R. Frazier Photolibrary; Inc./Alamy; p. 60 Mike Goldwater/Alamy; p. 62 NASA/ MODIS/Science Photo Library; p. 63 Horizon International Images Limited/Alamy; p. 65*l* imagebroker/Alamy; p. 65*r* Christian Brown/AFP/Getty Images; p. 67 Sipa Press/Rex Features; p. 69*bl* Islandstock/Alamy; p. 69*br* WoodyStock/Alamy; p. 72*t* Worldsat International/ Science Photo Library; p. 75*t* Earth Satellite Corporation/ Science Photo Library; p. 75*b* Shafiqul Islam Kajol/Majority/Still Pictures; p. 78 Thomas Enguehard/Wikimedia public domain; p. 79 John Quixley/Alamy; p. 80*t* NASA/Wikipedia public domain; p. 82*t* Stuart Chape/Still Pictures; p. 82*tc* David Ball/ Alamy; p. 82*bc* Ron Watts/Photolibrary.com; p. 82*b* Tetyana Kochneva/iStockphoto; p. 84 Jurgen Freund/naturepl.com; p. 85 Bruce Miller/Alamy; p. 88 Robbie Shone/Alamy; p. 91*l* Michael Fay/ National Geographic/Getty Images; p. 91*r* Jean-Leo Dugast/Still Pictures; p. 92 Huebi/Wikimedia; p. 93*l* Werner Bollmann/Photolibrary.com; p. 94*t* NASA; p. 94*b* Stuart Redler/Getty Images; p. 95*t* blickwinkel/Alamy; p. 95*b* Jon Arnold Images Ltd/Alamy; p. 97*tl* Claire Freebairn/iStockphoto; p. 97*tr* Caro/Alamy; p. 97*bl* NASA; p. 97*br* UNICEF; p. 99 NASA image courtesy Jeff Schmaltz, MODIS Rapid Response team, caption by Michon Scott.Instrument: Terra - MODIS; p. 101 Photolibrary/Alamy; p. 102*cl* Caro/Alamy; p. 102*cr* Tim E White/Alamy; p. 104 Yoav Lemmer/AFP/Getty Images; p. 105 Piero Pomponi/Liaison/Getty Images; p. 106 R1/Alamy; p. 113*t* Luiz C. Marigo/Still Pictures; p. 113*b* Hervé Collart/ Sygma/Corbis; p. 114 David Wall/Alamy; p. 115 Art Directors & TRIP/Alamy; p. 116*l* Ilene MacDonald/Alamy; p. 116*r* Borderlands/Alamy; p. 117 Eckstein Eckstein/Photolibrary. com; p. 119*t* Boris Heger/Das Fotoarchiv/Still Pictures; p. 119*b* Antony Njuguna/Reuters/Corbis; p. 123*t* Matt-80/Wikimedia; p. 123*b* Peter Titmuss/Alamy; p. 125*tl* Peter Turnley/Corbis; p. 125*tr* PCL/Alamy; p. 129 James L. Stanfield/National Geographic/Getty Images; p. 131 Map used by permission of Silicon Valley Map www.siliconvalleymap.com; p. 138 Peter Bowater/Alamy; p. 139*tl* Kumar Sriskandan/Alamy; p. 139*tr* Fabrice Bettex/Alamy; p. 139*tcl* Nicholas Pitt/Alamy; p. 139*bl* NASA; p. 139*br* NASA; p. 140*cl* Sinopix/Rex Features; p. 140*r* Alex Bartel/Science Photo Library; p. 142 Peter Treanor/Alamy; p. 143 Eitan Simanor/Alamy; p. 145*l* William S. Stevens/U.S. Navy/Getty Images; p. 145*r* Tom Hanley/Alamy; p. 147 Emil Thor Sigurdsson; p. 148*bl* SCPhotos/Alamy; p. 151 Sipa Press/ Rex Features; p. 152*tl* WaterAid/Marco Betti; p. 155 used by permission of George van der Merwe, TCTA; p. 157 Michel Setboun/Corbis; p. 158*t* John & Lisa Merrill/Getty Images; p. 158*b* Jorgen Schytte/Still Pictures; p. 159*t* James Green/ Robert Harding/Rex Features; p. 159*b* Photoshot Holdings Ltd/ Alamy; p. 160 MARKA/Alamy; p. 165*tl* Lisa Frias/iStockphoto; p. 165*c* logo used by permission of the Gorilla Organization; p. 165*b* John Isaac/UN Photo Library; p. 168 oversnap/ iStockphoto; p. 170*l* Frederic Soreau/Photolibrary.com; p. 177*tr* Paul Kingsley/Alamy; p. 182 Tsvangirayi Mukwazhi/AP/PA Photos; p. 191 Lew Robertson/iStockphoto; p. 195*t* Phil Kelly/ Alamy; p. 195 www.mbmp.org; p. 203 imagery © 2009 Digital Globe, GeoEye, Google Earth; p208*l* c./Shutterstock; p. 208*r* kaarsten/Shutterstock; p. 209*t* Andrew Fox/Alamy; p. 211 Phil Degginger/Alamy; p. 234*tr* Art Directors & TRIP/Alamy; p. 234*bc* Mark Boulton/Alamy; p. 234*c* Scott Bowman/Alamy; p. 234*bl* Brian Cosgrove/Dorling Kindersley Images; p. 234*br* GH Zeal Ltd; p. 235 Dorling Kindersley Images

The following photographs are used by kind permission of the authors, Steve Sibley and Gary Cambers, and colleagues: p. 5, p. 10*l*, p. 10*r*, p. 13*tl*, p. 13*tr*, p. 13*b*, p. 15*l* & 15*r* (photos by Mrs. C.R. Jones), p. 17*r*, p. 22*l*, p. 22*r*, p. 24*tl*, p. 24*tr*, p. 24*b*, p. 28*t*, p. 38*(all)*, p. 39 *(all)*, p. 41*(all)*, p. 49*tl*, p. 49*tr*, p. 49*bl*, p. 51*(all)*, p. 54, p. 55*l*, p. 55*r*, p. 56 *(all)*, p. 69*tl*, p. 69*tr*, p. 70*l*, p. 70*r*, p. 72*b* (photo by Stuart Currie), p. 76*t*, p. 76*b*, p. 80*b*, p. 81*tl*, p. 81*tr*, p. 81*b*, p. 86*tl*, p. 86*tr*, p. 86*b*, p. 93*r*, p. 95*c*, p. 102*(all* except 102*cl* & 102*cr)*, p. 108*t*, p. 108*b*, p. 110*l*, p. 110*r*, p. 120*tl*, p. 120*tr*, p. 120*b*, p. 121, p. 122, p. 124, p. 125*tc*, p. 125*b*, p. 127, p. 130*(all)*, p.132, p. 135 *(all)*, p. 136 *(all)*, p. 137, p. 139*bcl*, p. 139*bcr*, p. 140*l*, p. 140*cr*, p. 148*tl*, p. 148*tr*, p. 148*br*, p. 149, p. 152*tl*, p. 152*bl*, p. 152*br*, p. 156*t*, p. 156*c*, p. 156*b*, p. 161*t*, p. 161*b*, p. 165*tr*, p. 170*r*, p. 171*l*, p. 171*r*, p. 176, p. 177*l*, p. 177*br*, p. 179, p. 183*t*, p. 183*b*, p. 185, p. 188*l*, p. 188*tr*, p. 188*br*, p. 197*l*, p. 197*r*, p. 198, p. 206, pp. 209*b* & 242 (photos by Mark Birkenshaw), p. 210, p. 218, p. 219*tl*, p. 219*tr*, p. 219*b*, p. 226, p. 234*tl*, p. 234*cr*